David C. Cook
Bible Lesson
Commentary

The Essential Study Companion *for* Every Disciple

David C. Cook
Bible Lesson
Commentary

KJV

David C Cook®
transforming lives together

DAVID C. COOK'S KJV BIBLE LESSON COMMENTARY 2010–2011
Published by David C. Cook
4050 Lee Vance View
Colorado Springs, CO 80918 U.S.A.

David C. Cook Distribution Canada
55 Woodslee Avenue, Paris, Ontario, Canada N3L 3E5

David C. Cook U.K., Kingsway Communications
Eastbourne, East Sussex BN23 6NT, England

David C. Cook and the graphic circle C logo
are registered trademarks of Cook Communications Ministries.

Unless otherwise noted, Scripture quotations are taken from the King James Version of the
Bible. (Public Domain); or the New Revised Standard Version Bible, copyright 1989,
Division of Christian Education of the National Council of the Churches of Christ in the
United States of America. Used by permission. All rights reserved.

Lessons based on *International Sunday School Lessons: The International Bible Lessons for
Christian Teaching*, © 2007 by the Committee on the Uniform Series.

ISBN 978-1-4347-6489-8

© 2010 David C. Cook

Written and edited by Dan Lioy, PhD
The Team: John Blase, Doug Schmidt, and Jack Campbell
Cover Design: Amy Kiechlin
Cover Photo: iStockphoto

Printed in the United States of America
First Edition 2010

1 2 3 4 5 6 7 8 9 10

012510

CONTENTS

SEPTEMBER, OCTOBER, NOVEMBER 2010
THE INESCAPABLE GOD

UNIT I: GOD REVEALS

UNIT II: GOD SUSTAINS

UNIT III: GOD PROTECTS

DECEMBER 2010, JANUARY, FEBRUARY 2011
ASSURING HOPE

UNIT I: COMFORT FOR GOD'S PEOPLE

UNIT II: A FUTURE FOR GOD'S PEOPLE

UNIT III: JESUS, THE PROMISED SERVANT-LEADER

CONTENTS

A Word to the Teacher

A handful of teachers in a small rural church got together to share their concerns. They were worried because the congregation's budget could not afford the purchase of a large flat-screen television with a DVD player and a computer for accessing the Internet. "How can we teach if we don't have the latest equipment?" one woman bemoaned. Soon a sense of gloom began to pervade the meeting.

Then someone shared how he had been awakened to the meaning of the Savior while attending a large, affluent congregation years ago. The believer said, "Back then, we had film strips and tape recorders and all the fancy gadgetry that was in vogue. But do you know what really made a difference for me? It was Mr. Shewmaker, not the slide projectors and all the pricey stuff our church had bought. It was old Henry Shewmaker!

"Old Henry was told to use the expensive new set of slides, but he seemed to get them in upside down or out of focus the first few times he tried. Then he finally quit on all the new technology. Now I realize we don't have to worry about having a bunch of fancy electronics for our classes—as much as it might help. What's most important is being like Henry Shewmaker. Do you know why? Mr. Shewmaker had *enthusiasm* for us and for the Lord!"

What a superb way of describing the ideal teacher! We need to have *enthusiasm*! The word comes from a Greek verb that means "to be inspired." When a teacher like Mr. Shewmaker is filled with a genuine zeal for the Lord Jesus and the members of a class, faith is nurtured!

As you teach a class of adults this year, you initially may feel inadequate because of a perceived lack of skills, tools, or learning. But if you have enthusiasm for the gospel, you will have the essential ingredient you need for successful teaching. And you will find that your study of Scripture and the material in this year's edition of the *Cook Bible Lesson Commentary* can help you communicate God's truth in a relevant way. As you faithfully do your part in teaching the Word, your students will spiritually grow as Jesus' disciples. They may even find your enthusiasm for the Lord contagious!

Your fellow learner at the feet of the Master Teacher,
Dan Lioy

USING DAVID C. COOK'S KJV BIBLE LESSON COMMENTARY WITH MATERIAL FROM OTHER PUBLISHERS

Sunday school materials from the following denominations and publishers follow the International Sunday School Lesson (ISSL) outlines (sometimes known as the Uniform Series). Because *David C. Cook's KJV Bible Lesson Commentary* (formerly *Tarbell's*) follows the same ISSL outlines, you can use the commentary as an excellent teacher resource to supplement the materials from these publishing houses.

Nondenominational:
Standard Publishing—*Adult*
Urban Ministries—*All ages*

Denominational:
Advent Christian General Conference—*Adult*
American Baptist (Judson Press)—*Adult*
Church of God in Christ (Church of God in Christ Publishing House)—*Adult*
Church of Christ Holiness—*Adult*
Church of God (Warner Press)—*Adult*
Church of God by Faith—*Adult*
National Baptist Convention of America (Boyd)—*All ages*
National Primitive Baptist Convention—*Adult*
Presbyterian Church (U.S.A.) (Bible Discovery Series—Presbyterian Publishing House or P.R.E.M.)—*Adult*
Progressive National Baptist Convention—*Adult*
Union Gospel Press—*All ages*
United Holy Church of America—*Adult*
United Methodist Church (Cokesbury)—*All ages*

GOD'S REVELATION TO MOSES

BACKGROUND SCRIPTURE: Exodus 3
DEVOTIONAL READING: Luke 20:34-40

KEY VERSE: [The Lord] said, "I am the God of thy father, the God of Abraham, the God of Isaac, and the God of Jacob. And Moses hid his face; for he was afraid to look upon God." (Exodus 3:6)

KING JAMES VERSION

EXODUS 3:1 Now Moses kept the flock of Jethro his father in law, the priest of Midian: and he led the flock to the backside of the desert, and came to the mountain of God, even to Horeb. 2 And the angel of the LORD appeared unto him in a flame of fire out of the midst of a bush: and he looked, and, behold, the bush burned with fire, and the bush was not consumed. 3 And Moses said, I will now turn aside, and see this great sight, why the bush is not burnt. 4 And when the LORD saw that he turned aside to see, God called unto him out of the midst of the bush, and said, Moses, Moses. And he said, Here am I. 5 And he said, Draw not nigh hither: put off thy shoes from off thy feet, for the place whereon thou standest is holy ground. 6 Moreover he said, I am the God of thy father, the God of Abraham, the God of Isaac, and the God of Jacob. And Moses hid his face; for he was afraid to look upon God. . . .

13 And Moses said unto God, Behold, when I come unto the children of Israel, and shall say unto them, The God of your fathers hath sent me unto you; and they shall say to me, What is his name? what shall I say unto them? 14 And God said unto Moses, I AM THAT I AM: and he said, Thus shalt thou say unto the children of Israel, I AM hath sent me unto you. 15 And God said moreover unto Moses, Thus shalt thou say unto the children of Israel, The LORD God of your fathers, the God of Abraham, the God of Isaac, and the God of Jacob, hath sent me unto you: this is my name for ever, and this is my memorial unto all generations.

NEW REVISED STANDARD VERSION

EXODUS 3:1 Moses was keeping the flock of his father-in-law Jethro, the priest of Midian; he led his flock beyond the wilderness, and came to Horeb, the mountain of God. 2 There the angel of the LORD appeared to him in a flame of fire out of a bush; he looked, and the bush was blazing, yet it was not consumed. 3 Then Moses said, "I must turn aside and look at this great sight, and see why the bush is not burned up." 4 When the LORD saw that he had turned aside to see, God called to him out of the bush, "Moses, Moses!" And he said, "Here I am." 5 Then he said, "Come no closer! Remove the sandals from your feet, for the place on which you are standing is holy ground." 6 He said further, "I am the God of your father, the God of Abraham, the God of Isaac, and the God of Jacob." And Moses hid his face, for he was afraid to look at God. . . .

13 But Moses said to God, "If I come to the Israelites and say to them, 'The God of your ancestors has sent me to you,' and they ask me, 'What is his name?' what shall I say to them?" 14 God said to Moses, "I Am Who I Am." He said further, "Thus you shall say to the Israelites, 'I Am has sent me to you.'" 15 God also said to Moses, "Thus you shall say to the Israelites, 'The LORD, the God of your ancestors, the God of Abraham, the God of Isaac, and the God of Jacob, has sent me to you':

This is my name forever,
and this my title for all generations."

9

HOME BIBLE READINGS

Monday, August 30	Luke 20:34-40	*A God of the Living*
Tuesday, August 31	Numbers 23:18-26	*God Has Spoken*
Wednesday, September 1	Psalm 62:5-12	*Waiting for God to Speak*
Thursday, September 2	John 3:31-36	*God Speaks through the Son*
Friday, September 3	Exodus 3:7-12	*God Knows Our Suffering*
Saturday, September 4	Exodus 3:16-22	*God Will Relieve Our Misery*
Sunday, September 5	Exodus 3:1-6, 13-15	*God Speaks and Reveals*

BACKGROUND

Despite its historical significance, the exact location of "Horeb" (Exod. 3:1) remains unresolved. Several suggestions have been made to identify the mountain. One possibility is that Horeb is just another name for Mount Sinai, the place where God met Moses after the Red Sea crossing and gave the Hebrews the law. If that is true, then Horeb may be one of the many mountains on the Sinai peninsula suggested as Mount Sinai. These include Jebel Serbal, Jebel Helal, and Jebel Musa ("mountain of Moses").

Since the fourth century of the common era, a continuous Christian tradition has identified Jebel Musa (which is 7,363 feet at its peak) as the site of Mount Sinai. Just to the north of this mountain is a valley that is two miles long and opens into a plain that is about one mile wide. This area would have served well as a camp for the Hebrews while Moses visited the mountain to receive the law (Exod. 19). Another related tradition says that Horeb and Sinai are separate peaks close to each other. Ras es-Safsaf, a mountain peak (which is 6,540 feet at its summit) connected by a ridge to Jebel Musa, is then identified as Horeb. Still another suggestion is that Horeb and Sinai are the same names for one mountain called Jebel al-Lawz. Support for this idea comes from the apostle Paul's identification of Mount Sinai as "in Arabia" (Gal. 4:25) and from the mountain's possible nearness to where Moses was tending Jethro's flocks (Exod. 3:1).

NOTES ON THE PRINTED TEXT

When he was about 80, Moses apparently drove his flock into the wilderness far from Jethro's camp in an attempt to find sufficient grazing land for the animals. Moses stopped at Horeb, "the mountain of God" (Exod. 3:1). Little did Moses know that though he was now leading Jethro's little flock to this mountain, he would one day lead the much larger flock of God (the Israelites) to the same mountain. As Moses watched over Jethro's sheep, the "angel of the LORD" (vs. 2) manifested himself. The original can also be rendered "the messenger (or representative) of Yahweh." Previously, this designation was used in Genesis (see 16:7-13; 21:17; 22:11-18). Some think the expression refers to the Lord, for it often seems to be used interchangeably with the name of God. Others suggest the phrase refers to the Messiah before His birth at Bethlehem.

Moses also noticed a strange sight—a blazing bush (Exod. 3:2). As he scrutinized the bush from a distance, he realized that, though the bush was engulfed in flames, it was not consumed. In the desert, the wild acacia or thornbush is generally dry and brittle. A single spark can ignite such a bush, and it will burn rapidly with a great crackling. But because this particular bush continued burning, Moses decided to move closer and investigate the phenomenon (vs. 3). The Lord's messenger saw Moses coming to take a closer look at the amazing sight unfolding before his eyes. Suddenly, a voice from within the burning bush called out, "Moses, Moses" (vs. 4). The repetition of his name was intended for emphasis. It underscored that the divine appeal was immediate, personal, and direct. Moses, no doubt surprised to hear a voice, simply responded, "Here am I." This reply shows trust and availability. It was the same response that Abraham gave when the Lord asked him to sacrifice Isaac (Gen. 22:1, 11), and that Jacob gave to God when He spoke in a nighttime vision (46:2).

God then gave Moses two instructions. The Lord told him not to come any closer toward the bush and to remove his sandals (Exod. 3:5). The symbolic act of removing sandals would have been meaningful to one living in Old Testament times. People often removed sandals when entering a house, because sandals could bring dust and dirt into the home. Taking off one's sandals would be a way of recognizing one's personal uncleanness in the presence of holiness. In the current situation, the reason for the instructions was that the ground on which Moses stood was holy due to God's presence. Moses obeyed the instructions given to him, even though the voice from the bush had not yet identified itself. Then the speaker told Moses that He was the God of Moses' ancestors (vs. 6). He learned that Abraham, Isaac, and Jacob worshiped the Lord as their covenant God. With this statement, God instructed Moses about eternal life. The ancestors of the Hebrews still lived, even though their bodies had been dead for hundreds of years.

Jesus used this passage from Exodus when confronting the Sadducees over their disbelief in the resurrection. Because of God's words to Moses at the bush ablaze with fire, Jesus argued that they should have believed in the resurrection. The itinerant preacher from Nazareth explained that the Lord is the God of the living, not the dead (Matt. 22:32). In short, the deceased ancestors of God's people were alive with Him, even when He spoke to Moses. The mention of the patriarchs also brought to mind the covenant God had made with Abraham, Isaac, and Jacob. The Lord still honored that covenant and would rescue His people because of it, and He would do so through Moses. The latter, upon hearing the Lord's revelation of His identity, covered his face with his hands, for he was afraid to cast his gaze on the divine (Exod. 3:6). Moses' acting on his fear was well-founded in view of the ancient belief that no one can see God and live (see 33:20). Moses no doubt feared for his life when he realized he was in God's presence.

God next revealed to Moses the purpose of His appearing. He intended to deliver His people from their Egyptian taskmasters. God would use Moses to bring about the rescue and lead them to the rich and fertile land of Canaan (3:7-12). In short, the Lord would prove His care for His people by delivering and redeeming them from bondage. Despite these truths, Moses still wasn't quite convinced that he should be God's instrument. Moses proposed a hypothetical situation in which the Israelites asked him the name of the God who had dispatched him. Moses inquired of God as to how he should answer (vs. 13). Moses' proposed question—"What is his name?"—probably had little to do with learning God's identity. The latter had already been revealed when the Lord had called Himself the God of Abraham, Isaac, and Jacob (see vs. 6). Moses wanted to know what God's new revelation of Himself would mean to the oppressed Israelites. They would be more concerned about God's character than about His title or name.

In response to Moses' question, God said, "I AM THAT I AM" (vs. 14). This verse can also be rendered "I will be what I will be." Though the name "I AM" may seem odd to the modern ear, Moses apparently understood what God was saying to him. The name "I AM" comes from a Hebrew verb that means "to exist" or "to be" and is the basis for the proper noun *Yahweh*, which is translated "LORD" in verse 15. The latter was God's unique, deeply personal name that carried implications of the covenant relationship between Himself and the people of Israel.

Verse 14 is the only place in the Old Testament where the significance of the divine name is touched on. In essence, the name *Yahweh* signifies that God is pure being. Moreover, He is the self-existent one. God never came into being at any point in time, for He has always existed. To know God—the "I AM"—is to know the eternal one. This knowledge of God's nature and character would be Moses' strength. Because the divine name has historically been held in such awe and reverence, English translators printed the rendering of Yahweh in small capital letters, so that it appears in many Bibles as "LORD" (vs. 15). Thus, when we see the English word "LORD" in the Bible, we know that the Hebrew term in the original text was Yahweh.

Next, God directed Moses to tell the Israelites that Yahweh, the God of their ancestors—including the patriarchs Abraham, Isaac, and Jacob—had dispatched Moses to them. The patriarchal names would have captured the attention of the Israelites, for it was to Abraham, Isaac, and Jacob that God had revealed His covenant. From one generation to the next, God would be known and memorialized as "the LORD," who was faithful to His covenant promises made to the people of Israel. Then God instructed Moses to go back to Egypt and bring together the elders (or leaders) of Israel. Moses was to tell these leaders was that "the LORD" (vs. 16) had seen their misery and would deliver them from bondage. Indeed, God planned to lead them to a rich and fertile land (vs. 17; see vs. 8).

SUGGESTIONS TO TEACHERS

Anyone becoming a naturalized citizen of the United States is required to learn the basic history of the nation. Citizenship means knowing and appreciating the events that brought the U.S. into existence. The same is true with our faith. To be members of God's family, we must understand the account of His dealings with His people. For example, Israel's departure from Egypt was a pivotal event. Although we will be discussing Moses as the key human leader in this great drama, we should remember that God was the central character.

1. INEXPLICABLE REVELATION. Moses' encounter with the Lord through the burning bush cannot be explained away by stating that it was a species of brilliant thornbush found in Sinai or the reflection of the sunlight on the bush. No, Moses had met the living God, and His holy presence defied explanation. Ask your students to share why they think God's presence in their lives sometimes is beyond explanation.

2. UNEXPECTED ROLE. God said that He was sending Moses to Pharaoh to lead the Israelites out of Egypt. This suggests that God's encounters with us usually include a call to serve. The tasks that He gives us to do sometimes are not what we might expect or desire. Discuss with the class members some of the unexpected jobs God has had them do in the past.

3. UNDERSTANDABLE RELUCTANCE. Moses had no wish to go back to Egypt, where he was a wanted fugitive for murdering an Egyptian official. At times, we might drag our feet or plead that we are unable to carry out what the Lord wants us to do. But God sweeps aside our excuses!

4. UNMISTAKABLE REALIZATION. When Moses balked at appearing before Pharaoh, the Lord reassured him that he would not be alone. Regardless of how difficult or unpleasant the situation might get, God would give him success. Let the students know that God continues to help believers to do His will. With His strength and companionship, they can serve Him with confidence!

FOR ADULTS

■ **TOPIC:** No Excuses

■ **QUESTIONS:** 1. What was extraordinary about the blazing bush that Moses saw? 2. Why did Moses, upon hearing the Lord's revelation of His identity, cover his face with his hands? 3. What prompted God to set in motion a plan to deliver the Israelites from bondage? 4. In what ways did God deal with Moses' sense of inadequacy? 5. How can the promise of God encourage you to do tasks for Him that seem too difficult to handle?

■ **ILLUSTRATIONS:**

Hearing Requires Listening! Moses, Israel's liberator, did not have a business card when he introduced himself to Pharaoh after a 40-year flight. Moses did have a striking introduction: "I AM hath sent me unto you" (Exod. 3:14). Moses listened to it and heeded it.

The account behind Moses' "calling card" (of sorts) began with a flaming desert bush that was not consumed. Then God spoke to Moses. Initially, Moses concocted excuses about his alleged unsuitability for the task. Eventually, though, he accepted God's call to free His people.

Believers of all generations have also learned that God intervenes to establish His authority in their lives. They have been sufficiently impressed, as Moses was, to discover, listen to, and obey what God Himself has in mind.

Burning but Not Consumed. Many of our Protestant forebears in Europe identified closely with God's call to Moses to serve Him obediently. In fact, many in the Reformed tradition—such as the Scots, the Irish, the Huguenots, and the Magyars—depict a burning bush on their church's official seal or insignia.

The latter often has the Latin inscription, *Nec Tamen Consumebatur*. This means, in effect, "burning but not consumed." The phrase refers to the Lord's mysterious call to His people and His holy, indescribable presence among them. God's fire was understood to burn on without end, and continued to confront them. As Hebrews 12:29 says, "our God is a consuming fire."

God Will Not Forsake Us. Henry Jacobsen tells the story of six Scottish miners who were forced to make a life-and-death decision. They were trapped about 1,500 feet below ground when the shaft in which they were working collapsed.

A seventh miner was caught in the debris from the cave-in, but their attempts to rescue him were hampered by the mud and water that was pouring into the shaft. There was still a way out, but it would soon be closed off. Reluctantly and with great agony, the miners chose to leave their co-worker to die in the shaft rather than lose their own lives trying to save him.

God is never forced to forsake one of His children. No matter how desperate the situation may be or how great the problems we face, He stays beside us, hearing our prayers and meeting our needs in His time and in His way. We may feel abandoned, but we will never really be abandoned.

FOR YOUTH

■ TOPIC: Name Calling

■ QUESTIONS: 1. How did God make His presence known to Moses, and what was unusual about it? 2. How do you think you would have responded if God revealed Himself to you in a burning bush? 3. In what way did Moses' initial response show that he wanted to hear and heed the Lord? 4. Why do you think Moses felt inadequate when God directed him to appear before Pharaoh and liberate the Israelites? 5. What are some ways that God cares for believers today?

■ ILLUSTRATIONS:

Burning Questions. Life is filled with issues and decisions that can perplex us. Perhaps one of the most baffling is discerning the call of God. What is it like? Is it a voice from a flaming bush repeating our name? A voice out of a dazzling, blinding light? A voice from God's holy throne? A voice calling our name at night? That's what it was like for Moses, Paul, Isaiah, and Samuel, but not necessarily for us.

On some occasions, God might get our attention in a spectacular way, but that's not the norm. The important issue is not the setting, but the deep-seated assurance that we really can discern the call of God. But how? It occurs when we read the Bible and contemplate its words; when we worship; when we do what we know we are supposed to do; when we obey God's moral and spiritual precepts; when we pray; and when we talk with other believers.

We can ask "What should I do, Lord?" with the complete assurance that God will show the way. The one essential ingredient to discern God's call is a commitment to do His will.

Unexpected Call. A number of years ago in Atlanta, a young businessman named Jack Stephens got a call from a friend heading a local boys' club. The man asked Jack to drive a youngster and his mother to the hospital. Jack agreed, and met the mother and her boy at their house, which was not far from his home. (Jack learned that the boy had leukemia and that the disease was in its final stages.)

Early the next day as the three rode to the hospital, the boy was stretched out on his mother's lap, and his feet extended over to Jack. Jack glanced down at the child, and their eyes met. "Are you God?" the boy asked. Though startled by the question, Jack answered, "No, son. Why do you ask?" The boy responded, "My mother said that God would come and take me away with Him."

Jack was shaken by the reply. Even more distressing was the fact that a week later, the boy went home to be with the Lord. Despite the sadness of the boy's death, Jack found himself drawn to God in a way that he had not expected. The question, "Are you God?" was like a voice from the "burning bush" in Jack's life. He realized that he had to do more for the Lord with his life. Eventually, Jack became the director of the Joseph B. Whitehead Memorial Boys' Club in Atlanta, Georgia.

Perhaps the voice of God is calling from the "burning bush" in your life. The Lord might be summoning you to do more than just enjoy a life of ease with other believers in your church. God might be calling you to be His representative to those in this world who are suffering and spiritually lost. Perhaps the Lord wants you to be His agent among the helpless and forgotten, whom He remembers.

Do you feel overwhelmed by such a prospect? You don't need to be, for God will remain with you every step of the way, especially as you listen to and heed Him.

Sacred Ground? Tourists pass at a rate of 1,200 people per hour. Often they leave flowers or teddy bears and—much to the chagrin of the caretakers—even peel the bark off of nearby trees where they write messages in red ink. The spot is the bronze plaque marking Elvis Presley's grave at Graceland. Karen Christ of Canton, Ohio, called the ground "sacred." Fay Mathany of Richmond, Virginia, feels close to Elvis at this spot.

When Moses stood before the burning bush, he was filled with awe, but not because he was near the spot where a dead person had been buried. Rather, he knew that he was in the presence of the holy and living God. The ground was sacred because God had made His presence known there. At different times in your life you will sense God's holy presence. In those moments, you should show Him respect, sincerity, and reverence.

GOD'S COVENANT WITH ISRAEL

BACKGROUND SCRIPTURE: Exodus 20
DEVOTIONAL READING: John 1:14-18

KEY VERSES: I am the LORD thy God . . . Thou
shalt have no other gods before me. (Exodus 20:2-3)

KING JAMES VERSION

EXODUS 20:1 And God spake all these words, saying,
2 I am the LORD thy God, which have brought thee out
of the land of Egypt, out of the house of bondage.
3 Thou shalt have no other gods before me. 4 Thou shalt
not make unto thee any graven image, or any likeness of
any thing that is in heaven above, or that is in the earth
beneath, or that is in the water under the earth: 5 Thou
shalt not bow down thyself to them, nor serve them: for I
the LORD thy God am a jealous God, visiting the iniquity
of the fathers upon the children unto the third and fourth
generation of them that hate me; 6 And shewing mercy
unto thousands of them that love me, and keep my commandments. 7 Thou shalt not take the name of the LORD
thy God in vain; for the LORD will not hold him guiltless
that taketh his name in vain. 8 Remember the sabbath
day, to keep it holy. 9 Six days shalt thou labour, and do
all thy work: 10 But the seventh day is the sabbath of the
LORD thy God: in it thou shalt not do any work, thou,
nor thy son, nor thy daughter, thy manservant, nor thy
maidservant, nor thy cattle, nor thy stranger that is within thy gates: 11 For in six days the LORD made heaven
and earth, the sea, and all that in them is, and rested the
seventh day: wherefore the LORD blessed the sabbath
day, and hallowed it.

NEW REVISED STANDARD VERSION

EXODUS 20:1 Then God spoke all these words:
2 I am the LORD your God, who brought you out of the
land of Egypt, out of the house of slavery; 3 you shall
have no other gods before me.
4 You shall not make for yourself an idol, whether in
the form of anything that is in heaven above, or that is on
the earth beneath, or that is in the water under the earth.
5 You shall not bow down to them or worship them; for I
the LORD your God am a jealous God, punishing children for the iniquity of parents, to the third and the
fourth generation of those who reject me, 6 but showing
steadfast love to the thousandth generation of those who
love me and keep my commandments.
7 You shall not make wrongful use of the name of the
LORD your God, for the LORD will not acquit anyone
who misuses his name.
8 Remember the sabbath day, and keep it holy. 9 For
six days you shall labour and do all your work. 10 But
the seventh day is a sabbath to the LORD your God; you
shall not do any work—you, your son or your daughter,
your male or female slave, your livestock, or the alien
resident in your towns. 11 For in six days the LORD
made heaven and earth, the sea, and all that is in them,
but rested the seventh day; therefore the LORD blessed
the sabbath day and consecrated it.

Monday, September 6	Psalm 119:73-77	*Your Law Is My Delight*
Tuesday, September 7	Proverbs 7:1-5	*The Tablet of Your Heart*
Wednesday, September 8	John 1:14-18	*The Law with Grace and Truth*
Thursday, September 9	Romans 10:5-13	*Righteousness That Comes from Faith*
Friday, September 10	Galatians 2:15-21	*Justified through Faith*
Saturday, September 11	Exodus 20:12-21	*God's Claims on Our Relationships*
Sunday, September 12	Exodus 20:1-11	*God's Claims on Us*

BACKGROUND

The Ten Commandments, or Decalogue, are regarded by many as the ethical directives that God spoke to Moses and which God wrote on stone tablets at Mount Sinai (see Exod. 19). Like many other ancient political treaties and royal covenants, the Decalogue begins with a preamble in which the great King identified Himself (Exod. 20:1-2; Deut. 5:6). Yahweh declared that He was the Lord and God of Israel.

The preamble is followed by a brief historical prologue. In this section, Yahweh summarized the gracious acts He had displayed toward His covenant people. He noted that He had rescued them from Egypt, the land of slavery (Exod. 20:2; Deut. 5:6). The Lord was not just reviewing Israel's past to give a history lesson. Rather, He recounted the past to instill a sense of gratitude in His people. God also used the epic events of the past to form the foundation for the Israelites' obligations to remain obedient to the stipulations of His covenant with them. Yahweh next delineated the stipulations of the covenant He was making with His people. The Lord expected His subjects to obey these directives, which were ten in number (Exod. 20:3-17; Deut. 5:1-3, 7-21).

NOTES ON THE PRINTED TEXT

The Lord began the Ten Commandments by identifying Himself (Exod. 20:1) and declaring how He graciously redeemed His chosen people from bondage in Egypt (vs. 2). Verse 3 (see Deut. 5:7) records the first stipulation of the Decalogue. In short, it is a prohibition against serving false gods. The Hebrew can be rendered "before My face," "against Me," or "in hostility toward Me." The idea is that the Lord had exclusively claimed the Israelites as His own. Thus He would permit no rivals—whether real or imagined—in His presence. Such would create a hostile dynamic, one that would go against God and His relationship with His people.

The second commandment of the Decalogue is a prohibition against venerating idols. Whereas the first commandment deals with the issue of who is the true and living God, the second commandment focuses on how He is to be worshiped. Put another way, while the opening injunction discloses the true object of the believers' worship, the subsequent injunction reveals the correct way in which worship is to be undertaken. The latter emphasis is seen in the Hebrew noun rendered "graven image" (Exod. 20:4), which means "to carve out" or "to hew." It refers to a variety of idols one may cut or carve from wood, stone, metal, and pottery for use as an object of veneration. In ancient times, many people believed gods could reside in these materials. Jewelers and other workers would make miniature amulets and scarabs from a variety of stones. Idols made from silver and gold might be cast hollow because of the value of the metal. Bronze or lead images were often overlaid with silver or gold.

The Hebrew noun rendered "likeness" can also be translated "form" or "representation." The idea is that God banned the Israelites from making idols that bore the resemblance of anything God had created. This included whatever was seen in the sky (such as the sun, moon, stars, and birds), on the earth (such as animals), and in the waters below (such as fish, crocodiles, and other aquatic life). All these entities were worshiped by people in ancient times. The Lord prohibited the Israelites from serving these things and from falling prostrate before them in worship (vs. 5). Those who worshiped crude approximations of the Creator reduced Him to the substance of creation, for the image was made from it, not Him. Thus idol-worship fundamentally undermined the concept of God as the transcendent Lord. The object gave the devotees the false idea that they were physically close to the deity and that they could somehow harness its power.

The Lord declared that to create a false impression of Him would be to misrepresent Him. He wanted no challengers to compete with Him for His people's love and loyalty. Their reverence and respect were to be placed in Him alone—just as a relationship between a husband and wife. These truths are borne out by the Hebrew adjective translated "jealous." It comes from a verb that means "to act zealously" or "to be zealous." Emotional intensity forms the backdrop of both the verb and the adjective. While envy is a concept associated with these terms, such a notion is alien to God. The Lord's exclusive claim on His people is being stressed in verse 5. The idea is that Yahweh maintained a burning zeal and passion for them and would deal with all rivals firmly.

Thus, any Israelites who violated the second commandment or encouraged its infraction among others would bring disastrous consequences upon themselves and their loved ones. The Hebrew verb rendered "visiting" carries the sense of seeking something out to bring about affliction. In Exodus 20:5 and Deuteronomy 5:9, the term conveys the idea of God, in His righteousness, bringing punishment upon the transgressors of the second commandment. The noun translated "iniquity" can also be rendered "sin" and "transgression." The ideas of perversion and evil were closely related to the noun. The verb translated "hate" connotes such strong emotions as disdain, ill will, and abhorrence between two parties. Expressed differently, the noun conveys the ideas of opposing, detesting, or despising others. The objects of this emotion are avoided at all costs. Whereas love attracts and joins together, hatred repudiates and divides.

The preceding observations indicate that those who venerated false deities instead of God were rejecting His ownership and rulership in their lives. Such individuals spurned the covenant that the Lord had made with the Israelites. The transgressors also disdained the moral fabric of Israelite society and culture. The penalty for such idolatry was divine punishment among family members living in close proximity to one another and spanning up to possibly three or four generations. Exodus 20:6 spotlights a different outcome for God's people, to whom He shows "love." The latter renders a Hebrew noun that includes the notions of fidelity, loyalty, faithfulness, commitment, and mercy. When used in reference to God, the term points to Him providing for His people's needs, watching over them, and protecting them. In turn, they respond in service, reverence, and devotion.

Such commitment is evident in the Hebrew verb rendered "keep." The latter can also be translated "to watch over," "to take care of," "to preserve," and "to protect." With respect to God's people, they were to give heed to the ordinances and decrees of His covenant with them. In fact, such obedience formed the foundation of their worship and service. This mindset can be found in the noun translated "commandments." Depending on the context in which the term is used, it can refer to a "commission" (as in to carry out an assigned task), an individual directive, or an entire set of edicts. With respect to the Lord's decrees, the noun denotes the specific stipulations of the Mosaic covenant. In a more general sense, the verse teaches that those who maintained their wholehearted loyalty to God experienced the same from Him for generations to follow. For instance, a person's example of complete allegiance, continuing trust, and consistent obedience could influence many physical descendants to live in a similar manner. If these descendants devoted themselves to the Lord, they too would experience His unfailing love in their lives. The "thousands" mentioned in verse 6 stands in sharp contrast to the "third and fourth generation" referred to in verse 5.

The third commandment of the Decalogue is a prohibition against misusing the Lord's name (vs. 7). In Old Testament times, the names of people were not simply a convenient form of identification, but practically equivalent to the bearer of the title (see 1 Sam. 25:25). Likewise, there is an essential identity between God and His name (see Ps. 18:49; Isa. 25:1; Mal. 3:16). Furthermore, the Lord's name is characterized by sacredness and reflects the fact that He is infinitely exalted as well as set apart from His creation. In addition, He is morally pure and perfect in the most unsurpassed way. The holiness of God dictated that any reference the Israelites made to Him had to be done in a manner that expressed reverence and respect. This truth is evident in the Hebrew noun rendered "take . . . in vain" (Exod. 20:7). The word can also be translated "worthless," "deceit," "emptiness," and "falsehood."

People in the ancient Near East commonly believed that what someone said could either positively or negatively affect the outcome of a situation. Correspondingly, to utter the divine name meant invoking all that it represented in terms of God's identity and will. The third commandment banned the practice of associating Yahweh's powers and purposes with what someone declared and the objective connected with it. To do otherwise would represent a false claim to God's endorsement of what one intended to do. To sum up, Exodus 20:7 and Deuteronomy 5:11 forbid the use of God's name in false worship, for incantation or divination, as well as for attesting falsehood or speaking irreverently (see Lev. 19:12; Deut. 28:58). The Lord regarded the knowledge of His name to be a privilege, for it meant that the Israelites did not venerate an unknown, remote deity, but rather someone whose personal name they knew.

Since God's name represents the essence of His person (which is holy), to use it carelessly, thoughtlessly, or by rote was an offense to Him. The Israelites were not to regard God's reputation as being empty, meaningless, or worthless. Anyone who displayed such a reckless attitude toward the Lord would be held guilty of dishonoring Him and would one day be punished by Him. This truth is stressed by the Hebrew verb rendered "guiltless" (Exod. 20:7), which can also be translated "leave unpunished." The idea is that God would not acquit the violator of the third commandment. He would charge transgressors with wrongdoing and discipline them accordingly.

The fourth commandment of the Decalogue is an injunction to remember the Sabbath and observe it as a holy day (Exod. 20:8-11; Deut. 5:12-15). Because being holy means being distinct, keeping the Sabbath day holy involved observing or celebrating it differently than the other six days of the week. This was done by everyone in an Israelite household ceasing from their labor on the Sabbath. (The Hebrew noun translated "Sabbath" means "to cease" or "to rest.") The foundation for this commandment was that God created the universe in six days and rested on the seventh (Gen. 2:2-3). God did not intend for the Sabbath to be a day in which His people slept all day and refused to do anything. Rather, it was meant to be a day of spiritual service on which His people diligently focused on the Lord and worshiped Him.

SUGGESTIONS TO TEACHERS

How many of the Ten Commandments can your students recite? You may be surprised at what they might list. This week's lesson offers a long-overdue opportunity for the class to review God's ethical injunctions.

1. REMINDER OF THE DIVINE DELIVERANCE. God established the covenant at Mount Sinai after He reminded the people how He had redeemed them from slavery in Egypt. Our covenanted relationship with the Lord stems from His gracious acts on our behalf, particularly His sacrificial love through Christ. We should respond by exclusively worshiping and serving the Lord.

2. REITERATION OF THE DIVINE DECISION. God called the Israelites to be a kingdom of priests and a holy nation. Have your students explain what these words should mean to God's people today (see 1 Pet. 2:9-10).

3. RESPONSE TO THE DIVINE DICTATES. Have your students spend time exploring some of the ways in which God's ordinances and decrees apply to believers today.

4. RESPECT FOR THE DIVINE DEMANDS. Jesus said that loving God was the first commandment, and that the second was loving other people (Mark 12:29-31). Have your class members consider where their relationships with others might be frayed and what they can do to bring reconciliation.

FOR ADULTS

■ TOPIC: Who's the Boss?

■ QUESTIONS: 1. Why did the Israelites need to be reminded that God was their Lord? 2. Why did the Lord prohibit His people from serving false gods? 3. What might motivate people today to venerate things in creation rather than the Creator? 4. What are some ways that the Lord's name can be misused? 5. What does it mean for believers to "remember the sabbath day" (Exod. 20:8)?

■ ILLUSTRATIONS:

Accepting Rules for Living. Scientists have gone to great efforts in establishing precise standards for determining the exactness of measurements we use every day. For example, in the metric system, the meter is now precisely based on the speed of light, and the second is based on the oscillation of a cesium atom. The international standard for the kilogram is a platinum-iridium cylinder kept in the Bureau International des Poids et Measures (The International Bureau of Weights and Measures) in Paris.

The fine-tuned orderliness of the universe is due to the work of the Creator. He not only brought everything into existence, but also sets the rules for living. Because He is in charge, it is appropriate for Him to expect saved adults to heed His ethical precepts, which are recorded in the Ten Commandments. Indeed, the latter reflects His unchanging standard, against which human conduct must be measured. Any deviation from these basic norms brings eventual problems and a flawed existence.

Expectations Defined. Cecil B. DeMille, creator of the films *The Ten Commandments*, *Ben-Hur*, and *Cleopatra*, was one of Hollywood's directing geniuses. He was also known for his religious devotion and his interest in biblical archaeology. So strong was his conviction that each menu in the commissary carried the message: "Cecil B. DeMille says, 'Don't just act the Ten Commandments. Live them.'" Underneath this line was printed each of the commandments.

DeMille knew that all people search for meaning and purpose in life—and boundaries to behavior. The limits must be defined. With this understanding, DeMille acted to daily remind his employees of God's law, much as Moses reminded the people of God's expectations.

God's Promise to Israel. On January 20, 2009, Barack Obama was sworn in as the 43rd president of the United States. In contrast to his predecessors, he was the first African American to be elected to the highest office in the land. Nothing is quite as solemn as the swearing in of a new president. The newly elected official takes important vows that all citizens expect him or her to keep.

From an eternal perspective, our most solemn vows are those we make to God and His people. Throughout the Bible, God called the Israelites to obedience. For instance, those encamped at the base of Mount Sinai pledged to do all that the Lord commanded them. They willingly did so because of the promises that God made to them.

The apostles also consistently taught that Jesus' followers are expected to obey Him. They knew that coming to faith in the Messiah was not just a religious formality. Rather, if we take the promises and exhortations of God's Word seriously, we pledge to follow Him exclusively. That is the only sure way to find the Lord's blessing and joy.

FOR YOUTH

■ TOPIC: The Big Ten

■ QUESTIONS: 1. Why was it important for the Israelites to recall God's deliverance of them from Egypt? 2. What are some ways that people today worship false gods? 3. In what sense is God "jealous" (Exod. 20:5)? 4. How can we, as believers, encourage respect for the Lord's name among our peers? 5. Why was the Sabbath so important to the Israelites?

■ ILLUSTRATIONS:

What Are the Limits? The only restrictions on youth used to be the age of driving, drinking, and voting. No more. The rules now extend to what they can't wear to school, the weapons and drugs they can't carry into school, the hours they can't keep, the music they can't listen to, and the substances they can't abuse.

It's no use arguing that the reason for some of these rules is the safety and well-being of adolescents. If some youths had not started to carry habits of adult lawbreakers into school, the rules would not be necessary. In somewhat the same way, God saw the moral dangers the Israelites faced. He knew the world was filled with idolaters, murderers, thieves, and adulterers. Therefore, His people needed a set of rules called the Ten Commandments. He set the limits so they would know what holiness means.

For Christian youth, their allegiance is to the Savior, for He atoned for their sins at Calvary and rescued them from ungodly lifestyles. To get off to a good start, they need to know and obey the Ten Commandments.

Only the Best? Humorist and editor Bennett Cerf enjoyed telling about a book titled *The Ten Commandments,* which was supposed to be distributed among service personnel during World War II. When the manuscript arrived, it was too long. One of the editors looked at the weighty tome, smiled, and joked, "I know what we can do. We'll pick out five of them and call the book *A Treasury of the World's Best Commandments!*"

But we aren't permitted to select the commandments we may like while ignoring the rest. We can't create our little treasury of favorites, or pick and choose the duties we like or dislike the most. All 10 commands are from the Lord.

Mistaken Understanding. Tim Robbins, the film director who has produced several acclaimed movies, was interviewed at the Berlin Film Festival in 1996 about his motion picture entitled *Dead Man Walking*. When asked about the place of God and faith, this director mumbled, "I believe in . . . er . . . that there are people who live highly enlightened lives and who achieve a certain level of spirituality in connection with a force of goodness. And because these people have walked the earth, I believe that they have created God."

Nothing could be further from what the Bible teaches! Scripture reveals that God created the universe and humankind, not the other way around. This means that He is the sovereign Lord and that people exist to worship and serve Him. They show their love for Him by obeying the moral injunctions of His Word and loving others. They can do so only in His power and wisdom. Their motivation is not to exalt themselves but rather to glorify the Lord.

GOD VERSUS "GODS"

BACKGROUND SCRIPTURE: Exodus 32
DEVOTIONAL READING: John 5:39-47

KEY VERSE: [The Israelites] have turned aside quickly out of the way which I commanded them: they have made them a molten calf, and have worshipped it, and have sacrificed thereunto. (Exodus 32:8)

KING JAMES VERSION

EXODUS 32:1 And when the people saw that Moses delayed to come down out of the mount, the people gathered themselves together unto Aaron, and said unto him, Up, make us gods, which shall go before us; for as for this Moses, the man that brought us up out of the land of Egypt, we wot not what is become of him. 2 And Aaron said unto them, Break off the golden earrings, which are in the ears of your wives, of your sons, and of your daughters, and bring them unto me. 3 And all the people brake off the golden earrings which were in their ears, and brought them unto Aaron. 4 And he received them at their hand, and fashioned it with a graving tool, after he had made it a molten calf: and they said, These be thy gods, O Israel, which brought thee up out of the land of Egypt. 5 And when Aaron saw it, he built an altar before it; and Aaron made proclamation, and said, To morrow is a feast to the LORD. 6 And they rose up early on the morrow, and offered burnt offerings, and brought peace offerings; and the people sat down to eat and to drink, and rose up to play.

7 And the LORD said unto Moses, Go, get thee down; for thy people, which thou broughtest out of the land of Egypt, have corrupted themselves: 8 They have turned aside quickly out of the way which I commanded them: they have made them a molten calf, and have worshipped it, and have sacrificed thereunto, and said, These be thy gods, O Israel, which have brought thee up out of the land of Egypt. 9 And the LORD said unto Moses, I have seen this people, and, behold, it is a stiffnecked people: 10 Now therefore let me alone, that my wrath may wax hot against them, and that I may consume them: and I will make of thee a great nation.

NEW REVISED STANDARD VERSION

EXODUS 32:1 When the people saw that Moses delayed to come down from the mountain, the people gathered around Aaron, and said to him, "Come, make gods for us, who shall go before us; as for this Moses, the man who brought us up out of the land of Egypt, we do not know what has become of him." 2 Aaron said to them, "Take off the gold rings that are on the ears of your wives, your sons, and your daughters, and bring them to me." 3 So all the people took off the gold rings from their ears, and brought them to Aaron. 4 He took the gold from them, formed it in a mold, and cast an image of a calf; and they said, "These are your gods, O Israel, who brought you up out of the land of Egypt!" 5 When Aaron saw this, he built an altar before it; and Aaron made proclamation and said, "Tomorrow shall be a festival to the LORD." 6 They rose early the next day, and offered burnt offerings and brought sacrifices of well-being; and the people sat down to eat and drink, and rose up to revel.

7 The LORD said to Moses, "Go down at once! Your people, whom you brought up out of the land of Egypt, have acted perversely; 8 they have been quick to turn aside from the way that I commanded them; they have cast for themselves an image of a calf, and have worshipped it and sacrificed to it, and said, 'These are your gods, O Israel, who brought you up out of the land of Egypt!'" 9 The LORD said to Moses, "I have seen this people, how stiff-necked they are. 10 Now let me alone, so that my wrath may burn hot against them and I may consume them; and of you I will make a great nation."

HOME BIBLE READINGS

Monday, September 13	1 Corinthians 10:1-11	*Warnings against Idolatry*
Tuesday, September 14	1 Corinthians 10:14-21	*Flee from Idol Worship*
Wednesday, September 15	Psalm 135:13-18	*Idols—The Work of Human Hands*
Thursday, September 16	1 John 5:13-21	*Keep Yourselves from Idols*
Friday, September 17	Exodus 32:15-24	*Confronting Idolatry*
Saturday, September 18	Exodus 32:30-35	*The Consequence of Idolatry*
Sunday, September 19	Exodus 32:1-10	*The Infidelity of Idolatry*

BACKGROUND

An examination of the chapters leading up to Exodus 32 indicates that Moses had been on Mount Sinai—and had not been seen by the Israelites—for 40 days (24:18). During that time, God promised to give Moses tablets of stone containing the law while He met with him. So Moses, accompanied by Joshua, climbed farther up Mount Sinai and remained there 40 days and nights. There God revealed to Moses the materials that would be needed to put together the tabernacle. God also told Moses how to construct the various furnishings that would be placed in the shrine. When God had finished speaking with Moses on Mount Sinai, He presented him the two tablets of stone on which He had inscribed the Ten Commandments (see Deut. 9:9).

The biblical text states the tablets were "written with the finger of God" (Exod. 31:18; Deut. 9:10). Some Bible scholars say the Lord wrote on the tablets using supernatural phenomena. Others say He did so using a natural phenomenon, such as lightning. Still others say the "finger of God" simply represents the Lord's might and power. In ancient times, both parties making an agreement usually kept a copy of the covenant. For this reason, many Bible scholars think the two tablets given to Moses were actually duplicates. Though the stone tablets with the Ten Commandments inscribed on them have never been recovered, we do have God's Word to us as recorded in the Bible. And just as the ancient Israelites were responsible to obey laws of God inscribed on stone, so we are responsible to obey God's Word as it is recorded in Scripture.

NOTES ON THE PRINTED TEXT

Perhaps toward the latter part of Moses' extended absence (see Deut. 9:11), the Israelites grew anxious and impatient. They incorrectly concluded that the lawgiver would not be returning to guide them into the promised land. They dismissively referred to him as "this Moses" (Exod. 32:1) and seemed to minimize the fact that God had used him to bring the Israelites out of Egypt. Thus, the tribal and clan leaders went to Aaron, Moses' brother and the first high priest of Israel (see 4:14; 28:1-5). Aaron was married to Elisheba, the daughter of Amminadab (see

6:23). We can only imagine how intimidated Aaron must have felt when his Israelite peers gathered around him and demanded that he make new "gods" (32:1) to lead them into Canaan. Having lived in Egypt for a long time, the Israelites apparently could not get used to the truth that "God is a Spirit" (John 4:24) and dwells in "light which no man can approach" (1 Tim. 6:16). The people wanted something they could see with their own eyes, a deity with a face, one like all the other nations had.

Surprisingly, Aaron immediately granted the Israelites' request. He told the people to collect and give him their "golden earrings" (Exod. 32:2), which were probably part of the plunder they had taken from the Egyptians at the beginning of the Exodus (see 12:35-36). Just as personal items were to be contributed for the building of the tabernacle (25:1-7), now a collection was made for an idolatrous cause. It's difficult to know why Aaron proposed to use the gold earrings to make an idol. Perhaps he did not have the resolve of his brother to keep the wayward tendencies of the Israelites in check. It may also be that Aaron was stalling for time, especially if a group of malcontents were beginning to incite the people to rebel. Exodus 32:3 leaves the reader with the impression that it did not take the Israelites long to collect their gold jewelry and bring them to Aaron. In turn, he melted down the metal and poured the gold into a mold that was shaped like a young bull (vs. 4). In ancient Egyptian culture, the latter was a symbol of strength and vigor.

Some think that the calf-shaped idol was primarily made out of wood rather than solid gold. If so, Aaron plated the image with gold leaf and then used an engraving tool to further shape and form the exterior. Some Bible scholars claim this idol may have been of the Egyptian bull-god, Apis. Since the Israelites had spent more than four centuries in Egypt, they would have been familiar with this figure of a god. Others, however, assert the idol may have represented the bull into which the god Baal allegedly transformed himself on occasion. In any case, when the Israelites saw the idol, they proclaimed it to be their "god," who was responsible for rescuing them from Egypt. Both their statement and the statue violated the first two of the Ten Commandments (see Exod. 20:1-6; Deut. 5:6-10).

Once Aaron had completed the calf idol, he built an altar in front of it. Most likely, the platform was a crude structure hastily made out of field stones and dirt. Aaron proclaimed that a festival was to be held the following day in honor of the Lord (Exod. 32:5). The people, however, had a far different intention. The Israelites were so enthusiastic that they got up early the next morning and made sacrifices to their new idol. "Burnt offerings" (vs. 6) could have included bulls, rams, or male birds (see Lev. 1; 6:8-13; 8:18-21; 16:24). "Peace offerings" (Exod. 32:6) could include a variety of animals without physical defects from the people's flocks and herds (see Lev. 3; 7:11-34).

Next, the people sat down to consume their festive meal. Then, after they finished eating, Exodus 32:6 says the Israelites "rose up to play." Most likely, the latter included the practice of sexual immorality in the midst of the celebration. This type of orgy would have mirrored some of the ancient fertility rites practiced among the pagan Canaanites. Because God is omniscient, He knew His people were engaging in pagan revelry, even though He was talking with Moses at the time. In Egypt the enslaved Israelites had been indoctrinated with the idea of localized gods and goddesses who were not all-powerful or all-knowing. Despite the Lord's many miracles, the Israelites still had not grasped the concept of the one true God's infinite power and knowledge.

God directed Moses to descend from the mountain and return to the Israelite camp. Interestingly, the Lord referred to the group as "thy people" (vs. 7; see Deut. 9:12), rather than as His chosen people. God also stated that it was Moses who led the Israelites out of Egypt. Most likely, the Lord, in His anger against the people's sin, preferred not to acknowledge them as His own people. Tragically, in such a short span of time, the Israelites had "corrupted" (Exod. 32:7) themselves. The underlying Hebrew verb means "to spoil," "to ruin," or "to destroy." It's the same term used in Genesis 6:12 to describe the perversion of the earth's inhabitants living in Noah's day.

The issuance of the Ten Commandments was intended to prohibit the Israelites from practicing idolatry and immorality. Amazingly, though, in the span of a few weeks, the people abandoned what the Lord had declared in the Decalogue. They deliberately chose to make a bull calf out of melted gold. Then they prostrated themselves in veneration before the idol and offered sacrifices to it. They even had the audacity to declare that the statue was the embodiment of the deities who supposedly had led them out of Egypt (Exod. 32:8). The Lord declared to Moses that the Israelites were a "stiffnecked people" (Exod. 32:9; Deut. 9:13). In a figurative sense, it's as if God's chosen people were walking in His presence when He called out to them to head in a specific direction. Sadly, though, they refused to turn their necks to hear and heed what He declared. Because of their pride, they refused to submit to His will, choosing instead to resolutely travel down a sinful path. The Lord threatened to punish their rebellion by destroying them and building a new nation with Moses as its patriarch (Exod. 32:10; Deut. 9:14).

Moses, showing his love for the Israelites, reminded God of all He had done for them. Moses acknowledged that his peers were rebellious, but he also pointed out that in spite of their insurrection, they were God's chosen people (Exod. 32:11). Moses then pleaded for God's mercy, basing his appeal on two factors. First, if God destroyed the Israelites, the Egyptians and their false gods would be vindicated. The destruction of the Israelites would be cause for the Egyptians to mock the one true God, even calling Him evil (vs. 12). Second, God would be delaying His own plan for establishing His chosen people in the land of Canaan. Moses reminded the Lord of His promise to make Abraham's descendants innumerable and to bring His people into the promised land. For God to wipe out the Israelites and start over with Moses would be to delay that promise for many generations (vs. 13; see Gen. 12:7; 22:17).

Thanks to Moses' intercession, God did not bring the judgment He had threatened.

The Hebrew verb that is translated "repented" (Exod. 32:14) denotes a change in the response of God as a result of the action of those with whom He is dealing. In this case, it was Moses' intercession that made the difference. From this outcome we learn that God is not inflexible in His relationships with human beings. In this chapter, we clearly see the efficacy of intercession. Moses' petition on behalf of the Israelites should be an incentive to us regarding our intercessory prayers for others. After all, as James 5:16 says, "the effectual fervent prayer of a righteous man availeth much."

As we contemplate the nature of God's relationship with the Israelites, we discover several characteristics about Him. First, the Lord is sovereign over human affairs. He acted on behalf of His people to deliver them from oppression. Second, God cares for His people. He had seen His people suffering and this led Him to raise up Moses as a deliverer for the Israelites. Third, the Lord makes daily provisions for His people. During the Exodus, God satisfied the Israelites' needs for food and water. They could not have survived in the desert otherwise.

SUGGESTIONS TO TEACHERS

Being adults in our society, we are blessed with an incredible amount of independence. However, as wonderful as that freedom is, it also creates a minefield for us. It seems every direction we turn, temptations to our eyes, ego, and flesh confront us. "Just say no" may make for great advertising, but it is certainly difficult to do when we're trying to stare down an enticement to sin.

1. SMUGNESS LEADING TO VULNERABILITY. We all know believers who would never commit idolatry, adultery, theft, or murder, and yet their tempers are abominable or their tongues wag at both ends. They think their lives are holy and righteous, but observers would disagree. Satan gets a charge out of their self-satisfaction, but God grieves over them.

2. WISDOM IN BEING SELF-AWARE. Scripture often cautions believers to be aware of temptations around them. For instance, in 1 Corinthians 10:7, Paul warned against being idolaters by quoting Exodus 32:6. The apostle understood that believers tend to be even more vulnerable to temptation when they feel spiritually strong. If truth be told, some Christians incorrectly think that because they are spiritually mature, they won't be enticed to sin.

3. ADMITTING OUR WEAKNESSES. Believers who are thoroughly biblical in their theology and determined to please God in their lifestyles face temptations just as anyone else. Godly living is no more a matter of knowledge and willpower than is salvation. In fact, Satan probably takes particular delight in tripping up believers who think they are impervious to temptation.

4. TURNING TO GOD FOR HELP. We not only need to be more aware of the enticements we face, but even more important, we need to seek God's help in overcoming them. Mere knowledge of how we are being tempted will only make the enticement more desirable and us less resistant.

■ TOPIC: Keeping Faith

■ QUESTIONS: 1. Why do you think the Israelites would quickly abandon the Lord to venerate idols? 2. What could Aaron have done to resist the pressure from the Israelites to make an idol for them? 3. Which of the Ten Commandments did the Israelites violate? 4. Why would God propose to Moses that He wipe out the Israelites? 5. What kinds of false religions grip people today?

■ ILLUSTRATIONS:

Living Faith. How much faith is enough faith? Biblical insight into this matter can be found in Hebrews 11. Faith is never seen as a lever to demand things from God or a pretext to circumvent His will (which we find in the incident involving the Israelites' worship of the golden calf). Rather, faith is exemplified as enduring trust in God's promises, which prompts us to heed His commands.

Moreover, faith drives us to believe that eternal values are the most important. We keep looking for the city with eternal foundations and for a heavenly country. While that city and country are our eternal reward, we live by faith now according to God's standards of justice and holiness.

This means that our faith moves us out from the proclamation of the Gospel to help people in need. We bring help in the here and now because our hope is firm in God's promises. Faith prompts obedience, hope, love, and hard work.

Sin's Fatal Attraction. Dave was driving to work on an unusually cold winter morning when his engine temperature gauge suddenly shot into the danger zone. He eased the car to the side of the road and shut it off. He stared blankly at the gauge. He knew nothing about fixing cars. For the moment it seemed best to wait for a good Samaritan to drive by.

Thirty minutes later Dave wondered why it was that the longer he was stuck out in the cold, the better he felt. "It must be warming up outside," he decided as he snuggled down in his seat and closed his eyes. When Dave woke up, he was in a hospital emergency room, being treated for the early stages of hypothermia.

Dave was fortunate a helpful motorist had stopped to help him, the physician explained. Another hour and Dave might have simply frozen to death in his sleep. "But I felt great," Dave said. "The warmth you felt is one of your body's warning signs," the physician responded. "When the cold becomes so pervasive that it makes you feel warm and sleepy, you're in serious danger."

Sin can be like that. When we become so used to a sin—or a particular sinful environment—that we no longer recognize it as harmful, we can easily be drawn deeper in deplorable actions. This is what happened to the Israelites as they became panicky over the extended absence of Moses. So what's the solution? We should open our hearts and souls to the warmth of God's truth and turn from sinning.

Gap in Faithful Living. Americans claim that they are solidly attached to their Bibles. For instance, 93 percent of all homes contain at least one Bible. One of the country's largest religious publishing houses reports selling 8 million copies of the Bible every year. An astonishing 33 percent of American adults say that they read the Bible at least once a week.

But surveys show surprising gaps between reading and retention. Over 54 percent cannot name the authors of the four Gospel accounts. Nearly 63 percent don't know what a Gospel is. Fifty-eight percent cannot name five of the Ten Commandments. And one out of ten Americans thinks that Joan of Arc was Noah's wife!

What kind of commitment do these statistics suggest? What would Moses have to say to religious people in America?

FOR YOUTH

■ TOPIC: A Golden Mistake

■ QUESTIONS: 1. Why do you think the Israelites became so impatient when they felt Moses had been gone too long? 2. What might have prompted Aaron to go along with the request of the Israelites? 3. Why would God refer to the Israelites as the people who belonged to Moses? 4. How had the Israelites demonstrated by their actions that they were headstrong? 5. How can we help people to trust completely in the Savior without leaning on superstition or false religions?

■ **ILLUSTRATIONS:**

The Success Trap. Print and electronic media entice teens with false messages of what it means to be successful. From an early age they learn that the idea of success means climbing the corporate ladder, owning the largest home, driving the sportiest car, and drawing the biggest paycheck. While success in and of itself isn't bad, too often it is accompanied by a self-reliant attitude that ignores God.

This is precisely what happened to the Israelites as they waited for Moses to come down from Mount Horeb and return to their desert camp. When he didn't show up right away, they began to worry. And in their anxiety, they smugly determined they could ignore the lawgiver and the God whom he served. Tragically, the people ended up venerating a golden calf-shaped idol.

Saved teens are not called to avoid success. Instead, God wants to use their successes to glorify Him. The key is for them to rely on Him completely and worship Him exclusively.

An Idolatrous Allure. In the movie *Citizen Kane*, a reporter interviews the friends and associates of newspaper tycoon Charles Foster Kane to find out, after his death, what really made Kane tick. Each interview adds a piece to the Kane puzzle. Yet they all are summed up in a single sentence uttered by one of Kane's longtime business partners. The reporter expresses some surprise to the partner that Kane isn't more respected. After all, the reporter says, Kane was able to grow his newspaper business and become quite wealthy. Kane's old business partner looks at the reporter from behind his big desk and says simply, "It isn't hard to make a lot of money, if all you want is to make a lot of money."

Many young people who would like to be rich don't believe that statement. It sounds too simple. But Kane took it literally and made it his idol. Nothing else really mattered to him—not family, friends, ethics, or even God. The problem isn't money. Rather, it's the love of money, or power, or success (to name a few contemporary "idols").

When the allure of those things sounds stronger in the ears of young people than the summons of God, they'll likely make the mistake of venerating the things of the world rather than the one who created all things. The goal for saved youth is to seek to succeed in those things that will further God's kingdom and thereby please Him.

False Gods. Many people come to a tragic end because they worship false gods. Some are wicked people, having made a god out of sensual pleasure. Others are upstanding people, yet they too have worshiped false gods. I wonder if this was true of a young farmer who committed suicide when his venture in farming failed. I say this because of a comment made by his wife. She remarked, "Farming wasn't just a job with Floyd. It was his identity, his nationality, his religion."

Whenever an occupation or anything temporal takes number one priority in life, it becomes our idol. John admonished us not to love the things of the world, for it breeds arrogance and selfish desires (1 John 2:15-16). Let us ensure that we don't love anything more than the true and living God revealed in the Bible. Only He can help us when our plans are shattered, our health fails, or death beckons. Be sure you love and worship only Him.

AN AWESOME PROMISE

BACKGROUND SCRIPTURE: Exodus 34:1-10
DEVOTIONAL READING: Acts 3:19-26

KEY VERSE: The LORD passed by before him, and proclaimed, The LORD, The LORD God, merciful and gracious, longsuffering, and abundant in goodness and truth. (Exodus 34:6)

KING JAMES VERSION

EXODUS 34:1 And the LORD said unto Moses, Hew thee two tables of stone like unto the first: and I will write upon these tables the words that were in the first tables, which thou brakest. . . . 4 And he hewed two tables of stone like unto the first; and Moses rose up early in the morning, and went up unto mount Sinai, as the LORD had commanded him, and took in his hand the two tables of stone.

5 And the LORD descended in the cloud, and stood with him there, and proclaimed the name of the LORD. 6 And the LORD passed by before him, and proclaimed, The LORD, The LORD God, merciful and gracious, longsuffering, and abundant in goodness and truth, 7 Keeping mercy for thousands, forgiving iniquity and transgression and sin, and that will by no means clear the guilty; visiting the iniquity of the fathers upon the children, and upon the children's children, unto the third and to the fourth generation. 8 And Moses made haste, and bowed his head toward the earth, and worshipped. 9 And he said, If now I have found grace in thy sight, O Lord, let my Lord, I pray thee, go among us; for it is a stiffnecked people; and pardon our iniquity and our sin, and take us for thine inheritance.

10 And he said, Behold, I make a covenant: before all thy people I will do marvels, such as have not been done in all the earth, nor in any nation: and all the people among which thou art shall see the work of the LORD: for it is a terrible thing that I will do with thee.

NEW REVISED STANDARD VERSION

EXODUS 34:1 The LORD said to Moses, "Cut two tablets of stone like the former ones, and I will write on the tablets the words that were on the former tablets, which you broke. . . . 4 So Moses cut two tablets of stone like the former ones; and he rose early in the morning and went up on Mount Sinai, as the LORD had commanded him, and took in his hand the two tablets of stone. 5 The LORD descended in the cloud and stood with him there, and proclaimed the name, "The LORD."
6 The LORD passed before him, and proclaimed,
"The LORD, the LORD,
a God merciful and gracious,
slow to anger,
and abounding in steadfast love and faithfulness,
7 keeping steadfast love for the thousandth generation,
forgiving iniquity and transgression and sin,
yet by no means clearing the guilty,
but visiting the iniquity of the parents
upon the children
and the children's children,
to the third and the fourth generation."
8 And Moses quickly bowed his head toward the earth, and worshipped. 9 He said, "If now I have found favour in your sight, O Lord, I pray, let the Lord go with us. Although this is a stiff-necked people, pardon our iniquity and our sin, and take us for your inheritance."

10 He said: I hereby make a covenant. Before all your people I will perform marvels, such as have not been performed in all the earth or in any nation; and all the people among whom you live shall see the work of the LORD; for it is an awesome thing that I will do with you.

33

Monday, September 20	Psalm 57:1-5	*God's Mercy*
Tuesday, September 21	Lamentations 3:22-26	*God's Faithfulness*
Wednesday, September 22	Psalm 103:1-5	*God's Forgiveness*
Thursday, September 23	Psalm 103:6-10	*God's Justice*
Friday, September 24	Psalm 103:11-16	*God's Compassion*
Saturday, September 25	Psalm 103:17-22	*God's Steadfast Love*
Sunday, September 26	Exodus 34:1, 4-10	*God's Inheritance*

BACKGROUND

Exodus 34:1-10 recounts the provision of replacement stone tablets for the ones Moses broke at the foot of Mount Sinai (see 32:19). Once the new tablets were ready, the Lord pledged to inscribe on them the commands that were recorded on the preceding pair of tablets. It remains unclear how God actually did this. One possibility is the Lord worked through the hands of Moses to bring it about. In any case, the act symbolized God's renewal of His covenant with His people.

According to Deuteronomy 10:1-2, the new stone tablets would be placed in the ark of the covenant. The latter, in turn, would be reside in the tabernacle, where the Lord would manifest His presence. An examination of Exodus 34 indicates that some of the laws God wanted to be recorded on the replacement tablets were chosen with Israel's recent fall into idol worship in mind. In addition, there were a number of edicts dealing with the inevitable temptation to worship the pagan deities of the Canaanites. God also reminded the people to keep the Sabbath holy, to remember that the firstborn were God's own possession, and to offer their firstfruits to God since it was He who made the promised land fruitful.

NOTES ON THE PRINTED TEXT

Exodus 33:7-23 recounts an incident in which the Lord permitted Moses to see the afterglow produced by His glorious presence. This was followed by God's command that Moses "hew" (34:1) two new tablets of stone. The pair would replace the first stone tablets, which Moses had previously smashed. The Hebrew verb rendered "hew" can also mean "to cut," "to carve," or "to chisel." Interestingly, this is the same term from which the noun translated "graven image" (or "idol," 20:4) is derived. Exodus 34:2 reveals that Moses had to prepare himself for his encounter with the Lord on Mount Sinai. This mirrors the consecration God required the entire Israelite community to go through back in 19:10-15. "Sanctify" comes from a Hebrew verb that means "to consecrate" or "to be separate." The Israelites were to separate themselves from anything that would make them ceremonially unclean. Part of this purification ritual included washing clothes, which symbolized spiritual cleansing.

With respect to Moses, he was to be ready in the morning to climb to the summit of the mountain, station himself there, and wait for the Lord to communicate with him. This appearance would put God in stark contrast to pagan deities, who were thought to dwell in the mountains. Because God is spirit (see John 4:24), and He makes His dwelling in the heaven He created, He would have to come down (in a manner of speaking) in order to meet Moses on the mountain. To accentuate the seriousness of the matter, God forbid any other person from coming with Moses as he made his way up Mount Sinai. Furthermore, no one was to be seen anywhere on the mountain. Even flocks of sheep and herds of cattle were banned from grazing at the foot of the mountain (Exod. 34:3).

In accordance with the Lord's directive, Moses cut out two more stone tablets (vs. 4). Deuteronomy 10:3 adds that the lawgiver also made an ark out of acacia wood, which was subsequently used to hold the pair of stone tablets. Early the next morning, Moses carried the tablets in his hands to the summit of Mount Sinai (Exod. 34:4). As God had promised, He manifested His glorious presence before Moses "in the cloud" (vs. 5) and stood beside the lawgiver on the mountain. In addition, God proclaimed His special, covenant name—Yahweh.

God allowed the glory of His presence to pass in front of Moses, and as God did so He made a proclamation concerning His attributes (see Num. 14:18; 2 Chron. 30:9; Neh. 9:17; Pss. 86:15; 103:8; 145:8; Joel 2:13; Jon. 4:2; Nah. 1:3). The repetition of the covenant name for Israel's God was intended to emphasize its connection with the truth of His generous nature. "Merciful" (Exod. 34:6) renders a Hebrew adjective that spotlights the Lord's abundant compassion. "Gracious" translates an adjective that points to His undeserved favor. The adjective rendered "longsuffering" stresses God's willingness to be slow to anger with His wayward people. His patience is seen in His decision to be filled with "goodness and truth." "Goodness" renders a noun that draws attention to the unfailing love and kindness of the Lord, while "truth" translates a noun that emphasizes His reliability and faithfulness.

God not only abounds in unfailing "mercy" (vs. 7), but also lavishes it to a thousand generations of His people. Expressed differently, He keeps His covenant promises to His people forever. He even goes so far as to forgive His people when they stray from the injunctions of His Word. The Hebrew verb rendered "forgiving" literally means "to lift up," "to carry off," or "to take away." It's as if the Lord were removing all the trespasses of His people forever from His sight. His pardon includes "iniquity." The latter renders a noun that denotes the presence of wickedness and wrongdoing. "Transgression" renders a noun that refers to violations of the law and acts of insurrection against the ruling authorities. Collectively, these terms point to a range of offenses and crimes.

While the Lord is willing to forgive repentant transgressors, He does not excuse the guilty. "Clear" translates a Hebrew verb that means "to acquit," "to exonerate," or "to treat as innocent." When multiple generations of an extended family living together become entangled in idolatry, immorality, and injustice, God pledged to punish the offenders. Indeed, He would do so to the "third and to the fourth generation," if necessary. A superficial reading of the verse might leave believers with the incorrect impression that God might unfairly punish one person or group for the sins committed by another person or group. A more informed understanding of the biblical text indicates that God holds each individual accountable for his or her own behavior.

The latter truth is reiterated in Ezekiel 18:2-18. God's people living in exile went around saying that the sour grapes eaten by the parents left a foul taste in the mouths of their children (vs. 2). The proverb meant that because of the sins of previous generations, the present one was suffering. According to this logic, one generation could blame their troubles on the misdeeds of previous generations. The exiles were quoting this maxim so they could excuse themselves of responsibility. In essence, the adage insinuated that God was unfairly punishing the captives. Granted, the effects of sin can be cumulative (see Exod. 20:5-6; Matt. 23:35-36). The moral and spiritual decay of one generation may have profound, long-lasting effects upon those who follow. But "the word of the LORD" (Ezek. 18:1) that came to Ezekiel revealed that each person is responsible for his or her own sin.

Moses, in response to the truths the Lord had declared about Himself, immediately fell prostrate to the ground in an act of worship (Exod. 34:8). Then, he reiterated the fact that the Lord was pleased with him. Indeed, because Moses had "found grace" (vs. 9) with God, the lawgiver petitioned Him to travel with the Israelites to the promised land. Moses acknowledged that his peers were headstrong. That truth notwithstanding, Moses petitioned the Lord to pardon the Israelites' iniquity and transgressions and claim them as His "inheritance." In effect, Moses was saying, "Take us back as your inalienable and special possession." We learn from Deuteronomy 7:7-8 that God did not favor and choose the Israelites because they were more numerous than other nations. Instead, it was simply because He unconditionally loved them. Moreover, in faithfulness to the oath He had solemnly vowed to their ancestors, God redeemed them from slavery in Egypt and accompanied them to the promised land.

The Hebrew noun translated "covenant" (Exod. 34:10) refers to a formal agreement made between a superior and subordinates. In this case, the Lord was reinstating the compact He had previously enacted at Mount Sinai before the episode involving the Israelites' worship of the golden calf idol. As His chosen people trekked through the wilderness and made their way into Canaan, God pledged to perform unprecedented "marvels." The latter renders a Hebrew verb that refers to miraculous deeds. These would be extraordinary acts never before done anywhere on the planet. Neighboring nations would witness and be awestruck by the Lord's wonderworking power and recognize that it was done solely by Him.

Joshua 2:8-11 enables us to see just how terrified the Canaanites were over the miracles God performed on behalf of His people. Not long before Jericho's fall, a prostitute named Rahab told two Hebrew spies what she knew about God's purpose for the

Israelites' future and how that purpose had given rise to much dread on the part of the people of Canaan. The inhabitants knew the Israelites intended to dispossess them by force. The Canaanites' fear was a fulfillment of Moses' prophecy recorded in Exodus 15:15-16. Rahab's knowledge of Israel's history from the Exodus to the encampment on the plains of Moab indicates that information about the Israelites had spread into the land of Canaan.

The prostitute told the Israelite spies that she had specifically heard about the way God had parted the Red Sea to allow His people to cross it on dry land, and how the Hebrews had conquered the land of the Amorites east of the Jordan River (Josh. 2:10; see Exod. 14:21-29; Num. 21:21-35). After telling how the Canaanites feared the Israelites' arrival, Rahab made her own statement of faith: "The LORD your God, he is God in heaven above, and in the earth beneath" (Josh. 2:11). Rahab spoke as though God had already engineered the defeat of Jericho. The Lord had put the so-called gods of Canaan to shame with His obvious control over natural and military forces.

SUGGESTIONS TO TEACHERS

Even today God calls us to live according to His values. We need to place our lifestyles and priorities under the focus of His Word and see what is reflected before Him and the world. If we are true to His teachings, then we will please our Lord and draw others to Him. If we are not true, then we need to change our lifestyles, or like the people of Moses' day, we will incur His displeasure.

1. A NEW HONESTY. God does not accept blame shifting for anyone's sin. He wanted the Israelites to know that He responds to individuals on the basis of their own behavior. Urge your students to examine their lives to see whether they tend to blame their past or their situation for their mistakes or sin. God understands the influences that affect people, but He doesn't accept excuses for sin.

2. A NEW ACCOUNTABILITY. Moses taught that each individual must account for his or her actions before God. Help your students explore the significance of that truth for themselves. Adults are not responsible before God for the mistakes of their children. Also, young people are not limited in God's eyes by the failures of their parents.

3. A NEW START. Moses taught that a person's spiritual condition can change. It isn't determined by one's parents and it isn't locked in by one's past or present behavior. A great sinner can repent of his or her sin, commit to obeying God, and enjoy the eternal life that God gives. You can expand on the idea of turning from one's sin by relating it to faith in the sacrificial death of Jesus as the payment for those sins.

FOR ADULTS

■ TOPIC: Steadfast Love

■ QUESTIONS: 1. Why was it significant that the Lord wanted Moses to chisel out two replacement stone tablets? 2. Why do you think God wanted only Moses to meet with Him on Mount Sinai? 3. In what ways have you seen the Lord be compassionate and gracious to you and other believers? 4. How is it possible for the sinful tendencies of parents to adversely affect their children and grandchildren? 5. What are some of the promises of God that you fully expect to be fulfilled in your life?

■ ILLUSTRATIONS:

The Lord Forgives Sinners. We should be thankful that the Lord forgives sinners, for otherwise none of us would be saved. Yet once we become Christians and settle down among the nice people in church, we often forget that God's steadfast love is for every lost person. Sometimes those whom He calls to salvation embarrass us, and we feel uncomfortable in their presence. We don't approve of the way they look and the things they do. Would we ever sit down to dinner with people like them?

The church's hardest task is to expand its vision to unlikely candidates for salvation and fellowship. Once our lives get cleaned up, we don't want to get dirty again. But if we refuse to reach sinners as a demonstration of God's compassion and grace, then the church becomes a holier-than-thou club. It fails to fulfill its divine mission. Perhaps once in a while we need to put a banner behind the pulpit that says THE LORD FORGIVES SINNERS.

No Love Experienced. Late in her life, actress Marilyn Monroe was asked how often she felt love. She replied that she felt love only once in her life when one of her foster mothers was putting on her makeup and stopped and touched her on the top of her nose with her powder puff and gave her a smile. Just for a moment, the blonde screen star said, she felt love.

Small wonder that Monroe's life ended tragically. On the other extreme, Exodus 34:6-7 describes the abounding compassion of God for His people. We learn that His kindness and forgiveness endure to a thousand generations. Now that's steadfast love!

God's Awesome Power. Frank was on a ladder painting his house when a child's cry cut the air. "Somebody, help me!" the child screamed. As Frank quickly made his way down to the ground, he realized it was Melissa, the six-year-old daughter of Derek and Jessica, his next door neighbors. But Frank knew Derek had gone out for a quick trip to the grocery store. And Jessica was probably working out of earshot in the house.

"Mommy!" Melissa cried out again, as Frank reached her backyard. Frank looked up. There sat Melissa, high in the branches of a tree, clinging tightly to a thick limb. Frank brought his ladder and climbed up toward the frightened youngster. "That's as close as I can come," he told her, stretching out his arms to reach her. "You're too far away," Melissa said. "I can't make it." "Sure you can. Just grab that branch beside you, put your foot on that limb . . . good," said Frank. "You're still not close enough," Melissa blurted. "Just trust me, Melissa. Can you swing a little bit this way?" Frank asked. "I—I'll try," Melissa quivered. She did, and within minutes Melissa was safely back on the ground—with a stern warning not to climb so high in the future.

Perhaps like Melissa, the Israelites initially felt unsure about wanting to grab the "branch" of God's awesome power or put their foot on the nearby "limb" of His help. Yet they did so in faith and were eventually able to take control of the promised land. Similarly, just as Frank's presence reassured Melissa, we can enjoy the reassuring presence of God through prayer. In a way, the Spirit of the Lord comes up alongside of us, which is what we need to have courage to move forward.

As we continue our journey with God, He asks us to step out and risk new behaviors. Sometimes God speaks in gentle nudges, other times through the harsh words of a friend. We may resist, as Melissa resisted Frank's help to get out of the tree. But also like Melissa, we see how much better off we'd be if we stood safely on the ground by appreciating and depending on God's awesome power to sustain us.

FOR YOUTH

■ **TOPIC:** The Big Ten, Part Two

■ **QUESTIONS:** 1. Why was it necessary for Moses to chisel out two new stone tablets? 2. How do you think Moses got himself ready to meet the Lord on Mount Sinai? 3. What is the basis for God being patient with believers, even when they sin against Him? 4. What are some ways that God's people can work to break the destructive cycle of sin that grips so many communities these days? 5. How can you encourage others to more fully appreciate God's awesome power?

■ **ILLUSTRATIONS:**

Rejected Love. The father tried to show his young son how to untangle his fishing line. But the boy snarled, "I can do it myself!" Those are the times that can try a parent's soul. Should the father grab the line from his son? Or should the father let the child struggle while the line gets hopelessly knotted?

How should God treat us when we tell Him to buzz off? Would He be right to allow us to struggle with the consequences of our pride? Or should He shove us in the right direction (so to speak)?

When we neglect the disciplines of our faith, we are prone to ignore God. In some cases, He allows us to get into deep trouble, so deep in fact that eventually we cry out to Him for help. If we are wise, we will be careful not to drift away from Him.

Moses knew that the nation of Israel had gotten into deep trouble. But the lawmaker also knew that God's love would eventually triumph. Our faith in Jesus tells us to keep on believing in God's love, no matter what.

Be All That You Can Be. Shug Jordan used to coach football at Auburn. The story goes that he sent a former player out to scout high school teams. The young man asked the old coach, "What kind of player are you looking for?"

"Well, Mike," Coach Jordan said, "you know there's that fellow, you knock him down, and he stays down."

Mike said, "We don't want him, do we, Coach?"

"No, that's right. Then there's that fellow, you knock him down and he gets up, but you knock him down again and he stays down."

"We don't want him either, do we, coach?"

"No. But, Mike, there's a fellow, you knock him down and he gets up. Knock him down, he gets up. Knock him down, he gets up. Knock him down, he gets up."

"That's the guy we want, isn't it, Coach."

Shug Jordan answered, "No, we don't want him either. I want you to find the guy who's knocking everybody down. That's the guy we want!"

Through God's Word we learn that the Lord wants His people to follow all His ways with total commitment. Expressed differently, we should not be half-hearted Christians. Rather, the Father wants us to "be all we can be" (as the slogan says) for the Son.

No Insolence! The people of Moses' day were so insolent that they had a hard time submitting to God's will. They were like the naval officer who realized his lifelong ambition when he was given command of a battleship. One stormy night, as the powerful vessel sailed toward a harbor, the lookout spotted a strange light rapidly closing with them.

Immediately the captain ordered his signalman to flash the message, "Alter your course ten degrees to port." Almost instantly the reply came, "Alter *your* course ten degrees to port."

Determined to take a back seat to no one, the officer sent this message: "Alter course ten degrees. I am a highly decorated captain." Back came the reply: "Alter *your* course ten degrees. I am a third-class seaman."

Infuriated, the captain grabbed the signal lamp and flashed, "Alter your course. I'm a battleship." Back came: "Alter *your* course. I'm a lighthouse."

The moral of this story is that we shouldn't be insolent with God, for He knows where the "rocks" are (metaphorically speaking). He doesn't want anybody to end up spiritually shipwrecked. Also, He wants everyone to trust in the Messiah. Of course, they have to heed His warnings about death and life and do what He says.

MAJESTY AND DIGNITY

BACKGROUND SCRIPTURE: Psalm 8
DEVOTIONAL READING: Genesis 1:26-31

KEY VERSE: Thou madest him to have dominion over the
works of thy hands; thou hast put all things under his feet. (Psalm 8:6)

KING JAMES VERSION

PSALM 8:1 O LORD our Lord, how excellent is thy name in all the earth! who hast set thy glory above the heavens. 2 Out of the mouth of babes and sucklings hast thou ordained strength because of thine enemies, that thou mightest still the enemy and the avenger.

3 When I consider thy heavens, the work of thy fingers, the moon and the stars, which thou hast ordained;
4 What is man, that thou art mindful of him? and the son of man, that thou visitest him? 5 For thou hast made him a little lower than the angels, and hast crowned him with glory and honour. 6 Thou madest him to have dominion over the works of thy hands; thou hast put all things under his feet: 7 All sheep and oxen, yea, and the beasts of the field; 8 The fowl of the air, and the fish of the sea, and whatsoever passeth through the paths of the seas.
9 O LORD our Lord, how excellent is thy name in all the earth!

NEW REVISED STANDARD VERSION

PSALM 8:1 O LORD, our Sovereign,
how majestic is your name in all the earth!
You have set your glory above the heavens.
2 Out of the mouths of babes and infants
you have founded a bulwark because of your foes,
to silence the enemy and the avenger.
3 When I look at your heavens, the work of your fingers,
the moon and the stars that you have established;
4 what are human beings that you are mindful of them,
mortals that you care for them?
5 Yet you have made them a little lower than God,
and crowned them with glory and honour.
6 You have given them dominion over the works of
your hands;
you have put all things under their feet,
7 all sheep and oxen,
and also the beasts of the field,
8 the birds of the air, and the fish of the sea,
whatever passes along the paths of the seas.
9 O LORD, our Sovereign,
how majestic is your name in all the earth!

5

HOME BIBLE READINGS

BACKGROUND

Of the 150 psalms, only 34 do not have titles. For the hymns that have them, these superscriptions indicate such things (in various combinations) as the author, type of psalm, musical notations, liturgical notations, and historical context. The psalms attributed to David contain many references to his life that seem to be taken from 2 Samuel. Believing scholars are divided as to the reliability of the headings. Some think the titles were added at a later time, and there is some evidence that these titles did change over time. Others, however, maintain that the superscriptions were part of a psalm and should be regarded as an integral portion of the sacred text.

According to the title of Psalm 8, it was written by David. The psalms were penned over a long period of time and collected for worship as early as the reign of David. The titles at the beginning of most psalms identify several writers, though the Hebrew can also mean that the hymn belonged to the person or was about that person. David's ability as a musician, his interest in corporate worship, and the subject matter of some of the psalms make him the likely author of some of the hymns, including Psalm 8. The phrase "to the chief Musician" suggests that this song is from an early collection of hymns used in temple worship. It's also possible that when the psalm was used in the Hebrew liturgy, the leader of the Levitical choir spoke it before the assembly of worshipers.

The term rendered "Gittith" (which is also found in the headings of Psalms 81 and 84) was probably a liturgical word and may have referred to a musical style or type of stringed instrument. One suggestion is that it was a guitar-like harp associated with Gath in Philistia. Some manuscripts have the word translated as "winepress." This has led some to suggest that Psalm 8 was associated in some way with the vintage festival at the Feast of Tabernacles. The beginning and ending of this song suggests that it was a hymn of praise. The interior of the psalm, however, focuses on the Lord's sovereign ordering of the creation. It's for this reason that some classify this hymn as a nature psalm (or song of creation).

David's hymn extols both God's glory and the God-given dignity of human beings. Unlike the anonymously written Psalm 104, David did not draw upon the six days of creation to form the structure for his song. Rather, he wrote out of his own present experience of reality. Throughout the nine verses of Psalm 8, David praised God, all the while referring to his own sense of wonder over the Lord's powerful ordering of creation. One discerns that David composed this hymn while standing on his balcony and gazing into the sky at night—the same sky he no doubt had studied and pondered while tending his father's sheep or while on the run from King Saul. The occasion may have pushed to the back of David's mind the day-to-day affairs of administering the Israelite kingdom, while bringing to the forefront deeper thoughts such as the majesty of God and the origin of life.

NOTES ON THE PRINTED TEXT

In Old Testament times, there was no pollution or bright lights from nearby cities to deter a person's view of the sky. Thus, while King David did not have the benefit of a powerful telescope, he no doubt could grasp something of the vastness of space. Even today, scientists speak of stars as being trillions of miles away from us and describe the universe in terms that at times can seem hard to comprehend. Admittedly, we don't know the original circumstances leading up to David's writing of Psalm 8, but it's not hard to imagine. Many of us can recall times when we gazed up into the sky on a clear night and saw countless stars extending from one end of the horizon to the other. If this was the case for David, we can only infer how puny he must have felt against the immense expanse of the heavens above which God had set His glory (vs. 1).

Two different Hebrew words are rendered "Lord" in this verse. The first term is *Yahweh*, and underscores the everlasting quality of His self-existence (Exod. 3:14-15). The second term is *Adonai*, and places emphasis on God's supreme and unchallenged authority. It's no wonder that David declared that the name of the all-glorious one was "excellent . . . in all the earth!" (Ps. 8:1). (In Scripture, the name of the Lord was considered a reflection of His character, encompassing all His attributes.) "Excellent" renders a Hebrew adjective that can also be translated as "glorious," "powerful," or "delightful." Since in Old Testament thought the name of the Lord is often equated with His presence, this verse could be loosely rendered, "Yahweh, our Lord, how delightful is your Presence throughout the entire globe!"

This psalm ends with the same words as it begins. These words of praise to the name of God form a frame for its central subject—praise from humankind, whom God has made to reflect His majesty. Here we see that people count for something in God's eyes. We are important and valuable to Him—not just because He created us, but also because He sent His Son to redeem us and give us eternal life. When we visibly give thanks to God for His goodness, we declare to the unsaved that He is our Creator and Sustainer. We bear witness to the truth that every person needs God for present life and future hope. Our words of praise and gratitude to the Father might encourage the unsaved to consider the truths of the Son and turn to Him in faith for new life and eternal joy.

David recognized that whenever God reveals Himself, whether above the heavens or upon the earth, He is majestic. His praise is chanted on high and echoed from cradle and nursery. This praise is a sufficient answer to God's opponents. What is sweeter than the songs of children? Our hearts are lifted when we hear them singing the Lord's praises. He is worthy of such adoration, and He sees to it that even helpless "babes and sucklings" (vs. 2) draw the world's attention to Him. The unbelieving world rejects the rule of God, but the forces of darkness cannot silence His praise.

David gazed into the heavens once again and considered his place in the grand scheme of creation. Did he matter to God? Was he important and valuable compared to the heavenly bodies? He recognized that what he could see in the sky was the work of God's "fingers" (vs. 3). Of course, David knew that God did not have literal fingers, but in lavish poetic style the composer used a powerful figure of speech to describe God's creative power. Verse 4 indicates that the heavens belonged to God, for He had made them. We also learn that He set all the solar bodies in exactly the right place for our benefit. Ultimately, it takes faith to acknowledge that even the universe with its infinite distances is the work of God.

Two specific thoughts especially impressed David as he penned the words of Psalm 8. One was the magnificent glory of God as it was reflected in the clear, starry night. The other thought was the utter amazement that God, in all His glory, would even be mindful and considerate of the human aspect of His creation—so much so as to crown human beings with distinction and eminence and to give them lord-like stewardship over the rest of His creation. For the most part, David admitted that these two thoughts were practically beyond his comprehension. To respect God's majesty, we must compare ourselves to His greatness. That's what David did when he asked, "What is man, that thou art mindful of him?" (vs. 4). Here "man" refers to all human beings regardless of gender (see Gen. 1:26-27). David's use of the phrase "son of man" (Ps. 8:4) looks upon people as mere mortals who are insignificant and transitory. If the entire universe appears microscopic in the sight of the Creator, how much less must be the significance of humanity?

Because humans are the only creatures on earth made in God's image, God put us in charge of the rest of creation (Gen. 1:26-30). As Psalm 8:6-8 reminds us, we have dominion over the animal world. The implication is that we have the right to use nature to meet our needs, while at the same time fulfilling our responsibility to take care of nature. This truth is reinforced by the Hebrew verb translated "dominion" in verse 6. The word conveys the idea of oversight, administration, and government, with the extent of the authority dependent on the context in which the term is used. David concluded his psalm with another powerful affirmation of God's glory. The writer's prelude put him in the proper frame of mind to consider God's creation works. And his postlude moved him to exclaim "how excellent" (vs. 9) God's name was "in all the earth." Although the bulk of Psalm 8 describes humanity and its dominion over the earth, the first verse as well as the last make it clear that David wrote this psalm as an act of worship and praise to God, the Creator.

SUGGESTIONS TO TEACHERS

Seeing God as He is has a humbling effect on a person. When Isaiah beheld God's glory in a vision, he felt doomed (see Isa. 6:5). And when John had a vision of the risen Christ on the Isle of Patmos, the apostle felt overwhelmed (see Rev. 1:17). Isaiah and John recognized their own insignificance when they witnessed God's glory. But though David did not have a vision of the Lord's splendor, Israel's king did see God's glory and majesty displayed in the created universe. David was amazed that God would be both "mindful" (Ps. 8:4) of and caring for the people whom He had created.

1. STAND IN AWE OF GOD'S MAJESTY. Just as a person can stand in awe before a great painting for hours at a time and admire its beauty—taking in every detail, observing every stroke of the brush, and appreciating every choice of color— so a Christian can follow David's example and contemplate and admire the greatness of God's universe. And just as an artist deserves praise for his or her creative work, so the Creator of the universe rightly deserves our praise, adoration, and worship in response to His magnificent creation.

2. WITH CHILDLIKE FAITH. Sometimes as we grow older, we lose that sense of childlike awe for things that are beautiful, magnificent, awesome, or huge! Perhaps we would do well to reclaim not only our childlike eyes but also our childlike faith in our Creator. Most children seem able to put their trust in God and praise Him without holding anything back. This was certainly David's approach. No one would accuse him of holding anything back in the writing of Psalm 8.

3. FOR WE ARE HIS CREATION. Psalm 100:3 says, "Know ye that the LORD he is God; it is he that hath made us, and not we ourselves; we are his people, and the sheep of his pasture." When aligned beside the greatness of God, we pale in comparison! Recognizing this ought to cause us to be both humble and worshipful. We are humbled because we are a tiny part of His creation. We are worshipful because we are His creation, and He has granted to us a special status—being made in His image.

4. A LITTLE LOWER THAN THE ANGELS. Not only are we stamped with the image of God, but also we have been created "a little lower than the angels" (Heb. 2:7). So if you ever feel tempted to question your worth as a person, just remember how valuable God considers you!

5. TO EXERCISE DOMINION. God has ultimate rule over the earth, and He exercises His authority with loving care. When God delegated some of His authority to the human race, He expected us to take responsibility for the environment and the other creatures that share our planet. We should not be careless or wasteful as we fulfill this charge. After all, God was careful how He made this earth. Likewise, we should not be careless in our care of the planet.

<table>
<tr><td rowspan="4">FOR ADULTS</td></tr>
</table>

FOR ADULTS

■ TOPIC: Caring for Creation

■ QUESTIONS: 1. What effect did David's understanding of God's greatness have on his view of humanity? 2. As those who have dominion over God's creation, do we have an obligation to be careful about how we use the earth's resources? Why or why not? 3. How should we go about deciding which aspects of God's creation can be used and which aspects can be protected? 4. How is your faith in God affected by observing the created universe? 5. How can knowing that God is all-powerful, all-knowing, and always present help you make it through difficult times?

■ ILLUSTRATIONS:

Responsible to Care. Each generation discovers new wealth in God's creation. These discoveries show how prolific are the mighty acts of God. But each discovery brings new challenges and responsibilities. The more God gives us, the greater our responsibility to exercise wise stewardship according to His commands recorded in Scripture.

Our greatest failure seems to be our lack of gratitude. Simply put, we take God's gifts for granted. Many times we do not even acknowledge His daily provision of our needs. This is sad, for we could not survive without the air we breathe, the food we eat, or the water we drink, all of which come from God.

Psalm 8 reminds us that God is supremely praiseworthy. Wherever we look, we find reasons to praise Him. Most of all, when we consider what the Father has done for us in the Son, we should submit to our Lord. After all, He's the author of life, whether physical or spiritual in nature.

The Work of Your Fingers. William Beebe was no armchair naturalist. His extensive knowledge of nature was gained from exploring the jungles of Asia and South America and the ocean in the world's first bathysphere.

Beebe had much in common with his friend Theodore Roosevelt, who also loved nature and exploring. Often during a visit to Sagamore Hill, Beebe recalled, he and the president went outdoors to see who could first locate the Andromeda galaxy in the constellation of Pegasus.

Gazing at the tiny smudge of distant starlight, Beebe would say something like this: "That is the spiral galaxy of Andromeda. It is as large as our Milky Way, and is one of a hundred million galaxies. It is 750,000 light-years away and consists of one hundred billion suns, each one larger than our sun."

After that thought had sunk in, Roosevelt would flash his famous toothy grin: "Now I think we are small enough." And the two men would go inside, put in their place by the limitless universe that God created.

Our Lord, Our Sovereign. Louis XIV of France was the monarch who pompously called himself "Louis the Great" and made the famous statement "I am the state!" In his eyes, he had created something grand and glorious and deserved to be exalted. At the time of his death in 1715, his court was the most magnificent in Europe.

To dramatize his greatness, Louis XIV had given orders prior to his death that at the funeral, the cathedral was to be lit by a single candle set above his coffin. When that eventful day arrived, thousands of people packed into the cathedral. At the front lay Louis XIV's body in a golden coffin. And, per his instructions, a single candle had been placed above the coffin.

The congregation sat in hushed silence. Then Bishop Massilon stood and began to speak. Slowly reaching down, he snuffed out the candle and said, "Only God is great!"

Massilon recognized that even the greatest human accomplishments are insignificant when compared to the actions of the infinite Creator of the universe. Measured against God's glory, majesty, and greatness, no human can lay claim to greatness. Louis XIV had built a government, but God had created the entire universe!

FOR YOUTH ■ TOPIC: An Awesome Name
■ QUESTIONS: 1. In what ways do the "mouths of babes and sucklings" (Ps. 8:2) silence the foes of God? 2. When was the last time you felt the night sky declare God's majesty and power? 3. How does creation indicate that it must have had a master designer? 4. Why do some people deny God's existence while studying the details of His creation? 5. Why do you think David ended this psalm the same way he began it?

■ ILLUSTRATIONS:
Truly Awesome! Advertisers pandering to youth outdo themselves to make their products more attractive than their competitors'. For example, when we consider teen fashions, we can see how important it is for adolescents to stand out in a crowd. Yet no matter how impressive our clothes, computers, and cars might be, they are nothing compared to the magnificence of God's creation. We need to be careful lest in the many things that are supposed to make us happy, we lose sight of the glory of God's name.

The world has a way of dominating our time, and it tries to shape our desires and values. But as Christians, we are wise to step back and ask why God made us. What does He desire of us? Also, how can we strengthen our faith in Him and not be compromised by the world's values? Meditating on God our awesome Creator, as David did, is a step in the right direction.

Unwitting Praise. Sir Isaac Newton kept a miniature replica of the solar system in his study. In the center of the replica was the sun, with the planets revolving around it. A scientist who did not believe in God entered Newton's study one day and took notice of the replica. "My! What an exquisite object this is!" he exclaimed. "Who made it?" "Nobody," replied Newton to the questioner. "You must think I am a fool," the scientist responded. "Of course somebody made it, and he is a genius."

Laying his book aside, Newton explained, "This object is but a puny imitation of a much grander system, whose laws you and I know, and I am not able to convince you that this mere toy is without a designer and maker. Yet you profess to believe that the great original from which the design is taken has come into being without either designer or maker. Now tell me, by what sort of reasoning do you reach this conclusion?"

The unbelieving scientist had offered unwitting praise to the creator of the humanly made model of the solar system. How much more deserving of praise is the majestic Creator of the universe! Psalm 8 reminds us that God is worthy of our praise because He both created and sustains us.

How Majestic Is Your Name. In his book *Your God Is Too Small*, J. B. Phillips pointed out that many Christians have a less-than-majestic concept of God. They seem to doubt that God is all-powerful, all-knowing, and always present. They live their lives as if God has been weakened by stress and strain. They do not rely on Him as the powerful Ruler over all the universe.

When we read the writings of saints such as Martin Luther, Jonathan Edwards, and George Whitefield, we realize that these people were intimately acquainted with the mighty God who created the world. They knew the same God extolled by David in Psalm 8—the one true God whose name is majestic in all the earth. Their God was not "too small."

There is no limit to God's power, so there should not be a limit to our perception of His power. God has provided us ways to see a glimpse of His omnipotence. He has allowed us to observe His power reflected in the lives of His people as well as in the created universe.

GOD'S LAW SUSTAINS

BACKGROUND SCRIPTURE: Psalm 19

DEVOTIONAL READING: 1 Chronicles 22:7-13

KEY VERSES: The law of the LORD is perfect, converting the soul: the testimony of the LORD is sure, making wise the simple. The statutes of the LORD are right, rejoicing the heart: the commandment of the LORD is pure, enlightening the eyes. (Psalm 19:7-8)

KING JAMES VERSION

PSALM 19:7 The law of the LORD is perfect, converting the soul: the testimony of the LORD is sure, making wise the simple. 8 The statutes of the LORD are right, rejoicing the heart: the commandment of the LORD is pure, enlightening the eyes. 9 The fear of the LORD is clean, enduring for ever: the judgments of the LORD are true and righteous altogether. 10 More to be desired are they than gold, yea, than much fine gold: sweeter also than honey and the honeycomb. 11 Moreover by them is thy servant warned: and in keeping of them there is great reward. 12 Who can understand his errors? cleanse thou me from secret faults. 13 Keep back thy servant also from presumptuous sins; let them not have dominion over me: then shall I be upright, and I shall be innocent from the great transgression. 14 Let the words of my mouth, and the meditation of my heart, be acceptable in thy sight, O LORD, my strength, and my redeemer.

NEW REVISED STANDARD VERSION

PSALM 19:7 The law of the LORD is perfect,
   reviving the soul;
the decrees of the LORD are sure,
   making wise the simple;
8 the precepts of the LORD are right,
   rejoicing the heart;
the commandment of the LORD is clear,
   enlightening the eyes;
9 the fear of the LORD is pure,
   enduring forever;
the ordinances of the LORD are true
   and righteous altogether.
10 More to be desired are they than gold,
   even much fine gold;
sweeter also than honey,
   and drippings of the honeycomb.
11 Moreover by them is your servant warned;
   in keeping them there is great reward.
12 But who can detect their errors?
   Clear me from hidden faults.
13 Keep back your servant also from the insolent;
   do not let them have dominion over me.
Then I shall be blameless,
   and innocent of great transgression.
14 Let the words of my mouth and the meditation of
    my heart
   be acceptable to you,
   O LORD, my rock and my redeemer.

6

Monday, October 4	Psalm 19:1-6	*The Testimony of Creation*
Tuesday, October 5	Psalm 105:1-11	*An Everlasting Covenant*
Wednesday, October 6	Deuteronomy 29:25-29	*The Law as Revelation*
Thursday, October 7	Deuteronomy 30:1-10	*The Law as Obedient Love*
Friday, October 8	Deuteronomy 31:19-26	*The Law as Witness*
Saturday, October 9	Jeremiah 31:31-37	*The Law as Covenant*
Sunday, October 10	Psalm 19:7-14	*The Testimony of the Law*

BACKGROUND

The heading to Psalm 19 states that David was its author and that he originally intended the composition to be used by music directors or song leaders in the corporate worship conducted within the precincts of the Jerusalem temple. Specialists have categorized the poem as a wisdom psalm, especially in light of its celebration of the greatness of God's creation (vss. 1-6), its extolling the beauty of the law (vss. 7-11), and its emphasis on believers experiencing God's forgiveness (vss. 12-14). David began by commenting on the way in which the "heavens" (vs. 1) silently bear witness to God's "glory." The latter term, when applied to God in Scripture, refers to the brilliant revelation of Himself to humanity. This definition is borne out by the many ways the word is used in the Bible. For example, "glory" is often linked with verbs of seeing (Exod. 16:7; 33:18; Isa. 40:5) and of appearing (Exod. 16:10; Deut. 5:24), both of which emphasize the visible nature of God's majesty and power.

The ongoing testimony to God's presence and power is also made by the sky, especially as it showcases God's craftsmanship (Ps. 19:1). Verses 2-6 draw attention to the splendor of the celestial objects that parade themselves across the heavens day and night. Each day the Lord's glory is announced to the following day, while each night repeats the same proclamation to the next night (vs. 2). Though the sun, moon, and stars do not literally speak, their testimony to God's royal majesty echoes throughout the planet and journeys to the distant horizon (vss. 3-4). The sun was of particular interest to David. The place where this fiery ball seems to rest at night is compared to a tent. At dawn, the sun appears like a bridegroom emerging from his chamber after spending a joyous night with his bride. The sun is comparable to a mighty warrior who proceeds with enthusiasm and vigor along the path set out before him (vs. 5). At the start of a new day, the sun emerges at one end of the sky and makes it circuit to the other end. Throughout the cycle, nothing is able to escape its heat (vs. 6).

NOTES ON THE PRINTED TEXT

Psalm 19:7 shifts the readers' attention from God's revelation in nature to His disclosure of Himself in His Word. "Law" renders a Hebrew noun that means "direction," "instruction," or "edict." The noun appears 220 times in the Old

Testament and is the most comprehensive term used for law. It appears in narrative accounts, speeches, poems, and genealogies. Moreover, the noun denotes ethical imperatives that are more concerned with how people should live, rather than with abstract concepts about morality. David declared the law to be "perfect." The latter translates an adjective that denotes what is whole, complete, and sound. The idea is that God's decrees are entirely in accord with fact and truth. It's no wonder that David found his study of the Word to be spiritually nourishing and strengthening. As the king grew increasingly familiar with the law, it helped him to better understand the will of God. In the process, David discovered how to live in a way that pleased the Lord and preserve his life from mortal danger (see vs. 11).

The second half of verse 7 reiterates these truths by commenting on God's "testimony." The latter renders a Hebrew noun that concerns the statutes and regulations made by the Lord in His Word. These commands are "sure," in which the underlying verb refers to what is reliable, believable, and trustworthy. Those who allow themselves to be instructed by the teachings of the law obtain wisdom. The emphasis here is on becoming increasingly discerning and prudent. The "simple" person refers to those who are ignorant and inexperienced. They have much to gain by becoming familiar with God's decrees and avoiding the pitfalls that can trip up those who are naïve and misinformed about life.

"Statutes" (Ps. 19:8) renders a Hebrew noun that denotes commandments and precepts. In this case, David observed that God's mandates are "right." The latter includes the notion of being accurate, correct, and appropriate. Rightness also involves being fair, objective, and imparting a knowledge of such to the faith community. Those who heed the teachings of God's Word experience true "rejoicing" and lasting satisfaction in their innermost being. The upright discover that God's ordinances are "pure." The latter renders an adjective that refers to what is radiant, sincere, and lucid in character. Because God's decrees reflect His ethical priorities, they give insight to the faithful and impart understanding to those who seek to live in a judicious manner.

What does it mean to "fear . . . the LORD" (Ps. 19:9; see Job 28:28; Ps. 111:10; Prov. 1:7; 3:7; 9:10; 31:30; Eccl. 12:13)? On the one hand, it is not an irrational feeling of dread and impending doom. On the other hand, it is more than courteous reverence. Fearing the Lord involves a deep awareness of His sovereignty and power. It also includes holding God in awe and unconditionally obeying Him. This is demonstrated in doing what is right and refusing to involve oneself in wickedness. We can appreciate why David would say that God's commands for believers to demonstrate a proper reverence for Him are wholesome and right (see Ps. 111:10). Indeed, worshiping the Lord is a sacred act, one that will continue forever. "Judgments" (19:9) translates a Hebrew noun that refers to God's ordinances and judicial decisions. To assert that the latter are "true" means His determinations are reliable, certain, and unchanging. Moreover, His edicts are absolutely just, and there's no trace of unrighteousness in His judgments.

David had a clear understanding of human nature. For instance, he knew that people valued precious metals such as gold and devoted large amounts of time and energy to acquire these. The king declared that the law of the Lord was worth more than the finest gold (vs. 10). In fact, God's Word was beyond valuing. In a parallel thought, David declared that Scripture was sweeter than the most delicious honey. Even honey dripping from the comb could not compare with the joy and satisfaction to be found in heeding the Bible. Understandably then, believers find moral guidance in Scripture. Likewise, by obeying its ethical injunctions the upright are eternally blessed (vs. 11). In contrast, those who spurn the divine statutes experience bitterness, frustration, and disillusionment. If we want our soul nourished, our spirit invigorated, and our hope strengthened, we will focus our attention on what God has revealed in His Word.

"Errors" (vs. 12) translates a Hebrew noun that refers to faults and shortcomings in one's life. David acknowledged that no one was able to recognize and admit all the sins lurking within them. Jeremiah 17:9 affirms this truth when it declares that the human heart is capable of unimaginable deceit and evil. Even the upright commit sins without being aware of it. Likewise, 1 John 1:8 says if we claim to have no sin, we are only deceiving ourselves. In short, not even the more pious and virtuous of individuals have perfect moral discernment. For that reason, David petitioned the Lord to pardon him when he sinned without knowing it. "Cleanse" (Ps. 19:12) renders a verb that denotes being forgiven of wrongdoing and released from punishment. From the New Testament, we understand that the Father acquits believing sinners on the basis of His Son's redemptive work at Calvary (see Rom. 3:25-26).

David also asked God to keep him from committing deliberate sins. "Presumptuous" (Ps. 19:13) renders a Hebrew noun that denotes acts of wrongdoing which are willful in nature. These are the sorts of flagrant misdeeds that enslave the wicked (see John 8:34). Regrettably, those enmeshed in the snare of sin find the latter to be comparable to a merciless and cruel taskmaster (see Rom. 6:11-23). David was wise to ask God to keep him from such a fate. Moreover, the leader of Israel did not want to let sin have control over his life. As a result, he would be "upright" (Ps. 19:13). The latter renders a verb that points to those who have demonstrated their trustworthiness by dealing with others in an blameless, principled manner. David also envisioned himself being cleared of guilt associated with blatant "transgression." The latter renders a noun that points to acts of rebellion against God (for example, idolatry, injustice, and immorality).

David summarized his previous statements with the prayer that his words would be acceptable and his thoughts would be pleasing to the Lord. The king's unwavering commitment to God was the only rational course. After all, the Lord was comparable to a rocky cliff that provided one with shelter. Moreover, God, as the "redeemer" (vs. 14) of His people, was like a prominent family member who defended the rights of the clan and protected its members in times of extreme need. We learn from the New

Testament that the Father provides redemption for the lost through the shed blood of His Son (see Eph. 1:7; Col. 1:14).

SUGGESTIONS TO TEACHERS

People want meaning and satisfaction in their lives. They also want their lives to count for something. The Bible tells us how to achieve those goals. We obtain direction and value to our lives through God's Word.

1. GOD'S LAW REVIVES US. The mere knowledge of God's law—and therefore, His will—goes beyond helping us to distinguish between right and wrong. It also provides for us a measure of strength to do what is right and to turn away from what is wrong. David said that the law of God had a way of reviving him—physically, mentally, emotionally, and spiritually. It can have the same effect on us today.

2. GOD'S LAW MAKES US WISE. From the time when it was first given, God's law has always helped those who have learned it and studied it to discern what is true, right, and lasting. It not only reveals what God desires from His people, but also discloses much about the character and heart of God.

3. GOD'S LAW BRINGS JOY TO OUR HEART. God's law does not chain us down physically, mentally, emotionally, and spiritually. Rather, it provides for us boundaries within which we realize that it is safe and secure to work and play. That protection has the long-term effect of introducing the staying power of joy in our hearts. Just as a sheep is truly happy when it is safe within the fold of its shepherd, so too we are full of joy when we are safe within the fold of our Shepherd and Lord.

4. GOD'S LAW GIVES US INSIGHT. In the same way that God's law reveals much about the character and heart of God, it also gives us insight into our own character and heart. And because it does so, it provides us the insight of our dire need for God and His love, grace, and mercy. The law's guidelines are like lights that help us see the pathway for our life's journey. The law indicates what God's ultimate will is for the lives of those who put their faith in Him.

5. GOD'S LAW WARNS US AGAINST SIN. Going beyond teaching us right from wrong, the law promises certain rewards for right living and certain consequences for wrong living. Thus it warns us of the dangers of a life of sin.

6. GOD'S LAW BRINGS US FULFILLMENT. A common thread of all humanity is the lifelong yearning for fulfillment. God's law has the capability to set us on the right path and then guide us toward a rich and fulfilling life.

FOR ADULTS

■ **TOPIC:** Seeking Wisdom

■ **QUESTIONS:** 1. In what ways can the perfection of God's Word be seen in your life and the lives of other believers you know? 2. How is it possible to find true and lasting joy by heeding the ethical injunctions recorded in

Scripture? 3. How has the enduring value of the Bible proven true for you, especially when you encounter difficult circumstances? 4. What are some of the warnings recorded in Scripture that you have found to be especially pertinent and why? 5. What might be some hidden faults and willful sins you would like to pray to God about?

■ ILLUSTRATIONS:

Vital Checkpoints. All of us have our favorite sweets. If we were writing Psalm 19 today, we might say that God's Word is sweeter than a chocolate bar. In fact, many people are "chocoholics." They like chocolate bars and chocolate syrup on their ice cream. They love rich chocolate ice cream and devil's food cake with fudge frosting. They think nothing of spending money for imported chocolate truffles.

Whatever our passions, as believers we realize they must take second place to our love for Scripture and our search for the treasures of wisdom recorded on its pages. Sometimes believers get slack in their time with God in His Word and prayer. As a result, their spiritual lives decline. Sometimes they fall for lesser loves and their love for Jesus grows cold.

These possibilities underscore the reason why the truths recorded in Psalm 19 (the focus of this week's lesson) are important to study and apply. They serve as vital checkpoints of our spiritual vitality.

O Worship the King. Sir Robert Grant was acquainted with kings. His father was a member of the British Parliament and later became chairman of the East India Company. Following in his father's footsteps, young Grant was elected to Parliament and then also became a director of the East India Company. In 1834 he was appointed governor of Bombay, and in that position he became greatly loved. A medical college in India was named in his honor.

Late in his life, Grant wrote a hymn based on the wisdom found in the Psalter. The progression of titles for God in the last line of that hymn—"O Worship the King"—is interesting. We know God first as our Maker or Creator (see Ps. 19:1-6). Then, even before our conversion, He is our Defender. We know Him then as "Redeemer" (vs. 14), and finally, as we walk day by day with Him, we know Him also as Friend.

God Created Wonderful Things. In the late 17th century a philosophy emerged called deism, which saw God as a kind of clockmaker who created the universe with a set of unchanging laws, then left it to run by itself until the end of time. This was the period when scientists such as Sir Isaac Newton (1642–1727) were discovering and describing those "laws" of the universe.

Thomas Paine (1737–1809), the great American patriot whose pamphlet *Common Sense* helped inspire the Revolutionary War, also wrote a pamphlet on the deist philosophy called *The Age of Reason*. In it he stated that he did not believe in a God who was still involved in every aspect of His creation.

When we read Psalm 19, however, we obtain a different perspective. We discover that God is very concerned about His creation. He not only brought the world into existence, but lovingly governs it. Moreover, He has made Himself known through the silent witness of creation. But above all, the wisdom of the Father is unveiled in all its glory through the incarnation of His Son. Indeed, Jesus has become "for us wisdom from God" (1 Cor. 1:30 NRSV).

FOR YOUTH

■ **TOPIC:** Glory Revealed
■ **QUESTIONS:** 1. How might those who are naïve and inexperienced gain understanding by studying God's Word? 2. In what ways can the decrees of Scripture prove enlightening for younger and older believers? 3. What do you think it means to have a healthy fear of the Lord? 4. How can understanding God's revelation in His Word positively affect your life? 5. How is it possible for believers to live in a way that is blameless before God?

■ **ILLUSTRATIONS:**

The Best Course to Take. Youth reflect the character of individuals they admire but have never met. Adolescents also exemplify the behavior, dress, and habits of family members, friends, neighbors, and coworkers. Imitating others can be a good thing if those who serve as role models are upright people.

This week's lesson will challenge Christian teens to consider the path of the Lord as the best course to take in life. Psalm 19 begins by reminding them of the magnificent beauty of God's handiwork in creation. Next, they are urged to show appreciation for the glory of the Creator by taking time to follow and keep the ethical injunctions recorded in His Word.

Moreover, saved adolescents are encouraged to become godly examples for others to follow. The more class members focus their attention on the Lord and His Word and behave in ways that are characteristic of Him, the more they will set a godly example in their words and deeds.

Passing the Faith Along. My grandmother—I called her "Mammaw"—was one of the best horticulturists that I've ever known. Her springtime and summertime flowers were the subject of many photographs, not to mention the number of people who slowed down or stopped just to look. She didn't know the names of all her flowers because she often made Pappaw stop along the roadside for her to dig up some wild plant she thought was especially glorious in its beauty.

And Mammaw didn't limit herself to flowers either. Her garden was always something special, too. Perhaps the most special item to ever come out of her garden was her purple-hulled green beans. These were beans that were purple until you cooked them, and then they turned green. After cooking them, you couldn't tell them from any other green beans.

I recently learned that this variety of beans are called Royalty Purple Pod beans, and they were developed by Elwyn M. Meader. Meader introduced more than 60 varieties of plants—from beets to peaches to kiwi fruit to chrysanthemums. At least half of his introductions came after he "retired" from a distinguished 18-year career as a plant breeder at the University of New Hampshire. He could have gotten rich from royalties on all his releases, but instead he gave them away "as payment for his space on the planet." As a man of faith, Meader's dedication and unselfishness in sharing germplasm ideas with colleagues throughout the world may have been an even greater contribution than his plants.

Mammaw liked to pass plants and seeds on to others, too. Throughout the area many people still have some of Mammaw's flowers and plants growing in their gardens. Like Mammaw, Elwyn Meader passed on his ideas and his plants. By the way, Meader credited his development of the Royalty Purple Pod bean to his wife's suggestion that it would be easier to pick beans if the pod color differed from the vine color. Now you know the rest of the story!

Mammaw and Elwyn Meader were both a little like David in Psalm 19. Like him, they wanted to pass along the wisdom of their faith in God and what He has revealed about Himself, both in creation and in His written Word. May we seek to do the same!

GOD PROVIDES REFUGE

BACKGROUND SCRIPTURE: Psalm 46:1-7
DEVOTIONAL READING: Hebrews 6:13-20

KEY VERSE: God is our refuge and strength,
a very present help in trouble. (Psalm 46:1)

KING JAMES VERSION
PSALM 46:1 God is our refuge and strength, a very present help in trouble. 2 Therefore will not we fear, though the earth be removed, and though the mountains be carried into the midst of the sea; 3 Though the waters thereof roar and be troubled, though the mountains shake with the swelling thereof. Selah. 4 There is a river, the streams whereof shall make glad the city of God, the holy place of the tabernacles of the most High. 5 God is in the midst of her; she shall not be moved: God shall help her, and that right early.

6 The heathen raged, the kingdoms were moved: he uttered his voice, the earth melted. 7 The LORD of hosts is with us; the God of Jacob is our refuge. Selah.

NEW REVISED STANDARD VERSION
PSALM 46:1 God is our refuge and strength,
 a very present help in trouble.
2 Therefore we will not fear, though the earth should change,
 though the mountains shake in the heart of the sea;
3 though its waters roar and foam,
 though the mountains tremble with its tumult. *Selah*
4 There is a river whose streams make glad the city of God,
 the holy habitation of the Most High.
5 God is in the midst of the city; it shall not be moved;
 God will help it when the morning dawns.
6 The nations are in an uproar, the kingdoms totter;
 he utters his voice, the earth melts.
7 The LORD of hosts is with us;
 the God of Jacob is our refuge. *Selah*

7

Monday, October 11	Isaiah 40:6-11	*Our Strong Yet Gentle God*
Tuesday, October 12	Deuteronomy 7:7-11	*Our Faithful God*
Wednesday, October 13	2 Corinthians 1:3-7	*Our Comforting God*
Thursday, October 14	2 Corinthians 1:8-11	*Our Rescuing God*
Friday, October 15	Isaiah 52:7-12	*God before and after Us*
Saturday, October 16	Psalm 68:4-10	*God's Provision for the Needy*
Sunday, October 17	Psalm 46:1-7	*God's Help in Times of Trouble*

BACKGROUND

Psalm 46 is one of the "Songs of Zion" (along with Pss. 48, 76, 84, 87, and 122) due to its confident affirmation of God as the faith community's source of help and strength in times of trouble. It remains debated who wrote this poem and when. It's also unclear whether the author was referring to specific events in Israel's history or was just making a general statement. One suggestion is that the deliverance of Jerusalem from Sennacherib in 701 B.C. (see 2 Kings 18-19; Isa. 36—37) provides the chronological setting for the psalm. While there is nothing specific in the biblical text to support this conjecture, it remains likely that Psalm 46 was written in Jerusalem sometime before the nation's exile in 586 B.C. Additionally, the hymn maintained an enduring relevance for God's people, especially with its emphasis on Jerusalem as the royal "city of God" (vs. 4) and the epicenter of His triumphant kingdom on earth.

The psalm's heading reads "to the chief Musician." This suggests the piece was originally meant to be a part of the worship liturgy performed in the temple by the leader of the Levitical choir. The members of the latter included the "sons of Korah." Korah was a Levite who, along with Dathan, Abriam, and On, participated in a failed revolt against the leadership of Moses and Aaron while the Israelites were camped in the wilderness of Paran (see Num. 16:1-49). This treasonous act notwithstanding, David later appointed some of Korah's descendants to serve as ministers of music within the tabernacle and temple (see 1 Chron. 6:31-37).

NOTES ON THE PRINTED TEXT

Psalm 46 is composed of three symmetrical stanzas, with each containing three verses (vss. 1-3, 4-6, and 8-10). There are also two refrains, with each containing one verse (vss. 7 and 11). One proposed musical arrangement has the members of the Levitical choir singing the opening stanza (vss. 1-3) and the two refrains (vss. 7, 11), while the music director sang the second and third stanzas (vss. 4-6 and 8-10). Part of the superscription says "A Song upon Alamoth," in which the last term literally means "young women." However, the specific connotation here remains uncertain. One possibility is that "alamoth" designates a specific style of music—for example, one that called for female voices singing in the soprano range (see 1 Chron. 15:20). Another suggestion is that the term referred to young women who played timbrels (similar to modern-day tambourines) as they traveled with a procession of singers and other musicians heading to the temple for worship.

In Psalm 46:1, "refuge" translates a Hebrew noun that denotes a place of shelter from rain, storm, or other perils. Also, "strength" renders a noun that points to what is fortified and secure. Together these words depict God as the believers' impenetrable defense. Regardless of the adverse situation or anguishing circumstance, the Lord is always ready to help. Psalm 9:9 likewise declares that God provides safety for the oppressed and is a refuge in times of trouble. Moreover, we learn in 37:39 that the Lord protects the faithful even in the most challenging dilemmas. According to 61:3, God is comparable to a strong tower where the upright may flee when danger lurks. Even when the health of believers begins to fail and their spirit weakens, the Lord empowers them to cope with seemingly overwhelming conditions (see 71:23). Because He is their place of safety, they can find rest in the shadow of the Almighty (see 91:1-2) and have their eternal needs fully met (see 142:5).

Because the believers' stability is found in God, the faith community deliberately chooses to forsake fear and completely trust in Him. A series of convulsions of nature are described in 46:2-3. Some think these probably were meant to symbolize the ferocity of a war. Another option is that a doomsday scenario involving naturally occurring disasters is being portrayed. The latter included a violent series of earthquakes that cause the mountains (the epitome of all that is stable and enduring) to crumble into the sea (vs. 2).

Furthermore, there's a succession of massive tsunamis that cause ocean-sized tidal waves to inundate the land. The "roar" (vs. 3) and foam of water is so intense that it even seems to cause the mountains to be shaken by the violence. The creation myths of many ancient Near Eastern cultures told about gods who subdued a chaotic ocean and formed the world from it. These people viewed large bodies of water as evil. While Israelite religion denied the reality of such myths, God's people nonetheless were familiar with them. Thus it was natural for the psalmists to compare encroaching evil with water that seems to engulf the land.

The Hebrew verb *Selah* literally means "to lift up" or "to exalt." It is found 71 times in the Psalter and 3 times in Habakkuk. Despite this frequency of usage, the significance of this technical musical term remains uncertain. According to ancient Jewish tradition, the verb is understood to mean "forever," "always," or "everlasting." A more recent proposal understands the verb to be a cue for the choir to sing louder, to repeat a verse, or to fall prostrate in homage to God. Others think the verb is used to show accentuation, signal an interruption, or mark a pause (possibly through the sounding of cymbals). In the case of the latter, it might have provided an opportunity for different groups to take up the song being performed.

After a violent tidal wave at sea, the peaceful river of Psalm 46:4 comes as a welcome change. The verse's references to "the city of God" and "the holy place" where the "most High" dwells clearly point to Jerusalem, which is otherwise known as Zion. The latter is first mentioned in 2 Samuel 5:7 as a Jebusite fortress on a hill. After being captured by King David, this fortress was called the City of David. Here David brought the ark of the covenant, thereby making the hill a sacred site (6:10-12). In the Old Testament, Zion not only is called "the city of God" (Ps. 46:4), but also the place where God dwells (132:14), God's "holy hill" (2:6), "the holy city" (Isa. 48:2), and "the glorious holy mountain" (Dan. 11:45). Eventually, Zion came to stand for the whole city of Jerusalem. In early Christian thought, Zion also represented "the city of the living God, the heavenly Jerusalem" (Heb. 12:22).

Interestingly, Jerusalem occupies a dry hilltop, and it has never had a permanent river. So what did the poet mean about a "river" (Ps. 46:4) there bringing joy to God's holy city? The answer to that question is found in verse 5. It seems that, while there is no actual river coursing through the sacred home of God, He lives within it. Expressed differently, the presence of the "most High" (vs. 4) flows into the lives of His people like a river and makes their hearts glad (see Isa. 33:21; 51:3). "Most High" (Ps. 46:4) is a divine title that depicts the Lord as the exalted Ruler over the entire creation. As its moral governor, He judges the wicked and vindicates the upright (see 7:17; 9:2; 18:13; 21:7; 47:2). Zion needed the presence of the Lord against its enemies. "Right early" (Ps. 46:5) was the time when armies normally attacked. But when Jerusalem was assaulted as the morning dawn approached, God would come to the city's aid and prevent it from being destroyed. Even though the mountains might tumble into the sea and the nations of the world might be upended, God rescues His people from such tumult and protects them from experiencing devastation.

The imagery of upheaval introduced in verses 2-3 reappears in verse 6. This time, however, it is used with respect to nations and kingdoms of the world being locked in mortal conflict. Fallen humanity and its leaders might rage, but their dominions are doomed to one day fail. Moreover, when chaos ensues, their fiefdoms will crumble. God is the cause of this turmoil. The poet depicts His thunderous shout as the battle cry uttered by a mighty warrior that terrifies the nations and causes the kingdoms to be shaken (see 18:13; 68:33). In point of fact, at the sound of His voice, the entire planet dissolves (see Amos 9:5).

Psalm 46:7 reveals God to be full of power and grace. The verse can be translated "The Lord who commands heaven's armies is on our side." The poet was indicating that God is like a mighty warrior-king who leads the forces of heaven into battle on behalf of His chosen people (see 24:10). The name translated "God of Jacob" (46:7) evokes the memory of one of the nation's greatest ancestors. The Lord—who graciously chose Jacob for a blessing instead of his older brother, Esau—protects the faith community (20:1). The Hebrew word translated "refuge" (46:7) refers to a high place or elevated stronghold. The imagery is that of a mountaintop citadel that cannot be overcome by an army of invaders (see 9:9; 18:2). Because the mighty God is on the side of the upright, they experience His gracious hand of protection.

The final portion of Psalm 46 invites us to use the eyes of our imagination to examine the aftermath of a tremendous battle. The field is strewed with the broken and smoking instruments of warfare. This is a scene of terrible destruction. But this is not just the result of one group of armed fighters overcoming another. God Himself entered the fray on the side of His people. Thus the desolation on the battlefield is His work (vs. 8). He brought peace, but He did it by carrying the battle to a decisive end. This scene cannot represent only the conclusion of a battle in Israel's history. The psalm says God "maketh wars cease to the ends of the earth" (vs. 9). Therefore, it would seem that the scene must be a preview of God's final victory over evil. Above the din of earth's wicked people, God cries "Be still" (vs. 10), meaning "Enough! Stop!" He calls all people to recognize Him as God, and He confidently declares that He will be exalted throughout the entire globe.

SUGGESTIONS TO TEACHERS

One fact we can be sure of is that all of us go through times of trouble. Our experiences of difficulty often come unannounced and catch us off guard. The way in which we cope with these blows will be determined by the strength of our faith and the depth of our commitment to God. Despite the possible adversities facing the author of Psalm 46, he turned to God for help and strength.

1. GOD KNOWS HIS PEOPLE. One of the marvels of our heavenly Father is that He knows us completely. Being the eternal God, He has our total lives spread out before Him, from beginning to end. He rejoices when we are strong, and He understands and is ready to help us when we falter.

2. GOD PROTECTS HIS PEOPLE. Though God allows trials and testings to come into our lives at times that seem almost impossible to endure, He knows our breaking point. He will not permit a temptation that is beyond our ability, in Him, to bear (1 Cor. 10:13).

3. GOD GIVES WISDOM TO HIS PEOPLE. God has promised wisdom to His people that will help them endure overwhelming situations that come into their lives (see Jas. 1:5). The context of the preceding verse suggests James' readers needed wisdom to handle the trials of their lives. Biblical wisdom consists of the intellectual, moral, social, and spiritual skills necessary for successful living. Ultimately, this wisdom springs from the fear of the Lord (see Prov. 1:7; 9:10; 15:33).

FOR ADULTS

■ TOPIC: Seeking Refuge

■ QUESTIONS: 1. What sorts of troubles have you faced that God has helped you to handle? 2. How can the truths of Scripture reassure believers in times of turmoil? 3. How has God been like a mighty warrior to you when you felt threatened by others? 4. Why is it important to look to God for hope when life feels chaotic? 5. In what ways can believers contribute to God's exaltation in the world?

■ **ILLUSTRATIONS:**

Holding on Firmly. Ann was blind from birth. Everything she knew and accomplished in life she owed to her parents' sacrifice and dedication. When her mother fell ill, Ann was distraught. She had never seen her mother. She knew only her voice and touch. For months Ann sat with her mother in a nursing home, holding her hands and talking to her. But her mother had lost her speech and could not respond. Nevertheless, Ann held on firmly every day, speaking words of comfort and hope.

In times of suffering we hold on firmly to each other and especially to God. Even when God does not seem to reply to our cries, we continue to find refuge in Him. Faith drives us to prayer and worship every day. Despite the darkness, we believe that the all-powerful Lord is with us. We also claim God's promise that nothing can separate us from His love (see Rom. 8:31-39).

A Mighty Fortress. Perhaps one of the best-loved hymns of the church is "A Mighty Fortress Is Our God." The author, Martin Luther, wrote the words and composed the melody sometime between 1527 and 1529. The song has been translated into English from the German original over 72 times. It has also been translated into numerous other languages.

During the turmoil of the Reformation, Luther drew inspiration for his hymn from Psalm 46. For instance, the title of the song is his paraphrase of verse 1, "God is our refuge and strength." Today we sing Frederick Hedge's rendering of Luther's canticle, which includes the following familiar words:

A mighty fortress is our God, A bulwark never failing;
Our helper He, amid the flood of mortal ills prevailing.

How to Handle Troubles. Three women were talking about how they had handled worry and trouble in their lives. One said, "I have had lots of troubles. I have lain awake nights wrestling with them. Then I discovered that those things that worried me most never happened!" The second woman said, "I was once told that we carry 'three bags of troubles'—those we really have, those we had in the past, and those we are sure we are going to have."

The third lady chuckled and said, "Right now, I can't seem to remember my troubles. The Lord said for us to cast all our cares on Him. He gives me strength for each day's work, and helps me over the hard places. At night, by the time I've finished thanking Him for His goodness, I'm always so tired that I just fall asleep."

■ **TOPIC:** We Are Safe!

■ **QUESTIONS:** 1. What does it mean to you that God is the refuge and strength of believers? 2. How is it possible for believers to remain calm when their life circumstances feel out of control? 3. What are some things you can do to make your worship of almighty God a time filled with joy? 4. Why would God allow once-powerful nations to someday fall? 5. What are your greatest fears? How can God help you cope with those fears?

■ **ILLUSTRATIONS:**

Remaining Faithful. One of the basic therapies for strengthening hand, wrist, and arm muscles is to tightly squeeze a rubber ball several times a day. At first we feel the tension and pain, but gradually our muscles respond and we are able to function normally. This exercise is prescribed after injuries or surgeries—incidents and events we would prefer to avoid. In cases like these, holding tightly to a rubber ball is a discipline that produces results.

God sometimes takes us through tough times to strengthen our spiritual muscles (so to speak). He knows how flabby we get when we neglect our worship and obedience to His good and perfect will. But when He gets our attention, we respond with therapies that give us new love and zeal for Him.

Psalm 46 reminds us that it is possible to be faithful to God, even when we frightened by hard times. We overcome our fears by finding safety and strength in God, who is our eternal refuge.

The Only Hope. One day an artist sought to depict on canvas the meaning of the Gospel. He began by painting a storm at sea. Black clouds filled the sky. A flash of lightning illuminated a little boat, which could be seen disintegrating under the pounding of the ocean. People were struggling in the swirling waters, their anguished faces crying out for help.

The only glimmer of hope appeared in the foreground of the painting, where a large rock protruded out of the water. There, clutching desperately with both hands, was one lone seaman. It was a moving scene. As one looked at the painting, one could see in the tempest a symbol of humankind's hopeless condition. And, true to the Gospel, the only hope of salvation was "the Rock of Ages," that is, Jesus, our shelter in the time of storm.

The Tunnels of Life. Corrie ten Boom once said, "When a train goes through a tunnel and it gets dark, you don't throw away the ticket and jump off. You sit still and trust the engineer." Johnny was 14 years old and was en route to visit his grandparents in Switzerland. He had flown nonstop from New York to Geneva. There, a travel agent helped him transfer to a train on which he would ride to his final destination in the

Oberland region of central Switzerland.

Johnny had a window seat on the train, and enjoyed the fabulous scenery—the beautiful lakes, the towering, snow-covered Alps, and the quaint Swiss villages with their colorful flowers and chateaus. Then came the first tunnel. As the train entered the tunnel, suddenly it became pitch dark. In a moment, the train stopped. No one spoke. There was not a glimmer of light. There had been a temporary interruption in the electrical system that drove the train.

Johnny almost panicked. "Are we going to get off? How can we see how to walk? What is going to happen?" In a few moments, the lights came on in the train, the journey resumed, and it wasn't long until they emerged from the tunnel into a burst of sunlight.

Perhaps the author of Psalm 46 had a life experience that seemed at the time to be as unnerving as a dark tunnel. We, too, have experiences in life that are frightening. But there is a heavenly engineer who controls the train and who will safely bring us through.

GOD IS IN CHARGE

BACKGROUND SCRIPTURE: Psalm 47
DEVOTIONAL READING: Jeremiah 10:6-10

KEY VERSES: Sing praises to God, sing praises: sing praises unto our King, sing praises. For God is the King of all the earth: sing ye praises with understanding. (Psalm 47:6-7)

KING JAMES VERSION

PSALM 47:1 O clap your hands, all ye people; shout unto God with the voice of triumph. 2 For the LORD most high is terrible; he is a great King over all the earth. 3 He shall subdue the people under us, and the nations under our feet. 4 He shall choose our inheritance for us, the excellency of Jacob whom he loved. Selah.

5 God is gone up with a shout, the LORD with the sound of a trumpet. 6 Sing praises to God, sing praises: sing praises unto our King, sing praises. 7 For God is the King of all the earth: sing ye praises with understanding. 8 God reigneth over the heathen: God sitteth upon the throne of his holiness. 9 The princes of the people are gathered together, even the people of the God of Abraham: for the shields of the earth belong unto God: he is greatly exalted.

NEW REVISED STANDARD VERSION

PSALM 47:1 Clap your hands, all you peoples;
  shout to God with loud songs of joy.
2 For the LORD, the Most High, is awesome,
  a great king over all the earth.
3 He subdued peoples under us,
  and nations under our feet.
4 He chose our heritage for us,
  the pride of Jacob whom he loves.   *Selah*
5 God has gone up with a shout,
  the LORD with the sound of a trumpet.
6 Sing praises to God, sing praises;
  sing praises to our King, sing praises.
7 For God is the king of all the earth;
  sing praises with a psalm.
8 God is king over the nations;
  God sits on his holy throne.
9 The princes of the peoples gather
  as the people of the God of Abraham.
For the shields of the earth belong to God;
  he is highly exalted.

BACKGROUND

The heading to Psalm 47 states that it was originally intended for the "chief Musician" and that it was part of the collection of songs attributed to the descendants of Korah. As with Psalm 46 (which we studied last week), this poem was originally meant to be a part of the worship liturgy performed in the temple by the leader of the Levitical choir. The references in Psalm 47:1 to the clapping of hands and the raising of joyous shouts to God reinforce the impression that the ministers of music within the temple performed the hymn with enthusiasm and energy. This celebration might have also included the blowing of trumpets along with a procession of worshipers making their way to the temple, where the ark of the covenant lay (see 2 Sam. 6:12-19; Ps. 24:7-10). Some think the ancient Israelites used the collection in ritual ceremonies during an autumn festival or in conjunction with a new year festival to commemorate God's enthronement as ruler over creation.

Evidently, the underlying historical circumstance of Psalm 47 is a great military victory over one of Judah's enemies (for example, Sennacherib, the Assyrian monarch; see 2 Kings 19:35-37). The poem most likely was written in Jerusalem sometime before the nation's exile in 586 B.C. The Hebrew noun in the superscription translated "psalm" refers to a melody or a poem set to notes that was to be accompanied by instrumental music. The hymn has been categorized as one of the kingship or royal psalms because it explicitly refers to God as the sovereign monarch over the entire universe. The communal hymn also rehearses the jubilation of God's people over His ending of evil in its various forms (for example, iniquity, injustice, idolatry, and immorality; see Isa. 11:3-5). The early church picked up on the prophetic, end-time aspect of these themes to celebrate the ascension and rule of the Messiah, whom they proclaimed as the all-powerful warrior-king (see Matt. 24:30-31; 25:31; John 1:49; Rev. 19:16).

NOTES ON THE PRINTED TEXT

Concerning the literary structure of Psalm 47, verses 1-4 draw attention to the magnificence of God, both in terms of His awesomeness (vss. 1-2) and His love and care for His people (vss. 3-4). Then, verses 5-9 showcase the sovereignty of God.

It's easy to imagine a chorus of worshipers praising the ascension of God to His throne (vs. 5), announcing His rule over all the earth (vss. 6-7), and affirming His ownership of every nation (vss. 8-9). Indeed, verse 1 summons all the nations—here personified as individuals—to clap their hands to express their joy. Likewise, they were to utter exuberant praises with their mouths to God in anticipation of His kingship over all the earth at the consummation of the present era. These activities mirror the jubilant clapping and shouting that accompanied coronation ceremonies in ancient times (see 1 Sam. 10:24; 2 Kings 11:12-13). Psalm 29:1-2 calls upon heavenly beings to acknowledge the Lord's majesty and power and to worship Him in the splendor of His holiness. Similarly, 33:1-4 invites the righteous to shout their praises to God for His just decrees and equitable actions.

In 47:2, the poet referred to God as the "Lord most high." As was noted in last week's lesson, this divine title depicts God as the exalted Ruler over all the universe, who vindicates the upright and judges the wicked. Centuries earlier, Melchizedek (the king of Salem), in the blessing he spoke to Abraham, affirmed God as "most high" (Gen. 14:19) and the "possessor of heaven and earth." Moses also declared to the generation of Israelites living in his day that the Lord reigns as "God in heaven above, and upon the earth beneath" (Deut. 4:39). Moreover, Rahab the prostitute affirmed this same truth to the Israelite spies whom she sought to protect from the rulers of Jericho (Josh. 2:11). Psalm 47:2 reveals that the all-powerful Lord is "terrible." The latter renders a Hebrew verb that denotes the presence of intense fear. With respect to God's foes, they are filled with dread when He defeats them. Meanwhile, the godly respond with reverence, especially as they witness the royal splendor connected with the Lord's powerful deeds (see 66:3, 5; 68:35; 76:7, 12; 89:7; 96:4; 99:3; 111:9). When He decisively acts, there is no doubt that the great King reigns supreme "over all the earth" (47:2).

Verses 3-4 review God's love and care for His people during the previous years of their history. This includes the Lord freeing the Israelites from Egypt, leading them through an extended period of wandering in the wilderness of Sinai, and enabling them to enter and occupy Canaan. Particular attention is given to God's using Joshua to lead the chosen people in the conquest of the promised land. The Israelites were awe-inspired as they watched the Lord subdue the surrounding nations. It was God who enabled His people to establish their rule over the pagan inhabitants (vs. 3). The idiomatic expression rendered "nations under our feet" can be traced to the practice of the victor in battle placing his foot on the necks of his vanquished foes (see Josh. 10:24; Pss. 8:6; 110:1). In looking back on those eventual days, the covenant community acknowledged that the Lord was responsible for picking out a special land for His people as their abiding inheritance (see Gen. 12:7; 17:8; Exod. 3:8; Deut. 1:8; Jer. 3:18). Then when the Israelites established their claim over Canaan, it became a source of pride for Jacob's rightful heirs. Indeed, to Jacob and his descendants God pledged to give His covenantal love and unwavering devotion (Ps. 47:4).

Verse 5 depicts God ascending His throne while His subordinates affirm the action with joyous shouts. Then, as the Lord takes His seat as the all-powerful sovereign of the universe, He does so amid the blair of a "trumpet." The latter renders a Hebrew noun that is literally translated "ram's horn." Down through the centuries, this item became the preeminent ritual instrument used by God's people. Though the musical intonation produced by the ram's horn was limited in range, the Israelites still used it musically in worship. The loudness of the trumpet made it especially well suited in times of war as summon fighters to battle (see Jer. 4:19), to herald the commencement of an attack (see Judg. 3:27; 6:34), to signal the end of a military campaign (see 2 Sam. 2:28; 18:16; 20:22), to warn combatants of an impending assault (see Jer. 6:1, 17; Ezek. 33:3-6; Hos. 5:8; Joel 2:1), and to announce the achievement of victory in battle (see 1 Sam. 13:3). There were even occasions when ram's horns were blown to proclaim the installment of a new king (see 2 Sam. 15:10; 1 Kings 1:34, 39; 2 Kings 9:13).

What is the proper response of the covenant community to the ascension of God to His throne? It is for the upright to sing praises filled with thanksgiving to their King. The repetition of the exhortation in Psalm 47:6 emphasizes the joy and enthusiasm that are to accompany this important act of worship. In its original context, the exhortation would have been addressed to the musicians and singers in the temple. Verse 7 reiterates the truth that God is not only Israel's monarch, but also the ruler of everyone and everything in the universe (see Isa. 52:7). Accordingly, believers are to "sing . . . praises with understanding" (Ps. 47:7). "Understanding" renders a Hebrew noun that is derived from a verb that means "to be prudent" or "to be wise." This has led interpreters to suggest that in this context, the noun refers to a song that is well-written, contemplative, and able to impart moral wisdom to the faithful.

In ancient times, when a new ruler was coronated as king, his loyal subjects would acclaim him as their monarch using a standardized declaration. Verse 8 reflects this practice with the proclamation that the God of Israel had mounted His sacred throne and from it reigned supreme over every nation on earth. The emphasis on God's throne being holy reminds us that the Lord is distinct from His creatures and infinitely exalted above them. He alone is morally pure and upright in whatever He thinks, plans, and does. Only He is devoid of evil desires, aspirations, and initiatives. Moreover, because the Lord is holy, He is the standard for all that is good and right (see Lev. 19:2; Exod. 15:11; 1 Sam. 2:2; 1 Chron. 16:29; Ps. 99:3; 110:3; Isa. 6:3; Rev. 4:8).

Psalm 47:9 anticipates a future day when the rulers of the world will gather together with the people belonging to the God worshiped by Abraham (see Isa. 2:1-5; Mich. 4:1-5). The reason this will happen is that all the earth's leaders, regardless of their stature or power, "belong unto God" (Ps. 47:9). The Hebrew noun rendered "shields" is a reminder that in a metaphorical sense, the rulers of the world, like shields, shouldered the task of protecting and safeguarding their people (see 84:9). Because the Lord is more powerful than all the armies on the planet, He is highly exalted, honored, and praised throughout the universe (see 46:10; 97:9). Philippians 2:9-11 reveals that this truth applies just as much to the Son as to the Father. We learn that the place of honor that Jesus willingly forsook was given back to Him with the added glory of His triumph over sin and death.

SUGGESTIONS TO TEACHERS

We learn from Psalm 47 that God is the supreme ruler over all the earth. He is pleased when people praise Him as their eternal King. Moreover, the Lord of life is honored when humankind rejoices in His goodness and greatness. Indeed, this is one humble way for people to express their infinite debt of gratitude to Him.

1. THE KING'S UNENDING CONTROL. Without the sustaining hand of the Most High God, life would become intolerable. It would be impossible to find adequate food, water, or clothing. The environment would become unbearably hostile and we would not be able to protect ourselves for long from its ravages. Eventually our world would degenerate into chaos, putting our long-term survival in jeopardy.

2. THE KING'S ABUNDANT PROVISION. The exalted Lord is so faithful and consistent in providing our needs that we tend to forget He is present. We arrogantly think we have control over what happens to us. We imagine that we are self-sufficient and can survive solely by means of our will and strength. We know, however, from this week's lesson that our lives are in God's hands. Thus He is to be praised for the marvelous world He created and for the wonderful life He gives to us.

3. THE KING'S PROVIDENTIAL CARE. The students should be encouraged to reflect on how the Lord of life has faithfully provided for them throughout their earthly existence with food, shelter, good health, friends, and family. These are all evidences of God's providential care that they might take for granted and for which they might fail to give Him thanks. The students can also praise God for helping them overcome hardships and endure difficult times.

4. THE KING'S WITNESS THROUGH US. When we give thanks to the eternal King for His goodness, we declare to the unsaved that He is our Creator and Sustainer. We bear witness to the truth that every person needs God for present life and future hope. Our words of praise and gratitude to God might encourage the unsaved to consider the truths of Christ and turn to Him in faith for new life and eternal joy.

FOR ADULTS

▨ **TOPIC:** Good Leaders
▨ **QUESTIONS:** 1. What do you think the poet felt as he summoned the nations to clap their hands and shout joyfully to God? 2. In this day

and age, how might the Lord show Himself to be the great King of the entire world? 3. What was the basis for the Israelites taking pride in the fact that God had given them Canaan as their inheritance? 4. How can we derive comfort in the truth of God's universal sovereignty, especially when life feels overwhelming? 5. What are some reasons why we should praise God as the supreme Lord of the earth?

▪ ILLUSTRATIONS:

Certainty in an Uncertain World. Watching just 30 minutes of a nightly news broadcast is enough to convince most people that we live in uncertain times. There are reports about rogue leaders across the globe who have brought anguish and loss to many people. We also learn about floods, tornadoes, earthquakes, and wildfires that leave untold destruction and death in their wake.

And as we get older, we are eventually touched (either directly or indirectly) by disease and loss of loved ones. Other personal hardships we may encounter include financial loss, marital upheaval, and deep psychological turmoil. What are we to do in a world filled with so much uncertainty? To whom should we turn for guidance and help?

Psalm 47 (which is the focus of this week's lesson) urges us to put our hope in God, who reigns over the nations. Even in our moments of crisis, we can draw strength and encouragement from the King of all the earth. When we rest our confidence in Him, we will never be disappointed.

A Personal Fiefdom. John's computer company had prospered beyond his wildest dreams. In less than 10 years, he had gone from a salary in the $50,000 range to a net worth of more than $60 million. However, that huge excess didn't just go to his bank accounts. Much of it went to his head.

Year after year, John became more prideful of the empire that he had created. He was no longer the creative genius behind the product line, but simply relaxed in luxury, especially as the company continued to grow. He often bragged that there was no end in sight.

Imagine what John must have felt like the morning he awakened with no feeling below his waist. Consider the shock when the tests confirmed that inoperable tumors would take his life within weeks. Tragically, his personal "fiefdom" had taken precedence over God's kingdom.

All earthly domains—whether personal or corporate—will fall one day. Some leaders will be judged as God-fearing, while others will not. Praise God that our final and eternal ruler will be our Lord Jesus!

Global Financial Scam. Joe Bruno, a correspondent for the *Associated Press*, reported that on December 11, 2008, a former Nasdaq stock market chairman was arrested on a securities fraud charge. His name is Bernard L. Madoff, and he is said to have operated a "phony investment business that lost at least $50 billion" and "amounted to nothing more than a . . . massive deception."

Madoff was able to get his hands on so much money because people trusted his financial leadership and judgment. Indeed, he was a "respected, venerable figure on Wall Street." The names of the investors who said they were misled by Madoff were extensive and reached around the globe. According to Bruno, the victims included the "world's biggest banking institutions and hedge funds, the super rich and the famous, pensioners and charities."

The author of Psalm 47 belonged to a nation that had seen both honest and unscrupulous leaders. He understood that the covenant community would follow the wrong leaders just as easily as investors would entrust their assets to a con artist. The poet would exhort all people—both leaders and their subordinates—to yield control of their lives to God, the King of all the earth, and follow the ethical imperatives He has recorded in His Word.

■ TOPIC: King of the Earth

■ QUESTIONS: 1. In what ways has the Lord shown Himself to be awesome in your life? 2. How do you think the Israelites felt about the truth that their God had subdued other nations? 3. Why is it important for believers to affirm that the Lord is the eternal King of the universe? 4. During times of corporate worship, what sorts of praise songs do you enjoy singing to God? 5. Why is it sometimes hard to give the King of our lives the praise He deserves?

■ ILLUSTRATIONS:

It Keeps On Going and Going and Going. There's a certain company in the United States that markets its product by claiming that it can keep battery-operated devices going, and going, and going. This self-assured optimism is reflected throughout society in the West. It doesn't seem to matter whether we're talking about young people, middle-aged individuals, or those heading into retirement. People from each age group seem to have a durable confidence that they can do whatever they want, however they want, and whenever they want.

Our studies this week expose the folly of such thinking. People are not the captains of their own destiny, though they like to think they are. Ultimately the course of our lives falls under the rule of God. The King of the earth determines when we are born and when we will die. Even such things as the shape of our hands and the size of our feet are controlled by Him. Isn't it time we begin to acknowledge this in the way we live?

The Eternal Kingdom of Christ. Volumes have been written about Napoleon Bonaparte (1769–1821). Historians have detailed his career as a general during the French Revolution and his tenure as the emperor of the first French empire. Moreover, across the globe, military academies study his campaigns. Indeed, many regard him as one of history's greatest commanders.

The once-mighty Napoleon is reported to have made this statement: "Alexander, Caesar, Charlemagne, and myself founded empires; but on what foundation did we rest the creatures of our genius? Upon force. But Jesus Christ founded an empire upon love; and at this hour, millions of persons would die for Him. I die before my time, and my body will be given back to the earth to become food for the worms. Such is the destiny of him who has been called the 'great Napoleon.' What an abyss between my deep misery and the eternal kingdom of Christ, which is proclaimed, loved, adored, and is still existing over the whole earth."

Assyria Is Back! They have a national anthem, but they have not had a country since the seventh century B.C. Their population is over three million. They share a common language (Aramaic), and many have a common faith—Christianity. In fact, they were one of the first people groups to become Christian in the first century of the common era. For hundreds of years they have been dispersed around the world by war and persecutions, but now a modern invention has helped bring them together: the Internet.

Assyria is back—in cyberspace. The Assyrians created one of the greatest empires of the ancient world, until the Babylonians and Persians sacked and destroyed it. Now, the Assyrian homeland includes parts of northern Iraq, northeastern Syria, northern Iran, and southeastern Turkey. People of Assyrian ancestry have banded together online to call for a recognition of their rights by the countries that now control the Assyrian homeland, countries that have often ignored, persecuted, or even killed Assyrians.

Over the centuries, countless empires of such places as Rome, Spain, England, France, Greece, Turkey, Russia, Germany, Japan, and even Mongolia and Mali have risen and fallen. Even the United States is a mere speck on the timeline of history, existing for less than 250 years. Who knows whether it will exist even 50 years from now? Only one person knows—the one whose kingdom "is not of this world" (John 18:36), but who controls the destiny of all nations and peoples.

COMFORT AND ASSURANCE

BACKGROUND SCRIPTURE: Psalm 63
DEVOTIONAL READING: Psalm 3:1-6

KEY VERSE: O God, thou art my God; early will I seek thee: my soul thirsteth for thee, my flesh longeth for thee in a dry and thirsty land, where no water is. (Psalm 63:1)

KING JAMES VERSION

PSALM 63:1 O God, thou art my God; early will I seek thee: my soul thirsteth for thee, my flesh longeth for thee in a dry and thirsty land, where no water is;
2 To see thy power and thy glory, so as I have seen thee in the sanctuary.
3 Because thy lovingkindness is better than life, my lips shall praise thee. 4 Thus will I bless thee while I live: I will lift up my hands in thy name. 5 My soul shall be satisfied as with marrow and fatness; and my mouth shall praise thee with joyful lips: 6 When I remember thee upon my bed, and meditate on thee in the night watches.
7 Because thou hast been my help, therefore in the shadow of thy wings will I rejoice. 8 My soul followeth hard after thee: thy right hand upholdeth me. 9 But those that seek my soul, to destroy it, shall go into the lower parts of the earth. 10 They shall fall by the sword: they shall be a portion for foxes. 11 But the king shall rejoice in God; every one that sweareth by him shall glory: but the mouth of them that speak lies shall be stopped.

NEW REVISED STANDARD VERSION

PSALM 63:1 O God, you are my God, I seek you,
    my soul thirsts for you;
my flesh faints for you,
    as in a dry and weary land where there is no water.
2 So I have looked upon you in the sanctuary,
    beholding your power and glory.
3 Because your steadfast love is better than life,
    my lips will praise you.
4 So I will bless you as long as I live;
    I will lift up my hands and call on your name.
5 My soul is satisfied as with a rich feast,
    and my mouth praises you with joyful lips
6 when I think of you on my bed,
    and meditate on you in the watches of the night;
7 for you have been my help,
    and in the shadow of your wings I sing for joy.
8 My soul clings to you;
    your right hand upholds me.
9 But those who seek to destroy my life
    shall go down into the depths of the earth;
10 they shall be given over to the power of the sword,
    they shall be prey for jackals.
11 But the king shall rejoice in God;
    all who swear by him shall exult,
    for the mouths of liars will be stopped.

9

Home Bible Readings

Background

The heading of Psalm 63 identifies the poem as a "psalm of David." The Hebrew noun translated "psalm" refers to a melody set to notes that was to be accompanied by instrumental music. As with other hymns we have studied thus far, the ministers of music within the temple would have performed Psalm 63 with enthusiasm and energy. There is some uncertainty regarding the significance of the phrase "of David." The range of possible meanings include "belonging to," "dedicated to," "with reference to," "concerning," and "for the use of." The title locates the setting of the song somewhere in the "wilderness of Judah."

The entire region was a dry and inhospitable place. The topography included barren mountain cliffs, rock-covered valleys, and sandy dunes. Aside from the infrequent wadi, the region had little vegetation. Only the hardiest of desert plants survived the arid climate. There are two periods in David's life in which his time in the wilderness of Judah had historical significance. The first was when David fled from Saul around 1008 B.C. (see 1 Sam. 22—25). The second incident occurred around 980 B.C. when David and a group of his loyal officials left Jerusalem right before the king's son, Absalom, and his fellow insurrectionists temporarily seized control of Israel's capital (see 2 Sam. 15—17). Undoubtedly, during each of these episodes David was reminded of how fleeting and distressing life can feel.

Notes on the Printed Text

In Psalm 63, David expressed his ardent desire to be in the presence of God. Throughout David's harrowing experiences, the Lord remained faithful in protecting His servant from danger. David was not only confident that the Lord would safeguard him, but also that God would judge his enemies. This helps explain why David declared Israel's God to be the object of his worship and the source of spiritual strength. David, even as the nation's king (see vs. 11), longed for God. Indeed, Israel's monarch sought after the Lord "early" (vs. 1), in which the biblical text is more literally rendered "at dawn" or "in the morning." David portrayed the Judean wilderness as an arid place that brought fatigue, isolation, and gloom to those who were forced to inhabit it. During the king's sojourn in the desert, his soul thirsted for God and his whole being desired Him (see 143:6).

David stated that he had caught a glimpse of the Lord's holy presence in His "sanctuary" (63:2). The poet may have been referring to symbols of God's presence, such as the ark of the covenant. Furthermore, Israel's king recalled witnessing displays of God's might and splendor within the Jerusalem shrine (see 27:4). In the wilderness of Judah, David felt as if he were far from God's presence. Despite that, he was certain that he would again be able to return to the sanctuary and stand in worship before the Lord. The king's motivation for doing so was God's "lovingkindness" (vs. 3), in which the latter renders a Hebrew noun that refers to the unfailing compassion of the Lord for His chosen people. The nation's monarch considered the experience of God's love to mean more to him than life itself. It was for this reason that David wanted to utter praises to God and in that way glorify His name. Regardless of whether the poet was at the Jerusalem shrine or languishing in the Judean desert, he was committed to giving thanks to God throughout his life. In ancient times, raising one's hands toward God (who is in heaven) was regarded as a gesture to signal prayer (see Ps. 28:2; Lam. 2:19), adoration (see Ps. 134:2), dependence (see 77:2), and respect (see 119:48).

In 63:4, David said he looked forward to performing these acts of worship in God's "name." The Israelites considered the latter to be the supreme expression of the Lord's righteous character and holy presence (see Exod. 3:14-15; 34:6-7). This explains why they regarded the sanctuary in Jerusalem to be the earthly residence for the divine name (see Deut. 12:5, 11; 2 Sam. 7:13; Ps. 74:7). As well, the people could pray to the Lord by calling on His name (see Pss. 79:6; 80:18; 99:6; 105:1; 116:4, 13, 17). The Israelites believed God used His name to offer protection (see Ps. 20:1; Prov. 18:10) and deliverance to them (see Ps. 54:1), and to signal that His saving presence was near (see 52:9). For the upright, God's name was the focus of their trust (see 20:7; 33:21), hope (see 52:9), praise (see 7:17; 9:2; 18:49), and expression of joy (see 89:16). To love and fear God's name was considered to be the same as esteeming and reverencing the Lord Himself (see 61:5; 69:36; 86:11; 102:15; 119:132).

The beginning of Psalm 63:5 is literally rendered "like fat and fatness" and idiomatically refers to the choicest meat or more generally the finest food set out at a sumptuous banquet (see Gen. 45:18; Isa. 25:6). David saw his time of intimate communion with God as an opportunity for his soul to dine and be "satisfied" (Ps. 63:5). The latter renders a Hebrew verb that denotes someone who is completely satiated from the food and drink consumed at a feast. This information helps us to understand why Israel's king wanted to express thanks to God by singing to Him songs of praise.

In verse 1, David expressed his earnest desire to seek God, and in verse 11 he ended his poem with a declaration of joy-filled anticipation. At the thematic center of the hymn is David's statement of contemplating God during the nighttime hours (vs. 6). Doing this intensified the poet's desire to commune with the Lord and see Him vindicate His servant by silencing his foes. Undoubtedly, overseeing the entire Israelite nation could have easily dominated the king's thoughts throughout the day and during the night. Even so, David took the opportunity while resting in bed to direct his attention to God and meditate on Him until the early hours of the morning. (In those days, the Israelites divided the nighttime into three or four "watches"; see Judg. 7:19; 1 Sam. 11:11; Lam. 2:19; Ps. 119:48.) Instead of waking up feeling disconcerted and grumpy, Israel's monarch came away refreshed and reinvigorated to shoulder the tasks facing him at the start of a new day.

Perhaps many of David's contemporaries looked to military might as their source of help. In contrast, the king of Israel trusted in God as his deliverer. The poet compared God's protective presence to that of an adult bird sheltering its young under the shade provided by its wings (see Pss. 17:8; 57:1; 36:7; 91:4). Because David was assured that the Lord watched over and safeguarded him, he could sing for joy (63:7). The preceding statements did not mean David never struggled with anxiety about his situation. Instead, the poet acknowledged that when life felt overwhelming, he pursued with determination his relationship with God. Moreover, the king knew that clinging to the Lord was not a wasted effort, for His strong "right hand" (vs. 8) securely held His servant (see Deut. 4:4; 10:20; 11:22; 13:4; Josh. 22:5; 2 Kings 18:6). The latter is a picturesque way of saying that God kept David safe, even while he was in the wilderness of Judah.

David did not mince any words concerning the fate of his adversaries, whom he referred to for the first time in Psalm 63. Because God was the poet's source of help and protection, he was confident that those who sought to kill him would be brought to ruin. According to verse 9, they would end up in the "lower parts of the earth." This phrase depicts the underworld as the dwelling place of the dead (see Ezek. 26:20; 31:14, 16, 18; 32:18, 24). David's vindication would come when God, the divine warrior, caused the king's foes to die in battle by the "sword" (Ps. 63:10). The ultimate disgrace would be for the corpses of David's enemies to be eaten by "foxes." In contrast, the poet looked forward with all the upright to being spiritually satisfied at the Lord's heavenly banquet (see vs. 5).

David not only longed for God (vs. 1), but also anticipated being able to sing for joy in His presence once again at the Jerusalem sanctuary (vs. 11). Furthermore, Israel's king looked forward to the day when the Lord would give him victory and in doing so enable him to celebrate the triumphant occasion. More generally, the monarch awaited the day when everyone who took an oath of loyalty to God in His name would have the opportunity to join the king in singing praise songs to the Lord (see Deut. 6:13; 10:20; Jer. 12:16). In contrast, David was confident that God would shut the mouths of those who spoke lies and thereby prove them to be wrong (see Pss. 5:6, 9; 58:3; 101:7; 107:42). The latter would include those who were unsuccessful in their attempts to undermine the nation's king through the spread of malicious rumors. Ultimately, such treasonous acts were not only against the monarch, but also against God, whom he served as His ruling representative over the chosen people.

In several psalms, the writers urged God to strike down the wicked. Sometimes these curses appear as brief statements, while at other times they take up a large part or the whole of a psalm. Because these curses can seem shocking to Christians, we should remember three points. First, the curses were honest expressions of human emotion. Second, the curses were directed against severe cases of injustice. Third, the psalmists left it up to God to deliver judgment. Present-day believers should hate injustice as much as—if not more than—believers in ancient times did. But we should not curse people (see Luke 23:34).

SUGGESTIONS TO TEACHERS

Initially, David felt isolated from God in the Judean wilderness, and that prompted the king to depend on God to satisfy his spiritual thirst and hunger. When we face situations in which there seems to be no way out, we would do well to take a cue from the psalmist, who declared that he would "rejoice in God" (Ps. 63:11).

1. REJOICE IN GOD IN THE MIDST OF DESPERATION. When David wrote this song, he clearly felt separated from both his home and his God. But in the midst of his desperation, he renewed his faith in the Lord and this became the basis for his spiritual joy. Even as desperate as his situation seemed to be, the king was all the more fervent about his relationship with God. When we face difficult situations, may we, too, rejoice in the fact that we have a saving relationship with God.

2. REJOICE IN GOD IN THE MIDST OF DISCOURAGEMENT. While languishing in a place far away from his Jerusalem home and the temple, David must have struggled with discouragement. Perhaps he even found it hard to hold onto his memories of worshiping God at the sanctuary in Jerusalem. But then the king refocused his attention on the truth of God's abiding presence and care. By choosing to rejoice in God, David found renewed strength in the Lord. We, too, will face discouragement. In those times, may we, too, take courage by rejoicing in God.

3. REJOICE IN GOD IN THE MIDST OF DEPRESSION. Who can blame David for dealing with moments of depression while in isolation in the desert of Judah? Perhaps this is one reason why he talked about thirsting for God and longing for Him with his entire being (vs. 1). As well, the king affirmed his commitment to praise God throughout the remaining years of his life (vs. 4). The poet's decision to rejoice proved to be the right therapy for any despondency he may have felt. In the midst of depressing circumstances, may we also remember that rejoicing in God will help us focus our thoughts on His ability to deliver us and save us.

FOR ADULTS
■ TOPIC: Filling Our Emptiness
■ QUESTIONS: 1. What do you think motivated David to earnestly seek after God? 2. In what ways had David experienced the power and

glory of God in his life? 3. If you had the opportunity to praise God, what would you say to Him? 4. Do you have any memorable occasions when you communed with God all night long? 5. How has God upheld you in times of extreme difficulty?

■ ILLUSTRATIONS:

Live in Hope. A middle-aged man, along with his wife, went to Florida to recover from cancer treatments. The couple hoped to walk along the beach and soak up the sun's rays, and in this way help the man to regain his strength. But sadly, the man's health did not improve. As a result, his wife had to push him to the beach in a wheelchair, for he was not strong enough to walk the beach on his own.

Despite these difficulties, this couple continued to be people of faith. They did not give up their trust in the living God. Rather, their experience drove them to a deeper level of commitment. They came to know God in ways they had not known Him before. He filled whatever emptiness in life they might have felt with the joy of His presence and power.

The testimony of this couple illustrates the power of the hope that we have in God. None of us has any guarantees of long life and perfect health. But we do have the assurance of God's abiding love and care. As Psalm 63 reminds us, even when life seems dismal, putting our hope in God is the wisest thing we can do.

God's Abiding Presence. In the book *A Window to Heaven: When Children See Life in Death*, Diane M. Komp writes how Ann and her husband were typical married baby boomers. Well-off financially, they had no time for church, and they each became busy in their respective lives. Their romance faded early, but neither wanted to give up their lifestyle. Besides, both adored their children, and their youngest son, T.J., was a special favorite of his mother.

Although the children were never sent to Sunday school and God was never mentioned in their home, one day T.J., out of the blue, said, "Mama, I love you more than anything in the world, except God. And I love Him a little bit more!" Ann was surprised but told him it was okay. But why would he speak about God? she wondered.

Two days later, on a bitterly cold day, while his sister was horseback riding, T.J. crossed a snow-covered creek, fell through the ice, and died. Ann remembers saying, "I hate you God!" But even then she felt herself held in loving arms. Ann's world shattered. She remembered the Christmas gift T.J. had bought her that week. He had kept trying to give it to her before Christmas. Each time she had laughed and told him to put it away until Christmas Day. When she got home from the stables where he had died, she hurried upstairs to open it. Inside was a beautiful necklace with a cross.

Ann says that in that moment the Lord filled her emptiness with the abiding presence of His love. This gave Ann the strength to reach out to others rather than become lost in herself. "Helping others helped me." Ann's husband also changed, and together they became new creatures in Christ. Through her ordeal, Ann discovered a gift for spiritual hospitality, bringing healing to other parents.

By now, this young mother has reached out to help hundreds of families who have lost children in accidents. She calls her efforts T.J. Ministries, not only after her T.J., but to emphasize how she's made it since then: "Through Jesus."

A Deep Spiritual Hunger. Some years ago, there was a strike at Pittsburgh-based J & L Specialty Steel. One of the men from a nearby church was a supervisor at the mill on Second Avenue. Like other management personnel, he was shut in the mill, unable to leave because of the picket line, but busy turning out steel as part of a crew of supervisors and management, in spite of the strike.

The company paid these individuals handsomely for staying on in the plant. The cafeteria served free meals, and went out of its way to make them tasty. The company even arranged for movies to be brought in to entertain the crew in the plant. Everything seemed to be as comfortable as possible under the circumstances.

One day, after three weeks of confinement in the plant, a big Irish supervisor named Mike came to the man in the local congregation who worked with him. "Jack," Mike said, "I'm sick." "Then you'd better go to the infirmary," Jack said. Superintendents in the hot strip mills aren't in the soul business, and Jack was ready to dismiss Mike's complaint. But Jack saw that Mike was serious. Mike continued, "Look, I haven't been to church for weeks. I miss it. Something's wrong. I don't feel good. And I mean it!"

Like David in Psalm 63, Mike was saying that he had a deep spiritual hunger for the things of God. A few days later, Mike's request was honored when arrangements were made for a minister to come through the picket line to conduct worship services in the plant. If we found ourselves in the same situation as did Mike, would we feel the same way about our relationship with God?

FOR YOUTH

■ TOPIC: A Comforting Presence

■ QUESTIONS: 1. In what sense did David thirst after God? 2. How is it possible for the experience of God's love to mean more to believers than life itself? 3. What would motivate David to want to praise God throughout his life? 4. In what ways has God brought satisfaction and joy to your life? 5. What does it mean to cling to God, and why is this important for believers to do?

■ ILLUSTRATIONS:

Someone to Watch Over Me. What an encouragement it is to read accounts of God's comforting presence and care. In this regard, the psalms of the Bible function as recitals of how God has helped and protected people such as David. We all can benefit from the spiritual reinforcement these memorable passages offer.

That's why it's valuable to take time to recall what the Lord has done down through the centuries. Such accounts need not focus just on hair-raising rescues. Even what seems to be unimportant can help us recognize the hand of God at work in the lives of the upright.

When we reflect on these things, we quickly come to understand that God watches over all we do. He will uphold us when we feel spiritually weak and He will guide us when we feel morally confused. We never need to feel alone when the great God of the universe is ever present to lead and strengthen us.

Materialistic Mantra. Some time ago, the following message was seen printed on a sweatshirt of a passerby at the Mall of America (a large retail and entertainment complex located in Bloomington, Minnesota). The communication was a parody of Psalm 23:4:

> Though I walk through
> The Mall of America
> I shall fear no evil
> For with time and plastic in my pocket
> There's nothing to FEAR anyway.

What a contrast this materialistic mantra is to the God-centered perspective of David. While experiencing isolation and discouragement in the wilderness of Judah, the king did not turn to the things of the world to give him hope. Instead, he looked to God for temporal and eternal satisfaction. David compared his relationship with God to being at a banquet with the richest of foods and experiencing total satisfaction (see 63:5). Our walk with the Lord is just as special. Accordingly, we can join with David and all believers in singing praise to God as long as we live (see vs. 4).

No Substitutes. A monarch butterfly is as beautiful as a viceroy butterfly. A bird, looking for a light lunch, might snatch either, expecting a pleasurable meal. God designed both with beautiful orange and black wings. In fact, the only major differences are the viceroy's slightly smaller size and a black stripe along its hind wings.

The viceroy would be a feathered diner's delight, but a monarch would not. Poison ingested from the milkweed plant while the monarch was a caterpillar makes the butterfly taste bitter. Once a bird eats a monarch, it won't repeat the mistake.

All around us, there are subtle counterfeits. The most dangerous are religious frauds. When Jesus declared Himself to be the true bread from heaven (John 6:32), He identified Himself as the only healthful food for the soul.

GOD IS AWESOME

BACKGROUND SCRIPTURE: Psalm 66
DEVOTIONAL READING: Psalm 40:1-5

KEY VERSE: Come and see the works of God: he is
terrible in his doing toward the children of men. (Psalm 66:5)

KING JAMES VERSION

PSALM 66:1 Make a joyful noise unto God, all ye lands: 2 Sing forth the honour of his name: make his praise glorious. 3 Say unto God, How terrible art thou in thy works! through the greatness of thy power shall thine enemies submit themselves unto thee. 4 All the earth shall worship thee, and shall sing unto thee; they shall sing to thy name. Selah. 5 Come and see the works of God: he is terrible in his doing toward the children of men. 6 He turned the sea into dry land: they went through the flood on foot: there did we rejoice in him. 7 He ruleth by his power for ever; his eyes behold the nations: let not the rebellious exalt themselves. Selah.

8 O bless our God, ye people, and make the voice of his praise to be heard: 9 Which holdeth our soul in life, and suffereth not our feet to be moved. 10 For thou, O God, hast proved us: thou hast tried us, as silver is tried. 11 Thou broughtest us into the net; thou laidst affliction upon our loins. 12 Thou hast caused men to ride over our heads; we went through fire and through water: but thou broughtest us out into a wealthy place.

NEW REVISED STANDARD VERSION

PSALM 66:1 Make a joyful noise to God, all the earth;
2 sing the glory of his name;
  give to him glorious praise.
3 Say to God, "How awesome are your deeds!
  Because of your great power, your enemies cringe
    before you.
4 All the earth worships you;
  they sing praises to you,
  sing praises to your name."   *Selah*
5 Come and see what God has done:
  he is awesome in his deeds among mortals.
6 He turned the sea into dry land;
  they passed through the river on foot.
There we rejoiced in him,
7 who rules by his might for ever,
whose eyes keep watch on the nations—
  let the rebellious not exalt themselves.   *Selah*
8 Bless our God, O peoples,
  let the sound of his praise be heard,
9 who has kept us among the living,
  and has not let our feet slip.
10 For you, O God, have tested us;
  you have tried us as silver is tried.
11 You brought us into the net;
  you laid burdens on our backs;
12 you let people ride over our heads;
  we went through fire and through water;
yet you have brought us out to a spacious place.

10

Monday, November 1	Judges 10:10-16	*Deliver Us This Day!*
Tuesday, November 2	1 Samuel 7:3-13	*Direct Your Heart to the Lord*
Wednesday, November 3	1 Samuel 17:31-37	*The Lord Will Save Me*
Thursday, November 4	Psalm 40:1-5	*God Gives a New Song*
Friday, November 5	Psalm 66:13-20	*God Hears My Prayer*
Saturday, November 6	Psalm 22:19-28	*God Rules over the Nations*
Sunday, November 7	Psalm 66:1-12	*God Rules Forever*

BACKGROUND

Psalm 66 is a hymn of praise in which the Lord receives thanksgiving and adoration. Verses 1-12 praise God for His redemptive acts on behalf of the nation, while verses 13-20 record the poet's personal thanks to God for delivering him from a troubling circumstance. As the song unfolds, the writer praises God for who He is and what He does. The poet also exalts God for specific answers to prayer. The hymn restates some of the miraculous ways the Lord intervened in Israel's history and affirms that He has remained faithful to His chosen people regardless of the nature of their difficult circumstance. Some themes found in the song include triumph through God's awesome intervention, divine blessing to worshipers around the globe, and bringing offerings to the Jerusalem temple.

In terms of the chronological setting, it remains unclear whether the poet is talking about incidents that were occurring in the present or the past. Because its context is quite general, it is difficult to date the psalm. Most likely, the poem was written in Jerusalem sometime before the Exile (586 B.C.). Some think the song commemorates the Lord's deliverance of Judah from the Assyrians (see 2 Kings 19; 2 Chron. 32:1-23; Isa. 37). Others maintain the hymn praises God for rescuing the author from the undermining schemes of his foes, just as He came to the aid of the Israelites when He freed them from Egypt. In either case, just as the faith community prayed to the Lord in their time of need, so they corporately and individually thanked Him for delivering them from their enemies.

NOTES ON THE PRINTED TEXT

The heading of Psalm 66 indicates it is both a lyrical "song" and a melodious "psalm" that was intended to be accompanied by instrumental music. In addition to worshipers in Israel, all people of the world are entreated to raise a joyful shout of praise to God for what He has done (vs. 1; see 98:4; 100:1). The Hebrew verb rendered "sing" (66:2) can also be translated "to make music." It's not difficult to imagine the presence of energy and enthusiasm, especially as vocalists and musicians sang about the Lord's glorious name. Through the corporate worship experience, the participants sought to honor God by acclaiming the majesty of His reputation. They also wanted everyone to know how glorious He is.

The Hebrew verb rendered "terrible" (vs. 3) literally means "to inspire reverence" or "to instill godly fear." In a general sense, it is as if the poet was exhorting the entire world to declare to God that everything He did was both fearsome and wonderful. The psalmist explained that the warrior-king's displays of power were so overwhelming that it caused His foes to cower in fear before Him (see Deut. 33:39; Ps. 81:15). Before the awe-inspiring demonstrations of God's might, every inhabitant on the planet worships Him. They not only utter praises to the Lord, but also to His glorious name (Ps. 66:4). As was noted in lesson 7, the Hebrew verb "*Selah*" literally means "to lift up" or "to exalt." Imagine that after the cue was given, an entire sanctuary full of worshipers would fall prostrate in homage to God.

The poet invited all the people of earth to witness the fearsome exploits of God. Indeed, His miraculous acts done on behalf of the people was a testament to His awesome, glorious nature (vs. 5). Whatever He does is infinitely superior to anything people can do and defies human comprehension (see 1 Chron. 16:25; Pss. 89:7; 96:4; Zeph. 2:11). Implicit in the author's summons is the truth that the Lord's saving acts performed on behalf of Israel not only give the covenant community but also every person living on earth sufficient reason to worship God. One prime example would be the Israelites' crossing the Red Sea on foot. The episode immediately became an opportunity to rejoice because of what the Lord had done (Ps. 66:6). Another pertinent example was the Israelites' crossing the Jordan River about 40 years later (see Josh. 3—4; Ps. 114:3, 5).

The Hebrew verb translated "ruleth" (Ps. 66:7) can also be rendered "to have dominion" or "to reign" and points to the Lord's sovereign control over the nations of the earth. The poet declared that there is no limit to God's power and no end to the power He exercises over His creation and its inhabitants. He is aware of all that happens on earth. Indeed, every person, regardless of their station or status in life, is accountable to Him. For this reason, the rebellious are warned against exalting themselves in a defiant act against the rule of the Lord.

In light of God's mighty acts of redemption and sovereign, eternal reign, the poet entreated all earth's inhabitants to offer "praise" (vs. 8) to God. The underlying Hebrew verb literally means "to bless" and conveys the idea of declaring the Lord to be the source of the chosen people's deliverance from their calamity. So great were His displays of power that every corner of the globe was to hear the "voice of his praise." For instance, when the Israelites crossed safely through the Red Sea, the Lord prevented their "feet" (vs. 9) from being "moved." Furthermore, He enabled them to steadily make their way across the dry surface of the ground. This historical incident became a prominent example of how the lives of God's people were in His hands. He even prevented them from experiencing an untimely death.

Exodus 15 commemorates that momentous occasion in a hymn of praise to the Lord (see vs. 1). At a pivotal point in the song, the Israelites asked, "Who is like unto thee, O LORD, among the gods? who is like thee, glorious in holiness, fearful in praises, doing wonders?" (vs. 11). The purpose of this question was to point out the inability of pagan deities to act. The hymn accomplishes this by showing the Egyptian gods' impotence in contrast to the power of the one true God. After all, the Lord had caused the Egyptians to be gulped down into the earth, figuratively speaking (vs. 12). Having retold what had occurred, the remainder of the Israelites' song tells about the future results of God's deliverance.

Psalm 66:10-12 draws the reader's attention to the horrendous circumstance for the chosen people that preceded their exodus from Egypt. It was during that extended period of time that God "proved" (vs. 10) them, in which the underlying Hebrew verb can also be rendered "to examine," "to scrutinize," or "to evaluate." In a parallel thought, the poet compared the refining process to the purification of silver. The procedure involved the smelting of lead ore to separate the dross (lead oxide) from the silver. Just as impurities were removed from precious metal to purge it, similarly God used anguish and hardship to put His people to the test (see 17:3; 26:2).

Psalm 66:11 adds further details concerning what God allowed His people to endure. The poet said that God brought His people "into the net." It's as if the Lord allowed the Israelites to fall into a trap laid by their captors, which led to feelings of isolation and constraint. Moreover, the latter part of the verse says "thou laidst affliction upon our loins." The idea is that God permitted the Israelites' cruel taskmasters to lay the burden of slavery on the backs of His people. Verse 12 adds that the Lord let Israel's foes trample them. Perhaps the imagery is that of war chariots trying to crush the skulls of the downtrodden. The poet candidly acknowledged that God allowed the covenant community to pass through episodes involving fire (for instance, when flames engulfed a city besieged by foreign invaders) and floods (for example, when a torrent of water overwhelmed an entire region). These experiences included the nation's wandering in the Sinai desert and the subsequent conquest of Canaan (see Isa. 43:2; 45:7; Amos 3:6).

In those moments when the situation seemed completely unbearable and hopeless, the Lord brought relief to His chosen people by leading them into a wide open space. Indeed, the promised land proved to be a place filled with unimaginable abundance (Ps. 66:12). These truths form the backdrop of Joshua's farewell address to the Israelites living in his day. He appealed to the nation's elders because they had been eyewitnesses to God's work in the people's midst (Josh. 23:1-2). Though the Hebrews had fought bravely during the conquest of Canaan, the ultimate credit for the victory was given to the Lord (vs. 3). In one sense it was almost as if the people were spectators to the events God had brought about during the past several decades. Apart from the Lord, the Israelites could do nothing, as they had painfully learned at Ai (see 7:4-26).

SUGGESTIONS TO TEACHERS

What fears tend to paralyze your students and keep them from pursuing God's will for their lives? How do their terrors affect their personal lives, spiritual lives, families, work, and health? What pressures seem about to crush them? Do any of their responsibilities feel too great to handle? Regardless of their response to any of these questions, this week's study of Psalm 66 can give them the opportunity to contemplate both the awesomeness of God and His ability to deliver them from their trials.

1. BEING PREOCCUPIED WITH SELF. The terrors and tight places of life often take our primary focus off the Lord and put it on ourselves. When we are preoccupied with ourselves, we tend to pull back from total commitment to the Lord, especially in order to protect the vulnerable places in our lives. Terrors and tight places might also cause us to replace prayer and Bible reading with worrying.

2. RECOGNIZING INHIBITING FACTORS. Pride always makes it hard for us to admit we're struggling. Likewise, our position in the church or community can make us hesitate to admit our fears. Moreover, our upbringing or family attitudes can inhibit self-awareness as well as admission of problems to others. Even shyness, suspicion, or other negative personality traits can make it hard for us to seek help with our problems.

3. REMEMBERING GOD'S PRESENCE AND POWER. A breakthrough in attitude comes when we shift our focus from our limitations and liabilities to God's awesome ability to bring us through whatever hardships we're facing. We learn from Psalm 66 that He is so great in power that His enemies cower in fear before Him. When life feels overwhelming, it is helpful for us to recall that God never panics and He is always ready to guide us safely through the terrors and tight places in our lives.

4. THANKING GOD FOR DELIVERANCE. When God intervenes in amazing ways to deliver us, it is fitting for us to express gratitude to Him. Indeed, being thankful is one of the most important attitudes of the Christian life. We can express our gratitude directly to God. We can also praise Him in the presence of others. Finally, we can encourage others to become grateful praise-givers, too. People of praise readily discover that the Lord is ever present to safeguard them through the storms of life.

FOR ADULTS

■ **TOPIC:** Wholly Dependable

■ **QUESTIONS:** 1. Why did the poet summon all the earth to shout joyful praises to God? 2. What are some specific ways you can tell others how glorious God is? 3. Why were the exodus from Egypt and the crossing of the Jordan River such pivotal events for the Israelites? 4. How do you feel during times when you know God is testing you? 5. How has the Lord preserved you from danger?

ILLUSTRATIONS:

A New Song. "Declare the glory of God's name among the nations" has been the theme of student missionary conventions (see Ps. 66:2). And thousands of young people have responded to the command. They have given their lives to serve Christ where His name is not known, loved, or obeyed. These dedicated young people have changed countless communities and brought the hope of God's wholly dependable presence to innumerable people.

When we sing a new song of praise to God for the awesome things He has done for us (see vs. 3), we should also think about people locally and around the world who have no reason to sing. Some have never heard the good news of Jesus, while others have rejected it. In either case, we should continue filling our hearts with the praises of Psalm 66 (the focus of this week's lesson). Doing this will keep us from hardening our hearts to the needs of the lost around us.

Tell of God's Salvation. Psalm 66 is a song celebrating the awesome, saving power of God at work in the lives of people. Down through the centuries, countless servants of the Lord Jesus have drawn strength from the hymn's timeless message. It has even emboldened some of them in their proclamation of the good news of salvation to be found in the Messiah.

Consider the Scottish evangelist, John Harper. He was born into a Christian family in 1872. He became a Christian thirteen years later and had already started preaching by age seventeen. He received training at the Baptist Pioneer Mission in London, and in 1896 he founded a church—now known as the Harper Memorial Church—which began with twenty-five worshipers but had grown to 500 members by the time he left thirteen years later. When asked about his doctrine, he stated it was simply "the Word of God."

While Harper's spiritual growth followed a fairly direct uphill path, his personal life wasn't so smooth. When he was only two and a half, he fell into a well and almost drowned. At twenty-six he was nearly swept out to sea, and at thirty-two he found himself on a leaky ship in the middle of the Mediterranean. Most tragically, his wife died after only a brief marriage, leaving him alone with their daughter, Nana. Despite these calamitous events, Harper found renewed hope in the truth of Psalm 66:3 that God's power is great to save.

In 1912, Harper, the newly called pastor of Moody Church in Chicago, was traveling on the Titanic with his six-year-old daughter. After the ship struck an iceberg and began to sink, he got Nana into a lifeboat but apparently made no effort to follow her. Instead, he ran through the ship yelling, "Women, children, and unsaved into the lifeboats!" Survivors report that he then began witnessing to anyone who would listen. He continued preaching even after he had jumped into the water and was clinging to a piece of wreckage. (He'd already given his lifejacket to another man.)

Harper's final moments were recounted four years later at a meeting in Hamilton,

Ontario, by a man who said the following:

> I am a survivor of the Titanic. When I was drifting alone on a spar that awful night, the tide brought Mr. Harper, of Glasgow, also on a piece of wreck, near me. "Man," he said, "are you saved?" "No," I said, "I am not." He replied, "Believe on the Lord Jesus Christ and thou shalt be saved." The waves bore him away, but, strange to say, brought him back a little later, and he said, "Are you saved now?" "No," I said, "I cannot honestly say that I am." He said again, "Believe on the Lord Jesus Christ, and thou shalt be saved," and shortly after he went down; and there, alone in the night, and with two miles of water under me, I believed. I am John Harper's last convert.

This man was one of only six people picked out of the water by the lifeboats; the other 1,522, including Harper, were left to die.

■ **TOPIC:** The Noise of Praise

■ **QUESTIONS:** 1. Among your acquaintances, who might welcome an invitation to sing praises to God in corporate worship? 2. What are some of your favorite Scripture passages that recount the awesome deeds of God? 3. When is it likely that all the earth will one day worship the Lord? 4. Why is it unwise for the rebellious to rise up in defiance against God's rule? 5. In what ways has God watched over you in difficult circumstances?

■ **ILLUSTRATIONS:**

Shout for Joy. The men's rooming and boarding house had a weekly meeting convened by the owner. The residents were expected to attend. More than that, they were expected to tell about something that God had done in their lives. Of course, a few attendees were not too keen about this idea. But something always happened after those meetings. The stories about fresh encounters with God's awesome power were like blood transfusions. The accounts injected spiritual vitality into those who were just going through the same old religious routines.

Every convocation of believers can benefit from testimonies of how God has delivered His people from trials. That's why Psalm 66 (the focus of this week's lesson)—which is a hymn of worship and praise—is so invigorating and life-changing. We all need to contemplate ways we can shout for joy to God (see vs. 1), for doing so keeps our love for the Lord from growing cold.

Salvation Comes from God. We live in an age that some describe as "new." While the technology of this day may be different than anything that the world has ever seen or barely imagined, the fundamental spiritual truths remain the same. To many, salvation or a relationship with God is seen as a mountain to be climbed, with any number of equally valid paths that lead to its summit.

This dilemma of knowing and understanding the ways of God has been contested for thousands of years. An early church leader, Tertullian, tells us of one such debate: "The (then) richest man in the world, Croesus, once asked the wisest man in the world, Thales, this question: 'What is God?' The philosopher asked for a day to consider. Then, he asked for another day, and then another. Finally, he returned to Croesus and confessed that the longer he pondered the question, the more difficult it became, until finally Thales became totally confused."

When the fiery church leader Tertullian heard about this, he quickly seized upon it and said it was an example of the world's ignorance of God outside of Christ. "There," Tertullian exclaimed, "is the wisest man in the world, and he cannot tell you who God is. But the most ignorant person among the Christians knows God and is able to make him known to others." While the world continues to look for paths to ascend to the mountain of God, let us remember that Christ has not only shown the way, but delivers us to our heavenly home. Even in this life we can depend on Him to bring us through the trials we experience.

Never Alone. In *Our Daily Bread*, Clair Hess recounted one of his earliest memories of hearing good music when a male quartet rehearsed at his parents' home. Hess was ten years old at the time, and he remembered being especially attentive to his father, who sang first tenor. One of the favorites of the quartet was titled "I Am With You." Hess notes that "even at that tender age, I not only appreciated the music, but also I 'got the message.'"

Psalm 66 contains at least two historical references to God's abiding and saving presence with His people during challenging times—the Israelites' journey through the Red Sea and the nation's later crossing of the Jordan River. Verse 9 is especially poignant in noting that the Lord was close at hand to preserve the lives of His chosen people. He did not even allow their feet to slip.

A similar promise of God's abiding and saving presence can be found in the New Testament. In Hebrews 13:5, the author conveyed this assurance: "I will never leave thee, nor forsake thee." Hess, reflecting on this verse, offered this comment: "Wherever you may be today, you are not alone. If you've placed your trust in Jesus for your eternal salvation, you can be certain that He will never leave you."

GOD IS FOREVER

BACKGROUND SCRIPTURE: Psalm 90
DEVOTIONAL READING: 1 Timothy 1:12-17

KEY VERSE: Before the mountains were brought forth, or ever thou hadst formed the earth and the world, even from everlasting to everlasting, thou art God. (Psalm 90:2)

KING JAMES VERSION

PSALM 90:1 Lord, thou hast been our dwelling place in all generations. 2 Before the mountains were brought forth, or ever thou hadst formed the earth and the world, even from everlasting to everlasting, thou art God. 3 Thou turnest man to destruction; and sayest, Return, ye children of men. 4 For a thousand years in thy sight are but as yesterday when it is past, and as a watch in the night. 5 Thou carriest them away as with a flood; they are as a sleep: in the morning they are like grass which groweth up. 6 In the morning it flour- isheth, and groweth up; in the evening it is cut down, and withereth.

7 For we are consumed by thine anger, and by thy wrath are we troubled. 8 Thou hast set our iniquities before thee, our secret sins in the light of thy counte- nance. 9 For all our days are passed away in thy wrath: we spend our years as a tale that is told. 10 The days of our years are threescore years and ten; and if by reason of strength they be fourscore years, yet is their strength labour and sorrow; for it is soon cut off, and we fly away. 11 Who knoweth the power of thine anger? even according to thy fear, so is thy wrath.

12 So teach us to number our days, that we may apply our hearts unto wisdom.

NEW REVISED STANDARD VERSION

PSALM 90:1 Lord, you have been our dwelling place
  in all generations.
2 Before the mountains were brought forth,
  or ever you had formed the earth and the world,
  from everlasting to everlasting you are God.
3 You turn us back to dust,
  and say, "Turn back, you mortals."
4 For a thousand years in your sight
  are like yesterday when it is past,
  or like a watch in the night.
5 You sweep them away; they are like a dream,
  like grass that is renewed in the morning;
6 in the morning it flourishes and is renewed;
  in the evening it fades and withers.
7 For we are consumed by your anger;
  by your wrath we are overwhelmed.
8 You have set our iniquities before you,
  our secret sins in the light of your countenance.
9 For all our days pass away under your wrath;
  our years come to an end like a sigh.
10 The days of our life are seventy years,
  or perhaps eighty, if we are strong;
even then their span is only toil and trouble;
  they are soon gone, and we fly away.
11 Who considers the power of your anger?
  Your wrath is as great as the fear that is due you.
12 So teach us to count our days
  that we may gain a wise heart.

Monday, November 8	1 Timothy 1:12-17	*The King of the Ages*
Tuesday, November 9	Nehemiah 9:1-5	*Stand Up and Bless the Lord*
Wednesday, November 10	Ephesians 3:7-13	*God's Eternal Purpose*
Thursday, November 11	Romans 1:18-24	*God's Eternal Power*
Friday, November 12	2 Corinthians 4:13-18	*An Eternal Weight of Glory*
Saturday, November 13	Psalm 90:13-17	*All Our Days*
Sunday, November 14	Psalm 90:1-12	*From Everlasting to Everlasting*

BACKGROUND

The heading of Psalm 90 refers to Moses as the "man of God," that is, a person who was inspired by the Lord and who represented hope and faithfulness to the Israelites. At times this title was used in the Old Testament as a designation for a true prophet (see Deut. 33:1; Josh. 14:6; 1 Sam. 2:27; 9:6, 9-10; 1 Kings 13:1; 17:24; 2 Kings 4:9; 1 Chron. 23:14; Ezra 3:2). Psalm 90 is regarded as a communal lament, that is, a hymn initially composed to express the grief and sorrow of God's people over a distressing circumstance. The precise nature and cause of the anguish remains unknown, being sketched only in the broadest of terms.

Most likely, toward the end of the Israelites' 40-year period of wandering in the desert, Moses reflected on the brevity of human life, especially against the backdrop of the Lord's eternal existence. The fragility and transience of humankind is brought into sharp relief through a variety of chronologically oriented terms and phrases, including "years," "our days," "our years," "watch in the night," and "morning." The Lord's decision to consign an entire generation of Israelites (including Moses) to wander for forty years and then die in the Sinai desert mirrors the hardship and anguish that typifies the broader human experience. The godly recognize that ultimately life is fleeting and largely undermined by the presence of decay and death throughout creation (see Rom. 8:20-22).

NOTES ON THE PRINTED TEXT

Moses opened Psalm 90 with the affirmation that throughout each and every generation, the Lord has been the "dwelling place" (vs. 1) of His people. The underlying Hebrew noun can also be rendered as "habitation" or "refuge" (see 71:3). Metaphorically speaking, God is like an oasis in the desert around which the faithful encamp. Also, in a sense, the Lord has been and always will be the place of safety for His people and the one who protects them from all sorts of danger (see 91:9). Moses revealed that the Lord brought the mountains into existence and enabled them to pierce through the crust of the earth and dominate its landscape (90:2). The Israelites regarded the mountains, which God created, as being the most ancient and abiding part of the planet. The noun that is rendered "everlasting" in connection with God denotes an unlimited duration of time. Its repetition in this verse stresses the profound truth that before the mountains and the earth were ever created, the Lord eternally preexisted (see Pss. 93:2; 145:13; Isa. 40:28; Jer. 10:10; Rev. 1:8).

Psalm 90:3 refers to the reality of death, which hangs over everyone like an ominous storm cloud. All it takes is God's simple command to end the lives of His mortal creatures. At His directive, their brief existence suddenly ends. The Hebrew noun that is rendered "destruction" points to material that has been pounded, crushed, or pulverized. The prime example of God's judgment is seen in the faithless generation of Israelites whose miserable end was to return to the arid soil of the Sinai desert after spending forty years aimlessly wandering in it (see Num. 13—14).

Mere mortals cannot begin to fathom the truth that to the everlasting God a thousand years are as fleeting as a single day and as momentary as yesterday after it has quickly passed (Ps. 90:4). The ancient Israelites divided their days into two 12-hour periods—day and night, respectively. Furthermore, as noted in lesson 9, depending on the season of year, they divided the night into three or four equal periods of three to four hours. Nighttime watching was an important profession in ancient Israel. In the cities, men posted on walls and towers were given the responsibility to sound the alert if danger appeared either inside or outside the city. In rural areas, watchmen would spend the night in towers to prevent theft from field or flock. Moses stated that to the Lord an entire millennium seems as short-lived as a night watch (see 2 Pet. 3:8).

The Hebrew of Psalm 90:5 can be rendered as "You flood them with sleep" or "you bring them to an end with sleep." Perhaps the imagery is that of a torrent of water that devastates everything in its path, whether animate or inanimate. In the end, nothing survives the onslaught of the deluge. Against the backdrop of God's eternal preexistence, mere mortals last no longer than a dream before the years of their lives are engulfed and swept away by the arrival of death. Moses also used the analogy of tender grass that sprouts up at daybreak to represent the potential of youth. In the coolness of the dawn, it glistens and bursts into bloom. But by dusk the grass has dried up and withered in the unrelenting heat of the sun (vs. 6). For Moses and his peers, the arid climate of the Sinai desert at times must have felt this way. More generally, the existence of every living entity—including human beings—is just as ephemeral and cursory (see Pss. 102:25-28; 104:29-30; 144:3-4; 129:6; Isa. 40:6-8; Jas. 1:10-11).

Psalm 90:7 vividly refers to God's anger wiping out the lives of people through death. The Hebrew verb that is rendered "consumed" denotes something that has wasted away, failed, or perished. The noun that is translated "anger" literally refers to the nose or nostrils of the face. The image is that of a snorting sound that is produced by intense annoyance or dissatisfaction over some circumstance. With respect to the Lord, His anger is an expression of His righteous indignation over humanity's sins, including those involving His chosen people (see 2:5; 7:11; 39:11). The second part of 90:7 completes the thought begun in the first part. When people experience God's "wrath," they are "troubled." The first term renders a noun that denotes the hot displeasure associated with God's indignation. "Troubled" renders a verb that draws attention to the alarm and anxiety that people feel. In a manner of speaking, they are overwhelmed by the Lord's fury, which brings about their demise.

It is easy for people to imagine that no one knows about transgressions they commit in their heart, such as greed, arrogance, and resentment. But before the penetrating light of God's holy presence, nothing is hidden. Moses depicted the Lord as spreading out our "iniquities" (vs. 8) before Him. Every form of mischief is transparent and all our perversities are exposed. Even the sins people try to hide are ever-present before the light of His countenance. In a manner of speaking, God's face is comparable to a lamp that dispels the surrounding darkness to reveal what would otherwise remain hidden (see Matt. 10:26; Mark 4:22; Luke 8:17; 12:2; John 3:19-21).

In Psalm 90:9, the Hebrew verb that is rendered "passed away" conveys the image of something that is moribund and close to dying. Under the heat of God's raging fury, a person's existence withers and feels as if it is cut short prematurely. Life itself tends to be filled with unending struggles, which cripple the ability of people to deal with a successive series of afflictions. At the end of countless misfortunes, weary earthbound travelers end their pain-filled years with a sigh.

Such a perspective is often lost on youth, for whom seven or eight decades of life seem like a long time. In antiquity, the numbers 7 and 70 epitomized completion and perfection. The parallel construction of verse 10 reinforces this impression with the observation that some people, due to their God-given strength, live to be 80 years old. Even more impressive is the fact that the span of Moses' life reached 120 years. Indeed, Deuteronomy 34:7 notes that the eyesight of the lawgiver was still good, and his body remained strong. All the same, he did not escape death. Likewise, it does not matter how long people might live. Against the backdrop of God's eternal existence all the days of their life are too few.

"Strength" (Ps. 90:10) renders a Hebrew noun that literally means "arrogance" or "pride." The focus is on the prime of life, when young people are filled with confidence at what they imagine they can accomplish in their zeal and vitality. Yet even the best years of their life are scarred by "labour and sorrow." The more literal rendering is "destruction and wickedness," which points to the grief, disappointment, and loss that typifies human existence. After a lifetime of toil and heartache, one's existence suddenly ends. Moses compared the abrupt onslaught of death to a bird that quickly flies away as a result of being scared from its nest.

Moses wanted the covenant community to recognize that life's afflictions and brevity were manifestations of God's judgment on sin (vs. 11). The lawgiver admitted that no one, regardless of how wise and informed he or she might be, has ever fathomed the full extent of God's anger or even the duration of its intensity and severity. The second half of this verse is literally rendered "and like your fear is your wrath."

The Hebrew noun rendered "fear" denotes a reverential trust in the Lord that is the basis for His people knowing Him, doing His will, and fully appreciating His unfailing love (see Pss. 111:10; 147:11; Prov. 1:7). One possible meaning is that God's wrath causes humans to fear Him. Another likely sense is that the awesomeness of God's raging fury mirrors the fear He deserves to receive from human beings.

In either case, Moses petitioned God to teach the covenant community to "number [their] days" (Ps. 90:12). The idea is that in becoming more aware of how short existence really is, God's loyal followers will value the time He has given them, recognize it as His gracious gift to them, and seek to accomplish His will. The prudent, as a result of being so inclined, obtain a wise heart. The Hebrew noun that is rendered "hearts" denotes the center of a person's thoughts, will, and ethical character. The noun that is translated "wisdom" refers to God-given prudence in all areas of life. Together these terms point to those who astutely use all the allotted time they have on earth to bring glory to the Lord.

SUGGESTIONS TO TEACHERS

An entire generation of Israelites perished in the Sinai desert because of their rebellion against God. Even Moses, the nation's great lawgiver, failed to enter the promised land because at one point he too failed to do God's will. We learn from Moses' gloomy observations in Psalm 90 that our sins can have tragic, life-altering consequences.

1. THE REALITY OF DEATH. Every day people throughout the world experience the brevity and impermanence of their earthly existence. Their physical and mental capabilities, which might have held tremendous promise earlier in their lives, diminish and ebb away with the passing of the years and decades. This is a consequence of God's judgment of sin in the human race and throughout the universe. A testament to this truth is the monotony and misery the Israelites experienced while wandering in the wilderness, only thereafter to be greeted by death (see Deut. 4:25-28; 11:16-17).

2. THE MORAL DECLINE OF SOCIETY. As with the ancient Israelites, modern Western societies have moral standards that are no longer God's but our own. The consequences of this trend are clearly visible. We have been losing respect for human life. "Right" has started to become anything that a person can get away with. Any social practice is becoming acceptable as long as it doesn't hurt anyone.

3. THE CERTAINTY OF FUTURE JUDGMENT. God's moral standards are absolute. Furthermore, His ethical norms never change. Indeed, one day He will judge the nations. Jesus referred to the latter as a separation of the sheep from the goats, with the sheep receiving eternal life and the goats eternal punishment (Matt. 25:31-46). When people face God's judgment, the slogan "I only did what everyone else was doing" will not be a valid defense.

4. THE NEED FOR SELF-EXAMINATION. Throughout Israel's history, God's people failed to listen to His call to acknowledge their sins, receive His forgiveness, and change their lives. We, too, need to examine ourselves and receive forgiveness for personal sin. In the light of experiencing God's grace, we should reevaluate and, if necessary, adjust our life priorities to reflect the wisdom recorded in Scripture (see Ps. 90:12).

FOR ADULTS

■ TOPIC: Life Is Short

■ QUESTIONS: 1. How can knowing about God's eternal existence be a source of comfort to believers in uncertain times? 2. Why would God, who created people, allow them to die? 3. In what ways can believers encourage one another in the face of life's brevity? 4. Since God knows everything people do, why do some act as if He is unaware of their wrongdoing? 5. How have you seen God help you and other believers make it through times of sadness?

■ ILLUSTRATIONS:

Hope Born out of Despair. Most, if not all, of your students are probably Christians. No doubt most of them have been exposed to God's love. Despite the many ways God has shown His love to us, we all have areas in our lives where we stubbornly insist on doing what we want to do rather than what God expects us to do.

Although your students are adults, in many ways they may act like little children who are self-centered and spoiled. Remind your students that God views us in the same way as parents view their young children. Just as we expect our children to develop into mature adults, so God wants us to mature as Christians.

Of course, as we grow in the Lord, we will make many childish mistakes and even rebel sometimes. One important truth is that though we often act selfishly and behave stubbornly, God continues to love and nurture us. It's the presence of His compassion that gives us hope in the midst of life's brevity and the despairing circumstances that occur throughout life.

Trust God When Things Look Bad. An American man and an Irish woman who had been pen pals since childhood finally realized they had fallen in love. John scraped together enough money to fly to Dublin where Maureen was to meet him wearing a green scarf, a green hat, and a green carnation.

John stepped from the plane and scanned the crowd in the terminal. When he spotted the green scarf, green hat, and green carnation on the homeliest woman he had ever seen, his heart sank. But Maureen was John's dearest friend, so he approached her with a smile to give her a hug.

"Hey! Get away from me," the homely woman cried out when John embraced her.

"Is this airport full of crazy people today? That girl over there just paid me 20 pounds to wear all this green." The prettiest girl John had ever seen stepped forward and held out her hand. "I'm so pleased that you came, John. Please forgive my little trick. I'm just so tired of shallow men who only care about my looks."

How tired God must get of people who claim to love Him as long as their lives are going well but who desert Him as soon as anything ugly happens to them. This proved to be the case with an entire generation of Israelites. And it led to the tragic circumstance Moses alluded to in Psalm 90. If we trust the Lord's love and mercy in the bad times, we will find out how true a friend He can be—both in this life and in the one to come.

Choose Hope and Find Life. Back in the days of the Cold War, Woody Allen observed, "Civilization stands at the crossroads. Down one road is despondency and despair, and down the other is total annihilation. Let us pray that we choose the right road."

Moses could have said, "Civilization is at a dead end. We went down the road of total annihilation and ended up at despondency and despair. It's all the same." But the lawgiver didn't say that. Instead, in Psalm 90 he stopped looking at his dark circumstances and faced the bright sun of God's love and compassion. There Moses found hope. Likewise, when we turn our face to God and choose hope, we will find life.

FOR YOUTH

■ TOPIC: Only Dust

■ QUESTIONS: 1. What does it mean to you that the Lord is the believers' dwelling place? 2. How does our experience of the passage of time differ from what God experiences? 3. In what ways can a reminder of life's brevity encourage us to rethink our priorities? 4. Why would God, who is characterized by love, be filled with indignation over the sins committed by people? 5. What steps can we take now to ensure that the course of our lives is characterized by wisdom?

■ ILLUSTRATIONS:

Grief and Hope. A high school student lost his older brother in an automobile accident. At the funeral, the adolescent wept when he heard the minister say, "Earth to earth, ashes to ashes, dust to dust" (from the *Book of Common Prayer*; see Gen. 3:19).

The teen struggled for three years to find hope. During that time, he could not talk about his grief. Meanwhile, after the accident, some other students who were not Christians came to faith because of the older brother's witness on campus. They found that the only way to deal with the tragedy was to commit themselves to Jesus.

The explorer and missionary Wilfred T. Grenfell left us with some sound advice when we think about grief and hope. He wrote, "The faith that Christ asks for is not to understand Him, but to follow Him. By that and that alone can we convert the tragedy of human life—full of disappointments, disillusionments, and with death ever looming ahead—into the most glorious field of honor, worthy of the dignity of a son of God."

Which Way Will You Go? C. S. Lewis once observed, "Every road into Jerusalem is also a road out of Jerusalem." He meant that every circumstance in life is intended by God to lead people to Him, but no circumstances of life are one-way streets. People can travel away from God on the very paths meant to take them to Him.

In Psalm 90, Moses described the tragic consequences of sin and grieved over the demise of a generation of his fellow Israelites. The lawgiver also described God as the eternal dwelling place of His people. This reminds us that now is the time to turn away from sin and return to the Lord—our everlasting home—in unswerving devotion. The longer we wait to do what is right, the harder it might be for us to abandon our sinful ways.

Taste and See! Years ago an atheist was touring the country giving lectures about the folly of religion. At the end of his presentation, the atheist always challenged the audience to pose any questions they wanted, and he would take the opportunity to overpower any who dared oppose his conclusions.

In one audience the town drunk was present. He had recently come to faith in Christ at the local rescue mission and was enjoying his sobriety and his walk with the Lord. When the atheist issued his usual challenge, the former drunk ambled to the podium, took out an orange, peeled it, and started to eat. The audience laughed and hooted, figuring the guy was drunk again. The speaker was unsure what to do.

Finally the rescue mission convert smiled at the atheist and asked, "Was my orange sweet or sour?" The flustered lecturer bellowed, "You idiot, how would I know? I never tasted the orange. You tell me." "Well, how can you know anything about Jesus when you never tried Him neither?" asked the former drunk.

Many people might say that it makes no sense to trust God when life falls apart and seems near its end. But the people who do trust Him at the worst moments discover that He tastes sweet indeed!

GOD DELIVERS AND PROTECTS

BACKGROUND SCRIPTURE: Psalm 91
DEVOTIONAL READING: Isaiah 52:7-12

KEY VERSE: Because he hath set his love upon me, therefore will I deliver him: I will set him on high, because he hath known my name. (Psalm 91:14)

KING JAMES VERSION

PSALM 91:1 He that dwelleth in the secret place of the most High shall abide under the shadow of the Almighty. 2 I will say of the LORD, He is my refuge and my fortress: my God; in him will I trust. 3 Surely he shall deliver thee from the snare of the fowler, and from the noisome pestilence. 4 He shall cover thee with his feathers, and under his wings shalt thou trust: his truth shall be thy shield and buckler. 5 Thou shalt not be afraid for the terror by night; nor for the arrow that flieth by day; 6 Nor for the pestilence that walketh in darkness; nor for the destruction that wasteth at noonday. . . .

9 Because thou hast made the LORD, which is my refuge, even the most High, thy habitation; 10 There shall no evil befall thee, neither shall any plague come nigh thy dwelling. 11 For he shall give his angels charge over thee, to keep thee in all thy ways. 12 They shall bear thee up in their hands, lest thou dash thy foot against a stone. 13 Thou shalt tread upon the lion and adder: the young lion and the dragon shalt thou trample under feet. 14 Because he hath set his love upon me, therefore will I deliver him: I will set him on high, because he hath known my name. 15 He shall call upon me, and I will answer him: I will be with him in trouble; I will deliver him, and honour him. 16 With long life will I satisfy him, and shew him my salvation.

NEW REVISED STANDARD VERSION

PSALM 91:1 You who live in the shelter of the Most High,
  who abide in the shadow of the Almighty,
2 will say to the LORD, "My refuge and my fortress;
  my God, in whom I trust."
3 For he will deliver you from the snare of the fowler
  and from the deadly pestilence;
4 he will cover you with his pinions,
  and under his wings you will find refuge;
  his faithfulness is a shield and buckler.
5 You will not fear the terror of the night,
  or the arrow that flies by day,
6 or the pestilence that stalks in darkness,
  or the destruction that wastes at noonday. . . .
9 Because you have made the LORD your refuge,
  the Most High your dwelling place,
10 no evil shall befall you,
  no scourge come near your tent.
11 For he will command his angels concerning you
  to guard you in all your ways.
12 On their hands they will bear you up,
  so that you will not dash your foot against a stone.
13 You will tread on the lion and the adder,
  the young lion and the serpent you will trample
    under foot.
14 Those who love me, I will deliver;
  I will protect those who know my name.
15 When they call to me, I will answer them;
  I will be with them in trouble,
  I will rescue them and honour them.
16 With long life I will satisfy them,
  and show them my salvation.

12

HOME BIBLE READINGS

BACKGROUND

Psalm 90 emphasizes the frailty and mortality of people in a sin-cursed world. This profound truth notwithstanding, the poem's somber depiction of human life should not remain detached from the rest of God's Word. In point of fact, the canonical arrangement of the Hebrew Psalter pairs Moses' communal lament with the more hope-filled declarations recorded in Psalm 91. Here one finds a temple worshiper (possibly a priest or Levite) expressing categorical trust in the Lord despite the trials and tribulations of life. The references to shelter, refuge, protection, and so on, emphasize that God watches over and preserves the covenant community from a multitude of perils that often threaten humanity. Most likely, the unnamed poet wrote the hymn while living in Jerusalem sometime before the Exile (586 B.C.).

Verses 1-8 and 9-16 complement one another in their thematic emphases. Though these sets of verses are distinct literary units within the song, they jointly describe God safeguarding His people. Here believers find a hymn for their seasons of danger, especially when their physical or spiritual well-being seems at risk. Some think the poem's original setting was a wartime circumstance, including the battles and plagues that accompanied such conflicts in ancient times. Others conjecture the psalm was originally part of the liturgy used by worshipers as they entered and departed from the Jerusalem temple. Despite the song's unqualified declarations of God's protection and guidance for the righteous, it is unclear how metaphorical the language is to be understood. In any case, the poet wrote it to assure the faith community of their security in God.

NOTES ON THE PRINTED TEXT

Specialists have classified Psalm 91 as a didactic or wisdom poem. In it, the writer declared confidence in the Lord and encouraged His loyal followers to go to Him for habitation and safety. Verse 1 depicts them as living in the shelter of the Most High (perhaps originally a reference to the protective precincts of the temple; see 23:6; 27:4-5; 31:20), who alone is the one, true, and sovereign God. Like an attentive parent eagle who covers its young under the shadow of its outspread wings (or alternatively, like the pinions of the cherubim on either side of the ark of the covenant in the Holy of Holies of the temple), so too the Almighty tenderly provides sanctuary for His people to shield them from harm (see 36:7; 57:1; 61:4; 63:7; 91:4). "Almighty" (91:1) renders a Hebrew noun that also can be translated as "most powerful king" or "sovereign judge." With respect to God, He is the one who gives and takes away life. He also is the moral governor of the universe. Because of these unchanging truths, the faithful can look to the Lord as their defender and protector, the true and living God in whom they have placed their trust (vs. 2).

The believers' confidence in the Lord is not misplaced, for as verse 3 relates, God rescues His people from every secret trap (whether human or demonic in origin). The poet depicted these as the snare used by a fowler to hunt birds. Not even a deadly plague would overtake the righteous remnant. Amid the hidden dangers of life (including war, disease, wild animals, and demons), they are safe in the Lord's care. God does not always protect His people from perils such as war and disease. But He can and frequently does protect us.

Therefore, when dangers threaten God's spiritual children, they can know that they are not alone. After all, God's metaphorical "feathers" (vs. 4) protect the righteous and His "wings" give them refuge. His faithfulness is comparable to a shield or a rampart that protects the covenant community. The reference to God having "feathers" is an example of a literary technique that attributes a creaturely quality or feature (in this case, a body part) to a nonhuman being (in this case, God). In this verse, the poet was not saying that God is a literal bird with feather-covered wings. Instead, the psalmist was speaking figuratively to convey an important truth about the Lord safeguarding the upright. Other examples in the Hebrew Psalter include references to God's face, eyes, ears, arms, and feet.

God watches over His own at all times and in all places. Thus, rather than be plagued by fear, they experience His abiding peace. The Lord safeguards the upright from the terrors of the night and sudden attacks during the day (for example, originating from arrows shot by an enemy; vs. 5). Not even an epidemic—such as a dreaded communicable disease that strikes in the dark or a scourge that ravages at noon— would harm the Lord's chosen people (vs. 6). Even if a thousand persons fell dead beside God's loyal followers and ten thousand perished around them from the wasting disease, they would remain safe and secure (vs. 7). In contrast, they would see with their own eyes the retribution of the Lord on the wicked, namely, those who refuse to trust in and obey God (vs. 8).

The second half of Psalm 91 has a two-verse introduction, as does the first half. And like verses 1 and 2, verses 9 and 10 teach that those who seek God's shelter find it. Verse 9 depicts the righteous taking refuge in the Lord and making the Most High their dwelling place. Because they do, they have the assurance that no affliction or adversity will overtake them. Similarly, no calamity would be permitted to approach their home (in this case, a "dwelling" or tent; vs. 10).

In verses 11-13, the poet gives us one way by which God protects His people. He sends "angels" (vs. 11) to guard them. By drawing on the many biblical references to angels, we can piece together a partial description of them. They are supernatural beings whom God created before He brought human beings into existence. Angels possess some divine-like characteristics, such as being spirit creatures. They also possess some human characteristics, such as being limited in knowledge. Angels normally live in heaven, but God sometimes uses them on earth as mediators between Himself and people. When angels appear on earth, they look like humans. God has sent angels to people to announce, to warn, to guide and instruct, to guard and defend, to minister, and to assist in judgment.

In verse 12, the writer poetically represented the angels' intervention in the lives of the righteous as the act of raising pedestrians over a stone in their path so that they would not trip over it. Expressed differently, angels help safeguard God's people from many of the dangers that come into their lives. They may feel that they have to endure a lot of trouble, but if it were not for angels the upright might have to endure much more. Angels not only guard the faithful from dangers, but they also help them win victories over their enemies (vs. 13; compare vs. 8). The poet symbolized the enemies by a lion and a poisonous serpent, two creatures that posed real dangers in ancient Israel.

In Jesus' encounter with Satan, the tempter cited verses 11 and 12. We learn in Matthew 4:5 and Luke 4:9 that the devil supernaturally escorted Jesus to Jerusalem and stood Him on the highest point of the temple. Then Satan invited Jesus to prove in a spectacular way that He was God the Son. Couldn't He throw Himself down from the apex of the temple and trust the Father to protect Him (Matt. 4:6)? A common interpretation of Malachi 3:1 held that the Messiah would appear in the sky, descend to the temple, and proclaim deliverance. Apparently the Devil wanted Jesus to combine such an appearance with a sensational descent, complete with angels, to win popular approval for His kingdom.

Next, the tempter cleverly misquoted Psalm 91:11-12 by leaving out the phrase "to keep thee in all thy ways" (see Luke 4:10). As noted earlier, this passage teaches that God provides His angels to watch over His people when they live in accordance with His will. Satan claimed that God would protect Jesus as He plummeted to the ground. But since such a stunt would not be within the will of God, the promise of divine protection would not apply. Rather than yield to the devil's suggestion, Jesus quoted from Deuteronomy 6:16, saying, "Thou shalt not tempt the Lord thy God" (Matt. 4:7; Luke 4:12). We humans cannot dictate the terms of divine intervention by arranging situations of need. This would be foolish presumption, an attempt to deny the mutual accountability and responsibility woven into our personal relationship with God. Yet He freely grants what we need in order to grow in Him.

Psalm 90:1 affirms that the Lord has been the dwelling place of His people since time immemorial. In corresponding fashion, 91:9 encourages the righteous to take refuge in the covenant-keeping God of Israel and to find shelter in the one who reigns sovereign over all the earth. Verse 14 further notes the Lord's pledge to rescue those who cling to Him in love. He even promises to keep safe those who acknowledge Him as Lord and live according to His Word (see Rom. 8:28). In their time of trouble, He will answer their prayer for help by delivering and honoring them (Ps. 91:15). Verse 16 serves as a fitting response to 90:17. What Moses requested, the Lord declared to do for His loyal followers. He would let them live to a ripe old age and show them His salvation.

The picture of God's protection could hardly be more comprehensive than the poet presented in Psalm 91. The New Testament similarly teaches that the Father safeguards those who trust in His Son (see Rom. 8:31-39). For example, 1 Peter 1:5 says that God's power protects and preserves believers to receive salvation in Christ, which is ready to be revealed at the end of time. The Greek verb that is rendered "kept" conveys the idea of vigilantly defending a fortress. Believers can count on God's protection regardless of the hardships they might encounter. The "salvation" the apostle mentioned refers to the believer's complete deliverance from sin in the future. When the Messiah returns, He will raise His people from the dead and give them glorified bodies. They will then enjoy the riches of heaven.

SUGGESTIONS TO TEACHERS

The reason believers will endure to the end is that they belong to God. He included them in His gracious purpose of salvation, and He is working according to His grace to bring them to the eternal glory. A study of Psalm 91 reminds us of certain assurances we have as God's spiritual children.

1. ASSURED OF SUFFERING. Being the recipients of God's grace does not alleviate us from enduring persecution and hardships. Indeed, as is evident from Scripture and history, the people of God go through times of anguish.

2. ASSURED OF GOD'S HELP IN OUR DISTRESS. God never abandons us in our distress. He is always present to guide and watch over us. The Spirit will bring us comfort, stamina, and help when we need it. And even if we seem to have lost our way and don't know what to pray for, the Spirit is still with us, praying in our stead and in harmony with the will of God.

3. ASSURED OF SALVATION. Opposition will try to separate us from God, but He holds onto and safeguards His own so that no power of any kind has the ability to undo what Jesus has accomplished for us. What a word of encouragement we have!

4. ASSURED OF GLORY. This glory is the complete fulfillment of God's plan for redeemed humanity since the inception of creation. Not only will all creation attain its fullest potential, but all of redeemed humanity will also attain its fullest potential when those who are in Christ are resurrected to enjoy their ultimate salvation.

■ **TOPIC:** Where Is My Security Blanket?

■ **QUESTIONS:** 1. Why do you think believers are sometimes reluctant to ask God to safeguard them in times of peril? 2. What are some ways God helps us in moments of turmoil? 3. Why should believers not be filled with fear when life seems to be out of control? 4. When have you witnessed the presence and power of God deliver you out of agonizing situations? 5. What good things can God bring out of the grief and loss you experience?

■ **ILLUSTRATIONS:**

Source of Security. In his well-known *Peanuts* comic strip, Charles Schulz popularized the notion of a "security blanket." The phrase refers to a familiar object, person, or circumstance used by others to provide comfort or assurance.

We all know adults who use a "security blanket" to help them manage their anxieties. We also realize that excessive and prolonged worrying is not good for our health. In fact, worrying can rob us of peace and contentment. It should come as no surprise, then, that Jesus wants us to stop worrying and find our source of security in Him. But how can we do this?

Many books and sermons give us good practical advice. The simplest answer is to focus our attention on the Lord. When we start the day with praise and thanks to the Savior as well as meditate on His Word, we are in good shape to deal with the problem of worrying.

It also helps to have some good friends. These would not be people who dream up more stuff for us to worry about, but rather those who are good listeners and who can point us back to Jesus, our caring and protecting Shepherd. We all need encouragement to let go of our worries and give them to the Lord.

Secure in God's Protection. Annie swung her feet over the side of the empty bed. She felt the heaviness of having to tell each of her children as they woke that morning, "Daddy won't be living here with us anymore."

In some ways, Annie thought reporting that her husband had been killed in car accident would be easier than saying, "Your father is involved with another woman and does not want to live with us anymore." But Annie knew she had to be honest. They lived in a small city, and she didn't want her children to find out from the town gossip.

Annie worried about her children's immediate response. They would be so hurt. They loved their dad. They might blame themselves or their mother. Annie could feel the anger rising as she thought through what she was going to say: How could he do this to us? The children are only five and eight years old.

As the time drew near for the dreaded conversation with her children, the hot tears slid down Annie's cheeks, forming a little pool at her chin. Her lip quivered, and she wondered how she could make it through the conversation.

As Annie reviewed her little speech for the hundredth time, a verse came to mind: "I will say of the LORD, he is my refuge and my fortress: my God; in him will I trust" (Ps. 91:2). At first Annie was doubtful. "Even in this case?" she could hear herself arguing with God. "Even in this case," the distraught single parent could hear God assuring her.

It would be months, but eventually Annie could see the truth of that verse at work in her life. And as she reminded herself of it, she felt increasingly secure in God's protection. To Annie's surprise, good things arose from her terrible situation. And through it all, she realized that God was close by to safeguard her and her children.

Jesus Guides and Protects Us. Recently, when I typed the word *map* in my favorite Internet search engine, I obtained thousands of listings to help me look for locations, get directions, and so on. One typical Web site claims users can not only find addresses and phone numbers, but also obtain directory listings for airports, hotels, post offices, restaurants, and schools (to name a few items).

In the spiritual realm, there is no substitute for the Lord Jesus in navigating through life. At times we might feel directionless and vulnerable. In those moments, Christ is present to guide and protect us. On other occasions, we may struggle with depression or anxiety. In those dark times, the Savior will watch over and comfort us with His abiding presence and love.

FOR YOUTH

■ TOPIC: Sure Protection

■ QUESTIONS: 1. How can trusting God to watch over believers give them inner peace? 2. What insights from Psalm 91 can you glean to help you make it through difficult circumstances? 3. What are some of the ways that Psalm 91 says God safeguards the faithful? 4. What do you think is the right way and the wrong way for believers to respond to threatening situations in their lives? 5. Why is it important for believers to focus on the abiding presence and power of God in times of hardship?

■ ILLUSTRATIONS:

Perfect Security. There is such a thing as false security. In *At Dawn We Slept*, Gordon Prange noted the report made by journalist Clarke Beach on September 6, 1941, just a few months before the enemy bombardment of Pearl Harbor: "A Japanese attack on Hawaii is regarded as the most unlikely thing in the world, with one chance in a million of being successful. Besides having more powerful defenses than any other post under the American flag, it is protected by distance."

True security is not found in any human person, earthly object, or philosophical idea. Jesus alone offers it freely to all who trust in Him. He is the believer's sure protection in the storms of life. Even when God's children feel as if they are under spiritual attack, they can find sanctuary in their relationship with the Savior. When their faith is anchored in Him, they will remain perfectly secure.

A Reason to Hold On. Imagine what it would be like to be a prisoner in a foreign land, or under a tyrant ruler. In the early centuries of the common era, many Christian families were split apart, especially as fathers were taken from their homes and cast into dark dungeons. And it wasn't only the heads of households that suffered these imprisonments, tortures, and death. History records many accounts of Christian children and teenage boys and girls being carried away as well.

From accounts such as *Fox's Book of Martyrs* and others, we see that it was the inward assurance of God's presence and power that enabled Jesus' followers to endure unthinkable hardships. In a metaphorical sense, He spread His wings of protection over the saints and kept them secure in His love (see Ps. 91:4). Though their bodies were tortured and imprisoned, in their hearts they were free.

History records that there have been more martyrs for the Savior in the last 50 years alone than in all the preceding centuries of Christianity's existence combined. What made it worthwhile for these millions of men and women to give their lives for the gospel? Their reason for holding onto their faith was the assurance of being with Jesus forever in the life after death. And this is a hope that will not disappoint.

Looking Past the Pain. A couple of years ago, Pastor Jeff Wallace discovered an incident at the parsonage that left his daughter, Gracie, in tears. Jeff had left a little lavender-colored ceramic planter out on the deck. But this little planter was special. It had "Baby" molded into the side, and when he wound it up, a music box inside played a lullaby.

Some dear friends of Jeff had given this planter to him eleven years before, just after Gracie was born. It must have been the rising and falling of the temperatures over several seasons that somehow shattered that little treasure into multiple pieces. Gracie glared at the pieces in her hands, tears streaming from her eyes at her sense of the loss.

Admittedly, we all feel saddened when an earthly treasure is taken from us. But nothing this world has to offer can compare in value with the truth of Psalm 91:9 that the Lord is our refuge and the Most High is our dwelling. Indeed, the assurance of future glory in heaven can go a long way toward helping us look past the pain connected with a trying situation.

GOD IS ALL-KNOWING

BACKGROUND SCRIPTURE: PSALM 139
DEVOTIONAL READING: Psalm 42

KEY VERSE: There is not a word in my tongue, but, lo, O LORD, thou knowest it altogether. (Psalm 139:4)

KING JAMES VERSION

PSALM 139:1 O LORD, thou hast searched me, and known me. 2 Thou knowest my downsitting and mine uprising, thou understandest my thought afar off. 3 Thou compassest my path and my lying down, and art acquainted with all my ways. 4 For there is not a word in my tongue, but, lo, O LORD, thou knowest it altogether. 5 Thou hast beset me behind and before, and laid thine hand upon me. 6 Such knowledge is too wonderful for me; it is high, I cannot attain unto it. . . .

13 For thou hast possessed my reins: thou hast covered me in my mother's womb. 14 I will praise thee; for I am fearfully and wonderfully made: marvellous are thy works; and that my soul knoweth right well. 15 My substance was not hid from thee, when I was made in secret, and curiously wrought in the lowest parts of the earth. 16 Thine eyes did see my substance, yet being unperfect; and in thy book all my members were written, which in continuance were fashioned, when as yet there was none of them. . . .

23 Search me, O God, and know my heart: try me, and know my thoughts: 24 And see if there be any wicked way in me, and lead me in the way everlasting.

NEW REVISED STANDARD VERSION

PSALM 139:1 O LORD, you have searched me and known me.
2 You know when I sit down and when I rise up;
    you discern my thoughts from far away.
3 You search out my path and my lying down,
    and are acquainted with all my ways.
4 Even before a word is on my tongue,
    O LORD, you know it completely.
5 You hem me in, behind and before,
    and lay your hand upon me.
6 Such knowledge is too wonderful for me;
    it is so high that I cannot attain it. . . .
13 For it was you who formed my inward parts;
    you knit me together in my mother's womb.
14 I praise you, for I am fearfully and wonderfully made.
    Wonderful are your works;
    that I know very well.
15 My frame was not hidden from you,
    when I was being made in secret,
    intricately woven in the depths of the earth.
16 Your eyes beheld my unformed substance.
    In your book were written
    all the days that were formed for me,
    when none of them as yet existed. . . .
23 Search me, O God, and know my heart;
    test me and know my thoughts.
24 See if there is any wicked way in me,
    and lead me in the way everlasting.

13

Monday, November 22	Matthew 6:1-8	*God Sees and Knows All*
Tuesday, November 23	Proverbs 15:1-7	*God Keeps Watch over All*
Wednesday, November 24	Job 23:8-13	*God Knows Our Ways*
Thursday, November 25	Psalm 139:7-12	*The Expanse of God's Presence*
Friday, November 26	Psalm 147:1-6	*The Expanse of God's Understanding*
Saturday, November 27	Psalm 139:17-21	*The Expanse of God's Knowledge*
Sunday, November 28	Psalm 139:1-6, 13-16, 23-24	*The Intimacy of God's Knowledge*

BACKGROUND

We learn from Psalm 139 that God is *omniscient*, a term that literally refers to "all knowledge." Scripture teaches that God has unlimited awareness, understanding, and insight. Put differently, His knowledge and grasp of all things is universal and complete. His awareness is instantaneous, exhaustive, and absolutely correct. Even though all things are eternally present in God's view, He still recognizes them as successive, finite events in time.

The Lord is aware of every thought people have and every action they perform (2 Chron. 28:9). He can objectively and fairly evaluate the actions of people because He knows everything (2 Sam. 2:3). All wisdom and counsel reside with Him (Job 12:13), and His understanding is unbounded (Ps. 147:5). There is nothing in the entire universe that is not hidden from God's sight. Everything is exposed by His penetrating gaze (Heb. 4:13). God's awareness of all things serves two purposes. First, everyone is accountable to the Lord for his or her actions. No one will be able to do evil and get away with it. Second, God's omniscience reminds us that He is intimately aware of our circumstances. He not only sees our plight but also reaches out in love to care for us (Gen. 16:13).

NOTES ON THE PRINTED TEXT

The original historical context of Psalm 139 seems to be a situation involving some danger. Perhaps David exposed his life to God as a way of proving that he did not deserve divine punishment through his enemies. But before we get any hint of earthly peril, Israel's king eloquently described God's complete awareness of him. The Hebrew verb rendered "searched" (vs. 1) can also be translated "to investigate" or "to examine thoroughly." The poet stated that this was the basis for God's knowledge of him. The Lord's knowledge of David was not abstract, but specific and detailed. Verse 2 mentions when the king sat down and stood up, which is a general reference to his daily activities as Israel's head of state. Even though God was in heaven, He remained completely aware of David's thoughts and understood his motives. Moreover, the Lord carefully observed when the monarch traveled and when he lay down to rest. God was familiar with every aspect of David's life, whether public or private (vs. 3). The Hebrew verb rendered "compassest" literally refers to the winnowing of grain. Like the sharp-eyed farmer who scrutinizes the harvest and evaluates what is to be saved or thrown aside, God examines the human heart.

Concerning David, the Lord knew what His servant would say before he uttered it. God did not miss a single one of the poet's thoughts. In a manner of speaking, David's life was like an open book to the Lord. God knows everything about us, too. We might think that the people closest to us—a spouse, family members, and friends—know us pretty well. But no one, not even ourselves, knows us the way God does. Remembering this truth should make us more careful about what we think, say, and do. There was no doubt in David's mind that before his mouth framed a word, the Lord was already fully aware of what the king would say (vs. 4). Regardless of the dangers Israel's monarch might face, God went before him and followed him. Metaphorically speaking, the Lord squeezed David in from behind and in front. The idea is that God used His powerful arm to protect His servant from every side. Moreover, the Lord had placed His hand of blessing on David (vs. 5). The king admitted that God's awareness of him was so extraordinary that it went far beyond his comprehension. In fact, what the Lord knew about David was so infinite that he was unable to fathom it (vs. 6).

We know enough about our personal thoughts and actions to realize that God is not totally pleased with what He sees. To be sure, we may even wonder why God is so patient with our imperfections. Yet rather than casting us aside, the Lord constantly hems us in with His merciful care. The realization that God knows everything and still loves each person filled the poet with awe. If God knows our thoughts, some will wonder, then why pray? But prayer is not a news hotline to provide the Almighty with a breaking development taking place on earth. After all, He is fully focused on everything that is occurring and even understands the motives and implications for everyone involved.

As human beings we are limited by boundaries of time and space. For example, we cannot occupy two places simultaneously. However, God is not subject to such restrictions. He is *omnipresent*, meaning present everywhere at once. Nor is He divided, like minerals that may be scattered over a wide expanse of terrain. At all times, all that is God is totally present everywhere. David did not arrive at this truth easily. In his imagination he pondered several ways one might try to evade the presence of God (vs. 7). First, the poet thought about ascending to heaven or sprawling out in the realm of the dead (vs. 8). Together these places represented the most extreme vertical distances. It's as if David was saying, "If I ascended as high as I could, or descended to the lowest thinkable depth, I could not escape Your reach."

But what about the horizontal extremes? Suppose the poet made the rising sun his chariot and raced to the utmost reach of the western horizon (vs. 9)? Even if David could somehow settle down on the other side of the Mediterranean Sea (which lies west of Israel), the Lord would still be there to afford support every hour of every day (vs. 10). In contrast to idols, there is no point on any map where God is not fully present to protect and guide His people. David considered another possibility: hiding (vss. 11-12). Adam and Eve tried to hide from God among the trees of Eden. Here David thought about using the night as a screen to hide himself from God. However, he rejected this possibility as well, since God can see in darkness as well as in light. David had to give up the idea of escaping God.

The king had reached the point of spiritual maturity at which he had come to accept God's knowledge of him. The poet realized that every day of his life, from the first to the last, was known to God. In David's day, people knew little about how a human fetus forms in its mother's womb. But David understood that God knows about this, for He is the one who causes it to happen. The Lord is in charge of each individual's genetic code and brings together the substances that make up a human being. And since the result is obviously a remarkable creation, David considered the making of a child a sign of God's wisdom.

The process that takes place in the "mother's womb" (vs. 13; also called "in secret" and "the lowest parts of the earth" vs. 15) is like the creation of a work of art. David compared the formation of a human child to the skilled weaving of cloth on a loom. Figuratively speaking, children are knit together and woven by God inside the womb. Both the mind and the heart, the intellect and emotions (as well as the will) are the handiwork of God. David exclaimed that the Lord's deeds are awesome. And just as amazing is God's thorough knowledge of every human being from the moment of their conception (vs. 14). We who have seen photographs of fetuses at different stages of growth should be even more amazed than David was.

In verse 15, David commented on the formation of his bones in the womb of his mother, a place characterized by utter seclusion. He poetically described the gestation process for all human beings as one involving being stitched together deep in the earth below. Israel's king declared that before we were born, God knew everything that would happen on every one of our days as though all of the events were written in a book (vs. 16). As we look ahead, our future may appear cloudy to us, but it is as plain as day to God. Therefore, we can march ahead confidently, knowing that whatever awaits us, God will be with us.

The Lord's thoughts were far beyond David's ability to number (in other words, to comprehend). Nevertheless, God's thoughts were "precious" (vs. 17) to the king, for they meant that God had the ability and the willingness to care for His spiritual children. And even though we may lose consciousness of the Lord when we are asleep, He never loses consciousness of us (vs. 18). At our awakening from sleep (even the sleep of death), we will be with God and He with us. He will never leave us.

Verse 19 marks an abrupt transition. Suddenly, David began talking about wicked people who were his enemies and foes of God. These men, said David, were "bloody." Furthermore, they misused God's name, probably by calling down curses on the Lord's faithful servants. They hated God and opposed Him. Though abrupt, the transition makes sense. The earlier part of the psalm revealed that God's knowledge demonstrates His ability to care for His people and that it makes them love Him. Verses 19-22 reveal the psalmist's confidence that God could deal with his enemies. Those verses also reveal the poet's zeal for the Lord and for His standards of righteousness. Though zealous for God, David knew better than to think that he was perfect in God's sight. The poet's anxious "thoughts" (vs. 23) may have been caused by the idea of God searching him. But the king invited God to examine him anyway, probe his thoughts, and assess his concerns.

David believed there was no "wicked way" (vs. 24) in him, as there was in his enemies. This process of God sifting through David's life would bring up some impurities for cleansing. And this cleansing would open the way to greater progress in "the way everlasting." So the psalmist asked God to test him, cleanse him, and thereby vindicate him. David's exercise of freely opening his life to God is one each Christian could profitably adopt. Sometimes we try to keep parts of our lives hidden from God. We don't acknowledge before Him some of our most cherished sins. Therefore, we need the courage and the faith to show Him everything about us, realizing that afterward will come the healing and sanctifying work of the Spirit.

SUGGESTIONS TO TEACHERS

In Psalm 139, David expressed grief at the sins of the wicked (vss. 19-22). Then he wanted to be sure that his own sins were not grieving God (vss. 23-24). Since the Lord is everywhere present and knows everything, He becomes the perfect counselor to advise His people about issues that need to be resolved in their lives. Admittedly, it is hard for us to get a handle on the truth of God's absolute understanding of our thoughts, words, and actions. The great Bible teacher G. Campbell Morgan echoed David's sentiments when he wrote, "When all my attempts at [Bible analysis] fail, I worship."

1. GOD OF LIGHT AND DARKNESS. Perhaps several members of the class have experienced the darkness of a cave. In fact, David may have had his cave ordeals in mind when he wrote this hymn. Ask your students for words that describe how they felt when encompassed by deep darkness. Listen for such words as "helpless," "afraid," and "alone." Be sure to focus on how a person in darkness might become more aware of God's presence. You may want to suggest such things as praying to God, affirming statements about God, and quoting favorite Bible promises or hymns.

2. GOD OF ENCOURAGEMENT. Members of the class may recall periods of David's life when he was lonely or in danger. Also, David may have been grateful for God's presence when important decisions had to be made. There is evidence in

Scripture that David looked to God for guidance when preparing for battle, and also during his years as king. While it may seem unsettling to realize that God is always present in our lives, we can know that He understands and cares. We need never take a step in our journey without Him.

3. GOD OF HUMAN EXISTENCE. Let your students know that we do not serve a detached, uninvolved God. The Lord, who is far greater than us, is ever-present to watch over us. Even at the moment of our conception He was constantly attending to our human development. No one said it better than David. We are "fearfully and wonderfully made" (vs. 14).

4. GOD OF OUR WORSHIP. Until God is the sole object of our adoration and praise, life will be hopelessly chaotic and destructive. Our reverence for Him must not be left to our moods or whims. Rather, we must worship Him "in spirit and in truth" (John 4:24).

FOR ADULTS

■ TOPIC: Comforting Awareness

■ QUESTIONS: 1. How does God's intimate knowledge of every person prove to be both sobering and reassuring at the same time? 2. What does it really mean that God is present everywhere at all times? 3. Why should we want the Lord to know our every thought? 4. Why is it important for us to lean on God to avoid the way of wickedness? 5. How can we encourage others to follow the everlasting way?

■ ILLUSTRATIONS:

Searched and Known by God. At a recent funeral I conducted, one of the surviving children gave me a little booklet of prayers titled, *Adventures in Prayer.* One petition speaks of the comforting awareness of God's intimate knowledge of us as well as His loving care for us.

"Lord, I have been so defeated by circumstances. I have felt like an animal trapped in a corner with nowhere to flee. Where are You in all this, Lord? The night is dark. I cannot feel Your presence.

"Help me to know the darkness is really the 'shade of Your hand, outstretched caressingly'; that the 'hemming in' is Your doing. Perhaps there was no other way I would allow You to demonstrate what You can do in my life."

Known by Others. Thanks to advances in technology, more is known about each citizen than at any time in history. All of us are in somebody's data bank, and various organizations can produce detailed information about our lifestyles. What television shows do we watch? What are our reading preferences? What products are we likely to purchase? Someone somewhere knows. Researcher George Barna says that marketing agencies can produce information on about 92 percent of America's households.

One evidence of this is the electronic and postal mail we receive from people and companies we've never heard of. Read junk mail carefully and you'll be startled at what these groups know about your interests and spending patterns. As the information highway gains more and more traffic, the volume of unsolicited material will increase.

Yet despite being known by so many agencies, many adults are still searching for intimacy—to be really known by a few friends who care about them. One common denominator in growing churches is their ability to make newcomers feel cared for, especially through small groups. As Psalm 139 declares, God knows everyone's inward thoughts and outward actions and cares deeply for each individual.

Hallelujah! When Queen Victoria had just ascended her throne, she went, as was the custom of royalty, to hear George Frederick Handel's *Messiah*. The queen had been instructed as to her conduct by her royal advisers and was told that she must not rise when others stood at the singing of the "Hallelujah" chorus.

When that magnificent chorus was being sung, the choir shouted "Hallelujah! Hallelujah! Hallelujah! for the Lord God omnipotent reigneth." Meanwhile, the queen remained seated with great difficulty. Despite the custom of monarchs, several times it seemed as if she would rise.

Finally, the performance came to that part of the chorus where, with a shout, the choir proclaims God to be "King of Kings and Lord of Lords." At this point, the young queen rose to her feet and stood with her head bowed, signifying that she too would take her crown and cast it at the feet of her all-knowing Creator. This is the same God that David recognized. Israel's king rested in the assurance of God's intimate awareness of him. And so can we, for the Lord is above all others and knows everything.

■ TOPIC: You Can Run, but You Can't Hide

■ QUESTIONS: 1. In what ways do you think the Lord had searched and known David? 2. Why do you think David was contemplating God's intimate knowledge of him? 3. Why is it futile to try to hide from God's presence? 4. Why do you think David wanted the Lord to search and know his heart? 5. How might God lead us in everlasting paths of uprightness?

■ ILLUSTRATIONS:

God Knows Us like a Book. Many teenagers experience strong emotions when they find out someone of the opposite gender likes them. Some of these feelings include amazement and excitement. Perhaps it's a little like that for saved adolescents with respect to their relationship with God.

Even for young people who have little more than a passing knowledge of God's name, He still loves and cares for them. His heart must ache when they do not recognize His care, unseen protection, or concern. Even in the darkest times of their lives He is doing what He knows is best for them. In those overwhelming moments, when it is most difficult to praise Him, still there is cause since He knows them better than they know themselves. And even if they try to hide from His presence, He is always near to offer His comfort.

The Fear of Being Abandoned. In the *Search for Silence*, Elizabeth O'Connor notes that she was once part of a group that was asked to name the fear that filled them with the most dread. O'Connor studied a list of possible fears, then circled "The fear that one day I will be left alone."

The leader then asked everyone to become part of a small circle and urged each person to share his or her number-one fear. Someone mentioned being old and being alone. Another person declared, "I have that fear, too, but mine is really the fear of being abandoned." A third member added, "I fear too much committing myself to a cause, and as we go down the road, people drop out, and at last I'll be left holding the bag. I fear that there won't be anybody else there but me."

O'Connor thought she would be the only person who feared being alone, yet others felt this anxiety. It was a common concern even for the younger people in the group. And the answer to that issue was the One who said, "I am with you always."

The Human Heart. Your students may have some knowledge about specific organs of the human body that speak of our Creator's genius. The heart serves as one example. According to the Yale University School of Medicine, the heart, which is the size of two clenched fists, pumps one million barrels of blood during an average lifetime. This only takes into account its work at rest. During exercise or stress, the heart may pump 10 times as much blood as it does at rest.

Stretched end to end, the vessels of the circulatory system—arteries, arterioles, capillaries, and veins—would measure about 60,000 miles. The oxygen and nutrients transported in the bloodstream and delivered with each beat of the heart nourish 300 trillion cells. What an awesome Creator we serve! He knows us better than we can ever know ourselves. He will never forsake us, but promises to travel with us through the journey of life (see Heb. 13:5).

GOD'S PROMISED ONE

BACKGROUND SCRIPTURE: Isaiah 40
DEVOTIONAL READING: Ephesians 2:11-22

KEY VERSE: [God] giveth power to the faint; and to them that have no might he increaseth strength. (Isaiah 40:29)

KING JAMES VERSION

ISAIAH 40:1 Comfort ye, comfort ye my people, saith your God. 2 Speak ye comfortably to Jerusalem, and cry unto her, that her warfare is accomplished, that her iniquity is pardoned: for she hath received of the LORD's hand double for all her sins.

3 The voice of him that crieth in the wilderness, Prepare ye the way of the LORD, make straight in the desert a highway for our God. 4 Every valley shall be exalted, and every mountain and hill shall be made low: and the crooked shall be made straight, and the rough places plain: 5 And the glory of the LORD shall be revealed, and all flesh shall see it together: for the mouth of the LORD hath spoken it. . . .

25 To whom then will ye liken me, or shall I be equal? saith the Holy One. 26 Lift up your eyes on high, and behold who hath created these things, that bringeth out their host by number: he calleth them all by names by the greatness of his might, for that he is strong in power; not one faileth. . . .

29 He giveth power to the faint; and to them that have no might he increaseth strength. 30 Even the youths shall faint and be weary, and the young men shall utterly fall: 31 But they that wait upon the LORD shall renew their strength; they shall mount up with wings as eagles; they shall run, and not be weary; and they shall walk, and not faint.

NEW REVISED STANDARD VERSION

ISAIAH 40:1 Comfort, O comfort my people,
  says your God.
2 Speak tenderly to Jerusalem,
  and cry to her
that she has served her term,
  that her penalty is paid,
that she has received from the LORD's hand
  double for all her sins.
3 A voice cries out:
"In the wilderness prepare the way of the LORD,
  make straight in the desert a highway for our God.
4 Every valley shall be lifted up,
  and every mountain and hill be made low;
the uneven ground shall become level,
  and the rough places a plain.
5 Then the glory of the LORD shall be revealed,
  and all people shall see it together,
  for the mouth of the LORD has spoken." . . .
25 To whom then will you compare me,
  or who is my equal? says the Holy One.
26 Lift up your eyes on high and see:
  Who created these?
He who brings out their host and numbers them,
  calling them all by name;
because he is great in strength,
  mighty in power,
  not one is missing. . . .
29 He gives power to the faint,
  and strengthens the powerless.
30 Even youths will faint and be weary,
  and the young will fall exhausted;
31 but those who wait for the LORD shall renew their strength,
  they shall mount up with wings like eagles,
they shall run and not be weary,
  they shall walk and not faint.

HOME BIBLE READINGS

Monday, November 29	Deuteronomy 5:22-27	*God's Glory Revealed*
Tuesday, November 30	1 Chronicles 16:28-34	*God's Glory Declared*
Wednesday, December 1	2 Chronicles 5:11-14	*God's Glory Praised*
Thursday, December 2	Psalm 79:5-10	*God's Glory Beseeched*
Friday, December 3	Isaiah 40:12-17	*God's Glory above the Nations*
Saturday, December 4	Isaiah 40:18-24	*God's Glory above the Earth*
Sunday, December 5	Isaiah 40:1-5, 25-26, 29-31	*God's Coming Glory*

BACKGROUND

In Isaiah 40:3-5, a procession is described. Initially, we are told of a voice calling. (It's not clear whether this is the voice of God, an angel, or Isaiah.) The voice was "in the wilderness," namely, land of a dry and desolate nature and made up mostly of rock and sand. This passage has an immediate and a distant application. In the immediate context, Isaiah commanded that a path be cleared for the Lord to lead a procession of His people from Babylon to Jerusalem. Isaiah said that in Judah's deliverance, the glory of the Lord would be visible to everyone. All the nations would know that God had rescued His people from exile, and this deliverance would bring great honor to Him. The faithful remnant could derive much consolation from the knowledge that God stood behind His promises of deliverance and restoration.

In its more distant application, verses 3-5 serve as a fitting introduction to the ministry of John the Baptizer (see Matt. 3:3; Mark 1:2-3; Luke 3:4-6; John 1:23). He was the son of an elderly couple named Zechariah and Elizabeth. At the divinely appointed time, John traveled throughout the rural areas of the Jordan River Valley and urged people to repent and be baptized. John was helping the people of his day get ready for the advent of the Messiah. Within a short time after John began his ministry, the Lord Jesus would begin His public ministry. The people needed to know that God was sending them the Redeemer and that they would receive either salvation or judgment from His hands. John attuned the people to their spiritual need and built up an expectancy for the Savior, who could meet their need.

NOTES ON THE PRINTED TEXT

The translation of the initial verses of Isaiah 40 from Hebrew into English can shroud the fact that God was speaking to a group, such as the heavenly hosts, and not to the prophet Isaiah alone. For instance, note that the Hebrew verb rendered "comfort" (vs. 1) is a plural-form command. It's an order given to a multitude (perhaps an entourage of heavenly attendants), all of whom are assigned the same task, namely, to collectively announce the end of the Babylonian exile. Also note that "comfort" is repeated twice to emphasize that there would be an end of punishment and the coming of a new day of freedom.

The promise of a brighter future could be found only in the faithfulness of God. Accordingly, the goal of this second half of the Book of Isaiah was to convince God's people not only that the Lord would allow them to return home, but also that He desired that they do so. The necessity of this message was mandated because not all the people of God would be unhappy in Babylon. Many of them would assimilate into the Babylonian culture. And for them, the prospect of returning to a homeland in ruins was not their idea of a bright future.

The Lord directed Isaiah to speak "comfortably" (vs. 2) to "Jerusalem," which is here personified as a woman and refers to the people of Judah. The prophet was to address God's people as a mother would speak to her children. This was not the time for the inhabitants to hear harsh words of censure and condemnation. Instead, speaking prophetically, Isaiah was to tell the people that their appointed time of hardship was soon to be over. Like felons in prison, the people had served their term, and God accepted their punishment as being sufficient. Indeed, the Lord made His people pay "double for all [their] sins." Now, instead of having to endure more of God's judgment, they received His full pardon.

The previous statement does not mean that the people were overpunished but rather that as a result of their exile, they had been penalized as much as they deserved. Isaiah's promise of the Lord's comfort would bring renewed hope and assurance into the hearts of the Jews, whom God would not leave in an alien land. Here we find both God's holiness and grace at work. Because of continuous idolatry in Judah and Jerusalem, God would exercise His holy, righteous judgment and send His people into captivity. The Babylonian exile was not just the sad outcome of war. More importantly, it was directed by God's hand. The Lord, however, refused to abandon His people. Once they had endured enough suffering, He declared that He would release them from their captivity. With the ending of their exile, the faithful remnant could start fresh with God in the land of promise. This was the message of comfort and hope the people needed to hear.

According to verse 3, the heavenly voice directed God's people to prepare for His coming. In ancient times a herald was often sent ahead of a royal procession to make sure the path was sufficiently smooth. All obstacles were cleared off the road, and the general direction of the route was straightened to make travel easier for the visiting monarch. Admittedly, creating a road for the arrival of a king in ancient times periodically required extensive construction and reconstruction. Nonetheless, Isaiah used hyperbole (purposeful exaggerations) to describe an unprecedented leveling and smoothing process. For instance, he said that all the valleys would be elevated, the mountains and hills would be flattened, and the rugged landscape would be transformed into a wide valley (vs. 4). Then the royal splendor of the Lord would appear for the entire human race to see. This was not an idle promise, for the Lord stood behind His decree (vs. 5).

We learn from Isaiah 40 that God is greater than false gods and idols. Of course, the people of Israel should have been aware of God's great power and sovereignty (vs. 21). After all, prophets throughout the nation's history had emphasized these themes time and again. Isaiah reminded his forgetful people that God sits enthroned above the "circle" (vs. 22; or horizon) of the earth. Also, from God's perspective, the people are so puny that they are like mere grasshoppers. Isaiah portrayed the heavens as being a vast tent in which the Lord dwells—emphasizing His exaltation over people. Isaiah also said that God is sovereign over earth's rulers (vs. 23). This would have been quite meaningful to the exiles in bondage to Babylon's king. As easily and as quickly as a plant can die, God can remove rulers according to His sovereign choice (vs. 24). In view of all that had been said, God asked whether it was really possible to compare Him with any earthly power. The answer was no, for no one in all the universe resembled Him or was His "equal" (vs. 25). As the "Holy One," He is the sovereign monarch who reigns over His chosen people and exercises the right to judge them.

Verse 26 shifts our attention to the vast number of stars in the heavens. The Lord is the Creator of all these. The heavenly lights within them are comparable to an enormous army whose ranks are summoned and led out by God. He uses His absolute power and infinite strength to ensure that none of the stars are ever overlooked. This point is significant, for people throughout the ancient Near East believed in astrology. Whereas the Babylonians had made a false religion out of the stars, Isaiah affirmed that God is the Creator of the cosmic hosts. Moreover, the same power that brought these celestial objects into existence would deliver the chosen people from exile. The reason Isaiah spoke so much about God's power is that the prophet knew it would strengthen the faith of his peers.

The prophet noted that unlike humans, the all-powerful King never grows tired or becomes weary. Furthermore, there is no limit to His wisdom. Indeed, His "understanding" (vs. 28) is inscrutable. Rather than be filled with doubt and discontent, the exiles were to affirm the infinite sovereignty, power, and prudence of the Lord, especially in fulfilling His promise to deliver them from captivity. When they felt "faint" (vs. 29), they could look to Him for "strength." Likewise, He was to be their source of "power" whenever they felt weary. The sobering fact is that even the most vigorous of young people become exhausted (vs. 30). Similarly, the strongest of youth stumble and "fall." In contrast, when God's spiritual children patiently wait for His help, their "strength" (vs. 31) is renewed.

The Hebrew verb translated "renew" involves the idea of exchange. The Hebrew verb is used elsewhere to refer to a change of clothes (Gen. 35:2). The point is that those who hope in the Lord exchange their weakness for His strength. In context, Isaiah 40:31 seems to refer to the renewal of vitality that would be required for the journey from Babylon to Palestine. Those who trusted in the Lord would find all the strength they needed for this 900-mile journey. Eagles can soar for a long time on thermals (rising currents of warm air), and thus they are a symbol of power and endurance. The weary exiles would gain strength to soar above their circumstances, like eagles. Furthermore, they would run and walk without tiring, unlike the young in their prime who clumsily stumble.

SUGGESTIONS TO TEACHERS

Regardless of our current circumstances, regardless of our stressful situations, and regardless of our times of trial and testing, God is in our presence. And when we commit to trusting and obeying Him, He promises us that His peace and comfort will remain with us.

1. COMFORT IN ADVERSITY. Not everyone is going to go along with or agree with our faith in and commitment to God. We will face opposition and adversity. Though we cannot avoid hardship, as we face it we can find and experience God's comfort. As long as we're living for Him, we will be able to find promises and encouragement in His Word and in His presence.

2. COMFORT IN TRIALS. We will face trials and sufferings that we cannot explain. There will seem to be no purpose or reason for them. Although we are not immune to distress, our faith need not be hindered by them. In the midst of affliction—even when our life seems to be falling apart—we can call on God to comfort us.

3. COMFORT AGAINST THE FLOW. As believers, we will feel as though we are swimming upstream while striving to live the Christian life and obey God's Word. All around us, opinions and perceptions will change. We must remember that "the word of our God shall stand for ever" (Isa. 40:8). Only in God's Word will we find lasting solutions to each of our problems and needs.

4. COMFORT THROUGH REDEMPTION. At one time, our sin separated us from God. We were trapped in sin's clutches and held captives as exiles from God. But our Redeemer, Jesus Christ, has delivered us! And because He has, we can find great comfort for our minds, hearts, and souls through Him and His mercy and grace.

FOR ADULTS

■ **TOPIC:** Receiving Comfort and Strength

■ **QUESTIONS:** 1. Why do you think God issued words of comfort to Judah long before the nation was punished by being exiled to Babylon? 2. How would these words comfort God's people who were facing hard times but had not yet faced the worst of times? 3. What does God say to the people to assure them that He will, indeed, forgive them? 4. In what ways does the vast number of stars in the sky point to the awesome, creative power of God? 5. In what ways can believers renew their strength by hoping in the Lord?

■ ILLUSTRATIONS:

The Gift of Comfort. Different things represent comfort to different people. Some perceive a soft chair, an expensive car, warm temperatures, stretchy clothes, or a large bank account as something that can make them comfortable. Others think they would be more comfortable and stronger if they had good health, no pressure, or no money problems. Nevertheless, adults are rarely satisfied with the circumstances that surround them. There is always something about which they can complain.

Our level of comfort has much to do with what we have experienced. That's why we need to understand that God's comfort may not come in ways that we want. However, that does not mean God is trying to make our lives miserable.

People tend to be comfortable when they receive the things they want. That's why it is hard for them to thank God for difficult times. It is even more challenging for them to see the ways God seeks to comfort and strengthen them, for He may choose to do so in ways that they don't expect. His approach, though, is always best.

God for the Pressured. Lloyd J. Ogilvie, in his book *Life without Limits*, tells the story of a pastor who, in the space of one week, heard the following comments from various people:

A woman said, "I'm under tremendous pressure from my son these days. I can't seem to satisfy him, however hard I work. He really puts me under pressure."

A husband said, "My wife is never satisfied. Whatever I do, however much I make, it's never enough. Life with her is like living in a pressure cooker with the lid fastened down and the heat on high."

A middle-aged wife said, "My husband thinks my faith is silly. When I feel his resistance to Christ, I wonder if I'm wrong and confused. As a result, I've developed two lives; one with him and one when I'm with my Christian friends."

An elderly woman said, "My sister thinks she has all the answers about the faith and tries to convince me of her point of view. I feel pressured to become her brand of Christian, but I keep thinking if it means being like her, I don't want it at all. When she calls, I just put the phone on my shoulder and let her rant on while I do other things. A half hour later, she's still on the line blasting away, but I still feel pressure."

A young pastor at a clergy conference said, "I hardly know who I am anymore. There are so many points of view in my congregation, I can't please them all. Everyone wants to capture me for his camp and get me to shape the church around his convictions. The pressure makes me want to leave the ministry."

All of these individuals have two things in common. They are being pressured by other people, and they are in need of comfort. As Isaiah 40 makes clear, it is the Lord who consoles the frazzled (vs. 1), speaks tenderly to the downcast (vs. 2), and gives strength to the weary (vs. 29).

Comfort for the Raging. Two shoppers in a supermarket got into a fistfight over who should be first in a newly opened checkout lane. An airline flight returned to a major American city after a passenger was accused of throwing a can of beer at a flight attendant and biting a pilot. One father in an eastern state beat another father to death in an argument over rough play at their sons' hockey practice. A high school baseball coach in the South turned himself in to face charges that he broke an umpire's jaw after a disputed call. All these events were reported by *USA Today* over the span of a few months.

"Bad tempers are on display everywhere," wrote reporter Karen S. Peterson. The media is constantly reporting incidents of road rage, airplane rage, biker rage, surfer rage, grocery store rage, and rage at youth sporting events. This had led scientists to say the United States is in the middle of an anger epidemic. This epidemic rattles both those who study social trends and parents who fear the country is at a cultural precipice.

"We have lost some of the glue holding our society [together]," Peterson quoted one parent as saying. "We have lost our respect for others. The example we are setting for our kids is terrible."

Experts searching for causes blame an increasing sense of self-importance, the widespread feeling that things should happen "my" way. Other factors, they say, include too little time, overcrowding, intrusive technology, and too many demands for change in a society that is reeling from the effects of a global economic downturn. In the midst of our rage, we are desperately in need of comfort—and of the Comforter spoken about in Isaiah 40:1-2.

FOR YOUTH

■ TOPIC: The Road to Hope

■ QUESTIONS: 1. Why was it important for God's people to hear comforting words from Him? 2. How do you think the people felt when God told the nation of Judah that He would pardon her? 3. What do you think you would have done to "prepare . . . the way of the LORD" (Isa. 40:3)? 4. How would the "glory of the LORD . . . be revealed" (vs. 5) through the coming of the Messiah? 5. What are some ways you can encourage your saved peers to look to God for strength in their times of difficulty?

■ ILLUSTRATIONS:

Making a Fresh Start. What do you do with a broken-down car that needs repairs and paint? You see beyond the wreck and envision a sparkling new paint job and a motor that purrs sweetly down the road. You give that car all the sweat you can muster because you have high hopes for it and yourself.

Perhaps if we were writing Isaiah's sermons today, rather than comparing God to a tender shepherd, we would compare Him to a sensitive, careful, hardworking, and loving mechanic. That's because we bestow the same kind of love on our cars that shepherds do on their sheep.

The main point is that God can bring about restoration and healing in the lives of youth, especially if they submit to His will. He has wonderful plans for them that they can't even imagine. Metaphorically speaking, God can take their dings and dents, and all the misfirings of their cylinders, and make a beautiful automobile out of their lives. Through faith in His Son they can make a fresh start down the road to hope!

Comfort through Redemption. A year after brutally attacking a pastor, a gang member became a Christian. Patrick Shikanda Lokhotio apologized for attacking Timothy Njoya, pastor of a large Presbyterian church in Nairobi, Kenya, *Ecumenical News International* reported. Lokhotio beat Njoya with a wooden club outside the Parliament building, as the pastor led a political protest.

Lokhotio sought forgiveness from Njoya and his congregation in an address to the church. Njoya publicly forgave him months earlier and asked the authorities to stop criminal proceedings against him. These reassuring words of forgiveness greatly consoled Lokhotio. Indeed, he responded by saying he was ashamed for "beating up a man of God" and promised to live a Christian lifestyle.

Lokhotio's dramatic change "shows God's miracles have worked in this church," Njoya said. Lokhotio had been a member of a youth gang. During his talk, he introduced six members of the gang who also pledged to mend their ways. Not long after that about 100 additional members of the gang pledged to come to the church.

Comfort for the Needy. In an attempt to bring comfort to Vietnamese children without parents, Christian workers are running an orphanage under difficult conditions in Vietnam. They have received inspiration for their work from Isaiah 40:1, which says, "Comfort ye, comfort ye my people."

The religious group opened a home for children from the minority Cham population, according to Zenit, a Christian news agency. Bethany House, northeast of Ho Chi Minh City, houses fifty boys three to nineteen years old, many of whom have lost both parents. Cham fathers normally abandon their children and remarry if the mother dies, according to the news agency.

The orphans attend school and also are instructed in the faith. The Christian workers often are confronted by local authorities, since the Cham people embrace their own traditional religion, a local version of Hinduism, according to Zenit. However, some Cham adults have converted to Christianity and been baptized. Their reason is the consoling message of hope contained in the Gospel.

I AM YOUR GOD

BACKGROUND SCRIPTURE: Isaiah 41:1—42:9
DEVOTIONAL READING: 1 John 4:13-19

KEY VERSE: Fear thou not; for I am with thee:
be not dismayed; for I am thy God. (Isaiah 41:10)

KING JAMES VERSION

ISAIAH 41:8 But thou, Israel, art my servant, Jacob whom I have chosen, the seed of Abraham my friend. 9 Thou whom I have taken from the ends of the earth, and called thee from the chief men thereof, and said unto thee, Thou art my servant; I have chosen thee, and not cast thee away.

10 Fear thou not; for I am with thee: be not dismayed; for I am thy God: I will strengthen thee; yea, I will help thee; yea, I will uphold thee with the right hand of my righteousness. . . . 17 When the poor and needy seek water, and there is none, and their tongue faileth for thirst, I the LORD will hear them, I the God of Israel will not forsake them. 18 I will open rivers in high places, and fountains in the midst of the valleys: I will make the wilderness a pool of water, and the dry land springs of water. 19 I will plant in the wilderness the cedar, the shittah tree, and the myrtle, and the oil tree; I will set in the desert the fir tree, and the pine, and the box tree together: 20 That they may see, and know, and consider, and understand together, that the hand of the LORD hath done this, and the Holy One of Israel hath created it.

NEW REVISED STANDARD VERSION

ISAIAH 41:8 But you, Israel, my servant,
    Jacob, whom I have chosen,
    the offspring of Abraham, my friend;
9 you whom I took from the ends of the earth,
    and called from its farthest corners,
saying to you, "You are my servant,
    I have chosen you and not cast you off";
10 do not fear, for I am with you,
    do not be afraid, for I am your God;
I will strengthen you, I will help you,
    I will uphold you with my victorious right hand. . . .
17 When the poor and needy seek water,
    and there is none,
    and their tongue is parched with thirst,
I the LORD will answer them,
    I the God of Israel will not forsake them.
18 I will open rivers on the bare heights,
    and fountains in the midst of the valleys;
I will make the wilderness a pool of water,
    and the dry land springs of water.
19 I will put in the wilderness the cedar,
    the acacia, the myrtle, and the olive;
I will set in the desert the cypress,
    the plane and the pine together,
20 so that all may see and know,
    all may consider and understand,
that the hand of the LORD has done this,
    the Holy One of Israel has created it.

Monday, December 6	1 John 4:13-19	*A God of Love*
Tuesday, December 7	2 Chronicles 30:6-9	*A God of Grace and Mercy*
Wednesday, December 8	Nehemiah 9:16-21	*A God Ready to Forgive*
Thursday, December 9	Psalm 71:1-6	*A God of Hope*
Friday, December 10	Isaiah 41:1-7	*The Lord, First and Last*
Saturday, December 11	Isaiah 41:11-16	*Do Not Fear*
Sunday, December 12	Isaiah 41:8-10, 17-20	*The Lord's Promise to Protect*

BACKGROUND

In Isaiah 41, God declared that He alone was in control of human history. Indeed, it would be He who "raised up" (vs. 2) a king "from the east." An examination of other passages in Isaiah indicates that this verse is referring to Cyrus, the great king of Persia (see 44:28–45:6, 13; 46:11; 48:14-16). He reigned from 559–530 B.C., and founded the Persian Empire by combining the Medes and Persians into a powerful and unified nation. In 539 B.C., he conquered Babylon and the following year announced that the Jews could return to their homeland (Ezra 1:1-4; 6:3-5; Isa. 13:17-22; Dan. 5:25-31). Cyrus lived about two centuries after Isaiah wrote about him and correctly identified him by name. The ruins of the tomb of Cyrus indicate that he tended to be a humble monarch, in contrast to most ancient kings. He did not make great claims or boast about himself, even though he conquered much of the ancient Near East.

God, as the Lord over all creation, had the right to summon and commission Cyrus for service (Isa. 41:2). Also, it was God who sovereignly enabled the Persian king to conquer such powerful foes as Babylon and subdue its rulers. Moreover, the armies commanded by Cyrus trounced their potential opponents with such weapons of warfare as the sword and the bow. Before the Persian's seemingly invincible military machine all opponents were reduced to "dust" and windblown "stubble." The warriors commanded by Cyrus "passed safely" (vs. 3) as they hunted down and routed the troops belonging to other nations. Indeed, the Persians advanced into new regions with such great speed that it seemed as if their feet did not have enough time to touch the ground.

NOTES ON THE PRINTED TEXT

The amazing rise of Cyrus was not an accident of fate. It was the Lord, the eternal Creator (see Isa. 44:6; Heb. 13:8; Rev. 1:8, 17; 2:8; 21:6; 22:13), who decisively acted and brought to pass His decree. More generally, God is the one who controls all events and determines the course of history. He summoned forth each successive generation of humanity. In truth, He was present when He brought the first generation of people into existence, and even to the end of time He would still be there (Isa. 41:4). The inhabitants of faraway places were filled with fear as they witnessed the Lord's great acts. It seemed as if the whole earth trembled at the sight of God's awesome deeds (vs. 5). In response to the military threat that Cyrus posed, nations throughout the ancient Near East mobilized for war and turned to their pagan deities for help. The worshipers of idols urged each other not to worry (vs. 6). Also, skilled workers such as wood-carvers and metalsmiths exchanged compliments as they assembled their idols and nailed them down to prevent these powerless and lifeless objects from falling over (vs. 7).

Despite such efforts, the surrounding nations could not rely on their pagan deities to thwart God's will in connection with Cyrus and the way in which the Lord would use the Persian monarch to end the Babylonian exile. The descendants of the patriarchs had nothing to fear as God brought His will to pass. He encouraged them with the reminder that collectively they were His "servant" (vs. 8), whom He had "chosen" (see 14:1). Out of them the Lord forged a nation, the members of whom were descended from Abraham, God's "friend" (41:8; see Isa. 51:2; Heb. 2:16; Jas. 2:23). The latter reference implies that the Patriarch was a trusted and highly valued individual of God's royal administration. God's care for and protection of His chosen people are evident from the fact that centuries earlier He brought their ancestors out of Mesopotamia and Egypt and established them in the land of Canaan (see Gen. 11:31; 12:1; 15:7, 13; Ps. 114:1-2; Jer. 31:32). Moreover, the all-powerful Lord would once again bring the exiles back from the farthest regions of the Fertile Crescent and reestablish them in their homeland. After all, God regarded the righteous remnant as His "servant" (Isa. 41:9), whom He had chosen and whom He pledged to not reject.

The Hebrew noun rendered "servant" also can have the meanings of doer, tiller, or slave. It is a significant term in chapters 41—53, in which it sometimes refers to Judah and other times to an individual. In the royal terminology of the ancient Near East, "servant" meant something like "trusted envoy" or "confident representative." In chapter 41, the title refers to one who occupies a special position in God's royal administration. Cyrus is first introduced as such a servant, in which he was the divinely appointed liberator of the Jews from Babylonian captivity about 150 years later (539 B.C.). But Cyrus is also represented as a symbolic type of the future Messiah, and sometimes there is a blending of the two servants with a clear, overarching purpose of offering hope and comfort for the future.

For instance, in 41:8-20, we have unequivocal pledges of protection, of deliverance from enemies, and of blessing upon the promised land. Then in verses 21-29, we find God summoning idols themselves and effectively challenging, "Let's see if you can do that!" The Lord demands that they comparably interpret, predict, or even act in history. Of course, they could do none of these things. God, however, would not only predict, but also He Himself would raise up a Deliverer and announce this long beforehand through Isaiah. Apparently, some aspects of the Servant's ministry relate to delivering the exiles from Babylon; other aspects relate to Christ's earthly ministry;

and still other aspects may relate to His work in the end times. Ultimately, He is the standard toward which every one of God's servants is to strive.

When the Jews were permitted to return to their homeland, many chose to stay in Babylon (Ezra 1:5-6). Those who were young and strong enough to travel the distance to Judah had been born and raised in Babylon. They had never seen Judah. Many of them would have been reluctant to leave familiar surroundings to travel to a strange place that had yet to recover from the ravages of a bygone war. Unquestionably, the exiles had fears about their present circumstance and future prospects for survival. Nonetheless, the Lord encouraged them not to be afraid, for He promised to remain with them. Furthermore, He urged them not to be frightened, for He was their God. When they felt weak, He would strengthen them. And when they felt powerless, He would help them. Even when it seemed as if their survival was at stake, God pledged to rescue and protect them. By means of the "right hand of [God's] righteousness" (Isa. 41:10), He would vindicate their faith in Him (see Exod. 15:6, 12; Ps. 63:8).

As the Jews began the 900-mile journey back to promised land, they would feel oppressed, impoverished, and homeless. During this difficult period, they would encounter river-flooded plains, mountainous areas, and desert regions. Their will to survive the arduous trek would be tested by the constant need to find water and quench their parched throats. They would not be alone in their ordeal, for the Lord promised to hear and respond to their cries for help (see Isa. 30:19). Furthermore, the "God of Israel" (41:17) pledged not to abandon them. They could rely on the centuries-old declaration that the Lord would never leave them (see Deut. 31:6; Heb. 13:5). Indeed, He would be their constant companion and guide to offer help, allay their fears, and meet their most basic needs (see Ps. 118:6-7; Heb. 13:6).

Isaiah 41:18-19 describes paradise-like conditions that awaited God's people as they made the return journey to their homeland. For instance, rivers would cascade down once barren mountain peaks, and springs would flow in formerly parched valleys. Deserts, which were previously arid, would be transformed into a "pool of water" (vs. 18). Even land once thought to be too dry to sustain life would become a lake. Verse 19 draws attention to a variety of trees that were native to Canaan and Lebanon in ancient times—cedars, acacias, myrtles, and olive trees. These perennial woody plants required a lot of water to survive and thrive. The same held true for evergreens, firs, and cypresses. Regardless of whether it was a "wilderness" or a "desert," God would enable the environment to support a wide variety of vegetation. To the Jews returning to Canaan, trees were not only an image of nature, but also a symbol of life and vitality. Moreover, God's people associated such qualities as majesty, beauty, and power with trees (see Gen. 2:8-9; Pss. 1:3; 104:16-17; Song of Songs 2:3; 7:7; Jer. 17:8; Ezek. 31:3; 47:7, 12; Rev. 22:2).

The lush conditions described in Isaiah 41:18-19 would serve as a reminder of the Lord's unlimited ability to provide for the righteous remnant. Indeed, the holy God of

Israel would create for His people a homeland that was lush and fertile. The surrounding nations would also recognize that God was responsible for blessing His people with material abundance. This emphasis is conveyed through the usage of several key terms. The Hebrew verb rendered "see" (vs. 20) can also be translated "to take note of" or "to observe." "Know" renders a verb that can also be translated "to perceive" or "to discern." The verb rendered "consider" can also be translated "to contemplate" or "to ponder." "Understand" renders a verb that can also be translated "to instruct" or "to teach." As others grew in their awareness of the Lord's existence and comprehension of His ways, they might be inclined to turn to Him in faith and experience the joy of living in communion with Him and His people.

SUGGESTIONS TO TEACHERS

Isaiah 41 concerns the needs of God's people and the challenges they would face as they made the long journey from Babylon to their homeland. Verse 17 is especially poignant in reminding believers that the Lord not only hears, but also responds to their petitions. The class members will benefit from considering the following elements of effective prayer.

1. PRAYING IN HARMONY WITH GOD'S WORD. We sometimes forget that God listens to and understands our petitions. The Jews who embarked on a return to the promised land offered prayers to God, which He in turn answered—some right away, and others further down the road. They understood that petitions based upon God's Word and will are prayers that especially please the Lord.

2. RECOGNIZING GOD'S UNCHANGING NATURE. When we pray, we benefit from recalling that our Lord is "the same yesterday, and to day, and for ever" (Heb. 13:8). The implication is that He is ever faithful and all-powerful to respond to our requests. Indeed, the same God who reached out to His chosen people on their journey back to Judah thousands of years ago is the one who will help your students today.

3. AFFIRMING GOD'S INFINITE KNOWLEDGE OF US. We may wonder how God is able to understand our prayers when we feel so confused about ourselves. The teaching of Scripture is that the Lord knows our petitions better than we do ourselves. Even when we're not sure what the right prayers should be or the best method of prayer to use, God actively searches our "hearts" (Rom. 8:27). Moreover, due to the intercessory work of the Spirit, the Father is able to see the motive of our petitions and respond in kind.

4. UTILIZING ONE-MINUTE PRAYERS. Motivational speakers routinely emphasize how much can be accomplished in small spans of time. Let the students know that the same principle is true with prayer. An example of this would be petitions limited to one minute. Encourage them to work at developing the habit of offering a quick prayer for someone when they see that person in need, even though the class members may not know exactly what the need is. Also, when they come to a problem or dilemma in their daily routine, they can take a minute to ask the Lord for specific wisdom and then listen for His direction.

FOR ADULTS	■ TOPIC: Not Forsaken

■ TOPIC: Not Forsaken

■ QUESTIONS: 1. If you were an exile living in Babylon, how would you feel to know that God considered you as His "servant" (Isa. 41:8)? 2. Why would God not reject His people, despite the many ways they had sinned against Him? 3. How can the abiding presence of God calm believers when they feel afraid? 4. How has God quenched your spiritual "thirst" (vs. 17) when you felt inwardly parched? 5. Why is it important for believers to testify to others about the grace and goodness of God?

■ ILLUSTRATIONS:

Felt Supported. Perhaps years ago you saw *The Karate Kid*. It's a film about Daniel, a lonely, fatherless boy who is bullied by a gang called the Cobras. Daniel is aided by Mr. Miyagi, who teaches him karate. Through this benevolent but firm instructor, Daniel gets a new outlook on life.

In the climax, Daniel is involved in a karate match. Because he is physically abused by his archenemy in the Cobra gang, Daniel wants to quit. The odds of winning seem too great, and he doesn't believe he can possibly win. However, Mr. Miyagi offers him support. Through Mr. Miyagi's reassuring presence and gentle direction, Daniel finds hope and perseveres, and this enables him to finally win the match.

Perhaps there are adults in your class who are struggling with loneliness and dejection. They can benefit from the reminder in Isaiah 41:17 that God has not forsaken them, just as He did not abandon the Jews who were returning to their homeland after years of captivity in Babylon. His supporting, guiding presence can give them the strength to serve Him with renewed hope and vigor.

Take It to the Lord in Prayer. When the Baker Street Church felt the time was right to move ahead on a building project, congregational leaders made plans to develop a monthly prayer calendar for the parishioners. It was God's faithful answers to prayer that had made the project possible. The church had no desire to move forward without making prayer a reality.

Sometimes it may seem that our prayers reach no higher than the ceiling. Sometimes we may fear that there is really no one on the other end. But Isaiah 41:10 reveals that God cares about us enough to remain with us. We need not feel dismayed, for He hears our prayers. In fact, He understands our deepest needs—even those we can't bring ourselves to voice.

God's commitment to respond to our petitions is why Baker Street lists prayer concerns in the weekly bulletin. It is also why every meeting begins and ends with prayer.

And it is why some of the church members believe there is no sweeter sound than someone saying, "I'll remember you in my prayers."

God Listens and Understands. Have you ever prayed a "ridiculous" prayer to the Lord? Be honest! I define a ridiculous prayer as one that focuses exclusively on my will instead of God's.

Yes, I've prayed ridiculous prayers. Let's think of some that might fit the bill: the elimination of all personal suffering; the miraculous recovery of every terminally ill person I've ever known; having more money; enjoying less stress; obtaining more free time; and experiencing a ministry that is more effective. Here's the summary: "More gain, less pain."

Does God understand my penchant for the comfortable? I think so—much like my beagle's preference for a sprawl upon our old but comfy couch rather than the cold, hard kitchen floor. Do I let my furry friend take over people seating? No, but I did buy her a cozy dog bed, placed lovingly on the floor.

I'm thankful that God does not treat my prayers as His personal to-do list. And I'm also grateful that He listens to and understands all of my petitions.

FOR YOUTH

■ **TOPIC:** Got Fear? Trust God!

■ **QUESTIONS:** 1. How can knowing that God has "chosen" (Isa. 41:8) you be encouraging when you feel down? 2. How did God's love reach far across the earth to restore His people to their homeland? 3. What areas of your life do you feel could benefit from the strengthening hand of God? 4. What are some requests you can bring to God right now so that He can "hear them" (vs. 17)? 5. How might God use you to help others to "understand" (vs. 20) Him better?

■ **ILLUSTRATIONS:**

Someone You Can Count On. Her shoulders slumped as she waited to talk with me after church. Deep worry lines tugged her face into a furled, dejected expression of grief and fear. A three-year-old swung from her coat sleeve like a pint-sized Tarzan, whining so loudly that I could hardly hear the "secret" spoken from her despondent lips: "My husband is an alcoholic." Crushing despair overwhelmed Barb. She was trapped in a meaningless vortex. Life had become dismal, depressing, and seemingly hopeless.

As I listened to Barb's story, I thought about the eternal Creator and Lord, who raised up King Cyrus of Persia to restore the exiles to their homeland (see Isa. 41:2-4). Just as God had urged His people to dispel their fear and trust in Him (see vs. 10), so too He could give Barb the hope to dispel her heavy clouds of gloom. Regardless of the saved teens' circumstances, the Lord is someone they can always count on to help them through their ordeal.

More Than Enough. When Pastor Jim began to feel the need for the expansion of the sanctuary of his church, he faced one giant hurdle: There was no property available that was adjoining the congregation's building. On two sides were major roadways, and on the third was a large company. The fourth side was home to a corporately owned golf course.

When the parishioners voted on building new facilities on property eight miles away, the majority indicated that they did not want to relocate. That decision left few options to Paster Jim and the church leadership. It was then that they began to pray. Seven months after their weekly prayer meetings had begun, a representative of the golf course's owner called the church for an appointment. Through an acquaintance, the corporate CEO had heard about the congregation's interest in expansion, and he had a proposition to make.

By the time papers were signed, the golf course had acquired an ingress easement from the church and an acre of land from their back parking lot. In exchange, the golf course closed one of its two driving ranges and gave eight acres of adjoining land to the church. It was more than enough for their needed expansion!

God had moved in wonderful and mysterious ways as a result of many prayers being offered to Him. Think about the amazing things He wants to accomplish in your life as a result of you bringing your petitions to Him. As you depend on Him, His purposes will be achieved no matter what the difficult circumstances you might experience.

True Love and Care. In *Run With the Vision*, written by Bob Sjogren, Bill Stearns, and Amy Stearns, a Muslim student living in New Zealand explained his initial understanding of Christianity and Christians this way:

> When I first came to New Zealand, I thought this was a Western Christian nation and I associated immorality, violence, and pornography with Christianity. However, I have come to understand that this is not a Christian nation, but it is secular with Christians living here. Christians are different. They really love and care and have a different lifestyle and are very easy to pick out from other people.

How did this student find out about the *real* Christianity? Real Christians chose to rub shoulders with him. When he felt lonely and fearful, Christians prayed for his needs. They talked about the impact the Lord had made in their lives and answered questions the student had about the Savior and Christianity. They also gave him a Bible and the Jesus video. Additionally, one of his Christian friends had gone home with him to Pakistan to visit his family.

In short, through the sensitive witness of Jesus' true followers, someone outside the household of faith learned about the Son's love and care for him. The process involved prayer, but it did not end there. Who knows how God might use you to lead others to faith in Him, especially as you begin to bring their needs before Him in prayer.

THE SERVANT'S MISSION

BACKGROUND SCRIPTURE: Isaiah 9:1-7; 11:1-8; Matthew 1:18-25

DEVOTIONAL READING: John 4:19-26

KEY VERSE: Righteousness shall be the girdle of his loins, and faithfulness the girdle of his reins. (Isaiah 11:5)

3

KING JAMES VERSION

ISAIAH 9:7 Of the increase of his government and peace there shall be no end, upon the throne of David, and upon his kingdom, to order it, and to establish it with judgment and with justice from henceforth even for ever. The zeal of the LORD of hosts will perform this. . . .

11:1 And there shall come forth a rod out of the stem of Jesse, and a Branch shall grow out of his roots: 2 And the spirit of the LORD shall rest upon him, the spirit of wisdom and understanding, the spirit of counsel and might, the spirit of knowledge and of the fear of the LORD; 3 And shall make him of quick understanding in the fear of the LORD: and he shall not judge after the sight of his eyes, neither reprove after the hearing of his ears: 4 But with righteousness shall he judge the poor, and reprove with equity for the meek of the earth: and he shall smite the earth: with the rod of his mouth, and with the breath of his lips shall he slay the wicked. 5 And righteousness shall be the girdle of his loins, and faithfulness the girdle of his reins. 6 The wolf also shall dwell with the lamb, and the leopard shall lie down with the kid; and the calf and the young lion and the fatling together; and a little child shall lead them. 7 And the cow and the bear shall feed; their young ones shall lie down together: and the lion shall eat straw like the ox. 8 And the sucking child shall play on the hole of the asp, and the weaned child shall put his hand on the cockatrice den.

NEW REVISED STANDARD VERSION

ISAIAH 9:7 His authority shall grow continually,
   and there shall be endless peace
for the throne of David and his kingdom.
   He will establish and uphold it
with justice and with righteousness
   from this time onward and forevermore.
The zeal of the LORD of hosts will do this. . . .
11:1 A shoot shall come out from the stump of Jesse,
   and a branch shall grow out of his roots.
2 The spirit of the LORD shall rest on him,
   the spirit of wisdom and understanding,
   the spirit of counsel and might,
   the spirit of knowledge and the fear of the LORD.
3 His delight shall be in the fear of the LORD.
He shall not judge by what his eyes see,
   or decide by what his ears hear;
4 but with righteousness he shall judge the poor,
   and decide with equity for the meek of the earth;
he shall strike the earth with the rod of his mouth,
   and with the breath of his lips he shall kill the
      wicked.
5 Righteousness shall be the belt around his waist,
   and faithfulness the belt around his loins.
6 The wolf shall live with the lamb,
   the leopard shall lie down with the kid,
the calf and the lion and the fatling together,
   and a little child shall lead them.
7 The cow and the bear shall graze,
   their young shall lie down together;
   and the lion shall eat straw like the ox.
8 The nursing child shall play over the hole of the
      asp,
   and the weaned child shall put its hand on the
      adder's den.

Monday, December 13	Romans 15:25-33	*The God of Peace*
Tuesday, December 14	Ephesians 6:13-17	*The Gospel of Peace*
Wednesday, December 15	Romans 5:1-5	*Peace with God*
Thursday, December 16	John 14:25-31	*Peace Given to You*
Friday, December 17	Isaiah 9:1-6	*A Child Is Born*
Saturday, December 18	Matthew 28:16-20	*His Mission—Our Mission*
Sunday, December 19	Isaiah 9:7; 11:1-8	*The Prince of Peace*

BACKGROUND

Isaiah foretold the birth of someone who would one day be the King of kings. The prophet envisioned this birth as having been already accomplished: "A child is born . . . a son is given" (Isa. 9:6). God's promises would be fulfilled no matter how far-fetched they might seem. The prophecy pointed to the Lord Jesus' incarnation. He was born in the normal human way as a baby in Bethlehem. Isaiah next noted that Israel's Redeemer would carry the government "upon his shoulder." This may be a reference to the royal robe worn by ancient kings. Such robes hung on the shoulders and represented authority to rule. Down through the years, Israel had suffered through the reigns of many wicked, apostate kings. The coming Messiah, however, would rule uprightly for the good of God's people and be His just and faithful King.

Isaiah gave the Messiah several names or descriptions. As "Wonderful" and "Counsellor," He brings the words of life to His people. Humanity undoubtedly would be less besieged by psychological problems if it seriously acknowledged Christ as a wonderful counselor. The Messiah also is the "mighty God." The image in verse 6 is that of a valiant and stout fighter who is without equal. The emphasis is on the Messiah's ability to defend the cause of His people and protect their interests. With Him on their side, no foe would overcome them or threaten their existence.

Furthermore, the Lord Jesus is the "everlasting Father." The word "Father" refers to the Messiah's role as an ideal king. His rule is eternal and filled with compassion. When He reigns on the throne of David, the Messiah will provide for and watch over His people. Not one of their temporal or eternal needs will be overlooked or neglected by Him. Additionally, the Messiah is the "Prince of Peace." This indicates more than the absence of war. The Messiah will bring peace in the fullest sense of the word—peace between God and people as well as between person and person. Also, during the reign of the Lord Jesus, spiritual healing and wholeness will prevail throughout society. When we look at these majestic, descriptive titles, we conclude that no human emperor has ever come close to living up to them. Many rulers and kingdoms have come and gone, but none of them has achieved what Isaiah prophesied. The fulfillment will only come when Jesus returns. Celebrating His birth at Christmas means we can look to the future with confidence.

NOTES ON THE PRINTED TEXT

The child mentioned in Isaiah 9:6 will reign on "the throne of David" (vs. 7). This is an important prophecy in light of the New Testament's numerous references to David, many of which actually pertain to his greatest descendant, Jesus Christ. We learn from Isaiah 9:7 that the reign of the Messiah will be characterized by peace. His government will be ever expanding and never ending. Fairness and justice will be the hallmarks of His rule, and His passionate commitment for His people will guarantee that all the divine promises to them will be fulfilled. This verse also mentions "the zeal of the LORD of hosts." This phrase depicts God as a jealous lover who refuses to desert His people. His zeal is filled with devotion and single-minded allegiance, and this is the reason why His promise to the Israelites concerning the Davidic kingdom would be fulfilled (37:32; 42:13).

In 11:1, the Lord promised that a new branch would sprout from the old root of Jesse's family line. This tender shoot would be none other than the Messiah. One day He would rule the earth with an iron scepter (Ps. 2:9; Rev. 19:15), rescue the righteous, condemn the wicked (Rev. 20:11-15), end all war (21:1-4), and break down the barriers that divide people from one another and from God Himself (Eph. 2:14-22). Isaiah 11:1 says that a shoot will spring up from the "stem of Jesse." Scripture reveals that Jesse was the father of King David and an ancestor of Jesus (1 Sam. 16:1; Matt. 1:5-6). Jesse, whose name possibly means "man" or "manly," belonged to the tribe of Judah and lived in Bethlehem (1 Sam. 16:18). He was the son of Obed and the grandson of Boaz and Ruth (Ruth 4:17). Jesse had eight sons—Eliab, Abinadab, Shimma (Shammah), Nethaneel, Raddai, Ozem, Elihu, and David—and two daughters, Zeruiah and Abigail (1 Chron. 2:13-16; 27:18).

The Holy Spirit would be the basis for the Messiah's effectiveness (Isa. 11:2). In fact, the sixfold naming of God's Spirit indicates that He would empower the Messiah fully and perfectly and enable Him to carry out His royal tasks. The Spirit would give the Branch understanding, wisdom, and insight. Because of the work of the Spirit in the Messiah's life, He would know the Lord intimately and honor Him in all that He did. And the greatest joy of the Branch would be to obey the Lord. A review of the New Testament indicates that Isaiah 11:2 is fulfilled in the Messiah. Jesus was conceived by the Holy Spirit (Matt. 1:20). After Jesus' baptism, the Spirit came down on Him like a dove (3:16). The Spirit then led Jesus into the desert, where Satan tempted Him (Luke 4:1). During Jesus' public ministry, He taught with the Spirit's wisdom and power (Matt. 12:18; Luke 4:18). Jesus drove out demons by the Spirit's power (Matt. 12:28) and lived totally under the Spirit's control (Luke 4:14; Acts 10:38). Clearly, the Spirit's presence and grace marked Jesus' life, work, and teachings.

According to Isaiah 11:3, the Messiah would be totally submitted to the will of God. The Redeemer's submission was not grudging, but rather willing and cheerful. More than anything else, the Son delighted in pleasing the Father (John 4:34; 5:30;

6:38; 14:31). The Branch, originating from Jesse's roots, would rule over a righteous, peaceful kingdom based on immediate and unerring reverence for the Lord and His will. This statement is confirmed by Isaiah 11:3-5, which tells us that the Messiah would rule with perfect integrity. In contrast with the rulers of Isaiah's day, equity and virtue would characterize the Messiah. He would not judge merely by external appearances. Indeed, some clever trial witness would never fool Him with false evidence. The Messiah would judge with perfect equity because He Himself is faultless in every way.

As 11:4 says, the Messiah's word of judgment against the wicked would be powerful and active. In fact, the wicked would die at His command. The hand of God's discipline reflects His goal of bringing about justice for wrongs that people have committed. Because God is holy, He cannot allow evil and wickedness to prevail. Unlike the wicked, the Messiah would be perfectly righteous. In ancient times, people tied up their loose garments with a belt before engaging in vigorous action. The belt or sash worn by the Messiah would be one of righteousness and fruitfulness (vs. 5). These two virtues would characterize all His activities. When people vent their rage, it often leads to more violence, suffering, and bitterness. Conversely, when the Messiah displays His anger, it leads to peace and equity. This is because He seeks to eliminate unrighteousness and replace it with true justice.

Scripture reveals that, in the divine Kingdom, a golden age of peace and faithfulness will prevail. Wolves will rest with lambs, leopards will lie down with young goats, and calves and lions will eat together peacefully. Even more amazing is the idea of cows and bears sharing the same pasture, and lions and oxen eating straw. But that's the way things will be during the Messiah's righteous, peaceful reign (vss. 6-7).

Basic to the righteousness and peace of the messianic era would be the quality of the judgments issued by the Messiah to uproot evil and firmly implant holiness. The outstanding characteristic of His judicial rulings would be that they would not depend on deceptive outward appearances. He would not be limited to what can be seen with human eyes and heard with human ears. He would perceive the motives and intentions of every heart and yield judgments upholding the poor against their oppressors and the meek against the arrogant. Thus, from what has been noted, it's clear that the Messiah's character is incomparable. No one has ever fit this description except Jesus. He alone is the epitome of righteousness and faithfulness. He was sinless and completely obedient to His Father's will. And Jesus continues to be trustworthy and righteous to all who come to Him in faith.

The reign of Messiah will make the world a perfectly safe place for the most vulnerable of children. Isaiah described nursing children playing by the hole of a cobra, and weaned children placing their hands in a nest of deadly snakes (vs. 8). In each case, no harm would come to these little ones. This reflects the peace and protection they would enjoy in the golden age. Down through the centuries, evangelical scholars have interpreted these verses with varying degrees of literalness. Some who take this passage less literally say this prophecy depicts what happens in the environment now when Christ reigns. Others say these verses poetically represent the harmony that exists imperfectly in the church and perfectly in heaven. Some who understand this passage more literally say these verses are yet to be fulfilled quite concretely in an earthly messianic kingdom. Others (who don't go as far as this) say there really will come a time when aggression and hostility will be absent from people and animals on the earth after Christ's return.

To sum up his description of tranquility, Isaiah said that animals "shall not hurt nor destroy in all [God's] holy mountain" (Isa. 11:9). The Lord's holy mountain is also known as Mount Zion. Zion is first mentioned in 2 Samuel 5:7 as a Jebusite fortress on a hill. After being captured by King David, this fortress was called the City of David. Here David brought the ark of the covenant, thereby making the hill a sacred site (6:10-12). Perhaps most stunning of all was Isaiah's prophecy of a world filled with the knowledge of the Lord. This does not refer to mere intellectual knowledge. It includes the idea of living according to God's Word (Jer. 31:34). Because God's Word will be obeyed everywhere, there will be no place for harm and destruction. The preeminence of war in human relations will be removed forever. The tragic outcomes of battles (especially in terms of death and desolation) will never again tarnish the world.

SUGGESTIONS TO TEACHERS

Isaiah earlier referred to the coming Messiah as the "Prince of Peace" (Isa. 9:6). In chapter 11, Isaiah showed what the Messiah's rule and dominion would look like. Indeed, His would be a kingdom of peace in which judgment would be fair and compassion would be actively poured out. This kingdom is already active in the hearts of His people, and so, with God's help, we can seek to exhibit the traits of His dominion to the world around us.

1. GIVE WHAT YOU'D LIKE TO GET. How often have we said, "It's just not fair"? We desperately long for fairness from other people, and so we ought to show fairness to others. We rightfully get upset with those who base their judgments on appearance, false evidence, or rumors, and so we ought to refrain from judging others by such inadequate standards. Only Christ can be the perfectly fair judge. Thus only as He governs our hearts can we learn to be as fair in our treatment of others as we expect them to be toward us.

2. GIVE A HELPING HAND. Righteousness and faithfulness would be the basis for the coming Messiah's vigorous action on behalf of His people. Isaiah said with "righteousness shall he judge the poor, and reprove with equity for the meek of the earth" (11:4). These two essential concepts of the faith should be the basis for our vigorous action as well. The righteousness and faithfulness that God values are much more than just refraining from sin. They are actively turning toward others and offering them the help they need.

3. GIVE THOUGHT TO THE FACT THAT GOD IS IN CONTROL. "Desperate situations call for desperate measures," quipped Winston Churchill. Though God's people were in a desperate situation, Isaiah reminded them that the behavior of nations is well within the realm of God's rule. God's plan was being fulfilled, and God's plan would be fulfilled. And the most critical part of His plan was a coming King, a promised Messiah, who would deliver His people and rule with justice. Beyond keeping our faith in God, we need to keep the faith that God is in control.

4. GIVE YOUR NATION THE BENEFIT OF PRAYER FOR REVIVAL. Just as in Judah the leadership of the nation and its people desperately needed a revival of righteousness, justice, and faithfulness, so, too, we need revival. Be a part of making the conditions right for revival by seeking to live a holy life and praying that God would bless us with a spiritual reawakening.

FOR ADULTS

■ TOPIC: Hope for Good Leadership

■ QUESTIONS: 1. In what ways was the Messiah's advent like a "rod" (Isa. 11:1) that had "come forth" from the "stem of Jesse" and a "Branch . . . out of his roots"? 2. What evidence from Jesus' life demonstrates that He was the fulfillment of the prophecy recorded in verse 2? 3. Why was it important that the coming Messiah's "understanding" (vs. 3) be in the "fear of the Lord"? 4. In what ways would Jesus "judge the poor, and reprove with equity for the meek of the earth" (vs. 4)? 5. How does seeking to follow the Lord help us pursue righteousness and faithfulness in our lives?

■ ILLUSTRATIONS:

The Wrong Type of Captain. When the new church softball team was formed, Ted volunteered to be the captain. In previous years, he had been on other teams and had always thought he would make a fine captain. After all, he was a good player, he knew the game, and he was assertive with people.

It turns out that while Ted was good at being a member of the team, he was terrible at leading his peers. To others his decisions seemed arbitrary and his personal style seemed abrasive. Over the course of the season, Ted's assertiveness and impulsivity led to many hurt feelings and misunderstandings. By the end of the season, Ted had quit the team.

No matter how dedicated or qualified human leaders may seem, they are no substitute for the Savior's leadership in our lives. We learn from Isaiah 11:3-5 that His guidance over us is characterized by compassion, insight, and equity. When we put our total faith in Him as our leader, we end up winning in the things that matter most from an eternal perspective in the game of life.

Perfect Peace. "Maybe all dogs do go to heaven," reported *Newsweek*. But first, they might want to drop by the Episcopal Church of the Holy Trinity on Manhattan's Upper East Side, where parishioners and their pooches are regulars at Sunday-morning services. As long as they behave, dogs and their masters are welcome to sit side by side and even accompany each other to the altar during Communion.

"It's like being with a family member," says Judith Gwyn Brown, who attended the early Sunday morning service with her puli sheepdog, Cordelia. "We both get a lot out of it." But can a pet really be pious? Church spokesman Fred Burrell wouldn't touch the question, saying, "I don't think I'll go there."

So is this the peaceful kingdom prophesied in Isaiah? No. Perfect peace will come to all creation when the Messiah reigns supreme. Then the wolf will live with the lamb, the leopard will lie down with the goat, and no harm will come to any creature (see Isa. 11:6-9).

Backed into a Corner. Pastor Richard Exley, author of *Strength for the Storm*, noted that "sometimes God has to allow us to be backed into a corner before we truly rely on Him." Often throughout their history, God's chosen people found themselves backed into that sort of a corner. As one powerful force after another kept them in that corner, they weakly cowered. But Isaiah 11:1 promised them the Messiah, who would give them hope. And 9:7 declares that their King one day would lead them in righteousness and faithfulness and establish peace in their hearts.

FOR YOUTH

■ TOPIC: A Lineage of Leaders
■ QUESTIONS: 1. Why do you think Isaiah introduced the Messiah as a new shoot sprouting from the roots of an old stump? 2. Why was it important that the coming Messiah's judgment be based on righteousness and faithfulness? 3. What does it mean that the Messiah would have "the spirit of wisdom and understanding, the spirit of counsel and might, [and] the spirit of knowledge" (Isa. 11:2)? 4. How would you describe a kingdom of perfect peace? What do you think it would look like? 5. What responsibility do you have to contribute to Jesus' kingdom of peace?

■ ILLUSTRATIONS:
Follow the Leader. Throughout the week, my stern, bespectacled first-grade teacher had had difficulty quieting her happy "chatterboxes." Having been unable to accomplish what she had planned for the first week of school, she determined that the second week would not follow suit. Her solution was to assign detention to six of her students. Her tactical error was lining up the detainees behind those who would be excused with the sounding of the bell. When the bell sounded, I was the first to bolt

out the door! And five freedom-loving first graders followed my lead!

Our human nature desires leadership that seems more lenient and convenient than God's. But an examination of Israel's history reminds us that indulgent leadership is never in our best interest. The best example of godly leadership is found in the Lord Jesus. During the holiday season, we are encouraged by our study of Isaiah 9:7 and 11:1-8 (the focus of this week's lesson) to pray that our leaders will emulate the wisdom, discernment, and integrity modeled by the Messiah.

God Is in Control. Gladys Aylward, a missionary to China in the twentieth century, was forced to flee when the Japanese invaded Yangcheng. But she could not leave her work behind. With only one assistant, she led more than 100 orphans over the mountains toward Free China.

During her harrowing journey out of the war-torn city, Gladys grappled with despair as never before. After a sleepless night, she faced the morning with no hope of reaching safety. Then a 13-year-old girl in the group reminded her of their much-loved story of Moses and the Israelites crossing the Red Sea.

"But I am not Moses!" Gladys cried in desperation.

"Of course you aren't," the girl said, "but the Lord is still God."

When Gladys and the orphans made it through, they proved once again that no matter how inadequate we feel, the Lord Jesus is still God, and we can trust in Him. After all, He is the "Prince of Peace" (Isa. 9:6) and the one who brings justice and righteousness to the world (vs. 7).

Peaceful Acceptance. Isaiah 11:6-9 pictures a future idyllic scene of peaceful acceptance in the Messiah's kingdom. Children with severe skin diseases continue to find acceptance at a Christian summer camp. These children, who are socially excluded because of their deformities, are unconditionally welcomed and make lifelong friends at Camp Knutson, near Cross Lake, Minnesota, run by Lutheran Social Services.

Most of the children have never been able to go to the beach or for a walk without getting stares or rude comments, *The Lutheran* magazine reported. Some are covered head to toe with bandages or use a wheelchair, and others require as much as five hours of medical treatment a day.

The campers get absorbed without self-consciousness in activities such as swimming, waterskiing, tubing, and horseback riding, or sitting around a campfire. These are big steps for the young people, who have been closely monitored since birth by parents and schools. "All we believe in at Camp Knutson are compliments," camper and junior counselor Shauna Egesdal said. "No putdowns are allowed." We can imagine that the "Prince of Peace" (9:6) is smiling with approval from heaven.

I AM WITH YOU

BACKGROUND SCRIPTURE: Isaiah 43
DEVOTIONAL READING: Isaiah 63:7-14

KEY VERSE: When thou passest through the waters, I will be with thee; and through the rivers, they shall not overflow thee. (Isaiah 43:2)

KING JAMES VERSION

ISAIAH 43:1 But now thus saith the LORD that created thee, O Jacob, and he that formed thee, O Israel, Fear not: for I have redeemed thee, I have called thee by thy name; thou art mine. 2 When thou passest through the waters, I will be with thee; and through the rivers, they shall not overflow thee: when thou walkest through the fire, thou shalt not be burned; neither shall the flame kindle upon thee. 3 For I am the LORD thy God, the Holy One of Israel, thy Saviour: I gave Egypt for thy ransom, Ethiopia and Seba for thee. 4 Since thou wast precious in my sight, thou hast been honourable, and I have loved thee: therefore will I give men for thee, and people for thy life. 5 Fear not: for I am with thee: I will bring thy seed from the east, and gather thee from the west; 6 I will say to the north, Give up; and to the south, Keep not back: bring my sons from far, and my daughters from the ends of the earth; 7 Even every one that is called by my name: for I have created him for my glory, I have formed him; yea, I have made him. . . .

11 I, even I, am the LORD; and beside me there is no saviour. 12 I have declared, and have saved, and I have shewed, when there was no strange god among you: therefore ye are my witnesses, saith the LORD, that I am God.

NEW REVISED STANDARD VERSION

ISAIAH 43:1 But now thus says the LORD,
  he who created you, O Jacob,
  he who formed you, O Israel:
Do not fear, for I have redeemed you;
  I have called you by name, you are mine.
2 When you pass through the waters, I will be with
    you;
  and through the rivers, they shall not overwhelm
    you;
when you walk through fire you shall not be burned,
  and the flame shall not consume you.
3 For I am the LORD your God,
  the Holy One of Israel, your Savior.
I give Egypt as your ransom,
  Ethiopia and Seba in exchange for you.
4 Because you are precious in my sight,
  and honored, and I love you,
I give people in return for you,
  nations in exchange for your life.
5 Do not fear, for I am with you;
  I will bring your offspring from the east,
  and from the west I will gather you;
6 I will say to the north, "Give them up,"
  and to the south, "Do not withhold;
bring my sons from far away
  and my daughters from the end of the earth—
7 everyone who is called by my name,
  whom I created for my glory,
  whom I formed and made." . . .
11 I, I am the LORD,
  and besides me there is no savior.
12 I declared and saved and proclaimed,
  when there was no strange god among you;
  and you are my witnesses, says the LORD.

137

HOME BIBLE READINGS

BACKGROUND

In Isaiah 42:1, God introduced His ultimate servant. This is the Messiah—the one who would bring true deliverance, not merely from national slavery, but also from humanity's more tragic eternal bondage to sin (vs. 7). Some aspects of the Servant's ministry that are described in verses 1-9 do relate to rescuing the exiles from Babylon, while other aspects deal with Jesus' earthly ministry. Still other aspects concern His work at the end of the age. From Isaiah's perspective, thousands of years blend into a single, prophetic vision. Clearly, though, the primary reference to the Servant here is the Messiah, whose divine mission included bringing justice and salvation to people.

Verses 8-9 suddenly shifts the emphasis from the Servant back to God the Father. Here we find Isaiah's affirmation that the prophecy about the Servant was given by the Lord and not by the false gods of evil nations. Earlier predictions had already come to pass for the chosen people, and similarly, new prophecies—such as those about the Servant—would come to pass as well. The Lord declared in advance that these oracles would happen (vs. 9). To commemorate the new events announced in this verse, the entire world was invited to sing a new song of praise to the Lord. Creation would celebrate His victory over His enemies and His deliverance of His people (vss. 10-13). During the long years of Israel's humiliation in exile, God had refrained from taking action against the enemy of His people (vs. 14). But the day God had long awaited would come. As a pregnant woman anticipates the day of delivery, the Lord looked forward to the rebirth of His people. He assured the faithful remnant that their captivity would end and that He would lead them back to their homeland, as contrasted with the tragic stillbirth of the idolatrous (vss. 15-17).

Ever mindful of the context from which God's people would need to be delivered, Israel—also a servant of the Lord—is juxtaposed here as an ironic contrast to the messianic Servant. Collectively, the chosen people, as a "kingdom of priests" (Exod. 19:6) in service to the Lord, were supposed to bring the knowledge of God to the world (Deut. 4:6). Tragically, however, the chosen people had miserably failed. This is why the Lord wanted His imperfect servants to recognize and understand the truth of His Word. But due to their own volition, the nation would remain spiritually blind and obstinate (Isa. 42:18-20). It's no wonder the Lord would allow the Assyrians and Babylonians to oppress Judah. In fact, to decide differently would make Him something other than perfectly upright and just. So as the holy one of Israel, God punished His people with the fires of war. Sadly, they still paid no attention to the calamities, refusing in the least to take them to heart (vss. 21-25).

NOTES ON THE PRINTED TEXT

Isaiah 43:1 is directed specifically to Israel, whom God in His grace had chosen to be His special and holy people (see Deut. 7:6-8). He reminded the nation, whom He referred to by the parallel and synonymous names of Jacob and Israel (Isa. 43:1), that He was responsible for their creation and formation as a nation. The Hebrew verb rendered "created" means "to fashion anew," and the same term is used in Genesis 1:1 (see Isa. 40:26; 41:20; 45:12, 18; 65:17-18). The verb translated "formed" refers to a potter shaping or fashioning a lump of clay (see Gen. 2:7).

Throughout Israel's existence, the nation had been buffeted by internal and external forces. But rather than be frightened, they were to respond in faith to their Creator. After all, Yahweh, their covenant God, pledged to rescue and protect them. God, Israel's true Kinsman-Redeemer, would never vacillate in His commitment, for He had called the Israelites by name. This truth spotlights the Lord's intimate relationship with the Israelites. Because they belonged to Him, He would protect them. Isaiah 43:2 contains several metaphors that stress the idea of going through times of hardship. The Lord pledged that His people would not drown, even in the deep waters of difficulty. This is an allusion to Israel's crossing the Red Sea and Jordan River (see Exod. 14:21-22; Josh. 3:14-17; Ps. 66:6). Similarly, God would prevent them from being consumed by the flames of oppression (see Ps. 66:12; Dan. 3:25-27).

The many names and titles of God found in Isaiah 43:3 were intended to encourage the exiles in Babylon not to fear. After all, it was the infinitely powerful Lord who had created them. Moreover, it was the holy God of Israel who had formed them as a nation. They were not to be afraid, for their "Saviour" would enable them to overcome every obstacle hindering them from returning to the promised land. The Hebrew verb rendered "Saviour" means to rescue from danger or deliver from bondage. God declared that the ransom price He paid to liberate the captives included allowing Persia to conquer Egypt, Cush, and Seba. Cush (also called Nubia) was a region south of Egypt that included parts of the present-day countries of Ethiopia and Sudan. Seba was either a region in northeastern Africa or an area in southwest Arabia (see Gen. 10:7; Ps. 72:10; Isa. 45:14; Ezek. 27:21-22). Together, Egypt, Cush, and Seba represented the southwestern limits of Persian power (see Est. 1:1).

Isaiah 43:4 reminded the exiles how much the Lord valued them as His chosen people. "Precious" translates a verb that means "to esteem" or "to prize." "Honourable" renders a verb that means "to acclaim" or "to hold in high regard." The idea is that

God considered the faithful remnant to be like a special, cherished treasure in His sight (see Exod. 19:5; Deut. 26:18). The Lord's abiding commitment and devotion to His people is seen in the verb translated "loved" (Isa. 43:4). Because of His unfailing compassion for the exiles, He would hand nations over to Persia. Indeed, God would allow other countries to be conquered by Cyrus in exchange for the freedom of the captives. The message for modern-day believers is no different. At times we may feel overwhelmed by circumstances in our lives, but we need not fear. After all, the Lord—who created and rules over all things—is with us in every situation.

The Lord knew that the captives faced daunting challenges as they journeyed back to their homeland. He urged them to rid themselves of whatever apprehensions they had by trusting completely in Him. He pledged to be with them every step of the way and to gather them together from the farthest eastern and western stretches of the Fertile Crescent (vs. 5). The Lord, who created heaven and earth (see Gen. 1:1), had the power to command the nations to the north to hand over His people. Likewise, God had the authority to direct the countries to the south not to prevent any of the exiles from returning to their homeland. The Lord would work through King Cyrus of Persia to bring God's "sons" (Isa. 43:6) from distant lands and His "daughters" from the remote regions of the earth. The emphasis here is on the chosen people being set free from their captivity in Babylon. They are the ones whom God "called by [His] name" (vs. 7), which is another way of saying that they personally belonged to Him. The Lord created the faithful remnant to bring Him glory. Expressed differently, He formed them individually and forged them collectively into a distinct nation. Their successful return to Judah would bring honor to their covenant-keeping God.

Verses 8-13 present a courtroom speech against the nations and the idols they worshiped (see 1:2; 41:1, 21). Isaiah 43:8 seems to be an oblique reference to those among God's chosen people who persisted in disbelief (see 6:10). They were summoned to the Lord's imaginary court. Also, all the nations of the world were subpoenaed to stand trial before His holy presence. Yahweh urged everyone to consider His claim to be the only true God. The Lord asserted that the idols worshiped by pagans were impotent in revealing Cyrus's future deliverance of Israel from Babylon. The false gods could not foretell something even a short time in advance.

The situation was far different, however, for the Israelites. As a nation they had experienced the great works the Lord did on their behalf. Thus they were a logical choice to be God's witnesses; and it was reasonable to expect them to serve their Maker (43:10). After all, the Lord had graciously chosen the Israelites to know and trust in Him as well as to understand that He alone is God. None of the false deities worshiped by the pagans ever existed before Yahweh, and no entity would ever outlive Him. Only the eternal, living God was the Redeemer of Israel. No other entity could claim to be the Lord, and no other could assert to be the Rescuer of Israel. Their deliverance rested in Him alone (vs. 11).

The Israelites were constantly tempted to abandon their faith in Yahweh and give their allegiance to false gods. And yet none of the idols the pagans venerated had ever foretold and executed the deliverance of the Israelites. Only God declared what He would do and then successfully brought it to pass. Israel knew this to be true and was called upon to affirm it. In particular, the nation was to testify that Yahweh alone is God (vs. 12). Before time ever began, the Lord eternally existed as God. And He will eternally remain as such long after time ends. In light of this, no creature in heaven or on earth could ever oppose what Yahweh decreed He would do. In the case of Israel, He would redeem and restore the nation. No entity would be able to thwart or reverse His plan.

Verses 14-17 stress that the Lord would prepare the way for His people's return. Their Creator and King would send an army against Babylon. In the past, God allowed powerful nations to overrun His people. Now, in a comforting gesture, He urged them to let the past evils go, for a new day would come, and they should focus on His promise to defeat the oppressor. After the Israelites' exodus from Egypt and conquest of the promised land, they established themselves as a nation. Despite the glories associated with this time period (especially under David and Solomon), it would pale in comparison to the glories of the new kingdom the Lord would establish in the future.

In light of this wonderful prospect, God urged His people to think no longer about the past prophecies of judgment (vs. 18). The command of Cyrus for the Jewish exiles to return to their homeland is the "new thing" (vs. 19) being referred to here. From the eternal perspective of the Lord, the fall of Babylon and the restoration of Israel had already begun. When the promised act of deliverance occurred, the people of God were to recognize it as such. When the prophesied moment arrived, the Lord would give the exiles a free and clear route back to the promised land. It would be as if God created a pathway for His people to travel and a river for them to refresh themselves along the journey.

SUGGESTIONS TO TEACHERS

A key theme of Isaiah 43 is God's loving plans for His people, which are fulfilled when believers offer a committed response to Him. Many in our churches need to remember that God is still at work in His world.

1. PLEA FOR REMEMBERING. Isaiah called upon God's people to remember the Lord's goodness in their lives in the past and to remember the importance of God. During times of apparent hopelessness, God's people can recall instances of His goodness and guidance in their lives. Invite your group members to tell about times when remembering God's workings in the past helped them get through difficult days. Then remind them of the words inscribed on many altars and communion tables, "Do this in memory of me" (see Lk. 22:19). Recalling the death and resurrection of the Savior is the central act of worship in every Christian congregation.

2. PREDICTION OF RETURN. Isaiah assured his hearers that God would enable them to return to Judah. He based his confidence in God's Word, contrasting his insight to that of astrologers, fortunetellers, and all others who claimed special wisdom. God's people may rest assured that the Lord will bring new beginnings because of His faithfulness. While many look for guidance in the occult or through so-called "psychics," we need to hear Isaiah's words ringing out clearly.

3. PROMISE OF REBUILDING. Jerusalem would be rebuilt and the temple restored. In other words, God's purposes would be fulfilled. God bestows hope upon those who trust and serve Him. For those who are committed to Him, He introduces a future even in the worst of circumstances.

4. PREPARATION OF A RULER. Isaiah stated that Cyrus, the powerful ruler of Persia and conqueror of Babylon, would be God's instrument in history. Cyrus was a pagan. Nonetheless, he was used by the Ruler of all history. With God-given insight, Isaiah realized that his Lord could call the most unlikely persons and employ them as His agents. Cyrus would be the leader to carry out God's purposes and permit the exiles to rebuild. God's intentions will not be thwarted forever. He remains in charge of the world, despite the grim destruction of human violence, greed, and rebelliousness.

FOR ADULTS

■ TOPIC: Whom Shall I Follow?

■ QUESTIONS: 1. Why did God's people need to be reminded that He was their all-powerful Creator? 2. How could the exiles know with certainty that the Lord would be with them as they returned to Judah? 3. In what ways had God demonstrated to the faithful remnant that they were "precious" (Isa. 43:4) and "honourable" in His sight? 4. In an imaginary courtroom scene, what did the Lord urge Israel and the nations to consider? 5. What are some tangible ways in which the Lord has shown His unfailing compassion to you?

■ ILLUSTRATIONS:

A Guide for Life. For people who are blind or visually impaired, daily tasks that others don't even think about can be a real challenge. That's why at its inception, the concept of a guide dog was revolutionary. The seeing-eye dog has helped to enhance the independence, dignity, and self-confidence of people who are blind by enabling them to travel safely and independently.

In the spiritual realm, we are all born blind. Left on our own, we would stumble about in the darkness of sin. Thankfully, the Father has sent His Son to be our spiritual guide. He alone understands us, for He created and redeemed us (see Isa. 43:1). He is the one we should follow, for He promises to be with us when we pass through the deep and trying waters of life (see vs. 2). Indeed, only He can lead us in paths of righteousness and help us avoid the pitfalls of sin.

God at Work. Two men were forced to accept early retirement from their company. George and Henry both felt hurt and angry at being terminated unexpectedly after 30 years' faithful service. Both were also concerned about their finances in the days ahead.

George, however, was a man of faith. Certain that even an unforeseen early retirement could be used by God for good, he faced the future knowing that God was still in control. Henry, on the other hand, grew increasingly bitter. When George tried to share about his trust in the Lord, Henry snapped, "Don't give me any of that God stuff! What does God or anyone care?"

Although George faced over nine months of uncertainty, he started his own business by buying a carpet-cleaning franchise. Now, seven years later, he looks back on his life and sees that God had been involved more than he ever suspected. Meanwhile, Henry has become more bitter, brooding over "my bad breaks" and complaining about "the unfair system." Henry's wife is concerned that his attitude and inactivity are affecting his health.

Do you rely on God to be with you and guide you even during the toughest times? Isaiah 43:1-5 encourages all believers to do so. And countless people like George can testify that God cares and stays close—no matter what the situation.

Predictions. French physician and astrologer Michel de Notredame is better known by his Latin name, Nostradamus. In the sixteenth century he penned a book of rhymed prophecies entitled *Centuries*.

The book is chiefly known for correctly predicting the manner in which Henry II of France would die. Many people, though, have credited Nostradamus for predicting various events in European history, including the rise of Adolf Hitler. Yet the predictions are extremely vague and open to a variety of interpretations.

Contrast this with a true prophet! Isaiah's prophecies about Israel's true Savior would find historical fulfillment. God was working for the sake of Israel, and not one word about the coming Messiah was spoken in vain.

FOR YOUTH

■ TOPIC: Follow the True Leader
■ QUESTIONS: 1. What was significant about the fact that the Lord had summoned His people by name? 2. What sort of "ransom" (Isa. 43:3) did God pay to secure the freedom of His people? 3. How had the Lord demonstrated His love for the exiles (see vs. 4)? 4. Why were the Israelites a logical choice to be God's witnesses? 5. What are some ways we can encourage our peers to trust the Lord with their concerns and fears?

Following the Leader. "Simon Says" is a traditional children's game that can be played with any number of participants. It starts with a leader, or person at the head of the line, being chosen. Then the rest of the children line up behind the leader and agree to do whatever the leader does.

Leaders are encouraged to try a number of interesting and unusual movements in which they skip, jump, hop, walk, run, and so on. All the children in the group have fun mimicking the leader's actions. Any participants who make a mistake in trying to imitate the leader are out of the game. Aside from the leader, the last child standing becomes the new leader.

In the game of life, there is only one true leader for saved adolescents (as well as all other believers). He is the Lord Jesus. The Savior promises to be with teens throughout their life journey (see Isa. 43:2, 5). With Him at their side, they have nothing to fear.

Wary and Worried. Consider the romantic view of the life of a college freshman: four years of stimulating academic growth—and enjoyable parties—should prepare him or her for entry into the adult world. But is that how it really is?

Actually, today's freshmen feel great stress and anxiety. The American Council on Education surveyed 200,000 college freshmen. The majority of respondents indicated a growing anxiety about the cost of attending college. They were afraid they wouldn't be able to finish college because of tuition costs and expressed hopelessness about the potential job market. These 18-year-olds are wary and worried.

Isaiah spoke to a similar group of people. He urged them to have hope and promised them a blessed future. His message speaks to anyone worried about the next four years—or even the next day.

Our Redeemer

Background Scripture: Isaiah 44
Devotional Reading: Psalm 106:40-48

Key Verse: I have blotted out, as a thick cloud, thy transgressions, and, as a cloud, thy sins: return unto me; for I have redeemed thee. (Isaiah 44:22)

KING JAMES VERSION

ISAIAH 44:21 Remember these, O Jacob and Israel; for thou art my servant: I have formed thee; thou art my servant: O Israel, thou shalt not be forgotten of me. 22 I have blotted out, as a thick cloud, thy transgressions, and, as a cloud, thy sins: return unto me; for I have redeemed thee. 23 Sing, O ye heavens; for the LORD hath done it: shout, ye lower parts of the earth: break forth into singing, ye mountains, O forest, and every tree therein: for the LORD hath redeemed Jacob, and glorified himself in Israel. 24 Thus saith the LORD, thy redeemer, and he that formed thee from the womb, I am the LORD that maketh all things; that stretcheth forth the heavens alone; that spreadeth abroad the earth by myself; 25 That frustrateth the tokens of the liars, and maketh diviners mad; that turneth wise men backward, and maketh their knowledge foolish; 26 That confirmeth the word of his servant, and performeth the counsel of his messengers; that saith to Jerusalem, Thou shalt be inhabited; and to the cities of Judah, Ye shall be built, and I will raise up the decayed places thereof.

NEW REVISED STANDARD VERSION

ISAIAH 44:21 Remember these things, O Jacob, and Israel, for you are my servant;
I formed you, you are my servant;
O Israel, you will not be forgotten by me.
22 I have swept away your transgressions like a cloud,
and your sins like mist;
return to me, for I have redeemed you.
23 Sing, O heavens, for the LORD has done it;
shout, O depths of the earth;
break forth into singing, O mountains,
O forest, and every tree in it!
For the LORD has redeemed Jacob,
and will be glorified in Israel.
24 Thus says the LORD, your Redeemer,
who formed you in the womb:
I am the LORD, who made all things,
who alone stretched out the heavens,
who by myself spread out the earth;
25 who frustrates the omens of liars,
and makes fools of diviners;
who turns back the wise,
and makes their knowledge foolish;
26 who confirms the word of his servant,
and fulfills the prediction of his messengers;
who says of Jerusalem, "It shall be inhabited,"
and of the cities of Judah, "They shall be rebuilt,
and I will raise up their ruins."

5

Monday, December 27	Job 19:23-27	*My Redeemer Lives!*
Tuesday, December 28	Genesis 28:10-17	*Know That I Am with You*
Wednesday, December 29	Isaiah 44:1-5	*Do Not Fear*
Thursday, December 30	Psalm 106:40-48	*God's Steadfast Love*
Friday, December 31	Galatians 4:1-7	*Redeemed to Be Heirs*
Saturday, January 1	Isaiah 44:6-8	*Assured of the Future*
Sunday, January 2	Isaiah 44:21-26	*Rejoice in Redemption*

BACKGROUND

Isaiah 44 begins with a reminder that the Lord considered Israel to be His chosen servant (vs. 1). Also, as implausible as it may have seemed to them at that time, He pledged to restore the righteous remnant to their homeland and pour out His Spirit on their descendants (vss. 2-5). Then all of God's chosen people would finally worship and serve Him faithfully. By appreciating the scope of these prophecies, an honest reader must realize that no human scheme could bring to pass what God had in store for His chosen people. Certainly none of the idols that people worshiped could do such a great thing. These pathetic objects were nothing in the eyes of the Lord, and those who venerated them were spiritually blind and senseless. We can understand why Scripture exhorts us to keep ourselves from idols (1 John 5:21).

Isaiah 44:6 reveals that Israel's King was also the nation's Redeemer and the Lord of heaven's armies. In declaring Himself to be "the first" and "the last," Yahweh was stating that He is the one and only God. Should any entities be presumptuous enough to think otherwise, the all-powerful Lord challenged them to step forward and make their case. This included being able to predict all that would happen since the day He established the nation of Israel, including the accurate foretelling of future events (vs. 7). The shepherd and guide of the captives encouraged them not to panic or be frightened about what the future might bring, especially as they relocated to Judah. They could testify to the fact that Yahweh is the true and living God and that He alone was their source of redemption (vs. 8).

NOTES ON THE PRINTED TEXT

In contrast to the Lord were the powerless and lifeless idols worshiped by pagans. These treasured objects were utterly worthless, and those who venerated them were spiritually blind, ignorant, and foolish (Isa. 44:9). Nothing was gained by casting a metal image to worship as a god (vs. 10). Humiliation awaited those who revered idols and disgrace was the payment to artisans of these objects (vs. 11). The latter included metalworkers, who used their tools to forge metal over hot coals and in the process grew tired, hungry, and thirsty (vs. 12). There were also carpenters, who measured blocks of wood and drew outlines on them. Then they used chisels and planes to carve out a human-like figure that would be placed in a shrine (vs. 13). Artisans might cut down cedar, cypress, or oak, trees from the forest (vs. 14). Some of the wood was used to make a fire to heat a home and cook food. The remainder of the supply was used to fashion idols that people worshiped and looked to for deliverance (vss. 15-17).

The Lord considered these actions to be the epitome of ignorance and stupidity. The idolaters demonstrated that their eyes were blinded to the truth and their minds were so "shut" (vs. 18) that they could not recognize their folly. The skilled workers never stopped to consider that the idols they made were just blocks of wood, half of which they used for heating and cooking purposes. The artisans did not have enough sense to figure out that the "abomination" (vs. 19) they created from the remainder of the material was nothing more than dry timber. Those with insight realized that only a deceived mind would mislead a person to trust in an object that was powerless to offer any deliverance and could be easily burned to "ashes" (vs. 20).

Tragically, idolaters could not bring themselves to ask whether the objects they held in their hands and venerated were false gods. The Lord urged the exiles not to make the same mistake. He enjoined the descendants of Jacob to pay attention to the truth and to recognize that He had chosen them to worship and serve only Him. This response was appropriate, for Yahweh had brought the nation of Israel into existence. Moreover, despite their skepticism over His continuing commitment to the covenant (see 40:27), He did remember the exiles and would free them from their captivity in Babylon (44:21).

It was due to the spiritual blindness of God's people that He previously allowed them to be exiled. Yet even though Judah and Jerusalem continued to sin against Him, God urged His people to repent or "return" (vs. 22) to Him in faith. Just as clouds disappear in the morning with the rising of the sun, so the Lord pledged to cause the "transgressions" and "sins" of His people to completely vanish. The Hebrew noun rendered "transgressions" can also be translated "offenses" or "rebellious deeds." Furthermore, the noun translated "sins" can denote the guilt and punishment associated with the trespass committed. Yahweh assured the exiles that He offered them a full and complete pardon for their past sins. In turn, the provision of forgiveness was intended to encourage the captives to come back to Him and experience the joy of their redemption. The verb translated "redeemed" signifies that God not only had paid the price to set His people free, but also would watch over and protect them as they made the long and perilous journey back to Judah.

All of creation—from the heights of heaven to the deep places of the earth, and including every mountain and forest and tree—was commanded to shout for joy that God would redeem His people from captivity (Isa. 44:23). Underlying God's restoration of the exiles to the promised land was His fidelity to the covenant relationship He had with them. It was based on His steadfast love. This was neither an inconsistent nor volatile emotion, as it might be among humans. Instead, God's love was unselfish and unconditional, being prompted more by will than by feeling. God's love reached out to His needy people, even though they were unworthy of His affection (Deut. 7:8-9). It was because of His love that the Lord paid the price to rescue His people from slavery in Egypt (4:37). At the consummation of the age, God in His great love will deliver His people from their enemies (Isa. 43:4). And in the future day of redemption, the God of love will also gently lead His people and provide for their every need (Hos. 11:4).

Isaiah 44:24 refers to the Lord as Israel's "Redeemer." It renders a Hebrew verb that means "to act as a kinsman." In Israelite tradition, a kinsman-redeemer was a person who would help out a needy relative. The law made provision for a kinsman-redeemer to do the following: buy back the family land that had been sold (Lev. 25:25); buy back a family member who had been sold as a slave (vss. 47-49); avenge the death of a murdered relative (Num. 35:19); and marry a childless widow of a deceased brother (Deut. 25:5-10). Israel's Redeemer was also the nation's Creator. Like a mother who had conceived and would bring forth a child, God had formed the nation "from the womb" (Isa. 44:24). This was not too hard for the Lord to do. After all, He long ago made everything. As the first chapter of Genesis reveals, He alone stretched out the sky and made the earth (see Isa. 40:22; 51:13). In short, everyone and everything can trace their origin to God.

Not only did God demonstrate His power in the past, but He also showed His authority in Isaiah's day as the only one who could accurately predict the future. He frustrated the omens announced by "liars" (Isa. 44:25; that is, false prophets) and humiliated "diviners." The latter referred to people who tried to discover the unknown by means of idolatry and magic. God said He overturned the counsel of those who claimed to be discerning and insightful by making their advice seem foolish (see 29:14). Isaiah 44:25 most likely refers to Babylonian wise men who gave their rulers glorious and hopeful predictions of the future. The God who controls history turned their counsel into absurdity, and He did this despite their attempts to perform signs to back up their claims.

In contrast to the frauds who worshiped idols, God would fulfill the oracles of His prophetic servants. He would also bring to pass the announcements made by His "messengers" (vs. 26). He alone had the ability to accomplish His purpose on earth. Earthly wisdom could not have imagined that Jerusalem and its temple would be rebuilt 70 years after the Babylonians had destroyed them. Yet the Lord declared through Isaiah that the holy city would once again "be inhabited." Likewise, the towns of Judah would "be built." God would even raise up the nation's "decayed places." The Lord was not only able to reveal Himself, but also powerful enough to fulfill His promises.

Only the all-powerful Lord of the Exodus could command the world's deepest oceans and mightiest rivers to dry up (vs. 27). And only the all-knowing God of Israel could identify the name of the conquerer who would, about two centuries later, restore the chosen people to their homeland. "Cyrus" (vs. 28) would give the orders to rebuild Jerusalem and lay the foundation for the temple (see Ezra 1). Because Cyrus would not come to power for another two hundred years, some think his name was later inserted into Isaiah's prophecy. However, people of faith maintain that the all-powerful, all-knowing God is perfectly capable of naming Cyrus so far in advance. And doing so is a fitting climax to a passage in which the Lord was demonstrating His ultimate power to predict the future. Indeed, what better way was there for Him to confirm the authority of His messengers?

What a great comfort it is to have God as our Lord. He is eternal, unchanging, and is as mighty today as He was in the day of Creation. He does not grow weak with the passing of time, and He is not tired from having to sustain the universe. And most remarkable of all, we can trust the Lord to give us strength for His purpose in our lives. God has never failed in His promise to strengthen us in difficult times. Pleasures and powers of this world may offer temporary comfort, but they fade like flowers (Isa. 40:6-8). In contrast, God's love and care for us are everlasting.

SUGGESTIONS TO TEACHERS

God chose Cyrus, who did not even acknowledge Him, to be used for His purposes. We can therefore be confident that God delights to have us, His children, participate in carrying out His will.

1. SPOTTING ERRONEOUS THINKING. At times, we may think of our usefulness to God in terms of our own ability. Our circumstantial limitations—physical, mental, emotional, financial—can look overwhelming, and we may begin to believe that God cannot use us. Or perhaps a personal failure leads us to imagine that God has written us out of His plan and purpose.

2. AFFIRMING GOD'S UNLIMITED POWER. God's will is never thwarted by our limitations. His power is above and beyond our shortcomings. For example, a man out of whom Jesus cast demons became a missionary to the people of the Decapolis (Mark 5:18-20). Also, Jesus, the Savior of the world, was born and raised in a poor carpenter's family in a commonplace location (Mark 6:1-3; John 1:43-46).

3. RECOGNIZING GOD'S DESIRE TO WORK THROUGH US. Since God invites us to be a part of His great plans and purposes, where do we sign up? According to Ephesians 2:1-10, anyone who has experienced God's saving grace is already on the list. What, then, can we expect as participants in God's plans? We know that God will cause us to will and to act according to His good pleasure (Phil. 2:13). Also, He will be working through us to make His love and greatness known to others (1 Pet. 2:9-10). God can and will use us in extraordinary ways to carry out His purposes.

■ TOPIC: Experiencing Redemption

■ QUESTIONS: 1. How would the exiles be encouraged by the reminder that God had chosen them to serve Him? 2. Why would God want to sweep away all our "transgressions . . . as a cloud" (Isa. 44:22)? 3. How can we let others know that the Lord is their Creator and Redeemer? 4. In Isaiah's prophecy, how did the Lord remind the exiles of His power? 5. As you reflect on your own background, what factors might be considered major obstacles to serving God? How can He enable you to overcome them?

■ ILLUSTRATIONS:

Carrying Us. There once was a minister's child who had been born with a severe deformity in her legs and feet. Handicapped, the youngster hobbled painfully with crutches and braces. Though everything medically possible was done, the lovely little girl could only drag her virtually useless legs.

Near Christmas one day, the minister came in with a poinsettia for his wife, who was upstairs in bed recovering from an illness. The handicapped daughter was delighted to see her father and the lovely plant. She said, "Oh, Daddy! Let me carry it up to Mommy!" The man looked at the youngster and sighed. Trying to suppress his own weariness and sadness, he said, "Honey, I wish you could. I'd give anything to have you do it. But you know you can't." The little one gleefully replied, "Oh, but I can, Daddy! I'll carry the plant and you'll carry me!"

We may feel burdened with problems. But our Redeemer and Creator can bear us up (see Isa. 44:24). He can also carry us through our most difficult experiences (see vs. 26).

Presidential Example. John Quincy Adams served as the sixth president of the United States from 1825 to 1829. But unlike some modern politicians who seem to strive for increasing power and prestige, Adams thought in terms of how he could best serve God and his fellow citizens. This leader became the only former president to get himself elected to Congress after leaving the White House.

Incredulous inquirers asked how Adams could possibly step down and run for a lesser office, especially after experiencing the glory of the highest office in the land. The former president gave evidence of his faith by indicating that he cared nothing about honors and acclaim, but only service and justice.

In 1837, as a member of congress, Adams continued to set an example by vigorously opposing Andrew Jackson's policy of relocating Native Americans living in the eastern part of the United States to the western part of the nation. In 1844, while still in congress, Adams stated, "We have done more harm to the Indians since our Revolution than had been done to them by the French and English nations before. These are crying sins for which we are answerable before a higher Jurisdiction." (This statement brought him harsh criticism from his colleagues.) Adams also declared that slavery was "an outrage upon the goodness of God."

Perhaps God is calling us to be as humble as Adams was in his attitude. The Lord may also be encouraging us to be as sacrificial in our service to others as Adams was in his day. We can do so, for we know that God has not forgotten us and will empower us to be effective as His servants (see Isa. 44:21).

Something to Celebrate. When Angela goes out for a walk, she, like many others, takes her dog with her when she hikes the trails behind her family farm. However, taking the dog for a walk is a necessity for Angela, not just a choice, because she is blind.

Angela recalls that it was a bitter day when she finally submitted to the knowledge that, without a supernatural miracle, her failing eyesight would soon leave her in total darkness. Though her physicians had tried to prepare her for it, blindness still felt like an unbearable shock.

Now, seven years after the curtain's final fall on God's beautiful creation, Angela is still enjoying it. With Leonard, her seeing-eye dog, she takes at least a half-dozen walks each week into the forest. In the early days, Angela was still able to "picture" from her memory the changing scenery of the forest landscape. Now, she no longer needs the memories to enjoy God's spectacular creation around her.

Angela believes, more than most, that Isaiah was correct when he said, "The whole earth is full of his glory" (Isa. 6:3). As God carries out His will in extraordinary ways in Angela's life, each day for her becomes an opportunity to "break forth into singing" (44:23), especially as she celebrates the fullness of God's grace around her.

FOR YOUTH

■ TOPIC: Forget Me Not

■ QUESTIONS: 1. When you are discouraged, how can the truth that God has not forgotten you uplift your spirit? 2. How is it possible for God to forgive all our sins? 3. What are some ways we can "break forth into singing" (Isa. 44:23) because of the redemption we have through faith in Christ? 4. What would prove that God's prophecies are true, exactly as His messengers said? 5. In what ways can God work in your life for good to accomplish His will?

■ ILLUSTRATIONS:

The "Yea, God!" Party. I recently learned about a church youth group that is planning a "Yea, God!" party to celebrate all the marvelous things the Lord has done through them in the past year. The inspiration behind the group's decision was Isaiah 44:23, which commands the heavens to shout for joy and for the world's mountains and forests to praise the Lord for displaying His glory among His people.

This group of young believers recognizes the mighty acts of God that have blessed their existence. And they see these as an indication that He has not forgotten them (vs.

21). In fact, these adolescents are excited about giving God credit and praise for His gifts and blessings.

From what I hear, this won't be a small, quiet church service. It is going to be an all-out youth event. There will be a video presentation highlighting many things God has done, special music, testimonials, singing, and great food. What a wonderful way to celebrate and honor God for His mighty works among His people!

God Will Take Care of Us. As a result of the severe economic downturn that hit the U.S. in the latter part of 2008, Joann's husband, Ray, was laid off from his job. For 18 years prior, his work life had been stable. If anyone's professional circumstance had been predictable, it was Ray's.

In early 2009, Ray's 16-year-old nephew approached him, quietly and on the side, to ask with genuine concern, "How will you take care of your family?" No unemployed person particularly likes that question. It can resurrect feelings of inadequacy. A person can think, *What good am I? I can't even hold down a job!* But God provided the adolescent with an answer, and it came from Ray's lips. The teenager's uncle gently replied, "God will take care of us. He has, and He will."

This is the same God who declared to the captives in Babylon that He had not forgotten them (Isa. 44:21) and that He would work through their difficult circumstances to bring Himself glory (vs. 23). He is also the Creator and Redeemer of believers today (vs. 24). Just as He promised to take care of the exiles, and just as He is watching over Ray in his time of uncertainty, so too God pledges to take care of us. Indeed, His doing so enables us to do extraordinary things in accordance with His will.

A Clear Sense of Purpose. On September 30, 1998, Dan Quisenberry, the star relief pitcher for the Kansas City Royals, died of a brain tumor. "Quiz" (his nickname) had a 12-year career, and he led the American League in saves five different years. His 45 saves in 1983 was a major-league record at the time.

The shy, pale, skinny, and physically unimposing kid from Laverne College was ignored by every major league team in the draft. Sensing that he was destined to play baseball, he drove to the home of John Schuerholz—who was the head of the Royals' scouting department—and pleaded for a tryout.

Isaiah had a similar sense of purpose. He knew that God had called him to do a great work, and he never seemed to regret it. The Lord has also called you to live for Him and serve Him (see Isa. 44:21). Like Isaiah, accept God's will for your life, and pursue it with a clear sense of purpose.

FINDING SALVATION

BACKGROUND SCRIPTURE: Isaiah 45
DEVOTIONAL READING: Exodus 15:11-18

KEY VERSE: Look unto me, and be ye saved, all the ends of the earth: for I am God, and there is none else. (Isaiah 45:22)

6

KING JAMES VERSION

ISAIAH 45:18 For thus saith the LORD that created the heavens; God himself that formed the earth and made it; he hath established it, he created it not in vain, he formed it to be inhabited: I am the LORD; and there is none else. 19 I have not spoken in secret, in a dark place of the earth: I said not unto the seed of Jacob, Seek ye me in vain: I the LORD speak righteousness, I declare things that are right.

20 Assemble yourselves and come; draw near together, ye that are escaped of the nations: they have no knowledge that set up the wood of their graven image, and pray unto a god that cannot save. 21 Tell ye, and bring them near; yea, let them take counsel together: who hath declared this from ancient time? who hath told it from that time? have not I the LORD? and there is no God else beside me; a just God and a Saviour; there is none beside me. 22 Look unto me, and be ye saved, all the ends of the earth: for I am God, and there is none else. 23 I have sworn by myself, the word is gone out of my mouth in righteousness, and shall not return, That unto me every knee shall bow, every tongue shall swear. 24 Surely, shall one say, in the LORD have I righteousness and strength: even to him shall men come; and all that are incensed against him shall be ashamed.

NEW REVISED STANDARD VERSION

ISAIAH 45:18 For thus says the LORD,
who created the heavens
   (he is God!),
who formed the earth and made it
   (he established it;
he did not create it a chaos,
   he formed it to be inhabited!):
I am the LORD, and there is no other.
19 I did not speak in secret,
   in a land of darkness;
I did not say to the offspring of Jacob,
   "Seek me in chaos."
I the LORD speak the truth,
   I declare what is right.
20 Assemble yourselves and come together,
   draw near, you survivors of the nations!
They have no knowledge—
   those who carry about their wooden idols,
and keep on praying to a god
   that cannot save.
21 Declare and present your case;
   let them take counsel together!
Who told this long ago?
   Who declared it of old?
Was it not I, the LORD?
   There is no other god besides me,
a righteous God and a Savior;
   there is no one besides me.
22 Turn to me and be saved,
   all the ends of the earth!
For I am God, and there is no other.
23 By myself I have sworn,
   from my mouth has gone forth in righteousness
   a word that shall not return:
"To me every knee shall bow,
   every tongue shall swear."
24 Only in the LORD, it shall be said of me,
   are righteousness and strength;
all who were incensed against him
   shall come to him and be ashamed.

Monday, January 3	Exodus 15:11-18	*The People God Redeemed*
Tuesday, January 4	1 Kings 18:17-29	*Two Different Opinions*
Wednesday, January 5	1 Kings 18:30-38	*Answer Me, O Lord*
Thursday, January 6	James 5:13-18	*The Prayer of Faith*
Friday, January 7	2 Chronicles 36:15-23	*Building God a House*
Saturday, January 8	Isaiah 45:1-8	*The Lord Creates Weal and Woe*
Sunday, January 9	Isaiah 45:18-24	*A Righteous God and Savior*

BACKGROUND

We learned in last week's lesson that God provided remarkable proof of His sovereignty by specifying long in advance the name of the conqueror who would come onto the world scene and free the exiles from captivity (see Isa. 44:28). Even more remarkable is the fact that only the Lord had the power to use a pagan ruler such as Cyrus to lead the faithful remnant back to Judah so they could rebuild Jerusalem and the temple (see 45:1-8). God could do this, for He alone was all-powerful and uniquely able to rescue His chosen ones from danger.

Verse 9 contains a warning against disbelief, as if any imaginary skeptic (either the exiles themselves or possibly the nations of the world) might try to argue with the Lord over His decision to use Cyrus to end the exile of the Jews. The inappropriateness of the situation would be similar to a fragment of pottery disputing with its maker over the way the raw material was being shaped. The impropriety of the circumstance would also be akin to children haranguing their parents for making their offspring in an allegedly deficient way (vs. 10).

The larger setting is a trial proceeding in which the Lord cross-examines His detractors. As Israel's holy God and Creator, He had the authority to determine the way in which He would bring about His will for the exiles. Likewise, no one had the right to question His decisions, especially what He planned to do with His "sons" (vs. 11). After all, Yahweh reigned supreme as the Creator of heaven and earth. He alone used His infinite power to stretch out the "heavens" (vs. 12) and control the sun, the moon, and the stars that filled the nighttime sky. Moreover, it was part of His divine prerogative to commission Cyrus and stir him into action to fulfill God's righteous purpose. The Lord would guide the actions of the Persian conqueror and ensure that nothing would hinder him from freeing the Jewish exiles, restoring them to their homeland, and enabling them to rebuild Jerusalem (vs. 13).

NOTES ON THE PRINTED TEXT

In the outworking of God's will for His people, He would give Cyrus great success over his foes, including Egypt, Cush, and Seba (Isa. 45:14). In turn, the people of these vanquished nations would hand themselves over to the Lord and His chosen people (see 14:1-2; 49:23; 54:3; 60:11-14). God's purpose in one day allowing the faithful remnant to exercise dominion over their former enemies was so that the latter would come to a correct knowledge of Yahweh, specifically that He is the one true and living God (see Ps. 68:31; Isa. 2:2-4; 19:23-25; 45:23; Zech. 8:20-23). Even though the Lord—the "God of Israel, the Saviour" (Isa. 45:15)—had disclosed His remarkable plan for the redemption of His people, His actions still remained a mystery and were difficult to fully comprehend.

The preceding truth notwithstanding, one fact remained clear, namely, that embarrassment and humiliation awaited all the artisans who made idols (vs. 16). In contrast, Yahweh pledged to deliver His people once and for all. Indeed, their deliverance would be permanent, with no prospect for them ever again being ashamed or humiliated throughout everlasting ages (vs. 17). Verse 18 reiterates a number of truths appearing in verses 9-17. Yahweh once again declared that He, the God of Israel, created everything in heaven and on earth. The Lord, who alone is the sovereign Creator, not only formed the earth, but also firmly established it. At the end of the process, the planet was not a desolate wasteland, but a habitation perfectly suited for humankind (see Gen. 1:31).

The oracles announced by pagan diviners were notorious for being vague and obscure. Isaiah 45:19 depicts mediums and spiritists whispering ambiguous statements in secluded, dimly lit corners. In contrast, what the Lord declared about the redemption of the exiles was clear and heralded openly for everyone to hear. Furthermore, when God invited the faithful remnant to seek Him, He wanted their efforts to be fruitful, not "in vain." That is why Yahweh spoke honestly, sincerely, and truthfully about His plans for His chosen people. Indeed, His pronouncements of deliverance for the captives and the establishment of justice throughout the planet were reliable and accurate (see Pss. 96:10; 98:9; 99:4).

The Hebrew noun translated "escaped" (Isa. 45:20) refers to fugitives and refugees who have survived the onslaught of war, persecution, or natural disaster. In this case, the focus is on the exiles from Judah who were living throughout the ancient Near East after the Babylonian conquest of Judah and destruction of Jerusalem. In the aftermath of Babylon's fall to Cyrus of Persia, the Lord directed the captives to "assemble" and "draw near together"in preparation for their return to their homeland. They were wise to believe that the Lord would fulfill His promise to restore them to Judah, for He is the true and living God. In contrast were pagans who, in their ignorance, hauled around lifeless idols made from wood, stone, and metal and who offered their petitions and praises to objects that were powerless to rescue anyone from their dilemma.

Before an imaginary trial proceeding, Yahweh challenged the false gods of the surrounding nations to come and present the evidence of their ability to precisely foretell the future centuries in advance (see 41:21-22). The all-knowing, all-powerful Lord gave the defendants the opportunity to consult with one another to decide what they wanted to say. The faithful remnant would learn that these false gods were unable to do what only Yahweh had done (see vs. 26). He alone had made known "from ancient time" (45:21) that Cyrus would conquer Babylon and liberate the exiles. Furthermore, only the Lord successfully demonstrated His ability to announce from the distant past an epochal event with pinpoint accuracy. The exiles could see that Yahweh had no peer and that there was no other God but Him. He alone brought about justice and had the power to save. Indeed, by redeeming His people from captivity, He vindicated their decision to trust in Him.

We find recorded in Isaiah the promise that at the end of the age the Lord will finally establish Himself in the eyes of all races and nations as the only true and living God (see 37:16). At the consummation of the age, all the nations of the earth will stream to the Lord's temple to worship and serve Him (2:2-3). Both Gentiles and Jews will want to learn His ways and walk in His righteousness. Indeed, God's law will go "out of Zion," and everyone will want to obey Him. In the future kingdom, virtue and equity will prevail. Also, justice will characterize the Lord's settling of disputes between nations. Peace, not war, will typify the relationship between all races and peoples. In perhaps the most famous and vivid illustration of the coming peace under the Lord's reign, Isaiah saw that nations will convert their weapons used for war into tools used for peaceful, productive purposes (vs. 4). Undoubtedly, it was with this future scenario in view that the Lord urged the inhabitants of the earth to turn to Him in repentance and faith and be "saved" (45:22). Unlike the pagan deities they venerated, only the God of Israel had the power to deliver.

Isaiah 45:23 draws attention to the Lord's exalted position over all the earth as the one, true, and living God. Yahweh solemnly made an oath, which He declared to be true and reliable (see Gen. 22:16; Heb. 6:13). Consequently, it could not be changed or broken. One day, Yahweh will compel everyone's "knee" (Isa. 45:23) to "bow" in worship to Him. Likewise, the "tongue" of every person will "swear" their allegiance to Him (see Rom. 14:11; 1 Cor. 15:24-25).

In Philippians 2:10-11, Paul made reference to these verses when he taught that one day everyone everywhere would worship and serve the Messiah. The apostle noted the place of honor that Jesus willingly forsook was given back to Him with the added glory of His triumph over sin and death (see vss. 6-8). In response to Jesus' humility and obedience, the Father supremely exalted the Son to a place where His triumph will eventually be recognized by every living creature (vs. 9). Paul emphatically tells us that every person who has ever lived will someday recognize Jesus for who He is. The "name of Jesus" (vs. 10) signifies the position God gave Him, not His proper name. By bowing their knees, every human being and angel will acknowledge Jesus' deity and sovereignty. Everyone will confess that Jesus is Lord—some with joyful faith, others with hopeless regret and despair (vs. 11).

Isaiah 45:24 looks ahead to the end of the age in which all humanity will affirm the sovereignty and wisdom of the Lord. The Hebrew noun translated "righteousness" can also be rendered "justice," "deliverance," or "vindication." Moreover, the noun translated "strength" denotes the presence of might and power. Taken together, these terms emphasize that everyone from all walks of life and every corner of the globe will declare Israel's God to be a powerful deliverer. As for those who were incensed against Yahweh, one day they will suffer disgrace. Their decision to challenge the Lord's authority will reap utter humiliation for them. In contrast, the people of Israel will triumph in God and find their decision to trust and obey Him vindicated. Likewise, He will be the source of their honor and the reason for their praise to Him (vs. 25).

SUGGESTIONS TO TEACHERS

We discover in the Book of Isaiah that, even before Christ and the New Testament, salvation was being preached to humankind (see 45:22, 24). God called people to receive His gift of restored relationship with Him. This timeless message is as urgent and relevant for us today as it was for those who first heard Isaiah's declarations.

1. THE EVER-PRESENT REALITY OF SALVATION. Though we may have experienced salvation and begun our relationship with God, in one sense we are continuing to be saved from sin. This remains true even after our initial encounter with God's saving grace. Someone once said that we have been saved (in our initial conversion experience); that we are being saved (in our continued relationship with God); and that we will be saved (when our relationship with Him is completely restored in His presence).

2. THE THREAT OF SIN. For both saved and unsaved, sin is a constant threat to our ongoing relationship with God. For the unsaved, sin can be a distraction from seeking the Lord and accepting His salvation. For the saved, sin can stifle our relationship with Him.

3. THE IMPERATIVE TO REMAIN VIGILANT. Like our relationships with others, our relationship with God must be nurtured and maintained to stay healthy and thrive. If we are not vigilant, we may get sidetracked and deceived by sin. We may neglect spending time with the Lord and so lose the closeness we need with Him. Then we will not experience all the good things God intends for us as His children.

4. THE IMPORTANCE OF TURNING TO GOD IN FAITH. The Lord invites us to seek Him, to turn away from sin, and to experience a deep and fulfilling relationship with Him. But we must actively and intentionally turn to Him in faith while we have the opportunity. By His goodness and grace, we have that chance right now.

■ **TOPIC:** Hope for the Future

■ **QUESTIONS:** 1. How can the truth that God is the Creator give believers hope in times of uncertainty? 2. Why would God emphasize to the exiles that He openly proclaimed His promises to them? 3. What assurance did the Lord give to the captives in Babylon that He would restore them to their homeland? 4. What are some modern-day idols that adults might be tempted to revere? 5. Why do you think some believers tend to downplay the importance of encouraging the lost to trust in the Lord for salvation?

■ **ILLUSTRATIONS:**

Finding Hope. An unbeliever turned to his Christian friend and challenged him to explain the apparent unfairness of God's judgments. The Christian made no attempt to justify God's ways, though he knew that God was eminently fair. The believer simply said to his friend, "How many people do you know who are genuinely looking to God for hope?"

It's so easy to throw metaphorical "bricks" at God without admitting that many people want no part of Him. They prefer to ignore Him and to flout His laws. They also prefer to blame Him, rather than accept responsibility for not finding hope in Him.

The Bible makes clear in many ways that God welcomes and saves all those who turn to Him in faith (see Isa. 45:22). When their hope is anchored to Him, they find true deliverance (see vs. 24). Best of all, the prophet made it clear that anyone can come without any special credentials. God welcomes the spiritually needy, not people who think they don't need Him.

God's Great Invitation. Billy Graham is hailed as the greatest evangelist of the modern era. During his many years of ministry, he has preached the Gospel to hundreds of millions of people. Graham's messages have always been clear, biblical invitations for people to repent and accept the Lord Jesus as their Savior. According to Graham, the Gospel is the only hope for the world.

One of Graham's most memorable challenges made evangelistic history. A special intercontinental satellite network enabled him to attempt to speak to 2.5 billion people in 42 languages and 160 countries. Many of these individuals had never heard the good news of salvation.

In this week's lesson, we learn how God called all people to repentance and faith through the ministry of Isaiah (see Isa. 45:22). God's great invitation is still extended today to all who will openly and humbly accept it.

Emboldening Others. Roger was light and salt in the college dorm where he lived as a student. With a warm smile and genuine concern, he shared his faith with others. He was never ashamed of the Redeemer, who saved him, and never too proud to tell about the life he had led before his conversion.

Roger didn't hide his past from others because he knew it could function as an object lesson for them. He knew that if God could save him out of a lifestyle of dependency on drugs and alcohol, God could save anyone. Roger found hope in the exhortation recorded in Isaiah 45:22, "Look unto me, and be ye saved."

Roger was convinced that if others heard his testimony, they, too, might invite the Lord Jesus into their lives as Savior. While Roger's admonitions encouraged non-Christians to consider the claims of the Messiah, they also encouraged complacent believers to begin sharing their faith. Who knows how many people Roger helped to understand the meaning of salvation in Christ and to lead lives wholly committed to Him.

FOR YOUTH

■ **TOPIC:** Hope for the Future

■ **QUESTIONS:** 1. How is the power of God evident in forming the earth and making it habitable for people? 2. Why is it important for believers to affirm the truth that the Lord alone is the one true God? 3. In a world filled with misstatements and falsehoods, how can the inspired truth of God's Word give you encouragement? 4. How do you think the faithful remnant felt when they heard the Lord declare through Isaiah that He was going to restore them to their homeland? 5. What are some ways you can encourage your unsaved peers to turn in faith to the Lord for salvation?

■ **ILLUSTRATIONS:**

The Promise Is Real. The order placed on the company's website was simple enough, but when the package arrived, it did not contain what the customer wanted. In this case, what was promised in the advertisement proved to be false.

When God spoke to His chosen people, He made a real promise, one that He had the power to fulfill. The Lord declared that the anticipated hope of deliverance could be found in Him (see Isa. 45:24). So what was the catch? People had to turn to God in repentance and faith.

Sadly, many youth refuse to turn to the Lord. In fact, they want nothing to do with God. Thankfully, there are some adolescents who want the eternal hope the Lord has to offer. Through faith in His Son, they find true and lasting salvation (see vs. 22).

How You Look at It. A comic strip depicts a little bird lying on the ground, with its wings and beak all splayed out. The caption reads, "Worms are hard to find this time of year, the high winds make it hard to fly, and it's predicted we will have an early, long winter."

The next frame shows a picture of another little bird dancing and singing along.

The caption reads, "I've been able to find one worm every day, just enough to feed my little chicks. The high winds have made it easier for me to teach them how to fly, and we are just going south a little earlier to escape the cold winds. Isn't life great!"

These two birds had the same problems, but one bird allowed its concerns to undermine its energy. The other saw its problems from a more positive point of view. As the reading from this week's Scripture passage emphasizes, the way we look at things can mean the difference between having hope and feeling hopeless. Doubt leads us to disbelieve God's promise of salvation. In contrast, when we put our faith in the Lord and trust in His promises, we have a bright future to anticipate.

The Best Good News. Until recently, I had never taken great consolation in the advice to cheer up because things could get worse. Somehow just the hint that a bad situation could deteriorate used to crush all hope of a brighter day. Doubt would pervade my thinking and rob me of the joy I knew God wanted me to have. Recently, however, I have been seeing strong rays of God's bright love and grace pierce some ominously dark clouds. For example, I was encouraged to hear the good news about Matt, a 14-year-old hockey player who has emerged from a long bout with a serious illness and is sharing his personal good news with others.

Matt felt desperately ill during a hockey training camp last summer and was hospitalized for an emergency appendectomy (the surgical removal of his appendix). While awaiting surgery, Matt received disturbing news. An deadly virus was raging through his body, and he had a collapsed lung and pneumonia. That was terrible news! But it got worse. Soon, the physicians informed Matt that cancer had invaded his lymphatic system and that he required nine months of chemotherapy.

In the nine months that followed the terrible news, Matt's body was racked with pain. He lost his hair, his strength, and his immunity, but not his faith. At times he doubted God's fairness. But more often Matt just wondered whether he would ever play hockey again. Finally, light appeared at the end of the long ordeal. Matt received good news. He had survived and would grow strong again. More good news arrived. His hair was beginning to grow back. Then, tremendously good news lifted him higher still when he strapped on his skates, picked up a hockey stick, and won the admiration of his fellow players and coach.

However, Matt would be quick to tell you that the very best news he ever heard has nothing to do with being restored to health and hockey. Rather, it is the good news that the Father forgives and gives eternal life to all who turn to His Son in faith (see Isa. 45:22, 24). That news is the "best" good news that we are privileged to pass along to others.

DIVINE REASSURANCE

BACKGROUND SCRIPTURE: Isaiah 48
DEVOTIONAL READING: 1 Kings 8:33-40

KEY VERSE: Go ye forth of Babylon, flee ye from the Chaldeans, with a voice of singing declare ye, tell this, utter it even to the end of the earth; say ye, The LORD hath redeemed his servant Jacob. (Isaiah 48:20)

KING JAMES VERSION

ISAIAH 48:14 All ye, assemble yourselves, and hear; which among them hath declared these things? The LORD hath loved him: he will do his pleasure on Babylon, and his arm shall be on the Chaldeans. 15 I, even I, have spoken; yea, I have called him: I have brought him, and he shall make his way prosperous.

16 Come ye near unto me, hear ye this; I have not spoken in secret from the beginning; from the time that it was, there am I: and now the Lord GOD, and his Spirit, hath sent me. 17 Thus saith the LORD, thy Redeemer, the Holy One of Israel; I am the LORD thy God which teacheth thee to profit, which leadeth thee by the way that thou shouldest go. 18 O that thou hadst hearkened to my commandments! then had thy peace been as a river, and thy righteousness as the waves of the sea: 19 Thy seed also had been as the sand, and the offspring of thy bowels like the gravel thereof; his name should not have been cut off nor destroyed from before me. . . . 21 And they thirsted not when he led them through the deserts: he caused the waters to flow out of the rock for them: he clave the rock also, and the waters gushed out. 22 There is no peace, saith the LORD, unto the wicked.

NEW REVISED STANDARD VERSION

ISAIAH 48:14 Assemble, all of you, and hear!
    Who among them has declared these things?
The LORD loves him;
    he shall perform his purpose on Babylon,
    and his arm shall be against the Chaldeans.
15 I, even I, have spoken and called him,
    I have brought him, and he will prosper in his way.
16 Draw near to me, hear this!
    From the beginning I have not spoken in secret,
    from the time it came to be I have been there.
And now the Lord GOD has sent me and his spirit.
17 Thus says the LORD,
    your Redeemer, the Holy One of Israel:
I am the LORD your God,
    who teaches you for your own good,
    who leads you in the way you should go.
18 O that you had paid attention to my
        commandments!
    Then your prosperity would have been like a river,
    and your success like the waves of the sea;
19 your offspring would have been like the sand,
    and your descendants like its grains;
their name would never be cut off
    or destroyed from before me. . . .
21 They did not thirst when he led them through the
        deserts;
    he made water flow for them from the rock;
    he split open the rock and the water gushed out.
22 "There is no peace," says the LORD, "for the
        wicked."

7

Monday, January 10	1 Kings 8:33-40	*God Hears Confession*
Tuesday, January 11	Acts 9:3-6, 10-18	*God's Chosen Instrument*
Wednesday, January 12	Jeremiah 15:19-21	*God Will Deliver*
Thursday, January 13	Isaiah 48:1-5	*God Spoke Long Ago*
Friday, January 14	Isaiah 48:6-8	*God Discloses New Things*
Saturday, January 15	Isaiah 48:9-13	*God, the First and the Last*
Sunday, January 16	Isaiah 48:14-19, 21-22	*God Leads the Way*

BACKGROUND

Isaiah 48 shines the spotlight of attention on God's chosen people, especially His foretelling long ago of their defeat and captivity. In verse 1, the Lord used various parallel references to draw attention to the distinguished pedigree of those He sent into captivity. They comprised the "house of Jacob," were "called by the name Israel," and were descended from the tribe of "Judah." During their time in the promised land, they swore by the "name of the Lord" and made their petitions to the "God of Israel." When they did so, though, it wasn't in an honest and just manner, for they failed to keep their pledges. They proudly claimed to be citizens of Jerusalem, their "holy city" (vs. 2), and to trust in the all-powerful Lord and God of Israel. Yet despite their assertions, they had a long history of violating the stipulations of the Mosaic covenant.

Yahweh "declared" (vs. 3) the exile of Judah's inhabitants to Babylon centuries before it actually occurred. He not only issued decrees, but also made error-free predictions. After a considerable amount of time had passed, God "suddenly" acted and performed what He had declared. The initial delay was to give His chosen people time to abandon their evil ways and renew their commitment to Him. The Lord was not caught off guard, though, by their refusal to repent. After all, they had a well-deserved reputation for being obstinate. It's as if their necks were as rigid as "iron" (vs. 4) and their heads were as unyielding as "brass." God commissioned spokespersons such as Isaiah to deliver messages of judgment well in advance so that the Israelites would not conclude that the idols they worshiped brought about these calamities (vs. 5).

NOTES ON THE PRINTED TEXT

The context of Isaiah 48 is a trial proceeding in which the Lord cross-examined His chosen people. On the one hand, He exhorted them to acknowledge the fulfillment of His oracles. On the other hand, He knew they would refuse to admit the truth (vs. 6). In keeping with God's past dealings with His people, well in advance He foretold the return of the Jewish exiles from Babylon. The announcement He made to them concerned a series of events that had never before been revealed. Since the release of the captives from Babylon was a completely new development, they could not allege they already knew about it (vs. 7).

The Lord took note of His people's tendency to be deceitful and rebellious. That's why He waited until that time to disclose His plan to raise up Cyrus to free the exiles and restore them to Judah (vs. 8). Admittedly, God could have completely wiped out His people for their treachery. Nonetheless, for the sake of His reputation and prestige, He held back His "anger" (vs. 9). Instead, He used the crucible of the exile to spiritually refine the captives. It was in this symbolic "furnace of affliction" (vs. 10) that He removed their moral impurities (see Deut. 4:20; Jer. 11:4).

The Lord's decision to free His people was to preserve the honor of His name. He announced the momentous event long beforehand and brought it to pass to ensure that the credit did not go to any pagan deities. In short, God refused to allow His name to be defiled and His reputation tarnished by false claims (Isa. 48:11). Even though the chosen people were stubborn, Yahweh had not given up on them. He enjoined them to heed His pronouncements, again referring to them collectively as "Jacob" (vs. 12) and "Israel." The one who summoned them was the only true and living God. As "the first" and "the last," He emphasized His status as the eternal Creator and sovereign Lord. Like a master builder, He alone created the earth and stretched out the "heavens" (vs. 13). And when He issued His command to the stars, they immediately appeared and presented themselves to Him.

Before His celestial court, the Lord directed everyone to assemble and listen to His words. He challenged those who venerated idols to identify any who had predicted that the God of Israel would use Cyrus to liberate His people. The Hebrew verb translated "loved" (vs. 14) indicates that the Persian conquerer was like a loyal friend, covenant partner, or ally in fulfilling the Lord's will concerning Babylon. God would use Cyrus to defeat the Babylonian armies and obliterate the empire they swore to defend. Yahweh, Israel's God, had issued His decree, and no one could thwart His will concerning Cyrus. No one would undermine the Lord's summoning and commissioning of this renowned warrior. God would lead Cyrus and enable him to be successful in his mission (vs. 15). The Persian juggernaut would pave the way for the return of the exiles to Judah, the rebuilding of Jerusalem, and the restoration of the temple.

We learned in last week's lesson that pagan mediums and spiritists of the day were prone to issue cryptic mutterings in hidden places (see 45:19). Supposedly, doing so increased the allure of what they whispered. In 48:16, the Lord declared that He operated differently. He invited the exiles to approach Him and listen attentively to what He declared. From the very first time He announced His intentions to use Cyrus to end the captivity of His people, God openly disclosed His intentions. He never kept it a "secret" reserved only for a select few to know. Moreover, when the predicted event occurred, He would be there to ensure that His oracle came true. It's unclear to whom the last part of this verse refers. The options include Cyrus, Isaiah, and the Lord's messianic "servant" (42:1). Concerning the latter, He is filled with the divine Spirit and enjoys the approval of almighty God (see 11:2; 61:1).

In the Lord's continuing address to His people, He referred to Himself as the "Redeemer" (48:17), or covenant protector and deliverer, of His people. Moreover, in calling Himself "the Holy One of Israel," He indicated that He was their sovereign King and the one to whom they were morally accountable. Through the provision of the Mosaic law, the Lord instructed the exiles how to be spiritually successful. In addition to the written Word, the Lord used the rites and rituals of their faith, along with the input from their religious leaders, to guide them along the path of ethical uprightness. In short, they had all the resources they needed to obey God and carry out His will for them.

Tragically, the Israelites had a long history of disregarding the Lord's injunctions, and it was the root cause for Him sending them into exile. According to verses 18-19, the situation could have been far different for the chosen people. In return for their obedience to the covenant, God would have blessed the Israelites with abundant prosperity and peace. It would have been comparable to an overflowing river that never ran dry. Moreover, instead of foreign enemies oppressing the Israelites, deliverance would have come to a righteous remnant like the waves that roll on a shoreline from the sea (vs. 18). The Lord reiterated promises made elsewhere in the Old Testament to stress the extent to which He was prepared to bless His people (see Gen. 13:16; 22:17; Jer. 33:22). The descendants of the chosen people would have been as many as grains of sand along a seashore. Furthermore, God would not allow their family name to be cut off or eliminated from His presence (Isa. 48:19).

Isaiah 48:20 looks to the time when the Lord would use Cyrus to overthrow Babylon and free the Jewish exiles. When the fall of Babylon came, the faithful remnant was urged to quickly leave the place of their captivity. The good news that their long-awaited freedom had arrived was to be heralded with joy and declared to the farthest reaches of the globe. Messengers were to proclaim that the Lord had redeemed His servants, the descendants of Jacob. The return of the chosen people to their homeland would be like a second Exodus in which they would have plenty to drink, despite their trek "through the deserts" (vs. 21). In the wilderness wanderings, Moses struck a rock, and water gushed out of it for the Israelites to drink (see Exod. 17:6; Num. 20:11). Similarly, God pledged that when the exiles returned to Judah from Babylon, they would not suffer thirst (Isa. 48:21; see 32:2; 35:6; 43:19; 49:10).

The Hebrew noun translated "wicked" (Isa. 48:22) refers to evil people, namely, those who are guilty of committing crimes. In this verse, the focus is on those who defy the will of the Lord and transgress His covenant. In declaring that they would have "no peace," God indicated that those who were unjust and immoral would never prosper (see 57:21). Similarly, in 1 Corinthians 6:9-11, Paul wrote that evildoers would not inherit the kingdom of God. They include people who practiced illicit sexual activity, idol worshipers, adulterers, male prostitutes and homosexual offenders, thieves, people greedy for material gain, drunkards, people who use abusive language, and people who use violence to take other people's belongings.

SUGGESTIONS TO TEACHERS

As the exiles languished in captivity in Babylon, they had a lot of time to reflect on their past mistakes. But the Lord did not want them to remain stuck there. Through the exhortations of Isaiah, God promised to help His people move beyond the misjudgments they made in the past and begin to experience the life-transforming power of His grace. The adults in your class can also benefit from this message of hope originally given thousands of years ago.

1. PUTTING THE PAST ASIDE. It would have been easy for the exiles to indulge in their past mistakes and allow these to be a convenient excuse not to get back on track with their lives. Thankfully, the Lord nudged them in a better direction by pledging to meet their needs, especially as they made the journey back to Judah (see Isa. 48:21). A similar truth holds for believers today. In order for them to move forward with God's plan for their lives, they must first put aside the past with all its failures.

2. GETTING BACK ON THE RIGHT TRACK. The Lord did not ignore the shortcomings of His chosen people. He acknowledged that their lives could have been far better had they paid attention to His commands (see vss. 18-19). That truth notwithstanding, His primary concern was to get their lives back on track, beginning with setting them free from exile. The Lord's agenda for us is no less momentous. He wants us not only to learn from our past mistakes, but also to get on and stay on the path of righteousness.

3. RECOGNIZING THE IMPORTANCE OF FAITH. God enjoined the exiles to have faith in His promise to teach them what to do to succeed and to guide them in the way in which they should go (see vs. 17). Even today, faith in the Lord remains paramount in importance. In fact, it is only through faith in Him that we, as believers, can thrive in our spiritual journey.

4. REMAINING DEPENDENT ON THE LORD. Scripture teaches that our faith is the victory that overcomes the sinful influences of the world (see 1 John 5:4). We may try other means, such as willpower, accountability, support groups, human thought or philosophy, rituals or routines, aversion techniques, or shame and guilt. We may even find that some of these things offer limited success in helping us curb certain behaviors or keeping them in check temporarily. But it is only through faith in the Son that we can be sensitive to His will, our mind can comprehend His Word, and our actions can become joyful acts of worship.

FOR ADULTS

■ **TOPIC:** Putting the Past Aside

■ **QUESTIONS:** 1. How does the fact that God knows what will happen in the future affect your faith? 2. Why would the Lord choose a pagan conqueror, such as Cyrus, to free His people from captivity? 3. What are some ways God has enabled you to be successful in your service for Him? 4. Why is it best for believers to do all they can to discern and follow God's will for them? 5. What can believers do to urge the wicked to abandon their evil ways and turn to God in faith?

■ ILLUSTRATIONS:

Moving Beyond the Past. In his book *Don't Park Here*, C. William Fisher reminds us that the transforming power of the risen Christ can help us put aside our past mistakes. The key is to not allow ourselves to wallow in self-pity over our previous errors in judgment.

Fisher says that too many believers are like piano players who use only one or two "notes." Their testimonies to the power of Christ in their lives begin and end with "I was saved 40 years ago and I know I'm going to heaven." Yet there are so many other life-transforming melodies Jesus wants to "play" in our lives.

According to Fisher, "why, with all the rich, wide range of the keyboard of spiritual insight and truth, do so many Christians play only on one note? Why should we be content to be a dull monotone when God intends this life to be a rich, harmonious symphony?" As we allow the Lord to teach and direct us, we can begin to experience the sorts of life changes He wants to bring about in us (see Isa. 48:17).

An Attitude of Gratitude. Maya Angelou, poet laureate and author of many books including *I Know Why the Caged Bird Sings*, spoke about a conversation that she had in her younger days with her grandmother. It describes the attitude of gratitude we should have toward God in helping us to move beyond mistakes we have made in our lives.

Many of the old woman's friends complained about bills, disappointments, frustrations, problems, crises, and failures. They constantly grumbled and fussed. Life seemed to have no joys. Noting their ungrateful hearts to her young granddaughter, the old woman asked, "How many people went to bed and their beds became a funeral bier? How many of the bed sheets became a burial shroud? Many of those people would have given anything to have five more minutes of life about which they complained so bitterly. Life should be an occasion to offer gratitude to God."

This is the attitude that Isaiah wanted the exiles to maintain. It reflects an appreciation for the help the believer receives from the Lord. Give thanks to God for all that you enjoy from His bountiful hand (see Isa. 48:21).

Moving Triumphantly Forward. A cynic asked a new Christian, "You don't really believe that Jesus changed water into wine, do you?" The believer, a recovering alcoholic, responded, "All I know is that, in my home, Jesus has changed fear into peace, anger into love, and beer into furniture."

The power of God that would enable Cyrus to succeed in his mission of overthrowing Babylon would also pave the way for the exiles to be freed from captivity. It's the same divine power that rolled away the stone of Jesus' tomb and even changed the church's most vicious persecutor into one of the most ardent apostles.

The Lord pledges to be no less powerful in our lives. Our first transforming encounter occurs when we put our faith in Christ for salvation. It continues as we eagerly tell others about our life-altering experience. Then, as we fight life's spiritual battles, God supplies the power we need to move triumphantly beyond the mistakes we have made in our lives.

FOR YOUTH	■ **TOPIC:** On the Right Track

■ **TOPIC:** On the Right Track

■ **QUESTIONS:** 1. How does the knowledge that God is fully in control of the future increase your trust in Him? 2. How do you think the Jewish exiles in Babylon felt when God used Cyrus the Great to free them from captivity? 3. Why would the Lord openly make known to the exiles His plans for Cyrus? 4. What are some ways the Lord has led you in making important decisions in your life? 5. Why do you think some people, despite knowing what God has commanded in His Word, intentionally disregard His will?

■ **ILLUSTRATIONS:**

A New Beginning. Radical turnarounds command attention. When people known for profanity and immorality, for example, suddenly act differently, others want to know why. Consider the young man who was addicted to drugs. When his friends found out he had successfully stopped doing this, they wanted to know how it was possible. This gave the teenager an opportunity to tell them how Christ's resurrection had made a difference in his life.

The Lord announced to the exiles in Babylon that He was going to redirect their lives and put them on the right track. As a result of God freeing them from Babylonian captivity, they would experience a new beginning. Regardless of the challenges they faced and the mistakes they had made in the past, the Lord would help them to move forward in their lives.

Jesus can also transform the lives of the young people in your class. He can give them the courage to begin exercising better judgment and making wiser choices. With His help, they can succeed in carrying out His will for their lives (see Isa. 48:15).

A Life Preserver from Heaven. At his first meeting with his pastor, Bobby sat uncomfortably on a very comfortable couch. Like so many before him—those with broken lives seeking counsel—he had come to his minister searching for a life preserver as he felt himself struggling to get his life back on track.

Bobby had been a professional soccer player with a promising career, but drugs, alcohol, and a steady stream of lies and deceit had finally brought him down. After losing his dream, a wife, and a young daughter, Bobby was now in danger of losing his freedom. At this moment, only the judge knew for sure.

Bobby's pastor shared the Gospel with him and the power of the Lord to help people to move beyond mistakes they have made in their lives. As the minister continued to share, Bobby immediately took hold of this life preserver from heaven. He experienced a glorious conversion that day—plucked out of the kingdom of darkness and transplanted into the kingdom of God's Son.

It's exciting to see a genuine conversion lead people to repentance and then take them into the fullness of restitution. Following that initial encounter, Bobby walked through circumstance after desperate circumstance—all the while seeing God's delivering power continuing to go before him. This young man prayed that God would soften the hearts of several key people, especially as he began to put his life back together again.

And the Lord did. Bobby knew firsthand that the same God who had freed the exiles from captivity in Babylon could enable him to put aside his troubled past. Likewise, the Lord makes His power available for you to be victorious in your Christian walk.

Eradicating Sin. Imagine a bubbling, rushing stream, glistening in the mid-day sun. Beside it grow stately, gentle willows and wide-trunked, far-reaching cottonwoods. Animals come for drink and shade. Birds also find shelter and ample food supply. Nature, in beauty and balance, beckons humans to come and enjoy.

Then enters the tamarisk, a life-sucking weed. Its insatiable appetite for water (it often uses 10 to 20 times more water than native plants) spells certain ruin. Like a sponge, it will sop up the water required for the willows and cottonwoods, for the grasses beneath them, and for all the birds and wildlife that call the streamside home. Left unchecked, tamarisks will overtake the landscape. And they will pollute it with high concentrations of salt from their falling leaves.

Sin is a lot like the tamarisk (also called the salt cedar). Given a foothold—in this case, a root hold—there will be no retreat. Damage control is only possible through eradication. And what are the tools? They include bulldozers, chains, saws, and controlled burning.

So what tool eradicates sin? It's death to our old self, but life returned through faith in the risen Christ. Just as the Lord promised to provide for the exiles as they made a perilous journey back to the promised land, so too our Savior pledges to guide us through the difficult stretches of our lives and quench our spiritual thirst (see Isa. 48:21; John 6:35). Because of Jesus, the power of sin has been permanently uprooted. Praise God that the life-giving water will continually flow!

THE SERVANT'S MISSION

BACKGROUND SCRIPTURE: Isaiah 49:1-6
DEVOTIONAL READING: Hebrews 10:19-25

KEY VERSE: I will also give thee for a light to the Gentiles, that thou mayest be my salvation unto the end of the earth. (Isaiah 49:6)

KING JAMES VERSION

ISAIAH 49:1 Listen, O isles, unto me; and hearken, ye people, from far; The LORD hath called me from the womb; from the bowels of my mother hath he made mention of my name. 2 And he hath made my mouth like a sharp sword; in the shadow of his hand hath he hid me, and made me a polished shaft; in his quiver hath he hid me; 3 And said unto me, Thou art my servant, O Israel, in whom I will be glorified. 4 Then I said, I have laboured in vain, I have spent my strength for nought, and in vain: yet surely my judgment is with the LORD, and my work with my God. 5 And now, saith the LORD that formed me from the womb to be his servant, to bring Jacob again to him, Though Israel be not gathered, yet shall I be glorious in the eyes of the LORD, and my God shall be my strength. 6 And he said, It is a light thing that thou shouldest be my servant to raise up the tribes of Jacob, and to restore the preserved of Israel: I will also give thee for a light to the Gentiles, that thou mayest be my salvation unto the end of the earth.

NEW REVISED STANDARD VERSION

ISAIAH 49:1 Listen to me, O coastlands,
  pay attention, you peoples from far away!
The LORD called me before I was born,
  while I was in my mother's womb he named me.
2 He made my mouth like a sharp sword,
  in the shadow of his hand he hid me;
he made me a polished arrow,
  in his quiver he hid me away.
3 And he said to me, "You are my servant,
  Israel, in whom I will be glorified."
4 But I said, "I have labored in vain,
  I have spent my strength for nothing and vanity;
yet surely my cause is with the LORD,
  and my reward with my God."
5 And now the LORD says,
  who formed me in the womb to be his servant,
to bring Jacob back to him,
  and that Israel might be gathered to him,
for I am honored in the sight of the LORD,
  and my God has become my strength—
6 he says,
"It is too light a thing that you should be my servant
  to raise up the tribes of Jacob
  and to restore the survivors of Israel;
I will give you as a light to the nations,
  that my salvation may reach to the end of the earth."

8

Monday, January 17	Isaiah 49:7-11	*The Lord Has Chosen You*
Tuesday, January 18	Matthew 24:45-51	*Faithful or Unfaithful Servants*
Wednesday, January 19	Matthew 23:2-12	*The Greatest as Servant*
Thursday, January 20	1 Corinthians 9:19-23	*Made a Slave to All*
Friday, January 21	Matthew 10:16-24	*A Testimony to the Gentiles*
Saturday, January 22	Matthew 12:15-21	*Hope for the Gentiles*
Sunday, January 23	Isaiah 49:1-6	*A Light to the Nations*

BACKGROUND

Four passages in the Book of Isaiah are called the "Servant Songs"—Isaiah 42:1-7; 49:1-13; 50:4-11; and 52:13—53:12. This week's Scripture lesson is the second of the four "Servant Songs." The focus is upon God's Servant as a source of grace and hope to both Jews and Gentiles. The Lord offered comfort for His chosen people. Unfathomable blessings awaited them in the kingdom of the Servant. Also, His redemption and restoration of His people to their homeland would dispel all their doubts and give them reason to not only celebrate, but also to spread the good news of a glorious future because of the ministry of God's Servant.

Some consider the Servant to represent Israel as a collective, namely, an ideal Israel that is fully submissive to the will of God. Others say the Servant represents a corporate personality of sorts, where an individual (like a king or father figure) represents Israel as a nation. Despite the possible attractiveness of these views, the one with the most merit is that the Servant represents a historical individual who acts as a representative of God's people. This person is more than just an obedient follower of God. The Lord called and empowered Him to carry out a unique mission, one that fulfilled God's eternal purposes in a significant way. In this view, the Servant of God is the Messiah. He would deliver the people of God—not only from their enemies but also from their sinful condition.

NOTES ON THE PRINTED TEXT

Isaiah 49:1 reveals that before the Servant, the Messiah, was born, God had chosen Him to bring the light of the Gospel (namely, the message of salvation) to the world. The verse refers to the "isles" and "people," that is, Gentiles. Although the table of Gentile nations listed in Genesis 10 includes specific ethnic groups, a Gentile is a member of any race who is not Jewish. In the Bible, the terms *goyim* in Hebrew and *ethnoi* in Greek are translated "Gentile." In some English versions of Scripture (particularly, the King James Version), the term "Greek" is basically interchangeable with "Gentile."

Clearly, the Servant's mission was not a self-created one, but rather a uniquely God-crafted assignment. His work would affect far-off lands. The language of Isaiah

49:1 suggests that God would be with His Servant in whatever He did. Because of God's blessing on the Servant, He was assured of unqualified success in His mission. God always intended the Gospel to be for all people, whether Jews or Gentiles. This is reflected in God's promise to Abraham that through him all nations would be blessed (Gen. 18:18). This pledge came true in the Messiah. He now calls the church to shine His light on those who are in darkness so that they might hear the truth and be saved.

God not only called His Servant, but also completely and perfectly provided Him with spiritual equipment for His ministry. Using graphic metaphors, the Servant described each part of His preparation. The penetrating character of the Servant's message is compared to "a sharp sword" (Isa. 49:2) and "a polished shaft." The imagery reflects that the Servant's ministry would be powerful and true. In fact, His messages would be so powerful that they would cut through every defense. By speaking the words of God, the Servant would accomplish the purpose for which God had called Him. Also, in declaring the message of God to people, the Servant would bring honor and delight to the Lord.

The sword of the Servant was hidden in His hand, and His arrow was concealed in His quiver. This suggests that the Servant would be revealed for action at just the right time. In fact, His coming would be timed according to the plan of God, who loves all nations. This last point reminds us that Jesus was under His Father's continual care. The Lord's Servant did not trust His own strength, but rather He trusted in God to meet His needs. Even when Jesus hung on the cross, He was doing the Father's will.

Originally, God made the nation of Israel holy and set apart from the Gentile cultures, which were filled with idolatry and immorality. And unlike their neighbors, the Israelites were strongly monotheistic. In other words, they worshiped the one true God and no one else. This distinction was supposed to serve as a magnet to draw the other nations to God. Tragically, however, things didn't turn out that way. Whereas God intended His people to be a light to the nations, Gentiles became despised among the Israelites. And in the struggle to remain pure from the false religions of their neighbors, the ancient Israelites became elitist and racist. After the Israelites drifted from Yahweh, He ironically used the Gentile nations to discipline His people and bring them back to Him.

The naming of the Servant as Israel does not undercut the view that Jesus is the Servant. God ordained a servant role for Israel, but the nation largely failed at it. So Jesus came as the ideal "Israel" and perfectly fulfilled the role of the Servant. Thus, shortly before His death He could declare to God, "I have glorified thee on the earth: I have finished the work which thou gavest me to do" (John 17:4). The reference to "Israel" (Isa. 49:3), then, is not to the nation as it was but as it should have been. Though national Israel fell far short of doing what God originally intended, the Messiah perfectly accomplished the Lord's redemptive plan. When people saw the

Servant, they witnessed God's splendor. Jesus was so "full of grace and truth" (John 1:14) that those who walked with Him could say, "We beheld his glory, the glory as of the only begotten of the Father."

Isaiah 49:4 reveals that the Servant felt as if He had "laboured in vain." The text gives the impression that the Servant was completely worn out from toiling so hard. Despite all His efforts, it seemed as if His time had been wasted and His strength had been spent for nothing. Though conflict seems to lurk beneath the Servant's words in verse 4, God would widen, not narrow, His mission. No longer would the message of hope be limited to the Jews. God would also give His Servant as a "light to the Gentiles" (vs. 6). In this way, the Jewish rejection of the divine message would lead to the inclusion of both Jews and Gentiles into the restorative purposes of God. Through His Servant, the Messiah, God would proclaim "salvation unto the end of the earth." Perhaps this is why, even in the midst of disappointment, the Servant could express faith and hope. He knew that He had been serving the Lord, not people, and that He would leave His work in God's hands. The Servant announced He could do this because He trusted God to be just and to give Him the reward He desired for all His strenuous labor (vs. 4).

Verse 5 echoes verse 1 by noting that, even before the incarnation of the Servant (in other words, when God the Son became a human being), the Lord had chosen Him for His divine mission. It was God's intent for His Servant to bring the people of Israel back to Him in repentance and faith. This mission was necessary because the nation had wandered away from God. Israel had committed spiritual adultery by consorting with pagan deities. The nation's gross disobedience was the reason for God's righteous judgment.

Thankfully, God did not stop loving His chosen people. He sent His Servant to restore the relationship that the Lord had wanted when He first called the tribes of Israel out of bondage in Egypt. The Father's love and mercy were so great that He sent His Son as His emissary to offer forgiveness, salvation, and restoration to His wayward people. Like a shepherd rounding up a dispersed flock, the Servant was to call back these exiles, not merely from Babylon, but also from sin and rebellion. While sin divides and disperses, God's Servant unites. This is why He would be honored in God's sight and would be empowered by Him. The Servant had determined He would faithfully serve God, especially in reuniting Israel with the Lord. With God as His strength, the Servant was certain to succeed in His mission.

The goal of the Servant was to bring salvation and restoration to Israel for the fulfillment of the covenant promises God made to His people. The Servant's mission, though, was not limited to Israel. The Lord wanted Him to be a "light to the Gentiles" (vs. 6). Here "light" is parallel in thought to "salvation" and refers to the work of the Messiah to make redemption available to all humankind. Israel's mission had always been to bring the nations to God (19:24; 42:6). The Servant fulfills the call of

Abraham and the nation of Israel to be a blessing to the nations (Gen. 12:1-3; Exod. 19:5-6). After Jesus' death and resurrection, the Great Commission of global evangelism is carried on by His disciples (Matt. 28:18-20; Acts 13:47; 26:23).

SUGGESTIONS TO TEACHERS

When we delve into a study of Isaiah's prophecy, we find several comparisons being made to get across its message about the Servant's redemptive mission to the world. We soon learn that things aren't always what they seem. In Isaiah 49:1-6, we find an old covenant that points to a new one, a grand success that initially looks like a failure, a missionary nation that gets exiled because it refused to leave home, and a light that is a mirror-image reflection of the original.

1. WHEN AN OLD COVENANT LOOKS LIKE A NEW ONE. Hidden between the lines of these verses is a message about the nation of Israel's lackluster approach to its mission. God had made a covenant with Israel so that this chosen nation might show the rest of the world the rewards of intimacy with and obedience to the one true God. But when Israel either kept God to itself or forgot Him completely, thus breaking the covenant, God turned to His Servant, His own Son, the Messiah, to see to it that the mission of proclaiming the news of His salvation to the "end of the earth" (Isa. 49:6) might be accomplished. This established a new covenant for all who would believe.

2. WHEN SUCCESS LOOKS LIKE FAILURE. When Jesus hung on the cross, His lifeblood dripping to the ground, executed like a common criminal, it looked to the world as if His mission was a failure. But God turned what looked like a "failure" into a great success. Jesus' sacrificial death made a way for the lost from every nation and culture to be saved.

3. WHEN A MISSIONARY LOOKS LIKE A HOMEBODY. In eternity past— before the Servant, Jesus Christ, was born—God had chosen Him to bring the light of the message of salvation to the entire planet. The Messiah offered salvation to all nations, and His disciples began the missionary effort to take the Gospel to the ends of the earth. Today's missionary work continues Jesus' desire to take the light of the Gospel to all nations. But to fulfill His will, we cannot be homebodies. Though we may not be called or in the position to take His Gospel to the farthest regions of the globe, we are all called and in the position to take the message of truth around the block to those who are near to us.

4. WHEN A REFLECTION LOOKS LIKE THE LIGHT. Jesus said, "I am the light of the world: he that followeth me shall not walk in darkness, but shall have the light of life" (John 8:12). And Jesus also said, "Ye are the light of the world. A city that is set on an hill cannot be hid" (Matt. 5:14). God's Servant, Jesus Christ, is the Light of the World. And as Christians, we are called to reflect His light of salvation wherever we encounter spiritual darkness.

■ TOPIC: Pay It Forward

■ QUESTIONS: 1. Why is it significant that God called the Servant from His birth? 2. Why did the Servant compare His mouth to a sharp sword? 3. How does the example of the Servant encourage you about the burdens you may have to bear? 4. Why is the Servant glorious in the Lord's eyes? 5. In light of the Servant's mission, what do you think your mission is as His follower?

■ ILLUSTRATIONS:

Shine the Light! On January 20, 2009, after Barack Obama was sworn in as the 44th president of the United States, he gave a pointed inaugural address. He talked about a "new era of responsibility" in which he reminded Americans that "we have duties to ourselves, our nation, and the world." By this he meant that addressing the needs of others requires a commitment of service from us.

What is possibly the greatest gift of service the adults in your class can give to others? Simply put, it is for believers to spread the light of the Gospel through their words and actions. The more we labor to let others know about the good news of salvation, the greater are the eternal dividends the Gospel pays.

Sharing the truth of Christ with others is never easy, and sometimes it can feel like a thankless effort. We realize, though, that it is not a waste of our time to shine the light of Jesus in a world shrouded in moral and spiritual darkness. Indeed, our labor in the Lord is never in vain (see 1 Cor. 15:58).

Siberia: To the End of the Earth. Siberia in winter isn't April in Paris! But it was the right place at the right time for Russian Christians looking for a warm welcome several years ago.

Teams of Russian missionaries braved subzero temperatures to take the Gospel to the impoverished and spiritually bereft people of Siberia, Hannu Haukka of International Russian Radio/TV told *Religion Today*. The missionaries covered 9,000 miles and spoke in dozens of towns that dot the frozen tundra from the Siberian capital of Yakutsk to the Bering Sea. Many people became Christians in the towns. Residents thronged to see the visitors and hear what they had to say, since the isolated towns get few visitors and even fewer missionaries.

A tribal chief in Borulah called everyone who had a telephone and told them to invite their neighbors and come hear the missionaries speak. "The assembly hall was packed," the team leader said. "We spoke for two hours and nobody wanted to leave." When the missionaries invited people to trust in Christ, "everyone came forward. Now these people need a pastor to work with them."

Citizens begged a team of Christians traveling through Deputatsk to preach. The team had stopped to have its vehicle serviced when people noticed a sign on the bumper proclaiming the Gospel. "We too are human beings. Many of our townfolk want to hear about God," they said. The team held an impromptu service that ran late into the night. In Topolin, a "great spiritual hunger" caused services to extend for eight hours.

The rugged landscape and brutal climate isolate Siberians. Travel is difficult because of its few airports, nearly impassible roads, and swampy terrain. Winter is the best time to travel because swamps freeze, allowing vehicles to reach otherwise inaccessible places. Some towns are separated by hundreds of miles, but even nearby towns took hours to reach in the teams' four-wheel-drive vehicles. Such isolation makes Siberia one of the most spiritually desolate places in Russia, Haukka related. Poverty, spiritual oppression, and extended periods of winter darkness cause depression, alcoholism, and suicide.

Northern Siberia has "a big alcohol problem," said Stanislav Yefimov, a Yakut Eskimo who became a Christian through the broadcast ministry of IRR/TV. "People are continually drunk because they are looking for an escape from their problems," and others delve into witchcraft, he reported.

IRR/TV began Christian broadcasts to the Yakuts several years ago. It opened a facility to produce television programs in 15 languages all over Russia, including the Chinese and Mongolian borders, Caucasus Mountain region, and republics of the Commonwealth of Independent States (CIS). The ministry's Moscow training center teaches Christians how to produce radio and television broadcasts, which reach millions of Russians a week on 50 channels. Special broadcasts reach 70 million Muslims, 10 million Jews, and 17 million hearing-impaired people in Russia and the CIS.

Haukka, a Canadian minister, founded IRR/TV in Finland during the Soviet days. He signed a historic deal with Soviet television in 1989, which allowed the Christian Broadcast Network's Superbook animated Bible-on-video to be broadcast to the country. Some 200 million people saw the broadcast, and the response to a follow-up questionnaire was overwhelming. Here is a concrete way in which the Servant of the Lord continues to be a "light to the Gentiles" (Isa. 49:6) and whose message of hope is reaching to the "end of the earth."

FOR YOUTH

■ TOPIC: Light Up Your World

■ QUESTIONS: 1. In what ways do you think God would hide the Servant in the "shadow of his hand" (Isa. 49:2)? 2. When have you ever felt like God was hiding you in the shadow of His hand? 3. How should the Israelites have fulfilled their role as God's servants? 4. In what ways does Jesus Christ fulfill this mission of being God's Servant? 5. What are some things you can do to make sure that God's salvation may reach to the "end of the earth" (vs. 6)?

■ ILLUSTRATIONS:

Mission Possible! Every play in a football game is a mission for success. On the chalkboard everyone blocks his opponent and we score a touchdown. But in the real game the touchdown mission succeeds far less frequently because people keep getting in the way. Our blockers don't connect, our runners get tackled, and our quarterback gets sacked.

Long ago God used Isaiah the prophet to reveal His game plan (so to speak) for us. Seven hundred years before Jesus was born, the Lord declared what Jesus would be like and what He would do for us. The fulfillment of this prophecy is one of the strongest building blocks of our faith.

God's eternal plan has been to make redemption possible through faith in Christ. And the Lord wants us, as His spiritual children, not only to believe in Jesus but also to light up our world with the message of salvation. This is possible, not in our strength, but rather in the grace and power of God.

On a Mission. Several years ago more than 30,000 college students prayed and worshiped together at a large park in Memphis, Tennessee. Organizers said almost 24,000 people had registered in advance, and the rest arrived at the gate for the prayer rally, which was carried live on the Internet.

According to *Christ Notes*, organizer Louie Giglio prayed, "From north, south, east, and west, we come to stand before You to affirm that You are our God. This day belongs to You. Everything belongs to You." Giglio is the founder of Passion Conferences and its daylong worship, music, and prayer service, called OneDay.

The students stood with their hands raised above their heads, praising God, or knelt in the field with their heads bowed, praying for revival, praying that the light of Jesus' salvation might extend to the end of the earth. "It was unbelievable—tens of thousands of students from all over the world spending the entire day on Saturday praising God and praying for revival in their generation," Jocelyn Scott, a Campus Crusade for Christ staff member who traveled from Edison, N.J., told *Religion Today*.

Students started arriving Thursday afternoon and pitched hundreds of tents. More than half camped out in the 4,600-acre park, event coordinator Matt Morris said. Rain threatened, but held off, and only a slight drizzle fell briefly on Saturday.

In between prayers and speeches, people listened to Christian music as they watched the broadcast on three giant screens. Hay-wagon shuttles took participants around the park. Students added their individual artwork or written comments to a 40- by 50-foot banner, which was hoisted like a sail for all to see. Exhibitors from missions organizations were taking the names of interested students as fast as they could.

The event concluded on Sunday with a commissioning service during which students promised to spread the Gospel to the "end of the earth" (Isa. 49:6). More than 10 percent stood when asked to make a commitment to serve a year or more on a mission field. For months afterward, Morris was receiving hundreds of e-mails a day from students relating how they wanted to get involved in various ministries, pray, or reach out to someone with the "light" of the Gospel.

THE SERVANT SUFFERS

BACKGROUND SCRIPTURE: Isaiah 53
DEVOTIONAL READING: 2 Corinthians 5:16-21

KEY VERSE: He was wounded for our transgressions, he was bruised for our iniquities: the chastisement of our peace was upon him; and with his stripes we are healed. (Isaiah 53:5)

KING JAMES VERSION

ISAIAH 53:4 Surely he hath borne our griefs, and carried our sorrows: yet we did esteem him stricken, smitten of God, and afflicted. 5 But he was wounded for our transgressions, he was bruised for our iniquities: the chastisement of our peace was upon him; and with his stripes we are healed. 6 All we like sheep have gone astray; we have turned every one to his own way; and the LORD hath laid on him the iniquity of us all. . . .

10 Yet it pleased the LORD to bruise him; he hath put him to grief: when thou shalt make his soul an offering for sin, he shall see his seed, he shall prolong his days, and the pleasure of the LORD shall prosper in his hand. 11 He shall see of the travail of his soul, and shall be satisfied: by his knowledge shall my righteous servant justify many; for he shall bear their iniquities.
12 Therefore will I divide him a portion with the great, and he shall divide the spoil with the strong; because he hath poured out his soul unto death: and he was numbered with the transgressors; and he bare the sin of many, and made intercession for the transgressors.

NEW REVISED STANDARD VERSION

ISAIAH 53:4 Surely he has borne our infirmities
  and carried our diseases;
yet we accounted him stricken,
  struck down by God, and afflicted.
5 But he was wounded for our transgressions,
  crushed for our iniquities;
upon him was the punishment that made us whole,
  and by his bruises we are healed.
6 All we like sheep have gone astray;
  we have all turned to our own way,
and the LORD has laid on him
  the iniquity of us all. . . .
10 Yet it was the will of the LORD to crush him with
    pain.
When you make his life an offering for sin,
  he shall see his offspring, and shall prolong his
    days;
through him the will of the LORD shall prosper.
11 Out of his anguish he shall see light;
he shall find satisfaction through his knowledge.
  The righteous one, my servant, shall make many
    righteous,
  and he shall bear their iniquities.
12 Therefore I will allot him a portion with the great,
  and he shall divide the spoil with the strong;
because he poured out himself to death,
  and was numbered with the transgressors;
yet he bore the sin of many,
  and made intercession for the transgressors.

9

HOME BIBLE READINGS

BACKGROUND

Both in ancient times and in our day, everyone knows that something is wrong with our world, but what is it? Isaiah's answer is remarkably direct and simple. Sin is the problem. It is humans turning away from God to their own way. And the only solution is the substitutionary death of the Messiah. But in 53:1, Isaiah rhetorically asked whether anyone had believed this Good News of salvation. The implied answer is that the message and Messenger had gone unnoticed. What kind of person would the Messenger be? Isaiah gave a detailed description, first of His humble origins. The prophet compared the Servant of the Lord to a young plant or a root that sprouts in dry ground. This means that new life would spring out of the dead, dry religion of Judaism (vs. 2).

Unlike the alluring grandeur of earthly royalty, the Servant would appear ordinary or lowly. And clearly the Gospels' depiction of Jesus presents a person of humble origins and means. He was born in a stable, rejected by nearly all the important people, and prone to associate with the outcasts of society. The Epistles affirm such a characterization as well. For instance, Paul urged believers to imitate Christ's humility. The apostle also said they should consider others better than themselves (Phil. 2:1-4). Interestingly, Jesus was by all appearances well-accepted in society before He began His ministry, having grown "in wisdom and stature, and in favour with God and man" (Luke 2:52). But as Luke recorded only two chapters later, when Jesus began His ministry, that situation changed dramatically.

After Jesus read from Isaiah in the synagogue and claimed to be the fulfillment of the prophecy, the people became infuriated and nearly killed Him (Luke 4:16-30; see Isa. 58:6; 61:1-2). That negative experience was among the first of what would be persistent rejection for the remainder of Jesus' life. He knew grief, suffering, and rejection all too well. Isaiah predicted this circumstance centuries before it actually unfolded. The prophet revealed that people would despise and reject the Servant, for they would fail to recognize His exalted nature (Isa. 53:3). The Hebrew verb translated "despised" carries the idea of "to treat with contempt." Tragically, the Messiah would be disdained by the very people whom He came to save (see John 1:10-11).

Suffering was commonly viewed by Jews as a sign of God's displeasure (see Deut. 21:22-23; Gal. 3:13). Therefore, it is understandable that people would assume that God punished and afflicted the Servant for His own transgressions. But they would be mistaken. The Messiah—who was sinless—would be suffering for the iniquities of others. Isaiah 53:4 describes this phenomena in terms of the Servant lifting up our pain and bearing our afflictions. The Septuagint (or ancient Greek translation) of this verse is quoted in Matthew 8:17 to indicate that Jesus' healing ministry fulfilled what Isaiah foretold. There is a sense in which the Messiah bore the sicknesses of others by empathizing with their weaknesses (see Matt. 9:36; 14:14; 20:34; Mark 1:41; 5:19; Luke 7:13). Be that as it may, Jesus also carried our infirmities by His vicarious suffering for sin at Calvary (see Isa. 53:12).

Isaiah 53:5 tells us the result of the Servant's suffering. He was wounded because of our "transgressions." This term renders a Hebrew noun that can also be translated "rebellious deeds" or "acts of insurrection." Moreover, the Servant was "bruised" because of our "iniquities." The reference here includes the guilt and punishment connected with our trespasses. In short, the holy one of God allowed Himself to be profaned and brutalized to bring us "peace" with God. The noun rendered "peace" comes from a term that means health, wholeness, and well-being in every area of life, including people's relationship with God. Moreover, the "stripes" inflicted on the Servant from being beaten would bring spiritual healing to people's sin-sick souls (see Ps. 22:16; Zech. 12:10; John 19:34).

The truth is our best attempts at righteousness are no more than filthy rags (see Isa. 64:6). Certainly, God wants us to do righteous works, but these cannot satisfy the demands of His holy justice. Our morally upright standing before God is based solely on the finished work of the Messiah (see Rom. 3:21-26; 5:1). For that reason, Isaiah 53:6 aptly describes people as sheep that have wandered from and abandoned God's path. These domesticated animals were important to the economy of ancient Israel. Their tendency to stray was an appropriate illustration of the sinner's waywardness. We need someone to rescue us, because on our own we are defiant—morally and spiritually. Consequently, the Father caused the Son to shoulder the penalty associated with our "iniquity." The Messiah's task would be painful, for the verb rendered "laid" has the connotation of "hitting" or "striking violently."

First Peter 2:24 refers to Isaiah 53:5 to affirm that believers are healed by the wounds others inflicted on the Messiah. The Greek noun translated "stripes" refers to bruises and welts caused by being whipped or beaten. Based on this verse, some think that physical healing is included in Jesus' atonement. Probably the majority believe that Peter was referring to spiritual healing. The apostle stressed that those who trust in the Son are delivered from their spiritual sickness. In conjunction with Isaiah 53:6, Peter declared that his readers had once been like straying sheep (1 Pet. 2:25).

Furthermore, the apostle explained that though the recipients of his letter had once wandered far from the Son, they had returned to Him when they got saved. Indeed, He was their good Shepherd, the one who laid down His life for them (see John 10:11, 14; Heb. 13:20; 1 Pet. 5:4; Rev. 7:17). Jesus is also their Overseer. This means He looks out for their temporal and eternal welfare.

Isaiah 53:10 reveals that the Servant's treatment would be horrible. And yet—amazingly enough—it was the Lord's will (see Acts 2:23). God intended that the Messiah would be crushed and experience unimaginable suffering. Through His death on the cross, He became a substitute guilt offering for sinners and in this way made restitution to the Father for their wrongdoing and accompanying punishment. Previously, Isaiah had said of the Messiah that no one could speak to His descendants. However, now the prophet was saying that the Servant would "see his seed, [and] he shall prolong his days" (Isa. 53:10). In ancient times, having many descendants and having a long life were regarded as signs of God's blessing (see Job 42:12-16). Isaiah 53:10 is declaring the Servant's restoration to divine favor. In turn, this is the basis for the purpose of the Father prospering, or being accomplished, through the Son. Resurrection is the clear implication of prolonged days, especially after the Messiah had already been made a blood offering. And all of us who trust in the Son for salvation are His spiritual offspring, having been born into new life as a direct result of His resurrection.

Verse 11 reveals that the "soul" of the Lord's Servant will experience anguish for a limited period of time. In the Old Testament, the concept of the soul was not as well defined as in the New Testament. The Hebrew noun translated "soul" was often used to refer to that which animated the person. In this sense, animals also possessed a soul (as in the Hebrew of Gen. 1:20). In the Old Testament, when people were counted, they were often added up as souls (see Exod. 1:5). Admittedly, our clear-cut distinction of soul and body is not always plain in the Old Testament.

Isaiah 53:11 further develops the resurrection theme found in verse 10. In particular, once the travail of the Lord's Servant has ended, He will reflect on what He accomplished through His redemptive work. He will be satisfied by the truth that He did not suffer in vain, for His atoning sacrifice became the basis for a multitude of believing sinners being justified (see Rom. 5:19). Expressed differently, because God's "righteous servant" (Isa. 53:11) bore the punishment connected with the iniquities of the lost, they are acquitted or pronounced innocent. In turn, their legal standing of being declared not guilty prompts them to grow increasingly virtuous in their character and upright in their lifestyle. Just as a successful emperor would apportion captured land and possessions to his nobles and troops, so the Lord would reward His Servant's victory over sin by lavishing Him with honor. Likewise, the multitudes of redeemed sinners will share in the blessings of acquittal and peace connected with His victory (see Eph. 4:8).

It was for the eternal benefit of transgressors that the Messiah "poured out his soul" (Isa. 53:12) as a sacrifice to atone for their sins. Also, despite His innocence, He allowed Himself to be condemned and executed with insurrectionists and indeed prayed that they might be forgiven (see Luke 22:37). When Jesus hung on the cross, though He had been tormented and crucified, He refused to hold a grudge or seek revenge. Instead, He asked His Father to forgive those who executed Him (see 23:34). Some of the fruit of this prayer can be seen in the salvation of thousands of people in Jerusalem at Pentecost (Acts 2:41). The people who crucified Jesus had no idea they were murdering the Lord of glory (1 Cor. 2:8). In executing Him, they fulfilled the words of the prophets (Acts 13:27-28). For instance, the Roman soldiers casting lots for Jesus' clothes was foretold in Psalm 22:18. This reminds us that the Father remained in control of what happened to His Son (Acts 2:23).

SUGGESTIONS TO TEACHERS

Isaiah 53 takes us into the very holy of holies, presenting the Servant of the Lord in a way that leaves us speechless with amazement. We are overwhelmed at the significance of what is revealed here concerning the purpose of God, the infinite love that motivated Him, and the manner in which He has accomplished His will through the life, death, and resurrection of His Servant.

1. THE SERVANT SHUNNED AND SORROWFUL. Isaiah depicted the suffering of God's Servant in graphic terms. The Messiah would be grossly marred and disfigured, despised and rejected. These descriptions suggest that the Servant would be humble and unassuming.

2. THE ADVENT OF THE MESSIAH. Part of the Gospel account centers around the miraculous way in which the Father would send His Son, Jesus, to become the Savior of the world. This work of redemption would begin with Jesus' birth as a baby into the world that He had created. And it would end with His death on the cross and resurrection from the dead.

3. THE IMPORTANCE OF APPRECIATION. How sad it would be if we either disdained, ignored, or downplayed the overwhelming significance of Jesus' atoning sacrifice at Calvary. We honor His redemptive work on our behalf by expressing our appreciation in a variety of ways. This includes giving thanks to the Lord in prayer. We can also express gratefulness by joining with other believers in singing hymns of praise to God.

4. THE PROCLAMATION TO OTHERS. The truth of Jesus' vicarious suffering on our behalf has the power to appeal to people from any background and with any temperament. It is up to us, as Christians, to clarify for unbelievers the significance of Jesus' victory over sin and the awesome nature of the pardon He makes available. Who knows how many spiritual children might be saved for eternity as a result of the witness of the students in your class!

■ TOPIC: Suffering for Others

■ QUESTIONS: 1. Why would the Lord's Servant endure great pain and suffering for us? 2. In what ways has the punishment Jesus experienced at Calvary brought spiritual healing to you? 3. Why are we, like sheep, so prone to stray from the Lord? 4. What motivated the Father to make His Son an offering for our sin? 5. In what sense does the Lord's Servant "justify many" (Isa. 53:11)?

■ ILLUSTRATIONS:

The Suffering Servant. We cannot read Isaiah's description of the Suffering Servant without sensing that a great miscarriage of justice occurred. We know from the Gospels that the compelling reasons for Jesus' affliction were entrenched religious hatred and the ruling elite's fear of losing their power. They condemned Jesus to die for having exposed their heartless, rigid hypocrisy.

This reminds us to be careful about the inroads that ungodly ways of thinking and acting can have on us. We should also remember that Jesus was punished for our transgressions and pierced for our iniquities. He was the innocent Lamb of God who was sacrificed to atone for all our sins (see John 1:29).

Adults need to know that Jesus allowed Himself to be sentenced to death at the hands of hypocritical authorities so that His saving grace might be made known through the proclamation of the Gospel (Rom. 1:16). Adults also need to understand that it's only through faith in the crucified, risen Savior that they can be forgiven and receive eternal life (Acts 4:12).

The Offer of a Pardon. The Constitution of the United States grants the nation's president the authority to issue pardons: "The President . . . shall have power to grant reprieves and pardons for offenses against the United States, except in cases of impeachment."

Perhaps one of the most controversial pardons was made by President Gerald Ford on behalf of his predecessor, Richard Nixon, who resigned in disgrace in the wake of the Watergate scandal. When Ford announced the pardon on live television on September 8, 1974 (a little over a year after Nixon left the White House), he explained that it was to end "an American tragedy in which we all have played a part."

This week's Scripture passage from Isaiah declares the Lord's offer of salvation and pardon through faith in the Suffering Servant. John Bunyan, author of *Pilgrim's Progress*, imagined Christ coming after him "with a pardon in His hand." When Jesus' pardon comes to us, how will you or others you know respond? All people need to seek God's forgiveness for their sins by receiving the awesome pardon the Father offers through the Son's atoning sacrifice. This is the message we need to embrace by faith and declare to the lost around us.

Just Plain Jesus. Mystery writer G. K. Chesterton said about one of his fictional villains: "The man we must follow was by no means conspicuous. . . . There was nothing notable about him" (*The Innocence of Father Brown*). British novelist Thomas Hardy wrote that a character named Joseph Bowman had "no distinctive appearance beyond that of a human being" (*Under the Greenwood Tree*). In *The Moon and Sixpence*, Somerset Maugham's narrator recounted, "I confess that when first I made acquaintance with Charles Strickland [the chief character of the book] I never for a moment discerned that there was in him anything out of the ordinary."

All three of the above quotations from illustrious writers could be applied to the description in Isaiah 53:2 of the Lord's Suffering Servant. No one was ever impressed by Jesus' physical appearance on a street in Nazareth. And yet, this is the person through whom a sacrifice of atonement was made for the sins of the world (see 1 John 2:2).

■ **TOPIC:** The Sacrifice of Serving
■ **QUESTIONS:** 1. Why did the people in Jesus' day incorrectly assume that His afflictions were a sign of God's punishment? 2. What are some of your sins for which Jesus allowed Himself to be wounded and crushed? 3. How can the Father be just in letting His Son bear the punishment for our sins? 4. In what way has the Father bestowed honor on His Son for dying on the cross for us? 5. During Jesus' time of suffering, how did He make "intercession for the transgressors" (Isa. 53:12)?

■ **ILLUSTRATIONS:**

Suffering to Save. When the Son died on the cross, He endured both physical torture and spiritual separation from the Father (see Isa. 53:9-10). This is because God "hath made him to be sin for us, who knew no sin; that we might be made the righteousness of God in him" (2 Cor. 5:21).

Jesus' willingness to suffer in order to make salvation available to the lost shows young people that obedience to God is costly. This should come as no surprise, for Jesus said that no one can follow Him without taking the path of self-denial (Luke 9:23). Whenever Christian youth think they can't endure a severe test of their faith, they should recall how Jesus suffered for them (Heb. 12:2-3).

Jesus was far more than a martyr. He was God's sacrificial Lamb (1 Pet. 1:18-19). The one who atoned for our sins was genuinely humble and gracious, even to His enemies (2:23). No one else can enable young people to go through trials with a peace that surpasses "all understanding" (Phil. 4:7). And He alone can keep them from spiritually stumbling (see Jude 24).

A New Remedy. In *The Healing of Persons*, Paul Tournier describes an incident involving a Christian physician who had heard from an old friend suffering from Parkinson's disease. The man wrote a note in which he told the physician, "Come only if you have some new remedy. I've had enough of doctors who say they cannot cure me."

The physician decided to accept the challenge. After arriving at his friend's home and greeting him, the physician said, "I brought you a new remedy—Jesus Christ!" As the physician talked, his friend gradually started to soften in his attitude. It took several more visits before the man began to show a remarkable change in the way he thought and spoke. Because of his decision to trust in the Lord's Suffering Servant for salvation, he became less irritable and more pleasant.

This week's Scripture passage reveals that all of us are characterized by rebellion, self-centeredness, bitterness, and self-pity—just as the afflicted man who is mentioned above. And like him, we all have an incurable disease called sin. We learn that only the atoning sacrifice of the Messiah can enable us to win the battle against this ailment.

Carrying Our Sins and Sorrows. A Hebrew scholar named Delitzsch observed that the term for "borne" in Isaiah 53:4 combines the meaning of two Latin words—*tollere* and *ferre*. The first (*tollere*) makes us think of a tollgate. In a manner of speaking, Jesus paid the toll for our sins.

The second word (*ferre*) in its first four letters is the same as in ferry. Imagine our sins as a great garbage heap being ferried out on a barge in order to be dumped into the deepest ocean. In truth, our sins were dumped on the Suffering Servant and carried away by Him.

A folksinger named Noel Paul Stookey, in his song titled "Building Block," intoned, "There is a man who has collected all the sorrow in our eyes." Just as Atlas in Greek myth was pictured as carrying the weight of the world on his shoulders, so the Lord's Suffering Servant "carried our sorrows." Indeed, our corporate "griefs" were weighted upon Him. Likewise, He shouldered our suffering for our eternal benefit.

JESUS, THE MESSIAH

BACKGROUND SCRIPTURE: Mark 8:27—9:1
DEVOTIONAL READING: Luke 3:7-18

KEY VERSE: [Jesus] saith unto them, But whom say ye that I am?
And Peter answereth and saith unto him, Thou art the Christ. (Mark 8:29)

KING JAMES VERSION

MARK 8:27 And Jesus went out, and his disciples, into the towns of Caesarea Philippi: and by the way he asked his disciples, saying unto them, Whom do men say that I am? 28 And they answered, John the Baptist; but some say, Elias; and others, One of the prophets. 29 And he saith unto them, But whom say ye that I am? And Peter answereth and saith unto him, Thou art the Christ. 30 And he charged them that they should tell no man of him. 31 And he began to teach them, that the Son of man must suffer many things, and be rejected of the elders, and of the chief priests, and scribes, and be killed, and after three days rise again. 32 And he spake that saying openly. And Peter took him, and began to rebuke him. 33 But when he had turned about and looked on his disciples, he rebuked Peter, saying, Get thee behind me, Satan: for thou savourest not the things that be of God, but the things that be of men. 34 And when he had called the people unto him with his disciples also, he said unto them, Whosoever will come after me, let him deny himself, and take up his cross, and follow me. 35 For whosoever will save his life shall lose it; but whosoever shall lose his life for my sake and the gospel's, the same shall save it. 36 For what shall it profit a man, if he shall gain the whole world, and lose his own soul? 37 Or what shall a man give in exchange for his soul? 38 Whosoever therefore shall be ashamed of me and of my words in this adulterous and sinful generation; of him also shall the Son of man be ashamed, when he cometh in the glory of his Father with the holy angels.

9:1 And he said unto them, Verily I say unto you, That there be some of them that stand here, which shall not taste of death, till they have seen the kingdom of God come with power.

NEW REVISED STANDARD VERSION

MARK 8:27 Jesus went on with his disciples to the villages of Caesarea Philippi; and on the way he asked his disciples, "Who do people say that I am?" 28 And they answered him, "John the Baptist; and others, Elijah; and still others, one of the prophets." 29 He asked them, "But who do you say that I am?" Peter answered him, "You are the Messiah." 30 And he sternly ordered them not to tell anyone about him.

31 Then he began to teach them that the Son of Man must undergo great suffering, and be rejected by the elders, the chief priests, and the scribes, and be killed, and after three days rise again. 32 He said all this quite openly. And Peter took him aside and began to rebuke him. 33 But turning and looking at his disciples, he rebuked Peter and said, "Get behind me, Satan! For you are setting your mind not on divine things but on human things."

34 He called the crowd with his disciples, and said to them, "If any want to become my followers, let them deny themselves and take up their cross and follow me. 35 For those who want to save their life will lose it, and those who lose their life for my sake, and for the sake of the gospel, will save it. 36 For what will it profit them to gain the whole world and forfeit their life? 37 Indeed, what can they give in return for their life? 38 Those who are ashamed of me and of my words in this adulterous and sinful generation, of them the Son of Man will also be ashamed when he comes in the glory of his Father with the holy angels." 9:1 And he said to them, "Truly I tell you, there are some standing here who will not taste death until they see that the kingdom of God has come with power."

10

185

Monday, January 31	Jeremiah 33:14-18	*The Messiah Promised*
Tuesday, February 1	Luke 3:7-18	*The Messiah Expected*
Wednesday, February 2	Matthew 2:1-6	*The Messiah Sought*
Thursday, February 3	Luke 22:66-70	*The Messiah, Are You the One?*
Friday, February 4	John 4:16-26	*The Messiah Disclosed*
Saturday, February 5	John 1:35-42	*The Messiah Found*
Sunday, February 6	Mark 8:27—9:1	*You Are the Messiah!*

BACKGROUND

Jewish expectations about the Messiah reached all the way back to the time of David, whom God had chosen to be the first of many successive kings of Israel (2 Sam. 7:8-16). But the dynastic rule was broken when Jehoiakim died and his son Jehoiachin was carried away in exile to Babylon (2 Kings 24:15; 25:27-29; Jer. 36:30). Later, the prophets said that God would one day restore David's dynasty (Ezek. 37:24-25; Amos 9:11). By the second century B.C., there began to develop among the Jews a growing expectation for a future anointed leader. The Jewish group that wrote what are known as the Dead Sea Scrolls recorded on some of their documents their belief that three prominent figures would come instead of one—the prophet of Deuteronomy 18:15 and 18; a priestly figure named the "Messiah of Aaron"; and a kingly, Davidic figure called the "Messiah of Israel."

In the first century B.C., the Jews longed for an anointed, righteous king who would liberate God's people from their unpopular leaders. Some Jewish writings from this period linked this expected heavenly figure with the day of judgment. By the first century A.D., the Jews wanted freedom from Rome. Expectations ran high that God would raise up a warrior-prince who would throw off the yoke of Gentile rule and usher in a Jewish kingdom of worldwide proportions. John 6:15 and Acts 1:6 show traces of this hope among the people.

NOTES ON THE PRINTED TEXT

If Jesus had intended only to amaze people with sensational miracles and lofty ideals, His purpose would have been fulfilled. But astonishment was meaningless unless it led to faith in Him and to salvation. Because of this, His followers needed to understand who He was. Thus, Jesus left Galilee and went up the villages in the vicinity of Caesarea Philippi so that He could privately quiz His disciples about popular opinions of His identity (Mark 8:27). The Savior was being cautious to prevent others from misunderstanding and interfering.

Jesus chose this area, which the general populace identified with many gods, as the place to ask what His disciples really believed about His identity. Jesus hoped the Twelve would see the shallowness of widespread opinions as compared to what they knew about His ministry. While the people recognized the supernatural nature of His ministry, none of them recognized Jesus as the Messiah. Most saw Him as some kind of prophet but chose to identify Him with a figure of the past (such as John the Baptizer or Elijah), rather than regard Him as someone unique (vs. 28).

Jesus had not previously sought the disciples' acknowledgement of His person, but had rather impressed it upon them with His words and actions. But now, without responding to the popular opinions about Himself, Jesus asked their opinion. Peter, acting as the spokesperson for the group, replied, "Thou art the Christ" (vs. 29). The title *Christ* comes from a Greek word meaning "anointed one." It is equivalent to *Messiah*, a word derived from Hebrew. Both terms signify divine commissioning for a specific task.

The existence of distorted notions concerning the true identity of the Messiah explains why many failed to recognize Jesus, who fulfilled the most comprehensive definition of the Christ (John 1:10-11). It also explains why Jesus was careful not to give false impressions about the exact nature of His messiahship. He saw His future in terms of service to God and sacrificial suffering. Jesus accordingly urged His disciples to keep quiet regarding His identity (Mark 8:30). The popular idea of a Jewish Messiah would stir ideas of revolution and a glorious earthly kingdom. Jesus' followers needed to understand the suffering aspect of His work before they would be ready to proclaim the good news of the Messiah's arrival.

Some have seen Mark's Gospel as centered around three confessions of who Jesus is. This focus is stated in 1:1, where He is described as "Jesus Christ, the Son of God." The first confirmation of Jesus' identity came from the Father at Jesus' baptism (vs. 11). This confirmation was reaffirmed at the Transfiguration (9:7). The second confession was at Caesarea Philippi, at the midpoint of the Gospel, where Peter boldly stated who Jesus is. The third acknowledgment came at the cross, from a Gentile, a Roman centurion (15:39). At that point in the Gospel, Mark's Gentile readers would have surely agreed with these three statements and acknowledged who Jesus is.

Upon receiving the disciples' confession that He was the Messiah, Jesus immediately challenged their thinking by stating that He, the Son of Man, would suffer a violent death and then be raised from the dead. Jesus foretold that the Sanhedrin, made up of the three groups of Jewish leaders mentioned in 8:31, would repudiate His claims and sentence Him to death. The "chief priests" formed the leading component of the ruling council and represented the most important priestly families. "Elders" referred to the Jewish lay nobility, while the "scribes" or teachers were the experts in the law of Moses. Although answerable to the Roman governor, the Sanhedrin of Jesus' day did possess power in dealing with Jewish affairs as well as complete control in dealing with religious matters.

As Jesus predicted, the members of the ruling council did reject Him and sentence Him to death. But their decision apparently could not carry out that sentence without

Roman authority. The Savior foretold that despite His death on the cross, the "Son of man" would rise again on the third day. Jesus' most common self-description was "Son of man." He wanted to teach that, as the Messiah, He combined two Old Testament roles: Son of Man (Dan. 7:13-14) and Servant of the Lord (Isa. 52:13— 53:12). Daniel described a Son of Man to whom God gives an everlasting kingdom. Isaiah described a Servant of the Lord who suffers on behalf of others. Jesus knew that He must perform the role of the suffering Servant; but He also knew that eventually He would receive glory as the Son of Man.

This significant turning point in Jesus' teaching did not escape the notice of Peter, who took it upon himself to rebuke the notion of a suffering Messiah (Mark 8:32). The disciples did not fully comprehend Jesus' words about His death and resurrection until later. Jesus' rebuke, which made mention of Satan, must have stunned Peter and the other disciples (vs. 33). The term *Satan* comes from a Hebrew word meaning an adversary who lies in wait or someone who opposes. Revelation 20:2 identifies Satan as the devil, the primary opponent of God's purposes. Peter had not become Satan but had unwittingly become the devil's voice in encouraging Jesus to take the easy way out rather than go to the cross on our behalf.

Jesus summoned the crowd and His disciples to come closer and listen (Mark 8:34). He stressed to them the severe demands of discipleship. In particular, those who wanted to be associated with Him had to deny themselves, shoulder their cross, and follow Him. Bible students have long considered what it might mean to deny oneself. Suggestions include giving up control of our lives to the Lord, rooting out aspects of our sinful nature that are slowing down our spiritual growth, or being willing to give up our own comfort to serve others. It might mean all of these things.

When Jesus spoke about taking up one's cross daily and following Him, His hearers knew just what He was referring to. When the Romans crucified people, they often forced the condemned to carry the horizontal beam of their own crosses to the place of execution (see John 19:17). The idea is that Christians must be willing to follow the Lord's will even if it leads to pain and death. This historical backdrop sets the stage for one of the many paradoxes that pop up in Jesus' teaching. He said that people who tried to keep their lives for themselves were eternally lost. In contrast, those who surrendered their lives for the sake of Jesus and the Gospel were eternally saved (Mark 8:35). The cross is not an attractive object, so the natural reaction would be to recoil from it and avoid it. But Jesus said that to seek life by avoiding the cross would in the long run result in spiritual death. Eternal life is of much more value than success, prosperity, or even a long earthly life. Thus those who gain the whole world without the Messiah still lose their own soul (vs. 36). They have traded the joy of eternity with Jesus for the fleeting pleasures of the world (vs. 37).

The shame of the cross may cause some people to avoid Jesus and not want to be identified with Him (vs. 38). They prefer this adulterous and sinful world more than the Savior and His teachings. Accordingly, they will have to face His rejection when He, the Son of Man, comes in the glory of His Father and the holy angels. This statement prompted Jesus to declare that some of His hearers would not experience death before they saw that the divine kingdom had "come with power" (9:1). There are several views concerning what Jesus meant. Some think the arrival of God's kingdom "with power" refers to Jesus' resurrection and ascension. Others think the focus is on the coming of the Spirit at Pentecost. A third view is that Jesus was talking about His second advent and the establishment of His messanic reign. The most likely reference, though, is Jesus' transfiguration, which closely follows Peter's confession in Mark and other Gospel accounts (see Matt. 17:1-8; Mark 9:2-8; Luke 9:28-36).

SUGGESTIONS TO TEACHERS

Jesus remains the Messiah, just as He was two millennia ago. Today, He issues the call to potential disciples just as He did outside Caesarea Philippi. Why not use this week's lesson to encourage your students to adopt a fresh view of Jesus and renew their desire to follow Him?

1. THE SUFFERING MESSIAH. Jesus explained that it was necessary for the Messiah to suffer many things and be rejected by the religious leaders of His day. Jesus foretold a violent death and subsequent resurrection. Most knew about the glories associated with the Messiah, but few recognized His suffering.

2. THE SKEWED PERSPECTIVE. Peter viewed the Messiah's ministry from a skewed perspective. Peter did not understand the Father's purpose in letting His Son suffer and die on the cross. Indeed, Jesus could recognize Satan's voice behind Peter's words, especially as the confused disciple urged Jesus not to go to the cross.

3. THE CALL TO SURRENDER. Jesus explained in Mark 8:35 that if we try to keep, or preserve, our physical lives for ourselves, we will ultimately lose them. However, if we surrender our lives for the sake of Jesus and the Gospel, we will find true life. The questions appearing in verses 36 and 37 drive home the point that there is no benefit in losing what is of eternal value to gain what is of temporal value. Eternal life is of much more value than success, prosperity, or even a long earthly life. The one who wins without Jesus still loses in the end.

4. THE CALL TO CHANGE. Oswald Chambers said, "Our Lord's making of a disciple is supernatural. He does not build on any natural capacity at all. God does not ask us to do the things that are easy to us naturally; He only asks us to do the things we are perfectly fitted to do by His grace." When we commit to following the Messiah, we are responding wholeheartedly to His call to change. We remain faithful to our decision, not by trusting in ourselves, but by depending on Jesus to transform us to become more like Him morally and spiritually.

■ TOPIC: A Matter of Identity

■ QUESTIONS: 1. What was the popular opinion concerning Jesus' identity? How do these compare with common views today? 2. If you were Peter, what would you have declared concerning Jesus? 3. Why did Peter rebuke Jesus? 4. Why did Jesus then rebuke Peter? 5. What does it mean for us as believers to take up our cross?

■ ILLUSTRATIONS:

Committing Ourselves to Jesus. A group of young adults in an apartment complex got together to study the Gospel of Mark. When they came to Peter's confession of Jesus as the Messiah (see 8:29), several of the newcomers noted how this differed from the way they previously thought about Jesus' identity. That day they learned for the first time that He is not just an upstanding leader and famous teacher of morality. More importantly, He is the Savior of the world.

When the group concluded their study of chapter 8, one of them said, "This calls for a decision about the Messiah, doesn't it?" Two believers in the group nodded their heads. "Well, then," he said, "on the basis of what I've seen in this study, I'm ready to become a follower of Jesus. I want to commit my life to Him."

Today's culture militates against confronting people about their faith. But Jesus demanded a decision, and so must we. The Holy Spirit draws people to the Son through the record of His deeds, claims, and teachings. We cannot push people into becoming His disciples, but we can use the Spirit-inspired words of Scripture to help them on their way.

In Need of a Special Reminder. Do you post notes to yourself on your desk or refrigerator, that is, little reminders of what you need to do? Perhaps it's a grocery list in progress, a note about a meeting you have to attend, or a card from the dentist's office about your next appointment. Sometimes we also need to be reminded of exactly who Jesus is and what He wants us to do. We may forget the sacrifice He made for us and the discipleship He demands of us.

A commitment on our part to be Jesus' followers calls for 24-hour duty and constant vigilance. Sometimes we need a helpful rebuke from the Lord to keep us awake, a more-than-gentle push to continue faithfully in His service. Peter certainly did (see Mark 8:33)! Perhaps during our next time in prayer, we can ask the Lord what special reminder we might need from Him this week in order to live more fully for Him.

The Nicene Creed. Although the Bible clearly teaches that Jesus is God, influential teachers who claimed they were Christians argued against this central tenet of the faith. One person was Arius. He held that Jesus was not the same essence as God the Father, an idea the Council of Nicea repudiated in A.D. 325. Because the Arians continued to have the support of the Roman emperors, Athanasius (about 293–373), the leading opponent of Arianism and bishop of Alexandria, defended the decisions of the Nicene Council throughout his life. Because of the eventual triumph of his view of the Messiah, Athanasius is often called "the father of Christian orthodoxy."

Earlier, Emperor Constantine, who instituted Christianity as the state religion of the Roman Empire, had summoned the leading bishops of the church to Nicea to hold the first church council. The statement of faith produced at this council, which we know as the Nicene Creed, was later revised at the Council of Constantinople in 381. It condemns Arianism and affirms that Jesus the Messiah is truly God. Nevertheless, Christians did not universally affirm this doctrine until the fourth council in Chalcedon in 451.

FOR YOUTH

■ TOPIC: A Positive ID
■ QUESTIONS: 1. What response did Jesus receive from His disciples when He asked them about popular opinions concerning His identity? 2. Why did Jesus warn the disciples not to tell anyone about Him? 3. How would you explain to an unbeliever the reason why Jesus had to suffer and die on the cross? 4. What does it mean for us as believers to deny ourselves? 5. What will be the ultimate result of feeling ashamed of Jesus and His words?

■ ILLUSTRATIONS:

I'm Yours, Jesus. In a college fraternity discussion, a student in the back row stood up and demanded of the speaker, "I want to know why you bought this religious stuff." That was his way of asking why the speaker had become a Christian.

When we make clear where we stand in relation to the Messiah and His claims, others will want to know why. What makes Christians believe that Jesus is the Son of God and commit themselves to follow Him? We should be able to explain ourselves to others.

In effect, Jesus asked, "What do you believe is My true identity?" Or as the student might ask, "Why did you buy into Me?" When we can answer that question, we are well on the way to intelligent discipleship.

Knowing and Following Jesus. Ask three unsaved teens who Jesus was, and you might be surprised by their answers. "A really wise man and a wonderful teacher." "One of the greatest prophets ever to live." "A rebel who didn't mind causing trouble."

It's popular for adolescents to think of Jesus in these sorts of ways. But Jesus never claimed to be simply a prophet or a wise teacher. And it's hard to see Him agreeing to be called either a "rebel" or a "troublemaker." In short, Jesus claimed to be the Son of God, the Savior, and the Messiah.

This is a difficult hurdle of faith for many teens. To accept Jesus as He really is and then to follow Him, we first have to admit that there is no other way to the Father and that we need a Savior. Moreover, Jesus calls us to deny ourselves so we can be more like Him.

It is not easy for any of us to turn our eyes from ourselves and focus on Jesus. But it is the only way to truly be His disciples.

The Crucial Question. Alexis was only 11 when the power of communism began to crumble in his Russian homeland. He welcomed the changes that seemed to indicate greater freedom and prosperity for him and his family.

In the immediate years that followed the complete upheaval, and eventual overthrow, of all his country's systems and ideologies, Alexis was exposed to many new ideas and beliefs. In his teenage years, it seemed that Alexis could not go more than a few days without having a conversation with an "evangelist" of Islam, Mormonism, Jehovah's Witnesses, or Christianity. They seemed to be everywhere on the streets of Moscow.

Initially, Alexis was intrigued by the conversations and convictions that all these adherents of their religions expressed. But in the end, they left him more confused than convinced. They all had something to say about Jesus, but they all asserted different things about His identity. Who was correct? That was the crucial question.

At age 20, Alexis read Mark 8:27-30, which records Peter's affirmation of Jesus as the Messiah. Alexis finally believed in the Jesus who promised a salvation that came from grace, not one that, by his own merits, Alexis would have to work to attain. Now that he knew the truth, he felt led by the Savior to share the Good News with others.

A BELOVED SON

BACKGROUND SCRIPTURE: Mark 9:2-13
DEVOTIONAL READING: Malachi 4:1-6

KEY VERSE: There was a cloud that overshadowed them: and a voice came out of the cloud, saying, This is my beloved Son: hear him. (Mark 9:7)

KING JAMES VERSION

MARK 9:2 And after six days Jesus taketh with him Peter, and James, and John, and leadeth them up into an high mountain apart by themselves: and he was transfigured before them. 3 And his raiment became shining, exceeding white as snow; so as no fuller on earth can white them. 4 And there appeared unto them Elias with Moses: and they were talking with Jesus. 5 And Peter answered and said to Jesus, Master, it is good for us to be here: and let us make three tabernacles; one for thee, and one for Moses, and one for Elias. 6 For he wist not what to say; for they were sore afraid. 7 And there was a cloud that overshadowed them: and a voice came out of the cloud, saying, This is my beloved Son: hear him. 8 And suddenly, when they had looked round about, they saw no man any more, save Jesus only with themselves. 9 And as they came down from the mountain, he charged them that they should tell no man what things they had seen, till the Son of man were risen from the dead. 10 And they kept that saying with themselves, questioning one with another what the rising from the dead should mean. 11 And they asked him, saying, Why say the scribes that Elias must first come? 12 And he answered and told them, Elias verily cometh first, and restoreth all things; and how it is written of the Son of man, that he must suffer many things, and be set at nought. 13 But I say unto you, That Elias is indeed come, and they have done unto him whatsoever they listed, as it is written of him.

NEW REVISED STANDARD VERSION

MARK 9:2 Six days later, Jesus took with him Peter and James and John, and led them up a high mountain apart, by themselves. And he was transfigured before them, 3 and his clothes became dazzling white, such as no one on earth could bleach them. 4 And there appeared to them Elijah with Moses, who were talking with Jesus. 5 Then Peter said to Jesus, "Rabbi, it is good for us to be here; let us make three dwellings, one for you, one for Moses, and one for Elijah." 6 He did not know what to say, for they were terrified. 7 Then a cloud overshadowed them, and from the cloud there came a voice, "This is my Son, the Beloved; listen to him!" 8 Suddenly when they looked around, they saw no one with them any more, but only Jesus.

9 As they were coming down the mountain, he ordered them to tell no one about what they had seen, until after the Son of Man had risen from the dead. 10 So they kept the matter to themselves, questioning what this rising from the dead could mean. 11 Then they asked him, "Why do the scribes say that Elijah must come first?" 12 He said to them, "Elijah is indeed coming first to restore all things. How then is it written about the Son of Man, that he is to go through many sufferings and be treated with contempt? 13 But I tell you that Elijah has come, and they did to him whatever they pleased, as it is written about him."

11

Monday, February 7	Malachi 4:1-6	*Moses, Elijah, and the Coming Day*
Tuesday, February 8	Exodus 19:1-6	*Moses on the Mountain*
Wednesday, February 9	1 Kings 19:11-18	*Elijah on the Mountain*
Thursday, February 10	Ezekiel 40:1-4	*A Mountain of Revelation*
Friday, February 11	Isaiah 2:1-4	*Come Up to the Mountain*
Saturday, February 12	Psalm 48:9-14	*Ponder God's Love*
Sunday, February 13	Mark 9:2-13	*Listen to My Son!*

BACKGROUND

The literary context of Mark 9:2 and its reference to a "high mountain" seems to indicate that the Transfiguration occurred in the vicinity of Caesarea Philippi (see 8:27). Because Mount Tabor, the traditional site of the event, is some distance from the city and only 1,800 feet in height, it is unlikely that it took place there. Mount Hermon fits better in that it is close. Also, three different mountains to the southeast of Caesarea Philippi are each over 4,000 feet. Any of these could fit the context and provide the solitude Jesus desired for the Transfiguration.

Some see a parallel with the episode in which Aaron, Nadab, and Abihu accompanied Moses up Mount Sinai (see Exod. 24:1). This suggestion harmonizes with the truth that Jesus is the end-time prophet like Moses foretold in Deuteronomy 18:15. Why Jesus specifically chose Peter, James, and John is subject to debate. The Bible does describe Peter's special role because of his confession concerning Jesus (Matt. 16:16-19), John as the disciple whom Jesus loved (John 13:23), and James as the first of the Twelve to be martyred for the Lord (Acts 12:2). In general, Peter, James, and John enjoyed an especially close relationship with the Savior, and now they would be privileged to witness a special revelation of the Messiah's glory. In addition to this occasion, Jesus allowed only Peter, James, and John to accompany Him when He raised the daughter of Jairus from the dead (Mark 5:37; Luke 8:51) and while Jesus prayed in the Garden of Gethsemane (Matt. 26:37; Mark 14:33).

NOTES ON THE PRINTED TEXT

Jesus told His disciples that He would be executed and then rise from the dead (see Mark 8:31-32). Not even Peter, one of His closest followers, could prevent this from happening (see vs. 33). The Messiah stated that those who give Him complete control of their lives are His genuine followers and will be eternally blessed. On the other hand, those who reject Him will experience eternal loss (vss. 34-38). Mark 9:1 records Jesus' statement that some of His hearers would not "taste of death" before they saw "the kingdom of God come with power." About six days after making the preceding pronouncements, Jesus split up His group, taking three of the disciples with Him up the side of a "high mountain" (vs. 2).

While Jesus was praying on the mountain, He was "transfigured." The Greek word used is a form of *metamorphoo*, which means an essential change in form. This term is the origin of our English word *metamorphosis*. The glow on Jesus' face was translucent, coming from within, like a lampshade's luminance when the bulb inside is turned on. Mark noted that Jesus' garments became radiantly white—indeed, far more than any launderer on earth could bleach them (vs. 3). Matthew 17:2 adds that Jesus' countenance shone with the brightness of the sun. In the Bible, God's glory is often associated with light. Thus in the Transfiguration, Jesus' heavenly glory was being unveiled. It must have been a marvelous sight.

As if the Lord's transfiguration in glory was not enough, two former heroes of the faith—Moses and Elijah—appeared and began talking with Jesus (Mark 9:4). We know from another Gospel that the subject of their conversation was Jesus' approaching death (see Luke 9:31). It has been suggested that these two men, in particular, appeared because Moses (the nation's number one lawgiver) represented the Law and Elijah (a premier prophet) represented the Prophets. Their appearance was a visual reminder that Jesus fulfilled the Law and the Prophets, that is, the whole Old Testament revelation.

The Old Testament prophets had foretold the Messiah's suffering and glory to follow (1 Pet. 1:10-11). Peter, however, having just witnessed Jesus' glory during His transfiguration, evidently assumed that His glorification was immediately coming. Peter clearly didn't grasp the significance of Jesus' transfiguration, at least not while it was occurring. In fact, Mark 9:6 explains that Peter and his peers were so terrified that he was at a loss for words. According to verse 5, Peter spoke to Jesus on behalf of the other two disciples and offered to build "three tabernacles; one for [Jesus], one for Moses, and one for [Elijah]." It seems that Peter's intent in building huts was to prolong the experience. His wording shows that he was thinking of Jesus as being on a par with the other two. Peter failed to recognize that Moses and Elijah were secondary figures compared to Jesus. Furthermore, though Peter's motive seemed laudable (at least on the surface), his timing was out of sync with that of God and the Old Testament messianic prophecies. In short, Peter was eager to experience Jesus' promised glory without the suffering that Jesus had foretold.

Peter's mistake was pointed out to him by none other than the Father. While Peter was still speaking, a bright cloud (representing God's presence) enveloped the people on the mountaintop (Mark 9:7). In the Bible, God is often associated with clouds, such as when He led the Israelites in the Sinai wilderness. The Father, while speaking from the cloud that enveloped the mountain, gave the Son His stamp of approval. Incidentally, the Father made a similar declaration at Jesus' baptism, which signified the start of His earthly ministry (see 1:11). Now that Jesus was about to experience the Cross, the Father's voice saying, "This is my beloved Son" (9:7), affirmed Jesus' earthly ministry before His disciples.

It is worth noting that the Father, in making this pronouncement, rebuked Peter by pointing out that Jesus was not just another hero of the faith, but rather His very Son. Furthermore, the Father expressed His love and approval of Jesus. The Son had come to earth with a difficult mission, yet He was being completely obedient to God. In light of this, the three disciples—and all people—should have listened to and obeyed Jesus' words. Admittedly, the Twelve had often listened to Jesus' teachings, but frequently they did so without understanding or obeying His words. So now, the Father commanded that the Son's teachings were to be taken to heart and heeded. Doing so was especially appropriate in light of the difficult days that lay ahead.

According to Matthew 17:6, the three disciples were terrified by hearing the voice of God and fell prostrate. The ancient Israelites had felt the same kind of fear when they had heard the voice of God from the cloud on Mount Sinai. With genuine sensitivity and compassion, Jesus came, gave the disciples a reassuring touch, and said, "Arise, and be not afraid" (vs. 7). Jesus' actions reflected His deep affection for these three men. Mark 9:8 clarifies that suddenly when the disciples looked up, Jesus alone was with them. Moses, Elijah, and the cloud were gone, and the extraordinary experience was over.

As Jesus and His three followers descended from the mountain, the disciples were eager to tell the others what they had witnessed. But Jesus directed them not to tell anyone about it—not until after He, the Son of Man, was raised from the dead (vs. 9). One reason is that Peter, James, and John did not really understand the full import of what they had witnessed. They were especially perplexed by what Jesus meant when He talked about "rising from the dead" (vs. 10). It would only be after His resurrection that the disciples could correctly grasp the significance of the Transfiguration. And Jesus certainly didn't want to give the impression that He was about to establish a glorified earthly kingdom. On other occasions, Jesus had made a similar statement about not publicizing His messiahship (for example, when Peter said that Jesus is the Messiah; see Matt. 16:16-20; Mark 8:29-30). In each of these instances, the time was not right for the people at large to know Jesus' identity as the Messiah.

The Transfiguration was important for several reasons. First, it unveiled the splendor of the Redeemer, the Son of God, authenticating His messiahship. Second, the vision of Jesus confirmed and expanded what He had been teaching His followers about Himself. Third, the Transfiguration revealed the great depth to which the Savior had humbled Himself in becoming a human being. Fourth, the mountaintop experience encouraged the Twelve to remain faithful to one who would be executed on a cross because, despite the immediate prospect of suffering and shame, they could look forward to a future of unending glory with their almighty Lord.

Having been reminded that Jesus was going to die, the disciples asked why the scribes taught that Elijah would appear first, that is, before the advent of the Messiah (Matt. 17:10; Mark 9:11). It didn't make sense to the disciples that Jesus, whom they now knew to be the Messiah, would have to die, especially if Elijah came first and initiated widespread repentance (see Mal. 3:1; 4:5-6). Of course, the disciples had just seen Elijah, but they assumed that this was not the return of the prophet that Malachi had foretold. Understandably, then, the Twelve wondered why Elijah had not come to prepare the way for Jesus.

Jesus did not contradict the scribes' teaching about Elijah's coming, which was certainly part of God's eternal plan (see Rev. 11:3-6). Instead, Jesus affirmed that the scribes were correct in teaching that Elijah would precede the Messiah (Matt. 17:11; Mark 9:12). But Jesus pointed out that the scribes had failed to recognize that Elijah had already come (Matt. 17:12; Mark 9:13). Of course, Jesus was talking about John. The Baptizer was not a reincarnation of Elijah, but rather one who fulfilled the role of Elijah by preaching repentance and preparing the way for Jesus. The scribes had not only failed to recognize John for who he was, but they had gone even further and contributed to his persecution and eventual murder. This anticipated Jesus' own suffering at the hands of the nation's leaders.

When the Savior said these things, it became clear to His three disciples that the Elijah who had already come was John (Matt. 17:13). The Baptizer was the person whom the prophet Isaiah had promised would prepare the way of the Lord (Isa. 40:3). John's ministry also found fulfillment in what the prophet Malachi had described when he spoke of Elijah preparing the hearts of the people for the advent of the Lord (Mal. 4:5-6). Jesus, in confirming John's role, affirmed both the Baptizer's ministry and Jesus' own work as the Messiah.

SUGGESTIONS TO TEACHERS

In this week's lesson, we study a pivotal experience in the lives of Peter, James, and John. Since these followers of Jesus were committed to Him, He invited them to witness His transfiguration. The aftermath of the event became an opportunity for them to increase their commitment to the Savior and one another.

1. GENUINE COMMITMENT. Explain to the class that adults need genuine commitment in their relationships—not only receiving commitment but also giving commitment. Without genuine commitment, our relationships are shallow and meaningless. Point out that this is also true with regard to our relationship with Jesus. He has already committed Himself to us. But unless we are truly committed to Him, we can never have an intimate relationship with Him.

2. SELF-DENIAL. Mention to the class that the willingness to deny self measures a person's commitment. When we are truly committed, we have an unwavering desire to place our lives on the line at any time. Stress that few seem to have that level of commitment to Jesus. But those who do burn into history their devotion to the work of the Savior. Invite the students to discuss what it is about William Tyndale, Martin Luther, and the many Christian martyrs of history that caused them to be radically committed to Jesus.

3. WHOLEHEARTED OBEDIENCE. Emphasize to the class that there is more to spiritual intimacy than just the presence of God. Since Jesus demonstrated His love to us while we were repulsive to Him as sinners (see Rom. 5:6-8), we can at least demonstrate our commitment to Him by obeying His commands. Reinforce this truth by noting John 14:21, which says the following: "He that hath my commandments, and keepeth them, he it is that loveth me: and he that loveth me shall be loved of my Father, and I will love him, and will manifest myself to him."

FOR ADULTS

■ TOPIC: Follow the Leader

■ QUESTIONS: 1. How would you have felt if you were with Peter, James, and John as they went with Jesus up a high mountain? 2. What is significant about Moses and Elijah appearing and talking with Jesus? 3. What are some specific ways you can affirm your love for Jesus to others? 4. Why did Jesus direct Peter, James, and John not to tell anyone about the Transfiguration until after Jesus' resurrection? 5. In what way did Jesus' response to His disciples' question about Elijah actually refer to John the Baptizer?

■ **ILLUSTRATIONS:**

Whom Should We Follow? Not all leaders are worth following. Consider James Warren "Jim" Jones, who was the founder of the Peoples Temple. Throughout his checkered career, he gained notoriety as a captivating and controversial public figure. Then on November 18, 1978, Jones had over 900 members of his religious sect in Jonestown, Guyana, killed by means of cyanide poisoning. This tragedy was one of the largest mass suicides in modern times.

Unlike Jones, the Lord Jesus has brought new life and hope to countless numbers of people down through the centuries. Peter, James, and John were among the first disciples to experience the wonder of Jesus' glory and the power of His grace (see Mark 9:2-8). Even in the bleakest of times, Christians are able to see a future because of the Savior. He promised to one day transport us to the celestial "mount Sion, and unto the city of the living God, the heavenly Jerusalem" (Heb. 12:22).

Commitment to the Boss. John Kenneth Galbraith, a famous economist, devoted a page in his autobiography to a faithful housekeeper named Emily. There Galbraith described how, after a tiring day, he asked Emily to keep anyone from interrupting him. Galbraith wanted to take a nap. A few minutes later the phone rang. President Lyndon Johnson was calling from the White House.

The voice on the other end said, "This is Lyndon Johnson. Get me Ken Galbraith." "I'm sorry, Mr. President, but Dr. Galbraith is sleeping. He instructed me not to disturb him." "Well, wake him up. I need to speak to him now on an urgent matter." "No, Mr. President. I work for him, not you."

Later that evening, Galbraith called the President back. Was Johnson upset? No, he too praised Emily. "I need someone with that level of commitment here in the White House." As well, Jesus desires us, His followers, to be just as committed to Him. After all, during the Son's transfiguration, Peter, James, and John heard the Father say to them, "This is my beloved Son: hear him" (Mark 9:7).

A Deeply Flawed Leader. Charles Colson undoubtedly felt great pride when the new president of the United States invited him to serve on his staff. Few people ever receive this privilege—to have the opportunity to work in the White House, perhaps to impact the history of the nation or world.

Colson did receive fame, but not in the way he intended, for the path down which he followed Richard Nixon. Colson ended up in prison for his part in the Watergate scandal. But in jail, Colson found a new and far superior leader to follow. Colson's Prison Fellowship organization has done far more to impact eternity than any act for which any presidential adviser ever could hope.

FOR YOUTH

■ TOPIC: A Mountaintop Experience

■ QUESTIONS: 1. What sort of change in Jesus' appearance did the three disciples witness as He was transfigured before them? 2. If you were Peter, do you think you would have felt compelled to build three booths to shelter Jesus, Moses, and Elijah, or would you have responded differently? 3. Why were Peter, James, and John possibly terrified by the sound of the Father's voice? 4. What was it about the teaching of the scribes concerning the prophet Elijah that perplexed the disciples? 5. What explanation would you give to your peers for the reason why Jesus had to suffer at the hands of the religious and civil authorities?

■ ILLUSTRATIONS:

A Glimpse of Glory. John Denver was an American folksinger and songwriter and among the most popular acoustic artists of the 1970s. One of his highly acclaimed ballads is "Rocky Mountain High," which was first released in 1972. The song celebrates the grandeur and beauty of the Rocky Mountains, a portion of which are located in Colorado.

In one stanza, Denver used his soaring tenor voice to sing, "I've seen it rainin' fire in the sky." And this is followed by the words "The shadow from the starlight is softer than a lullabye." These lyrics are capped off by the ballad's refrain: "Rocky Mountain high . . . Colorado!"

The supreme mountaintop experience for Peter, James, and John came when they accompanied Jesus to the place of His transfiguration. There they caught a glimpse of His heavenly glory and discovered the importance of heeding Him (see Mark 9:2-8). Even today, the ultimate dream or hope of a believer, whether young or old, is one day to "see [Jesus] as he is" (1 John 3:2). Our confident expectation resides in His eternal kingdom, not in material wealth or earthly power.

A New Adventure. By the time she was seven, Elizabeth had lived on three different continents. Her parents, in Christian ministry, had taken her around the world. In the process, she experienced many new and different things. This increased her hunger to see more of the world and to serve people facing all kinds of needs.

As she approached her teen years, Elizabeth felt led by the Savior to ask her parents, on an international flight, to stop over in a third world country. Then when Elizabeth was in high school, the Lord opened a door for her to take a short-term mission trip to Russia. Later, travel with a college group took her to Honduras.

Elizabeth is convinced that Jesus has led her every step of the way. And in obedience to His will for her, Elizabeth is planning to take an entire semester in Tanzania. These adventures have "bitten" her. She now anticipates a career in international missions and relief work. Following the Savior wherever He leads can offer the greatest of adventures!

Seeing Things More Clearly. There once was a little girl named Beatrice who could not see very well. But the strange part is that she didn't know it. In fact, no one in her family knew that she had poor eyesight. Beatrice thought that everything around her had fuzzy edges, for that's the way things looked to her. She didn't realize that other children could see farther than her. She also thought that everyone saw exactly what she did.

Then, as Beatrice got older, her mother began to wonder why her daughter always sat so close to the television. Beatrice's grandmother noticed that when she read a book, she held it close to her face. When Beatrice started school, her kindergarten teacher noticed that she couldn't see the words on the chalkboard very easily.

Suddenly, it seemed as if everyone began to say, "Beatrice needs glasses." So her father took her to an eye doctor, and within a few days, Beatrice received a brand-new pair of glasses. At first, she was scared that her peers would tease her because she had to wear glasses. But when she put them on, the world looked different. Nothing had fuzzy edges. She could read a book, even if she held it away from her face. She could see her mother's face clearly, even when she was across the room. It was great!

Sometimes in our lives we can feel confused and not see things clearly. Jesus can help us to understand our lives better, just as He helped Peter, James, and John when they saw Him transfigured. Moreover, the Son enables us to know that the Father loves us and that there is nothing to fear. Jesus is with us at all times and can help us to make sense out of what confuses us in life.

COMING TO SERVE

BACKGROUND SCRIPTURE: **Mark 10:35-45**
DEVOTIONAL READING: **John 13:3-16**

KEY VERSE: For even the Son of man came not to be ministered unto, but to minister, and to give his life a ransom for many. (Mark 10:45)

KING JAMES VERSION

MARK 10:35 And James and John, the sons of Zebedee, come unto him, saying, Master, we would that thou shouldest do for us whatsoever we shall desire. 36 And he said unto them, What would ye that I should do for you? 37 They said unto him, Grant unto us that we may sit, one on thy right hand, and the other on thy left hand, in thy glory. 38 But Jesus said unto them, Ye know not what ye ask: can ye drink of the cup that I drink of? and be baptized with the baptism that I am baptized with? 39 And they said unto him, We can. And Jesus said unto them, Ye shall indeed drink of the cup that I drink of; and with the baptism that I am baptized withal shall ye be baptized: 40 But to sit on my right hand and on my left hand is not mine to give; but it shall be given to them for whom it is prepared. 41 And when the ten heard it, they began to be much displeased with James and John. 42 But Jesus called them to him, and saith unto them, Ye know that they which are accounted to rule over the Gentiles exercise lordship over them; and their great ones exercise authority upon them. 43 But so shall it not be among you: but whosoever will be great among you, shall be your minister: 44 And whosoever of you will be the chiefest, shall be servant of all. 45 For even the Son of man came not to be ministered unto, but to minister, and to give his life a ransom for many.

NEW REVISED STANDARD VERSION

MARK 10:35 James and John, the sons of Zebedee, came forward to him and said to him, "Teacher, we want you to do for us whatever we ask of you." 36 And he said to them, "What is it you want me to do for you?" 37 And they said to him, "Grant us to sit, one at your right hand and one at your left, in your glory." 38 But Jesus said to them, "You do not know what you are asking. Are you able to drink the cup that I drink, or be baptized with the baptism that I am baptized with?" 39 They replied, "We are able." Then Jesus said to them, "The cup that I drink you will drink; and with the baptism with which I am baptized, you will be baptized; 40 but to sit at my right hand or at my left is not mine to grant, but it is for those for whom it has been prepared."

41 When the ten heard this, they began to be angry with James and John. 42 So Jesus called them and said to them, "You know that among the Gentiles those whom they recognize as their rulers lord it over them, and their great ones are tyrants over them. 43 But it is not so among you; but whoever wishes to become great among you must be your servant, 44 and whoever wishes to be first among you must be slave of all. 45 For the Son of Man came not to be served but to serve, and to give his life a ransom for many."

12

201

HOME BIBLE READINGS

Monday, February 14	Luke 15:25-32	*Serving like a Slave*
Tuesday, February 15	Luke 10:38-42	*Choosing the Better Part*
Wednesday, February 16	Luke 22:24-30	*As One Who Serves*
Thursday, February 17	Mark 10:17-22	*Come, Follow Me*
Friday, February 18	John 12:20-26	*Serving and Following*
Saturday, February 19	John 13:3-16	*An Example Set*
Sunday, February 20	Mark 10:35-45	*Greatness through Service*

BACKGROUND

Slavery was common in biblical times (see Mark 10:43-44). By the first century A.D., perhaps as much as a third of the population in metropolitan areas such as Rome was slaves. At its worst, slavery was a hideous institution, for slaves often were physically abused and literally worked to death. At its best, slavery was not pleasant, even though it had been humanized somewhat by the first century in the Roman Empire. For instance, slaves could hold positions of some importance, such as in teaching or government service. Nonetheless, slaves were regarded as property to be owned, traded, or sold.

There were at least four ways people could acquire slaves. First, the victors in a battle could enslave the people they conquered. Second, a wealthy person could purchase a slave from other slave owners. Third, a slave owner could make slaves out of the children of a woman who was a slave. Fourth, the lender could enslave someone for failing to pay a debt. The slave in New Testament times owed obedience and allegiance to a master. This is the sense in which believers are to be servants to the Redeemer.

NOTES ON THE PRINTED TEXT

Jesus foretold that once He was in the custody of the religious authorities, they would sentence Him to die and hand Him over to the Gentiles (the civil authorities). The Romans, who ruled Judea at this time, would then mock Him, spit on Him, and flog Him severely (using a lead-tipped whip) before crucifying Him (Mark 10:34).

Despite what Jesus said, His disciples did not grasp the meaning of His words. While we cannot be sure of all that they thought and felt, we do know they were caught up in the popular idea that the Messiah would throw off foreign rule and establish a Jewish kingdom (see Acts 1:6). The notion of a suffering Messiah was alien to the disciples, as it was to most of the Jews of that day. They reveled in the prophecies from Daniel, the Psalms, and elsewhere that foretold a conquering Messiah-King. They overlooked those prophecies that also spoke of the Messiah as a suffering Servant.

Therefore, when Jesus talked about His crucifixion, the disciples failed to grasp the significance of it. This is seen in the request that James and John brought to Jesus (Mark 10:35). According to Matthew 20:20, it was the mother of the two (possibly Salome; see Matt. 27:56; Mark 15:40) who knelt down in front of the Savior and initially made the request. But Jesus evidently responded directly to James and John (Mark 10:36). The mother of the two disciples boldly asked the Messiah to agree to the request before she made it. Jesus, in response, simply asked what He could do for James and John, knowing the question would reveal the state of their hearts.

James and John asked that, in Jesus' glorious kingdom, they be allowed to sit at His right- and left-hand sides (vs. 37). In the palaces of that day, these were the places of highest honor. And the one on the right held the most importance. Even at Jewish banquets, the seating arrangement reflected the guests' degrees of distinction. Those whom the host wanted to honor were seated nearest him. The most privileged position was to the host's immediate right. And the second most privileged position was to the host's immediate left. This practice determined the way in which James and John asked the Messiah for the most privileged positions in His kingdom. Jesus, having just foretold His rejection, death, and resurrection, must have been disappointed that His disciples were so concerned with obtaining honored places. While their request showed great confidence in Him, it was motivated by selfishness.

Jesus' patience with James and John showed in His response. They had foolishly asked for something about which they had no knowledge. Jesus, in turn, queried whether they were able to drink from the bitter cup of sorrow He would soon drink. He also asked whether they were ready to be baptized as He would be in the suffering of the cross (vs. 38). With just James and John's words, it is difficult to know whether their positive response of "We can" (vs. 39) was with inflated assurance or the humility of having been sobered by Jesus' warning. In either case, the Messiah did not express doubt over their intentions. Instead, He assured them that they would share in His sorrow and suffering.

Jesus' reference to drinking from the cup reflected a Jewish expression for sharing one's end. In the Old Testament, the cup itself was a sign for both suffering and joy, but often symbolized God's wrath against sin. The added idea of baptism pictures someone totally immersed in calamities. James would be the first disciple martyred (Acts 12:2), while John would live a long life, enduring great persecution, banishment, and loneliness (Rev. 1:9). With respect to the issue of sitting in the places of highest honor in Jesus' glorious kingdom, the Savior told James and John that this decision did not rest with Him. Rather, it was for the Father to decide (Mark 10:40; see Matt. 20:23). He had prepared those positions for the ones He had chosen.

When the other 10 disciples heard about the bold request James and John had made, they resented the two for making it (Mark 10:41). But the other 10 were no better in their attitude, for they were motivated by self-centeredness, pride, and greed.

The strength of their emotional response, together with their involvement in a previous discussion about who was the greatest (see 9:33-37), shows their reaction for what it was—another desire for greatness. Jesus responded quickly to deal with the division among the Twelve and to teach them a valuable lesson. He began by drawing their attention to something they knew—the Gentiles saw leadership as an opportunity to exercise power, impress others, and take advantage of their subjects (10:42).

The phrase "exercise lordship over" described the way foreign rulers used their authority. The expression implies the imposition of power on the subjects, which the leaders used to their own advantage. It pictures these rulers as oppressing those under them. In Jesus' day, it was common for governing leaders, such as the Romans, to abuse their power and exploit those under them. Such a selfish style of leadership was opposite of what Jesus desired for His followers. He said that the one willing to serve and put the interests of others first would be great (vs. 43). Jesus used the word rendered "servant" (vs. 44) to depict the type of attitude that would put one ahead among His followers. Preeminence would be gauged by a willingness to give up personal rights for the sake of others.

Jesus Himself set the supreme example of humble and sacrificial service when He, the "Son of man" (vs. 45), laid down His life as a ransom for us from our sins. Although He was God, He came to serve and give Himself totally for us. This is a key verse, since it clearly states the purpose of Jesus' ministry. By His sacrifice, He would pay the price (the "ransom") to free the lost from the bondage of sin and death. The ransom offered is not said to be paid to anyone. But the Greek term it renders pictures the price given to release slaves.

Leviticus describes an elaborate system of sacrifices that began with God's covenant with His people on Mount Sinai. The old system, however, was not able to cleanse the human conscience. Also, access to God was limited to the high priest once a year. Moreover, the rituals and sacrifices were merely external regulations that had to be followed until Jesus' death (Heb. 9:8-10). Something more was needed—the blood of the Messiah. He offered His own blood as the sacrifice for sin (vs. 12). The Old Testament sacrifices only covered sins outwardly. But the New Testament sacrifice through the Son cleansed sin inwardly (vss. 13-15). When we trust in Jesus, we receive pardoning for sins and cleansing for our consciences (see Isa. 1:18). To experience true forgiveness, we must understand that the Redeemer freed us from the weight of our guilt and our slavery to sin. He alone ransomed Himself at the cross so that we can serve Him with our entire being.

People in Jesus' day regarded crucifixion as the Roman government's method of humiliating and defeating those who opposed their rule. But the cross on which the all-powerful Messiah died did not defeat Him. He triumphed over every evil it represented on Golgotha. Thus, when Jesus declared, "It is finished" (John 19:30), He meant His work of redemption was now completed. The Greek verb rendered "finished" was often used in the first and second centuries A.D. for paying, or "fulfilling," a debt. It appeared as such on receipts. This fact helps to explain why "It is finished" can literally be rendered "paid in full." From a theological standpoint, the Lamb of God paid humankind's debt of sin to the Father in full when the Son became "sin [or a sin offering] for us" (2 Cor. 5:21). To know the Son is to firmly bank on the sufficiency of His finished work at the cross for a right standing before a holy God. The cross was not where Jesus was victimized. It was where He was victorious over all that separates people from God.

SUGGESTIONS TO TEACHERS

Someone once said, "Life is like a game of tennis. The player who serves well seldom loses." In a way, this can be said for believers. While we serve our Lord, though we may suffer great losses, we will never lose what truly counts—Jesus' love. In fact, in the end we will hear Jesus' precious commendation: "Well done, thou good and faithful servant" (Matt. 25:21). Yet many people believe it is better to be in charge than to be a servant. It is better to be aloof and critical of those who are serving than to serve. It is better to strive for greatness than to labor for the needy. As you cover Mark 10:35-45 with the students, be sure to emphasize the following points:

1. DENYING A GREEDY REQUEST. James and John asked for a gift to be squandered only on themselves and to place themselves ahead of others. Jesus had no choice but to refuse such a selfish demand.

2. ADOPTING PROPER PRIORITIES. It's easy for us to embrace mixed-up priorities when we make our requests known to the Lord. For instance, instead of humbly seeking Jesus' will for our lives, in our hearts we are actually giving Him the answer we want to receive from Him. This is the same sort of mistake that James and John made. Another trouble is becoming so focused on our everyday dilemmas that we forget what is most important to Jesus. For example, we may be so worried about having enough money to buy something we want that we never think to ask Jesus how He wants us to use the money we have (which He gave us anyway).

3. RECOGNIZING THE TRUE NATURE OF GREATNESS. Being great does not mean standing in the spotlight and enjoying the world's adulation. It does not mean amassing a fortune or acquiring power. It does not mean having your biography listed at the end of the dictionary or your photograph appearing on the cover of a popular magazine. It does not mean what the world thinks being great means. Being great is living as a humble servant of the Lord Jesus.

FOR ADULTS

■ **TOPIC:** True Leadership

■ **QUESTIONS:** 1. Why did James and John insist that Jesus do whatever they asked? 2. Why do some believers want to share in Jesus' honor, but not in any sacrifice connected with being His disciple? 3. How does being great in God's kingdom differ from the world's concept of greatness? 4. What do you think sometimes prevents believers from wholeheartedly serving one another? 5. Why did Jesus deem it necessary to give Himself as a ransom for us?

■ ILLUSTRATIONS:

How Bold Is Your Faith? Jesus defined greatness in terms of serving others. Consider the example of Amy. She has been blind from birth. Yet every day she walks from her apartment to the nearby train station, takes the train to the city, and holds down an important job. To look at Amy, one would think that she is totally helpless. But in more than 40 years of blindness, she has learned how to take care of herself with remarkable ingenuity and courage.

Amy has moved from helplessness to boldness. She is a powerful witness in her church and community. Her commitment to Christ stands out in her life, her demeanor, and her values. Instead of whimpering and complaining, she accepts her life and gets on with it.

Amy shines as an example of bold faith. Her life illustrates the kind of courage we all need, especially if we want to be true spiritual leaders. God calls everyone of us to live by faith and to inspire other believers in their Christian service to do the same.

God Loves Them All. Every Friday evening, people gather for a special interdenominational musical service in Seattle's beautiful cathedral. Named for a Christian community in France, these events are called Taizé services. During most of the service, worshipers repeatedly sing a distinctive variety of prayer choruses.

I don't attend often, but when I do, I always head for the same set of seats. Sitting there, I wait for my friends. From a nearby home, caretakers accompany a group of mentally disabled adults. They sit in my section; more accurately, I sit in their section. One of them occasionally speaks out during a quiet moment, but that doesn't happen often.

These adults show as much respect for the cathedral and the God to whom we sing as anyone there. One young man kneels during a major part of the hour. An older woman, who has greater disabilities, tries to sing with the others. In most cases, I cannot recognize her words, but I appreciate her spirit. As we prayed the Lord's Prayer together, she could remember only the first three lines. She spoke those words clearly, "Our Father, who is in heaven, hallowed be Your name." The last time I attended, we closed with the simple chorus "Jesus, remember me when You come into Your kingdom." She knew those words. I could hear her giving, serving heart as she sang.

I could just as easily sit in another part of the cathedral. But sitting with my friends has become part of the Taizé experience for me. They remind me that Jesus does not listen to me pray because of anything I do for Him. Rather, He loves my challenged friends every bit as much as He loves me. Also, it wouldn't surprise me if God gave two of them the honored spots on Jesus' right and left in His glorious kingdom (see Mark 10:39-40).

The Problems of Greed. Americans make up only 5 percent of the world's population, but our machines use one-quarter of the oil the world refines each year. Per person, we go through far more water and own many more cars than the people of any other nation on earth. Per person, we waste more food than many Africans eat.

Because of how the media portrays the American lifestyle, people around the world now want to live at American levels of comfort. Everyone is competing for more. This worldwide greed may lead to major problems at some point when the supply of some necessary resource runs out. James and John fell into this trap two millennia ago, wanting the best only for themselves. Thankfully, Jesus emphasized a different mindset, one that lauds self-sacrifice and service to God and others as the benchmarks of genuine Christian leadership.

FOR YOUTH

■ TOPIC: A Selfish Request?
■ QUESTIONS: 1. Why did James and John want places of honor alongside Jesus in His kingdom? 2. How do you think you would respond if Jesus called upon you to suffer for the sake of His name? 3. Why were Jesus' other disciples indignant at the request made by James and John? 4. What did Jesus mean by believers wholeheartedly serving their fellow Christians? 5. What spiritual blessings do you receive when you serve others?

■ ILLUSTRATIONS:

Created to Serve. Over one holiday break a group of college students went to the Dominican Republic to help people rebuild their homes after a disastrous hurricane. However, one of the girls who planned to go with the group was detained by a family need, and so she traveled later by herself.

Lisa arrived in a village late at night after a bus ride from the capital to the interior. She walked by herself to a nearby house, where people took her in. Lisa told them about the camp and the project. The next day, they showed her the way. She came to a swollen river, which she crossed in a dugout canoe, and then walked to the camp.

Lisa's friends greeted her warmly, and when she described her journey, they were amazed at her courage and persistence. Very simply, her faith kept her going. Lisa knew God had called her to serve these poverty-stricken people. And she could not fail them or God. In contrast to James and John, who pitched a selfish request to Jesus (see Mark 10:35-40), Lisa's life epitomizes what it means to be great in God's eyes.

It's Not Fair. The disciples became angry when James and John asked for special treatment. How much better if the group's members had all supported one another! Consider an older sister in a large family remembering a key incident from her childhood.

> Back home in the autumn, for the annual ritual of canning apples for winter, Mom sat the whole family down. That included us five kids and Dad, too. Equipped with knives, it was our task to reduce a mountain of fruit to pots full of peeled apples. No one ever competed with anyone else. We made hard work into a family party. We all worked as hard as we could, knowing the winter's pies depended on that day's work.
>
> My youngest brothers probably didn't accomplish much. They spent more time eating apples and throwing apple cores at each other. But at the end of the day, my father always bought the same reward for each of us—the largest ice cream cone the corner store sold.
>
> Was it fair? Shouldn't those who peeled more apples have received more ice cream? No, this was a family, not a competition. In fact, one year the store ran out of ice cream and my youngest brother ended up with only a popsicle. All the rest of us felt sorry for him despite the fact that he had already eaten all the apples he'd peeled that day—both of them.

God wants all of us to serve to the best of our capacity, and then to reward us all, not just a select few. Isn't that the way it should be?

A Difficult Choice. Would you rather be Oscar the Grouch or Big Bird? That's the choice that Caroll Spinney faces when he heads for work. You guessed it. He works on the set of *Sesame Street*, where at various points in a day, he may be called upon to play both roles.

How did Big Bird become such a likable character? It's because one experience helped Spinney see the value of kindness. After work one day, Spinney was heading home. Walking down the sidewalk, minding his own business, Spinney passed an older man who looked drunk. Something told Spinney to go back and offer help. The man was not drunk, but merely in poor health. The man hoped someone would help him across a busy street. Reflecting back on that small deed, Spinney said, "Ever since, seeing how easy it is to help, we've had Big Bird doing good deeds."

If only James and John had learned from Jesus or even from Big Bird! If only they had learned that it's better to serve others than to grasp for themselves!

Jesus' Return

BACKGROUND SCRIPTURE: Mark 13
DEVOTIONAL READING: Isaiah 2:5-12

KEY VERSE: Then shall they see the Son of man coming
in the clouds with great power and glory. (Mark 13:26)

KING JAMES VERSION

MARK 13:14 But when ye shall see the abomination of desolation, spoken of by Daniel the prophet, standing where it ought not, (let him that readeth understand,) then let them that be in Judaea flee to the mountains: 15 And let him that is on the housetop not go down into the house, neither enter therein, to take any thing out of his house: 16 And let him that is in the field not turn back again for to take up his garment. 17 But woe to them that are with child, and to them that give suck in those days! 18 And pray ye that your flight be not in the winter. 19 For in those days shall be affliction, such as was not from the beginning of the creation which God created unto this time, neither shall be. 20 And except that the Lord had shortened those days, no flesh should be saved: but for the elect's sake, whom he hath chosen, he hath shortened the days. 21 And then if any man shall say to you, Lo, here is Christ; or, lo, he is there; believe him not: 22 For false Christs and false prophets shall rise, and shall shew signs and wonders, to seduce, if it were possible, even the elect. 23 But take ye heed: behold, I have foretold you all things.

24 But in those days, after that tribulation, the sun shall be darkened, and the moon shall not give her light, 25 And the stars of heaven shall fall, and the powers that are in heaven shall be shaken. 26 And then shall they see the Son of man coming in the clouds with great power and glory. 27 And then shall he send his angels, and shall gather together his elect from the four winds, from the uttermost part of the earth to the uttermost part of heaven.

NEW REVISED STANDARD VERSION

MARK 13:14 "But when you see the desolating sacrilege set up where it ought not to be (let the reader understand), then those in Judea must flee to the mountains; 15 someone on the housetop must not go down or enter the house to take anything away; 16 someone in the field must not turn back to get a coat. 17 Woe to those who are pregnant and to those who are nursing infants in those days! 18 Pray that it may not be in winter.

19 For in those days there will be suffering, such as has not been from the beginning of the creation that God created until now, no, and never will be. 20 And if the Lord had not cut short those days, no one would be saved; but for the sake of the elect, whom he chose, he has cut short those days. 21 And if anyone says to you at that time, 'Look! Here is the Messiah!' or 'Look! There he is!'—do not believe it. 22 False messiahs and false prophets will appear and produce signs and omens, to lead astray, if possible, the elect. 23 But be alert; I have already told you everything.

24 "But in those days, after that suffering,
  the sun will be darkened,
    and the moon will not give its light,
25 and the stars will be falling from heaven,
    and the powers in the heavens will be shaken.
26 Then they will see 'the Son of Man coming in clouds' with great power and glory. 27 Then he will send out the angels, and gather his elect from the four winds, from the ends of the earth to the ends of heaven.

13

Monday, February 21	Isaiah 2:5-12	*Terror for the Proud and Lofty*
Tuesday, February 22	2 Timothy 3:1-9	*Peril in Distressing Times*
Wednesday, February 23	2 Peter 3:3-10	*The Day of Judgment*
Thursday, February 24	2 Peter 3:11-18	*What You Ought to Be*
Friday, February 25	Mark 13:1-13	*Beware!*
Saturday, February 26	Mark 13:28-37	*Be Watchful!*
Sunday, February 27	Mark 13:14-27	*Coming of the Son of Man*

BACKGROUND

While in an outer court of the Jerusalem temple, Jesus praised the generosity of a widow (Mark 12:41-44). Then, as Jesus and His disciples were leaving the temple area, one of His followers drew attention to the shrine's huge stones and beautifully adorned buildings (13:1). In response, Jesus foretold that not a single stone of those magnificent structures would be left in its place (vs. 2). His statement looked ahead to the complete obliteration of the temple at the hands of the Romans in A.D. 70. Next, the group crossed the Kidron Valley and climbed the nearby Mount of Olives (vs. 3). There Jesus taught about the difficult days ahead for His followers.

Perhaps without intending to, one of Jesus' disciples supplied an opening for Him to introduce the subjects that were on His heart. The disciple merely drew Jesus' attention to the appearance of the temple. And His followers must have been shocked to learn that the impressive cluster of buildings and courtyards would be destroyed. Undoubtedly, while the disciples were with Jesus on the Mount of Olives, they had time to reflect on His ominous prediction. For them, any suggestion that the entire shrine complex would be destroyed was highly disturbing. In response to Jesus' prediction, the disciples asked Him to explain what He had meant by it. They specifically wanted to know when the catastrophic events would happen and what the sign would be to indicate they were about to occur (vs. 4).

Everything that follows in Mark 13 was Jesus' response to those two questions. His answer to the second question is found in verses 5-27, while His response to the first question is found in verses 28-32. The Savior pledged that those who endured "unto the end" (vs. 13) would be "saved." This promise does not mean that salvation is obtained as a result of good works, rather than received by grace (see 10:15). Instead, Jesus was declaring that those who are truly regenerate will demonstrate the genuineness of their faith by remaining loyal to Him even in the midst of the most distressing of circumstances.

What the Savior said to His followers provides us with additional information, not only about the destruction of the temple, but also about His own future return to earth in glory. Evidently, in Jesus' mind those two events were closely connected. That is probably because the destruction of the temple was, and the Second Coming will be, a time of God's judgment on humanity. Nonetheless, as we now know, the Roman's obliteration of the Jerusalem shrine and the Lord's second advent are separated by a long span of time.

NOTES ON THE PRINTED TEXT

If the disciples were to survive the time of great distress preceding the Second Coming, they would need a plan of action, and that's what Jesus gave them. He said they were to be on the lookout for the "abomination of desolation" (Mark 13:14). The preceding phrase comes from the Book of Daniel (see 9:27; 11:31; 12:11). One aspect of the prophecy's fulfillment occurred in 168–167 B.C. At that time a Syrian ruler named Antiochus Epiphanes profaned the Jerusalem temple by erecting an altar to the pagan deity Zeus and sacrificing a pig on the shrine's altar. But Jesus' warning related to a second aspect of the prophecy's fulfillment, which occurred at the time of the siege and subsequent destruction of Jerusalem by the Roman general (later emperor) Titus in A.D. 70. During that invasion, Jewish Zealots profaned the shrine through a number of acts, including murder. A third and final aspect of the prophecy's fulfillment will occur in connection with the atrocities committed by the future Antichrist during a period of unparalleled anguish at the end of the age (see Matt. 24:21, 29; Mark 13:19, 24-25; Luke 21:25-26; 2 Thess. 2:1-12; Rev. 3:10; 13:1-10).

In light of the dire nature of the future situation Jesus described in Mark 13:5-14, He urged those living in Judea at that time to "flee to the mountains." Running away to an elevated location to escape impending danger is a common Old Testament image (see Gen. 19:17; Judg. 6:2; Isa. 15:5; Jer. 16:16; Zech. 14:5). Aside from the surrounding elevation in the vicinity of Jerusalem, the nearest mountains were many miles away, across the Jordan River. Interestingly, the fourth-century church historian Eusebius wrote: "Before the war [that destroyed Jerusalem in A.D. 70], the people of the church of Jerusalem were bidden in an oracle given by revelation to [people] worthy of it to depart from the city and to dwell in a city of Perea called Pella. To it those who believed in Christ migrated from Jerusalem." Eusebius may have meant that Christians applied Jesus' words in Mark 13:14 to their situation and fled to distant Pella in some foothills of the mountains across the Jordan.

In verses 15-16, Jesus stressed the urgency of escaping as quickly as possible. The judgment would be so severe and sudden that no individuals on the roofs of their homes would have enough time to come down or even dart inside their houses to fetch anything they valued. Most Jews in Jesus' day lived in simple homes made of stone or brick. Inside were plain furnishings and utensils. Often the family shared the home with their animals. Outside, a sturdy wooden ladder or narrow stone stairway led to the roof. The latter was made from dried clay (sometimes mixed with lime or stones) and branches laid over heavy wooden beams. The roof was frequently used for working or sleeping. In the midst of the emerging crisis, Jesus cautioned against those working out in the nearby fields rushing back to their homes to grab a cloak. This typically was an outer garment made from two pieces of woolen material that had been sewn together, making it well-suited for use as a night covering. Moreover, Jesus noted that the future situation would be so awful that fleeing in distress would be difficult for pregnant women as well for mothers nursing their babies (vs. 17).

Jesus admonished His followers to petition the Lord that the time of great distress would not erupt during winter, that is, the rainy season when attempting to cross the swollen Jordan River would be especially treacherous (vs. 18). But in any event, Jesus urged His disciples to run for refuge in the mountains. After all, the anguish experienced in those days would be unlike anything that had ever previously happened since God brought the world into existence. Indeed, this future time of suffering would be unmatched in its severity by any circumstance to take place again (vs. 19).

The Savior's words are apocalyptic, which means they reveal information about the future. This chapter of Mark falls into the same category as large portions of Daniel and Revelation. Mark 13 is not an easy chapter, and we cannot hope to resolve all the disputes that exist among evangelical scholars over its interpretation. By its nature, prophecy becomes increasingly clear only at the time of its fulfillment. Some details will remain obscure even after we have made our best efforts to comprehend them. So we should not become distracted by speculations about the obscure parts. Instead, we can learn from and act upon that which is clear.

For Jesus' followers living during the future time of unprecedented calamity, the situation would seem never-ending. In fact, the circumstance would be so intense and hellish that no person would survive apart from the Lord reducing the number of days of distress. He would do so because of His love for and commitment to His chosen people (vs. 20). We learn in 1 Peter 1:2 that the Father chose believers for salvation in accordance with His foreknowledge.

Christians have different viewpoints on how God's sovereignty relates to human freedom, especially in the area of salvation. Some believe God used His foreknowledge to look down the corridor of time to see which human beings will respond favorably to His offer of salvation and then called those individuals to salvation. Others believe God does not base His calling on foreknowledge, but rather sovereignly calls or elects certain individuals to salvation for His own glory. In any case, the salvation of believers comes "through sanctification of the Spirit." By this the apostle meant that God the Spirit has made unholy people holy. Moreover, through the Son's death for sin, He purifies His disciples for the Father's service.

Jesus warned His followers not to allow themselves to be delayed from fleeing by anyone who claimed that the Messiah had appeared (Mark 13:21). The situation would be horrible, but it would not be the time for the Messiah to return. Anyone at that time who claimed to be the Messiah or a divinely appointed prophet, regardless of how impressive his proof might seem, would be a liar who sought to fool as many of God's chosen people as possible (vs. 22). The Savior urged His disciples to avoid this deception by keeping up their guard. That is why He told them all these things long before they actually happened (vs. 23).

Now Jesus seems to have turned from discussing the fall of Jerusalem to His own return to earth. To clarify the sequence of events, the Savior described the signs that will appear before His second coming ("in those days," vs. 24) but after the demise of the holy city ("after that tribulation"). In verses 25-26, He alluded to Isaiah 13:10; 34:4, and Joel 2:10 to emphasize the intervention of God in history. The celestial objects in the sky will appear to be adversely affected. For instance, the sun will become dark, the moon will no longer shine, the stars will fall from the sky, and even the planets will be driven from their courses. Some understand Jesus' reference to these celestial bodies as being representative of spiritual powers in the heavenly realms over which God exercises His supreme control (see Eph. 1:21; 3:10; 6:12).

SUGGESTIONS TO TEACHERS

Jesus urged His followers to be on guard and alert for His return. Our attitude should be the same as the Christians in the first century A.D. We should be prepared for Jesus' coming at any moment, both as a church and as individuals.

1. BEING PREPARED FOR THE WORST. Some believers are too prone to expect to find lasting peace within this world. That's not to suggest we should say or do anything to deliberately provoke disfavor from others. It only means that while we hope and work for the best, we need to be prepared for the worst. We cannot let opposition discourage or deter us from proclaiming the Gospel throughout the planet (see Mark 13:10; Acts 1:8).

2. REFLECTING ON GOD'S UNCHANGING NATURE. People of every age need to learn that only those who are faithful to Jesus can enjoy security in the midst of a crumbling world. No time or place is free from upheavals. For that reason we must rest our confidence on the eternal promises of God, which cannot change. When we see institutions, nations, and even religious organizations in which we have placed our trust begin to fall apart, we can reflect on the changelessness of God. Our first duty is to know Him and obey His Word. Then we need to recognize that the future holds no surprises for Jesus. He is completely aware of what lies ahead and is preparing His people to deal with the disturbing events they will encounter. Those events only come with His permission. And along with the trials He gives grace to deal with them.

3. FINDING REASON TO HOPE. Unfortunately, many sermons about the Second Coming unnecessarily frighten the faithful. That's a shame, for Jesus certainly did not intend to petrify His disciples. Admittedly, terrifying events will come to pass. Even so, Jesus wanted us to know that the very calamities that destroy the peace of unbelievers can give Jesus' followers reason to hope. When distress is upon the world, we can look to the Messiah's return. On that day when the Son appears in power and glory, the Father will vindicate the faithful and the values by which we have lived. We will see—indeed, everyone will see, once and for all—that faith is stronger than doubt, good is more powerful than evil, and love is more triumphant than hate.

FOR ADULTS	■ TOPIC: The Return!

■ TOPIC: The Return!

■ QUESTIONS: 1. What was Jesus talking about when He referred to the "abomination of desolation" (Mark 13:14)? 2. Why will the days preceding Jesus' return be characterized by great distress? 3. How does the Savior want us to respond when we encounter spiritual frauds? 4. Why should we keep watch for Jesus' return? 5. How can we avoid the tendency to set dates and times for Jesus' return?

■ ILLUSTRATIONS:

The Joy of Being Prepared. While attending seminary, Joe and his wife lived in a small apartment with a tiny yard. Joe paid little attention to the property, though, because he felt overwhelmed by his studies. But when graduation approached, he tore into that yard with a vengeance.

Why did Joe do so? It's because his father and mother were coming, and this was their first visit to their son's home. Joe's dad was a consummate gardener, and so Joe did not want to disappoint his father when he appeared. Joe knew the joy of being prepared.

This is similar to our being prepared for the return of Jesus. Because He is the most special friend we have, we want to be sure to welcome Him properly. We can only anticipate what it will be like to see Him face-to-face.

However, our meeting will not be joyful unless we are prepared. We have to trim the sinful edges of our lives and uproot the weeds of transgression that sap our holiness. It's a constant battle. Fortunately, Joe knew the date of his dad's arrival, so he could be prepared in advance. But Jesus won't tell us ahead of time when He's going to return. So we can't slack off. Instead, we have to be ready all the time.

Watch as Well! John McMillan was a noteworthy Presbyterian missionary, evangelist, and educator to frontier western Pennsylvania. On his way to a meeting of the Presbytery of Pittsburgh, McMillan and Pastor Joseph Patterson, a member of the Board of Trustees of Jefferson College, stopped at an inn.

Two glasses of refreshment were placed on the table before the two ministers. Patterson closed his eyes and prayed. His prayer was extremely long. When he opened his eyes, there were two empty glasses on the table. McMillan is reputed to have said, "My brother, you must watch as well as pray!"

Jesus also urged vigilance. Faithful disciples are to be watchful and prepared for His return.

A Sudden Arrival. Julia had not seen her brother Judd in over three years. Now that they each had their own families and lived a thousand miles apart, getting together was not easy.

Several times when Judd was in the area on business, Julia had hoped Judd would stop by, but things did not work out. Now he was coming for sure. He had called on Saturday to say that after he completed his business in town, he would drop by no matter what—probably next Thursday or Friday.

Julia was excited about seeing Judd again, yet she thought she had plenty of time to get ready. Julia wanted everything to be in perfect order, but other things kept stealing her time—garage sales, church, lunch with friends, a bike hike with the kids, and so on.

By Wednesday noon, Julia realized that time was running out. After sorting the dirty laundry on the kitchen floor, she sat down at the counter to get organized by starting a "to do" list: laundry, dishes, beds, floors, bathrooms, windows, groceries, baking . . . Sighing, Julia thought, Sure glad Judd's not coming till tomorrow or Friday! Just then the doorbell rang. It was Judd—one day early!

In a similar way, we cannot determine ahead of time when Jesus will return. But when He does, will we be prepared? The key to spiritual preparedness is faithfully doing the Lord's work in anticipation of His eventual arrival.

FOR YOUTH

■ TOPIC: I'll Be Back

■ QUESTIONS: 1. How is God's decision to cut short the future time of great distress a sign of His grace to us (see Mark 13:20)? 2. What are some ways we can be on our guard against religious charlatans? 3. How do you think people living on earth will react when they see the calamities Jesus described in verses 24-25? 4. How does being mindful of Jesus' return help you to be holy and obedient to His teachings? 5. How can the truth of Jesus' return be used to help bring someone to faith in Him?

■ ILLUSTRATIONS:

Jesus' Promise. In 1984, Arnold Schwarzenegger starred in the science fiction thriller film *The Terminator*. His character is a merciless cyborg assassin sent back from the year 2029 by artificially intelligent computer-controlled machines. The Terminator's mission is to kill Sarah Connor, whose future son leads a human uprising against the machines.

Perhaps one of the most memorable lines from the movie is the Terminator's deadpan assertion "I'll be back." He makes the statement after being blocked from entering a police station. In response, he uses a stolen car to smash through the doors of the building and begin a killing rampage.

In contrast to the Terminator, when Jesus returns, He promises to end the conflict, destruction, and death that have plagued the human race since Cain killed Abel (see Gen. 4:8). Jesus' Second Coming will also usher in an era of unprecedented peace and hope, especially for those who have put their faith in Him for eternal life. Their prayer, as recorded in Revelation 22:20, is "Amen. Even so, come, Lord Jesus."

A State of Alert. Jostling for time in front of the bathroom mirror. Looking for the perfect outfit. Hunting for matching socks. Spilling juice at the breakfast table. Fraying nerves as the family piles into the car. Welcome to the typical Sunday morning for many Christians.

Getting ready to leave the house for church (especially in households with younger children) often means rushing from crisis to crisis. It can be a struggle to slip into the sanctuary or Sunday school classroom somewhere near the actual time the activities begin.

While Christians might be able to get away with such behavior on Sundays right now, Jesus asks much more from us when it comes to getting ready for His eventual return. Because "that day and that hour knoweth no man" (Mark 13:32), it is our duty to be always on guard and alert for the Savior's arrival. We cannot leave spiritual preparations to the last minute.

Watching and Waiting. What would it be like to truly be ready for Jesus' return? Dr. Joseph M. Stowell, president of Cornerstone University, tells about a friend who operates a home for mentally challenged children. Though marginally educable, these young ones have been exposed to the Gospel and believe in Jesus. They've all been taught that one day Jesus will come again and take them to a better place.

Can you guess what the home's biggest maintenance problem is? It's smudges on the windows left by the fingers and noses of children who run to the windows each day to look for Jesus' return. When the Savior comes back, will our fingers and noses be pressed against the window, too?

INSTRUCTIONS ABOUT WORSHIP

BACKGROUND SCRIPTURE: 1 Timothy 2:1-6; 3:14-16
DEVOTIONAL READING: Hebrews 8:6-12

KEY VERSE: There is one God, and one mediator
between God and men, the man Christ Jesus. (1 Timothy 2:5)

KING JAMES VERSION

1 TIMOTHY 2:1 I exhort therefore, that, first of all, supplications, prayers, intercessions, and giving of thanks, be made for all men; 2 For kings, and for all that are in authority; that we may lead a quiet and peaceable life in all godliness and honesty. 3 For this is good and acceptable in the sight of God our Saviour; 4 Who will have all men to be saved, and to come unto the knowledge of the truth. 5 For there is one God, and one mediator between God and men, the man Christ Jesus; 6 Who gave himself a ransom for all, to be testified in due time. . . .

3:14 These things write I unto thee, hoping to come unto thee shortly: 15 But if I tarry long, that thou mayest know how thou oughtest to behave thyself in the house of God, which is the church of the living God, the pillar and ground of the truth. 16 And without controversy great is the mystery of godliness: God was manifest in the flesh, justified in the Spirit, seen of angels, preached unto the Gentiles, believed on in the world, received up into glory.

NEW REVISED STANDARD VERSION

1 TIMOTHY 2:1 First of all, then, I urge that supplications, prayers, intercessions, and thanksgivings be made for everyone, 2 for kings and all who are in high positions, so that we may lead a quiet and peaceable life in all godliness and dignity. 3 This is right and is acceptable in the sight of God our Savior, 4 who desires everyone to be saved and to come to the knowledge of the truth. 5 For there is one God;
there is also one mediator between God and
humankind,
Christ Jesus, himself human,
6 who gave himself a ransom for all
—this was attested at the right time. . . .

3:14 I hope to come to you soon, but I am writing these instructions to you so that, 15 if I am delayed, you may know how one ought to behave in the household of God, which is the church of the living God, the pillar and bulwark of the truth. 16 Without any doubt, the mystery of our religion is great:
He was revealed in flesh,
vindicated in spirit,
seen by angels,
proclaimed among Gentiles,
believed in throughout the world,
taken up in glory.

HOME BIBLE READINGS

BACKGROUND

The Pastoral Epistles and Philemon are the only biblical letters Paul wrote to individuals. (All of his other letters were addressed to entire churches.) The letters to Timothy and Titus are called pastoral because they contain instructions to two young leaders about the issues of pastoring and caring for churches. We learn from these ancient sacred texts that believers in leadership need to be spiritually mature and disciplined to withstand the attacks of Satan—attacks that often originate from the people in their own congregations.

Timothy was given charge of the church at Ephesus, while Titus was to oversee the churches in Crete. These congregations needed trustworthy leaders who were beyond reproach. False teachers were springing up everywhere, and they needed to be eliminated. Paul's purpose in writing these letters was to arm Timothy and Titus for the spiritual battle of leadership. The apostle wanted to provide them with the authority and tools necessary to teach and protect the flocks that God had entrusted to them.

NOTES ON THE PRINTED TEXT

In 1 Timothy 2:1, Paul stressed the centrality of public prayer to a church's worship service. Corporate acts of prayer were not to be seen as dead liturgical formalities. Neither were they something to be neglected or rushed to get to the other parts of the service. Instead, the apostle urged Timothy to make prayer a priority when believers assembled together. Paul illustrated the aspects of corporate entreaties to God by using several different Greek words for prayer.

At the end of verse 1 the apostle tells us for whom to pray: everybody! Family, relatives, friends, people at work, leaders, and the lost everywhere should be named in our prayers. Such prayer does make a difference. If it were not effective to intercede for the needs and salvation of other people, God would not command us to do it. Paul singled out one group to represent the scope of such universal praying. He asked that prayers be made for "kings, and for all that are in authority" (vs. 2). The Greek term rendered "kings" called attention to the Roman emperor as well as to lesser rulers.

Paul emphasized praying for rulers because their decisions affect our daily lives and the privilege to freely worship. The Greek noun Paul used for "godliness" occurs eight times in 1 Timothy, once in 2 Timothy, once in Titus, and nowhere else in Paul's writings. The word describes our attitude and conduct as measured by God's standards and depicts a way of life that shows reverence for God as well as respect for other people. The noun translated "honesty" (1 Tim. 2:2) denotes the presence of such virtues as dignity, piety, and holiness. Our ability to live calm and quiet lives depends on our national leaders. Paul believed that prayer made a significant impact on governmental matters, brought about opportunities to further the Gospel, and enabled greater reverence to be shown to God.

Verse 3 gives us the primary motive for praying for all people as well as for our leaders. We should do so because it is wholesome and commendable. Likewise, praying for others is welcomed by God and pleases Him. After all, our Lord and Savior recognizes that when we bring to Him our petitions about others, it can lead to a favorable evangelistic climate. When we pray for the salvation of our leaders, some may indeed come to a saving "knowledge of the truth" (vs. 4). The Greek noun translated "knowledge" refers to a deep and accurate understanding that occurs at salvation and continues to grow afterward. "Truth" renders a noun that denotes the teachings of the Gospel concerning the Father's redemptive plan involving His Son.

Paul discussed the basis of prayer in verse 5. Since there is only "one God," He is Lord of the entire human race. Moreover, there is only one way for sinful humanity to approach Him, that is, through the Lord Jesus Christ (see Deut. 4:35, 39; 6:4; Ps. 86:10; Isa. 44:6; Mark 12:29; John 14:6; 1 Cor. 8:4; Eph. 4:6). Accordingly, the Redeemer is the "one mediator" (1 Tim. 2:5) between God and people. The Greek noun rendered "mediator" does not refer to someone who searches for an ill-defined, indeterminate compromise between God and sinners. Rather, the term denotes an intermediary who stands between two hostile parties and seeks to bring about reconciliation on terms that God alone has established (see Rom. 5:1-2). The historical backdrop for this concept comes from the ceremonial worship stipulated in the Old Testament. Both in the tabernacle and temple, priests interceded on behalf of their fellow Israelites before God. The priests, by offering animal sacrifices, atoned for the sins of the people.

The Greek noun rendered "man" (1 Tim. 2:5) in the phrase "the man Christ Jesus" is not the specific word referring only to the male gender, but a term that represents all of humanity. Paul chose that noun to emphasize that in Jesus' role as mediator, He acts on behalf of all people regardless of their gender, race, or nationality. Because Jesus is God and man, He is able to bridge the gap between the Father's holiness and humanity's sinfulness. Without the Son's mediating work, we would have no hope of establishing peace with the Father. Thus not only is it appropriate to pray for the salvation of others, it is essential that we do so. If people reject the Messiah, there is no other way for them to receive eternal life (see Acts 4:12). We must not neglect to pray for our lost friends, as well as for missionaries who carry the Good News to the unsaved in foreign lands around the globe.

Jesus' primary act as mediator was giving "himself a ransom" (1 Tim. 2:6). In the first century A.D., a ransom was the payment given to free a slave. The Son, acting on our behalf, paid the debt for our sins by dying on the cross. His death frees us from the slavery of sin. It was the Father's will that His Son's atonement for the sins of humanity become available for all humankind (see vs. 4). This truth does not mean that all people will be saved (see John 1:12). The good news that the Son gave His life to pay the debt for our sins must be received personally in order for salvation to occur. There are two interrelated ways for us to understand the phrase "to be testified in due time" (1 Tim. 2:6). In one sense, the Son's death at Calvary was itself a declaration of the Father's unrelenting commitment to make salvation available to the lost (see John 3:16). His eternal plan of redemption came to light at the divinely appointed time (see Gal. 4:4; 2 Tim. 1:9-10; Titus 2:11-14; 3:4-7). In another sense, the Father has commissioned believers to proclaim the testimony about the Son's redemptive work to people across the planet (see Matt. 28:19-20; Acts 1:8).

After Paul left Timothy in Ephesus, he hoped he would be able to return to his colleague soon. When the apostle realized that circumstances could keep him away longer than anticipated, he wrote 1 Timothy to provide his faithful representative with instructions for the congregations under his care. These guidelines gave direction not only in the selection of church officers, but also in the matter of proper behavior within the church itself (3:14-15). The directions were important because Timothy was managing things in "the house of God" (vs. 15). This is not a literal reference to a congregational building, for at that time the church met in homes scattered throughout various cities. Paul's reference is to the believers themselves, who make up the church, and emphasizes the family nature of the Body of Christ. The apostle also described the church as "the pillar and ground of the truth." In ancient times, pillars were used as much for display as they were for support. The statue of a famous person was often placed atop a pillar so that it would stand out from its surroundings. As a pillar the church is to proudly display the truth of its faith so that others will be attracted to the saving message of the Gospel. Also, as the foundation and bulwark of the truth of God's Word, the church protects the faith entrusted to it from perversion and error.

The Greek noun translated "mystery" (vs. 16) refers to a truth that was once hidden but has now been revealed through the Messiah. The message of salvation is intended to promote "godliness" (or "piety"; 1 Tim. 3:16), that is, reverence for and devotion to God (see Rom. 1:5). The words recorded in 1 Timothy 3:16 probably came from a hymn that believers sung in the early church. There's no doubt that the Messiah is the central focus of these creedal statements. Paul described the Son as having been "manifest in the flesh," which referred to the event of His incarnation. Although the Son previously existed as God, He assumed humanity in order to fully accomplish our salvation (see John 1:14; Heb. 2:14). He took on a natural human body without diminishing His deity. The phrase "justified in the Spirit" (1 Tim. 3:16) points to the work of the Holy Spirit in confirming Jesus' person through His claims, miracles, and resurrection (see Rom. 1:4). Some commentators, however, see this as a reference to Jesus' Spirit and regard this as an allusion to Christ's righteousness.

The heavenly host witnessed every moment of Jesus' ministry, and in this way He was "seen of angels." Angels ministered to Jesus after His temptation in the wilderness, and during His anguish in the Garden of Gethsemane (see Matt. 4:11; Luke 22:43). Certainly prior to the Incarnation, Jesus was the object of worship for legions of angels. Paul spoke of how people from the various nations put their faith in the Messiah. The climax of the Son's ministry came after His death on the cross, when He was resurrected and taken up into heaven to be with His Father in glory (see Acts 1:2-9). While the Son's glory was veiled for most of His earthly ministry, the promise of His ascension into heaven is that He will one day come again in the same way He left (see vs. 11). He will return to share His glory with His church and to judge those who refused to believe on His name (see John 3:36; 5:24-30; 2 Thess. 1:5-10).

SUGGESTIONS TO TEACHERS

Imagine what life would be like if we rarely talked to our loved ones, had no opportunities to meet new people, and never took the time to learn new things. Eventually, we would become lonely, isolated, and dull individuals. In the spiritual realm, we need to talk with God every day, reach out to the lost with the Gospel, and increase our understanding of God's Word. Unless we take the time to do these three things as a church, we will become spiritually weak and insipid. When prayer, evangelism, and Bible learning are a consistent part of our corporate worship, we will become spiritually dynamic and effective servants of Christ.

1. MAKING PRAYER A PRIORITY. It has been suggested that the best way to get a sick church on its feet is to first get it on its knees. It has also been suggested that a healthy church can grow even stronger through regular and consistent prayer. In 1 Timothy 2:1-6, we learn that a church cannot spiritually prosper and grow unless its members engage in prayer. Paul recognized this, and thus urged Timothy to make it a priority in the corporate worship of the church at Ephesus.

2. REMEMBERING TO PRAY FOR OTHERS. Sadly, our prayers are often restricted to our loved ones and friends. In verse 2, Paul stated that we should also pray for rulers and other leaders in high positions of authority. The primary reason given is that God's people might be able to live in a quiet and peaceful manner. They will be free to worship Him fully and honor Him in all their activities. By praying for their leaders, believers set a noble example for others. God's people demonstrate their trust in Him to handle their nation's economic, social, and political problems.

3. EVANGELIZING AND THE ROLE OF PRAYER. Take a few moments to encourage the class members to think about how they came to faith in the Messiah.

Encourage them to write their testimony down on paper. They could memorize it along with some appropriate Scripture verses dealing with salvation. Urge them to pray for opportunities to witness to unsaved loved ones and acquaintances. When those opportunities arise, they can then use their testimonies along with Scripture to tell people about the Savior.

FOR ADULTS	■ TOPIC: The Search for Meaning

■ TOPIC: The Search for Meaning

■ QUESTIONS: 1. Why does God want us to pray for others? 2. What are some specific things you can do to bring others to a saving knowledge of the truth? 3. Why would the Father give His Son as a ransom for all people? 4. In what sense is your local congregation part of the "church of the living God" (1 Tim. 3:15)? 5. How does believing the "mystery" (vs. 16) about the Savior promote "godliness" in His followers?

■ **ILLUSTRATIONS:**

Centered in Christ. It's typical for adults to want their lives to count for something, that is, to have enduring significance. There are times, though, when a person's well-intended search for meaning becomes misguided.

Elyn Saks, in her book titled *The Center Cannot Hold*, describes a situation in which the very core of one's identity begins to unravel. This is a state of disorganization that is characterized by an inner sense of chaos and confusion. It doesn't really matter, either, whether the circumstance is real or imagined, to those who feel as if their existence is disintegrating.

Where do believers go when they sense they need to put their lives back together? The answer is the Lord Jesus Christ. He alone must become the true center of their identity. When He is the foundation of their existence, He gives genuine meaning and lasting relevance to their lives.

Answered Prayers. Clara, an elderly Christian woman, had many unsaved family members for whom she regularly prayed. Year after year, she continued to petition God, yet this saint never saw one of her prayers answered during her lifetime. She was inspired to pray because of 1 Timothy 2:4, which says that God wants "all men to be saved, and to come unto the knowledge of the truth."

One of these family members was a niece named Amy, who was only a teenager at the time of Clara's death. Several years after her aunt passed away, Amy, her husband, and their two young daughters moved into a house across the street from a family of Christians. These believers greeted their neighbors and helped them clear their property so that grass could be planted.

Eventually, Amy became curious about her neighbor's local church and asked whether she and her family could attend with them. The first time Amy heard the

Gospel, her heart was opened, and she received the gift of salvation. Soon afterward, her husband put his faith in the Messiah. Later, Amy's sister, aunt, uncle, and cousins also were saved in that church. Many months later, Amy came to realize that the church she and her family members were attending was the same congregation in which her Aunt Clara had prayed faithfully for their salvation!

A Godly Life. "You know, pastor, not everyone's cut out to be a Father Damien," Gil told his minister after the Sunday sermon. That morning's message had included the account of Belgian missionary, Father Damien, who, in the late 1800s, volunteered to oversee a leper colony on the Hawaiian island of Molokai.

Damien, whose given name was Joseph de Veuster, ministered to the lepers' spiritual needs but became their physician as well, since very few medical personnel would come to the island. Damien also worked with the Hawaiian government to improve the water supply, dwellings, and food supply of the settlement. After five years, Father Damien's actions inspired numerous others to devote themselves to the colony. But eventually the minister himself contracted leprosy and died on the island in 1889.

To Gil, it all sounded pretty incredible. "I'm no martyr," he told his pastor. "You don't have to be," Gil's minister replied. "God doesn't call everyone to go to an island and die for His sake. But He does call all of us to lead holy lives—wherever we are." Or, as this week's Scripture passage states, we are to "lead a quiet and peaceable life in all godliness and honesty" (1 Tim. 2:2).

■ **TOPIC:** Sing and Celebrate

■ **QUESTIONS:** 1. Who are some leaders in your community who could benefit from your prayers on their behalf? 2. In what ways can you give thanks to the Father for the saving gift of His Son? 3. Why is it important for believers to conduct themselves properly when they gather together for worship? 4. What is the basis for seeing local churches around the world as the "pillar and ground of the truth" (1 Tim. 3:15)? 5. What difference has the truth of the Gospel made in your life?

■ **ILLUSTRATIONS:**

A Goal Worth Celebrating. Spiritual retreats can be a wonderful experience for saved teens to sing to the Lord Jesus and celebrate with their peers their shared faith in Him. Often, adolescents devote a week or a weekend to read the Bible and evaluate their lives. However, what teen has time to do that on a daily, or even weekly, basis?

The answer can be found in an old hymn by William Longstaff. The song is "Take Time to Be Holy":

Take time to be holy,
The world rushes on.
Much time spend in secret
With Jesus alone;
By looking to Jesus,
Like Him thou shalt be;
Thy friends in thy conduct
His likeness shall see.

This hymn reminds younger believers that holiness is indeed a time-consuming activity. Yet the Savior calls them (and all His spiritual children) to set aside time in order to get to know Him better. When they make the sacrifice, they will gradually become more Christlike. Now that's a goal worth singing about and celebrating!

Who Needs Prayer? Samuel's daughter had been rebelling against God for quite some time. Lisa had abandoned her family by leaving home, and was living as far from God as she could. But one night, this teenager awoke with the distinct feeling that someone was praying for her.

In fact, a lot of people were praying for Lisa. The entire church family her father pastored was talking to God about her. During their midweek prayer meeting, a member recommended that they should pray for Lisa.

Two days later, Lisa came home. When she learned the details of who had been praying for her, Lisa turned her life over to the Lord. Later, during Lisa's time of study in Scripture, she learned from 1 Timothy 2:3 that her salvation reflected God's will for her life. Indeed, it was a "good and acceptable" outcome to the Savior.

Motivation for Prayer. A cartoon portrayed a tiny insect peering up at a monster insect. After staring at the monster for a while, the tiny insect said, "And what kind of bug are you?" "I'm a praying mantis," the monster said.

"That's absurd!" said the tiny insect. "Bugs don't pray!" With that, the praying mantis grabbed the tiny bug around the throat and squeezed. The bug's eyes bulged, and it screamed, "Lord, help me!"

Some people are like that tiny bug. They ignore—even ridicule—the sort of prayer enjoined in 1 Timothy 2:1 until they get squeezed. Then they scream, "Lord, help me!" What motivates you to keep praying?

QUALIFICATIONS FOR LEADERS

BACKGROUND SCRIPTURE: 1 Timothy 3:1-13
DEVOTIONAL READING: 1 Peter 5:1-5

KEY VERSE: Holding the mystery of the faith in a pure conscience. (1 Timothy 3:9)

2

KING JAMES VERSION

1 TIMOTHY 3:1 This is a true saying, if a man desire the office of a bishop, he desireth a good work. 2 A bishop then must be blameless, the husband of one wife, vigilant, sober, of good behaviour, given to hospitality, apt to teach; 3 Not given to wine, no striker, not greedy of filthy lucre; but patient, not a brawler, not covetous; 4 One that ruleth well his own house, having his children in subjection with all gravity; 5 (For if a man know not how to rule his own house, how shall he take care of the church of God?) 6 Not a novice, lest being lifted up with pride he fall into the condemnation of the devil. 7 Moreover he must have a good report of them which are without; lest he fall into reproach and the snare of the devil.

8 Likewise must the deacons be grave, not double-tongued, not given to much wine, not greedy of filthy lucre; 9 Holding the mystery of the faith in a pure conscience. 10 And let these also first be proved; then let them use the office of a deacon, being found blameless. 11 Even so must their wives be grave, not slanderers, sober, faithful in all things. 12 Let the deacons be the husbands of one wife, ruling their children and their own houses well. 13 For they that have used the office of a deacon well purchase to themselves a good degree, and great boldness in the faith which is in Christ Jesus.

NEW REVISED STANDARD VERSION

1 TIMOTHY 3:1 The saying is sure: whoever aspires to the office of bishop desires a noble task. 2 Now a bishop must be above reproach, married only once, temperate, sensible, respectable, hospitable, an apt teacher, 3 not a drunkard, not violent but gentle, not quarrelsome, and not a lover of money. 4 He must manage his own household well, keeping his children submissive and respectful in every way— 5 for if someone does not know how to manage his own household, how can he take care of God's church? 6 He must not be a recent convert, or he may be puffed up with conceit and fall into the condemnation of the devil. 7 Moreover, he must be well thought of by outsiders, so that he may not fall into disgrace and the snare of the devil.

8 Deacons likewise must be serious, not double-tongued, not indulging in much wine, not greedy for money; 9 they must hold fast to the mystery of the faith with a clear conscience. 10 And let them first be tested; then, if they prove themselves blameless, let them serve as deacons. 11 Women likewise must be serious, not slanderers, but temperate, faithful in all things. 12 Let deacons be married only once, and let them manage their children and their households well; 13 for those who serve well as deacons gain a good standing for themselves and great boldness in the faith that is in Christ Jesus.

225

Monday, March 7	1 Peter 5:1-5	*Tending the Flock of God*
Tuesday, March 8	Isaiah 9:13-17	*Leading God's People Astray*
Wednesday, March 9	Titus 1:5-9	*Leaders as God's Stewards*
Thursday, March 10	Hebrews 13:1-7	*Imitate Your Leaders' Faith*
Friday, March 11	Hebrews 13:17-25	*Obey Your Leaders*
Saturday, March 12	1 Peter 4:7-11	*Good Stewards of God's Grace*
Sunday, March 13	1 Timothy 3:1-13	*Qualifications for Leaders*

BACKGROUND

Perhaps the most extended image of the church is its representation as the body of Christ. This image emphasizes the connection of the church, as a group of believers, with the Messiah. After all, salvation, in all of its complexity, is in large part a result of union with the Son. In fact, Christ in the believer is the basis of belief and hope (see Gal. 2:20; Col. 1:27).

The image of the body of Christ also speaks of the interconnectedness between all the persons who make up the church. Here we see that Christian faith is not to be defined merely in terms of individual relationship to the Lord (see 1 Cor. 12:12-31). There is a mutuality in this understanding of the body in which each believer encourages and builds up the others (see Gal. 6:2; Eph. 4:15-16).

NOTES ON THE PRINTED TEXT

In order for our faith communities to grow and thrive, they need godly spiritual leadership. Paul applauded the desire of those who aspired to shepherd the flock of God, implying that ministry opportunities existed for such individuals (1 Tim. 3:1). The first qualification Paul mentioned is that overseers be "blameless" (vs. 2). That means that no one could bring a just cause for censure against them.

The next requirement specifies that an overseer be "the husband of one wife." Some suggest this means that overseers were not to be divorced and remarried and prefer the verse to be translated "a man married only once." Meanwhile, others think Paul was referring to monogamy and note that polygamy was widespread in the first century A.D. They think the rendering of the verse should be "devoted solely to his wife" (see 1 Tim 3:12; 5:9; Titus 1:6). Regardless of which option is preferred, it's clear that overseers were to be sexually pure in conduct and thought. If they were married, they were to have no romantic ties with any person but their spouse.

Paul stated that overseers were to be "vigilant" (1 Tim. 3:2), a word that refers to abstaining from the immoderate use of alcohol. "Sober" denotes the virtue of curbing one's sensual impulses and desires. The word translated "of good behavior" points to individuals who are appropriate and modest in their conduct. When present together in church leaders, these qualifications show that their lives demonstrate orderliness.

They seek to be Christlike in their thinking, Spirit-filled in their demeanor, and honoring to God in their words and deeds.

During the first century A.D., the inns throughout the Mediterranean world were often places of heavy drinking and fighting. As a result, it was essential that the overseer set an example for the rest of the flock by providing hospitality to strangers. Furthermore, because church leaders provided teaching in faith and doctrine to the members of their congregations, it was imperative that they have some skill in that area. While not all the overseers specialized in teaching, some did take time to prepare for this valuable ministry. Just the same, all shepherds of God's flock needed to have some ability in communicating the basic truths of the faith.

Paul said church leaders should not be addicted to alcohol, regardless of how common drunkenness might be in the surrounding culture. Also, the apostle forbade overseers from being "a striker" (vs. 3), a word that denotes someone who is contentious and pugnacious. Moreover, rather than being greedy and covetous, church leaders were to be "patient," a term that refers to those who are equitable and even-tempered in their behavior. The opposite disposition would be individuals who were prone to harshness and violence in their dealings with others. Overseers could undercut this tendency by cultivating a kind and peaceable demeanor, one in which they sought to be considerate of the feelings of those to whom they ministered.

Paul considered it important that an overseer be someone who managed "his own house" (vs. 4). This included his children, whether younger or older, respecting and obeying him. As he supervised family matters, he was to remain considerate and even-handed in his approach and thereby maintain his reputation as a godly parent. The apostle argued that such a testimony would demonstrate an ability to rule well in the church (vs. 5).

Paul insisted those chosen as overseers be mature believers and not new converts. An inflated sense of importance would cause a novice in the faith to fall and incur the same type of judgment imposed on Satan. This possibly refers to the overseer's loss of position due to pride (vs. 6). Others understand this verse to be referring to the condemnation exacted by the devil on arrogant believers. The idea is that Satan becomes the agent whom God uses to discipline conceited, wayward Christians and bring them to repentance and restoration in the Church (see Matt. 18:15-20; 1 Tim. 1:20; 2 Tim. 2:26). In any case, not only were overseers to be respected in the church, but they were also to be looked upon favorably by those outside the faith. A congregation that selects overseers with poor reputations for integrity would not only bring reproach upon itself but also leave the leaders open to Satan's attack (1 Tim. 3:7; see 1 Pet. 5:8). The devil seems able to make the most of incidents where Christian leaders fall.

In 1 Timothy 3:8, Paul insisted that deacons be believers known for their serious demeanor and honorable character. Likewise, they were not to be two-faced or deceitful. This meant they were not to give conflicting statements, depending on the situation. The service of the deacons probably took them to many different homes in the faith community. It was essential that they not tell contradictory stories, but be consistent in their speech.

Like the overseer, the deacon was not to excessively drink alcohol. While the consumption of liquor was prevalent in Paul's day, church leaders were to exercise care so as to not begin to come under its intoxicating influence (see Eph. 5:18). Interestingly, Timothy himself had totally abstained from wine and had to be instructed to drink some for his health (see 1 Tim. 5:23). Like the overseer, the deacon was not to be motivated by a desire for financial gain (3:3, 8). While Paul would have more to say later about lovers of money (see 6:6-10), here he stressed the need for church leaders to be free from greed. The deacons in particular, as distributors of goods to the poor, needed to be people who could be trusted with the material resources of the church.

Even though deacons normally did not teach, Paul literally insisted that they hold fast to the "mystery of the faith" (3:9). By this the apostle meant they were to remain doctrinally sound. In this regard, to possess a "pure conscience" meant to have a heart free from any awareness of overt sin. The idea is that not only did deacons remain committed to the revealed truths of the Christian faith, but also they reflected these teachings in their lives. While it is essential that our beliefs be free from doctrinal error, it is also imperative that our lives provide an example of what we believe. If we say that Jesus is Lord, we must act as though He is in charge of our existence. We must never forget that non-Christians are watching to see whether our lives measure up to what we profess to believe.

Like overseers, deacons were not to be recent converts (vss. 6, 10). The Greek verb rendered "proved" (vs. 10) refers to individuals undergoing a time of scrutiny to ensure they were blameless. In the case of those who aspired to be deacons, the period of examination was to verify they were spiritually mature and emotionally ready to assume their ministerial responsibilities. The same process of examination is implied in the long list of qualifications given for the overseers. When the prospective candidates had proven that they were serious about their faith, they were then to be considered for the position of elder.

The Greek noun rendered "wives" (vs. 11) refers either to the spouses of deacons or women who were deacons. The women under consideration were to be people of integrity and show the same strength of character as their male counterparts. Since these women would be involved in the ministry of the church, it was important that their character be examined. For instance, like the deacons, the women would be involved in many of the homes of the congregation. So it was essential that they not engage in gossip or malicious talk. If gossip separates the closest friends (Prov. 16:28), it can certainly divide an entire congregation. In addition to refraining from slander, the women were also to be modest and faithful in every area of their lives

(1 Tim. 3:11). Indeed, the one overriding point of this chapter is that those chosen for leadership offices must be of proven character. We would do well to keep that in mind in our congregations today. In our search for willing workers, it is easy to prematurely seize the opportunity to enlist someone who is anxious to help without taking the time to examine his or her character.

The requirements of faithfulness in marriage and well-managed households applied to deacons as well as to overseers (1 Tim. 3:12). For those overseers and deacons who served well, there was ample spiritual reward. The phrase "purchase to themselves a good degree" (vs. 13) most likely refers to the respect church leaders enjoyed among the members of their congregation as well as the approval of God. Those ministers who worked hard and did a good job could look forward to being esteemed by other Christians and laying up treasure for themselves in heaven.

SUGGESTIONS TO TEACHERS

Paul knew that the future of the church depended, to a great degree, on the quality of its leaders. Thus he selected others (such as Timothy and Titus) who could serve as good leaders. But beyond that, Paul described the type of people that ministers should desire as their successors. Should the standard in today's churches be any lower? God calls all of us, as believers, to evaluate our lives by these criteria so that we can serve Him in any way He sees fit.

1. QUALITY OF RELATIONSHIP WITH JESUS. Paul intended that church leaders not be new converts and that they be those whom the church had adequate time to test. The apostle wanted overseers and deacons to be those who had matured in their faith. No one can change the quantity of time that he or she has known Jesus. But each of us can seek, as time passes, to ensure that our relationships with Him not merely grow older, but deeper.

2. QUALITY OF RELATIONSHIP WITH FAMILY. Paul specifically stated that church leaders should be chosen from those who served first as good family leaders. Paul recognized that those who abused their spouse or their children would also abuse the church. All believers need to live in faithfulness to Christ not only before their broader communities, but also before those who see them the most and know them the best. If our spouses or children would not nominate us for church office, then perhaps we should not serve.

3. QUALITY OF RELATIONSHIP WITH FELLOW CHRISTIANS. Perhaps you have known people who moved into ministry for selfish reasons. Do such people serve God or His church fruitfully? Thankfully a person's human sinfulness does not prevent God from working through him or her, but the Lord works through people far more easily when they seek to live as servants, not bosses.

4. QUALITY OF RELATIONSHIP WITH THE NON-CHRISTIAN COMMUNITY. The church can neither let the world choose its leaders nor set the criteria by which good church leaders are known. But how can nonbelievers respect the church if its leaders do not live by the high standards the congregation itself proclaims? From this we see that even the world holds high expectations for church leaders.

FOR ADULTS

■ **TOPIC:** Choosing a Good Leader

■ **QUESTIONS:** 1. What can the existing leadership in your congregation do to encourage recruitment and training of future church leaders? 2. Among the virtues Paul listed for overseers, which ones do you most often see among the leaders in your congregation? 3. In what way is a person's relationship with family members a good test of his or her potential for church leadership? 4. Do you feel the standards for church leaders should be higher than those of other church members? Why or why not? 5. Why did Paul recommend that an otherwise highly qualified new Christian be given a time of testing before becoming an overseer or deacon?

■ **ILLUSTRATIONS:**

Foundations for Effective Leadership. From its earliest days, the church was an organized body of believers, not a collection of individuals doing as they pleased. Therefore, congregational leadership is critical. Godly, effective leaders are needed because, without them, there could be anarchy in which everyone does what is right in their own eyes.

Clearly, then, congregations need good leaders to responsibly carry out their missions. Also, churches need qualified leaders to facilitate their spiritual ministries. A well-organized congregation lacking spiritual vitality is just another organization. We must be certain that our churches are not cut off from the life of Christ.

Whitefield's Power. In the years just before the American Revolution, God used George Whitefield, an associate of John Wesley, to help bring revival to the colonies. Like Wesley, Whitefield possessed an amazing mind, a convincing preaching style, and most importantly, a heart for God.

On one occasion, Whitefield was preaching in Philadelphia. Benjamin Franklin, the great American statesman, chose to attend the service. Near the end of his sermon, Whitefield asked his hearers to make a contribution to an orphanage he had founded in Savannah, Georgia.

The appeal first upset Franklin. He thought to himself, "Why should I give money for children who live a thousand miles from here when there are plenty of poor children here in Philadelphia?" Whitefield continued to speak. Franklin felt moved and decided to put his copper coins in the offering plate. Whitefield continued. Franklin felt so convinced that he gave his silver coins, then a gold coin, and finally emptied his pockets for Whitefield's worthy cause!

What motivated Franklin to give? Whitefield certainly was "apt to teach" (1 Tim. 3:2). But was he "greedy of filthy lucre" (vs. 3)? No, none of the offerings he collected went into his own pocket. Whitefield was known and respected even among people outside the church (such as Franklin). Whitefield lived a life that was "blameless" (vs. 2).

A Little Maturity. When Jeff was born, his dad was a pastor. Ten years later, Jeff's dad was elected district superintendent. One year, Jeff's father asked him to serve as a page at the annual district business meeting. The pastors and elected lay delegates carried out their business in good form. Jeff knew then he was headed for the pastorate, and dreamed of the day when he would have the right to speak at such events.

The day came. Fresh out of seminary, Jeff was a pastor of his own church. He could hardly wait for the district conference when he could be seated within the official body, cast his ballot, and even speak. The first few years, Jeff must have driven other people crazy. He felt a need to speak (or at least ask a question) on nearly every issue. He felt that was his right, and nothing was going to hinder him from exercising it! Years later, as Jeff looked back on those early days of his ministry as a pastor, he recognized how foolish he must have looked.

Paul told Timothy to be wary of giving too much power to spiritual rookies. The apostle knew they weren't ready for it. A little maturity goes a long way.

FOR YOUTH

■ TOPIC: Everybody Can't Do It

■ QUESTIONS: 1. Do you have any desire to become a leader in your church, and if so, what is motivating you? 2. Why do you think a church leader needs to be a person of virtue? 3. What type of parents command the respect of their children? 4. Why did Paul emphasize the need for church members to honor their parish leaders? 5. What steps can young people take to prepare themselves for effective and faithful church leadership?

■ **ILLUSTRATIONS:**

Who Me, Lead? After one glance at Paul's high standards for Christian leaders, our first response might be that we are not qualified for the task. Of course, it is good to be humble rather than over-confident. But the Bible tells about great leaders—Moses and Jeremiah, for example—who felt unqualified for their tasks.

When we feel that way, we open the doors for God to exercise His love, wisdom, and power in our lives. Jesus sent the Holy Spirit to be our teacher and helper. He gives us all the wisdom and strength we need. In fact, Christ's power can be magnified in our weaknesses.

The Holy Spirit gifts the church with leaders to guide others in the enormous task of doing the work of the church. When we open ourselves to the Spirit, He uses us to help others come to saving faith in Christ. This is what it means to be a true spiritual leader!

A Girl of Remarkable Character. First Timothy 3:1-13 contains a formidable list of virtues that are to be found in overseers and deacons. Initially, we might assume that only those who have lived a long life could have such a remarkable character—that is, until we take the time to consider the testimony of Anne Frank.

Anne was a Dutch Jewish girl who died at the age of 15 of typhus in the Nazi concentration camp at Bergen-Belsen. She had some astonishing wisdom for one so young. For example, she said, "Parents can only give good advice or put them on the right paths, but the final forming of a person's character lies in their own hands." For saved teens, this implies that it's never too early to pursue godliness, especially if they want to be future leaders in their church.

Who knows what wisdom Anne might have passed on to her peers had the Nazis not ended her life while she was still an adolescent? Nevertheless, her diary expresses a person with unusual insights and maturity. Even as a young girl, she had a virtuous disposition. Despite horrors surrounding her in war-torn Amsterdam, Holland, she still wrote, "Whoever is happy will make others happy too. He who has the courage and faith will never perish in misery." May these sentiments be true of us, especially as we move into leadership positions in the church.

The Infection from a False Leader. Paul's admonitions to Timothy concerning the qualifications for overseers and deacons were intended to prevent sincere but misguided individuals from becoming church leaders. In his book, *The 17 Indisputable Laws of Teamwork*, John Maxwell relates the story of how incorrect leadership can drag people down.

At a football game, five people came to a first aid station feeling ill. The attending physician asked questions and found out that all five had bought drinks from the same stadium vendor. He quickly diagnosed food poisoning.

Just as quickly, the physician sent a messenger to the public address announcer to tell the entire crowd to avoid all stadium drinks. The physician thought his announcement would help reduce the problem, but, before too long, people all over the stadium were falling ill. They had heard the announcement and assumed that they too had consumed a tainted drink.

But further investigation revealed that the stadium drinks were harmless. The first five victims had each eaten a salad at the same problem restaurant on the way to the game. As soon as the public address system announced that people could return to purchasing drinks, a stadium full of people felt physically better. Erroneous information, spread even accidentally by one "false leader," infected thousands of people.

PREPARE FOR LEADERSHIP

BACKGROUND SCRIPTURE: 1 Timothy 4:6-16
DEVOTIONAL READING: Philippians 3:17—4:1

KEY VERSE: Take heed unto thyself,
and unto the doctrine. (1 Timothy 4:16)

KING JAMES VERSION

1 TIMOTHY 4:6 If thou put the brethren in remembrance of these things, thou shalt be a good minister of Jesus Christ, nourished up in the words of faith and of good doctrine, whereunto thou hast attained. 7 But refuse profane and old wives' fables, and exercise thyself rather unto godliness. 8 For bodily exercise profiteth little: but godliness is profitable unto all things, having promise of the life that now is, and of that which is to come. 9 This is a faithful saying and worthy of all acceptation. 10 For therefore we both labour and suffer reproach, because we trust in the living God, who is the Saviour of all men, specially of those that believe.

11 These things command and teach. 12 Let no man despise thy youth; but be thou an example of the believers, in word, in conversation, in charity, in spirit, in faith, in purity. 13 Till I come, give attendance to reading, to exhortation, to doctrine. 14 Neglect not the gift that is in thee, which was given thee by prophecy, with the laying on of the hands of the presbytery.
15 Meditate upon these things; give thyself wholly to them; that thy profiting may appear to all. 16 Take heed unto thyself, and unto the doctrine; continue in them: for in doing this thou shalt both save thyself, and them that hear thee.

NEW REVISED STANDARD VERSION

1 TIMOTHY 4:6 If you put these instructions before the brothers and sisters, you will be a good servant of Christ Jesus, nourished on the words of the faith and of the sound teaching that you have followed. 7 Have nothing to do with profane myths and old wives' tales. Train yourself in godliness, 8 for, while physical training is of some value, godliness is valuable in every way, holding promise for both the present life and the life to come. 9 The saying is sure and worthy of full acceptance. 10 For to this end we toil and struggle, because we have our hope set on the living God, who is the Savior of all people, especially of those who believe.

11 These are the things you must insist on and teach. 12 Let no one despise your youth, but set the believers an example in speech and conduct, in love, in faith, in purity. 13 Until I arrive, give attention to the public reading of scripture, to exhorting, to teaching. 14 Do not neglect the gift that is in you, which was given to you through prophecy with the laying on of hands by the council of elders. 15 Put these things into practice, devote yourself to them, so that all may see your progress. 16 Pay close attention to yourself and to your teaching; continue in these things, for in doing this you will save both yourself and your hearers.

HOME BIBLE READINGS

BACKGROUND

In 1 Timothy 4:10, Paul stated that the Father is the Savior of all people, and in particular those who put their faith in the Son. Paul's statement reflects the fact that Jesus died for all of humanity (see 1 John 2:2). Three differing views have been put forward regarding what the apostle meant: (1) *Universal-salvation interpretation.* Eventually all people will be saved from sin and punishment. But this view contradicts Scripture, which teaches that only those who respond to Jesus' work in faith will be redeemed (see John 1:12). (2) *Potential/actual interpretation.* Because Jesus died for all, all have the potential of being saved. However, only those who trust in the Son will actually be redeemed. (3) *Temporal/eternal interpretation.* Jesus is the Savior of all in the sense that He gives life to all. Unbelievers benefit from the earthly life He provides, while Christians additionally enjoy His gift of eternal life.

NOTES ON THE PRINTED TEXT

Paul, after describing the doctrinal error of the false teachers (see 1 Tim. 4:1-5), told his younger protege how to fortify himself and the churches under his care against the devious message of the impostors. Timothy's first responsibility was to inform believers about the deception of Satan. Also, Timothy was to teach proper doctrine in a calm and articulate manner. This would make him a "good minister of Jesus Christ" (vs. 6).

Paul repeated a warning he had given in regard to "profane and old wives' fables" (vs. 7; compare 1:4). These were the Jewish tales and legends that embellished the Old Testament chronologies and stories. The apostle instructed Timothy to avoid them and refuse to be pulled into discussions about them. His focus was to be solely on the sound teachings of the faith. Instead of concerning himself with Jewish myths, which were fit only for those who were irreverent and gullible, Timothy was to keep on training himself for godliness. The Greek verb rendered "exercise" (4:7) conveys the idea of disciplining oneself for a particular task. In this case, Timothy was to make piety the pursuit of his life.

Even today, believers have much more important things to do than listen to pointless stories told by misguided teachers. Jesus' followers are to exercise their spiritual muscles so they can continue to grow strong in their faith. Paul's reference to spiritual training prompted him to bring up the relative value of physical exercise. The apostle acknowledged that such discipline had little value (vs. 8). Paul was not seeking to discourage physical fitness. It does have its place. But the gain of physical training, while noteworthy, pales by way of comparison to what godliness can accomplish.

Spiritual exercise enriches our soul and spirit as well as our bodies. Godly living is usually much healthier than the way of the world. And not only is the scope of benefits wider, but also the spiritual benefits last for all eternity. Even if the results of physical exercise are temporarily advantageous, the eternal value of godliness still dwarfs them by comparison. Thus, without minimizing exercise, Christians need to set a more holistic standard than the world. We must find a balance that incorporates physical and spiritual development.

In verse 9, Paul highlighted his message by affirming it to be reliable, dependable, and meriting complete acceptance. Interpreters are split on whether the apostle's declaration goes with the statement in the previous verse or with the verses after it. In either case, the apostle used athletic metaphors to make his point. For instance, the Greek verb translated "labour" (vs. 10) pictures someone who works to the point of exhaustion. In the process, the evangelists suffered "reproach" to proclaim the Gospel with all their energy. Thankfully, persecution did not stop Paul and his colleagues from encouraging godliness among believers while protecting the Gospel against deceitful and futile thinking. Since their hope was firmly placed in the living God, the apostle and his associates could toil knowing that their efforts would not be in vain. This hope was not just for them but for all who had faith in the Son.

As Paul's representative to the churches in and around Ephesus, Timothy was to continue to command and teach the need for self-discipline and godliness. The apostle made Timothy's role clear: He was to pass on Paul's teaching to the churches under his care (vs. 11). There was, however, a perceived problem. Some regarded Timothy as being too young for such a task and had contempt for him. Perhaps the false teachers kept expressing this opinion, hoping to minimize his impact as Paul's representative. The apostle's remarks in verse 12 were meant not only to bolster Timothy's confidence but also to discourage anyone who might oppose him by using the issue of his age to question his competence. No one was to think less of Timothy because of his relative youth. While Timothy was considerably younger than Paul, he was old enough to carry out his ministerial responsibilities. The Greek noun rendered "youth" was used of those who were of military age, which extended to about 40. Timothy was most likely somewhere between 35 and 40 years of age at this time.

One way for Timothy to silence his critics was to continue being an example of the faith he proclaimed. As Timothy was steadfast in all aspects of Christian living, others would recognize his maturity in the faith and respect him for it. While we admire others who live consistently with what they believe, it is not always easy to obtain that consistency in our own lives. But regardless of our age, the best way to silence our critics is to carefully live out the Christian faith in the areas listed in verse 12 ("word," "conversation," and so on). Even if others disagree with us or refuse to believe in the Messiah, they will not be able to escape the impact of a sincere life.

While Paul was away, Timothy was to devote himself to three important tasks. The first item was the public "reading" (vs. 13) of Scripture. The early church copied the synagogue practice of reading the Hebrew sacred writings (that is, the Old Testament) at every synagogue service. Here the apostle encouraged that custom, which by this time also included reading some of the New Testament Scriptures. In the synagogues, after the Scriptures were read, the people were encouraged to carry out the commands of the reading. That sort of "exhortation" for others to obey was the preaching referred to in verse 13, and the second matter Timothy was to devote himself to. "Doctrine," which is the third detail, consisted of instruction in truth and appealed to the minds of the listeners.

Paul's personal teaching to Timothy included a reminder not to "neglect" (vs. 14) his spiritual gift. The underlying Greek verb implies an attitude of indifference. As elsewhere, the apostle's words should not be taken as an indication that Timothy had become careless. Paul's admonition was a reminder that God-given abilities require attention in order to be effective. The scene Paul described in this verse may have taken place at the time of Timothy's ordination (see Acts 16:1-3), but we cannot be certain. His gift was identified through a prophetic utterance by someone in attendance. The laying on of hands by the elders symbolized Timothy's reception of the gift as well as his call into the ministry. God, of course, was the one who gave him his special ability as well as the ministry in which to use it.

Timothy's spiritual life and ministry were to be his continual concern. Paul commanded him to "meditate upon" (vs. 15) these things and to give himself "wholly" to them. These words suggest that Timothy was to undertake his ministerial responsibilities carefully and absorb himself in them. As a result of giving himself wholeheartedly to the Savior and His work, others would recognize Timothy's progress in the faith.

Like a coach admonishing his star athlete, Paul kept encouraging Timothy to be conscientious about how he lived and what he taught. Moreover, he was to persevere in attending to his pastoral duties (vs. 16). The apostle had given his protege sound instruction, and now it was up to Timothy to remain loyal to the truth in both his life and ministry. As someone called upon to uphold the truth in the face of much false teaching, it was crucial that he guard his own thoughts and feelings. A failure would hurt both Timothy and the cause of Christ in the churches around Ephesus.

As Timothy remained faithful to his ministerial calling, he would save both himself and those who heard him preach. We know from Scripture that only God—ultimately— saves a person. Nevertheless, He graciously uses devout believers to lead people to believe. Through faith they enter justification and the assurance of redemption, yet there is still a lifelong journey of being conformed to the image of the Son. The growth of believers continues until they are finally glorified in heaven (see Phil. 2:12-13). Concerning Timothy, his faithful devotion to godliness and his ministry would not earn salvation for anyone, but would bring himself and others closer to the Lord.

SUGGESTIONS TO TEACHERS

Paul wrote 1 Timothy from a distance. In his letter, he expressed his concern for Timothy and for each member of the congregation he led. Today, this epistle still offers instructions for each of us, but also, through us, Paul offers his teaching to everyone we know. You can apply the following thoughts to your own role as a teacher, or perhaps the less formal role your students serve as their lives and words instruct others.

1. INSTRUCTIONS CHRISTIANS SHOULD HEAR. Paul wanted there to be no likelihood that Timothy would miss any of the apostle's important teaching. For that reason, Paul included sentences such as this one: "This is a faithful saying and worthy of all acceptation" (4:9). If this teaching was that important for a church leader thousands of years ago, then we need to hear it today. We cannot teach others what we ourselves do not know.

2. INSTRUCTIONS CHRISTIANS SHOULD AFFIRM. It would be wonderful if everyone under a godly pastor's teaching would accept sound doctrine, cling to it, and cooperate with that minister in serving the Lord. Sadly, many reject the truth to chase after what is false but palatable. In verses 1-6, we learn not only about the presence of corrupt teaching, but also how to combat it by affirming the truth.

3. INSTRUCTIONS CHRISTIANS SHOULD FOLLOW. Hearing and affirming are necessary first steps, but in themselves are inadequate. We must put into practice the biblical truths we have heard and affirmed (see vs. 15). Can we teach others what we do not do? If we try, our negative actions will always speak louder than our positive words.

4. INSTRUCTIONS CHRISTIANS SHOULD APPLY. The students can be encouraged to devote themselves to the work of the ministry. This is not restricted to preaching and teaching the Word. Faithful service for Christ also includes being a loyal spouse, a good parent, and a diligent employee. The Lord is honored when the salvation His people have in the Son permeates every area of their lives.

FOR ADULTS

■ TOPIC: Fitness for Leadership

■ QUESTIONS: 1. Why do you think it was important for the early church to be focused on adhering to apostolic truth? 2. In what ways have you found "godliness" (1 Tim. 4:8) to be profitable? 3. What can you do to encourage your fellow Christians to become more godly? 4. Why were some looking down on Timothy because of his age? 5. What would Timothy's devotion to godliness show the believers in the Ephesian church?

▧ ILLUSTRATIONS:

Putting Godliness First. Sara was known in her church as the person who had started and remained the leader of the congregation's weekly women's Bible study. One day, the Lord used the message of 1 Timothy 4:8 to teach Sara a valuable lesson during her battle with arthritis in her lower back. After her physician discovered her condition, he sent her to a physical therapist, who taught Sara a variety of exercises to alleviate the discomfort she was feeling. She responded by working diligently at her daily exercise routine, and this helped to relieve some of her pain.

As Sara continued to exercise, however, she discovered that she had not been giving as much attention to praying to God and reading her Bible. Sara began to wonder why she was willing to work so hard at physical therapy while neglecting activities having greater eternal value. She began to give godly training a higher priority in her life. And gradually, she sensed that this effort made her more spiritually fit to lead other women in the weekly study of God's Word.

An Enduring Heritage. For Derek, nothing was quite so enjoyable as spending an afternoon paddling out to his favorite fishing spot on a nearby lake. But on this day, there was a little snag. After digging through his worn metal tackle box, he could not find the lure he wanted. It had been his favorite—and the fish's favorite.

Now frustrated, Derek shifted lures and bobbins around and pulled out forgotten reels of fishing line. Then he found it—not the lure he had been looking for, but a lure he thought he had lost forever. It had belonged to his father, and to his grandfather. It was a family heirloom, and seeing it again reminded him of everything else right and good that had endured from generation to generation—including the family's faith in God.

Derek knew that God had richly blessed his grandfather and had been faithful to his father. Both of these family stalwarts had demonstrated by their lives what it means to be godly servant and leader to others. Derek also realized that the faith his father and grandfather had in the Lord is what carried them through the hard times they experienced. As Derek spent the remainder of the afternoon on the lake, he prayed that he too would be "nourished up in the words of faith and of good doctrine" (1 Tim. 4:6). In this way, he sensed that his own children would continue to serve God and experience His blessings.

A Living Legacy. Many believers have read, at one time or another, Andrew Bonar's celebrated *Memoir* of the young Scottish pastor, Robert Murray McCheyne. McCheyne died in March 1843, just shy of his thirtieth birthday, but left a legacy of godly leadership that continues to pay large dividends still today.

That fact is all the more striking because McCheyne wrote no important books. He was not the organizer of any movement. He was not even the founder of any great institution. McCheyne was loved in his own time and has been famous ever since almost entirely for what he *was*, not for what he *did*. In short, he invested his life in the pursuit of "godliness" (1 Tim. 4:8). He once said that he aspired to be as holy as a redeemed sinner can be. And he must have come closer to the mark than most Christians ever do, so great was the effect of his character on those who knew him.

Robert Candlish, a famed Christian minister and scholar, knew McCheyne and said this about him: "Assuredly he had more of the mind of his Master than almost any one I ever knew, and realized to me more of the likeness of the beloved disciple." Alexander Moody Stuart, a noteworthy Scottish minister of the period, remarked that what impressed him about McCheyne was that his holiness, his Christlikeness seemed so natural. He was a man who impressed virtually everyone who met him with his humility, his sincerity, his grace, and, especially, his devotion to Jesus Christ. McCheyne's testimony can inspire all of us to be an example to others "in word, in conversation, in charity, in spirit, in faith, in purity" (vs. 12).

FOR YOUTH

■ **TOPIC:** Are You Ready to Invest Yourself in Others?

■ **QUESTIONS:** 1. What was the nature of the false teachers' doctrinal error? 2. How can you demonstrate to others that you are a good servant of Christ? 3. Why is it important for you to train yourself for godliness? 4. What sorts of things was Timothy to insist on and teach? 5. How could Timothy be an exemplary role model to others?

■ **ILLUSTRATIONS:**

Teaching by Example. Teens reflect the character of individuals they admire but have never met. This includes music artists, entertainment celebrities, and talented athletes (among others). Adolescents also exemplify the behavior, dress, and habits of family members, friends, peers, and neighbors. Imitating others can be a good thing if those who serve as role models are upright people.

This week's lesson challenges your students not only to consider Jesus as a suitable role model, but also to become a Christlike example for others to follow. You can encourage the members of your class to consider it an opportunity to use their pursuit of godliness as a way of making a positive investment in the lives of their peers. The more saved adolescents focus their attention on Jesus and behave in ways that are characteristic of Him, the more they will set a Christlike example in their words and deeds to others.

Game Changer. Roynell Young is the founder and president of Pro-Vision, which is based in Houston, Texas. The nonprofit organization exists to give hope and purpose to youngsters by providing them with moral, cultural, and educational opportunities.

Roynell explains in his *Guideposts* article "Game Changer" that while growing up in New Orleans, Louisiana, he often challenged authority and broke the rules. It was his way of appearing as "one bad dude." While this got him a lot of attention from his peers, it also set a poor example for them to follow.

So what turned this troubled kid around to eventually become an all-pro cornerback for the Philadelphia Eagles and a model citizen? According to Roynell, it was an "act of faith from a line of people who went out of their way to rescue me from myself." The turning point for him came when he put his faith in Christ and found a new direction and purpose for his life.

In the years that followed, Roynell played nine seasons in football and had a career in business before starting Pro-Vision. These days, he uses his considerable leadership skills to encourage young people to "connect with one another for the good of society." It's his dream that his efforts to invest in the lives of adolescents will "benefit future generations."

Would you like to be a leader someday? If so, how might the Lord use you in a purposeful way to be a godly role model and positive influence in the lives of your peers?

A Family Matter. The Christian faith is a family matter. The Patons, John and Janet, believed that. In an inconspicuous Scottish thatch-roof cottage, they raised 11 children. We would never have heard their name, except that their son, John Gibson Paton, became one of Christendom's great missionary statesmen and evangelists. Behind the walls of that simple cottage, God molded a child to become His spokesman in the New Hebrides and Australia.

J. G. Paton often recalled what life was like in that humble home. As a boy, he often pressed his ear against the door of a tiny room where his father prayed. In his later years, J. G. testified, "Never in temple or cathedral, on mountain or in glen, can I hope to feel that the Lord God is more near, more visibly walking and talking with a man, than under that humble cottage roof. Eleven of us were brought up there. All of us came to regard the church as the dearest spot on earth and the Lord's day the brightest day of the week."

From this we see that the Christian faith is a family matter in which older loved ones can invest valuable time and effort to encourage younger members to spiritually grow and flourish. Who knows what the Lord is doing at your house through your godly example? Ultimately, only the Father does. Take courage, friend, and remain faithful to Him (see 1 Tim. 4:15). Eternity alone measures the full results of your steadfast walk with the Lord.

WORSHIP INSPIRES SERVICE

BACKGROUND SCRIPTURE: 1 Timothy 5:1-22
DEVOTIONAL READING: John 12:20-26

KEY VERSE: If any provide not for his own, and specially for those of his own house, he hath denied the faith, and is worse than an infidel. (1 Timothy 5:8)

KING JAMES VERSION

1 TIMOTHY 5:1 Rebuke not an elder, but intreat him as a father; and the younger men as brethren; 2 The elder women as mothers; the younger as sisters, with all purity.

3 Honour widows that are widows indeed. 4 But if any widow have children or nephews, let them learn first to shew piety at home, and to requite their parents: for that is good and acceptable before God. 5 Now she that is a widow indeed, and desolate, trusteth in God, and continueth in supplications and prayers night and day. 6 But she that liveth in pleasure is dead while she liveth. 7 And these things give in charge, that they may be blameless. 8 But if any provide not for his own, and specially for those of his own house, he hath denied the faith, and is worse than an infidel. . . .

17 Let the elders that rule well be counted worthy of double honour, especially they who labour in the word and doctrine. 18 For the scripture saith, Thou shalt not muzzle the ox that treadeth out the corn. And, The labourer is worthy of his reward. 19 Against an elder receive not an accusation, but before two or three witnesses. 20 Them that sin rebuke before all, that others also may fear. 21 I charge thee before God, and the Lord Jesus Christ, and the elect angels, that thou observe these things without preferring one before another, doing nothing by partiality. 22 Lay hands suddenly on no man, neither be partaker of other men's sins: keep thyself pure.

NEW REVISED STANDARD VERSION

1 TIMOTHY 5:1 Do not speak harshly to an older man, but speak to him as to a father, to younger men as brothers, 2 to older women as mothers, to younger women as sisters—with absolute purity.

3 Honor widows who are really widows. 4 If a widow has children or grandchildren, they should first learn their religious duty to their own family and make some repayment to their parents; for this is pleasing in God's sight. 5 The real widow, left alone, has set her hope on God and continues in supplications and prayers night and day; 6 but the widow who lives for pleasure is dead even while she lives. 7 Give these commands as well, so that they may be above reproach. 8 And whoever does not provide for relatives, and especially for family members, has denied the faith and is worse than an unbeliever. . . .

17 Let the elders who rule well be considered worthy of double honor, especially those who labor in preaching and teaching; 18 for the scripture says, "You shall not muzzle an ox while it is treading out the grain," and, "The laborer deserves to be paid." 19 Never accept any accusation against an elder except on the evidence of two or three witnesses. 20 As for those who persist in sin, rebuke them in the presence of all, so that the rest also may stand in fear. 21 In the presence of God and of Christ Jesus and of the elect angels, I warn you to keep these instructions without prejudice, doing nothing on the basis of partiality. 22 Do not ordain anyone hastily, and do not participate in the sins of others; keep yourself pure.

BACKGROUND

In 1 Timothy 5:3-16, Paul gave many guidelines for congregations to follow regarding the treatment of widows. In the early church, the death of a woman's husband could leave her in an abandoned and helpless state. Widowhood was viewed with reproach by many in Greco-Roman society. Thus, a widow without legal protection was often vulnerable to neglect or exploitation. If a woman's husband died when her children were adolescents, they were considered orphans. Unfortunately, it was far too common for greedy and unscrupulous agents to defraud a destitute widow and her children of whatever property they owned.

There were three primary ways a widow could provide for the financial needs of herself and her children. First, she could return to her parents' house. Second, she could remarry, especially if she was young or wealthy. And third, she could remain unmarried and obtain some kind of employment. The last prospect was rather bleak, for it was difficult in ancient times for a widow to find suitable work that would meet the economic needs of herself and her family.

NOTES ON THE PRINTED TEXT

The diligence with which Timothy was to attend to his personal faith (see 1 Tim. 4:15) needed to be matched by his caring treatment of people in the congregations under his supervision. The attitudes he displayed toward fellow members of the church family would set the tone for effective church ministry. There would be times when members of the church family needed to be admonished by Timothy. He was to handle them differently, depending on their gender and age, but he was to treat all of them as members of his own family.

In the first example, an older man had done something wrong. Timothy was not to rebuke such a person. The Greek verb translated "rebuke" (5:1) literally means to "assault with blows." The connotation is of pummeling others with words. Rather than verbally chastising an older man in this way, Timothy was to exhort him as his father. The idea behind "intreat" is calling aside to speak with privately. Thus while Timothy was not to ignore an older man's sin, he was to bring up the issue in a respectful, loving way. Loving exhortation is not for church leaders alone. In Ephesians 4:15, Paul said that believers were to speak "the truth in love." When it comes to admonishing others, we usually fail to say anything at all or fail to confront them respectfully. Paul's solution is that we humbly and gently counsel others with a careful eye on our own lives (see Gal. 6:1).

Next, Paul briefly mentioned three other types of people. When dealing with younger men, Timothy was to treat them as brothers, that is, to avoid any appearance of self-exaltation because of his ministerial position. As for older women, Timothy was to treat them as mothers, showing them respect, just as with older men. Concerning younger women, Timothy was to deal with them as with sisters, "with all purity" (1 Tim. 5:2) or complete chastity. Impropriety in that regard could bring reproach upon the church and ruin the ministry of Paul's representative.

Following the lead of the Jewish synagogue, the early church sought to provide for the needs of widows. Indeed, one of the first controversies in the church was over the distribution of food to widows (see Acts 6:1). The Greek verb behind "honour" (1 Tim. 5:3, 17) was used to describe the price paid for something. This word had the connotation of respect when used of people. It referred to the proper recognition that a person enjoyed in the community because of position or wealth. But the verb could also be used in the sense of financial compensation (like honorarium). Though some commentators think that Paul's intended meaning was limited to respect for the widow or elder, most hold that he intended some type of financial support as well.

While Paul desired to help widows who were genuinely destitute, he did not want the church's resources to be wasted on those who had other means of support. If a widow had children or grandchildren who could take care of her, then she was not really impoverished. In that instance, it was the congregation's duty to point out that obligation to her family members. Godly children would welcome the opportunity to please the Lord by paying back their parents for all they had done for them (vs. 4).

The type of widows Paul had in mind for support were godly women who depended upon the Lord to meet their needs. The congregation's responsibility rested with believing widows who displayed their godliness through faith and continual prayer (vs. 5). The church did not have an obligation, however, to maintain those widows who lived for pleasure rather than for God. Such women were spiritually dead (vs. 6). The implication is that widows who indulged in a wasteful, selfish, or sensual way of life were not to be honored in any sense. The limited resources of the church were not to be used to sustain that type of lifestyle. Timothy was to reiterate these directives (vss. 3-6) to the churches to prevent his peers from incurring reproach as a result of making poor decisions in supporting widows (vs. 7).

It appears that some in the early church were already taking advantage of the generosity of congregations by letting the church provide for their needy family members. Paul strongly denounced such an attitude by pointing out the necessity of taking care of one's own relatives. Men and women were responsible to provide for their immediate and extended families. To neglect impoverished members was a practical denial of the faith they claimed to believe (vs. 8).

In verse 17, Paul shifted his emphasis from the support of widows to the support of elders. While some contend that "honour" should be used exclusively in the sense of respect, most conservative evangelical scholars think that the context supports financial reimbursement for church leaders who provided effective leadership. In particular, those who excelled at preaching and teaching would need to spend considerable time in preparation for those activities. It was only fair that they receive some compensation for their labor. What did Paul mean by "double honour"? It may imply recognition for both the office and for the effort in performing its duties well. Or it may indicate generosity in their pay or in honor or in both. While this phrase is difficult to understand, Paul was making it clear that church leaders should be held in high regard for their position and for their hard work.

To support his contention of reimbursement for church elders, Paul quoted from Deuteronomy 25:4 as well as from Luke 10:7. Paul also used the Deuteronomy passage in 1 Corinthians 9:9, where he argued for the right of ministers to be financially supported by those who benefit from their ministry. The words of Jesus referring to the worker and wages also strongly indicate that Paul was seeking to build his case for financial support of elders (1 Tim. 5:18).

Deuteronomy 25:4 prohibits restraining an ox from eating as it treads out the grain. As farm animals, oxen were used for plowing and threshing. While threshing, oxen were often tethered to a post in the middle of the threshing floor. Sheaves of corn were laid on the floor, and the oxen were made to march round and round, pulling a threshing sledge over the grain. While the oxen were performing this service, the animals were allowed to feed on as much of the grain as they wished. If a farmer were especially stingy, he could muzzle the oxen so that they would not be able to eat. Usually this was considered unwise, since the animal's increasing frustration level would have a negative effect on its willingness to work.

Regrettably, there would be times when an elder had to endure the opposite of honor. In these cases, Timothy was not to consider any accusation against an elder unless it could be substantiated by two or three witnesses (1 Tim. 5:19). This Old Testament principle referred to bringing cases to judgment (see Deut. 17:6; 19:15). But in 1 Timothy 5:19 the witnesses were required to appear before any further action could be contemplated. Moreover, any action taken had to be based on established fact, not gossip or the careless slander of an adversary.

When it was proven that an elder was guilty of sinning, that person was to be rebuked or censured before the whole congregation to dissuade believers from making the same mistake (vs. 20). The "others" probably refers to the rest of the elders in the church, though some think that this refers to the entire church body. If the offense was serious enough to warrant removal from office, then the matter would need to come before everyone in the congregation.

In dealing with such serious matters, Timothy or any other church leader would be tempted either to prejudge a matter or show partiality before examining all the facts. Paul cautioned Timothy against letting his personal feelings dictate the outcome of an investigation. The apostle made his solemn affirmation by calling upon the Father, the Son, and the "elect angels" (vs. 21) as his witnesses. From this we see that when Timothy was dealing with such matters, he needed to be mindful of God's presence.

One way to avoid having to discipline elders was to exercise great care in choosing them. Paul's instruction to "lay hands suddenly on no man" (vs. 22) refers to ordaining or officially installing people to the ministry before they had an opportunity to establish themselves in the faith. Ordination assumes approval of a person for the ministry. Those who ordain unwisely share in the sins of spiritually immature candidates.

SUGGESTIONS TO TEACHERS

The church at Ephesus was made up of believers from various age groups and different social backgrounds. Christian love could surmount the obstacles such differences presented, and mutual respect could provide a foundation for cooperation in the Lord's work. Such love and respect would also provide a strong witness to the community. We thus can see why Paul wrote to Timothy regarding the church's responsibility to foster love and mutual respect.

1. COUNSEL FOR YOUNGER ADULTS. Paul's instructions to Timothy about honoring church leaders should be emphasized to young adults. This is because a pastor deserves the respect of the entire congregation. Young adults have a right to befriend the pastor. Nevertheless, they should not view the minister in a disrespectful manner. The esteem they give the pastor is an indication of the value they place on the teaching and shepherding ministry being provided.

2. COUNSEL FOR MIDDLE-AGED ADULTS. Paul's discussion concerning widows raises an important issue for middle-aged adults to discuss, namely, how they can plan ahead for their later years so that they will not be a financial burden to the church, their relatives, or society. Also, ask the students how planning for a financially secure future does not necessarily contradict the truth that the believer's eternal treasure is in heaven, not on earth.

3. COUNSEL FOR OLDER ADULTS. Older adults can be encouraged to show kindness and generosity to others, especially those in need. Explain that hospitality opens doors of communication and thereby strengthens the bonds of Christian fellowship. It is a virtue that is severely lacking today, but it can be revived. Perhaps a discussion of this topic will uncover ways in which the older adults can expand their efforts to be hospitable. In turn, their example might encourage younger members of the congregation to emulate their neighborliness to others.

■ TOPIC: All in the Family

■ QUESTIONS: 1. How do you think Timothy might have related to younger women in a virtuous manner? 2. What responsibility do extended family members today have toward relatives who are destitute? 3. How could believers discern whether a member of their congregation is truly impoverished? 4. Why was it important for the church to adequately compensate its hardworking leaders? 5. How is the church to deal with renegade ministers?

■ ILLUSTRATIONS:

God's Family. Edith Schaeffer, in her book entitled *What Is a Family?* relates that the family is an "ever-changing mobile of life, a center for the formation of human relationships, a perpetual relayer of truth, and a museum of memories." She also notes that these days the survival of the family as a living, loving unit is being threatened as never before.

Saved adults can help to create a biblically centered view of God's family by shunning such vices as arrogance and selfishness and embracing such virtues as humility, respect, and mercy. Moreover, they can do their part to enable Edith Schaeffer's vision of the family to become an increasing reality among believers.

Renewed Love. Michael Reagan, son of the former president, wrote a book entitled *On the Outside Looking In.* In it Michael poignantly related how he felt his love for his famous father was apparently rejected. On one occasion, young Reagan and two friends won the Outboard World Championship of 1967. Michael Reagan was featured in newspapers and on television as a winner.

Apparently Ronald and Nancy Reagan had never shown Michael much affection or appreciation. Despite this, Michael felt certain that they would hear about his accomplishment and finally welcome him because of his award. Longing for some word of love and appreciation, Michael waited expectantly to hear from his parents. He never heard from them, to his intense disappointment.

But by the time of Ronald Reagan's death on June 6, 2004, a dramatic change had occurred. The scene was a brief ceremony held on June 11 at the Ronald Reagan Presidential Library in Simi Valley, California. In the presence of a frail and tearful Nancy Reagan (the wife of the deceased former president), Michael lingered after others had departed to kiss his father's casket. Earlier in the service Michael had spoken lovingly of his relationship with his father and of the mutual faith they had in the Savior. Everyone present could tell that the bond of affection between President Reagan and his son had been renewed and would endure for eternity.

Fostering Restoration and Restitution. First Timothy 5:19-20 urges caution when trying to decide whether a church leader is guilty of sin. And even when a wayward minister is censured, the goal is to bring about spiritual correction and restoration. The same remedial intent extends to every member of the church family. Admittedly, while sometimes restoration and restitution are possible to diminish the consequences of sin, the process is often not quickly accomplished.

For instance, consider the story of John Allen. After he burglarized his uncle's home, he was sent to jail. When John got out, the Restorative Justice Project (RJP) contacted him and asked whether he was willing to meet with his uncle to have their relationship restored and to make payments for restitution. (The RJP is an initiative of the Center for Peacemaking and Conflict Studies at Fresno Pacific University.)

When John and his uncle met with an RJP volunteer, the uncle expressed his anger and fears. Despite that, John agreed to make the necessary payments. Says RJP worker Ron Classen, "Trust grows when agreements are made and kept. If a victim and offender make a constructive agreement, trust will grow between them, at least a little. If the agreement is kept, trust will grow more."

FOR YOUTH

■ TOPIC: Serving the Deserving

■ QUESTIONS: 1. What are some ways that younger believers can respectfully address older men and women within the church? 2. Why was Timothy to relate to younger women with absolute purity? 3. Why is it important for local churches today to reach out and assist those who are destitute? 4. How can the members of a church appropriately honor their leaders who excel in their service to the congregation? 5. Why was Timothy not to hastily ordain individuals as leaders?

■ ILLUSTRATIONS:

Humbly Serving Others. In *Love Beyond Reason: Moving God's Love from Your Head to Your Heart*, John Ortberg asserts the following: "Envy is wanting what another person has and feeling badly that I don't have it. Envy is disliking God's goodness to someone else and dismissing God's goodness to me. Envy is desire plus resentment. Envy is anti-community."

An envious heart is incapable of humbly serving those in need, for it is too preoccupied. And its seed of discontentment quickly grows into the weed of resentment. This weed can choke relationships—even among Christians. So how can younger believers eradicate this weed and become more sacrificial in their ministries to others among them who are struggling? Extermination begins with developing a right attitude toward God and the blessings He, in His wisdom, bestows. The result is the increased presence of compassion and generosity within the Body of Christ.

Rich Are Still Richer. According to *Forbes* magazine, there were about 140 billionaires worldwide in 1986. Yet despite the global economic downturn that emerged in 2008, the number of billionaires across the planet had grown to 793 by 2009.

Moreover, the gap between the wealthiest and the rest is widening. Currently, the richest fifth of the world's population accounts for 86 percent of all private consumption. But in Africa, the average household consumes 20 percent less than it did a generation ago. Meanwhile natural resources as well as household purchasing power are declining.

The richest fifth of the world's people buy nine times as much meat, have access to nearly 50 times as many telephones, and use more than 80 times as many paper products and motorized vehicles than the poorest fifth. Americans spend more than $8 billion annually on cosmetics, whereas it would cost only $6 billion to provide basic education for the children in developing countries who have no schooling. Europeans spend $11 billion yearly on ice cream. About $9 billion would provide water and basic sanitation to the more than 2 billion people worldwide who lack safe water or hygienic toilets.

Paul's words to Timothy about the responsibility of believers to help destitute people continues to be a challenge. May we take to heart the words of our Savior, "It is more blessed to give than to receive" (Acts 20:35).

Prophetic Stand. Congressman Tony Hall was concerned about helping the hungry. When the Select Committee on Hunger in Congress was terminated a number of years ago, Hall worried that his colleagues would neglect those who lacked enough to eat and adequate diets. His wife suggested that he fast. After praying and seeking the counsel of fellow Christians, he undertook a water fast to call attention to the urgent needs of those lacking sufficient food. "When I did that," Hall reported, "I separated myself from my colleagues. I felt like I was alone."

But Hall continued with the fast. It was difficult and also humbling. After two weeks of fasting, he felt that there was no hope that the Committee would be restored. But at that point, students and community groups heard about his commitment, and were impressed that a politician would fast. Shortly thereafter, the administration and the World Bank made strong suggestions about curbing world hunger. Congressman Hall spoke to the House of Representatives. The majority leader confessed, "I feel ashamed. You have embarrassed us in the right way."

Hall's lonely stand illustrates the kind of concern Paul enjoined all believers to have for the impoverished. Indeed, the apostle declared that those who refused to provide for the destitute, in effect had "denied the faith" (1 Tim. 5:8) and were "worse than an infidel."

REMEMBERING JESUS CHRIST

BACKGROUND SCRIPTURE: 2 Timothy 2:8-15
DEVOTIONAL READING: Titus 3:1-7

KEY VERSE: Study to shew thyself approved unto God, a workman that needeth not to be ashamed, rightly dividing the word of truth. (2 Timothy 2:15)

KING JAMES VERSION

2 TIMOTHY 2:8 Remember that Jesus Christ of the seed of David was raised from the dead according to my gospel: 9 Wherein I suffer trouble, as an evil doer, even unto bonds; but the word of God is not bound. 10 Therefore I endure all things for the elect's sakes, that they may also obtain the salvation which is in Christ Jesus with eternal glory. 11 It is a faithful saying: For if we be dead with him, we shall also live with him: 12 If we suffer, we shall also reign with him: if we deny him, he also will deny us: 13 If we believe not, yet he abideth faithful: he cannot deny himself.

14 Of these things put them in remembrance, charging them before the Lord that they strive not about words to no profit, but to the subverting of the hearers. 15 Study to shew thyself approved unto God, a workman that needeth not to be ashamed, rightly dividing the word of truth.

NEW REVISED STANDARD VERSION

2 TIMOTHY 2:8 Remember Jesus Christ, raised from the dead, a descendant of David—that is my gospel, 9 for which I suffer hardship, even to the point of being chained like a criminal. But the word of God is not chained. 10 Therefore I endure everything for the sake of the elect, so that they may also obtain the salvation that is in Christ Jesus, with eternal glory. 11 The saying is sure:

If we have died with him, we will also live with him;
12 if we endure, we will also reign with him;
if we deny him, he will also deny us;
13 if we are faithless, he remains faithful—
for he cannot deny himself.

14 Remind them of this, and warn them before God that they are to avoid wrangling over words, which does no good but only ruins those who are listening. 15 Do your best to present yourself to God as one approved by him, a worker who has no need to be ashamed, rightly explaining the word of truth.

5

Monday, March 28	Acts 3:11-16	*Raised from the Dead*
Tuesday, March 29	Romans 1:1-7	*Descended from David*
Wednesday, March 30	Titus 3:1-7	*Our Savior*
Thursday, March 31	Matthew 26:17-30	*Remembering Jesus' Sacrifice*
Friday, April 1	1 Corinthians 11:23-33	*Proclaiming the Lord's Death*
Saturday, April 2	2 Corinthians 6:1-10	*Now Is the Day of Salvation*
Sunday, April 3	2 Timothy 2:8-15	*Salvation in Christ Jesus*

BACKGROUND

Paul was writing from a Roman prison and seemed to know that the end of his life was near. The apostle spoke about how he had finished his work and completed the race (2 Tim. 4:6-8). However, he did not intend that this letter to Timothy would be his last contact with him. Instead, Paul hoped Timothy would be able to come visit him in Rome (vss. 9, 13). Church tradition states that the apostle was executed by the emperor Nero near the end of his reign of terror. Nero committed suicide in A.D. 68, so Paul probably wrote this last epistle around A.D. 67.

Second Timothy reveals some of Paul's personal concerns. In it he opened his heart to his younger colleague in the faith, expressing sorrow and anger about those who had turned their backs on the apostle and left the truth of the Gospel. In some ways Paul felt completely abandoned (1:15; 4:10). The apostle thus poured out his heart to Timothy. The bleak prison walls had cut Paul off from those he longed to be with. The lonely echoes of the dungeon heightened the intensity of his desire to see Timothy as soon as possible (1:8; 2:3; 4:9). Despite Paul's hardships, the Holy Spirit used him to minister greatly to others. The apostle's words are now part of Scripture and have continued to strengthen and encourage church leaders throughout the centuries. Pastors and lay leaders who have struggled against opposition—either from within the church or from without—have found comfort in Paul's words to Timothy as he ministered at Ephesus.

NOTES ON THE PRINTED TEXT

Paul directed Timothy's attention to their Savior. He was fully human, as His ancestry from King David testified. (The Redeemer fulfilled God's promise to grant to one of David's descendants an everlasting kingship.) Jesus was also fully divine, as His resurrection from the dead confirmed (2 Tim. 2:8). Because Jesus is human, He can serve as a substitutionary sacrifice for the lost. And because He is divine, His atonement is infinite in its saving value. The incarnation, death, and resurrection of Christ were the essential truths of the Gospel that Paul declared.

It should be clear that the apostle did nothing wrong in telling others about the Savior. Nevertheless, the Roman authorities locked up Paul and treated him like a criminal. Although the apostle was chained, the Gospel remained unshackled (vs. 9). For this reason, Paul was willing to endure all sorts of suffering. Indeed, he knew a number of prisons from firsthand experience. For instance, after being flogged in Philippi, he was imprisoned and put in stocks—until an earthquake shook the prison doors open (Acts 16:23-39). The apostle was kept briefly in the Fortress of Antonia in Jerusalem (22:23-29). Later, he was transferred to Caesarea, where he was kept under guard in Herod's palace (23:35). Paul said he had been beaten and imprisoned frequently (2 Cor. 11:23).

Primitive conditions characterized ancient prisons. Prisoners were at the mercy of their guards and often had to make their own arrangement for food and other necessities of life. Paul asked Timothy to bring the cloak the apostle had left behind (2 Tim. 4:13), very likely because he had little to ward off the cold of the dungeon. Even in such horrid conditions, the apostle was able to glorify God. Paul's desire was that the Lord's special people—the elect—might be saved and receive eternal glory in Christ (2:10). Paul was referring to the believer's final and complete salvation in which God bestowed a resurrection body and a completely transformed human nature. Through the Redeemer, the people of God would triumph over sin and death and experience the fullness of unending joy in the Lord's presence.

Many conservative evangelical scholars think verses 11-13 were part of an early Christian hymn. In this passage, Paul stressed the faithful and certain truth that eternal glory will follow a relatively short time of suffering for Christ. As Paul said, if we are spiritually united with Jesus in His death on the cross, we now have eternal life. (It is also true that we will be resurrected from the dead when Jesus returns for His church.) If we presently endure suffering for the sake of the Gospel, we will also reign with Christ in His kingdom. From the first through the third centuries A.D., believers were repeatedly slandered and accused of wrongdoing by their opponents. In such an environment, the behavior of Christians greatly affected the spread of the Gospel.

Evangelicals have interpreted verses 11-13 in various ways. Some think Paul was indicating that believers can choose to walk away from their commitment to Jesus—and suffer the eternal consequences of their choice. Others think this passage is a generic statement that describes those who reject Christ's offer of salvation, having never believed (see also Matt. 10:32-33). Some hold that despite a believer's unfaithfulness, God remains faithful to His promises. No matter which way 2 Timothy 2:11-13 is interpreted, the lesson is that Jesus can be trusted more than we can trust ourselves. He remains faithful even when people are faithless. In light of these truths, Paul urged Timothy to remain committed to the Lord and reminded him that Jesus had committed Himself to us. We should trust God's grace and give ourselves to the Lord, remaining faithful even if circumstances bring hardship or pain. Suffering can lead to great spiritual blessings.

Timothy was to remind the believers at Ephesus about the truths of the Gospel. This was imperative because some were teaching false doctrines. Paul's coworker was to call on God as his witness as he solemnly warned the troublemakers not to argue about inane philosophical matters that helped no one. In fact, those who listened were spiritually harmed by what the religious charlatans said (2:14).

Moreover, unlike the spiritual frauds at Ephesus, Timothy was to make every effort to present himself to God as one whom He had tested and approved. Timothy would have no cause for shame as long as he taught the message of truth, namely, the Gospel. He was to diligently study and accurately expound the Word so that others might know sound doctrine. Proficient use of the Scripture involves correctly handling it. In ancient Greece, the verb translated "rightly dividing" (vs. 15) was used to describe a father cutting meat into the exact proportions his family needed at mealtime. The term also was used to refer to a farmer plowing straight furrows. Finally, the verb was used to describe the careful slicing of animal hides into square sections so that a tentmaker could exactly fit and sew them together.

From these illustrations we can see how important it is to precisely interpret and apply Scripture. When Paul wrote 2 Timothy, the books of the Old Testament were the Scriptures used by the church. At that time, the New Testament did not exist as an authoritative and finalized collection of sacred writings. In fact, some of the New Testament books were probably not yet penned. Even though this is the case, what the apostle said about the origin and accuracy of the Old Testament would equally apply to the New Testament. In other words, both Old and New Testaments are the inspired and infallible Word of God.

In 2 Timothy 3:16, Paul declared that all Scripture is "given by inspiration of God." The apostle used a Greek adjective that means "God-breathed." Expressed differently, the Lord is the origin and ultimate author of Scripture. Though He supernaturally directed the biblical writers, He did not override their intelligence, individuality, literary style, personal feelings, or any other human factor. Nevertheless, God's own complete and coherent message to humankind was recorded with perfect accuracy.

Inspiration extends equally and absolutely to all portions of Scripture. All the books of the Bible are error-free in what they teach. This involves every aspect of them. It is not restricted to moral and religious truths but even extends to the statement of facts. This includes information of an historic or geographic nature. The doctrine of inspiration not only encompasses details of vital importance to Christian belief, but also anything that the sacred writers affirmed to be true.

As Paul talked about the origin and authority of Scripture, he stated that the study and application of it was eternally beneficial. For example, it was immeasurably useful for teaching sound doctrine and for showing people where they had strayed from the truth. The Bible was also useful for correcting sinful behavior and for training people how to live in an upright manner. We learn from verse 16 that God's Word is supremely authoritative. This means it possesses the absolute right to define what we should believe and how we should behave. When Scripture is consistently heeded, God's servants will be thoroughly prepared and equipped to do every kind of good work for His glory (3:17).

So then, there is no substitute for Scripture when it comes to combatting false teaching, learning the ways of the Lord, and ministering for Him. We insult God, deceive ourselves, and cheat others when we fail to study the Bible diligently and obey it wholeheartedly. If each of us fills our life to overflowing with God's Word, the spiritual benefits from this act will spill over to a world that needs the knowledge of salvation. There is no other infallible beacon to guide people to an eternally safe harbor.

SUGGESTIONS TO TEACHERS

As Paul's life and ministry were drawing to a close, he encouraged Timothy and all believers to draw close to the Savior in their times of hardship. Paul also urged his fellow Christians to remember the Messiah as the supreme example of suffering. Indeed, it was through the knowledge and power of the Son that believers such as Paul could continue proclaiming the Gospel to others.

1. THE EXAMPLE OF PAUL'S OWN MINISTRY. In an effort to encourage Timothy to remain faithful to the Savior, Paul asked his protege to consider the example of the apostle's own ministry. It's as if Paul were saying, "I have fought as a good soldier, but for now the only reward I have is this prisoner of war camp. I have kept all the rules as a good athlete, but for now the only crown I receive is made of thorns. But I am remaining faithful, as a good farmer does, so that I can receive my true reward at the time God has set" (see 2 Tim. 2:3-6). Moreover, despite Paul's hardships, he declared, "I endure all things for the elect's sakes" (vs. 10). The apostle set his own life as an example for Timothy and us to follow.

2. THE EXAMPLE OF THE WORKER. In verse 15, Paul implied a comparison between two types of workers, those that end their week with shame and those who can look back with feelings of legitimate pride. The latter have done their work to the best of their ability, in contrast to those who have knowingly offered shoddy labor. Some workers do only enough to get by. Faithful workers produce a quality product. Paul reminded Timothy and us that we cannot cut any corners in what we say or do. We need to offer our best to God and His people.

3. THE EXAMPLE OF CONTEMPORARY EXPERIENCE. Not long ago newspapers featured a story about a street gang that attacked and burned a young college student because he refused to take drugs. This student could have avoided the agony and embarrassment of this ordeal if he had gone along with his attackers. However, his moral and spiritual convictions prevented him from giving in to their coercion. This account emphasizes the level of commitment the Father calls us to have to His Son.

■ **TOPIC:** Communicating Personal Beliefs

■ **QUESTIONS:** 1. What are the essential truths of the Gospel the Lord wants us to share with others? 2. Why did Paul willingly submit to the hardships of suffering for the cause of Christ? 3. In what sense could Paul believe that the Word of God was "not bound" (2 Tim. 2:9)? 4. What can you do to improve your attitude about the prospect of suffering for the Savior? 5. How has the Lord proven Himself faithful to you?

■ **ILLUSTRATIONS:**

True Qualifications for Success. When we prepare our list of qualifications for church leaders, we often begin with their education and experience. These are important factors to consider.

It's much harder, though, to evaluate the qualifications Paul had in mind for success in ministry. He upheld virtues like our personal belief in the truths of the Gospel and our willingness to share the Good News with others even in the face of persecution. Although professional training such as we know it was not available in Paul's day, we can profit from such training.

At the same time, all of us—not just our leaders—must always put our adherence to the Gospel and devotion to the Lord Jesus above everything else. We may have many other recommendations, but without those qualities we will be able to fulfill God's vision for us.

A Committed Life. Paul shared with Timothy the sobering news that the apostle was languishing in a Roman prison for the cause of Christ. Despite this, the "word of God [was] not bound" (2 Tim. 2:9). This truth has been repeatedly confirmed by the testimony of countless believers down through the centuries who have suffered for the faith.

A case in point would be Eric Liddell, whose account is immortalized in the film *Chariots of Fire*. Liddell was a Scottish athlete in the 1924 Olympic Games who refused to run on a Sunday because of his religious convictions. Nonetheless, Liddell did win a gold medal in the 400-meter race.

Later, Liddell became a missionary to China and was eventually imprisoned by the Japanese during World War II. In the course of his two years at the internment camp, Liddell's committed life and genuine love for all people made a strong Christian witness among young and old alike. He died of a brain tumor on February 21, 1945, just months before the war ended.

David Mitchell, who was a young child in the same prison camp, was greatly influenced by Liddell's efforts to share his personal belief in the Savior. Mitchell later testified: "None of us will ever forget this man whose humble life combined muscular Christianity with radiant goodness."

Remembered as a Teacher. People who have done any reading on World War I (or have closely followed *Peanuts* cartoons) know the name of Baron Manfred von Richthofen, the great German air force ace. Far fewer people have heard about Oswald Boelcke, who may have had far more impact on the tactics used by fighter pilots to this day.

William Cohen, in his volume, *The New Art of the Leader*, tells Boelcke's story. Boelcke was himself a skilled fighter. But his goal went beyond winning glory for himself. Today he is remembered as a strategist and team-builder. He would not allow any pilot newly assigned to his squadron to fly with him until the rookie had adequately learned the system.

What system did Boelcke develop? It was that planes should fly together in squadrons supporting and protecting one another. Boelcke himself was shot down and killed in 1916, quite early in the war. Yet, his careful concern for training others has given him his own place in military history.

Paul encouraged Timothy and all future generations of Christians to openly share with others their personal belief in the Savior. This includes training inexperienced believers to communicate effectively the truth of His death on the cross and resurrection from the dead (see 2 Tim. 2:8). Who knows how many people will be encouraged through our ministry of training to find salvation in the Redeemer (see vs. 10)!

■ **FOR YOUTH**	■ **TOPIC:** It's All about J.C.

■ **QUESTIONS:** 1. Why is it important for believers to never forget what Jesus has done for them? 2. How do you think you would feel if others labeled you a criminal for believing in the Savior? 3. How can you encourage other believers in their times of hardship? 4. Over what types of words might Timothy and his congregation be tempted to argue? 5. If someone asked you to pen your own "faithful saying" (2 Tim. 2:11), what would you write?

■ **ILLUSTRATIONS:**

Serving Jesus. Career options have changed dramatically over the years. For example, young people today can anticipate challenging work using computer technology. New discoveries mean new opportunities in business and professional life.

It's hard for church leaders to compete with business and education when it comes to attracting young people to live for Christ and commit to serving Him. Reading what Paul said to Timothy leaves us cold, because he said nothing about advancing up the corporate ladder and making lots of money.

However, when we open our dreams to the Lord Jesus and center our lives on Him, He gives us the intense satisfaction of serving people in ministry. Like Timothy, we are called to think about what we can do for Jesus, not just professionally but with all of our interests and skills.

A Life Centered on Christ. An evangelical pastor named Ron opened his heart up to his congregation about the influence his parents had on him during his formative years. Ron shared that his dad had finally died after struggling with cancer on Sunday, July 27, 2008, and that his mom had passed away the previous summer on that same day. Ron noted that by the evening of his father's death, he and six siblings had gathered from around the country for a funeral, to support each other, and to begin caring for household details.

At one poignant moment the next day, Ron's oldest sister, the executor for the estate, called all the family members into the living room for the reading of the will. At first there were no great surprises. After gifts to Christian institutions that Ron's parents had valued, their worldly goods were to be divided as equally as possible among their seven children. But at the end of the document, Ron's dad spoke powerfully to the surviving family members one last time.

"I desire to leave the following message with my beloved children: 'The material inheritance which I have left you is small and insignificant. However, I trust that I have left you the memory of a faithful father, who honored Christ in his ministry and in his daily life. I would direct you "To an inheritance incorruptible, and undefiled, which fadeth not away, reserved in Heaven for you," which your Heavenly Father hath provided for you, "according to His abundant mercy," and "hath begotten us again into a lively hope by the resurrection of Jesus Christ from the dead." Don't miss it.'"

As Ron's sister read those words, with tears in her eyes, all the siblings reflected on the most important legacy their parents had left them. It was that they had made the Savior—who is "of the seed of David" (2 Tim. 2:8) and "raised from the dead"—the center of their earthly existence and their eternal hope.

Father and Son. Paul was not Timothy's biological father, but their relationship was perhaps as close as some sons enjoy with their fathers. Can you think of some adult, other than your own parents, who has had a significant positive influence on your development as a person?

In an article in the *Seattle Times*, King County executive, Ron Sims, gave loads of credit to a childhood Sunday school teacher and the teacher's wife. When Sims reflected on the influence of Sylvester and Pauline Lake, he ran out of words. "Mr. Lake helped make me. How do you measure the contribution of a person who helped shape your values, who helped teach me to be kind and to care? It's immeasurable."

What specifics does Sims remember? The Lakes had him to their home for meals. After an auto accident, Sims was housebound with a fractured skull, so the Lakes often brought him stacks of books to read. Lake not only taught his Sunday school class with words, but also with his life. Sims looks back and summarizes the Lakes' ministry as "a magnificent gesture of caring."

PRAISE BUILDS US UP

BACKGROUND SCRIPTURE: Jude 17-25
DEVOTIONAL READING: 2 Corinthians 4:1-12

KEY VERSES: Now unto him that is able to keep you from falling, and to present you faultless before the presence of his glory with exceeding joy, to the only wise God our Saviour, be glory and majesty, dominion and power, both now and ever. Amen. (Jude 24-25)

KING JAMES VERSION

JUDE 17 But, beloved, remember ye the words which were spoken before of the apostles of our Lord Jesus Christ; 18 How that they told you there should be mockers in the last time, who should walk after their own ungodly lusts. 19 These be they who separate themselves, sensual, having not the Spirit. 20 But ye, beloved, building up yourselves on your most holy faith, praying in the Holy Ghost, 21 Keep yourselves in the love of God, looking for the mercy of our Lord Jesus Christ unto eternal life. 22 And of some have compassion, making a difference: 23 And others save with fear, pulling them out of the fire; hating even the garment spotted by the flesh. 24 Now unto him that is able to keep you from falling, and to present you faultless before the presence of his glory with exceeding joy, 25 To the only wise God our Saviour, be glory and majesty, dominion and power, both now and ever. Amen.

NEW REVISED STANDARD VERSION

JUDE 17 But you, beloved, must remember the predictions of the apostles of our Lord Jesus Christ; 18 for they said to you, "In the last time there will be scoffers, indulging their own ungodly lusts." 19 It is these worldly people, devoid of the Spirit, who are causing divisions. 20 But you, beloved, build yourselves up on your most holy faith; pray in the Holy Spirit; 21 keep yourselves in the love of God; look forward to the mercy of our Lord Jesus Christ that leads to eternal life. 22 And have mercy on some who are wavering; 23 save others by snatching them out of the fire; and have mercy on still others with fear, hating even the tunic defiled by their bodies.

24 Now to him who is able to keep you from falling, and to make you stand without blemish in the presence of his glory with rejoicing, 25 to the only God our Savior, through Jesus Christ our Lord, be glory, majesty, power, and authority, before all time and now and forever. Amen.

6

Monday, April 4	2 Corinthians 4:1-12	*Treasure in Clay Jars*
Tuesday, April 5	Jeremiah 31:2-9	*Praise from the Restored*
Wednesday, April 6	1 Corinthians 10:23-31	*Live for the Glory of God*
Thursday, April 7	Acts 20:28-35	*A Message That Builds Up*
Friday, April 8	John 17:6-19	*Protection from Evil*
Saturday, April 9	1 Samuel 12:19-25	*The Good and the Right Way*
Sunday, April 10	Jude 17-25	*Build Yourselves Up in Faith*

BACKGROUND

Jude was a younger brother of James, who wrote the epistle bearing his name. Both were half-brothers of Jesus (Matt. 13:55; Mark 6:3). Neither brother drew attention to his family tie to the Lord (Jas. 1:1; Jude 1). Both called themselves Jesus' servants. Although Jude follows the letters of Peter and John in the New Testament, it precedes most or all of them in time of composition. Jude 4-18 and 2 Peter 2:1-22 are so similar that one must have relied directly on the other or both used a third source that no longer exists. Most New Testament scholars think Peter relied on Jude. If that is so, Jude had to be written long enough before Peter's death in the late A.D. 60s to have been recognized as authoritative. Assuming Jude precedes 2 Peter, it may have been written about A.D. 65.

Jude made extensive use of Old Testament allusions. This may indicate he wrote to an audience in Palestine. The false teachers Jude warned against seem to have interpreted the doctrine of salvation by grace to imply that sins were acceptable or even desirable as stimulants for more grace (Jude 4). The deceivers combated in John's epistles held false views about the full humanity and full deity of Christ. Jude's (and 2 Peter's) spiritual frauds primarily seem to have tried to join the gracious Gospel of Christ to immorality.

Jude's original intent was to write to his dear friends in the faith about their "common salvation" (Jude 3), and he was quite eager to offer pastoral counsel. The presence of false teachers, however, prompted Jude to redirect his attention. Charlatans were threatening believers with a counterfeit gospel. The danger was so great that Jude exhorted his readers to "earnestly contend for the faith." This refers to the body of apostolic truth the Lord had handed down to the faith community once for all time. God, in His grace, gave His inspired and infallible Word to His holy people, and they were to uphold and defend it against heretics.

NOTES ON THE PRINTED TEXT

In Jude's letter, he exhorted his readers to not let false teachers take advantage of them. The spiritual frauds were noted for their constant murmuring and complaining and for doing whatever their "lusts" (vs. 16) dictated. Such arrogance also manifested itself in speech characterized by boasting. Moreover, they were brash enough to flatter people to gain an "advantage." The godly, in contrast, seek to praise God and encourage His people. The righteous also shun evil desires and reach out to others in need. Thus, rather than exploiting and manipulating people, believers make great sacrifices to proclaim the truth so that the lost might be saved.

On the one hand, the false teachers were so wicked that the Lord was coming to judge them. On the other hand, believers should not be surprised to find such people in their midst. Jude reminded his readers that the apostles had foretold that scoffers would appear in the end times, and now the prediction was coming true (vs. 17). In the early church—before the New Testament was completed—the teaching of the apostles, whether communicated in writing or by word of mouth, provided the source for Christian beliefs. For instance, Paul referred to spiritual frauds as "grievous wolves" (Acts 20:29). Also, Peter called them "false prophets" (2 Pet. 2:1) who taught "damnable heresies." Jude's original readers apparently had heard some of the apostles in person. Perhaps at different times Peter, Paul, James, and others had come to their church (or churches). The readers would do well, Jude implied, if they held to the teachings of those godly ministers rather than to the teachings of the deceivers.

Jude reminded his readers of one warning in particular that the apostles had given. They prophesied that in the "last time" (Jude 18) the impious would deride God's truth and gratify their forbidden passions. As a matter of fact, we find many warnings like this one in the Gospels and other New Testament books (for example, Mark 13:22 and 2 Thess. 2:3). Jude 18, rather than presenting an exact quote, may have summarized statements made by several apostles on different occasions. In Jewish thought, history could be divided into two ages, often called "the present age" and "the age to come." Jews believed that the Messiah would usher in the age to come. Christians, who know Jesus as the Messiah, recognize that while the age to come has already broken in on the present era, the final era hasn't entirely come. That awaits the second advent of the Savior.

Jude believed that, in a sense, he was living in the last times, when impostors would arise. Also, he maintained that the false teachers were among the predicted scoffers. For instance, they disputed God's commands, preferring instead to follow their own unbridled lusts. Jude also pointed out that the mockers were guilty of causing divisions. This may simply mean that some people sided with the false teachers, while others sided against them. But if the charlatans were Gnostics (a heretical group claiming to have secret knowledge), this may mean that they were dividing people into two categories: the spiritual (meaning Gnostics) and the sensual (all others).

If the deceivers considered themselves the enlightened and spiritual ones, then Jude 19 is especially insightful. Despite the inflated claims made by the false teachers, they were devoid of the Spirit, which implies they were unregenerate (see Rom. 8:9). Even worse, they were worldly, for they operated on the level of their raw instincts and took their cues from the devil. Religious charlatans in our own day have the same characteristics as those in Jude's day. They cause divisions, they follow mere natural inclinations, and the Spirit does not abide in them. Bad theology and bad living usually go together. If we see the one, we should be on the lookout for the presence of the other (see Matt. 7:15-20).

In response to the threat posed by the spiritual frauds, Christians were to continually establish their lives on the bedrock of their "most holy faith" (Jude 20). In addition to adhering to apostolic truth, they were to keep praying "in the Holy Ghost." This probably means either to pray in communion with the Spirit or to pray in the power of the Spirit. The idea is that believers can only combat the false teachers in the power of the Spirit and the true teaching of God's Word. Furthermore, Jude urged his readers to keep themselves grounded "in the love of God" (vs. 21). With the love of the Father as the anchor of their souls, believers could remain united in their faith and committed to one another. They were also to wait eagerly for "the mercy of our Lord Jesus Christ." This is a reference to the Savior's return, at which time believers will be resurrected, resulting in their full and final reception of "eternal life."

Among Jude's readers were those who were wavering (vs. 22). This possibly refers to people who were genuinely vacillating in their faith. These sincere doubters deserved mercy from Jesus' followers. A second group appears to be those who were further entrenched in unbelief. Jude urged his readers to make every effort to show forbearance on them "with fear" (vs. 23). God was able to make the witness of believers so persuasive that unbelievers could be snatched "out of the fire" of judgment. A third group were the apostates, whose lives, like a "garment," were "spotted," or defiled, by moral filth. Believers, while abhorring the depravity of the false teachers, were to show mercy on them. The adage of "hating the sin but loving the sinner" seems applicable here.

Jude capped his letter with one of the Bible's most glorious doxologies (that is, passages of praise). While Jude recognized that the danger posed by the religious frauds was severe, he was not pessimistic. If it were up to his readers alone to combat the charlatans, they would have been in real trouble. But they were not alone. God would help them, specifically by preventing them from spiritually stumbling. The Lord would also bring the readers of Jude's epistle (along with all believers) into the "presence of his glory" (vs. 24). Indeed, they would stand before Him rejoicing and without blemish.

The false teachers wanted to see Jude's readers soiled with sin, as they themselves were. But the recipients of Jude's epistle had already been washed clean of sin by trusting in the Messiah. They could keep from sinning if they remained faithful and dependent on the Lord. Like those first-century believers, we too are presented with situations in which sinning seems the easiest thing to do. But we don't have to give in to that temptation. We can turn to God in prayer and say, "No, I just won't do it; I won't disobey the Lord, whom I love." The God who safeguards us and welcomes us into His presence is worthy of every honor we can give—or even think of. To the Father, our Savior, through the Son, our Lord, belongs all "glory and majesty, dominion and power" (vs. 25). This was true in the past (before all time), it is just as true now (in the present), and it will remain true for all eternity (beyond all time).

Romans 11:33-36 records a similarly glorious doxology. Paul was in awe because God's plan of salvation for all people—Jew and Gentile—demonstrated His infinite wisdom and knowledge. Truly, God's judgments are unsearchable and His paths beyond tracing out. The apostle quoted from Isaiah 40:13 to show that the Lord was the wise planner who brought all this about. No one counseled Him. God was under no obligation to repay anyone, because no one has ever provided Him with anything. Since God is the comprehensive source of all things, to Him "be glory for ever. Amen" (Rom. 11:36).

SUGGESTIONS TO TEACHERS

Christian faith, at a personal level, is a spiritual affirmation that the Father has revealed Himself in the Son, who died to atone for our sins. The Christian faith, at a corporate level, consists of the body of truth about God, humankind, and salvation revealed by the Lord in the Bible. It should be the goal of every Christian to be steadfast in personal and corporate faith. Jude focused primarily on corporate faith.

1. RECOGNIZE ERROR Jude knew that the best way to recognize a counterfeit is to become very familiar with the genuine article. He appealed to his readers to get in excellent spiritual condition so that they could "earnestly contend for the faith which was once delivered unto the saints" (Jude 3). If they knew the Gospel backwards and forwards, they could spot an intruder on sight.

2. RECOIL FROM ERROR. People steadfast in their commitment to the faith pull back from the worthlessness of false teachers. They try to prevent disharmony in the fellowship of believers. They avoid and warn about people who make empty promises and display fruitless lives. They confront blatant immorality and steer the immature away from those who would lead them astray.

3. RESPOND TO ERROR. Steadfast faith contrasts sharply with error in character and behavior. Error is self-centered, vain, and destructive. Steadfast faith is Christ-centered, holy, and constructive. Error has no contact with the power of God's Spirit. Steadfast faith has constant prayerful contact with God's Spirit (Rom. 8:26-27; Gal. 4:6; Eph. 6:18). Error establishes a pecking order that destroys unity. Steadfast faith expresses the love of the Father in such a way that unity is maintained in the Son.

4. RESCUE FROM ERROR. The "mercy of our Lord Jesus Christ" (Jude 21) compels people of steadfast faith to try to rescue fellow believers ensnared in error. Some can be convinced by calm reasoning. Others must be confronted sharply. Those deeply enmeshed in error must be approached with great caution, lest the rescuer be swept away with the victim in the tidal wave of sin.

■ **TOPIC:** Assurance for Daily Living

■ **QUESTIONS:** 1. What were some of the characteristics of the false teaching Jude warned about? 2. How did Jude graphically describe the false teachers? 3. What vices did Jude associate with the false teachers? 4. What actions did Jude recommend for believers to guard against false teaching? 5. How might we someday have to contend for the faith?

■ **ILLUSTRATIONS:**

Anticipating a Future Time of Great Joy. Some folks claim boldly that they plan to live their lives their own way and turn to God only at the last possible moment on their deathbed. This way, they figure, they'll be able to live life to the fullest, yet still set things straight with God before they pass away. Supposedly, it's the best of both worlds.

Moreover, these individuals assume that a happy life comes from following their own whims. Tragically, they overlook the incredible joy that comes from living for God in the here and now. They also fail to realize that assurance for living comes by building a relationship with Him over months and years, through good times and bad.

These procrastinators conjecture that this life is the only place for them to experience fun. Of course, there is fun in this life, but the here and now are not the sum total of human existence. Believers await an eternity with the Lord in which we will enter the "presence of his glory with exceeding joy" (Jude 24). Christians can—and should—live every day in expectation of that time to come.

The Triumph of Forgiveness. Gordan MacDonald was the pastor of a highly visible New England church, the president of an international campus ministry, and the author—sometimes along with his wife—of several Christian best sellers on marriage and pastoral leadership. His life seemed perfect, but it wasn't.

At the height of MacDonald's popularity and influence, he confessed to his congregation that he had been involved in an adulterous relationship. He was deeply apologetic and broken. He was repentant, truly sorry for what he had done and the damage to his marriage, his ministry, and his relationship with God.

MacDonald resigned his presidency of InterVarsity Christian Fellowship. He canceled a pending book contract. He recommitted himself to his wife. And MacDonald placed himself under the discipline of his church leadership. He knew that, biblically speaking, he needed to seek his congregation's forgiveness. Only as a result of receiving their mercy and compassion could he expect to be reconciled and brought back into meaningful fellowship (see Jude 22-23).

The church could have chosen not to forgive. They could have looked at the sin and decided that there was no place for adulterers in their congregation. But, as Jude understood, such a strategy is doomed to fail. If there is no room for adulterers, what about liars, people who have lustful thoughts, and people whose habits are out of control (to name a few categories of sinners)? At this rate, there would be an abundance of free seating in most of our churches!

No, the only realistic response—indeed, the only truly Christian action—is to forgive, to heal, and to grow. Thankfully, that's what Gordan MacDonald experienced. After more than four decades of service as a pastor in Massachusetts, New York City, Illinois, and Kansas, he most recently served as the interim president of Denver Seminary (from 2008-2009).

Have Mercy. Jude 22 and 23 direct believers to show mercy and compassion on others, regardless of where they find themselves in their faith journey. According to a fictional Hebrew story, one of the patriarchs was sitting outside his tent one evening when he saw an old man, weary from age and journey, coming toward him. The patriarch rushed out, greeted him, and invited him into his tent. There he washed the old man's feet and gave him food and drink.

The old man immediately began eating without saying any prayer or blessing. So the patriarch asked him, "Don't you worship God?" The old traveler replied, "I worship fire only and reverence no other god." When the host heard this, he became incensed, grabbed the old man by the shoulders, and threw him out of his tent into the cold night air.

When the old man had departed, God called to His friend and asked where the stranger was. The patriarch replied, "I forced him out because he did not worship You." God answered, "I have suffered him these 80 years, though he dishonors Me. Could you not endure him one night?"

FOR YOUTH

■ TOPIC: Plug into Power!

■ QUESTIONS: 1. Why must we, as Jesus' followers, take a stand for the faith? 2. What danger do religious frauds pose to us as believers? 3. What is the connection between what people believe and how they live? 4. What types of people did Jude think would need correction from false teaching? 5. How should the reality of divine judgment affect the way we live our lives?

■ ILLUSTRATIONS:

Power to Serve. On August 4, 2008, then presidential candidate Barack Obama delivered a speech in Lansing, Michigan, in which he described his new energy plan for America. Among other things, he talked about providing "short-term relief to American families facing pain at the pump." He also wanted to ensure that "10 percent of our electricity comes from renewable sources by 2012, and 25 percent by 2025."

Where do we go, as Jesus' followers, for power to serve Him? According to Jude, it is the Holy Spirit (see vs. 20). Just as we might plug in an electric car to reenergize its depleted batteries, so too we must spiritually plug in ourselves to the third person of the Trinity for strength to endure. Even when times feel hard and we get discouraged, the Spirit is always present in us to enable us to remain faithful to the Lord and to our fellow believers.

Life Under Construction. In her book, *Bird by Bird*, Anne Lamott tells about a report on birds that once overwhelmed her ten-year-old brother. He had had three months to write it, but kept putting it off. Now it was due the next day.

"He was at the kitchen table close to tears," Lamott recalls, "surrounded by binder paper and pencils and unopened books on birds, immobilized by the hugeness of the task ahead. Then my father sat down beside him, put his arm around my brother's shoulder, and said, 'Bird by bird, buddy. Just take it bird by bird.'" A seemingly overwhelming report came together, one piece at a time.

A faithful Christian life can be built in the same way, habit by habit. In Jude's brief letter, the author encouraged believers to build themselves up in godly habits like faith and prayer. He knew that living in a holy manner is a challenge for believers, whether they are younger or older. But, as Jude helps us understand, it is a challenge that can be met, godly action by godly action.

Make a Difference. In the biography, *Scully*, there is an account of a conversation between Steven Jobs, the founder of Apple Computer (along with Steve Wozniak), and John Scully, who at the time was president of Pepsi. Jobs was attempting to recruit Scully for the top job at Apple, and he asked Scully, "Do you want to spend the rest of your life selling sugared water or do you want a chance to change the world?"

Jude also challenged his readers to make a difference in their generation. They could do so by knowing and living their faith in such a vibrant way that what the false teachers were peddling would seem like sugared water by comparison.

HOSANNA!

BACKGROUND SCRIPTURE: Mark 11:1-11
DEVOTIONAL READING: 1 Chronicles 16:8-15

KEY VERSE: Hosanna; Blessed is he that
cometh in the name of the Lord. (Mark 11:9)

KING JAMES VERSION

MARK 11:1 And when they came nigh to Jerusalem, unto Bethphage and Bethany, at the mount of Olives, he sendeth forth two of his disciples, 2 And saith unto them, Go your way into the village over against you: and as soon as ye be entered into it, ye shall find a colt tied, whereon never man sat; loose him, and bring him. 3 And if any man say unto you, Why do ye this? say ye that the Lord hath need of him; and straightway he will send him hither. 4 And they went their way, and found the colt tied by the door without in a place where two ways met; and they loose him. 5 And certain of them that stood there said unto them, What do ye, loosing the colt? 6 And they said unto them even as Jesus had commanded: and they let them go. 7 And they brought the colt to Jesus, and cast their garments on him; and he sat upon him. 8 And many spread their garments in the way: and others cut down branches off the trees, and strawed them in the way. 9 And they that went before, and they that followed, cried, saying, Hosanna; Blessed is he that cometh in the name of the Lord: 10 Blessed be the kingdom of our father David, that cometh in the name of the Lord: Hosanna in the highest. 11 And Jesus entered into Jerusalem, and into the temple: and when he had looked round about upon all things, and now the eventide was come, he went out unto Bethany with the twelve.

NEW REVISED STANDARD VERSION

MARK 11:1 When they were approaching Jerusalem, at Bethphage and Bethany, near the Mount of Olives, he sent two of his disciples 2 and said to them, "Go into the village ahead of you, and immediately as you enter it, you will find tied there a colt that has never been ridden; untie it and bring it. 3 If anyone says to you, 'Why are you doing this?' just say this, 'The Lord needs it and will send it back here immediately.' "
4 They went away and found a colt tied near a door, outside in the street. As they were untying it, 5 some of the bystanders said to them, "What are you doing, untying the colt?" 6 They told them what Jesus had said; and they allowed them to take it. 7 Then they brought the colt to Jesus and threw their cloaks on it; and he sat on it. 8 Many people spread their cloaks on the road, and others spread leafy branches that they had cut in the fields. 9 Then those who went ahead and those who followed were shouting,

"Hosanna!
Blessed is the one who comes in the name of the Lord!
10 Blessed is the coming kingdom of our ancestor David!
Hosanna in the highest heaven!"

11 Then he entered Jerusalem and went into the temple; and when he had looked around at everything, as it was already late, he went out to Bethany with the twelve.

Monday, April 11	Psalm 55:16-22	*Call on God to Save*
Tuesday, April 12	2 Kings 19:14-19	*O Lord, Save Us*
Wednesday, April 13	Psalm 109:21-31	*At the Right Hand of the Needy*
Thursday, April 14	Psalm 22:1-8	*The Lord Rescues*
Friday, April 15	1 Chronicles 16:8-18	*Sing Praises to the Lord*
Saturday, April 16	Matthew 21:12-17	*Children Shout, "Hosanna!"*
Sunday, April 17	Mark 11:1-11	*Welcome the King*

BACKGROUND

In our lesson, we jump ahead in Mark's Gospel to what has commonly been called Jesus' "Passion Week." This refers to the final week of His earthly life. It began with a joyous event—Jesus' triumphal entry into Jerusalem as King. Set on a hill some 2,500 feet above sea level, Jerusalem is 33 miles east of the Mediterranean Sea and 14 miles west of the Dead Sea. Because access was difficult and the city lacked natural resources, it at one time enjoyed a relatively protected location. But when a major regional trade route developed through the city, Jerusalem became commercially and strategically desirable to every subsequent political force that came to power.

The following are some key facts about the holy city: It appears in the Bible as early as Abraham (Gen. 14:18), though the site had probably been inhabited for centuries before; it was captured by David and made the capital of Israel; Jerusalem was the site of Solomon's temple and, in the first century, Herod's temple; the city's estimated population in Jesus' day was probably 50,000 (though during Passover, it possibly grew to 120,000); Jerusalem was besieged and destroyed by the Romans in A.D. 70; and the city was relatively small geographically, but had a sizable metropolitan area with numerous suburban towns.

NOTES ON THE PRINTED TEXT

Jesus, having ministered in Perea and the Jordan River area, now headed westward with His disciples by the steep road leading uphill to Jerusalem. On Sunday, the first day of the week preceding Passover, they came to the towns of Bethphage and Bethany. Bethphage was near Bethany, which in turn was located on the southeastern slopes of "the mount of Olives" (Mark 11:1). Bethany was also about two miles east of Jerusalem near the road to Jericho. Because the Mount of Olives is approximately 2,700 feet in elevation and thus about 200 feet higher than the city of Jerusalem itself, it commanded a superb view of the city and its temple.

With Passover only a few days away, Jerusalem was already filling up with pilgrims from all over. Jesus, too, was expected to be there. On every hand there were high expectations and high tensions. Undoubtedly, some of Jesus' followers were hoping He would use the great national celebration to claim His place as king of the

Jews. The Jewish leaders were hoping to find an opportunity to arrest and execute Him. Knowing the danger, Jesus could have stayed away. Yet He chose otherwise. He decided to enter Jerusalem—but on His own terms.

Jesus instructed two of His followers to go into Bethphage. As soon as they entered the village, perhaps just inside the gate, they would find a mother donkey and her colt tethered there. The disciples were to untie the animals and bring them to Jesus (Matt. 21:2). The colt had never been ridden (Mark 11:2). Jesus would ride the colt, but the colt's mother could also have been taken along as a steadying influence, leading the way as the colt followed (Matt. 21:7). If the disciples were questioned by anyone (for instance, the animals' owner or onlookers), they were to explain that Jesus needed the donkeys (Mark 11:3).

We learn in Matthew 21:4-5 that Jesus' entry into Jerusalem on the back of a colt would fulfill Zechariah 9:9. Jerusalem, personified as the "daughter of Zion," was about to see its long-awaited King—the Messiah—humbly ride into the holy city. In Bible times, unused animals were often taken for religious purposes (Num. 19:2; 1 Sam. 6:7-8). Also, while donkeys were commonly used for transportation, they had come to be associated with royalty and with peace (2 Sam. 16:2; 1 Kings 1:33-34). The Son was unmistakably different from human conquerors. His claim to sovereignty did not rest on political and military subjugation, but on the strength of His character and His obedience to His Father's will. Nowhere did the Son's distinctiveness become more apparent than when He rode into Jerusalem.

The two disciples left and found the animals standing in a street and tied outside a house (Mark 11:4). As Jesus' followers were untying the animals, some bystanders questioned what they were planning to do (vs. 5). When the disciples repeated what Jesus had said, they were permitted to take the animals (vs. 6). It may be that the donkeys' owner was a follower of Jesus and by prearrangement had agreed to provide the animals to the Lord.

The two disciples successfully carried out Jesus' instructions by bringing the donkeys to Him (Matt. 21:6). To show Jesus honor and make Him more comfortable, they placed their cloaks on the animals as a makeshift saddle before Jesus took His seat (Mark 11:7). Presumably, while Jesus sat on the colt, the mother donkey walked beside to calm her offspring (Matt. 21:7). Next, the Messiah started the steep ascent into the valley, a route that for years was jammed with thousands of pilgrims coming to Jerusalem for the Passover. The climb from the valley into the city was more gradual. Jesus' ride was a living parable that set forth His claim to be the Messiah. His kingdom was at hand, a rule characterized by peace, love, humility, and gentleness. This monarch was considerate and compassionate, even to the extent of doing good to His enemies. For instance, He bore their persecutions with a tender, forebearing spirit, even on the cross.

As Jesus rode the donkey, a large crowd of people gathered at the Mount of Olives.

Apparently, they sensed that something dramatic was about to happen. Admittedly, the throng included critics (see Luke 19:39-40). Even so, the majority of the group was full of high hopes, especially as they came from all over Israel and various parts of the Roman Empire to celebrate the Passover. According to a census taken by Emperor Nero, nearly three million Jews came to Jerusalem for the event. A spontaneous outburst of adulation, welcome, and praise filled the air. People tore off their cloaks and spread them on the road (Mark 11:8).

As the triumphal procession made its way, other people cut branches off the trees and spread them on the road (Matt. 21:8). This action was a demonstration of respect such as might have been shown to royalty. From ancient times, people in the Middle East have valued the palm tree for its usefulness and beauty. Its branches and leaves are used as ornaments, while its sap is made into sugar, wax, oil, tannin, and dye. People in the Middle East eat its fruit and grind its seed for their camels. They use its branches in the production of mats, roofs, baskets, and fences. To desert travelers, the shade of a palm tree is a welcome sight.

Furthermore, in Bible times, the Jews applied religious symbolism to the palm tree. For example, the psalmist described the righteous as flourishing like the palm tree (Ps. 92:12). Also, in accordance with the Mosaic law, they celebrated the feast of tabernacles with palm branches (Lev. 23:40). In the time preceding the New Testament era, the Jews used palm branches in their observance of other feasts as symbols of national triumph and victory. Early Christians adopted this appreciation of the palm tree. John himself noted that people in heaven will pay homage to the Messiah with palm branches (Rev. 7:9), which became a symbol of His victory over death. In fact, the emblem of the palm leaf frequently accompanied the monogram of the Savior on Christian tombs.

The people demonstrated their respect for Jesus by word as well as deed. Accompanying Jesus on His journey, they hailed Him with such acclamations as "Hosanna!" (Mark 11:9) and "Blessed is he that cometh in the name of the Lord." These praises all come from Psalm 118:25-26. (Psalms 113–118 were usually sung at Passover.) Most likely, the crowds were thinking Jesus would liberate them from Rome. The word "Hosanna" (Mark 11:9) means "Save now!" or "Save, we pray!" The use of the expression "son of David" (Matt. 21:9) was a recognition of Jesus' royal lineage. The statement appearing in Mark 11:10 was a recognition that Jesus came with the authority and approval of God. "Hosanna in the highest!" implied that the angels of heaven were to praise Jesus. In short, the crowd's words proclaimed Jesus to be the Messiah. The irony is that within a week nearly all support for Jesus would melt away. These truths mirror what the shepherds heard on the night of the Savior's birth. They were greeted by a chorus of angels who gave glory to God and announced peace for all who received the Lord's favor (Luke 2:14).

By the time Jesus crossed from the Mount of Olives to Jerusalem, "the eventide was come" (Mark 11:11). With darkness soon to arrive, most of the people were beginning to leave the temple, the shops, and the gates, and were heading for their homes or inns. So all Jesus did in Jerusalem on this day was to stop briefly in the temple area. The phrase "he had looked round about" in the courts of the shrine complex holds more significance than may at first appear. As the Son of God, Jesus was examining His property to see how it was being used. He said nothing, but from the events of the next day we know He had an opinion (see vss. 15-17). For the time being, Jesus left Jerusalem and spent the night in Bethany, perhaps at the home of Mary, Martha, and Lazarus (see John 12:1-2). This withdrawal from the city may have been for safety's sake, since Jesus knew it was not yet time for Him to fall into His opponents' hands. It may also have been to dramatize His unwillingness to be a part of what was going on in the temple.

SUGGESTIONS TO TEACHERS

Up to this point, Jesus had tried to keep His identity veiled. But during the final week of His earthly ministry, and knowing that this was the divinely appointed time for His crucifixion, Jesus openly proclaimed His identity as the promised Messiah. As He did so, others around Him chose how they would respond. Still today, all people must choose how they view Jesus, who is the unique Son of God.

1. JESUS REVEALED WHO HE WAS. By fulfilling the specific prophecy of Zechariah and then by taking authority over the temple, Jesus announced His identity to the city and all its guests. Through His Word and power, Jesus still reveals Himself to our world today.

2. JESUS' FOLLOWERS ASSISTED THE ANNOUNCEMENT. One group, represented by two disciples who brought the donkey, and another group represented by its owner who released the animal, actively helped Jesus reveal Himself to the people of Jerusalem. How do we, as twenty-first century disciples, assist Jesus, especially as He offers Himself to our world? When our character shows that we love Jesus, other people will notice that we are different. Also, how we live should be consistent with the faith we profess. When we walk our talk (so to speak), God will give us many opportunities to tell others about Jesus.

3. SOME REJECTED JESUS IN ANGER. Those who saw Jesus as a threat to their security and to their control of the circumstances wanted to push Him away. Later in this same week, they would succeed in murdering Jesus. But even that strategy could not defeat Him. Are there those in your circle of acquaintances who are resisting Jesus?

4. OTHERS RECEIVED JESUS GLADLY. The enthusiasm of Jesus' followers attracted others who joined in worshiping Him. Perhaps there are members of your class who have been quietly hanging off to the side. This Sunday might be their day for joining the crowd of disciples.

■ **TOPIC:** Lavishing Praise

■ **QUESTIONS:** 1. How do you think the disciples felt about Jesus' plan to enter Jerusalem? 2. Why is it sometimes hard to understand and obey the Lord's instructions? 3. Why did Jesus choose this time to enter Jerusalem in a royal way and accept the praises of the crowds? 4. How can believers show their exuberant, uninhibited praise to the Savior? 5. What impresses you most about this occasion?

■ **ILLUSTRATIONS:**

Purifying the Worshiping Community. An old saying warns us, "If you find the perfect church, don't join it, because you'll wreck it." Due to our sinful natures, this is always a possibility. On the other hand, God calls His purified people to worship in a purified way. There's no room for ungodliness in Christ's Body.

When Jesus accepted praise from the crowd, He could have felt good about things. But then He witnessed the wretched conditions around the temple, and He decided to risk the crowd's fury. Yes, there was a time to challenge worship that had been corrupted by commercialism. Pure worship was a worthwhile goal that required drastic action.

How easy it is to slip over the line and make worship into a business. This danger lurks everywhere. Therefore, we need constant reminders to purify our hearts before we lavish our praise in worship to the Lord.

Worthy of True Worship. Many churches hand out palm branches as a symbol of the praise Jesus received as He triumphantly entered Jerusalem the week of His crucifixion. The Gospels say palm branches and cloaks were spread out on the ground, covering Jesus' path like a red carpet for a king. The symbolism was perfect. Jesus did not want a king's crown. He wanted people's humble hearts. Palms worked just fine to show the world what kind of king Jesus was.

Our palms work fine today, too. The palms of our hands can symbolize Jesus' kingship and authority to our world. Held out open, our palms can offer our possessions and hearts to His service. Clasped together, they show how we come into His presence in prayer, seeking forgiveness and strength and sharing our needs. Clapping together, our palms applaud Jesus' power. Placed over our hearts, our palms show allegiance to the only King worthy of worship.

This week's lesson explores people's responses to Jesus' kingship and authority in the first century A.D. Consider using the teaching time to suggest ways you can encourage your students to truly worship the Savior in the days ahead.

Overturned Expectations. Lorraine wondered why she hadn't heard from her mother since Christmas. She had made her mother's favorite candy—divinity fudge with walnuts—and shipped it to arrive just in time for the holidays. But except for a curt "Thank you for the box" postscript on a letter back in January, her mother hadn't mentioned it. It was now April. That wasn't like her mom.

Lorraine decided to call. After catching up on the latest family news, she asked her mother how she liked the Christmas candy. Her mom said, "I didn't get any, honey. I'd remember if you sent me fudge." Lorraine replied, "But you wrote back and said 'Thank you for the box,' so I know it arrived." After a long pause, her mother said, "What did you send it in?" Lorraine responded, "An old fruitcake tin we had in the cupboard." Upon hearing this her mom exclaimed, "Oh honey, I'm so sorry!" She explained that she hadn't even bothered to open the tin. When she assumed it contained fruitcake—which she didn't like—she threw the tin in the trash. By not even looking inside, she missed her daughter's wonderful surprise.

When Jesus arrived on the scene, many rejected Him because He didn't look like a "savior" or "king" to them. They expected trumpets, finery, riches, and other symbols of power. Instead, He came on a donkey. That was only one way that Jesus overturned people's ideas of what religion and true power should look like. His whole life and ministry was a series of surprises from God.

FOR YOUTH

■ TOPIC: A Praise Parade!

■ QUESTIONS: 1. What instructions did Jesus give to two of His disciples? 2. What was the significance of Jesus riding into Jerusalem on a colt? 3. Why were the crowds excited to see Jesus? 4. What would you have done, had you been among the throngs of pilgrims that day? 5. What is something Jesus has done for you that you want to praise Him for?

■ ILLUSTRATIONS:

A Time for Personal Examination. Pageantry excites young people, whether it's a sports event, a political rally, an art or music fair, or even a religious event. In Christendom, Christmas, Easter, and Palm Sunday call for pageantry, including processions, music, and colorful banners. For many years, until politics intervened, the Palm Sunday procession leading from the Mount of Olives into Jerusalem was one of the most exciting religious processions anywhere.

Jesus did not avoid a wild public demonstration when the time was right according to His purposes. His triumphal entry into Jerusalem—what we now call Palm Sunday—signified that He threw down the gauntlet to the nation of Israel. Would the people accept His coming as from heaven, from God above, or would they see Jesus simply as another impostor, a false messiah?

This week's lesson prompts your students to examine their motives in coming to Jesus. If they join the crowd in hailing Him, they must accept all He has to offer and the changes He wants to make in their lives.

Missing the Real Event. The story is told of a boy from the country who came to town many years ago to see the circus. He had never seen one before, and was excited at the prospect of watching the clowns, elephants, lions, and tigers. The boy got up early and rode his horse and wagon to town in time for the big parade. Standing at the curb, he clapped enthusiastically as the steam calliope tooted and the stream of gaudily painted circus wagons rumbled by.

The boy shrieked with delight at the clowns and acrobats, and he grew wide-eyed with wonder at the sight of the wild animals in their cages. He laughed at the shuffling lines of elephants and watched the jugglers with wonder. When the parade reached its end, the boy rushed up to the last man in the procession and handed him his money, and then the boy went back home. The lad didn't discover until later that he hadn't seen the circus but had merely watched the parade. He missed the acts under the big top and merely caught sight of the procession leading to the performance.

Some church members are a bit like that boy. They watch the Palm Sunday procession, but they never go any farther. They enjoy a brief emotional experience but miss the real action of the cross and the empty tomb. They enjoy the pageantry and watch the parade briefly, but they never participate in the meaning of the resurrection. Sadly, they never get beyond Palm Sunday's events.

The Cheering Stopped. When World War I ended, American President Woodrow Wilson was a hero across western Europe. The American forces had swung the battle to the Allies. Everyone felt optimistic. Maybe the nations had truly fought their last war and the world had been made safe for democracy. Everyone loved Wilson for his part in the flow of events.

After the war, when Wilson first visited Paris, London, and Rome, cheering crowds greeted him everywhere. Their enthusiasm lasted about a year. Then it gradually stopped. Europeans forgot what Wilson had done and focused their attention on resuming all facets of normal life. Back in Washington, D.C., the U.S. Senate vetoed Wilson's plan for an international peace organization, the League of Nations.

During the last days of his presidency, Wilson's health began to fail. His party lost the next national election. Within a short time, Wilson went from world hero to a broken man. How quickly the crowds turned on him! Jesus did not break under the strain, but He faced the same pattern. Crowds that welcomed Him as He entered Jerusalem on Palm Sunday deserted Him as He moved toward the end.

CHRIST IS RISEN!

BACKGROUND SCRIPTURE: Matthew 28:1-17

DEVOTIONAL READING: 1 Corinthians 15:1-8

KEY VERSE: As they went to tell his disciples, behold, Jesus met them, saying, All hail. And they came and held him by the feet, and worshipped him. (Matthew 28:9)

KING JAMES VERSION

MATTHEW 28:1 In the end of the sabbath, as it began to dawn toward the first day of the week, came Mary Magdalene and the other Mary to see the sepulchre. 2 And, behold, there was a great earthquake: for the angel of the Lord descended from heaven, and came and rolled back the stone from the door, and sat upon it. 3 His countenance was like lightning, and his raiment white as snow: 4 And for fear of him the keepers did shake, and became as dead men. 5 And the angel answered and said unto the women, Fear not ye: for I know that ye seek Jesus, which was crucified. 6 He is not here: for he is risen, as he said. Come, see the place where the Lord lay. 7 And go quickly, and tell his disciples that he is risen from the dead; and, behold, he goeth before you into Galilee; there shall ye see him: lo, I have told you. 8 And they departed quickly from the sepulchre with fear and great joy; and did run to bring his disciples word. 9 And as they went to tell his disciples, behold, Jesus met them, saying, All hail. And they came and held him by the feet, and worshipped him. 10 Then said Jesus unto them, Be not afraid: go tell my brethren that they go into Galilee, and there shall they see me.

11 Now when they were going, behold, some of the watch came into the city, and shewed unto the chief priests all the things that were done. 12 And when they were assembled with the elders, and had taken counsel, they gave large money unto the soldiers, 13 Saying, Say ye, His disciples came by night, and stole him away while we slept. 14 And if this come to the governor's ears, we will persuade him, and secure you. 15 So they took the money, and did as they were taught: and this saying is commonly reported among the Jews until this day.

16 Then the eleven disciples went away into Galilee, into a mountain where Jesus had appointed them. 17 And when they saw him, they worshipped him: but some doubted.

NEW REVISED STANDARD VERSION

MATTHEW 28:1 After the sabbath, as the first day of the week was dawning, Mary Magdalene and the other Mary went to see the tomb. 2 And suddenly there was a great earthquake; for an angel of the Lord, descending from heaven, came and rolled back the stone and sat on it. 3 His appearance was like lightning, and his clothing white as snow. 4 For fear of him the guards shook and became like dead men. 5 But the angel said to the women, "Do not be afraid; I know that you are looking for Jesus who was crucified. 6 He is not here; for he has been raised, as he said. Come, see the place where he lay. 7 Then go quickly and tell his disciples, 'He has been raised from the dead, and indeed he is going ahead of you to Galilee; there you will see him.' This is my message for you." 8 So they left the tomb quickly with fear and great joy, and ran to tell his disciples. 9 Suddenly Jesus met them and said, "Greetings!" And they came to him, took hold of his feet, and worshiped him. 10 Then Jesus said to them, "Do not be afraid; go and tell my brothers to go to Galilee; there they will see me."

11 While they were going, some of the guard went into the city and told the chief priests everything that had happened. 12 After the priests had assembled with the elders, they devised a plan to give a large sum of money to the soldiers, 13 telling them, "You must say, 'His disciples came by night and stole him away while we were asleep.' 14 If this comes to the governor's ears, we will satisfy him and keep you out of trouble." 15 So they took the money and did as they were directed. And this story is still told among the Jews to this day.

16 Now the eleven disciples went to Galilee, to the mountain to which Jesus had directed them. 17 When they saw him, they worshiped him; but some doubted.

Monday, April 18	1 Corinthians 15:1-8	*Good News of First Importance*
Tuesday, April 19	Matthew 26:1-5	*The Plot to Kill Jesus*
Wednesday, April 20	Matthew 27:15-26	*The Judgment against Jesus*
Thursday, April 21	Matthew 27:32-44	*The Crucifixion of Jesus*
Friday, April 22	Matthew 27:45-56	*Witnesses to Jesus' Death*
Saturday, April 23	Matthew 27:57-61	*Witnesses to Jesus' Burial*
Sunday, April 24	Matthew 28:1-17	*Witnesses to Jesus' Resurrection*

BACKGROUND

No one in the crowds at Golgotha the day Jesus was crucified expected Him to come back to life. Understandably, Jesus' friends were overwhelmed by fear, because they assumed that the high priest and the Sanhedrin would also ask the Roman authorities to arrest the Savior's followers and possibly have them executed. Of course, this concern disregarded the fact that Jesus had plainly told the disciples on several occasions that after He had been crucified He would be raised from the dead. Evidently, His words seemed like a fairy tale to the disciples.

Besides, Pilate had posted guards at the tomb where Jesus' body lay. The alliance of the political and religious leaders was to ensure that Jesus' crucifixion was the final blow to this popular movement of Galileans. At first, high hopes had risen in the hearts of Jesus' followers. But now they were all smashed, stained in the blood of Golgotha. A once-brilliant dream had been shattered. Against such a dark backdrop are the startling words about Jesus' resurrection recorded in Matthew 28. If this episode were part of a novel, readers would not expect such an amazing conclusion. Even in fiction, dead heroes and leaders of revolutionary movements do not experience resurrection. In that sense, the Gospel account has the strangest twist in all the world's literature.

NOTES ON THE PRINTED TEXT

Matthew 28 begins with the ending of the Sabbath, which had drawn to a close at sundown on Saturday. Jesus' followers were free to go to His tomb now, but of course they did not want to do so at night. Thus, at first light on Sunday, Mary Magdalene and Mary the mother of James and Joses went to the burial site (vs. 1). They had watched Jesus' entombment and so knew where to go (see 27:56, 61). An examination of Luke 24:1 indicates that the women who "came unto the sepulchre" were the same women previously identified as eyewitnesses of the Crucifixion: "the women that followed him from Galilee" (23:49; also vs. 55). Those same women are named in 24:10.

According to Matthew 28:1, the two Marys went to the tomb to look at it, perhaps because Jewish tradition called for loved ones of the deceased to visit a tomb for three days after the burial to be sure the person had truly died. Mark 16:1 additionally relates that the women hoped to anoint Jesus' body. This was a customary practice to mask the odor brought on by decay. It was also an act of devotion. At some point, perhaps shortly before the women's arrival at the tomb, a severe earthquake had occurred. An angel of the Lord had descended from heaven, rolled back the stone from the entrance, and "sat upon it" (Matt. 28:2).

The angel did not remove the stone to enable Jesus to leave the tomb; rather, the celestial being did it to permit others to enter the sepulcher and see for themselves that Jesus' body was gone. The angel had a glorious appearance. Verse 3 says his face beamed with the brightness of "lightning" and his clothes were brilliant like snow (perhaps to reflect his holiness). His awesome presence (after he had arrived at the tomb) caused the guards to tremble with fear. In fact, they were so terrified that they "became as dead men" (vs. 4), which possibly means they fainted. They evidently then fled in terror. Because the angel's appearance also frightened the women, the angel told them, "Fear not ye" (vs. 5). He then said he was aware that the women were coming to find the crucified Jesus. Next, the angel gave them the startling news that they would not find Jesus' body because He was alive. Jesus had risen from the dead, just as He had foretold (vs. 6; see 16:21; 17:23; 20:19). As proof that Jesus truly was alive, the angel invited the women to examine the spot where His body had been.

After the women had taken a little time to examine the empty tomb, the angel told them to deliver an important message to Jesus' disciples. The message was that He had "risen from the dead" (vs. 7) and would be going ahead of the disciples to Galilee. They would meet Him there, in fulfillment of an earlier promise to them (26:32). The statement "lo, I have told you" (28:7) implies that the message from the angel was extremely important and that the women were not to delay in reporting it. Matthew and Mark both mention that the angel directed the women to tell Jesus' disciples that they should meet Him in Galilee (Matt. 28:7; Mark 16:7). John also mentions another appearance by Jesus in Galilee to seven disciples by the sea (John 21). That Jesus would appear to His disciples in Galilee seems appropriate when we consider His earthly ministry. For all practical purposes, Galilee was His home (Matt. 21:11), and He summoned most of the disciples there.

The two Marys, having encountered the angel and heard the news of Jesus' resurrection, felt both fear and joy. They were afraid, for they stood in the presence of a supernatural being come from heaven. But the empty tomb and the angel's words also made them experience intense "joy" (28:8). In fact, the realization that the one they thought was gone forever had come back to life sent them running—not walking—to tell the disciples. Another surprise still awaited the women as they hurried on their way. They met the risen Lord. His "All hail" (vs. 9) was a common statement that expressed a wish for happiness and well-being in the recipients. Upon seeing the risen Lord, the women approached Him, fell at His feet, and worshiped Him. Paying such homage to God the Son was an entirely appropriate response. The sight of the Messiah was also a good reason to be filled with delight, for He had conquered death.

There evidently was a strong sense of fear in the women as they prostrated themselves in the presence of the glorified Savior. Like the angel, Jesus directed the women not to be afraid (vs. 10). In His presence, they were to be courageous. Jesus also repeated the same basic message the angel had given to the women. Perhaps this was to underscore the urgency of their telling the disciples to go to Galilee, where they would see Him. It was gracious of Jesus to call the disciples "my brethren," for just a few days earlier they had denied and abandoned Him (see 26:56). Despite what they had done, He was willing to forgive them and to allow them to serve Him. They were members of the Savior's spiritual family and would share in His inheritance. In accordance with Jesus' instructions, the women went to the rest of the disciples to report that they had seen the risen Lord.

Meanwhile, some of the soldiers who had been stationed at the tomb returned to Jerusalem and reported to the chief priests "all the things that were done" (28:11). This report probably included mention of the earthquake, the appearance of the angel, and the opening of the tomb. If the chief priests had considered the situation in an objective and unbiased manner, they would have realized that Jesus had indeed risen from the dead. Instead of believing the obvious truth, however, the chief priests assembled with the elders and devised a scheme to explain the empty tomb (vs. 12). The religious leaders bribed the soldiers with a large sum of money, telling them to claim that, while they were asleep, Jesus' disciples stole the body from the tomb (vs. 13). The chief priests and elders promised to intercede for the soldiers, if necessary, to prevent them from being punished for dereliction of duty. If Pilate were to hear an unfavorable report, the religious leaders would satisfy his concerns about the matter and keep the soldiers out of trouble (vs. 14).

The soldiers, being pleased with this arrangement, accepted the bribe and did as they had been instructed. Perhaps with the help of the Jewish authorities, they spread a rumor that Jesus' followers had stolen His body from the tomb to fake His resurrection. Matthew noted that this story, though false, was still being circulated at the time he wrote his Gospel (vs. 15). All four Gospels agree that Jesus' tomb was empty the first Easter morning and that the Messiah later appeared to His followers to prove that He had risen from the dead (1 Cor. 15:3-8). Even the religious leaders did not deny that the tomb was empty. They just invented the story that Jesus' disciples stole His body (Matt. 28:11-15).

There are numerous problems with the stolen-body theory worth mentioning. For example, how could sleeping guards know for sure that Jesus' body was taken? Why were the disciples not immediately arrested for the serious offense of desecrating a grave? Why would demoralized, frightened disciples confront armed guards in an attempt to steal the body? And why would these disciples, knowing that Jesus was dead, go into the next decades to preach the Gospel with power—and willingly accept martyrdom for themselves? These unanswered questions indicate that it is more intellectually satisfying to accept, rather than reject, the truth of the Messiah's resurrection from the dead.

Perhaps the strongest evidence for the truth of the Resurrection is what happened to Jesus' disciples afterward. They had seen Him after He rose from the dead and heard His instructions to tell all the world about Him. They did not need to see or hear anything else. They just went into all the world and did what He told them to do. That kind of courage and determination would not come from a deception or a myth. In the next segment of their journey, Jesus' disciples traveled north from Jerusalem to Galilee to meet with Him. These disciples were originally from Galilee, and Jesus had spent much of His earthly ministry there. So it was fitting for the risen Lord to meet His followers in Galilee at the "mountain where Jesus had appointed them" (vs. 16). We don't know which mountain this was.

When the disciples saw Jesus, their response was mixed. Some "worshipped him" (vs. 17), which means they recognized Him to be the risen Lord and paid Him homage as the Son of God. Others, however, doubted. They were uncertain about whether Jesus had truly risen from the dead or whether the person they were meeting was actually Jesus. Thankfully, these differing responses did not prevent Jesus from declaring that the Father had given Him all authority in heaven and earth (vs. 18). Jesus, by being completely faithful in His mission on earth, had proved His right to have such authority. Indeed, it was the basis for the commission He was about to give.

SUGGESTIONS TO TEACHERS

Someone has said about Easter, "Though each step to the cross was a step of agony, it was also a step of victory." Jesus was victorious over the enemy that all of us finally face—death. What happened that first Easter morning has profound implications for all Christians today. Four truths stand out.

1. THE EMPTY TOMB. There is no greater hope in this life than what comes from Jesus' resurrection. Because He lives, we too can live after the end of this lifetime. Note what Paul said: "If in this life only we have hope in Christ, we are of all men most miserable. But now is Christ risen from the dead, and become the first fruits of them that slept" (1 Cor. 15:19-20). Jesus was the "advance party" of those who will follow Him.

2. THE ETERNAL DESTINATION. Jesus rose from the dead to return to heaven and reign eternally. Heaven is also the destination of all believers. As Paul said, "we have a building of God, a house not made with hands, eternal in the heavens" (2 Cor. 5:1). That home is waiting for us even now.

3. THE DEFEATED ENEMY. While Satan may have believed that he had triumphed over the Son of God on the cross, the opposite was true. Jesus defeated Satan, and we can have victory over him as well. He cannot keep us from doing God's will unless we let him. If you "resist the devil, . . . he will flee from you" (Jas. 4:7).

4. THE EASTER MESSAGE. The good news about Easter is most of all a message that must be shared. It is, Paul told the Corinthians, a message of foremost importance (1 Cor. 15:3-4). Every person needs to hear that Jesus rose from the dead and offers those who trust in Him eternal life. Will everyone believe the truth? No. But that does not mean we should not share it, and especially share what it means to us personally.

FOR ADULTS	▨ TOPIC: Eternal Remembrance ▨ QUESTIONS: 1. Why did the women come to the tomb so early in the day? 2. If you were among the women, how do you think you would

have responded to the angel? 3. Why do you think Jesus appeared to the women, especially since He simply repeated what the angel had already said? 4. What response do you think you would give to the false report made by the guards? 5. Would you have gone to Galilee to see Jesus? Why?

▨ ILLUSTRATIONS:

Changing Defeat into Victory. Easter for Christians memorializes the resurrection of a rejected King. His resurrection brought victorious life out of dark death and despair. This is perhaps the greatest reversal in history!

Jesus was the only perfect human who ever lived. His contemporaries hated Him, but they could find no flaws in His life and teachings. Yet the greatest life ever lived suffered a terrible end.

Thankfully, the Father's love, wisdom, and power provided forgiveness, hope, and eternal life out of apparent defeat. The Son's incomparable triumph from tragedy stands as the greatest event of all time. But it is more than a historical incident. Jesus lives in the hearts of all those who trust in Him. And He empowers them to bear witness to others the truth of His resurrection.

The Power in a Seed. In a cemetery in Hanover, Germany, there is a grave where huge slabs of granite and marble are cemented together and fastened with heavy steel clasps. It belongs to a woman who did not believe in the resurrection of the dead. Yet strangely, she directed in her will that her grave be made so secure that, if there were a resurrection, it would not include her.

On the marker were inscribed these words: "This burial place must never be opened." In time, however, a seed covered over by the stones began to grow. Slowly it pushed its way through the soil and out from beneath them. As the trunk enlarged, the great slabs were gradually shifted so that the steel clasps were wrenched from their sockets. A tiny seed had become a tree that had pushed aside the massive stones.

The power seen at the Resurrection is the same power that can change a hardened heart toward God. The power seen at the Resurrection is the same power that will raise those who die in the Lord to eternal life with Him.

The Only Answer. Some of the hardest questions in life all have the same answer: What is it that gives a widow courage as she stands beside a fresh grave? What is the ultimate hope of the amputee, the abused, or the burn victim? How can the parents of a brain-damaged or physically handicapped child keep from living their lives totally depressed? Where do the thoughts of a young couple go when they finally recover from the grief of losing their newborn child? How about when a family receives the news that their dad was killed in a terrorist attack? How about when a son or daughter dies due to an overdose? What is the final answer to pain, mourning, senility, insanity, terminal diseases, sudden calamities, and fatal accidents?

By now, hopefully, you have guessed the correct answer. Because Jesus conquered sin and death through His resurrection, believers also have the assurance of one day being raised from the dead. Indeed, the saints in heaven have an eternity to praise Jesus for His victory!

FOR YOUTH

■ **TOPIC:** He Lives!

■ **QUESTIONS:** 1. How would you have felt at the tomb? Why? 2. What did the guards at Jesus' tomb experience while they were on duty? 3. Why did the angel invite the women to see the empty tomb for themselves? 4. What did Jesus tell the women to do? 5. If you were among the early disciples, how do you think you would have responded to the risen Jesus?

■ **ILLUSTRATIONS:**

Alive! On student trips to Washington, D.C., I used to stand in awe before the memorials to the United States' greatest heroes—Washington, Jefferson, and Lincoln. I admired their courage and wisdom. They spoke to me in their speeches and proclamations. I owe them a great debt.

Nevertheless, these greats from the past are dead and gone. We cannot know them personally. We cannot invite them into our hearts. In contrast, we can know Jesus in an intimate and personal way.

That's because Jesus is alive in heaven. There is a real person in heaven, the same person who came to earth two thousand years ago. Jesus invites our trust, worship, hope, and obedience. We can talk to Him in prayer. He is our supreme confidant and helper.

Surprise! A two-year-old girl could hardly wait for Easter to come. She had a new dress to wear and new shoes to go with it, but her father wondered whether she knew the true meaning of the holiday.

"Kara," he asked, "do you know what Easter means?"

"Yes, I do," she smiled.

"What does it mean then?"

With a smile on her face and her arms raised, she cried, "Surprise!"

What better word could there be to describe Easter? No one expected a crucified person to rise from the dead. Even the religious leaders, who put a guard on the tomb, did not do so because they expected a resurrection. The women came that morning to anoint a body, not find an empty grave. No one expected Jesus to be alive, but He was—and He still is! Surprise!

Waiting for Someone to Come. Marilyn Laszlo serves as a Bible translator in the jungles of Papua New Guinea. In the village of Hauna, she teaches the people to read and write their own language and has aided in the formation of a strong church.

One day, a canoe loaded with 15 people from a distant village arrived to receive medical help. They stayed for a week and attended services where they heard for the first time the good news of Jesus' resurrection. Before they returned home, the visitors asked, "Could you come to our village and give us God's Word so that we might know about Him, too?"

Several weeks later, some missionaries set out for the village. They arrived to find a new building, very different from all the other houses, standing in the center of the village. When the missionaries asked about the structure, they were told, "That's God's house. That's our church."

The missionaries were puzzled, knowing there had not been any Christian work in that part of the country. "What is that building for?" the missionaries asked. In response, the tribal leaders explained, "Well, we saw that church in your village, and our people decided to build a church, too. Now we are waiting for someone to tell us about God in our language."

Today, there are thousands of groups like this one waiting to hear in their language the saving message of Jesus' resurrection from the dead. Indeed, they are waiting for someone like you to respond.

THE CHRIST HYMN

BACKGROUND SCRIPTURE: Philippians 2:1-11
DEVOTIONAL READING: 1 Peter 2:18-25

KEY VERSE: Let this mind be in you, which
was also in Christ Jesus. (Philippians 2:5)

KING JAMES VERSION

PHILIPPIANS 2:1 If there be therefore any consolation in Christ, if any comfort of love, if any fellowship of the Spirit, if any bowels and mercies, 2 Fulfil ye my joy, that ye be likeminded, having the same love, being of one accord, of one mind. 3 Let nothing be done through strife or vainglory; but in lowliness of mind let each esteem other better than themselves. 4 Look not every man on his own things, but every man also on the things of others. 5 Let this mind be in you, which was also in Christ Jesus: 6 Who, being in the form of God, thought it not robbery to be equal with God: 7 But made himself of no reputation, and took upon him the form of a servant, and was made in the likeness of men: 8 And being found in fashion as a man, he humbled himself, and became obedient unto death, even the death of the cross. 9 Wherefore God also hath highly exalted him, and given him a name which is above every name: 10 That at the name of Jesus every knee should bow, of things in heaven, and things in earth, and things under the earth; 11 And that every tongue should confess that Jesus Christ is Lord, to the glory of God the Father.

NEW REVISED STANDARD VERSION

PHILIPPIANS 2:1 If then there is any encouragement in Christ, any consolation from love, any sharing in the Spirit, any compassion and sympathy, 2 make my joy complete: be of the same mind, having the same love, being in full accord and of one mind. 3 Do nothing from selfish ambition or conceit, but in humility regard others as better than yourselves. 4 Let each of you look not to your own interests, but to the interests of others. 5 Let the same mind be in you that was in Christ Jesus,
6 who, though he was in the form of God,
  did not regard equality with God
  as something to be exploited,
7 but emptied himself,
  taking the form of a slave,
  being born in human likeness.
 And being found in human form,
8 he humbled himself
  and became obedient to the point of death—
  even death on a cross.
9 Therefore God also highly exalted him
  and gave him the name
  that is above every name,
10 so that at the name of Jesus
  every knee should bend,
  in heaven and on earth and under the earth,
11 and every tongue should confess
  that Jesus Christ is Lord,
  to the glory of God the Father.

9

Monday, April 25	1 Peter 2:18-25	*Follow in Christ's Steps*
Tuesday, April 26	James 3:13-18	*Good Lives Shown in Works*
Wednesday, April 27	Matthew 10:34-39	*Being Worthy of Jesus*
Thursday, April 28	Ephesians 4:1-6	*Lives Worthy of Your Calling*
Friday, April 29	Colossians 1:9-18	*Lives Worthy of the Lord*
Saturday, April 30	Philippians 1:27-30	*Lives Worthy of the Gospel*
Sunday, May 1	Philippians 2:1-11	*Living the Mind of Christ*

BACKGROUND

In ancient times, the Greeks disdained the notion of "lowliness of mind" (Phil. 2:3). Indeed, they regarded humility as something to be avoided and overcome with positive thoughts and actions. Believers, however, operated differently. God wanted them to recognize their true sinful condition and need for His grace. This is in keeping with the Greek noun rendered "lowliness of mind," which means to think rightly about one's position in life.

Here we see that humility is a continual appreciation of our need for the Savior and of our need to always depend on Him. This was the opposite of the Greek concept of freedom, which called for a person not to be subject to anyone or anything, including God. For the Messiah, humility meant a recognition of His role as a servant in becoming human. Since He was sinless, recognition of His true condition did not involve sin. He did, however, demonstrate the need to depend daily on the Father for strength.

NOTES ON THE PRINTED TEXT

In Philippians 2:1-2, Paul called the recipients of his letter to unity, humility, and obedience. As long as the congregation remained divided, they would not be able to resist the opposition they faced from antagonists (see 1:28). Although the Jewish population in Philippi was small, the problems in the city could have been caused by Jews from other cities who sometimes followed Paul and made trouble for his ministry in the towns he visited (Acts 17:13). However, the opposition referred to in Philippians 1:28 was probably the resistance of the pagan populace in general. They had created a mob scene in which Paul and Silas were arrested on their initial visit to Philippi (Acts 16:16-24).

The persecution encountered by Paul's readers undermined their Christian unity. Well aware of how this problem was manifesting itself among his friends, the apostle appealed to them in four compelling ways. First, the apostle noted the united position of his readers in the Messiah (Phil. 2:1). In a manner of speaking, he was saying to his readers, "We are all in this together." Second, Paul reminded the Philippians about Jesus' love. The Son died for each one of them because He loved each one of them. Third, the apostle stressed the indwelling of the Holy Spirit in each of his readers.

Since there is one Spirit, there is one body of believers of which the Philippian believers were a part. Thus the sharing of the one Spirit of God should have compelled them to avoid any action or attitude that would divide the Body of Christ.

Finally, Paul spoke about the tender feelings and deep sympathy his readers were to have for one another. This was prompted by the apostle's strong desire for these believers to be drawn together. Yet, rather than command the Philippians to bury any resentment they may have toward one another and behave as good Christians should, Paul appealed to their hearts in such a way as to motivate them to be loving and forgiving toward one another. Though the apostle had zealously persecuted the earliest followers of Jesus Christ, the Lord still called this passionate Pharisee from Tarsus to be an important messenger to the Gentiles of the gospel of love and forgiveness. Paul accomplished his God-appointed mission by personally establishing churches throughout Greece and Asia Minor and by writing divinely inspired letters to Christians throughout the Mediterranean world—including those living in Philippi.

Just as the apostle made four appeals to his readers, so he listed four results from such an effort to be united. First, the Philippians would be of the same mind. This does not mean they would always think the exact same thoughts. Instead, Paul meant they would be in agreement about laboring together for the glory of Christ. Second, they would experience the love for one another they each had in the Savior. Third, they would be wholeheartedly of one accord. Finally, they would be of one mind in purpose as a church (vs. 2).

Paul warned his readers not to succumb to those spiritual viruses that damage Christian unity. "Strife" (vs. 3) and "vainglory" were evils that had evidently stricken some of the Philippian believers. Perhaps there were some who were engaging in party strife and petty squabbles because of their self-centeredness. Instead, the apostle admonished them to be humble, not like one who cringes before others, but like one who treats others as being more worthy than himself or herself. Paul advised that believers should look to the interests of other Christians as well as their own concerns (vs. 4).

The supreme example of humility was the attitude that Jesus had when He rescued us from sin (vs. 5). The apostle portrayed Jesus' disposition in what some scholars have suggested was originally a hymn sung in the early church. Those in favor of this view maintain that Paul quoted the song in verses 6-11 to provide an example of humility. These conservative evangelical scholars note the solemn tone of Paul's words, the way they fit together, and the manner in which they were carefully chosen. Read aloud in the Greek, the rhythmical quality of the words provides further evidence that this passage could have easily been sung.

There is no problem in seeing these verses as an incorporation of an early hymn. The words definitely reflect Paul's thought and support his point, which would make their inclusion natural. On the other hand, the apostle was capable of writing poetic passages (1 Cor. 13, for example), and he should not be dismissed as the author just because of style. Either way, Philippians 2:6-11 provides a wonderfully concise theology of the person of Christ and accurately reflects other statements of Scripture regarding the Savior. In particular, we learn about the humility and exaltation of the Redeemer, which Paul wanted to convey to his readers.

If we truly are to have the mind of the Messiah, then we should also have this attitude of loving humility in relationship with others and self-sacrificing obedience to God. This was the disposition Paul wanted the Philippians to embrace. He reminded them that prior to the Son's incarnation, He eternally existed as God with the Father and the Spirit (vs. 6). One of the key doctrines of the Christian faith is that Jesus is, always was, and always will be God. In fact, Paul declared in Colossians 2:9 that in the Messiah all the fullness of the Godhead dwelt in bodily form. Philippians 2:6 reveals that Jesus not only is God but also decided not to use His privileges as God to seize His share of divine glory and honor, but instead chose the path of lowly obedience.

The Son acted upon His decision to be obedient to the Father by emptying Himself, which is the literal meaning of the Greek phrase and which the KJV translates as "made himself of no reputation" (vs. 7). In this selfless act, Jesus did not give up His divinity, but laid aside His kingly privileges as God to become a human being. He also did not choose to be an earthly monarch, a wealthy merchant, a powerful military leader, an idolized athlete or entertainer, or even a renowned philosopher. Jesus became a servant. Once Jesus became fully human through His incarnation, people who knew Him could see that He possessed the full nature of a human being—except that He was without sin. He hungered as any human would. He felt the discomfort of hot and cold weather as any person would. He became tired after a long walk in the same way His fellow travelers became exhausted.

In verse 7, Paul described three steps in Jesus' mission. He emptied Himself; He "took upon him the form of a servant"; and He was "made in the likeness of men." From birth to death, Jesus lived in humility. He was born in a stable. His parents were refugees in Egypt. Jesus grew up in obedience to His parents. He worked at a humble trade as a carpenter. Jesus cried with those who grieved. He washed the feet of His disciples. Paul summarized the Messiah's self-emptying this way: "ye know the grace of our Lord Jesus Christ, that, though he was rich, yet for your sakes he became poor, that ye through his poverty might be rich" (2 Cor. 8:9).

Because of His sinlessness, Jesus could choose whether to die (see John 10:17-18). All people are subject to physical death unless God decrees differently, but Jesus could conceivably have rejected this final conclusion to His earthly life. The Son, however, chose to die—not to leave this life peacefully like Enoch, but to die on the cross in anguish and humiliation so that we might live in renewed and eternal communion with the Father (Phil. 2:8). Paul could not end his extended illustration with Jesus on the cross. The place of honor that Jesus willingly forsook was given back to

Him with the added glory of His triumph over sin and death. In response to Jesus' humility and obedience, the Father supremely exalted the Son to a place where His triumph will eventually be recognized by every living creature (vs. 9).

The apostle emphatically tells us that every person who has ever lived will someday recognize Jesus for who He is. The "name of Jesus" (vs. 10) signifies the position God gave Him, not His proper name. By bowing their knees, every human being and angel will acknowledge Jesus' deity and sovereignty. Everyone will confess that Jesus is Lord—some with joyful faith, others with hopeless regret and despair (vs. 11). Centuries earlier, the prophet Isaiah had announced the words of the Messiah: "unto me every knee shall bow, every tongue shall swear" (Isa. 45:23). Philippians 2:6-11 affirms that this universal acknowledgment of Jesus' lordship will ultimately come to pass.

SUGGESTIONS TO TEACHERS

In the world, aggression is seen as strength, while humility connotes weakness. Occasionally, a servant—such as a devoted minister of the Gospel—is honored. But for every one of these individuals, there are hundreds of arrogant athletes, actors, and others who count ego and pride as virtues. Few among them would be willing to tie on the apron of a servant (so to speak).

1. CHOOSING TO BE DIFFERENT. Being clothed with the humility of the Son means seeing ourselves as the Father sees us and respecting others by loving them unconditionally. Jesus did far more for us by leaving the glories of heaven to become a human being and eventually dying on the cross for our sins. Out of gratitude for Him, we should treat one another with kindness, sensitivity, and compassion.

2. TAKING THE LEAD TO BE DIFFERENT. Christian leaders are the role models for other believers. First, they must lead by example, as our Lord did. He did not call believers to do anything He Himself had not done or was not willing to do. He lived His life as a servant, died for the unrighteous, and loves the unlovely without limits.

3. BEING OTHERS-FOCUSED. In this way of thinking and acting, Christian leaders become role models of humility by submitting to Jesus, rather than advocating a personal agenda. These leaders also acknowledge the need for resources beyond themselves. Any church leader's burden will be lightened by casting his or her cares on the Lord.

4. AFFIRMING THE VALUE OF OTHERS. A godly leader respects every person in the congregation. If that happens, each member in turn will see others as people of value who are appreciated for what they contribute to the church. The world's theme song is "My Way." Every member of the Body of Christ should say, "I will do this the Lord's way, for the benefit of others."

■ TOPIC: Emulating Others

■ QUESTIONS: 1. What does unity in your congregation look like? 2. How do we develop humility and dispose of selfish ambition? 3. What effects does Jesus' humiliation have on the Christian's outlook on life? On the life of the church? 4. Why is it hard to live by the principle that exaltation follows humiliation? 5. How might your church's business meetings be different if Philippians 2:1-11 was read thoughtfully before the meeting started?

■ ILLUSTRATIONS:

What Me, Serve? We all need reminding that the Lord Jesus is number one. This remains true regardless of whether we are ministers, deacons, trustees, Sunday school teachers, or other church officers. This knowledge calls for us to emulate Him in humble servanthood to others in Christ's name.

Often, however, we are like the woman in a certain congregation who was asked to prepare a snack for her children and others in her church youth group for one evening. She retorted in a scalding tone, "You mean you are asking me to come up to the church and do the work of a servant?" Exactly! And in the process, we might encourage others to emulate a similar attitude by their actions.

Extending a Humble, Helping Hand. It was the most cluttered that David's 300-acre farm had ever looked. Fifteen combines, 24 grain trucks, and about 50 friends had converged on his land. By the end of the day, 60,000 bushels of corn would be harvested, then transported to a nearby grain elevator.

The oil company David used for years had provided the fuel. His local bank provided a catered lunch. Family and friends provided the labor—and kind words of remembrance. This is how the farm community in a Midwest town mourned the unexpected death of one of its own. For a day, everyone's usual priorities had been shelved. David's widow had needed a humble, helping hand—in fact, many hands!

When was the last time you dropped everything to help someone for a day? Right now, is there someone who needs you to put his or her needs ahead of your own (see Phil. 2:3-4)?

The Path of Humility. Several years ago, the Chinese government launched a plan to stamp out its country's notoriously bad customer service, a remnant of Communist rule. According to a report in *The New York Times*, "In China, it is common for clerks to abandon their post without notice, and to ignore—or even insult—customers who happen to come along."

To help store clerks deliver better service, the government has banned 50 of the most commonly used phrases, including these: "Buy it if you can afford it. Otherwise, get out of here." "Time is up. Be quick!" "Didn't I tell you? How come you don't get it?" "Why didn't you choose well when you bought it?"

It would be rare to hear such comments from clerks in the United States. But that doesn't mean they don't want to blurt out these kinds of remarks. And this observation points to a sobering truth. It's difficult to see others' needs as being equal to our own. If we aren't "looking out for number one," we tend to feel more like doormats than godly servants.

It doesn't have to be like that. In this week's Scripture passage, Paul pointed toward a better way of living through the example of the Messiah. The apostle reminded his readers that the Son, the Creator of the universe, humbled Himself to the extent of dying on a cross. In turn, His followers are to follow the path of humility by sacrificially serving one another.

■ TOPIC: Praise and Submission

■ QUESTIONS: 1. What reasons did Paul give the Philippians for pursuing oneness in the midst of being persecuted? 2. How is it possible for us, as Jesus' followers, to balance looking out for the interests of others while not neglecting our own legitimate concerns? 3. How was it possible for Jesus, who is fully God, to become fully human? 4. Why did the Father highly exalt the Son? 5. Why is it often challenging for us as believers to model the humble attitude of the Lord Jesus?

■ ILLUSTRATIONS:

Genuine Humility. Paul wanted the believers in the Philippian church to change. The apostle did not call for a conference on management. Instead, he called for a fresh look at the suffering Savior. Until His followers praised Him with their words and submitted to Him in their attitudes and actions, they would not discover genuine and joyful humility.

A Christian pastor said, "A person who profoundly changed my life was not a preacher or the leader of a big organization. She was a cheerful office worker at the local bus company. She never married. She used her home and her slim resources to develop Christian maturity among college students. Many of them—including myself—went into the ministry at home and abroad."

Few of us recognize the power of humble, exuberant, Christian service. But when the books are revealed, we may be surprised to learn that the major influences in God's kingdom come from unselfish, loving servants. Our own lives and our churches are immeasurably enriched when we follow the mind of Christ.

Considering the Needs of Others. *The Apprentice* is a reality television series that its producers have billed as "the ultimate job interview." On any given show a diverse group of candidates pit their wits and skills against one another to win the prize of being hired by the Trump Organization and earning a hefty six-figure salary.

During one season, it's men against women. Then the next season, those with "book smarts" go up against those with "street smarts." Regardless of the venue, the competitive atmosphere remains the same. And in the end, it's not about being nice or polite. It's about remaining on top at any cost.

If believers aren't careful, they can find themselves getting sucked into this cut-throat way of living in which ambition and conceit trample sensitivity and kindness. On the one hand, the Lord does not call His people to overtly seek to be mistreated by others. On the other hand, the example of Jesus reminds us that considering the needs of others is just as important as ensuring our own desires are satisfied.

A Heart of Concern. In *Our Daily Bread*, Bill Crowder recounts the story of Jason Ray, who was a student at the Chapel Hill campus of the University of North Carolina. For three years, Jason performed as the school mascot. This involved transporting a "giant ram's head costume to sporting events one day and children's hospitals the next."

Suddenly, however, Jason's life ended in March 2007. At the time, he was with his team for a basketball tournament when he was struck by a car. While Jason's family watched and waited at the hospital, the 21-year-old died from his injuries.

Just two years earlier, Jason had filled out the necessary paperwork to "donate organs and tissues upon his death." As a result of his forethought and concern, the lives of four people have been saved. Moreover, dozens of others have been helped. Understandably, the people and their families who benefited from Jason's selfless act of kindness are deeply grateful.

What Jason did, both in life and in death, "echoes the heart of Paul's words in Philippians 2." In that passage, the apostle encouraged his fellow Christians to "look beyond themselves and their own interests," especially as they considered the interests of others. Here we see that a "heart that turns outward to others" ultimately brings glory to the Savior.

HEAVENLY WORSHIP

BACKGROUND SCRIPTURE: Revelation 4
DEVOTIONAL READING: Psalm 11

KEY VERSE: And immediately I was in the spirit: and, behold, a throne was set in heaven, and one sat on the throne. (Revelation 4:2)

KING JAMES VERSION

REVELATION 4:1 After this I looked, and, behold, a door was opened in heaven: and the first voice which I heard was as it were of a trumpet talking with me; which said, Come up hither, and I will shew thee things which must be hereafter. 2 And immediately I was in the spirit: and, behold, a throne was set in heaven, and one sat on the throne. . . . 6 And before the throne there was a sea of glass like unto crystal: and in the midst of the throne, and round about the throne, were four beasts full of eyes before and behind. 7 And the first beast was like a lion, and the second beast like a calf, and the third beast had a face as a man, and the fourth beast was like a flying eagle.

8 And the four beasts had each of them six wings about him; and they were full of eyes within: and they rest not day and night, saying, Holy, holy, holy, Lord God Almighty, which was, and is, and is to come.
9 And when those beasts give glory and honour and thanks to him that sat on the throne, who liveth for ever and ever, 10 The four and twenty elders fall down before him that sat on the throne, and worship him that liveth for ever and ever, and cast their crowns before the throne, saying, 11 Thou art worthy, O Lord, to receive glory and honour and power: for thou hast created all things, and for thy pleasure they are and were created.

NEW REVISED STANDARD VERSION

REVELATION 4:1 After this I looked, and there in heaven a door stood open! And the first voice, which I had heard speaking to me like a trumpet, said, "Come up here, and I will show you what must take place after this." 2 At once I was in the spirit, and there in heaven stood a throne, with one seated on the throne! . . . 6 and in front of the throne there is something like a sea of glass, like crystal.

Around the throne, and on each side of the throne, are four living creatures, full of eyes in front and behind: 7 the first living creature like a lion, the second living creature like an ox, the third living creature with a face like a human face, and the fourth living creature like a flying eagle. 8 And the four living creatures, each of them with six wings, are full of eyes all around and inside. Day and night without ceasing they sing,

"Holy, holy, holy,
the Lord God the Almighty,
who was and is and is to come."

9 And whenever the living creatures give glory and honor and thanks to the one who is seated on the throne, who lives forever and ever, 10 the twenty-four elders fall before the one who is seated on the throne and worship the one who lives forever and ever; they cast their crowns before the throne, singing,
11 "You are worthy, our Lord and God,
to receive glory and honor and power,
for you created all things,
and by your will they existed and were created.

10

Monday, May 2	Psalm 11	*In the Holy Temple*
Tuesday, May 3	Isaiah 6:1-5	*Holy, Holy, Holy*
Wednesday, May 4	Exodus 6:2-8	*The Lord God Almighty*
Thursday, May 5	Psalm 24	*The King of Glory*
Friday, May 6	Psalm 10:12-16	*King Forever and Ever*
Saturday, May 7	Psalm 96	*Worship the Lord*
Sunday, May 8	Revelation 4:1-2, 6-11	*You Are Worthy, O Lord*

BACKGROUND

The phrase "which must be hereafter" (Rev. 4:1) echoes similar wording found in 1:19, in which the Messiah gave John specific instructions. The apostle was to write what he had seen, what was now taking place, and what would take place later. Some see here a possible threefold division of Revelation. The promises and vision of the Messiah recorded in chapter 1 would be what John had seen. The Savior's letters to the seven churches, which are recorded in chapters 2 and 3, could be what is taking place now. And all that is recorded in chapters 4 through 22 would be what will take place in the future.

Another possibility is that the clause "write the things which thou hast seen" (1:19) is Jesus' main directive and reiterates what He had commanded in verse 11. The remaining portion of verse 19, therefore, would give further details. In other words, as John wrote what he had seen, he was to comment on what was now taking place and what would take place later. Whether verse 19 contains a basic outline of Revelation remains a matter of debate. What is clear is that each portion of the book—including chapter 4—deals with issues relating to the past, the present, and the future. From this we can see that Revelation has continuing relevance for us as believers.

NOTES ON THE PRINTED TEXT

In John's unfolding vision, he saw a door standing open in heaven, and this allowed him to enter into the celestial realm. He heard the penetrating voice of the Son directing him to come up to heaven and receive special revelation concerning the future (Rev. 4:1). Some think Jesus' invitation is a symbolic reference to the rapture of the Church. More likely, John's experience parallels that of other believers in Scripture—for example, when Moses went up to Mount Sinai or when Paul was caught up to heaven to receive special revelations from God (see Exod. 19:3, 20; 2 Cor. 12:2). The phrase recorded in Revelation 4:1 may be an indication that chapters 6 through 20 of Revelation concern the final great conflict between God and the forces of evil. Satan and his demonic cohorts will neither immediately nor voluntarily surrender to the Messiah. Nevertheless, Jesus will be victorious in His mission of defeating the devil and condemning him to the lake of fire.

The Spirit immediately took control of John, perhaps putting him in a trance. The apostle found himself standing before a throne in heaven, and he saw the Lord sitting on it. In ancient times, thrones were symbols of power, sovereignty, and majesty. The throne of God radiated His glorious presence (4:2; see 1 Kings 22:19). It is interesting to note that John did not describe the details of God's appearance. This reminds us that His greatness and glory are beyond our ability to comprehend. First Timothy 6:16 says that the Lord dwells in such blazing glory that no human can approach Him. As the eternal and holy God, He could not be seen by the naked eye. Perhaps that is why John described his vision of the Lord by referring to the appearance of precious stones.

The apostle first mentioned jasper and carnelian. Jasper is usually clear or has a reddish hue, while carnelian is usually deep red or reddish-white. John also described seeing the glow of an emerald (light green) encircling God's throne like a rainbow. The picture was one of a transparent jewel radiating the splendor of God (Rev. 4:3). Ezekiel 1:26-28 contains another description of the Lord in brilliant splendor seated on His heavenly throne. His royal seat looked as if it were made out of sapphire (or lapis lazuli). Sapphire is a precious stone that is transparent and bright blue in color. From His waist up God appeared to be gleaming like bronze in the middle of a fire. Also, from His waist down the Lord was surrounded by what looked like a burning flame that emanated a dazzling light. The halo-like radiance that encompassed Him was comparable to all the colors of a rainbow shining in the clouds on a rainy day. Understandably, when Ezekiel saw the glory of the Lord, the prophet threw himself face down on the ground.

In ancient times, a king would permit lesser rulers (such as tribal judges) to sit on thrones next to his. In John's vision he saw 24 thrones surrounding God's royal seat, and 24 elders were on these thrones. They wore white clothes, which represent purity and uprightness. They also wore gold crowns, which symbolize honor, splendor, and victory (Rev. 4:4). These elders may have been exalted angels who served God in His heavenly court, or they could have been glorified saints in heaven. Some think the number 24 is a symbolic reference to the 12 tribes of Israel in the Old Testament and the 12 apostles in the New Testament. This suggests that all the redeemed of all time (both before and after the Savior's death and resurrection) are represented before God's throne and worship Him in His heavenly sanctuary.

John saw flashes of lightning and roars of thunder coming from God's throne (vs. 5). These storm phenomena symbolized the power and majesty of the Lord. The episode also recalled the natural disturbances on the summit of Mount Sinai in Moses' day (Exod. 20:18-19). Seven lampstands with burning flames—which represented the seven spirits of God—stood in front of the throne (Rev. 4:5). The lampstands symbolized the perfection, completeness, and fullness of the Holy Spirit. He worked through the redeemed in their various churches to shine the light of the Gospel to a lost world.

In 1:4, we also find a reference to the "seven Spirits." Some think this is an allusion to seven angels who stand before the throne of God (see 8:2). Most likely, though, John was symbolically referring to the totality and purity of the Holy Spirit and His ministry (see Isa. 11:2).

Furthermore, John saw in front of God's throne something that looked like a sea made of glass. It was clear and sparkling like crystal (Rev. 4:6). In New Testament times, glass was a rare item, and crystal-clear glass was virtually impossible to find. The celestial ocean in John's vision may symbolize the magnificence and sacredness of God. Another throne room scene is spotlighted in chapter 15. The apostle noted he saw something that looked like a sea of glass mixed with fire. And standing by this fire-glowing sea were those who had defeated the enemies of God (vs. 2) by the blood of the Lamb and the word of their testimony (12:11). The victors held harps, which God had given them (15:2), and they sang the song of Moses (God's servant) and of the Lamb (vss. 3-4). The idea is that the redemption symbolized by the Israelites departure from Egypt (see Exod. 15:1-18; Deut. 32:1-47) has reached its fulfillment in the salvation offered by the Messiah.

In John's vision, he saw four living creatures in the center around God's throne. The eyes covering the front and back of each creature may symbolize their unceasing watchfulness (Rev. 4:6). It's possible that these entities were representations of God's attributes or symbols of the natural order of creation. More likely they were angels, perhaps similar to the cherubim of Ezekiel 1 and 10 or the seraphim of Isaiah 6. The four living creatures guarded the throne of God, proclaimed His holiness, and led others in worship.

It is possible that these angelic beings portrayed various aspects of divine majesty. For instance, the first creature had the form of a lion, possibly symbolizing either mobility or majesty. The second creature had the form of an ox, perhaps representing either strength or faithfulness. The third creature had a human face, possibly symbolizing wisdom. And the fourth creature had the form of an eagle with its wings spread out as though in flight, perhaps representing either speed or control (Rev. 4:7; see Ezek. 1:5-10). Each of the living creatures had six wings, and their bodies (including the underside of their wings) were covered with eyes, which is suggestive of alertness and intelligence (Rev. 4:8).

Day after day and night after night, the angelic beings John saw repeated the chorus "Holy, holy, holy, Lord God Almighty, which was, and is, and is to come." In Scripture, triple repetition is often used to emphasize a truth. The angels' threefold repetition of the word "holy" underscored the fact that God is absolutely sinless. Their refrain also stressed that He is the all-powerful Ruler of the universe. Further they emphasized that He is not bound by the limitations of time. In Isaiah's vision, the prophet also noted that the seraphim he saw proclaimed the Lord's holiness (Isa. 6:3). The triple reference pointed to the fullness or completeness of God's holiness.

In addition to declaring God's holiness, the seraphim also declared His glory, which fills "the whole earth." This suggests that even though God is perfectly holy and glorious, He is not aloof from our world and our lives.

John saw that the living creatures never stopped praising, honoring, and thanking the Lord. The apostle also noticed that the 24 elders prostrated themselves before God's throne and placed their crowns at the base of His royal seat. These were fitting acts of worship to give to the one who controls all time and all people (Rev. 4:9-10). Whereas the living creatures praised God for His holiness, the elders lauded Him for His creative acts (vs. 11). He not only brought all things into existence, but also sustains them. The idea is not of some superhuman creature (such as the Greek god Atlas) holding up the world. Rather, it is of God maintaining the existence of the universe and bearing it along to its divinely ordained conclusion. We have life—both physical and spiritual—because of God's grace. And we exist to bring Him glory. We honor the Lord when our thoughts are virtuous, our words are wholesome, and our deeds are kind.

SUGGESTIONS TO TEACHERS

In John's vision of the heavenly throne room, all honor, praise, and worship is given to the Lord. Why is He worthy of praise? The reasons He is lauded in heaven are the same reasons why we should praise Him now with our own songs of celebration.

1. OUR GOD IS ABSOLUTELY HOLY. This week's lesson text draws attention to the infinite glory and uniqueness of the Lord over any other entity in the universe. Indeed, there is not a trace of sin within Him. For this reason He deserves our praise.

2. OUR GOD SAVED US. Because of His love for humanity, the Father sent His Son to die for us (see John 3:16). Jesus' death was not an accident of history. His blood "redeemed" (Rev. 5:9) us from the slavery into which sin has put us. We cannot save ourselves. We have been purchased with a price, Jesus' blood. Any time we think we are personally worthy of praise, we must remember who we are without the Lord.

3. OUR GOD ADOPTED US. God loved us so much that He brought us who have trusted in the Messiah into His kingdom. One day we will "reign on the earth" (vs. 10) with Jesus. But what does that mean for us today? It means that because the Savior has overcome the world (John 16:33), so also can we. The more we live for the Lord, the more His kingdom will come and His will be done, on earth as it is in heaven (Matt. 6:10).

4. OUR GOD PROVIDES FOR US. God is so faithful and consistent in providing for our needs that we tend to forget He is present. We arrogantly think we have control over what happens to us. We imagine that we are self-sufficient and can survive solely by means of our wit and strength. We know, however, from this week's lesson that our lives are in God's hands. As an echo of the praise God receives in heaven, we should sing the old hymn "When I Survey the Wondrous Cross"—and mean what it says: "Were the whole realm of nature mine, that were a present far too small; love so amazing, so divine, demands my soul, my life, my all."

FOR ADULTS

■ TOPIC: Communicating through Symbols

■ QUESTIONS: 1. How did John describe the glory of the sovereign Lord? 2. How would you feel if you suddenly found yourself standing before the presence of God's celestial throne? 3. What was the significance of the seven lampstands? 4. What was distinctive about each of the four living creatures? 5. What can you do to make your worship more God-centered, rather than self-focused?

■ ILLUSTRATIONS:

Worshiping God Alone. The Lord uses a variety of ways to communicate with us. For instance, Revelation 4 indicates that God used amazing sights and sounds to emphasize to John (and us) the importance worshiping Him as the glorious, holy, and all-powerful Lord.

Admittedly, worship is a difficult concept to define. Things are clarified by the observation that the word *worship* is drawn from the concepts of worthiness and repute. Another important point is that activity is central to many forms of worship. But too often we limit our worship of God to an hour on Sundays. In contrast, the Lord measures our worship, not only by what we do during one hour on Sunday, but also by how we live after we leave the doors of the church.

Many people debate at length over the "how" of worship. The more important issue is the object of our worship. We need to be reminded each time we gather to worship that we have an audience of one—namely, the Lord. And in the worship we offer, the goal is not to talk about God. Instead, it is to commune with Him every hour of every day. It is also an opportunity for us to offer our praise to the Lord for His glory and grace.

Charles's Choice. Charles was a promising young lawyer in Adams, New York. One day he decided to buy a Bible because his law texts frequently quoted from it. At first he didn't show anyone he was reading the Bible and hid it among his law books. But the more he read, the more convicted he became of the need to serve Christ instead of pursuing a law career.

On October 10, 1821, Charles made his choice. He accepted Christ as his Savior and told people that he had been given "a retainer from the Lord Jesus Christ to plead His cause." That same day Charles brought 24 people in town to know the Lord, including another lawyer and a distiller. Later Charles would preach revivals in New York City, Boston, and Philadelphia, with as many as 50,000 people converted in one week in Boston. It has been claimed that in his lifetime, the great American evangelist, Charles Finney, influenced over a half-million people to worship the Father through the Son, assuring them it was the wisest choice in life they would ever make.

Our lives are filled with choices, too, some of which are more pivotal than others. When the Lord is at the center of our decision-making and the sole object of our worship, we will make the right choices, those that count both for time and eternity.

Why God Gives Us Choices. Madeleine L'Engle notes the following in her book entitled *Walking on Water*: "The problem of pain, of war, and the horror of war, of poverty, and disease is always confronting us. But a God who allows no pain, no grief, also allows no choice. There is little unfairness in a colony of ants, but also there is little freedom. We human beings have been given . . . this ability to make choices, to help write our own story, is what makes us human . . . even when we make the wrong choices, abusing our freedom and the freedom of others."

Consider the following. If God gave you 70 years of life, you would spend:

- 24 years sleeping,
- 14 years working,
- 8 years in amusement,
- 6 years at the dinner table,
- 5 years in transportation,
- 4 years in conversation,
- 3 years in education, and
- 3 years reading.

If you went to church every Sunday and prayed to the Lord five minutes every morning and night, you would be giving God five months of your life in worship. That's only five months out of 70 years!

FOR YOUTH

■ TOPIC: Awesome Praise and Worship

■ QUESTIONS: 1. What did the voice from heaven command John to do? 2. How can the truth of the Father being all-powerful encourage you to remain faithful to the Son? 3. Who were the 24 elders that John saw? 4. What sorts of creatures were around the throne? 5. What are some ways you like to worship God?

■ ILLUSTRATIONS:

Sing Praise! Worship experiences for teens may come in a variety of forms and formats. One young person might think of the overwhelming sensation of adoration experienced by singing "Amazing Grace" amid thousands of people at an evangelistic crusade. A second adolescent might think of being moved to tears by the praise tape "The Greatest Thing" while viewing the Alpine Mountains. A third youth might recall a worshipful insight triggered during a quiet communion service.

The type of homage the students give to the Lord is not the main focus here. It is that they give Him praise, whether in words, deeds, or thoughts. God is worthy of their adoration because of who He is and what He has done for all people in Christ. For these reasons alone, every day can be a new opportunity for teens to devote time to worship the Lord both publicly and privately.

O Worship the King. Sir Robert Grant was acquainted with kings. His father was a member of the British Parliament and later became chairman of the East India Company. Following in his father's footsteps, young Grant was elected to Parliament and then also became a director of the East India Company. In 1834, he was appointed governor of Bombay, and in that position he became greatly loved. A medical college in India was named in his honor.

Late in his life, Grant wrote a hymn based on Psalm 104. The progression of titles for God in the last line of that hymn—"O Worship the King"—is interesting. We know God first as our Maker. Then, even before our conversion, He is our Defender. We know Him then as Redeemer, and finally, as we walk day by day with Him, we know Him also as Friend.

> Frail children of dust, and feeble as frail,
> In Thee do we trust, nor find Thee to fail;
> Thy mercies how tender, how firm to the end,
> Our Maker, Defender, Redeemer, and Friend.

God's Awesome Power. On May 18, 1980, Mount Saint Helens in the Cascade Range of Washington state exploded with what is probably the most visible indication of the power of nature that the modern world has ever seen. At 8:32 a.m., the explosion ripped 1,300 feet off the mountain, with a force of 10 million tons of TNT, or roughly equal to 500 atom bombs. Sixty people were killed, most by a blast of 300-degree heat traveling at 200 miles an hour. Some were killed as far as 16 miles away.

The blast also leveled 150-foot Douglas firs as far as 17 miles away. A total of 3.2 billion board-feet of lumber were destroyed, enough to build 200,000 three-bedroom homes. This incident is just a small reminder of the awesome power of God. As John caught a glimpse of the Lord's celestial throne, the apostle saw "lightnings and thunderings" (Rev. 4:5) coming from it. We should not be surprised that day and night the host of heaven offered praise to God (see vs. 8). Likewise, the Lord wants us to praise Him for His awesome power.

THANKFUL WORSHIP

BACKGROUND SCRIPTURE: Revelation 7:9-17
DEVOTIONAL READING: Psalm 23

KEY VERSE: [A great multitude] cried with a loud voice, saying, Salvation to our God which sitteth upon the throne, and unto the Lamb. (Revelation 7:10)

KING JAMES VERSION

REVELATION 7:9 After this I beheld, and, lo, a great multitude, which no man could number, of all nations, and kindreds, and people, and tongues, stood before the throne, and before the Lamb, clothed with white robes, and palms in their hands; 10 And cried with a loud voice, saying, Salvation to our God which sitteth upon the throne, and unto the Lamb. 11 And all the angels stood round about the throne, and about the elders and the four beasts, and fell before the throne on their faces, and worshipped God, 12 Saying, Amen: Blessing, and glory, and wisdom, and thanksgiving, and honour, and power, and might, be unto our God for ever and ever. Amen.

13 And one of the elders answered, saying unto me, What are these which are arrayed in white robes? and whence came they? 14 And I said unto him, Sir, thou knowest. And he said to me, These are they which came out of great tribulation, and have washed their robes, and made them white in the blood of the Lamb. 15 Therefore are they before the throne of God, and serve him day and night in his temple: and he that sitteth on the throne shall dwell among them. 16 They shall hunger no more, neither thirst any more; neither shall the sun light on them, nor any heat. 17 For the Lamb which is in the midst of the throne shall feed them, and shall lead them unto living fountains of waters: and God shall wipe away all tears from their eyes.

NEW REVISED STANDARD VERSION

REVELATION 7:9 After this I looked, and there was a great multitude that no one could count, from every nation, from all tribes and peoples and languages, standing before the throne and before the Lamb, robed in white, with palm branches in their hands. 10 They cried out in a loud voice, saying,

"Salvation belongs to our God who is seated on the throne, and to the Lamb!"

11 And all the angels stood around the throne and around the elders and the four living creatures, and they fell on their faces before the throne and worshiped God, 12 singing,

"Amen! Blessing and glory and wisdom
and thanksgiving and honor
and power and might
be to our God forever and ever! Amen."

13 Then one of the elders addressed me, saying, "Who are these, robed in white, and where have they come from?" 14 I said to him, "Sir, you are the one that knows." Then he said to me, "These are they who have come out of the great ordeal; they have washed their robes and made them white in the blood of the Lamb.

15 For this reason they are before the throne of God,
and worship him day and night within his temple,
and the one who is seated on the throne will
shelter them.

16 They will hunger no more, and thirst no more;
the sun will not strike them,
nor any scorching heat;

17 for the Lamb at the center of the throne will be
their shepherd,
and he will guide them to springs of the water of
life,
and God will wipe away every tear from their
eyes."

Monday, May 9	Psalm 23	*The Lord Is My Shepherd*
Tuesday, May 10	Ezekiel 34:11-16	*God, the True Shepherd*
Wednesday, May 11	John 10:11-16	*The Good Shepherd*
Thursday, May 12	Matthew 9:35-38	*The Shepherd's Compassion*
Friday, May 13	Matthew 25:31-40	*The Shepherd's Judgment*
Saturday, May 14	Psalm 107:1-9	*The Shepherd's Steadfast Love*
Sunday, May 15	Revelation 7:9-17	*The Lamb as the Shepherd*

BACKGROUND

In Revelation 7:17, Jesus is presented as the believers' good Shepherd (see John 10:11). In Bible times, shepherds performed numerous duties as they cared for their flocks. In addition to finding adequate shelter for sheep, shepherds also had to lead them to good pasturelands and ample supplies of water.

Knowing that their flocks were easy prey, shepherds spent part of their time warding off attacks from savage animals. If necessary, shepherds were willing to risk their own lives to ensure the safety of the flock. At night, several shepherds might bring their flocks into a protected area called a sheepfold. This was a cave, shed, pen, or courtyard that had one entrance and was enclosed by branches or stone walls. In addition to providing some protection from the weather, the walls also prevented the flock from getting out and wild animals from getting in and preying on the sheep.

NOTES ON THE PRINTED TEXT

Revelation 7:4-8 states that God placed His seal on the foreheads of 144,000 people from all the tribes of Israel. The Lord chose 12,000 people from each tribe. The identity of the 144,000 saints in Revelation is not clear. They could be a select group of people from the literal 12 tribes of Israel. Or they could be a specific number of believers whom God will in some way shield during a final period of distress. It could be that 144,000 (calculated using 12 as a multiple of 12) is a symbolic number for the fullness of the people of God. In other words, the Lord will bring all His followers safely to Himself. He will protect them either by removing them from the earth (this is called the Rapture) or by giving them the strength they need to endure persecution and remain loyal to Him. The encouraging aspect is that God has a plan for our lives and is able to spiritually protect us so that His purposes might be accomplished. The Lord does not leave anything to chance. We can rest assured that He is able to bring all His own people safely to their eternal destination.

We can only imagine how stirred John was as he saw in heaven a vast crowd that was too large to count. Certainly, the depth of their unity far exceeded any earthly counterpart. This throng was made up of people from every nation, tribe, people, and language, and they all stood before the throne of God and before the Lamb (vs. 9).

Many ideas have been suggested regarding the identity of this host of believers. They could be the saved of all the ages, only Gentile believers, or martyrs killed during a final period of great distress, to name three common views. One remarkable aspect of the scene John saw in heaven is the position of the believers before God. While the earth is about to feel the full force of God's wrath, all these different saints are standing before His throne, a place of safety and security. Understandably, John was impressed by the widespread representation of this group. No people group was excluded. The Lord has accepted and honored them as His true servants.

We see evidence here of the success of missionary work. Even in such a time of distress as the apostle described in the Book of Revelation, people in large numbers from all over the world have responded to the Gospel. We can all be encouraged by the rich harvest described in verse 9. It reminds us that when we serve the Lord in the proclamation of the Gospel, eternal fruit results. We may not always know the outcome of our attempts to share the Good News, but our efforts are never wasted, for the Lamb is glorified in the process.

The early readers of Revelation might have associated white clothing with the garb of Roman generals, who dressed in this fashion when celebrating their triumphs. The long white robes worn by the saints in heaven represent the purity, righteousness, and glory of the Messiah, all of which they received by faith. Many of the non-Christian religions of the world acknowledge that there is something morally wrong with humankind. And all non-Christian faith systems teach their followers that such things as self-discipline and fortitude are the keys to personal improvement. Only Christianity teaches that people are spiritually dead and unable on their own to free themselves from the shackles of sin. And only the Christian faith declares that people cannot save themselves. If the lost are to be rescued, they must trust in the Son, whom the Father sent to be an atoning sacrifice for their sins (see Eph. 2:1-10).

John noted that the multitude he saw in heaven were holding palm branches, which they used to pay homage to the Messiah. As noted in lesson 7, the early church regarded palm branches as a symbol of Jesus' victory over death. Moreover, they represent complete triumph and unending joy. Everything about the heavenly scene John saw points to the unconditional acceptance of God's spiritual children in His presence. They are celebrating victory in a place of honor before the Lord and the Lamb. The truths disclosed in this verse are reflected in the chorus that the multitude in heaven shouted before the throne. They acknowledged that salvation comes only from God the Father, who sits on His celestial throne, and His Son, the Lamb, who offered His life as an atoning sacrifice for sins (vs. 10).

John observed that all the angels who stood around God's throne knelt in front of it with their faces to the ground. And the elders and the four living creatures knelt there with the angels. Together they worshiped God and sang a chorus of praise to Him (vs. 11). "Amen" (vs. 12) introduces the sevenfold doxology, and

"Amen" closes it. The heavenly choir first used the term to register their approval of the cry of the multitude, and they shout "Amen" at the end to affirm the reliability of each quality of God. The angels, elders, and four living creatures ascribe seven different attributes to God. Each term in the doxology is accented in the original language by the definite article "the"—in other words, the blessing, the glory, the wisdom, and so forth. The idea is that God is perfect in every way, and thus He deserves unlimited praise from His creatures.

John was curious about the identity and origin of the vast number of people who were clothed in white robes and standing before God's throne. One of the elders evidently discerned this, and thus rhetorically asked the apostle about the multitude (vs. 13). Rather than try to bluff his way through an inaccurate response, John humbly admitted that he did not know the answer to the elder's question. The apostle looked to the speaker for clarification. Based on the elder's response, some identify the "great tribulation" (vs. 14) with a final period of persecution shortly before the return of the Messiah. Others, however, note that believers have endured affliction and grief throughout history, so that the entire church age can be seen as a time of tribulation (see 2 Thess. 1:5-6; 2 Tim. 3:1, 12).

Perhaps John intended to comfort both first-century Christians as well as God's people living during a time of final crisis. This aim is reinforced by the mention of "the blood of the Lamb" (Rev. 7:14). We learn that the people in this vast throng, like all believers, have been saved on the basis of Jesus' atoning sacrifice. The disputed identity of this group does not alter the hope we see here. Through faith in the Son we, too, can find acceptance before the Father and will someday experience His glory. In Romans 5:2, Paul likewise noted that through faith in the Son, we are the recipients of the Father's grace and rejoice in the confident expectation of sharing in His glory.

The elder revealed that the glorified state will include service for God in His heavenly sanctuary. But labor for the Lord will be a delight, performed without the fatigue and boredom that so often mark activities in this life. Scripture does not tell us what that service will entail, but surely it will involve worship, adoration, and continuous praise (Rev. 7:15). The Greek verb translated "dwell among them" has a rich Old Testament heritage. It comes from a term that also means "to abide" and was used for God's presence with Israel in the tabernacle and later in the temple. The term refers to God sheltering and protecting His people with His presence. In eternity, the Lord's glorious presence will never fade away from us as it did from Israel. This scene in heaven tells suffering believers that their struggles are worth the effort. Their oppressors may think they are the winners, but in actuality these victims are the real champions. Suffering believers can look forward to celebrating a tremendous victory in God's presence. The persecutors, however, will face God's wrath.

Verses 16 and 17 present a dramatic contrast to the death, famine, war, and sorrow of chapter 6. The believers who have endured hardship will find rest and relief from their pain. Specifically, John learned that one day God will wipe away all tears from the eyes of His people. Pain, suffering, sickness, grief, and death will never be experienced by them in heaven. In some way, the Lord will cause their past to never bring them remorse in the coming age. Having taken His people to heaven, the Lord will not abandon them. His presence will always be with them, bringing them happiness. God Himself will provide for the needs of Christ's followers in eternity. Those facing almost certain death at the hands of Roman authorities could take heart at this vivid glimpse of the glory that awaited them. Moreover, a vast number of Christians throughout history have also received courage to face life's trials by meditating on these words.

For all believers, heaven will be a blessed contrast to the suffering felt on earth. The Bible does not tell us all we'd like to know about the nature of life in eternity. But from what Scripture does say, we know that God will take care of our every need. In the Lord's presence we will experience joy, blessing, and comfort. As seen in Genesis 3:22-24, God expelled Adam and Eve from the Garden of Eden so they would not eat fruit from the tree of life. God did not want them to live forever in their sinful state. But in Revelation 7:17, the Messiah leads the redeemed to the waters of life. The imagery is that of a shepherd guiding his sheep to a freshwater spring in the desert. Salvation from the death that sin brought into the world will be complete. In heaven, the righteous will enjoy unending life.

SUGGESTIONS TO TEACHERS

What will heaven be like? Will we just be sitting on clouds all day playing harps and singing? We do not have all the answers to our questions that we may wish we did, but the Book of Revelation tells us what rewards believers will find when they reach paradise. Three stand out in this week's lesson.

1. NO MORE SEPARATION FROM GOD. Revelation pictures believers standing by the throne of God, worshiping Him "day and night in his temple" (7:15). There will be no barriers in heaven between God and His people, and no separation between believers due to nations, tribes, or languages. While we cannot exactly have that now, remind your students that we can see some of the glory of God reflected in our own lives when we faithfully serve Him, and we should work toward breaking down those barriers that separate believers here on earth.

2. NO MORE HUNGER OR THIRST. All our basic physical needs will disappear in heaven. We will no longer be hungry, tired, or thirsty. As the good Shepherd who leads His sheep to the greenest pasture, Jesus will guide us to the "living fountains of waters" (vs. 17), where we will not want. While physical needs may be paramount in our lives today, they will be nonexistent in heaven.

3. NO MORE SUFFERING. The Scripture that has comforted millions of believers who have lost loved ones tells us that one day "God shall wipe away all tears." The suffering of this life, and our heartbreaking separation from other believers who have died, will end in heaven one day. While it is sometimes hard for us to remember, our life today is only temporary. The everlasting joys of eternity are really just around the corner.

FOR ADULTS

■ TOPIC: Where We Look in Times of Trouble

■ QUESTIONS: 1. What sorts of people made up the great multitude John saw? 2. What can you do to ensure that as many people as possible from all walks of life have an opportunity to hear the Gospel and be saved? 3. What is the great tribulation mentioned in Revelation 7:14? 4. Why will the great multitude in heaven hunger no more? 5. What injustices in your life do your look forward to the Lord vindicating?

■ ILLUSTRATIONS:

Source of Security. It's common knowledge that excessive and prolonged worrying, especially in troubling times, is not good for our health. We also know that worrying can rob us of peace and contentment. It should come as no surprise, then, that Jesus wants us to stop worrying and find our source of security in Him. But how can we do this?

Many books and sermons give us good practical advice. The simplest answer is to focus our attention on the Lord. When we start the day with praise and thanks to the Savior as well as meditate on His Word, we are in good shape to deal with the underlying problems that lead us to worry.

It also helps to have some good friends. These would not be people who dream up more things for us to worry about, but rather those who are good listeners and who can point us back to Jesus, our caring and watchful Shepherd (see Rev. 7:17). Occasionally, we all need encouragement to let go of our worries and give them to the Lord.

No More Weeping. "God, where were you in Paris?" asked a church leader named Josef Homeyer, his voice quavering with emotion as he addressed 350 people at a worship service in Hanover, Germany, after a Concorde airliner burst into flames and crashed outside Paris on July 25, 2000, killing 113 people, most of them German tourists, Reuters reported. "Why have you deserted us? Our hearts are heavy."

Homeyer then reminded the mourners of the assurance of the resurrection. After him, a church leader named Horst Hirschler reminded the audience of a similar tragic incident two years earlier, when a high-speed train crashed near Hanover, taking the lives of more than 100 people. One minute vacationers were happily looking forward to the time of their lives, and the next minute they were faced with death, the pastor said. "What a tragic transformation."

The only real consolation is that even the Son of God had asked His Father in heaven, "Why hast thou forsaken me" before He died on the cross, Hirschler said. He assured his audience that Jesus, their good Shepherd, is with those who are feeling desperate and who mourn over the loss of their loved ones (see Rev. 7:16-17). "You will never fall deeper than into God's hand."

Blessed Assurance. Fanny Crosby (1820–1915) was one of the most prolific hymnists in history. Though blinded at six weeks of age, she wrote over 8,000 hymns. About her blindness, she said, "It seemed intended by the blessed providence of God that I should be blind all my life, and thank Him for the dispensation. If perfect earthly sight were offered me tomorrow I would not accept it. I might not have sung hymns to the praise of God if I had been distracted by the beautiful and interesting things about me."

In her lifetime, Fanny Crosby was one of the best known women in the United States. To this day, the vast majority of American hymnals contain her work. When she died, her tombstone carried the words, "Aunt Fanny" and "Blessed assurance, Jesus is mine. Oh, what a foretaste of glory divine." Such thoughts remind us of the joys of heaven, as foretold in Revelation 7:15-17.

FOR YOUTH

■ **TOPIC:** Thank you!

■ **QUESTIONS:** 1. How would you feel if your were part of the heavenly host singing praise to God? 2. Why is the Lord worthy of receiving all glory, honor, and praise? 3. Where did the great multitude come from? 4. What is the significance of what the multitude was wearing? 5. How has God's promise to watch over you been a source of encouragement for you?

■ **ILLUSTRATIONS:**

Steadfast Faith. When Ernest Shackleton, the famous British explorer, left 22 men behind on an island in the Antarctic Sea, they had to keep strong faith that he would return—despite the fact that Shackleton had to cross 800 miles of wild ocean in a lifeboat to reach a whaling station. To keep steadfast faith in Shackleton's return, every day the men packed their gear. This might be the day he comes back, they told themselves, and one day he did.

Living our Christian faith is something like that. We face rugged times and days of uncertainty. Sometimes our future appears to be hopeless. But because we are in Christ, we can trust Him to find us, as it were, and bring us through our darkest hours. For this He deserves our unending expression of thanks.

Jesus lives and encourages us to keep on hoping and believing. He also wants us to give a lift to our friends who are in the pits. Our faith gets stronger when the waves blow against us. And we are grateful that we can reach out and find that Jesus is there when we need Him most (see Rev. 7:17).

The Smallest Loaf. There was once a rich baker who sent for 20 of the poorest children in town and said to them, "In this basket is a loaf of bread for each of you. Take one and come back every day and I'll give you more." Immediately the youngsters began quarreling about who would get the largest loaf. Snatching from the basket, they left without even thanking the baker.

Gretchen, a poorly dressed little girl, patiently waited until the others had left. She then took the smallest loaf, which remained in the basket, kissed the old man's hand, and went home.

The next day the scene was repeated. But when Gretchen's mother sliced this loaf, she found many shiny gold coins inside. Gretchen took the money back to the baker, thinking there had been some mistake, but he said, "No, my child, it was not a mistake. I put them into the smallest loaf knowing you would be rewarded."

Faithfulness is shown in many character traits, including honesty and humility as little Gretchen showed the baker. Just as the baker felt compelled to bless Gretchen for her sweet spirit, our God wants to bless each of us for our actions and thoughts that are pure and unselfish. In this world we may not see a reward for every good thing we do, but we can be assured that God will not forget to reward us when we get in heaven with His abiding presence and consolation (see Rev. 7:15-17).

ALL THINGS NEW

BACKGROUND SCRIPTURE: Revelation 21
DEVOTIONAL READING: Colossians 4:2-9

KEY VERSE: He that sat upon the throne said,
Behold, I make all things new. (Revelation 21:5)

KING JAMES VERSION

REVELATION 21:1 And I saw a new heaven and a new earth: for the first heaven and the first earth were passed away; and there was no more sea. 2 And I John saw the holy city, new Jerusalem, coming down from God out of heaven, prepared as a bride adorned for her husband. 3 And I heard a great voice out of heaven saying, Behold, the tabernacle of God is with men, and he will dwell with them, and they shall be his people, and God himself shall be with them, and be their God. 4 And God shall wipe away all tears from their eyes; and there shall be no more death, neither sorrow, nor crying, neither shall there be any more pain: for the former things are passed away. 5 And he that sat upon the throne said, Behold, I make all things new. And he said unto me, Write: for these words are true and faithful. 6 And he said unto me, It is done. I am Alpha and Omega, the beginning and the end. I will give unto him that is athirst of the fountain of the water of life freely. 7 He that overcometh shall inherit all things; and I will be his God, and he shall be my son. 8 But the fearful, and unbelieving, and the abominable, and murderers, and whoremongers, and sorcerers, and idolaters, and all liars, shall have their part in the lake which burneth with fire and brimstone: which is the second death.

NEW REVISED STANDARD VERSION

REVELATION 21:1 Then I saw a new heaven and a new earth; for the first heaven and the first earth had passed away, and the sea was no more. 2 And I saw the holy city, the new Jerusalem, coming down out of heaven from God, prepared as a bride adorned for her husband. 3 And I heard a loud voice from the throne saying,

"See, the home of God is among mortals.
He will dwell with them
they will be his peoples,
and God himself will be with them;
4 he will wipe every tear from their eyes.
Death will be no more;
mourning and crying and pain will be no more,
for the first things have passed away."

5 And the one who was seated on the throne said, "See, I am making all things new." Also he said, "Write this, for these words are trustworthy and true." 6 Then he said to me, "It is done! I am the Alpha and the Omega, the beginning and the end. To the thirsty I will give water as a gift from the spring of the water of life. 7 Those who conquer will inherit these things, and I will be their God and they will be my children. 8 But as for the cowardly, the faithless, the polluted, the murderers, the fornicators, the sorcerers, the idolaters, and all liars, their place will be in the lake that burns with fire and sulfur, which is the second death."

12

BACKGROUND

In John's unfolding vision, the condemnation of the wicked (Rev. 20:11-15) is followed by the new creation that awaits believers (21:1). Throughout history, people have failed to create utopian communities. God, however, will ensure that the situation is far different in the eternal state for believers. They will dwell in the new Jerusalem and enjoy the beauty of the Lord. Moreover, those who are victorious in this life will enjoy unbroken fellowship with the Lord of glory.

What John saw is consistent with Isaiah's reference to the "new heavens and a new earth" (Isa. 65:17). The apostle, however, was not thinking of a world merely free of sin and hardness of heart. John's vision was of a creation new in all its qualities. Isaiah's final prophecies probably applied in part to the exiles returned from Babylon. But his language clearly goes beyond any fulfillment in ancient history. Earlier, while prophesying about end-time judgments, Isaiah had said, "The heavens shall vanish away like smoke, and the earth shall wax old like a garment" (51:6). Now Isaiah recorded God's declaration that in place of the old heavens and earth He would create "new heavens and a new earth" (65:17). So glorious would the new creation be that God said "the former shall not be remembered, nor come into mind." Those former things, such as weeping and crying, would give way to new things, including gladness, rejoicing, and delight. God, too, would find joy in the new creation. He would "rejoice in Jerusalem, and joy in [His] people" (vs. 19).

NOTES ON THE PRINTED TEXT

John stated that he saw "a new heaven and a new earth" (21:1). These are total replacements for their old counterparts, "the first heaven and the first earth," which God had destroyed. He evidently did this to eliminate any corrupting presence or influence of sin (2 Pet. 3:7, 10-13). God will also eliminate the vast and mysterious seas. In the Old Testament, the sea was a symbol for the agitation and restlessness associated with evil (Isa. 57:20; Jer. 49:23). In the Book of Revelation, the sea is the source of the satanic beast and a burial site for the wicked dead (Rev. 13:1; 20:13). In the eternal state, there can be no physical and symbolic place for this seething cauldron of wickedness.

In John's vision of the future, his attention quickly passed from the creation to the new heaven and earth and to "the holy city, New Jerusalem" (21:2), which God sent down out of heaven. The Lord magnificently adorned the new Jerusalem (the bride) for her husband (the groom). The implication here is that the city surpassed the beauty of everything else God had made. Some think the new Jerusalem in the Book of Revelation is a symbol of the Christian community in heaven. However, based on the detailed information recorded in verses 10-21, others maintain the new Jerusalem will be a literal city where God's people dwell for all eternity. In either case, the main point is that a new world is coming, and it will be glorious beyond imagination.

A loud voice from the heavenly throne declared that "the tabernacle of God is with men" (vs. 3); in other words, in the eternal state God will permanently dwell among the redeemed of all ages. They will be His people, and He will be their God. The voice also disclosed that five scourges of human existence will not exist in the eternal state—tears, death, sorrow, crying, and pain. The new order will eliminate all these forms of sadness (vs. 4).

In Isaiah 65:20-25, the prophet described what the glorious newly created Jerusalem would be like for God's people. This new creation will be so spectacular that any beauty of this present world—for instance, the Grand Canyon, the Alps, Victoria Falls, and all the other amazing sights people travel so far to see—will pale in comparison. Yet beyond the beauty, this set of verses contains four promises of great blessing: Those who would live in newly created Jerusalem (1) would have long lives, (2) would not labor in vain, (3) would be speedily answered by God when they pray, and (4) would live in an environment without hostility. When taken together, these blessings seem to indicate that the effects of the Fall would be reversed in the new heavens and new earth and new Jerusalem.

God declared that He was doing away with the old order and making "all things new" (Rev. 21:5). The Lord told John to write down what He had said, for His words were "true and faithful." Believers could stake their hopes for spending eternity with God in heaven, for they knew that the divine promise was accurate and reliable. At Jesus' final meal with His followers, He referred to heaven as a large house, which has many rooms, belonging to His Father. Though Jesus was leaving His disciples, He was going there to prepare a place for them. He told them that if this were not so, He would not have made this promise to them. But since this was so, they could count on being reunited with the Savior no matter what happened to Him or to them (John 14:2-3).

In Revelation 21:6, the phrase "It is done" could also be rendered "It has happened." The idea is that everything the Lord declared was finished and absolutely certain to occur. This was possible because God is the "Alpha and Omega" as well as "the beginning and the end." God's declaration of Himself as the "Alpha and Omega"—drawing upon the first and last letters of the Greek alphabet—is emphatic in the original. It's as if the divine were saying, "I and no other." It is similar in meaning to the expressions "the beginning and the end" and "the first and the last" (1:17; 22:13). The idea behind these statements—which are applied interchangeably to both the Father and the Son—is one of totality. Put another way, the Lord is the beginning and ending of all things. Also, His rule encompasses the past, the present, and the future. Furthermore, He is sovereign over all that takes place in human history and is directing its course to a final and proper conclusion (Col. 1:17; Heb. 1:3).

In John's continuing vision of the eternal state, God promised to give water from the life-giving fountain to everyone who was thirsty (Rev. 21:6). This pledge is a vivid reminder of the refreshment and satisfaction believers will enjoy in heaven. In eternity, God will permanently satisfy the yearnings of the soul. This assurance is grounded in the Lord's own nature. Those who overcome in this life will receive an everlasting inheritance and an abiding relationship. They will be the eternal people of the eternal God (vs. 7). Virtue and purity will characterize life for the redeemed in heaven. Also, the Lord will ban from heaven all who are characterized by the vices listed in verse 8. The habitually wretched actions of these people will be irrefutable evidence that they are not saved (see Matt. 7:21-23).

The angel that John mentioned in Revelation 21:9 is one of the seven who had emptied the bowl plagues (see 16:1). The celestial being may also be the same angel who had revealed to the apostle the judgment of the prostitute (see 17:1). The messenger of God invited John to see the bride, the wife of the Lamb (21:9). Suddenly, the apostle found himself being transported by the Spirit to a huge, majestic mountain. "Spirit" (vs. 10) could also refer to John's human spirit. In either case, the apostle seemed to have been in a trancelike state as he viewed the holy city—the new Jerusalem—descending out of heaven from God (vs. 10). This was the final dwelling place of those who followed the Messiah. John noted that the eternal abode of the redeemed was filled with the glory of God and its radiance was like an extremely precious jewel. Indeed, the holy city was crystal clear like a prized jasper stone (vs. 11). In Bible times, jasper tended to be mostly reddish in hue, though stones have been found that are green, brown, blue, yellow, and white in color. The new Jerusalem sparkling like a gem suggests that it radiated the majesty of the Lord.

The city was a gigantic cube and the same shape as the Most Holy Place in the tabernacle and temple. In ancient Israel, both the tabernacle and the temple were set apart for God and became the place where He manifested His presence among His people. Every detail of their exterior construction and interior contents were to correspond exactly with God's definitive instructions. The holy city had a massive, high wall with 12 gates. On the latter were the names of the 12 tribes of the nation of Israel, and there were 12 angels stationed at the gates (vs. 12). In terms of distribution, the east, north, south, and west sides of this magnificent abode each had three gates (vs. 13). Moreover, the wall of the new Jerusalem had 12 foundation stones, and on them were inscribed the 12 names of the 12 apostles of the Lamb (vs. 14). The length, width, and height of the new Jerusalem were equal (about 1,400 miles), making it perfectly symmetrical (vss. 15-16). The wall was about 200 feet thick (or high; vs. 17) and made of jasper. The pristine city was pure gold, like transparent glass (vs. 18), while its foundation stones were inlaid with 12 gems (vss. 19-20). Each of the 12 gates was made from just one pearl. The main street of the new Jerusalem was pure gold, as transparent as glass (vs. 21).

All the dimensions of the new Jerusalem were multiples of 12, which symbolically designates the fullness of God's people. Also, the Lamb was very prominent in the new Jerusalem, along with the Father and the Spirit. The splendor and opulence of the city reflected the beauty and majesty of God. The believers' eternal home was characterized by awesomeness and durability. Unlike the Jerusalem of Bible times, the new Jerusalem did not have a temple within it (vs. 22). The reason is that "the Lord God Almighty and the Lamb" were the city's temple. Similarly, the new Jerusalem had no need for the sun or the moon, for "the glory of God" (vs. 23) illuminated the city and "the Lamb" was the city's source of light.

John's reference to the Lord God as the "Almighty" (vs. 22) renders a Greek noun that means "all-powerful" or "omnipotent." Outside Revelation, this term is found only once in the New Testament (2 Cor. 6:18), but here it occurs nine times. The word conveys the sense of God being invincible. The idea is that no matter how fierce and wicked Satan and his demonic cohorts may be, they cannot defeat God. In the Lord's time and in His way He fulfills His promises and accomplishes His sovereign purpose in history. Consequently, while human rulers might claim total dominion over the world and have themselves celebrated as rulers of history, in reality it is God alone to whom dominion over the world and history belongs.

SUGGESTIONS TO TEACHERS

What will increase the sales of almost any product on the market? Add to the product's name the words "New and Improved!" People seem to be fascinated by new things, so John's vision of a new heaven, a new earth, and a new Jerusalem probably intrigues us. There are at least three reasons for our fascination, and these three reasons can also help us rethink our Christian lives on this side of eternity:

1. NEW THINGS ARE UNTARNISHED. The "new heaven" (Rev. 21:1) and the "new earth" that are coming will only faintly resemble what exists now. None of the problems that are here now will be found in eternity. In much the same way, Paul said, when we trust in Christ for salvation, we become new creations—"old things are passed away; behold, all things are become new" (2 Cor. 5:17). God wants to always be at work in our lives through the Holy Spirit, creating in us new people who are genuinely transformed (Rom. 12:2).

2. NEW THINGS ARE FRESH. New life in springtime brings fresh leaves and plants, not a recoloring or reworking of what was there last year. The old fall leaves, for example, do not suddenly change color and reattach themselves to the branches. Thus, a plant always has new opportunities to grow and flourish. Similarly, believers should always grow in Christ, continually looking for new opportunities to serve Him and to be more like Him.

3. NEW THINGS ARE UNCLUTTERED. Though the Holy Spirit makes us new creations in Christ, it's hard to be a completely new person in Him because we carry with us the "clutter" of what we once were or are still trying not to be. Thankfully, in the new heaven and new earth, the past will not even be a memory. The slate will be wiped clean. Though we have a start on that process now, we can only fully complete it with Jesus in eternity, for when we leave this earth to be with Him, we will "leave our baggage at the terminal before departing."

| **FOR ADULTS** | ■ **TOPIC:** New Beginnings
■ **QUESTIONS:** 1. How was John able to catch a glimpse of the new |

Jerusalem? 2. Why won't the new Jerusalem have any temple? 3. If you had the opportunity, what would you bring into the new Jerusalem? 4. In the new Jerusalem, what prominence is given to the Lamb? 5. What are some ways you can give praise to the Father for His goodness and grace made available through faith in the Son?

■ **ILLUSTRATIONS:**

A New Homecoming. "We've found the perfect house," some people say when they succeed in finding the home of their dreams. However, year after year they discover that what seemed like a perfect house needs repairs, upkeep, and even remodeling. They work hard to keep it livable and enjoyable.

Our journeys through life are something like that. We launch our relationship with God and then we find that discipleship is hard work. We can't fall behind in our worship and service. We need constant renewal and stimulation to keep walking with God.

For our sakes, God tells us that one day our struggles will be over. At the end of the age, the Father and Son will abide with us. We, in turn, will experience unimagined joy in their presence.

Let's Go to Your House. Tom was elderly, and for many years he had enjoyed taking long walks with the Lord each evening. On these walks, he would talk with the Lord about all kinds of things, especially about many of the important times in Tom's life, such as when he met his wife, the birth of his children, and special Christmases.

One day, while Tom was out walking with the Lord for an especially long time, Tom sensed the Lord conveying to him, "We are closer to My house than we are to yours. Why don't you just come home with Me?" Tom was glad to go.

I think that is the way God would like for all of us to view His house. In Revelation 21:7 God said, "I will be his God, and he shall be my son." Going to heaven is going home to be part of the everlasting family of God.

The Definition of Heaven. Robert Capon, author of *The Parables of the Kingdom*, says, "'Heaven' or 'heavenly' in the New Testament bear little relation to the meanings we have so unscripturally attached to them. For us, heaven is an unearthly, humanly irrelevant condition in which bed-sheeted, paper-winged spirits sit on clouds and play tinkly music until their pipe-cleaner halos drop off from boredom. But in Scripture, it is a city with boys and girls playing in the streets; it is buildings . . . that use amethysts for cinder blocks and pearls as big as the Ritz for gates; and indoors, it is a dinner party to end all dinner parties at the marriage supper of the Lamb. It is, in short, earth wedded, not earth jilted. It is the world as the irremovable apple of God's eyes."

This new city that God is creating for us will be more than we could ever hope for or imagine. God is eagerly awaiting the time when all believers will be gathered together at His table, having come to His house to stay.

FOR YOUTH

■ TOPIC: Something Really New
■ QUESTIONS: 1. What happened to the first earth and sea? 2. How would you describe the new Jerusalem to a friend? 3. Why will there be no more death or sorrow in the new Jerusalem? 4. How can the hope of your eternal inheritance in the Son give you inner strength to resist the temptations you encounter on a daily basis? 5. What sorts of things do you envision doing in the new Jerusalem?

■ ILLUSTRATIONS:

A New World Coming! Space missions no longer excite us like they once did. But among today's students could be those who someday will inhabit a new world in deep space. Something in human beings drives them to push back the old frontiers.

Jesus told us about a new world, that is, an entirely new creation. Our universe will be replaced by a new one—not just with new physical attributes, but also with moral and spiritual qualities, including freedom from sin, fear, sickness, and death.

God's picture of the future far surpasses anything we could ever imagine or achieve. We must listen to what He says, so that we will not miss the greatest adventure of all time.

Leaving the Old Behind. During Erin's growing up years, her family moved around a lot because of her dad's job as a soldier in the Army. Erin was in six different school systems by the time she graduated from high school.

While going to a new place was scary and hard for Erin, her mom always tried to help Erin and her brothers see the good things that could come from all things being new. Her mom told her children that it was their golden opportunity to change a bad habit or attitude they did not like about themselves. No one would know all of their past faults, and the new people would not be able to throw past mistakes up in their faces.

Erin especially remembered the family move during her middle school years. She went from a school with about 300 students to one with over 900 students. She decided she was going to be more outgoing and not as shy in this new school. It became fun for Erin to create a "new world" for herself. She was still true to herself—with the same likes, dislikes, and morals, for example—but she was "allowed" to talk more freely in class and to be more adventurous. She even tried out for the school play and joined several clubs!

As we look ahead to the new world God will create for believers in heaven, we can be excited to know that all old things will pass away. No one will care about the past mistakes and failures in our lives if our name is written in the Lamb's book of life.

A Happy Ending. Katie was offered the opportunity to select a dog for her birthday present. At the pet store, she was shown a number of puppies. From among them she picked one whose tail was wagging furiously. When Katie was asked why she chose that particular dog, she said, "I wanted the one with the happy ending."

Everyone will share in the ultimate "happy ending," if they make the choice now to follow the living Christ as Lord and Savior. Revelation promises us that a new world is coming for all believers and what a happy "beginning" it will be!

TREE OF LIFE

BACKGROUND SCRIPTURE: Revelation 22
DEVOTIONAL READING: Ephesians 3:14-21

KEY VERSE: On either side of the river, was there the tree of life, which bare twelve manner of fruits, and yielded her fruit every month: and the leaves of the tree were for the healing of the nations. (Revelation 22:2)

KING JAMES VERSION

REVELATION 22:1 And he shewed me a pure river of water of life, clear as crystal, proceeding out of the throne of God and of the Lamb. 2 In the midst of the street of it, and on either side of the river, was there the tree of life, which bare twelve manner of fruits, and yielded her fruit every month: and the leaves of the tree were for the healing of the nations. 3 And there shall be no more curse: but the throne of God and of the Lamb shall be in it; and his servants shall serve him: 4 And they shall see his face; and his name shall be in their foreheads. 5 And there shall be no night there; and they need no candle, neither light of the sun; for the Lord God giveth them light: and they shall reign for ever and ever.

6 And he said unto me, These sayings are faithful and true: and the Lord God of the holy prophets sent his angel to shew unto his servants the things which must shortly be done. 7 Behold, I come quickly: blessed is he that keepeth the sayings of the prophecy of this book. 8 And I John saw these things, and heard them. And when I had heard and seen, I fell down to worship before the feet of the angel which shewed me these things. 9 Then saith he unto me, See thou do it not: for I am thy fellowservant, and of thy brethren the prophets, and of them which keep the sayings of this book: worship God.

NEW REVISED STANDARD VERSION

REVELATION 22:1 Then the angel showed me the river of the water of life, bright as crystal, flowing from the throne of God and of the Lamb 2 through the middle of the street of the city. On either side of the river is the tree of life with its twelve kinds of fruit, producing its fruit each month; and the leaves of the tree are for the healing of the nations. 3 Nothing accursed will be found there any more. But the throne of God and of the Lamb will be in it, and his servants will worship him; 4 they will see his face, and his name will be on their foreheads. 5 And there will be no more night; they need no light of lamp or sun, for the Lord God will be their light, and they will reign forever and ever.

6 And he said to me, "These words are trustworthy and true, for the Lord, the God of the spirits of the prophets, has sent his angel to show his servants what must soon take place."

7 "See, I am coming soon! Blessed is the one who keeps the words of the prophecy of this book."

8 I, John, am the one who heard and saw these things. And when I heard and saw them, I fell down to worship at the feet of the angel who showed them to me; 9 but he said to me, "You must not do that! I am a fellow servant with you and your comrades the prophets, and with those who keep the words of this book. Worship God!"

13

Monday, May 23	Ephesians 3:14-21	*Bowing before the Father*
Tuesday, May 24	Exodus 33:17-23	*A Glimpse of God's Glory*
Wednesday, May 25	Psalm 47:5-9	*The Throne of God*
Thursday, May 26	John 4:7-15	*Living Water*
Friday, May 27	Revelation 2:1-7	*The Tree of Life*
Saturday, May 28	Revelation 22:10-21	*I Am Coming Soon*
Sunday, May 29	Revelation 22:1-9	*Worship God!*

BACKGROUND

In the last book of Scripture, we discover that many themes introduced in Genesis find their fulfillment in Revelation. For instance, God created the sun (Gen. 1:14-18), but in the eternal state it will no longer be needed (Rev. 21:23; 22:5). Sin long ago entered the human race (Gen. 3:1-7), and is expelled in the end (Rev. 21:8, 27; 22:15). Whereas before people tried to hide from God (Gen. 3:8), in the eternal state the redeemed enjoy intimacy with Him (Rev. 21:3; 22:4). The earth now languishes under the scourge of sin (Gen. 3:17) and is subjected to futility (Rom. 8:20). But one day the planet will join God's children in glorious freedom from death and decay (Rom. 8:21; Rev. 21:1, 4-5; 22:3). Whereas now tears are shed over sorrow from sin (Gen. 21:16; 27:34, 38), in the eternal state there will be no more tears and sorrow, because sin will be eliminated (Rev. 7:17; 21:4).

For the moment people are destined to die (Gen. 5:5-31), but the wonderful news is that Jesus has defeated death, and believers will live forever with Him in heaven (Rev. 21:4; 22:1-2, 17). In the new creation, the Father and the Son will be seated on the throne, and the redeemed will worship and serve God continually (22:3). Furthermore, at the end of the age, we will not only be like the Messiah but also see Him as He is (1 John 3:2). Now we view things imperfectly, like trying to see our reflection using an inferior mirror. But in the eternal state, we will understand our place in the universe with perfect clarity. Admittedly, we now know the Lord only partially. Nevertheless, we look forward to a time when we will know Him fully (1 Cor. 13:12).

NOTES ON THE PRINTED TEXT

John saw a pure river with the water of life (Rev. 22:1). The river was crystal clear, and it flowed from God's throne down the middle of the city's main thoroughfare. The river and its water are a symbol of the fullness of eternal life that proceeds from the presence of God. To those living in the hot and dry climate of Palestine this scene would be a vivid image of God's ability to satisfy a person's spiritual thirst (see John 4:7-14; Rev. 22:17). In Revelation 22:1, John mentioned "the throne of God and of the Lamb." The apostle's repeated reference to the Messiah suggests that John did not want us to miss the significance of the Lamb in the eternal state. In this vision of the future, God and the Lamb are joint owners of the heavenly throne. Also, the imperial role of the Father and the Son has become a functional unity. The fact that they share one single throne underscores the full divinity of the Son and His equality with the Father and the Spirit.

John observed that a tree of life grew on each side of the river. Some think the Greek noun rendered "tree" (vs. 2) should be taken in a collective sense to refer to an orchard lining both sides of the riverbank. In either case, the tree bears 12 different kinds of fruit, with a new crop appearing each month of the year. The fruit gives life, and the leaves are used as medicine to heal the nations. The presence of healing leaves does not mean there will be illness in heaven. Rather, the leaves symbolize the health and vigor that believers will enjoy in eternity (see Ezek. 47:12). A tree of life first existed in the Garden of Eden, and it must have been lush. After Adam and Eve had sinned, God did not allow them to eat the fruit of the tree. In eternity, however, the all-powerful Lord will allow the redeemed to partake fully of eternal life, which is symbolized by the tree and its fresh, abundant fruit (see Gen. 2:9; 3:22).

After the Fall, God placed everything under sin's curse. In the eternal state, however, He will remove the curse of sin and all its effects. Similarly, God will ban from the new Jerusalem anyone who is accursed because of wickedness (Rev. 22:3; see Gen. 3:14-19; Rev. 22:15). This truth is another reason for the wicked to abandon their evil ways and for the upright to avoid the path of sin. The presence of believers with the Lamb in heaven will enable them to see His face (Rev. 22:4). It would be incorrect to infer from this verse that the triune God, who is spirit (John 4:24), has a literal human face. Rather, John spoke figuratively to stress that the Lord will establish unbroken communion with His people. The apostle also used metaphorical language when he said that the name of the Lamb will be on the foreheads of His followers (Rev. 22:4). The idea is that He will claim them as His own.

The end of history will be better than the beginning, for a radiant city will replace the Garden of Eden, and the light of God's glory will drive out all darkness. There will be no idleness or boredom in the eternal state, for the Lord will give His people ruling responsibilities (vs. 5). The last book of Scripture assures us of God's final purposes. Revelation should also increase our longing for communion with the triune God. What we now enjoy is only a foretaste of grand and glorious things to come.

When someone recounts a fantastic story, it's natural for us to be skeptical—at least initially. If John had any doubts concerning the vision he had received, the interpreting angel dispelled them with words of reassurance. He declared that God's prophecies about the future—for instance, the Lamb's overthrow of evil and the joys awaiting His followers in the eternal state—were true, trustworthy, and certain to take place at the divinely appointed time (vs. 6).

One prominent, Christ-centered aspect of John's message was the return of Jesus at the end of the age (vs. 7). The certainty of His future appearing should have comforted His followers in times of hardship and motivated them to be obedient and faithful in times of temptation. Moreover, in this sixth statement of blessing found in Revelation—which mirrors the first statement of blessing recorded in 1:3—the upright are reminded that, by remaining devoted to the Son, they would be the privileged recipients of the Father's favor.

In Revelation 1:2, John affirmed his own testimony concerning the Messiah. The apostle again picked up on this theme in 22:8 when he said he was an eyewitness to the visions recorded in the last book of Scripture. John also affirmed that he faithfully wrote down what he saw so that future generations of believers could read and obey these unveiled mysteries. This statement emphasizes that a Christ-centered goal of John was to shift the focus of believers from themselves to the Lamb. Oddly enough, when John saw and heard what the interpreting angel had revealed to him, the apostle fell down to worship the celestial being. But the angel commanded him to stop and urged John to worship the Lord (vs. 9). Similarly, His people were to make Him the recipient of their homage and praise.

As we see in Daniel 12:4, an angel commanded Daniel to seal, or close up, the vision he had received so that it would remain confidential. In contrast, an angel told John not to keep the prophecies he had received a secret. The message he recorded was relevant not only for first-century Christians but also for believers today. As we study and apply the truths of Revelation, we will be better prepared for the return of the Savior (Rev. 22:10). People can respond either positively or negatively to the message of this book. A proper response includes repenting of sin, seeking to live uprightly, and desiring to become more like the Messiah. An improper response includes remaining entrenched in the world's evil system and taking God lightly. Those who respond this way will become spiritually hardened and more firmly set in their present course of wrongdoing (vs. 11).

At the end of the age, Jesus will reward people for what they have done. While eternal joy is the heritage of the righteous, eternal sorrow is the lot of the wicked. Ultimately, the way people live is an indicator of whether they are regenerate or unregenerate (vs. 14; see Matt. 7:15-20; 1 John 1:6-7). God will allow the faithful—namely, those who have not defiled themselves by the corrupt world system—to live with Him in heaven and enjoy the blessings of eternal life. However, God will ban from His presence the "dogs" (Rev. 22:15)—namely, people of immoral and unspiritual character (see Phil. 3:2).

Jesus assured His followers that what is recorded in Revelation is true and can be trusted. He could guarantee what He had declared, for He is the Messiah who came from the house and lineage of David. As the "bright and morning star" (Rev. 22:16), He ensures that a new day of salvation will dawn. With such promises from the Savior awaiting fulfillment, it's no wonder that God's Spirit and His people extend an invitation for everyone to come to Jesus in faith and experience the joys of redemption. All are welcome to drink from the water of eternal life, which the Lamb offers free of charge (vs. 17). Revelation—like the rest of Scripture—is to be distinguished from mere human words. The book's message is so important that God promises to judge those who might distort what it says (for example, by adding things to it or omitting things from it). This warning should prompt us to handle Scripture with care and respect, and to heed what it discloses (vss. 18-19; see Deut. 4:2; 12:32).

The good news is that Jesus will one day return. With John and all believers, we can affirm the certainty of this promise. Interestingly, the phrase rendered "come, Lord Jesus" (Rev. 22:20) is equivalent to the transliterated Aramaic expression *Maranatha*, which appears in 1 Corinthians 16:22 (and similarly means either "Our Lord, come!" or "Our Lord has come!"). John ended the last book of Scripture with a benediction of Jesus' abundant grace for God's people (Rev. 22:21; see 1 John 2:28). As we await Jesus' return, let us serve the Lord out of love and with deep devotion. By His grace we can resist any temptation to compromise our faith. Then when He appears, we will be able to face Him with joy and gladness. At that moment all of our deepest longings will finally be fulfilled.

SUGGESTIONS TO TEACHERS

While we do not know exactly when Jesus is coming again, we know He will one day return. Therefore, we live beyond the problems of today with the hope that comes from knowing the future belongs to Him.

1. THINGS WILL GET BETTER FOR US. Whatever pain, sorrow, or hurts that we have to face right now are merely tests of our endurance and perseverance. Our sole task is to keep our eyes on the Lord and listen to Him through His Word as He provides direction and protection for our individual lives. If we endure and persevere in our faith, we have the sure and certain hope of being rewarded—of being the recipients of God's ultimate and fantastic promises!

2. THINGS WILL GET BETTER FOR OUR CHILDREN. Past generations of people have been quite concerned about "making things better" for future generations. Much of this concern has been directed toward efforts at making future generations better physically, mentally, emotionally, and (especially) financially. God puts back in the hearts of His people the desire for their children to be better off spiritually. And if this is a concern of our present generation, God promises that He will bless future generations of our children with eternal peace.

3. THINGS WILL GET BETTER FOR GOD'S PEOPLE. The supreme hope for the culmination of the future kingdom of God is that His people will be better off because the effects of sin will be eliminated. God's grace will overrule all wickedness and His goodness and righteousness will create an atmosphere of peace and prosperity, where all the spiritual members of His family will be blessed.

■ **TOPIC:** Appreciating Abundance

■ **QUESTIONS:** 1. What do you think you would have felt if you were permitted to see the "river of water of life" (Rev. 22:1)? 2. In what sense will the "tree of life" (vs. 2) be for the "healing of the nations"? 3. How can knowing that the Lord's name will be written on our foreheads in eternity encourage us now (see vs. 4)? 4. Why did the angel who spoke to John stress that words he heard were "faithful and true" (vs. 6)? 5. How can we ensure that we give our worship only to God (see vs. 9)?

■ **ILLUSTRATIONS:**

Experiencing True Happiness. With the proliferation of legalized gambling, more and more people think they can find happiness by winning lots of money. Players envision an abundance of wealth to pay off their debts and buy a new home, car, or boat. They also dream of traveling to distant lands and enjoying idyllic vacations.

Occasionally, we read stories about the troubles that have plagued overnight millionaires. This should not surprise us, for as Christians we know that money cannot buy happiness. In the eternal state, spiritual abundance will come as a result of abiding with the triune God.

While we acknowledge the perils of money, we find it hard not to define our lives in terms of how much we have. It should come as no surprise, then, that we need the promises of dwelling with God found in Revelation 22. In these verses, the Lord addresses the heart of our deepest longings and values.

The Ultimate Master Builder. For over two decades, *This Old House* has televised home improvement stories. Each week, a group of experts—including a master carpenter, a general contractor, a heating and plumbing specialist, and a landscaper—share their tips and tricks on how to do home remodeling and renovation. Watching the crew perform their "magic" on a run-down house is both educational and entertaining.

In the grand scheme of things, our Lord is the ultimate master builder. After all, He commanded all that we know into existence. One day He will remake the universe—along with everything in it—so that our eternal dwelling place is infinitely pure and pristine. He will leave nothing undone and spare no expense (in a manner of speaking) so that we can live in our new home with Him for eternity (see Rev. 22:1-5).

Ready or Not. The wreckage of the luxury liner, *Titanic,* thought to have been "unsinkable," now rests 13,120 feet down on the Atlantic Ocean floor. In its day, the Titanic was the world's largest ship, weighing over 46 tons, being 882 feet long, and rising 11 stories high. The vessel employed a crew and staff of almost 1,000 and could carry nearly 2,500 passengers. The ship was ready for its passengers with a complete gymnasium, heated pool, squash court, and the first miniature golf course.

Even for all the elegant and luxurious extras this ship had, it still lacked some basic equipment needed for survival if something "unthinkable" happened. It was short the needed number of lifeboats for all of its passengers and crew, and on its first voyage it was short a simple pair of binoculars needed for the lookouts to spot icebergs. On its first trip, the ship received at least seven warnings about dangerous icebergs in its path. However, the captain and others were more concerned with getting to America in record time instead of watching out for the safety of the ship and its passengers.

The night of April 14, 1912, the "unthinkable" happened to the "unsinkable." Near midnight, the great *Titanic* struck an iceberg, ripping a 300 foot hole through 5 of its 16 watertight compartments. It sank in 2 1/2 hours, killing 1,513 people.

Sometimes we act as if Jesus is never coming back, despite the knowledge that He is. The *Titanic* supplies a lesson for us all. If the people in charge would have been more watchful and more diligent in doing the right things, many lives would have been saved, and possibly the entire ship would have made it to its destination on time. Jesus wants us to be ready and expectantly waiting for what He will bring us today or tomorrow (see Rev. 22:7).

FOR YOUTH

■ TOPIC: Source of Blessings

■ QUESTIONS: 1. What is significant about the celestial throne being associated with both "God and . . . the Lamb" (Rev. 22:1)? 2. What kind of service can you envision giving to the triune God in heaven (see vs. 3)? 3. How do you think it will feel in eternity when there is "no night there" (vs. 5)? 4. Why did Jesus emphasize the truth of His second coming (vs. 7)? 5. What might have led John to mistakenly worship the angel (see vs. 8)?

■ ILLUSTRATIONS:

What Is True Happiness? For many youth in the West, experiencing true happiness means wearing the right clothes, using the right words, having the right friends, and driving the right car. This is crass materialism, and it is of no eternal value.

An examination of Revelation 22 indicates that the triune God is the ultimate source of blessing for saved adolescents (as well as for all believers). In the eternal state, He promises to refresh them with life-giving water, to invigorate them with health-giving fruit, and to enable them to see Him face-to-face. Admittedly, there is nothing in this present life that can compare with what the Lord has in store for His people in eternity.

Fortunately, this world is not the truest home for believing teens. They are looking to Jesus' return to give them hope. The latter is not something they merely wish for either, but is absolutely certain to happen. This realization helps to put the focus of saved adolescents on the Savior and the eternal life He freely offers to all who trust in Him.

Extreme Makeover. The television series by this name showcases everyday people who undergo a series of cosmetic procedures and supposedly have their lives changed forever. One season included two sisters who struggled with cleft palettes and underwent nearly 40 surgeries; a colorful bull rider who had his teeth knocked out and wanted to be transformed into an urban cowboy; and a female rock musician who spent her days hiding behind her shocking stage appearance. These and other participants recuperated at the "Makeover Mansion," a luxurious residence tucked away in the Hollywood Hills, complete with stunning views, a swimming pool, fully equipped home gym, and plasma televisions.

This prime-time version of a new start on life is a far cry from what we find revealed in Scripture. God doesn't promise to revamp our dying physical bodies. And we aren't going to be deposited in a lavish manor that will eventually decay and fall apart. What the Lord has in store for us is far better and will be everlasting. Indeed, He will be our light, and we will rule with Him forever (see Rev. 22:1-5).

"Fish" for Life. A young boy stood idly on a bridge watching some fishermen. Seeing one of them with a basket full of fish, he said, "If I had a catch like that, I'd be happy." "I'll give you that many fish if you do a small favor for me," said the fisherman. "I need you to tend this line awhile. I've got some business down the street."

The young boy gladly accepted the offer. After the man left, the trout and bass continued snapping greedily at the baited hook. Soon the boy forgot everything else, and was excitedly pulling in a large number of fish. When the fisherman returned, he said to the young boy, "I'll keep my promise to you by giving you everything you've caught. And I hope you've learned a lesson. You mustn't waste time daydreaming and merely wishing for things. Instead, get busy and cast in a line for yourself."

This young boy made the most of his time, not realizing that he was really going to benefit the most from the amount of energy he put into catching the fish. He could have just as easily put out only enough effort to catch one or two fish. It's your life. What you get out of it depends greatly on what you put into it. As you think about being prepared for the second coming of Christ, "fish" as if your heavenly reward depends on it (see Rev. 22:7).

GOD'S PROMISES FULFILLED

BACKGROUND SCRIPTURE: Joshua 1:1-6; 11-12
DEVOTIONAL READING: Acts 26:1-7

KEY VERSE: As the LORD commanded Moses his servant, so did Moses command Joshua, and so did Joshua; he left nothing undone of all that the LORD commanded Moses. (Joshua 11:15)

KING JAMES VERSION

JOSHUA 1:1 Now after the death of Moses the servant of the LORD it came to pass, that the LORD spake unto Joshua the son of Nun, Moses' minister, saying, 2 Moses my servant is dead; now therefore arise, go over this Jordan, thou, and all this people, unto the land which I do give to them, even to the children of Israel. 3 Every place that the sole of your foot shall tread upon, that have I given unto you, as I said unto Moses. 4 From the wilderness and this Lebanon even unto the great river, the river Euphrates, all the land of the Hittites, and unto the Great Sea toward the going down of the sun, shall be your coast. 5 There shall not any man be able to stand before thee all the days of thy life: as I was with Moses, so I will be with thee: I will not fail thee, nor forsake thee. 6 Be strong and of a good courage: for unto this people shalt thou divide for an inheritance the land, which I sware unto their fathers to give them. . . .

11:16 So Joshua took all that land, the hills, and all the south country, and all the land of Goshen, and the valley, and the plain, and the mountain of Israel, and the valley of the same; 17 Even from the mount Halak, that goeth up to Seir, even unto Baalgad in the valley of Lebanon under mount Hermon: and all their kings he took, and smote them, and slew them. 18 Joshua made war a long time with all those kings. 19 There was not a city that made peace with the children of Israel, save the Hivites the inhabitants of Gibeon: all other they took in battle. . . . 21 And at that time came Joshua, and cut off the Anakim from the mountains, from Hebron, from Debir, from Anab, and from all the mountains of Judah, and from all the mountains of Israel: Joshua destroyed them utterly with their cities. 22 There was none of the Anakim left in the land of the children of Israel: only in Gaza, in Gath, and in Ashdod, there remained. 23 So Joshua took the whole land, according to all that the LORD said unto Moses; and Joshua gave it for an inheritance unto Israel according to their divisions by their tribes. And the land rested from war.

NEW REVISED STANDARD VERSION

JOSHUA 1:1 After the death of Moses the servant of the Lord, the Lord spoke to Joshua son of Nun, Moses' assistant, saying, 2 "My servant Moses is dead. Now proceed to cross the Jordan, you and all this people, into the land that I am giving to them, to the Israelites. 3 Every place that the sole of your foot will tread upon I have given to you, as I promised to Moses. 4 From the wilderness and the Lebanon as far as the great river, the river Euphrates, all the land of the Hittites, to the Great Sea in the west shall be your territory. 5 No one shall be able to stand against you all the days of your life. As I was with Moses, so I will be with you; I will not fail you or forsake you. 6 Be strong and courageous; for you shall put this people in possession of the land that I swore to their ancestors to give them. . . .

11:16 So Joshua took all that land: the hill country and all the Negeb and all the land of Goshen and the lowland and the Arabah and the hill country of Israel and its lowland, 17 from Mount Halak, which rises toward Seir, as far as Baal-gad in the valley of Lebanon below Mount Hermon. He took all their kings, struck them down, and put them to death. 18 Joshua made war a long time with all those kings. 19 There was not a town that made peace with the Israelites, except the Hivites, the inhabitants of Gibeon; all were taken in battle. . . . 21 At that time Joshua came and wiped out the Anakim from the hill country, from Hebron, from Debir, from Anab, and from all the hill country of Judah, and from all the hill country of Israel; Joshua utterly destroyed them with their towns. 22 None of the Anakim was left in the land of the Israelites; some remained only in Gaza, in Gath, and in Ashdod. 23 So Joshua took the whole land, according to all that the Lord had spoken to Moses; and Joshua gave it for an inheritance to Israel according to their tribal allotments. And the land had rest from war.

Monday, May 30	Acts 26:1-7	*Hope in God's Promises*
Tuesday, May 31	Romans 9:1-5	*God's Promises to Israel*
Wednesday, June 1	Romans 9:6-12	*Children of the Promise*
Thursday, June 2	Romans 9:22-26	*Children of the Living God*
Friday, June 3	2 Corinthians 6:14–7:1	*Since We Have These Promises*
Saturday, June 4	Romans 15:7-13	*Abound in Hope*
Sunday, June 5	Joshua 1:1b-6; 11:16-19, 21-23	*God's Promises to Moses Fulfilled*

BACKGROUND

Joshua 1:1 picks up where Deuteronomy 34:5 left off—with the death of Moses, the Lord's servant. In a sense, the events described in the Book of Joshua were the fulfillment of what God had done through and promised to Moses. Because it chronicles the way God provided for the Israelites' entrance into the promised land, Joshua reveals much about the character and nature of God. The traits of the Lord are portrayed and clarified, as this book shows how God interacted with His people, leading them, protecting them, teaching them, loving them, and making a way for them to fulfill His will for their lives.

Joshua was born in Egypt and lived a good part of his adult life as one of the hundreds of thousands of Hebrew slaves under Pharaoh. Joshua was appointed as Moses' lieutenant shortly after the Exodus and served in that capacity during the 40 years the Israelites spent in the wilderness (see Exod. 24:13; 33:11; Num. 11:28; Deut. 1:38). The Lord Himself told Moses to appoint Joshua as his successor, saying Joshua was "a man in whom is the spirit" (Num. 27:18). So with Moses' death, the Lord spoke to Joshua, commissioning him as the new Israelite leader.

NOTES ON THE PRINTED TEXT

The Lord directed Joshua (through what means remains unknown) to prepare the people to cross the Jordan and enter the land God had promised to the descendants of Abraham (Josh. 1:2; see Gen. 12:1, 7; 13:15; 15:18; 28:13; 50:24; Exod. 3:8; 23:31; Deut. 1:7-8). The Israelites must have known they were embarking upon a formidable task. Camped on the plains of Moab, the Israelites probably knew that their fierce Canaanite foes were by now expecting an Israelite attack. One could not blame God's people if they shied away from the tasks of attacking fortified cities and fighting well-trained, well-equipped warriors. Nonetheless, unlike the previous generation of Israelites, this new cohort believed God to be faithful to His promise. In response to the Lord's call and Joshua's leadership, the people prepared to overcome all the obstacles and enter the promised land.

The Lord's promise to Joshua was similar to the one He had earlier made to Moses (see Deut. 11:24-25). God pledged to the new Israelite leader that He would give the

Hebrews all the regions through which they walked during their military campaign in Canaan (Josh. 1:3). The Israelites' accomplishing this under Joshua's leadership would bring to completion the work initiated by Moses. Even so, the main emphasis is on the fact that the land was God's gift to the Israelites. Still, the land would be theirs only as they would appropriate it. The land promised to Joshua was broader than what was actually conquered under the Israelite general's leadership. Verse 4 says the territory would stretch from the wilderness in the south to Lebanon in the north. Moreover, the nation would control all the land from the Euphrates River in the east (including all of Syria, that is, the "land of the Hittites") to the Mediterranean Sea in the west. However, the land conquered by the Israelites under Joshua only stretched from Dan in the north to Beersheba in the south (compare Gen. 15:18; Num. 34:3-12; Deut. 34:1-4).

The Lord promised that throughout Joshua's life, no one would be able to resist his efforts to conquer Canaan. God's abiding presence was the key to the Israelites' military success. Indeed, just as God had promised Moses His constant presence, so He pledged to comfort and encourage Joshua with His presence. The Lord declared that He would never abandon or forsake Israel's general (Josh. 1:5). Shortly before his death, Moses commissioned Joshua a second time in the sight of all Israel. Moses' words to Joshua recorded in Deuteronomy 31:7-8 parallel those of the Lord found in Joshua 1:5-6. The Israelites' newly appointed general was to "be strong and of a good courage," for God, the divine King, had summoned Joshua to lead the people into the land promised to their ancestors (namely, Abraham, Isaac, and Jacob).

God pledged to give Joshua success in leading the Israelites into Canaan and ongoing combat. More generally, God's presence among the people of Israel was vital to their survival as a nation. Consequently, the presence (or absence) of the Lord is a recurring theme throughout the Old Testament. Of course, because the Lord is omnipresent, we can never escape His presence (technically speaking). The covenantal gift of God's presence, however, was promised to the Israelites. Only in God's presence could Israel maintain its sense of unity and well-being. When the Israelites spiritually and morally abandoned their commitment to the Lord, they were no longer able to experience His sustaining presence among them. The divine presence of God is seen in the Old Testament as His gift to those who have obedient and loving hearts toward Him. For God to withdraw the sense of His presence was a stifling thing. Perhaps for that reason, hell may best be described as the absence of God.

Joshua 10, 11, and 12 complete the account of the Israelites' conquest of Canaan. They are complete in the sense that these chapters record the major cities taken by Joshua and his soldiers. More than likely, many battles occurred that were not recorded. Much of the promised land had yet to be taken and occupied by the Hebrews even after the land was divided among the twelve tribes. As a matter of fact, in the time of Solomon's reign, descendants of the Amorites, Hittites, Perizzites, Hivites, and

Jebusites still remained in the land (see 1 Kings 9:20-21).

Joshua 11:16-17 gives a summary statement of what the Israelites achieved militarily in Canaan. They conquered the whole land: the southern desert (or Negev) and the surrounding hill country; the region of Goshen; the lowlands (or western foothills) and valley of the Jordan River (or the Arabah); the hill country of northern Israel with its lowlands; Mount Halak, which towered over the region of Seir; and Baal Gad in the Lebanon Valley at the foot of Mount Hermon. The Lord also enabled Joshua and his armies to overcome the rulers of these lands, strike them down, and execute them.

In order to take the cities of Canaan, Joshua employed common methods of conducting a siege. The typical siege, especially one that lasted for an extended period of time, was mostly a battle of wills. During a siege, the city was first encircled to prevent aid or supplies from reaching it. Cutting off supplies either accelerated the initiation of a battle or produced a surrender from the city. Trees surrounding the locale were often cut down to make battering rams and ladders to breach the walls. But the Israelites probably refrained from cutting down fruit-bearing trees for these purposes, especially since they intended to harvest these trees once the siege was complete.

Joshua campaigned against the rulers of Canaan for quite some time (vs. 18). In fact, at least seven years passed from the crossing of the Jordan River to the capture of Hebron. Aside from a peace treaty made with the Hivites living in Gibeon, the Israelites defeated all the cities they fought against in Canaan (vs. 19). Chapter 9 details the circumstances involving Gibeon, which was about six miles northwest of Jerusalem. The inhabitants of the city and its surrounding towns were Hivites, a people included on Moses' list of occupants of Canaan who were to be driven out of the country (see Deut. 7:1-6).

When news of the Israelites' initial victories spread through Canaan, the inhabitants of the land began to unite in hopes of staving off the Hebrews' conquest. Joshua 11:20 explains that the Lord determined to make the Canaanites obstinate, which resulted in the Israelites completely annihilating their foes. This included the Anakites—a formidable, warlike people who lived around Hebron (see Num. 13:33; Deut. 9:2). During the conquest of Canaan, the Israelites exterminated the Anakites living in Hebron, Debir, Anab, as well as the hill country of Judah and Israel (Josh. 11:21). While there were no Anakites left in the territory controlled by Israel, some of these ancient people remained in the non-Israelite cities of Gaza, Gath, and Ashdod (vs. 22).

Despite some setbacks, overall the military campaign that Joshua led was deemed to be a success. This was in accordance with the Lord's directive to Moses. Furthermore, Joshua oversaw the distribution of the conquered territory among the various tribes of Israel. By the end of his life, Canaan was largely free of war (vs. 23). Though decisive battles were won under Joshua, the Israelite general intended for the tribes to take the rest of the land on their own initiative. When Joshua died and the Israelites entered into the period of the judges, their spiritual infidelity kept them on the defensive rather than on the offensive and squelched their attempts to take all that God had given to them. Indeed, the early Israelites' disobedience and halfhearted devotion to God prevented them from conquering the entire area, at least not until King Solomon extended Israel's borders to their farthest reaches in the tenth century B.C. (see Judg. 2:1-4, 20-23; 1 Kings 4:21, 24; 2 Chron. 9:26).

SUGGESTIONS TO TEACHERS

When we were saved, many of us were filled with zeal to live in a godly fashion. It may have even seemed easy to do so, because we loved God so much. But somehow, over time, we fell away from a strict obedience to biblical morality. It's not a hopeless situation. We can get back to obeying God—and in fact, do better than ever at it.

1. EXAMINE YOUR COMMITMENT TO LIVING GOD'S WAY. Joshua knew from personal experience how ruinous it can be to rebel against God. Joshua spent 40 years with the rest of his peers wandering in the wilderness of Sinai before only he and Caleb from that generation were allowed to enter the promised land. In what areas of morality are you the weakest? Recommit to being true to God's commands in those areas. Start now! You'll be glad you did.

2. DON'T BE DISCOURAGED. Perhaps Joshua faced times of discouragement, so much so that God reminded him to be courageous (see Josh. 1:6). We, too, can feel demoralized by our shortcomings. On the one hand, it is important for us to face those shortcomings and realize that they displease God. On the other hand, we must never forget the grace of God, which is able to forgive our sin and help us to overcome the bad habits we've developed. In obedience is freedom.

3. UNDERSTAND GOD'S WILL AS REVEALED IN HIS WORD. Sometimes people never get beyond a devotional reading of Scripture. But there is a time for study—for doing the hard work of trying to understand this ancient, complex, and unique book. Joshua sought to understand and heed God's will for him. Likewise, we must make sure we comprehend and heed what Scripture says, for in it we find God's will revealed to us.

FOR ADULTS

■ **TOPIC:** A Job Well Done

■ **QUESTIONS:** 1. What do you think it means to be known as a "servant of the LORD" (Josh. 1:1)? 2. Why did God displace the Canaanites and give their land to the Israelites? 3. In what ways has God's promise to never forsake His people been a source of encouragement for you (see vs. 5)? 4. Why did the Israelites make a peace treaty with the Hivites living in Gibeon? 5. How have human action and divine intervention worked together in your life to bring about the fulfillment of God's will?

■ ILLUSTRATIONS:

Learning to Listen. The structure of the ear enables sound vibrations to pass from outside the head to the part of our brain that controls hearing. Sound waves cause the eardrum to vibrate, which then turns the sound waves into nerve impulses inside the cochlea. Twenty-four thousand fibers cause a vibration in the cells that make up the organ of Corti. These fibers send messages through the auditory nerve to the center of hearing in the brain.

God designed our ears so that we can hear sounds of infinite variety. God also designed our souls to hear what He has revealed in His Word. Indeed, it is the basis for hearing Him declare to us, "Well done, good and faithful servant" (Matt. 25:23). But just as physical problems can cause deafness, so, too, our spiritual ears can become plugged by selfishness, willful disobedience, and outright sin. As the life of Joshua demonstrates, only by obeying the Lord can we discern what's really important in our lives.

The Skill of Listening. It kept Barb away regularly, two or three nights a week. Once she was there, she spent hours at a time. While she was gone, she socialized with friends and made jokes that she'd better get home before her husband and children thought she'd abandoned them.

Was Barb attending a neighborhood bar? Did a gambling casino have her hooked? No. She was overcommitted at her local church. She convinced herself that this was the best way to remain obedient to God. Sadly, Barb's desire to be at church whenever its doors were open took a tremendous toll on her marriage. After 20 years, her husband finally ended their relationship.

How could this problem have become so severe? Over the years, Barb sensed that there was a conflict between what God was telling her about commitment to her marriage and what she thought she should be doing at church. Ultimately, God was ignored.

Listening to God is an acquired skill. This proved to be true in the life of Joshua. In fact, the basis for his successful leadership of the Israelites was his willingness to hear and heed God's commands. Likewise, when we endeavor to listen to God, we will find ourselves operating more in harmony with His will for us.

Do Something. Theodore Roosevelt, the twenty-sixth president of the United States, seemed to always display a vigorous determination to get involved. He was Assistant Secretary of the Navy in 1898 when the Spanish-American War broke out, and he resigned that post to form the Rough Riders, a volunteer cavalry group that was to become famous for its charge up San Juan Hill in Cuba. An advocate of a venturesome foreign policy, Roosevelt effected the construction of the Panama Canal, won the Nobel Peace Prize for his successful intervention in the Russo-Japanese War, and dispatched the U.S. Fleet on a round-the-world tour.

Roosevelt's famous motto was "Speak softly and carry a big stick." But he had another motto that he wrote as advice to himself and others but that sounds as if it could have come from the mouth of Joshua: "In a moment of decision, the best thing you can do is the right thing to do. The worst thing you can do is nothing." From this statement we recognize that a big part of remaining obedient to the Lord involves energetically doing His will. After all, little is accomplished if we refuse to act.

FOR YOUTH

■ **TOPIC:** Hearing and Obeying God

■ **QUESTIONS:** 1. How do you think Joshua felt as he prepared to lead the Israelites into Canaan? 2. What role did Moses serve in getting the Israelites ready to conquer Canaan? 3. How is it possible for believers to remain courageous when their Christian commitment is challenged by unbelievers? 4. Why were the Israelites so successful in taking control of the promised land? 5. What are some of the promises of God that you fully expect to be fulfilled in your life?

■ **ILLUSTRATIONS:**

Tuned Out. While walking through a supermarket one day, a man listened to a mother scream at her child, "Do you hear me?" Children soon get immune to that cry, and by the time they are teenagers they learn to tune it out. Of course they hear, but they don't obey. That's why we say, "Listen to me!" when we really mean, "Obey me!"

A study of the Book of Joshua indicates that in God's kingdom hearing equals obedience. The successes and failures of the Israelites in their conquest of Canaan remind us that we are not serious about following the Lord if we refuse to do what He commands. Of course, God keeps giving us ample reasons to hear and heed His Word. We have no excuses for being ignorant of what He wants us to do.

In worship, prayer, and Bible study, God says, "Listen to Me." When we do, He fills our lives with contentment, no matter what our circumstances might be.

Strange Petition. A mother, while listening to her little girl's bedside prayer, heard her say, "Dear God, please make Boston the capital of Vermont!" Astonished by the strange petition, her mother asked, "Why did you pray for that?" "Because," answered the child, "that's the way I wrote it down on my test at school today."

We often wonder whether God hears and answers our prayers. Some people, if posed with the question, would unhesitatingly answer, "I doubt it."

Perhaps we have difficulty acknowledging the efficacy of prayer because we find that we want to set the ground rules for it. In prayer, we often bombard God with petitions for this or that, and we neglect an important aspect of prayer, namely, letting God speak to our hearts. We expect God to hear our prayers, but we don't wait around for

His answer. It's like the person who prayed, "God, give me patience, and I want it now!"

If we commune with the Lord the way Joshua did—namely, with an attitude of openness, seeking it to be an offering of ourselves and our needs—God will answer our requests. His response might not be when we expect it. We might not always like the answer, for God gives His blessings according to His purposes, not ours. But He will answer, especially when we listen to and obey Him.

Listening Attentively. When Bill launched his own private investment company in the spring of 2005, he and his nine employees were overjoyed. Then, when he took the company public in 2006, he and his 50 employees were ecstatic. But just two years later, when the global economic crisis tore down business after business, Bill and his 200+ employees were somewhere in the middle of the heap.

Bill was forced to file for bankruptcy. Understandably, he felt despondent and broken. Before returning to work for his former employer, Bill asked his spiritual mentor, Jeff, to help him get perspective on what he had done wrong. Jeff helped Bill see that the business failure was not merely the result of the widespread economic decline.

Bill came to realize that the fast growth of his business had done three things. First, it made him lose focus on his spiritual renewal and growth. Second, it created an attitude of pride in him that obscured the character compromises he was committing. Finally, it gave him the feeling that he no longer needed to take the Lord's commands seriously or remain sensitive to His leading.

Though Bill lost a company, he now feels he's regained something much more important—his ability to listen attentively to the Lord. And much like the Israelites entering Canaan under the leadership of Joshua, he would have to listen more closely to the important things he needed to hear.

GOD HAS EXPECTATIONS

BACKGROUND SCRIPTURE: Joshua 1
DEVOTIONAL READING: Deuteronomy 5:22-33

KEY VERSE: Be thou strong and very courageous, that thou mayest observe to do according to all the law, which Moses my servant commanded thee: turn not from it to the right hand or to the left, that thou mayest prosper whithersoever thou goest. (Joshua 1:7)

KING JAMES VERSION

JOSHUA 1:7 Only be thou strong and very courageous, that thou mayest observe to do according to all the law, which Moses my servant commanded thee: turn not from it to the right hand or to the left, that thou mayest prosper whithersoever thou goest. 8 This book of the law shall not depart out of thy mouth; but thou shalt meditate therein day and night, that thou mayest observe to do according to all that is written therein: for then thou shalt make thy way prosperous, and then thou shalt have good success. 9 Have not I commanded thee? Be strong and of a good courage; be not afraid, neither be thou dismayed: for the LORD thy God is with thee whithersoever thou goest.

10 Then Joshua commanded the officers of the people, saying, 11 Pass through the host, and command the people, saying, Prepare you victuals; for within three days ye shall pass over this Jordan, to go in to possess the land, which the LORD your God giveth you to possess it. 12 And to the Reubenites, and to the Gadites, and to half the tribe of Manasseh, spake Joshua, saying, 13 Remember the word which Moses the servant of the LORD commanded you, saying, The LORD your God hath given you rest, and hath given you this land.
14 Your wives, your little ones, and your cattle, shall remain in the land which Moses gave you on this side Jordan; but ye shall pass before your brethren armed, all the mighty men of valour, and help them; 15 Until the LORD have given your brethren rest, as he hath given you, and they also have possessed the land which the LORD your God giveth them: then ye shall return unto the land of your possession, and enjoy it, which Moses the LORD's servant gave you on this side Jordan toward the sunrising.

16 And they answered Joshua, saying, All that thou commandest us we will do, and whithersoever thou sendest us, we will go.

NEW REVISED STANDARD VERSION

JOSHUA 1:7 "Only be strong and very courageous, being careful to act in accordance with all the law that my servant Moses commanded you; do not turn from it to the right hand or to the left, so that you may be successful wherever you go. 8 This book of the law shall not depart out of your mouth; you shall meditate on it day and night, so that you may be careful to act in accordance with all that is written in it. For then you shall make your way prosperous, and then you shall be successful. 9 I hereby command you: Be strong and courageous; do not be frightened or dismayed, for the Lord your God is with you wherever you go."

10 Then Joshua commanded the officers of the people, 11 "Pass through the camp, and command the people: 'Prepare your provisions; for in three days you are to cross over the Jordan, to go in to take possession of the land that the Lord your God gives you to possess.'"

12 To the Reubenites, the Gadites, and the half-tribe of Manasseh Joshua said, 13 "Remember the word that Moses the servant of the Lord commanded you, saying, 'The Lord your God is providing you a place of rest, and will give you this land.' 14 Your wives, your little ones, and your livestock shall remain in the land that Moses gave you beyond the Jordan. But all the warriors among you shall cross over armed before your kindred and shall help them, 15 until the Lord gives rest to your kindred as well as to you, and they too take possession of the land that the Lord your God is giving them. Then you shall return to your own land and take possession of it, the land that Moses the servant of the Lord gave you beyond the Jordan to the east."

16 They answered Joshua: "All that you have commanded us we will do, and wherever you send us we will go."

HOME BIBLE READINGS

BACKGROUND

Scripture reveals that Joshua was commanded six times to be strong and courageous: once by Moses (Deut. 31:7), four times by the Lord (Deut. 31:23; Josh. 1:6, 7, 9), and once by the people of Israel (Josh. 1:18). Undeniably, strength and courage would be essential assets for Joshua. Now that Moses was dead, the full burden of leading the Israelites was on Joshua's shoulders. It was an intimidating position to be in, for he was following in the illustrious footsteps of Moses (see Deut. 34:10-12). Such laudable truths notwithstanding, there were times when the Israelites challenged the authority of Moses as their intercessor and advocate. Joshua witnessed those unsavory instances when the Hebrews showed disrespect for Moses. To be sure, Joshua had no real assurance that the people would treat him any better.

Strength and courage were also vital because, while the people wandered in the wilderness, the elements of nature had been their greatest enemies. Now they were about to face some of the cruelest and most ruthless warriors in the region. The Israelites were outnumbered and ill-equipped to attack these inhabitants. Thus God's people could not afford to have a timid leader. There is no indication in Scripture that Joshua ever hesitated to take on any challenge God gave him. Even so, the courageous Joshua needed to know that God would be with him, at least in part because of the odds against the nation he led.

NOTES ON THE PRINTED TEXT

Joshua became Moses' successor in leading the Israelites. The "law" (Josh. 1:7) Moses gave to Joshua probably comprised most of the Book of Deuteronomy (see Deut. 31:24-26; Josh. 8:34-35; 23:6; 24:26). In fact, Joshua might have had the original manuscripts of the Pentateuch (the first five books of the Bible) at his disposal. The many parallels between the books of Deuteronomy and Joshua lead specialists to conclude that the author of Joshua was quite familiar with the contents of the last book of the Pentateuch. As far as the nation's obedience to God's injunctions was concerned, there was to be no deviation. The phrase "to the right hand or to the left" (Josh. 1:7) implied that the Hebrews were to strictly obey the commandment. They were to walk the fine line of obedience.

In verse 8, both a promise and a condition for the fulfillment of that pledge are included. Joshua's allowing the "book of the law" to leave his lips meant that he should remember, rehearse, and obey the teaching Moses had passed on to him. God also directed Joshua to "meditate" on the law. The Hebrew verb that is rendered "meditate" implies a barely audible muttering of the words recorded in Scripture while studying them or reflecting upon them. Such a practice assured that the Israelite general would be thinking about what he read as he repeated the words to himself. Nonetheless, God would not consider knowledge of the law to be enough. The Lord also demanded obedience. So the practice of Joshua repeating the law as he meditated on it also served to remind him to carefully obey all that was "written therein."

To focus one's mind on God's Word "day and night" does not mean one has to live the life of a hermit. Certainly this was not true of Joshua. God intended him to fulfill this command even as he was in the process of conquering the land. Thus Joshua was to keep God's law in mind as he entered into each battle. After all, God was fulfilling through Joshua what He had promised to Abraham. If Joshua kept the commandments and the history of his ancestors in mind as he led the people, he would be more likely to obey God's will and less likely to repeat the mistakes of previous generations. Since God had denied Moses entrance into the promised land because of his disobedience, Joshua could be sure that the Lord would not make an exception for him.

God's admonition to Joshua to "be strong and of a good courage" (vs. 9) was more than just a word of encouragement; it was a command. The promise of the Lord's presence would be enough for Joshua to act bravely despite any fear or insecurity that might have remained after the death of Moses, his leader and mentor of 40 years. Evidently, any trembling or hesitation on Joshua's part would cause the courage of the people to waver. Therefore, Joshua had to be a rock of bravery and faithfulness, especially if the Israelites were to succeed.

Joshua dedicated himself to following the command God had given him (vs. 2). Accordingly, the Israelite general summoned his officers (vs. 10), whom Moses evidently appointed before his death (see Exod. 18:21; Deut. 1:15). Joshua directed his subordinates to prepare the people for the start of the military campaign into Canaan (Josh. 1:11). Initially, Joshua anticipated that it would be no more than three days before the Israelites began the process of crossing the Jordan River as a prelude to entering and seizing the promised land. An examination of 2:22 and 3:1-2 indicates that the subsequent chain of events took longer to play out. One possibility is that in his enthusiasm, Joshua was a bit optimistic about how quickly the Hebrews could prepare to move into Canaan. A second option is that in 1:11, he used a common figure of speech that meant the people were to set out on their journey a few days later. A third alternative is that "three days" denotes a ritual period before the onset of the military operation (see Gen. 40:13, 19-20; Exod. 3:18; 19:11; Hos. 6:2). In any case, Joshua apparently did not meet any resistance from his subordinates.

After Joshua addressed the officials of all the Israelite tribes, he turned his attention to the Transjordan tribes, whose inheritance would lie east of the Jordan River (Josh. 1:12-15). At this point, Joshua probably had in mind two concerns (vs. 12). First, the Israelite general must have presumed that he would need every available fighting man in order to take the fortified cities of Canaan. He could not afford to let these tribes settle on their own land while their fellow Israelites, who had assisted them in gaining their land east of the Jordan, fought for land on the other side of the river. Second, he may have suspected that the natural boundary of the Jordan River could cause these tribes to drift apart from the nation of Israel as a whole. By being involved in the battles inside Canaan, they would not easily shirk their responsibility to the other tribes later.

Joshua acknowledged that God was going to give "rest" (vs. 13) to the tribes in the Transjordan region, as Moses had said. The concept of rest in the Old Testament was never meant to imply the absence of work. Even after the Israelites had achieved their aim of conquering the land, they would still have to labor in order to survive. God's promise of rest meant security from disruption or from the attack of outside forces. Again, God's promise of rest was conditional. The people had to remain obedient to Him to receive their promised rest. The Canaanites were being driven from the land because of their refusal to acknowledge the Lord. Despite hearing reports of the miraculous power of the Israelites' God, these people refused to repent and serve the one true Lord of the universe. Because of their disobedience, they were denied rest from war. Israel would be held to the same standard. Rest from war would be the reward for obedience.

Joshua stipulated that all fighting men from the tribes of Reuben, Gad, and Manasseh—that is, men over the age of 20 who could equip themselves for war and who were known for their courage—were to participate in the nation's upcoming military endeavors (vs. 14). Part of the agreement the Transjordan tribes had made with Moses was that they would fight alongside their fellow tribes until all tribes had secured their inheritance of land. Then the Reubenite, Gadite, and Manassite fighting men would return home to their families and begin building their lives in their new homeland (vs. 15; see chap. 22).

The Transjordan tribes vowed to heed whatever the Israelite general commanded (1:16). Wherever Joshua dispatched them, they pledged to go. In the same way they had "hearkened unto Moses" (vs. 17), they likewise promised to heed Joshua's orders. By and large, what the Transjordan tribes pledged reflected the sentiments of the entire nation of Israel at that time. This implies that Joshua achieved the unity for which he was hoping. It is ironic, however, that the people promised to obey Joshua just as much as they had obeyed Moses. Given the Israelites' history of rebellion against Moses' leadership, this might have caused Joshua a lot of concern. On numerous occasions recorded throughout the books of the Pentateuch, the Israelites are shown to have failed to obey Moses and to have been severely disciplined as a result. Joshua himself had spent the last four decades in the wilderness because an earlier generation of Israelites refused to enter the promised land. Given the character of Joshua, however, he probably accepted the people's vow without question.

SUGGESTIONS TO TEACHERS

The Lord promised to be with Joshua in all that he undertook (Josh. 1:9). We also have this promise of God's presence today (Heb. 13:5). Indeed, as we face the trials and temptations presented by the modern world, we have Jesus' full assurance that He is always present to comfort, encourage, and empower us (Matt. 28:20). After introducing these truths to the students, be sure to walk them through the following emphases.

1. GOD KEEPS HIS PROMISES. Based on our study of this week's Scripture passage, we learn about the ways God interacts with us today. For instance, we discover that God is a promise keeper. In many respects, the Book of Joshua is about the fulfillment of a promise more than 600 years old: God's pledge to give the land of Canaan to Abraham's offspring (Gen. 15:18-21; Josh. 1:11). After the generations of Abraham, Isaac, and Jacob, after 400 years under Egyptian oppression, and after 40 years of wandering in the wilderness, the time had finally come for God's chosen people to cross over into and conquer Canaan. God is faithful and keeps His promises, no matter how long it takes.

2. GOD EXPECTS OBEDIENCE. We also learn that God is holy and does not tolerate wickedness and rebellion against Himself. Even though the Canaanites were driven out of their land because of their sinfulness and because they were not willing to accept the Lord as the one true God, the Israelites could not rightly possess the land unless they themselves repented of their sinfulness. They also had to obey the commandments recorded in the Mosaic law. Even Joshua, the new leader of the Israelites, had to heed the divine injunctions. As a matter of fact, doing so was the key to his success as the nation's general (Josh. 1:7-8).

3. GOD WELCOMES ALL PEOPLE. An examination of Joshua indicates that God extended His grace to all people—not just the Israelites—who were willing to repent of their sins and acknowledge the Lord as their God. This truth reminds us that all creation is subject to God's control, and that He sometimes alters the course of nature for the good of His people. In fact, one of the main points of the Book of Joshua is that God works on behalf of His chosen people to bring about His will for His glory.

FOR ADULTS

■ **TOPIC:** Living by the Rules

■ **QUESTIONS:** 1. Why, at the outset of a major military campaign, would the Lord focus the attention of His people on obeying the Mosaic law? 2. What sorts of successes have you experienced in your life as a result of heeding God's Word? 3. How can meditating on God's Word help believers over-come discouragement? 4. What place is there for advance preparation in doing the work of the Lord? 5. Why is it important for believers to honor the commitments they have made?

■ **ILLUSTRATIONS:**

The Challenge of Choosing. Some time ago, my wife and I had to choose a new office chair. It soon became clear that her preferences did not match mine. After an hour or more consulting with a sales representative, we finally agreed on a suitable choice we both could enjoy.

Imagine how much harder it is to choose leaders for a Christian organization. Not only is the process more complex, but believers must also submit their preferences to biblical teaching. They should also bathe their decision-making in prayer and seek the counsel of seasoned Christians.

Believers may not always agree, but they can ensure that their deliberations are in harmony with God's Word (see Josh. 1:7-8). With this principle in mind, Christians can choose the right leaders, namely, individuals who live by the rules of Scripture. When this happens, the members of a congregation can be confident that God has led them to make the best decision for the organization.

Unconditional Surrender. Heidi has lived in the United States for 20 years, but she is not a U.S. citizen. Originally, she came to America from Germany looking for career opportunities. She found them, first by studying to be a physical therapist and then by taking a job she loves in the physical therapy unit of a local hospital.

Heidi thinks the United States is wonderful, and she may live in America the rest of her life. That said, she is reluctant to give up her German citizenship. "It's impor-tant to me," she explains. "I was born in Germany, and it's a part of me that I can't let go of."

There is nothing wrong with Heidi's choice to remain a German citizen while liv-ing in America. She understands that in her case, a nonnegotiable rule of becoming a citizen of the United States is to renounce her commitments to her homeland. In short, she would have to pledge her allegiance to the United States.

Similarly, Christians are called to be permanent citizens of one kingdom—God's. In this week's Scripture passage, the Lord directed Joshua and a new generation of Israelites to be unwavering in their commitment to Him. This included carefully obey-ing God's Word. The prescription for spiritual success, both then as now, has not changed (see Josh. 1:7-9).

God-Reliant or Self-Reliant? A passage in *Fundamentals of Marxism-Leninism*, a textbook that has been used by members of the Communist Party, reads as follows:

"Materialists do not expect aid from supernatural forces. Their faith is in man, in his ability to transform the world by his efforts and make it worthy of himself."

As believers, we may shake our head in disapproval at such a statement of arrogance and self-reliance. However, we might stop to consider whether, in practice, we don't sometimes subscribe to that very belief. Are we reliant on God, His abiding presence, and the directives of His Word or do we trust in other things for our spiritual success (see Josh. 1:7-9)? Whenever we fail to recognize our dependence upon God, whenever we try to manipulate circumstances to get what we want, whenever we put our personal priorities above what we know God is asking us as potential church leaders to give our attention to, we act out this fundamental principle of the materialists' belief system.

FOR YOUTH

■ TOPIC: What's in It for Me?

■ QUESTIONS: 1. What sorts of challenges did the Israelites face in their upcoming military campaign that would test their courage? 2. How are you spiritually benefitted when you spend time meditating on God's Word? 3. How can God's abiding presence boost your morale when life feels overwhelming? 4. If you were among the Israelites, how do you think you would have felt as they prepared to cross the Jordan River? 5. How is a church negatively affected when its members break promises they have made?

■ **ILLUSTRATIONS:**

What Really Counts? High school class elections are often decided on the basis of what candidates promise to do for their peers. In short, the latter want to know what they will get out of voting for one adolescent over another. Admittedly, the decision often comes down to beauty and brawn. In some cases, brains prevail, but usually the combination of good looks and popularity is hard to beat. Other qualities are rarely considered.

Perhaps this seems like innocent fun. But consider the following. Early in life we establish patterns that determine whom we elect to office and also whom we choose to emulate. That's why young people should be encouraged to cultivate within themselves hard work, honesty, and unselfishness, and to look for these qualities in their leaders.

Youth need to know that God has given them His Word so that they can make wise choices. For example, Scripture teaches that what really counts in life is neither popularity nor acceptance but rather faith in the Lord and obedience to His will. Indeed, this is the true basis for success (see Josh. 1:7-8).

Bringing Christianity to India. William Carey (1761–1834) is known as the "father of modern missions." Like Joshua, Carey's determination to follow the teachings of

Scripture was the reason for his success (see Josh. 1:7-9). From his study of God's Word, he concluded that the basis for missions included Christian obligation, wise use of available resources, and accurate information.

By the end of the 18th century, Carey became a missionary when there were no independent mission boards. Moreover, he founded his first church on foreign soil in India when the presence of Christianity was practically nonexistent among the native population. His stress on translating the Bible for the people to whom he was sharing the Gospel, and on planting indigenous churches, revolutionized missions abroad.

Carey's achievements, however, did not come easily. For instance, his young son died of dysentery and his wife became mentally ill. Also, for many years Carey had hardly any success in bringing any Indians to Christ. Despite these disappointments and setbacks, Carey continued to commit his life in service to Christ in India. "I can plod," he once wrote. "I can persevere in any definite pursuit." And it was Carey's pursuit in serving the Lord wholeheartedly and obediently that paved the way for the transformation of modern missions.

Always the Same Size. The late Woody Hayes was a legendary and much-loved football coach for the Ohio State Buckeyes. Between 1951 and 1979, he compiled an overall win-loss-tie record of 205-61-10. Before Hayes became great at Ohio State University (OSU), however, he had been coaching for some smaller football programs in the state.

After 24 years of coaching at OSU, Hayes talked to the Newark, Ohio, newspaper *Advocate* about what it had been like coming from the small-school teams he was used to coaching, to the much larger OSU: "The first time I stood in the middle of the OSU stadium with its 86,000 seats staring down at me, I was shook up. My young son was with me and had hold of my hand. He must have felt my reaction, for he said, 'But, Daddy, the football field is the same size.'"

We, too, can be equal to any challenge because God does not change with the size of the army, the sophistication of the weapons, or the complexity of the plan. He is always the same great God who will cause us to rise up to the challenges we meet, especially as we obey His Word and trust in His abiding presence (see Josh. 1:7-9).

GOD PROTECTS

BACKGROUND SCRIPTURE: Joshua 2
DEVOTIONAL READING: James 2:18-25

KEY VERSE: [The two spies] said unto Joshua, Truly the LORD hath delivered into our hands all the land; for even all the inhabitants of the country do faint because of us. (Joshua 2:24)

3

KING JAMES VERSION

JOSHUA 2:3 And the king of Jericho sent unto Rahab, saying, Bring forth the men that are come to thee, which are entered into thine house: for they be come to search out all the country. 4 And the woman took the two men, and hid them, and said thus, There came men unto me, but I wist not whence they were: 5 And it came to pass about the time of shutting of the gate, when it was dark, that the men went out: whither the men went I wot not: pursue after them quickly; for ye shall overtake them. 6 But she had brought them up to the roof of the house, and hid them with the stalks of flax, which she had laid in order upon the roof. 7 And the men pursued after them the way to Jordan unto the fords: and as soon as they which pursued after them were gone out, they shut the gate.

8 And before they were laid down, she came up unto them upon the roof; 9 And she said unto the men, I know that the LORD hath given you the land, and that your terror is fallen upon us, and that all the inhabitants of the land faint because of you. . . . 15 Then she let them down by a cord through the window: for her house was upon the town wall, and she dwelt upon the wall. 16 And she said unto them, Get you to the mountain, lest the pursuers meet you; and hide yourselves there three days, until the pursuers be returned: and afterward may ye go your way. . . .

22 And they went, and came unto the mountain, and abode there three days, until the pursuers were returned: and the pursuers sought them throughout all the way, but found them not. 23 So the two men returned, and descended from the mountain, and passed over, and came to Joshua the son of Nun, and told him all things that befell them: 24 And they said unto Joshua, Truly the LORD hath delivered into our hands all the land; for even all the inhabitants of the country do faint because of us.

NEW REVISED STANDARD VERSION

JOSHUA 2:3 Then the king of Jericho sent orders to Rahab, "Bring out the men who have come to you, who entered your house, for they have come only to search out the whole land." 4 But the woman took the two men and hid them. Then she said, "True, the men came to me, but I did not know where they came from. 5 And when it was time to close the gate at dark, the men went out. Where the men went I do not know. Pursue them quickly, for you can overtake them." 6 She had, however, brought them up to the roof and hidden them with the stalks of flax that she had laid out on the roof. 7 So the men pursued them on the way to the Jordan as far as the fords. As soon as the pursuers had gone out, the gate was shut.

8 Before they went to sleep, she came up to them on the roof 9 and said to the men: "I know that the Lord has given you the land, and that dread of you has fallen on us, and that all the inhabitants of the land melt in fear before you. . . .

15 Then she let them down by a rope through the window, for her house was on the outer side of the city wall and she resided within the wall itself. 16 She said to them, "Go toward the hill country, so that the pursuers may not come upon you. Hide yourselves there three days, until the pursuers have returned; then afterward you may go your way." . . .

22 They departed and went into the hill country and stayed there three days, until the pursuers returned. The pursuers had searched all along the way and found nothing. 23 Then the two men came down again from the hill country. They crossed over, came to Joshua son of Nun, and told him all that had happened to them. 24 They said to Joshua, "Truly the Lord has given all the land into our hands; moreover all the inhabitants of the land melt in fear before us."

Home Bible Readings

Background

The account of Rahab and her protection of the Israelite spies is one of the most endearing in all of Scripture. Of the people living in the land of Canaan, she and her family apparently were the only ones to turn away from idolatry and place faith in the God of the Israelites. Even though she was not an Israelite and her occupation could have made her an outcast, Rahab came to be highly regarded among Jews and later among Christians. According to some Jewish traditional writings, Rahab married Joshua sometime after the Israelites' capture of Jericho. As the wife of Joshua, she was said to have become the ancestor of at least eight priests. Jewish traditional writings also list her among the four women recorded in the Hebrew Scriptures who were of surpassing beauty. The others were Sarah, Abigail, and Esther.

In an attempt to play down or even deny Rahab's prostitution, many legends have evolved about her. One tradition promoted by the Jewish historian Josephus holds that Rahab was not a prostitute at all, but only an innkeeper. Though in Hebrew "harlot" and "innkeeper" are the same word (see Josh. 2:1), there is little evidence that Rahab was only an innkeeper and a lot of evidence that she was a prostitute. She may have been led into prostitution because of her family's poverty. Of course, this does not excuse the immorality of what she did. It only makes it more understandable. She and her family were probably supported financially while they were being absorbed into the nation of Israel. This would have eliminated any economic need for Rahab to continue her prostitution. In the New Testament, Hebrews 11:31 mentions her as an example of faith; James 2:25 speaks of her favorably; and Matthew 1:5 lists her in the genealogy of Jesus as the wife of a man named Salmon.

Notes on the Printed Text

Joshua 2 details Rahab's involvement in the Israelite reconnaissance mission. The latter was evidence of Joshua's foresight as a capable general. Keeping the mission secret was certainly part of his strategy (vs. 1). The spies set out from Shittim—a place whose name means "acacia trees"—on the plains of Moab. The two were instructed to "view the land, even Jericho." Thus their mission was to center on Jericho, which at that time was a seemingly unconquerable fortress keeping invaders from using the pass leading westward into the mountainous region of Canaan.

Once the two spies entered the city, they took up residence at the home of Rahab. Because of the number of men going in and out of the house, it would serve as a good place for the spies to gather information about the city. Staying there would also make their detection by city officials less likely. In addition, because the prostitute's residence was located on the city wall, the spies would have a ready means of escape should they be discovered. Moreover, as divine providence would have it, Rahab feared the God of Israel and acknowledged His sovereignty over the land. His will included witnesses spotting the two spies in Jericho and reporting this to the king of the city (vs. 2). At the time the Israelites began their invasion, most of the towns of Canaan were independent city-states ruled by kings. The monarch was usually the first to be informed of urgent matters concerning the safety of the city.

The fact that Israelites, about whom the people of Jericho had heard much, had infiltrated the city walls was frightful news to the king. Knowing Rahab's profession, the king apparently assumed Rahab had no treasonous motive in housing them. In fact, the king assumed that the prostitute was ignorant of the purpose of these men, because he told her the real reason for their visit to Jericho (vs. 3). But Rahab knew more about the spies' plans than the king realized. When faced with the decision of turning the spies over to the king's officers or continuing to hide them, Rahab chose the latter. She knew that by hiding the spies, she had put herself and her family in great danger. And yet she placed more trust in the God of Israel than in the fortified walls of Jericho.

Rahab hid the two spies beneath some flax on her roof (vss. 4, 6). During the time of Joshua, flax was being used in the manufacture of linen. It is one of the oldest textile fibers known. The flax plant grows to a height of nearly three feet and produces a lovely blue blossom. The stalk's shiny seeds are used to make linseed oil. It was common for poor farmers in the Near East to lay out stalks of flax on their roofs to dry. This is a possible indication that Rahab's family members had been conscripted as agricultural slave laborers. The oppressive landlords over these people kept them in a state of perpetual poverty. Rahab may have been led into prostitution in order to support her family. In light of the agreement she made with Joshua's spies, she obviously cared about her parents and family very much.

Thus, instead of revealing the true location of the Israelite spies, Rahab lied to those looking for the Israelite men. In fact, the prostitute told the king's officers four deliberate lies. First, she claimed that she did not know where the men were from (vs. 4). Second, Rahab claimed that the men left at dusk as the city's gates were closing. Third, she said that she did not know where they went. Fourth, the prostitute told the king's officers that if they hurried they would improve their chances of catching up with the spies (vs. 5). Rahab's lies to the king's officers have long been the focus of debates on biblical ethics. Not only is the prostitute never condemned in Scripture for her fabrications, but she is actually commended for demonstrating her faith in this manner.

It is interesting that the king's officers believed Rahab so quickly. They set out looking for the spies without conducting a search of Rahab's house (vs. 7). Had such a probe of her home been ordered, the two men would probably have been discovered, and both the spies and Rahab likely would have been executed. With a search party on their way toward the Jordan River to look for the Israelite spies, Rahab went up to the roof of her house to speak with the pair (vs. 8). The spies' intent may have been to settle in for the night on the prostitute's roof when she interrupted them. Rahab began by telling the spies what she knew about God's purpose for the Israelites' future and how that purpose had given rise to much dread on the part of the people of Canaan (vs. 9).

After Rahab made a pledge with the spies (vss. 10-15), she instructed them to go west, toward the barren hills outside of Jericho, rather than east, toward the Jordan River and the Israelite encampment on the plains of Moab. She had sent the king's officers toward the river. In the hills, the spies were to remain a few days until they were sure that the king's officers had returned to Jericho, and that their passage east would be a safe one (vs. 16). These instructions from Rahab and the ensuing conversation between her and the spies (see vss. 17-21) apparently occurred just before the spies escaped from the city. Rahab's house was built into part of Jericho's wall. Consequently, it provided a way for the Israelite spies to leave the city in a way other than through the city gate. Using a rope, the prostitute let the two men down from a window of her house, and they began their getaway (vs. 15).

The spies followed Rahab's instructions, staying in the hill country west of Jericho for a few days. In these hills there were cracks and crevices that made them a superb hiding place. In the meantime, the king's officers scrutinized the roads and countryside east of Jericho, assuming the spies were heading back to the Israelite encampment at Shittim. Having failed to find the two men, the posse returned home empty-handed (vs. 22). Once the Israelite spies realized that they were no longer being sought by the king's officers, they began their journey back to the Israelite encampment. After fording the Jordan River, the pair returned to Joshua and told him everything that had happened (vs. 23). This would have included, of course, the oath they had made to Rahab. When the Israelites did attack Jericho, Joshua made sure that the house of Rahab was spared (see 6:17).

After giving Joshua a positive report, the two spies confirmed that the prophecy of Moses was about to be fulfilled. They repeated to Joshua what Rahab had told them and what they had no doubt seen for themselves, namely, that the hearts of the Canaanites were melting in fear because of the Israelites' string of victories (2:24). The faltering morale of the people of Canaan served to heighten the morale of the Israelites. We can only speculate about what the people of Jericho thought about the scarlet cord hanging in Rahab's window. Perhaps many gave it little consideration.

Some may have regarded it as a poor family's attempt to decorate. Maybe a few people assumed it to be an indication that Rahab's home was a place of ill repute. Little did any of the people of the city know that the scarlet cord represented the newfound faith of a woman—and was a symbol of the imminent demise of Jericho.

SUGGESTIONS TO TEACHERS

As we continue our journey with God, He asks us to step out and risk new behaviors. Sometimes God speaks in gentle nudges, and at other times through the candid words of a friend. Initially, we may resist. But hopefully with each passing day, we will begin to see how much better off we are when we depend on God's awesome power to sustain us.

1. GOD'S AWESOME POWER. The worship services in some churches regularly feature what's called a "testimony time," when members of the congregation reflect on the awesome power of God in their lives. Those testimonies might describe events from years ago or something incredible that happened this past week—from miraculous healings, to new jobs, to doors opening where it seemed they never would.

Whatever is being described, those testimonies have one element in common: something amazing happened that only God could do. Those testimony times are a record of divine intervention in the everyday lives of people today. As this week's lesson concerning Rahab shows, the same Lord also intervened in a powerful way when the Israelites conquered Jericho.

2. GOD'S GOODNESS AND GREATNESS. Listening to testimonies given by believers can be a moving experience, especially as our focus is shifted from present difficulties to the goodness and greatness of God. As we remember what God has done in the past, we can face the future with a renewed hope and a proper focus. God has worked in the lives of others, such as Rahab and her family, and He can do so in our lives, even if the mountains around us seem impossible to climb or the floodwaters before us look impossible to cross.

3. GOD'S CONTINUOUS WORK. We need testimonies of divine intervention because they are the pages in our mental book of remembrance. And we can add to it the testimonies of God's continuous work in the biblical record. We can point to both to remind ourselves and others that our all-powerful Lord has never forsaken His people in the past and He will not abandon us now—or ever.

 FOR ADULTS ▦ **TOPIC:** Knowing Whom to Trust
▦ **QUESTIONS:** 1. Why did Joshua decide to send out the spies secretly? 2. If you were Rahab, would you have taken the risk of hiding the Israelite pair? 3. Why did the Canaanites have a great fear of the Israelites? 4. What reports concerning God's activity had the Canaanites heard? 5. What are some ways you can encourage other believers to more fully appreciate God's awesome power?

A College from Nothing. Where the rest of the world saw a garbage dump, Mary McCloud Bethune saw a college. In 1904, she started transforming the city dump of Daytona Beach, Florida, into an institution of higher learning. With a great dream but almost no money, she and a few other black women took the first step by building a shack for a classroom building and furnishing it with wooden packing crates for desks. Blackberry juice was the ink used to write reports.

The daughter of former slaves, Mary Bethune had been chosen from her 17 brothers and sisters to be the one to go to a Presbyterian school. Later, she graduated from Moody Bible Institute, and she wanted to use her education to help other African-Americans. The result was Bethune College (now Bethune-Cookman, a Methodist school). Like Rahab during the time of Joshua, Mary is a shining example of what can happen when someone steps out in faith and trusts God to act in awesome power to bring great blessing to many people.

Sure-footed Faith. Experts say that difficulty with money is the number-one cause of marital distress and division. For Bruce and Charlotte, that could have been the case, beginning with the severe economic downturn of 1981—but it wasn't.

Instead of letting their financial woes overtake an otherwise wonderful life together, this couple learned to commit their struggles to the Lord. Charlotte had great faith that Rahab had it right when she declared to the Israelite spies, "The LORD your God, he is God in heaven above, and in earth beneath" (Josh. 2:11).

So, though Bruce and Charlotte seemed to barely squeak by year after year, the couple not only stayed together, but they also grew closer to one another and to God each year. Financial pressures seemed to be a part of their life's burden. But through regular prayer, it was a burden that could be endured. Though they were lower-income by government standards, they felt rich by kingdom standards. And today, the two have raised five godly children and are mentors and trusted confidants to an ever-growing circle of friends.

The Object of Trust. When her husband, Larry, suggested dinner in Mt. Vernon, a town 20 minutes away, Gwen reluctantly agreed. "I could have fixed us something nice at home," she thought later as she stared out the car's rain-streaked windows.

But as the couple neared their destination, Gwen's thoughts suddenly turned from home cooking to utter surprise. There, flashing brightly in the rain, was a huge hotel marquee with the message "Happy 60th, Gwen!" That wasn't the end. Inside, Larry led his wife to a banquet room that erupted with cheers and warm wishes from family members and friends Gwen hadn't seen in ages. It was perfect. And Larry had arranged it all. "I had no idea you were making all these wonderful plans behind my back!" Gwen said through her tears of joy.

The two Israelite spies might have been just as surprised as Gwen when Rahab offered to help them during their reconnaissance mission (Josh. 2:6). And we can only imagine the shock the pair felt when they heard the prostitute declare that the Lord would hand over the land of Canaan to the Israelites (vs. 9). Perhaps at first the spies and their peers back at camp had some misgivings about trusting God to give them the victory over their formidable Canaanite foes. If so, Rabab's further comments must have erased all doubt (vss. 10-11). Then, as now, the Lord is the object of the believer's trust.

FOR YOUTH	■ TOPIC: Security in an Insecure World ■ QUESTIONS: 1. If you were one of the two Israelite spies, would you have agreed to enter the house of Rahab, the prostitute? 2. Why did

Rahab take the risk of hiding the spies? 3. How and by what means were you finally convinced to place your faith in the Lord? 4. How were the spies able to make it back safely to the Israelite camp? 5. What report did the spies bring to Joshua?

■ **ILLUSTRATIONS:**

A Sure Hope. On May 29, 1953, Edmund Hillary (from New Zealand) and Tenzing Norgay (from Nepal) were the first to ascend Mount Everest. As the world's tallest mountain, its summit is 29,029 feet. Today, expeditions routinely climb its peak. In fact, at present there have been around 3,700 ascents to the summit. Despite the risks, many people enjoy the challenge. Good health and climbing experience are required. Nevertheless, each individual attempting the trek arrives believing in the promise that this mountain can be conquered with enough effort.

Joshua promised the Israelites that the land of Canaan could be conquered. As the Israelite spies learned from a prostitute named Rahab, this was not an empty pledge but a sure hope (see Josh. 2:8-11). The people had to trust in God's presence, for it was only through His power, not their own strength, that they would succeed in occupying the land. Likewise, the Lord wants us to look to Him for grace and guidance to make it through the toughest of situations. We can do so, for He is our source of security in an insecure world.

Don't Underestimate God. Tara, a new Christian, was reading her Bible in the high school cafeteria during lunch. It wasn't long before her non-Christian friend Carol sat down. "What are you reading?" she asked. "It's the most incredible account," Tara responded. "It's about how God used a prostitute named Rahab to provide help to a pair of Israelite spies. Isn't it just amazing that God would work through such an unlikely person in this way?"

Carol put down her soda. "You know," she said flatly, "it didn't really happen like that. What you shared is just another made-up story that has been retold and exaggerated by religious people for thousands of years." She smiled, as if to say, "See? You can't put any stock in that Bible stuff." But Tara didn't take it that way. "What do you mean? I can't believe that God was powerful enough to bring blessing to the lives of others through one ordinary individual?"

Tara had entered into a relationship with the living God. And Tara wasn't about to let her friend's comments dissuade her from finding strength and stability in the Lord. Unlike Carol, Tara believed that God's work in the lives of His people is truly miraculous. Indeed, it is a mistake to underestimate Him!

The "Miracle" of Dunkerque. When Adolf Hitler's armies were overrunning Europe in May 1940, they trapped almost half a million British and French troops against the English Channel at Dunkerque, France. The British army estimated that they could safely evacuate no more than 30,000 to 40,000 of these troops to England. The rest would be captured or killed on the beaches by the German army and air force.

But then the situation changed. First, Hitler turned his tanks toward Paris, leaving the job of destroying Dunkerque mostly to his air force. Then, smoke from factories the Germans themselves had bombed began to blow across the beaches, hiding the escaping forces. Finally, the normally stormy English Channel became as calm as glass, and fog covered it for nine days. That grounded the German planes but allowed an armada of over 800 boats from England to rescue not 30,000, but over 338,000 troops to fight another day.

What was behind the "miracle" of Dunkerque? No one can say for certain. But perhaps the miracle came because in this time of crisis, Britain's King George VI called his country to a national day of prayer. The British people filled their churches, humbly asking God to save their troops and their nation from the Nazis.

Centuries earlier, Rahab looked to the Lord for security and strength, so much so that she was willing to take the risk of helping a pair of Israelite spies. Even today, when life can sometimes feel scary and uncertain, we can find hope in God, knowing that He is still just as powerful to work unexpected miracles in our lives.

GOD IS VICTORIOUS

BACKGROUND SCRIPTURE: **Joshua 5:13–6:27**
DEVOTIONAL READING: **Psalm 98:1-6**

KEY VERSE: It came to pass at the seventh time, when the priests blew with the trumpets, Joshua said unto the people, Shout; for the LORD hath given you the city. (Joshua 6:16)

KING JAMES VERSION

JOSHUA 6:2 And the LORD said unto Joshua, See, I have given into thine hand Jericho, and the king thereof, and the mighty men of valour. 3 And ye shall compass the city, all ye men of war, and go round about the city once. Thus shalt thou do six days. 4 And . . . the seventh day ye shall compass the city seven times, and the priests shall blow with the trumpets. . . .

12 And Joshua rose early in the morning, and the priests took up the ark of the LORD. 13 And seven priests bearing seven trumpets of rams' horns before the ark of the LORD went on continually, and blew with the trumpets: and the armed men went before them; but the reward came after the ark of the LORD, the priests going on, and blowing with the trumpets. 14 And the second day they compassed the city once, and returned into the camp: so they did six days. 15 And it came to pass on the seventh day, that they rose early about the dawning of the day, and compassed the city after the same manner seven times: only on that day they compassed the city seven times. 16 And it came to pass at the seventh time, when the priests blew with the trumpets, Joshua said unto the people, Shout; for the LORD hath given you the city.

17 And the city shall be accursed, even it, and all that are therein, to the LORD: only Rahab the harlot shall live, she and all that are with her in the house, because she hid the messengers that we sent. 18 And ye, in any wise keep yourselves from the accursed thing, lest ye make yourselves accursed, when ye take of the accursed thing, and make the camp of Israel a curse, and trouble it. 19 But all the silver, and gold, and vessels of brass and iron, are consecrated unto the LORD: they shall come into the treasury of the LORD. 20 So the people shouted when the priests blew with the trumpets: and it came to pass, when the people heard the sound of the trumpet, and the people shouted with a great shout, that the wall fell down flat, so that the people went up into the city, every man straight before him, and they took the city.

NEW REVISED STANDARD VERSION

JOSHUA 6:2 The Lord said to Joshua, "See, I have handed Jericho over to you, along with its king and soldiers. 3 You shall march around the city, all the warriors circling the city once. Thus you shall do for six days, . . . 4 On the seventh day you shall march around the city seven times, the priests blowing the trumpets. . . ."

12 Then Joshua rose early in the morning, and the priests took up the ark of the Lord. 13 The seven priests carrying the seven trumpets of rams' horns before the ark of the Lord passed on, blowing the trumpets continually. The armed men went before them, and the rear guard came after the ark of the Lord, while the trumpets blew continually. 14 On the second day they marched around the city once and then returned to the camp. They did this for six days.

15 On the seventh day they rose early, at dawn, and marched around the city in the same manner seven times. It was only on that day that they marched around the city seven times. 16 And at the seventh time, when the priests had blown the trumpets, Joshua said to the people, "Shout! For the Lord has given you the city. 17 The city and all that is in it shall be devoted to the Lord for destruction. Only Rahab the prostitute and all who are with her in her house shall live because she hid the messengers we sent. 18 As for you, keep away from the things devoted to destruction, so as not to covet and take any of the devoted things and make the camp of Israel an object for destruction, bringing trouble upon it. 19 But all silver and gold, and vessels of bronze and iron, are sacred to the Lord; they shall go into the treasury of the Lord." 20 So the people shouted, and the trumpets were blown. As soon as the people heard the sound of the trumpets, they raised a great shout, and the wall fell down flat; so the people charged straight ahead into the city and captured it.

4

Monday, June 20	Psalm 98:1-6	The Victory of Our God
Tuesday, June 21	Isaiah 25:6-10	A Victory to Anticipate
Wednesday, June 22	1 Corinthians 15:50-57	Victory through Christ
Thursday, June 23	1 John 5:1-5	The Victory of Faith
Friday, June 24	Psalm 20	A Petition for Victory
Saturday, June 25	Joshua 5:10-15	Assurance before the Battle
Sunday, June 26	Joshua 6:2-3, 4b, 12-20b	God's Victory over Jericho

BACKGROUND

Jericho is considered one of the oldest cities in the world. Some archaeologists date its beginnings back to perhaps 8000 B.C. The city is located in the Jordan River valley less than 15 miles east-northeast of Jerusalem. It may have been a major trading center, especially for perfumes and fragrances. Jericho was built near a bountiful freshwater spring, eventually called the fountain of Elisha (2 Kings 2:18-22). Because it was located on the edge of the desert just north of the Dead Sea, water was considered one of its most valuable assets. Its warm winter climate earned Jericho the nickname the "city of palm trees" (Deut. 34:3). This city on a hill was also a center of worship for the Canaanite moon-god. The name "Jericho" (Josh. 6:1) may mean "moon city" and sounds like the Hebrew word for moon. Thus by destroying Jericho, God was not only striking down an idolatrous people, but their pagan religion as well.

The defeat of Jericho was to be the Israelites' first military victory upon entering the promised land. This fortified city was therefore to be considered the firstfruits of Israel's inheritance from God. The result of this first military engagement would have a profound effect on the Hebrews' confidence as they prepared to take possession of the whole of Canaan. Forty years prior to crossing the Jordan River, the walls of Canaanite cities had caused the hearts of the Israelites to melt in fear (see Num. 13:28, 31). This time the courage and faith of a new generation of Hebrews would bring down the walls of Jericho.

NOTES ON THE PRINTED TEXT

As Rahab had reported to the spies, the residents of Jericho were trembling with fear because of the encroachment of the Israelites. However, despite Jericho's imminent defeat, the people (with the exception of Rahab and her family) refused to surrender to God and devote themselves to His service. The tightly closed city was evidence enough of their paralysis (Josh. 6:1).

Normally, a city under siege would send out soldiers to periodically provoke the enemy into combat. Sometimes they would send out spies to check for weaknesses in their enemies' ranks. But apparently the fear of infiltration prevented the inhabitants of Jericho from putting either of these strategies into practice. The closed gates also discouraged desertion. The Lord's proclamation of the Israelites' victory over the city of Jericho was made as if it had already occurred (vs. 2). Evidently, this was the first time the Hebrews had encountered such a well-fortified city, and Joshua, though seasoned in battle, had no experience in conducting a siege of such a fortification. Encouragement and explicit instructions from the Lord were necessary if this military strategy was to succeed.

In light of God's promise to defeat the king and warriors of Jericho, the Lord directed Joshua to have all the Israelite fighting men march around the city one time. Also, this procedure was to be repeated for six consecutive days (Josh. 6:3). Meanwhile, seven priests were to carry trumpets made from rams' horns in front of the ark of the covenant (vs. 4). Finally, on the seventh day, the Israelite army was to march around Jericho seven times, while the priests blew their trumpets. The people were to remain silent until they heard a long blast on the trumpets, and at that time they were to let out a high-pitched war cry. Then the walls of the fortified city would collapse, enabling the Israelite warriors to charge straight ahead (vs. 5).

The instructions Joshua received from the Lord may have seemed a bit strange to the Israelite leader. Normally, ladders and ramming logs would be used to enter a fortified city. Sometimes in situations like this one, tunnels could be dug under the walls at night. Or Joshua could have waited for the starving residents to eventually come out looking for food. Marching around a city for seven days, making a lot of noise, and waiting for the walls to collapse were certainly not in any of the military manuals of that day. Furthermore, the prominent place given to the ark of the covenant in the Israelites' march around Jericho clearly made this event a religious ceremony (vss. 6-7). Previously, the stranger Joshua met somewhere outside of Jericho had opened the general's eyes to the armies of the Lord, much like Elisha did years later for his servant (see 2 Kings 6:16-17). In essence, the host of heaven was ready to fight this battle for God's chosen people. This was not to be the Israelites' siege, but the Lord's.

Joshua 6:11-14 summarizes the Israelites' compliance with the Lord's instructions, beginning with the circuit the group made around Jericho on the first day. Then, early the next morning, Joshua and the rest of the group started marching around the fortified city in the same manner as the preceding day. The order of the procession was warriors, the seven priests blowing the trumpets, the ark of the covenant, and the rear guard. From the second through sixth days, the parade of Israelites returned to their camp after making one complete circuit around Jericho. At that time, the city occupied a plot of land large enough for the Israelites to completely encircle it.

Those looking down from the walls of Jericho saw that there was no chance of escape, and yet they must have hoped that their fortressed city could withstand any Israelite attack. The successive days of the Israelites' marching may have produced a tedium that slowly wore down the fighting spirits of those inside the city. On each of six successive days, the people of Jericho were awakened by the stamping of the

Hebrews' march and the blaring of the priests' trumpets. From the top of the city wall, the inhabitants could see the armed men leading the way for the seven priests blowing rams' horns, followed by the ark of the covenant, the rear guard, and the whole army of Israel. All of this pointed to the perfection, completeness, and consummation of God's plan.

After six days of slow, suspenseful marching, the seventh day of the Israelites' siege of the city dawned. On each of six previous days, the threatening troops had tramped around the city once, and then had headed back to their encampment. On the seventh day, however, the Israelites did not return to camp after a single trip around the city. They continued around Jericho a second time, and then a third, and so on (vs. 15). The columns of Israel's troops may have kept doubling themselves on each pass, creating several rows of soldiers all the way around the city. The people of Jericho must have suspected that this day was to be different somehow from the previous days. Perhaps they hurriedly prepared themselves for an Israelite invasion.

On the seventh time around the city, the priests blew the rams' horns and Joshua gave his command to "Shout; for the LORD hath given you the city" (vs. 16). The Israelite general reminded his troops that the city was to be treated as a type of first-fruits offering. Jericho and all that was in it were to be devoted to the Lord. "Accursed" (vs. 17) meant that the city and its inhabitants were to be irrevocably sacrificed to God—that is, totally destroyed. If any of the Hebrews failed to respect this curse, they themselves would reap its punishment. Joshua's warning had a twofold purpose. First, the Israelites were not to act like pagan plunderers and carry off everything for themselves. Second, there was deep spiritual peril in accumulating anything the Lord had designed for destruction.

Thankfully, Joshua did not forget the grace of God that was to be extended to Rahab and her family. According to the Israelite general, she was to be spared because she hid the two spies. Joshua warned his warriors to stay away from what had been devoted to the Lord. Joshua made it clear that even the compromise of a single individual could bring destruction down on the entire Israelite camp (vs. 18). All the items made out of silver, gold, bronze, and iron—which could not be burned—were to be set apart for use in the tabernacle. These metals would eventually be melted down and used by the priests to beautify the sanctuary of the Lord. In effect, the metals were to be considered the Lord's spoils of war (vs. 19).

In a single paragraph of punctuated action, the writer of the Book of Joshua described the demise of Jericho (vss. 20-21). Joshua followed the sequence of events exactly as God had ordered (see vss. 4-5). It is far-fetched to maintain that the acoustics of the trumpet blast and the shouts of the people were enough to raze the walls of the city. Some people have suggested that an earthquake shook the foundations of Jericho. Even if this were true, the destruction of the fortified city must still be considered miraculous. Whatever the cause, the hand of God knocked down the walls of Jericho as easily as a toddler might push over a stack of blocks.

With the walls of Jericho down, penetration into the city was easy. Rahab's house was part of the city wall, but obviously it was still standing when the Hebrews entered. Regardless of all the unexplained details, the Israelites could enter the city unhindered. Since the Israelites had the city surrounded at the time the walls fell, they were able to attack Jericho from all sides (vs. 20). Though the inhabitants were demoralized, they still put up a fight (see 24:11). When the Israelites entered the city, it must have been clear that Joshua intended to take no prisoners. We can assume that the king of Jericho met the same fate that the king of Ai and the five Amorite kings later met (see 8:29; 10:26). As Moses had instructed, Joshua killed everything that breathed, with the exception of Rahab and her family (6:21). Apparently, that family became fully accepted members of the Israelite community (vss. 22-25).

SUGGESTIONS TO TEACHERS

This week's lesson offers a powerful reminder of the way the Lord enables faithful members of His community to persevere in the face of obstacles. God stands with those who trust and obey Him!

1. GOD GAVE A PLAN. The invasion of Canaan and the capture of Jericho appeared to be impossible tasks, but God provided guidance and strength for the Israelite victory. Instead of focusing on the obstacles, Joshua and his army centered on the divine plan. God always offers possibilities when we listen and obey!

2. JOSHUA GUIDED THE ATTACK. Marching around Jericho's walls for six days with the ark of the covenant might have seemed silly and pointless to some. But Joshua faithfully followed God's orders. Joshua did not question the Lord's command, even when it might have been questioned by others. God often uses unorthodox ways to accomplish His purposes!

3. ISRAELITES CAPTURED THE CITY. Significant victories come when God's people cooperate, take courage, and act in obedience to the Lord.

4. GOD GOT THE CREDIT. Don't get bogged down in useless discussion in your class over the precise details of the fall of Jericho by trying to "explain" the collapse of the walls by an earthquake or pursuing other earthly causes. The credit for the miracle goes to the Lord!

5. VICTORS PROTECTED RAHAB. The protection of Rahab won safety for her entire family during the battle and an enduring place in the covenant community. Sometimes the most unlikely persons turn out to be the most faithful!

FOR ADULTS

■ **TOPIC:** The Thrill of Victory

■ **QUESTIONS:** 1. How do you think those living in Jericho reacted to the advancing Israelites? 2. What did God tell Joshua the priests should do? 3. What were the people told to do when they heard the priests blow the long blast of their trumpets? 4. How were the people to treat the items devoted to destruction (see Josh. 6:18)? 5. Why is God's judgment of sin so hard to accept?

■ ILLUSTRATIONS:

Overcoming Obstacles. Joshua's victory at Jericho was a great one, accomplished in a remarkable way. Today's heroes also return from battles basking in the glory of their victories. Grateful citizens show their appreciation with cheers and confetti. Thanks to various forms of broadcast media, all of us share the thrill of the moment, even though we're not on the scene.

Meanwhile, in ordinary lives the battles go on every day. Winners and losers go unnoticed by the media. These are not the battles that warrant major news coverage, but they are extremely significant to the participants: battles against cancer, old age, debts, loneliness, the difficulties faced by one's family members, unemployment, and so on.

In the local church, believers do not fight these sorts of battles alone. We know that while we are not spared life's struggles, we do have a unique companion who stands with us, that is, the Lord Jesus. We also know we can count on a committed band of friends who pray, counsel, and encourage one another to overcome life's obstacles.

Doing Your Best for God. Joshua is not the only person in history who has endeavored to do his or her best for God. Another individual is Jimmy Carter. As a young naval officer, he applied for an assignment in Admiral Hyman Rickover's nuclear submarine program. At the time, Rickover asked him, "How did you stand in your class at the Naval Academy?" "Sir, I stood 59th in my class of 820." Expecting to be congratulated, Carter was surprised to hear Rickover say, "Did you do your best?"

At first Carter was going to say yes, but then he remembered the times when he had not learned all that he could have in a class. So he answered, "No, sir, I didn't always do my best." Rickover then hit him with a stinger that touched a spot in the soul of a Christian striving to serve God: "Why not?"

We might learn something from the example of Jimmy Carter, who has lived by the conviction that all the Father expects of us is that by faith in the Son we do the best we can with what we have. Like Joshua in his service to the people of Israel, Carter was always starting over again, learning from his failures and moving on, trying to do his best with the God-given means at hand. Serving the Lord has driven Carter's career through a series of defeats and victories. Carter accepted his weaknesses, and determinedly drew on the power of the Redeemer at work within him.

Carter's greatest defeat as president came when his rescue mission failed to save the American hostages held in Tehran. But in the midst of a desperate campaign for re-election, which he also lost, Carter continued to negotiate for the safe return of the hostages. In his first act as a former president, Carter flew to Germany to welcome the released hostages.

Returning to Plains, Georgia, Carter found his farming business $1 million in debt. An even greater threat to his mental health was the realization that he was no longer president. Losing the presidency to Ronald Reagan might have led Carter into bitterness and recrimination. Instead, the former president launched the Carter Center in Atlanta, Georgia, as a base for his efforts to reconcile warring factions abroad, to eradicate diseases in developing countries, and to address domestic problems of housing and poverty. Like Joshua in the conquest of Canaan, Carter relied on his God-given ability to put setbacks behind him and focus only on the future. He received a letter from Rickover that said: "As long as a man is trying as hard as he can to do what he thinks to be right, he is a success regardless of the outcome."

Writing books and building houses for the poor have consumed the time of both Rosalynn and Jimmy Carter over the past three decades. But the former president's greatest legacy is still unfolding. He draws inspiration and strength from Scripture as he works for world peace and toward eliminating poverty and eradicating disease. Carter's faith in the Savior led him to strive for the same objectives by whatever means were at hand while he was in Georgia, during his tenure as president of the United States, and long after he left office.

Celebration. Returning from their surprising win of the Pennsylvania Class AA state championship on November 26, 1997, the South Park Eagles football team arrived at the high school at almost midnight. As the buses carrying the team came up the driveway, hundreds of students, parents, community people, teachers, and administrators began a joyous welcome and a victory celebration. For an unranked team to beat several of the state's ranked favorites had been quite a feat! Joy and pride exploded into a celebration.

This team was like any other team in that it was excited about the victory. Most people love to celebrate victories. The Israelites under Joshua's leadership were no different. The celebration of God's defeat of Jericho must have been combined with equal joy and enthusiasm.

FOR YOUTH

■ TOPIC: Obedience Leads to Victory
■ QUESTIONS: 1. What do you think the Israelites felt as they circled Jericho without attacking it? 2. Why is it often hard to be patient for God to act, and to wait for His will and way to become clear? 3. What temptations awaited the victorious Israelite army? 4. How do you feel when it seems as if God has denied you something you think you deserve? 5. Why is it difficult today to be uncompromising about God's truth and His commands?

■ **ILLUSTRATIONS:**

Sticking to the Plan. Competition excites youth, whether in sports, music, or academics. Tragically, in some institutions, competition can turn nasty and violent. Many young people lose their lives in violence caused by recklessness, drugs, and alcohol—all in the name of trying to be bigger, better, or more respected than the next person.

The task of believers is to direct the energy and enthusiasm of youth into acceptable channels, and to provide challenges that lead to worthy goals and outcomes. The Bible is full of accounts of people who accepted God's call, obeyed His will, and experienced victory over the challenges in their lives.

Joshua's march against Jericho is just one example of this. He succeeded because he knew God personally and stuck to the plan the Lord gave him. Though God's command might have appeared to be ridiculous, Joshua still obeyed the Lord. And in the end, the Israelite general led God's people to success over their foes.

Specific Directions. A story is told of an old hand-operated pump in the badlands of the American west. A thirsty visitor to the pump found a note with the following instructions and a bottle of water: "Do not drink the water in this bottle. Pour the contents down the hole at the top of the pump. Allow the washer and the packing a few minutes to soak up the water. Then pump and drink your fill. Before leaving, fill up the bottle, and leave it for the next person."

The instructions might have seemed absurd, particularly when an individual was thirsty. Why pour good water away when the precious liquid might be wasted? However, these were the instructions, and they worked.

The people of Israel heard what must have seemed like equally absurd instructions about capturing Jericho. No general or military leader in their right mind would have thought of such a scheme. However, the idea was God's plan. In faith, Joshua and his army were to follow the plan, and it was their key to achieve success.

Bold Plan. On the evening of May 1, 1863, Generals Lee and Jackson conferred in the woods. The situation looked grim. Hooker and the Union Army were at Chancellorsville, Virginia. He had outflanked the Confederate forces and moved 130,000 men across the Rappahannock River. Lee's army had 60,000. It appeared that the fighting force was caught in a trap and would be crushed.

Jackson proposed taking his corps of 26,000 men and slipping around the Union flank. It would be a ten-mile end sweep through dense woods at night. The plan seemed crazy. However, the execution of the plan was flawless. The Union line cracked in panic as Jackson's soldiers swept in, boxing in the Union forces.

Thousands of years earlier, another army listened to a plan that seemed absolutely crazy. Yet the Israelites, too, followed the plan with similar victorious results.

DISOBEDIENCE AND DEFEAT

BACKGROUND SCRIPTURE: **Joshua 7:1–8:29**
DEVOTIONAL READING: **Romans 6:1-11**

KEY VERSE: The children of Israel committed a trespass in the accursed thing: for Achan, . . . of the tribe of Judah, took of the accursed thing: and the anger of the LORD was kindled against the children of Israel. (Joshua 7:1)

KING JAMES VERSION

JOSHUA 7:1 But the children of Israel committed a trespass in the accursed thing: for Achan, the son of Carmi, the son of Zabdi, the son of Zerah, of the tribe of Judah, took of the accursed thing: and the anger of the LORD was kindled against the children of Israel. . . .

10 And the LORD said unto Joshua, Get thee up; wherefore liest thou thus upon thy face? 11 Israel hath sinned, and they have also transgressed my covenant which I commanded them: for they have even taken of the accursed thing, and have also stolen, and dissembled also, and they have put it even among their own stuff. 12 Therefore the children of Israel could not stand before their enemies, but turned their backs before their enemies, because they were accursed: neither will I be with you any more, except ye destroy the accursed from among you. . . .

22 So Joshua sent messengers, and they ran unto the tent; and, behold, it was hid in his tent, and the silver under it. 23 And they took them out of the midst of the tent, and brought them unto Joshua, and unto all the children of Israel, and laid them out before the LORD. 24 And Joshua, and all Israel with him, took Achan the son of Zerah, and the silver, and the garment, and the wedge of gold, and his sons, and his daughters, and his oxen, and his asses, and his sheep, and his tent, and all that he had: and they brought them unto the valley of Achor. 25 And Joshua said, Why hast thou troubled us? the LORD shall trouble thee this day. And all Israel stoned him with stones, and burned them with fire, after they had stoned them with stones. 26 And they raised over him a great heap of stones unto this day. So the LORD turned from the fierceness of his anger. Wherefore the name of that place was called, The valley of Achor, unto this day.

NEW REVISED STANDARD VERSION

JOSHUA 7:1 But the Israelites broke faith in regard to the devoted things: Achan son of Carmi son of Zabdi son of Zerah, of the tribe of Judah, took some of the devoted things; and the anger of the Lord burned against the Israelites. . . .

10 The Lord said to Joshua, "Stand up! Why have you fallen upon your face? 11 Israel has sinned; they have transgressed my covenant that I imposed on them. They have taken some of the devoted things; they have stolen, they have acted deceitfully, and they have put them among their own belongings. 12 Therefore the Israelites are unable to stand before their enemies; they turn their backs to their enemies, because they have become a thing devoted for destruction themselves. I will be with you no more, unless you destroy the devoted things from among you. . . .

22 So Joshua sent messengers, and they ran to the tent; and there it was, hidden in his tent with the silver underneath. 23 They took them out of the tent and brought them to Joshua and all the Israelites; and they spread them out before the Lord. 24 Then Joshua and all Israel with him took Achan son of Zerah, with the silver, the mantle, and the bar of gold, with his sons and daughters, with his oxen, donkeys, and sheep, and his tent and all that he had; and they brought them up to the Valley of Achor. 25 Joshua said, "Why did you bring trouble on us? The Lord is bringing trouble on you today." And all Israel stoned him to death; they burned them with fire, cast stones on them, 26 and raised over him a great heap of stones that remains to this day. Then the Lord turned from his burning anger. Therefore that place to this day is called the Valley of Achor.

5

Monday, June 27	Joshua 7:2-9	*Victory Turned to Defeat*
Tuesday, June 28	Joshua 7:12-15	*The Reason for the Defeat*
Wednesday, June 29	Joshua 7:16-21	*The Sin Revealed*
Thursday, June 30	Romans 6:15-23	*The Wages of Sin*
Friday, July 1	John 16:4b-11	*The Work of the Advocate*
Saturday, July 2	Romans 6:1-11	*Dead to Sin, Alive to God*
Sunday, July 3	Joshua 7:1, 10-12, 22-26	*The Outcome of Achan's Sin*

BACKGROUND

Joshua 7 reveals that Achan's greed and thievery resulted in Israel being defeated at Ai. The items Achan stole from Jericho included the following: (1) "a goodly Babylonish garment" (vs. 21). Such a robe was considered a valuable import at the time of Jericho's conquest. (2) "two hundred shekels of silver." This is equal in weight to about five pounds, which today would be worth around $1,000. (3) "a wedge of gold of fifty shekels weight." This is equal to about 1.25 pounds, which at today's prices would be worth about $16,000. All of these items could have been concealed easily. Achan probably wrapped the precious metals in the robe before placing them in a hole beneath his tent. For his act, the whole nation of Israel came face-to-face with God's anger.

Achan described the items he took from Jericho as "spoils," perhaps an indication that he was trying to rationalize his crime. Riches seized from an enemy were usually a legitimate reward for participating in a victorious battle. But the wealth recovered from Jericho was not plunder in this sense. Before the siege ever began, Joshua had made it clear that the riches of the fortress city were devoted to the Lord and to be completely destroyed (see 6:17-19). This meant the spoils of that battle belonged to God alone, and by keeping some of the plunder for himself, Achan had violated the Israelites' covenant with the Lord. As soon as he had committed his crime, Achan knew that what he had done was wrong. Indeed, his concealment of the items clearly proves his sense of guilt (7:21).

NOTES ON THE PRINTED TEXT

The Israelites had experienced a resounding victory at Jericho. The city had been offered as firstfruits to the Lord and supposedly everything within its walls had been sacrificed to Him. Every resident of Jericho who refused to acknowledge the God of the Hebrews had been killed. Everything that could be burned had been burned. Meanwhile, all the precious metals had been set aside for eventual use in the tabernacle—or at least that's what Joshua thought. Achan, one of the soldiers involved in the siege of Jericho, saw the riches of the city and decided he wanted to keep some of those things for himself, despite the restriction forbidding any of the Israelites from doing so. As part of the introduction to the account of Achan's sin, his family line is traced back three generations (Josh. 7:1). This was likely an attempt to emphasize the seriousness of Achan's crime. Furthermore, Achan's violation of the covenant was to affect more than himself. It was to affect the entire nation of Israel.

The contempt for the Lord shown by Achan's act caused God to be furious with the Hebrews. And yet, as God's anger against His people went unresolved, the Israelites prepared for a battle against the warriors of Ai. Little did the Israelites know that they were entering the conflict without the Lord's blessing. Nothing is said in the biblical text about Joshua seeking God's direction before sending spies and troops to Ai. Perhaps for the first time in his military career, the Israelite general ignored his accountability to the Lord. The Hebrews' routing of Jericho may have made Joshua overconfident. And so, as he had done at Jericho, the commander of Israel's armies dispatched spies to scout out Ai (vs. 2). When he commissioned the men, he was unaware of either Achan's hoarding or God's displeasure. If Joshua had consulted the Lord before making his plans, he certainly would have learned about both.

The journey of the spies from Jericho to Ai was about 15 miles as the crow flies. Also, it was an uphill trek, since Jericho is about 800 feet below sea level and Ai is about 2,500 feet above sea level. With a population of about 12,000 (see 8:25), a town the size of Ai could muster a fighting force of probably no more than 3,000 warriors. After the Israelites had handily defeated Jericho, the spies evidently thought that their soldiers could take this town man for man. Therefore, they suggested that Joshua send only a few thousand soldiers (7:3).

At Jericho, the hosts of the Lord were behind the Hebrews, but this time God withheld His support. Consequently, the Israelites were chased downhill from the city gate to the deep ravines and thrashed at the rocky bluffs surrounding Ai (vss. 4-5). Joshua sent the maximum number of soldiers recommended by the spies. Of course, 36 fatalities out of a 3,000-man fighting force does not seem like a significant loss in modern military terms. Psychologically, however, this was a devastating defeat for Israel's commander. The tide had seemed to turn, and now it was the Israelites rather than the Canaanites whose courage melted away like water.

God did not want Joshua to waste his time mourning over the military defeat suffered (vss. 6-9). Instead, he was to get up and take care of the situation (vs. 10). The Lord told Joshua that the nation of Israel had sinned. The third person plural "they" appears several times in the Lord's rebuke in verse 11, which indicates He held the entire nation accountable for Achan's iniquity. God called this transgression a violation of the people's covenant with God, and then specified that the nation was guilty of sacrilege, theft, lying, and deceitful hoarding. Moreover, because of these sins, the Lord had made His people subject to annihilation, as seen in their humiliating defeat at the hands of Ai's warriors. God's threat to leave Israel must have felt overwhelming to Joshua. Nothing could have seemed more dreadful to the Israelite commander than that the Lord would sever His relationship with His people. The condition for God's continued presence with the Hebrews was that the people must search out and destroy the materials looted from Jericho. There were to be no exceptions made to this ultimatum (vs. 12).

It is interesting that Achan did not admit his sin until he had been exposed. As it turns out, he probably would not have confessed if he had not been caught. Though Achan could have voluntarily come forward at any point during the search for the culprit, he held back each time the lots were cast. Perhaps he hoped that the lots would fall purely by chance and that someone else might be condemned. In any case, Achan avoided making a confession until he was clearly pinpointed as the felon. Once Achan had made his confession, Joshua acted quickly and decisively by sending messengers to Achan's tent. There they discovered the loot and confirmed Achan's confession (vs. 22). After the messengers returned to Joshua with the stolen material, they spread out the items "before the LORD" (vs. 23). What had been taken from God was now returned to His rightful ownership.

Joshua, along with the rest of the Israelites, led Achan, his family, and their possessions up to the Valley of Achor (vs. 24). The fact that Achan possessed cattle, donkeys, and sheep indicates that he was a wealthy man by the standards of the day. Thus Achan's theft was not inspired by need but by greed. If he had only waited until the eventual defeat of Ai, he could have taken whatever he wished with the Lord's blessing (see 8:2). Punishing Achan's sons and daughters along with the culprit himself may seem unjust to many of us who read this account. Indeed, though Achan's children may have known about the theft, it may seem unfair that they should lose their lives because of their father's greed.

These concerns notwithstanding, because this was the first act of theft by an Israelite upon entering the promised land, it was vital for the good of the nation that all those involved in breaking the covenant with God be severely punished. Moreover, Joshua's comment to Achan before the culprit was executed was not meant to be vindictive. The Israelite leader simply told Achan that he had caused all of Israel to fall in defeat and that he deserved the punishment he was about to receive. Representatives of the entire nation participated in stoning the offender, his family, and his livestock. Once Achan and all that belonged to him were dead, their bodies were cremated (7:25). Burning the felon's body may have also served as a symbol that the Israelites had purged themselves and the promised land of Achan's sin.

After the execution was complete, Achan's remains were buried under a pile of rocks as a type of memorial (vs. 26). In Hebrew "Achor" means "disaster" or "trouble." This explains why the site of Israel's defeat was called the Valley of Achor. The crude altar the people erected there became a reminder of the nation's disobedience and first military setback in the promised land. Because the nation's commander acted justly in righting Achan's wrong, the Lord "turned from the fierceness of his anger." Consequently, God would now be with His chosen people as they prepared to attack Ai a second time.

SUGGESTIONS TO TEACHERS

Joshua 7 explains why the Israelites suffered defeat at Ai. The Lord told Joshua that by stealing and lying, the Israelites had broken their covenant with Him. God said He would no longer be with them and that they would fall in battle unless they destroyed the items set apart for destruction. From this we see that the Hebrews were to purify themselves and come before the Lord so that He could identify the offending party, who was to be executed.

1. RECOGNIZNG ISRAEL'S CORPORATE SOLIDARITY. It may be difficult for those of us who have grown up in a Western culture to understand why God would hold a nation responsible for the sin of one man. To better comprehend the Lord's judgment, we need to realize that the Israelites were in a military situation in which corporate solidarity and strict discipline were essential for their success. In many modern boot camps, an entire platoon may be disciplined for the misconduct of one soldier. Though this may seem harsh and unfair, such discipline produces a strong sense of accountability in the platoon.

2. FAILING TO CONSULT THE LORD. It is important to clarify that the Israelites were defeated by the warriors of Ai because Joshua and his officials failed to consult God before the battle ensued. Herein lies an important lesson for believers living today. Perhaps many of our failures could be avoided if we first took our plans and concerns to God in prayer. Christians would do well to spend some time consulting with the Lord before making decisions that may have a major impact on their own and other people's lives.

3. HONORING GOD THROUGH THE CONFESSION OF SIN. According to Joshua 7:19, the commander of Israel's armies said to Achan, "My son, give, I pray thee, glory to the LORD God of Israel, and make confession unto him." The truth behind this exhortation is that the confession of sins honors God. When we admit our wrongdoing and take responsibility for it, we acknowledge the Redeemer's lordship and power, as well as His grace. Covering up sin, on the other hand, is actually a form of self-deceit.

4. OVERCOMING SIN'S DEVASTATING EFFECT. The psychological process of sin that Achan described is as old as Adam and Eve's transgression in the Garden of Eden. According to Achan's account, he saw, he coveted, and then he took (vs. 21; see Gen. 3:6). Sin still clouds our relationship with God. But through Jesus' sacrifice and the Spirit's power, we have the opportunity to go beyond our sin and experience a closer relationship with the Lord.

■ TOPIC: The Agony of Defeat

■ QUESTIONS: 1. In what way had the Israelites disobeyed the Lord's command? 2. Why do you think Joshua responded in a demoralized way when he first heard about the Israelites' defeat at Ai? 3. How had the sin committed by Achan violated the covenant Israel had with the Lord? 4. What emotions do you think you would have felt if you were among the messengers dispatched to Achan's tent? 5. What is the reason for the Israelites' decision to stone Achan and his family?

■ ILLUSTRATIONS:

The Curved Mirror of Temptation. Roses' Restaurant and Bakery in Portland, Oregon, is famous for its cakes. As customers approach the display case, they pass a mirror that is slightly curved to make people look thinner than they actually are. Viewers chuckle and laugh at the image, then suddenly realize there's a not-so-subtle message here: "Go ahead. Forget your waistline for a moment. Have a piece!"

Isn't this the human saga, especially as seen in the Israelites' defeat at Ai? One member of the covenant community allowed an enticing illusion to overtake reality, and it brought the agony of defeat on everyone. In a spiritual sense, the curved mirror of temptation distorts the way we should see ourselves. We become convinced that we can forget God's view. Our basic problem is sin—that is, seeing ourselves through the distorted reflection of deception.

Preventing the Rippling Effect of Sin. Things had been going so well. Every Saturday night, Carl and Joanne phoned in a pizza order and waited for the speedy delivery. Then one Saturday, Carl noticed that the pizza was 15 minutes overdue. He called the restaurant. "The driver just left with it," they told him.

Fifteen more minutes went by before Carl phoned again. "You told me the driver just left 15 minutes ago," he said. "I only live five blocks away." "I was wrong about that," he was told. "Your pizza's just coming out of the oven." Ten minutes later a pizza arrived, but it was not their order.

The next Saturday night, Carl and Joanne called a different pizza restaurant. "I know its a little thing," Carl says now, "but we just don't feel we can trust that restaurant anymore. Things were fine for a long time. But then they made some big mistakes. I don't think I could just call them and relax about it."

Perhaps the emotions Carl and Joanne felt about the pizza restaurant are remotely like God's reaction to the transgression that Achan committed during Joshua's tenure as Israel's military commander. When Achan willfully disobeyed God's ban on taking the objects set apart for destruction, the culprit disrupted the nation's covenantal relationship and broke God's trust. And the only way for the Israelites to restore their fellowship with God was by dealing forthrightly with the iniquity in their midst (see Josh. 7:12).

It is clearly pointed out in the New Testament that the Lord yearns for His church to have this same sense of unity and solidarity. For instance, in 1 Corinthians 5:6-13, Paul wrote about how undisciplined sin in a congregation can eventually contaminate the entire assembly. Remaining accountable to each other is one way we can prevent the rippling effect of sin.

Reckless Tinkering. Rushworth M. Kidder covered events in the former Soviet Union as a reporter for the *Christian Science Monitor*. He has shown that many moral lapses were responsible for the Chernobyl meltdown in April 1986. Perhaps the worst example was the reckless tinkering by two engineers who had decided to perform an unauthorized experiment. To do so, they had to override a computerized alarm. In other words, the pair shut down the warning system and kept going.

In a manner of speaking, these rogue staff members put themselves above the established codes and rules. Disaster followed, the effects of which continue to be felt. For instance, in 2009, *Scientific American* correspondent Brendan Borrell reported that "radiation is still hammering the region's insect, spider, and bird populations."

It's not hard to see a spiritual parallel between this debacle and the disaster the Israelites experienced in their defeat at Ai. A rogue member of their community decided to violate an important God-given rule. In turn, some of the nation's finest warriors died in battle. Tragically, Achan's entire family also lost their lives as the leadership of Israel dealt with the tragic incident.

 FOR YOUTH

■ TOPIC: Disobedience Has Consequences
■ QUESTIONS: 1. What specifically made the Lord furious with His chosen people? 2. If you were Joshua, how do you think you would have initially responded to the Israelite defeat at Ai? 3. Why did God hold the entire nation of Israel responsible for one man's sin? 4. Do you think you would have been angry or sympathetic with Achan over what he had done? 5. How could Achan's confession of his sin be honoring to God?

■ ILLUSTRATIONS:

Rx for Temptation. Madonna isn't exactly a poster child for family values. However, in a 2008 interview, she told the German magazine *KulturSpiegel* that she "doesn't let her kids watch television or eat lollies." She explained that she did not want them to be tempted. "I'm a tough mother," she admitted.

Like Madonna, you are aware of sin in the world and that indulging in it has consequences. It enters your life in a variety of ways, such as through certain kinds of music and television programming. Take a prescription from this unlikely source and wisely choose what you do.

Rather than ignore God's will, as Achan did during the Israelites' conquest of

Canaan, strive to resist the daily temptations coming your way. One way to spiritually fortify yourself is through daily Bible reading and prayer.

Tempted. A 12-year-old girl was looking for an online pen pal. So she posted a notice on a social networking Web site. What she thought was a 15-year-old boy responded. In reality, the lovesick "boy" was a 47-year-old man. He kept asking the lonely girl for inappropriate pictures, which she finally supplied.

The girl's mother discovered what was going on and alerted the authorities. When the city police searched the man's basement, they uncovered correspondence and pictures from a dozen teenage girls from various locales across the U.S. All of them had been lured via the Internet, having been tempted by the promise of friendship.

These adolescents, like Achan, fell to the power of temptation. Our temptations are indeed beguiling and often seem innocent. It takes enormous effort and faith to resist the evil one's attempts to beat us into submission. Are you prepared for the next round?

The Lure. Casinos across our nation do everything to lure families inside. Las Vegas gambling centers offer circus atmospheres and amusement parks. And dozens of gaming halls now boast child-care centers. A survey conducted at 11 casinos disclosed that three-quarters of the gamblers would have stayed home were it not for the day-care services.

One spokeswoman for a management company that runs some of these day-care facilities defended them. She argued that the parents would probably gamble anyway and cited examples in which children have simply been left in the parking lot. For instance, one 12-year-old Mississippi youth was locked in the car with a loaded pistol for his safety. The glitz and glamour of the casinos, coupled with the prospect of winning big money, is too great a temptation for some parents.

Achan's admission in Joshua 7:21 reminds us of how irresistible temptations can feel. The devil speaks to us with clever arguments and soothing words. However, we must recognize sin for what it is—anything that moves us away from close fellowship with God (see vs. 12).

HEED GOD'S LEADERS

BACKGROUND SCRIPTURE: Judges 2; 21:25
DEVOTIONAL READING: Psalm 78:1-8

KEY VERSE: [The Israelites] would not hearken unto their judges, but they went a whoring after other gods, and bowed themselves unto them. (Judges 2:17)

KING JAMES VERSION

JUDGES 2:11 And the children of Israel did evil in the sight of the LORD, and served Baalim: 12 And they forsook the LORD God of their fathers, which brought them out of the land of Egypt, and followed other gods, of the gods of the people that were round about them, and bowed themselves unto them, and provoked the LORD to anger. 13 And they forsook the LORD, and served Baal and Ashtaroth. 14 And the anger of the LORD was hot against Israel, and he delivered them into the hands of spoilers that spoiled them, and he sold them into the hands of their enemies round about, so that they could not any longer stand before their enemies. 15 Whithersoever they went out, the hand of the LORD was against them for evil, as the LORD had said, and as the LORD had sworn unto them: and they were greatly distressed. 16 Nevertheless the LORD raised up judges, which delivered them out of the hand of those that spoiled them. 17 And yet they would not hearken unto their judges, but they went a whoring after other gods, and bowed themselves unto them: they turned quickly out of the way which their fathers walked in, obeying the commandments of the LORD; but they did not so. 18 And when the LORD raised them up judges, then the LORD was with the judge, and delivered them out of the hand of their enemies all the days of the judge: for it repented the LORD because of their groanings by reason of them that oppressed them and vexed them. 19 And it came to pass, when the judge was dead, that they returned, and corrupted themselves more than their fathers, in following other gods to serve them, and to bow down unto them; they ceased not from their own doings, nor from their stubborn way.

NEW REVISED STANDARD VERSION

JUDGES 2:11 Then the Israelites did what was evil in the sight of the Lord and worshiped the Baals; 12 and they abandoned the Lord, the God of their ancestors, who had brought them out of the land of Egypt; they followed other gods, from among the gods of the peoples who were all around them, and bowed down to them; and they provoked the Lord to anger. 13 They abandoned the Lord, and worshiped Baal and the Astartes. 14 So the anger of the Lord was kindled against Israel, and he gave them over to plunderers who plundered them, and he sold them into the power of their enemies all around, so that they could no longer withstand their enemies. 15 Whenever they marched out, the hand of the Lord was against them to bring misfortune, as the Lord had warned them and sworn to them; and they were in great distress.

16 Then the Lord raised up judges, who delivered them out of the power of those who plundered them. 17 Yet they did not listen even to their judges; for they lusted after other gods and bowed down to them. They soon turned aside from the way in which their ancestors had walked, who had obeyed the commandments of the Lord; they did not follow their example. 18 Whenever the Lord raised up judges for them, the Lord was with the judge, and he delivered them from the hand of their enemies all the days of the judge; for the Lord would be moved to pity by their groaning because of those who persecuted and oppressed them. 19 But whenever the judge died, they would relapse and behave worse than their ancestors, following other gods, worshiping them and bowing down to them. They would not drop any of their practices or their stubborn ways.

6

Monday, July 4	Exodus 23:20-33	*The Snare of Other Gods*
Tuesday, July 5	Joshua 24:19-27	*A Covenant to Obey God*
Wednesday, July 6	1 Samuel 15:17-23	*Better to Obey and Heed*
Thursday, July 7	Ephesians 5:6-20	*God's Wrath for the Disobedient*
Friday, July 8	Judges 2:1-10	*An Ignorant Generation*
Saturday, July 9	Psalm 78:1-8	*Teaching the Next Generation*
Sunday, July 10	Judges 2:11-19	*A Cycle of Stubborn Sin*

BACKGROUND

Jewish tradition says that Samuel, the last judge, wrote the Book of Judges. Moreover, the frequent comment "In those days there was no king in Israel" (for example: 17:6) plainly suggests that the book was put in its finished form during the monarchy period, which began about 1050 B.C. Judges tells the history of the Israelite people during the period stretching from the death of Joshua to the beginning of the monarchy. Some argue that this period lasted only about a century and a half. The biblical evidence, however, seems to favor the view that the period of judges extended from about 1375 B.C. to about 1050 B.C., that is, nearly three centuries.

This was an era of tremendous political upheaval in the ancient Near East. The Hittite Empire, which had once controlled a region extending from southeastern Asia Minor to northern Lebanon, was overthrown by an influx of Sea Peoples, who included the Philistines. Though their southward advance was checked by the Egyptians, these Sea Peoples remained in Canaan and dominated the area for many years. During this time, Egypt's power and influence began to wane. The Assyrians were so preoccupied with other matters that they exercised only a marginal influence in the regions south of Lebanon. These circumstances gave the Israelites considerable freedom to strengthen their control of Palestine. Despite their military victories under the leadership of Joshua, the Israelites continued to wage war with various tribal groups in Canaan. They also were repeatedly attacked by nomadic groups from Moab, Ammon, and the eastern desert.

NOTES ON THE PRINTED TEXT

Joshua died when he was 110 years old and was buried at Timnath Heres, which was also known as Timnath Serah. The city was located north of Mount Gaash in the southern slopes of Ephraim (Judg. 2:8-9; see Josh. 19:50; 24:30). Joshua served God until the day of his death. The Israelites that followed in the next generation were quite different from their predecessors. The people born after the time of Joshua neither personally experienced the Lord nor acknowledged Him as God. They also ignored all that God had done to establish Israel in Canaan (Judg. 2:10).

The expression "did evil in the sight of the LORD" (vs. 11) signifies that the

Israelites engaged in practices that God detested. Rather than exclusively worshiping Him, they served the Baals. Baal, whose name means "lord," was the supreme storm and fertility god of the Canaanites and Phoenicians. He was venerated in different forms in various locations, which explains why the Bible sometimes refers to "the Baals" (a plural term). Yahweh, the Lord of Israel, had graciously rescued His people from slavery in Egypt. Yet the Israelites abandoned Him to bow down to the pagan deities of the Canaanites.

The Hebrews' unfaithfulness angered the Lord (vs. 12), especially their decision to revere Baal and the Ashtoreths (vs. 13). Ashtoreth was a popular goddess of the Canaanites. She was considered to be a consort (or wife) of Baal. The Israelites did not completely abandon the Lord. Instead, they worshiped Him alongside the deities venerated by the Canaanites. The sin of the Hebrews was not that they substituted these false gods for the Lord, but tried to worship Him and these pagan deities at the same time. But in Isaiah 48:11, God declared, "I will not give my glory unto another." The same principle holds true for believers today. The Lord will not share His glory with anyone or anything. Believers must remain single-minded in their devotion to Him (see Jas. 4:4-5).

Israel's apostasy deeply grieved the Lord, and He responded by allowing robbers to plunder His people. He turned the Hebrews over to their Canaanite enemies, and the Israelites were unable to withstand the attacks of their foes (Judg. 2:14). We can only imagine the dread felt by the chosen people when they realized they were no longer able to defend themselves against enemy raids. Each time the Hebrews fought their adversaries, God's people lost, for He was no longer on their side (vs. 15).

The unfaithfulness of the Israelites was the first part in a cycle that occurs throughout the Book of Judges. This cycle had four steps: disobedience, oppression, repentance, and deliverance. Each time the Israelites went through this recurring pattern, they seemed to sink deeper into alienation from God. Indeed, spiritual compromise was the norm. In the Bible, we discover that God gives us healthy boundaries for living. When we operate within those boundaries by keeping His commands, we find spiritual wellness and wholeness.

God's decision to allow harm to come to His people was in harmony with the promises He had made in the Mosaic covenant. The Lord pledged that if the Israelites rebelled against Him and served other gods, He would bring disaster on them (see Josh. 23:12-13; 24:19-20). Evidently, these warnings were forgotten by the Hebrews. God was always straightforward in His dealings with Israel. His goal was to urge, not force, His people to repent of their sin. The Lord deeply loved the Israelites and did not want them to wallow in their idolatry. The purpose of His loving discipline was to woo the hearts of His people back to Him. Tragically, the Hebrews kept giving in to the pagan ways of their neighbors, and each time, God sent powerful oppressors until His people cried out for deliverance. When the Israelites were ready to listen, the Lord raised a judge to lead and liberate them.

God used tribal chiefs called judges to rescue His people from their foes (Judg. 2:16). To a lesser extent, these individuals decided matters of law and justice. Though some of the judges were corrupt, many were virtuous and honest. These leaders tried to persuade the Israelites to remain faithful to the Lord. The narratives connected with the exploits of various judges reflect a theological interpretation of history. Together they emphasize the truth that disregard for God brought oppression and that a broken spirit brought deliverance.

The Book of Judges has a historical and a religious purpose. The former is to provide glimpses of Israel's history from the death of Joshua to the beginning of the monarchy—a period of significant transition. The religious purpose of Judges is to stress God's discipline of the Israelites when their hearts turned to pagan deities. After a time of peace, the Israelites refused to obey their leaders any longer. Instead, God's people returned to their evil ways. In particular, they committed spiritual adultery by following after pagan deities and bowing down to them. The previous generation of Israelites obeyed the commands of the Lord. In contrast, the next generation wanted little to do with righteousness. Tragically, they rejected the way of God for a path of idolatry and grief (vs. 17).

Apostasy is the repudiation of a faith in God as it was formerly confessed. It is the deliberate turning from the Lord to follow pagan deities, or merely a life of self-worship. When the Israelites settled into the land of Canaan, they were constantly tempted to compromise the monotheism of their ancestors—that is, the belief in a single supreme being. Most of the Canaanites were polytheistic—that is, believing that many gods coexisted peacefully as long as each was given its proper due. Later in the history of Israel, various groups of Hebrews tried to blend their faith with that of the Canaanites, and after that, with that of their captors. But this process—called syncretism—failed miserably. The Lord refused to coexist with any other object of worship.

Despite the despicable ways in which the Israelites acted, the Lord did not abandon them. He was moved with pity each time His people groaned under the tyranny of their enemies. In every instance, God appointed a leader to free His people. Throughout the lifetime of that judge, God enabled this liberator to rescue and protect the Israelites from their latest oppressor (vs. 18). Israel's unfaithfulness was kept in check as long as the judge lived. But when the leader-liberator died, the next generation became even more sinful and idolatrous than the preceding one. Rather than abandon the wicked practices of the Canaanites, the Hebrews obstinately clung to them (vs. 19).

The stipulations of the Mosaic covenant were intended to provide order in the lives of God's people. The religious, social, and economic life of the nation was woven into the fabric of the law. These decrees were repeatedly violated as the Israelites venerated pagan deities (vs. 20). Understandably, the Lord was furious with His people for their unfaithfulness. Scholars have noted the unique way God referred to the Israelites in this verse. Instead of calling them "My people," He referred to them indirectly as "this people." From the preceding observation it may be inferred that Israel's once-intimate relationship with God was jeopardized by the people's sin.

Time and again the anger of the Lord was kindled against His spiritually adulterous people. Their repeated acts of rebellion compelled God to back away from them. He would no longer defeat and expel the nations left in Canaan after Joshua died (vs. 21). The Lord would use the continuing presence of these idolatrous neighbors to test the loyalty of His people. Would they carefully walk in the way of righteousness, as their ancestors did, or follow the path of wickedness (vs. 22)? God is supremely wise in His sovereignty. He could have used Joshua's army to completely drive out the Canaanites from the promised land. However, the Lord knew that the Hebrews would waver in their devotion to Him. Because they compromised themselves, God allowed a variety of idolatrous groups to remain in the land. Their continued presence would constantly test the seriousness of Israel's commitment to the Lord (vs. 23).

SUGGESTIONS TO TEACHERS

Time after time, God's people forgot the lessons of the past. Disobedience led to disaster. One generation turned away from God by consorting with the Canaanite deities, then suffered the consequences before finally returning to the ancestral faith. But the following generation failed to remember the lesson. Your emphasis in this week's lesson will be to help your class grow more obedient to the Lord.

1. DEADLY ATTRACTIONS. The lure of the Canaanite religion throughout Israel's history was almost irresistible. These cults promised that the adherents would have good weather for bountiful harvests and healthy offspring of their sheep and goats. The rites assuring such fertility for the barley fields and livestock always involved sexual practices and often demanded human sacrifices. Each time the Israelites allowed themselves to become mired in these pagan ways, they sank increasingly deeper into spiritual darkness and eventually experienced the judgment of the Lord.

2. DIVINE INTERVENTION. The Israelites were repeatedly led astray by their ungodly neighbors, and God responded by allowing their enemies to afflict them. Despite the Israelites' infidelity, a message of hope emerges. Even though God's people were unfaithful, He did not abandon them. The Lord allowed the Israelites to experience not only the natural consequences of their sin, but also the joy of His mercy.

3. DISASTER AWAITS. Be sure to emphasize to the class that rebellion against God always leads to disaster. Whenever we value the things of the world (for instance, wealth, power, and recognition) more than the things of God, the result is frustration and disappointment. Our disobedience brings spiritual defeat and moral bankruptcy to our lives.

4. DIVINE PARDON. Let the students know that when we "own" our sin by taking personal responsibility for it, we experience the Lord's forgiveness and restoration. He wants us to examine our lives to make sure that nothing is more important to us than Him. If we discover that we value something more than the Lord, we should turn away from it immediately. When we do, we will find ourselves stunned by God's grace.

FOR ADULTS	■ TOPIC: Help Is on the Way

■ QUESTIONS: 1. Why did God's people decide to be unfaithful to Him? 2. If you were a member of the Israelite community, how might you have resisted the temptation to compromise your faith? 3. What justification does the Bible give for God allowing His people to be defeated by their enemies? 4. Why do you think the Israelites were so fickle in their commitment to God? 5. How might you have encouraged God's people to remain faithful to Him?

■ **ILLUSTRATIONS:**

Seeking Deliverance. There was once a minister's child who had been born with a severe deformity in her legs and feet. Pathetically crippled, the youngster hobbled painfully with crutches and braces. Though everything medically possible was done, the lovely little girl could only drag her virtually useless legs.

Near Christmas one day, the minister came in with a poinsettia for his wife, who was upstairs in bed recovering from an illness. The crippled daughter was delighted to see her father and the lovely plant. She said, "Oh, Daddy! Let me carry it up to Mommy!" The man looked at the youngster and sighed. Trying to suppress his own weariness and sadness, he said, "Honey, I wish you could. I'd give anything to have you do it. But you know you can't." The little one gleefully replied, "Oh, but I can, Daddy! I'll hold the plant and you'll help by carrying me all the way up!"

The adults in your class may feel burdened with problems. But the Lord of life can bear them up and carry them through their most difficult experiences.

Wretched Excess. Before the burst of the housing bubble in the U.S. in 2008, realtors asserted that a four-car garage was a "must" for many of the 40-something, "gotta have it all" generation. Likewise, bakers reported that the cake was the newest status symbol. Each party cake had to outdo the previous party's cake. Vendors and customers alike thought it was important how outrageous and garish each decorated cake was made.

During this era of extravagance, it is not unusual for a bakery to spend three weeks on an individual cake that would cost thousands of dollars. For instance, one man ordered a 40" by 16" three dimensional cake to replicate his metallic blue-gray sports car. The finished cake cost $2,200, according to the *New York Times*. Ironically, at the same time the homeless and hungry were being herded from the street corners of New York!

In the face of such excesses, what would the Lord have said? An examination of Judges 2 suggests He might have accused the people of misplaced priorities and unbridled greed. He also might have censured them for refusing to admit that real life is not measured by how much people own, but by how justly and humanly they treat others (see Luke 12:15).

How to Stay Pure. A minister who was visiting a coal mine noticed a pure white flower growing at one of the tunnel entrances. When he asked the miner with him how the flower stayed white, the worker said, "Throw some coal dust on it." When the minister did, the dust slid right off the flower's smooth surface, enabling it to remain white.

That's how believers should be in the world—people who remain holy in an unholy place. The devastating alternative is seen in the lives of the Israelites during the time of the judges. They allowed the pagan ways of the Canaanites to corrupt their thinking and soil their spiritual lives. The result was unrelenting hardship and grief.

 FOR YOUTH

■ **TOPIC:** You Need to Listen

■ **QUESTIONS:** 1. Why did the Lord consider the Israelites' veneration of pagan deities to be abhorrent? 2. How did the Israelites' apostasy compare with the way in which the previous generation under Joshua had lived? 3. What would have been your response to the Lord's decision to let Israel's pagan neighbors overrun them? 4. How did the Lord display His mercy to His people in their times of distress? 5. What virtues would you have liked to see in the judges God raised up for Israel?

■ **ILLUSTRATIONS:**

Judges Bring Justice. In the story of Superman, a fictional character named Clark Kent leads a double life. In one scene, he's a mild-mannered reporter working for a large metropolitan newspaper. Then in the next scene, he's a larger-than-life hero who brings relief to the oppressed and the long arm of justice to villains.

Of course, in the real world there is no Superman. Even so, the desire of saved teens for justice is worthy of commendation. Help them understand that justice comes in many forms and can be fostered by how they choose to live. For instance, when they renounce sin, choose to listen to and heed God's commands, and display kindness to others, they are championing the cause of justice and promoting goodwill in the world. Explain that God will eternally bless His people when they conduct themselves in this way.

Modeling Care. South Bend's Center for the Homeless helps dozens of people each day. What is surprising is that young alumni and students run it from the University of Notre Dame's Center for Social Concerns.

Consider Shannon Cullinan. She developed a landscaping business that employs homeless people for eight months of training and then places them in other landscaping companies, especially as it cares for the properties in the City of South Bend, Memorial Hospital, WNDU Broadcasting, and the University properties. Then there's Drew Buscarieno. He developed a medical clinic, early childhood center, and drug and alcohol treatment center. He also developed educational facilities, job training, and care for the mentally ill.

Praised by the executive director of the National Coalition for the Homeless as a model of collaboration between university students and the local community, the center seeks to find solutions to the problems of the homeless. Here is a group of young people working to implement what God requires in their lives. Imagine how different the period of the judges would have been if the Israelites decided to operate in such a compassionate, unselfish way!

Protected from Harm. In 1893, the mayor of Chicago was shot and killed in his home. That murder motivated a local minister, Casimir Zeglen, to invent an early bulletproof vest. To prove the effectiveness of his invention, Zeglen himself submitted to a test in Chicago. He put on a vest made of the special material and an expert fired a revolver at the garment from a distance of eight paces. Amazingly, not one of the bullets disturbed the minister at all.

In the spiritual realm, the evil one is always shooting his flaming arrows at believers. But without the armor of God, we are defenseless. It is only when we put on His protective armor that we can withstand Satan's attacks. Tragically, the Israelites during the era of the judges failed to realize these truths, and they languished under the heavy weight of their moral compromise.

Use God's Strength

BACKGROUND SCRIPTURE: Judges 3:7-31; 21:25
DEVOTIONAL READING: Psalm 27:7-14

KEY VERSE: When the children of Israel cried unto the LORD, the LORD raised them up a deliverer, Ehud the son of Gera, a Benjamite, a man lefthanded. (Judges 3:15)

KING JAMES VERSION

JUDGES 3:15 But when the children of Israel cried unto the LORD, the LORD raised them up a deliverer, Ehud the son of Gera, a Benjamite, a man lefthanded: and by him the children of Israel sent a present unto Eglon the king of Moab. 16 But Ehud made him a dagger which had two edges, of a cubit length; and he did gird it under his raiment upon his right thigh. 17 And he brought the present unto Eglon king of Moab: and Eglon was a very fat man. 18 And when he had made an end to offer the present, he sent away the people that bare the present. 19 But he himself turned again from the quarries that were by Gilgal, and said, I have a secret errand unto thee, O king: who said, Keep silence. And all that stood by him went out from him. 20 And Ehud came unto him; and he was sitting in a summer parlour, which he had for himself alone. And Ehud said, I have a message from God unto thee. And he arose out of his seat. 21 And Ehud put forth his left hand, and took the dagger from his right thigh, and thrust it into his belly: 22 And the haft also went in after the blade; and the fat closed upon the blade, so that he could not draw the dagger out of his belly; and the dirt came out. 23 Then Ehud went forth through the porch, and shut the doors of the parlour upon him, and locked them. 24 When he was gone out, his servants came; and when they saw that, behold, the doors of the parlour were locked, they said, Surely he covereth his feet in his summer chamber. 25 And they tarried till they were ashamed: and, behold, he opened not the doors of the parlour; therefore they took a key, and opened them: and, behold, their lord was fallen down dead on the earth. . . . 29 And they slew of Moab at that time about ten thousand men, all lusty, and all men of valour; and there escaped not a man. 30 So Moab was subdued that day under the hand of Israel. And the land had rest fourscore years.

NEW REVISED STANDARD VERSION

JUDGES 3:15 But when the Israelites cried out to the Lord, the Lord raised up for them a deliverer, Ehud son of Gera, the Benjaminite, a left-handed man. The Israelites sent tribute by him to King Eglon of Moab. 16 Ehud made for himself a sword with two edges, a cubit in length; and he fastened it on his right thigh under his clothes. 17 Then he presented the tribute to King Eglon of Moab. Now Eglon was a very fat man. 18 When Ehud had finished presenting the tribute, he sent the people who carried the tribute on their way. 19 But he himself turned back at the sculptured stones near Gilgal, and said, "I have a secret message for you, O king." So the king said, "Silence!" and all his attendants went out from his presence. 20 Ehud came to him, while he was sitting alone in his cool roof chamber, and said, "I have a message from God for you." So he rose from his seat. 21 Then Ehud reached with his left hand, took the sword from his right thigh, and thrust it into Eglon's belly; 22 the hilt also went in after the blade, and the fat closed over the blade, for he did not draw the sword out of his belly; and the dirt came out. 23 Then Ehud went out into the vestibule, and closed the doors of the roof chamber on him, and locked them.

24 After he had gone, the servants came. When they saw that the doors of the roof chamber were locked, they thought, "He must be relieving himself in the cool chamber." 25 So they waited until they were embarrassed. When he still did not open the doors of the roof chamber, they took the key and opened them. There was their lord lying dead on the floor. . . .

29 At that time they killed about ten thousand of the Moabites, all strong, able-bodied men; no one escaped. 30 So Moab was subdued that day under the hand of Israel.

HOME BIBLE READINGS

BACKGROUND

During the time of the judges, Israel's true form of government was a theocracy. This means that no matter who led the people, the Lord alone was their King. As the nation's leader, God raised up a number of judges between Joshua's death and the coronation of Saul. The book mentions 12 people who served in this capacity: Othniel, Ehud, Shamgar, Deborah, Gideon, Tola, Jair, Jephthah, Ibzan, Elon, Abdon, and Samson. Some of these were major judges, military leaders whose deeds and accomplishments are recounted at length. Others were minor judges, individuals about whom little is known apart from their names.

Judges 3:1-6 expands on the observations found in 2:21-23, namely, that the Lord left large groups of native peoples of Canaan to test the loyalty of the Israelites who had not fought in the wars to control the land. The Hebrew verb rendered "prove" (3:1) means to examine, assess, or test. In this case, God used the unsettled situation in Canaan to verify the true nature of Israel's commitment to abide by the stipulations of the Mosaic covenant (vs. 4). The Lord also wanted the new generation of Israelites—who had no previous battle experience—to learn the art of warfare (vs. 2). Tragically, God's people disobeyed Him by intermarrying with idolaters and venerating their pagan deities (vss. 3, 5-6).

NOTES ON THE PRINTED TEXT

During the period of the judges, the coalition of Moabites, Ammonites, and Amalekites routed the Israelites and captured Jericho, which was known as the city of date palm trees (Judg. 3:13). Then, for the next 18 years, God's people suffered under the oppressive rule of the Moabite king (vs. 14).

From a spiritual perspective, when believers disobey the Lord, they bring hardship and sorrow into their lives. Soon to follow is God's loving discipline to get His people back on track. In the case of the Israelites, their situation became so deplorable that they eventually cried out in distress to the Lord. In turn, He raised up a person named Ehud to liberate them (vs. 15). Ehud was the son of Gera the Benjamite, about whom we know nothing. Ehud was left-handed, a trait characteristic of some other Benjamites (see 20:16). The Israelites decided to send Ehud and some other men to bring a payment of tribute to Eglon.

Ehud devised a daring plot to murder Eglon. This judge of God made a dagger-sized sword that had two edges and was about 18 inches in length. He strapped the weapon to his right thigh and hid it underneath his outer garment (3:16). Because Ehud was left-handed, he could hide his blade on the side where it would not have been suspected by Eglon. The Moabite king received the tribute that Ehud brought. Verse 17 notes that the monarch was extremely obese. This would turn out to be a liability that Ehud would exploit to his advantage.

After Ehud had dismissed the men who carried in the tribute, he also left the presence of the Moabite king (vs. 18). Ehud traveled as far as some carved images (perhaps sculptured stones or sacred pillars) near the city of Gilgal. Some think this town was located about a mile east of Jericho, while others place Gilgal about two miles southeast of Jericho. In any case, Ehud decided to turn back, claiming that he had a secret message for Eglon. It may be that Ehud returned alone to the king's court because he did not want to risk the arrest of those who were with him. Eglon wanted to hear what Ehud had to say, so he ordered his attendants to stop talking and directed them to leave.

Once all the monarch's attendants had left, Ehud came near. At this time, Eglon was sitting all by himself in his well-ventilated upper room (vs. 20). This chamber on the flat roof of the building probably had a cool breeze blowing through the latticed windows. The Moabite king stood up from his chair in reverence. Just then, Ehud used his left hand to pull his dagger-like sword from his right thigh. Next, he forcefully drove the blade into Eglon's enormous stomach (vs. 21). The king was so obese that the fat in his abdomen covered the entire dagger. Apparently, so much damage was inflicted that Eglon's bowels began to discharge (vs. 22). Ehud did not waste any time trying to pull out the sword. Instead, he quickly went out into the vestibule, locked the doors of the roof chamber, and proceeded on his way (vs. 23). Clearly, this judge of God was a decisive man of action! The Lord used this quality to bring His people relief from a tyrant.

Shortly after Ehud left, the king's attendants discovered that the doors of the roof chamber were "locked" (vs. 24). They assumed Eglon was literally "covering his feet" with his outer garments while he relieved himself in a bathroom located either within or attached to the well-ventilated upper room. But after a considerable amount of time had elapsed, the servants became increasingly anxious about Eglon's well-being. Finally, after a sufficiently long delay, the attendants got a key, opened the doors, and found the lifeless body of their "lord' (vs. 25) sprawled out on the floor. It's not hard to imagine the shock the servants felt at the sudden death of their master.

The circumstances could not have worked out better for Ehud. Indeed, he took full advantage of this time to escape. He passed by the carved images near Gilgal and then fled to Seirah (vs. 26). The location of Seirah is not known, though evidently it was in the hill country of Ephraim. When Ehud arrived at Seirah, he blew a trumpet to muster and lead an army of Israelites down from the hills to battle (vs. 27). He enjoined the warriors to follow him, and declared that the Lord had given them victory over their enemies, the Moabites. Here we find Ehud being careful to acknowledge that the Lord would enable His chosen people to overturn their foes. The verb tense used in verse 28 emphasized the certainty of the adversary's defeat. This meant that even though the victory had not yet occurred, from God's perspective it was already an accomplished fact.

The Israelites traveled east to the banks of the Jordan River leading to Moab and took control of the spot where the water could easily be crossed. In ancient times, a large group of soldiers could safely traverse the Jordan River only at its fords. This made these shallow crossing points militarily strategic. When the Jordan reached its flood stage during the spring, the river stretched at some places to more than a mile wide. The current during that time of year was probably strongest near the place where the Israelites originally crossed the river into Canaan (see Josh. 3–4). Today, the southern portion of the Jordan is about 90 to 100 feet wide and about three to ten feet deep during the summer. The decision of the Israelites under Ehud to prevent the enemy from crossing over the Jordan kept the enemy from obtaining reinforcements.

The Israelites were able to strike down Moabites fleeing from Jericho. Ehud's men killed 10,000 valiant, capable warriors. The victory was so complete that not one enemy combatant survived (Judg. 3:29). The triumph that day gave Israel control over Moab and provided God's people with 80 years of peace in the land (vs. 30). Unfortunately, after the death of Ehud, the cycle of oppression and deliverance occurred again. Like their predecessors, the next generation of Israelites acted in ways that were abhorrent to the Lord (4:1). Consequently, God allowed Jabin, a Canaanite king who ruled in Hazor, to defeat the Israelites and tyrannize them (vs. 2).

When the Israelites cried out to the Lord for help, He told Deborah, a prophetess, to call Barak into His service. Barak accepted the command to lead the Israelites against Jabin and his top commander, Sisera. Deborah agreed to help him (vss. 3-10). Sisera moved his fighting men and nine hundred iron chariots in the Valley of Jezreel. Going before Barak into battle, the Lord threw Sisera's forces into a panic, and the Canaanite army abandoned its chariots and attempted to flee on foot. Barak pursued them and destroyed the army of Sisera (vss. 11-16). With his army conquered, Sisera fled to the tent of Jael. This woman welcomed him into the tent. Sisera commanded Jael to misdirect anyone who asked for him. But when Sisera fell asleep, Jael drove a tent peg through his temple. The Israelites continued to grow stronger against Jabin, the Canaanite king, and his kingdom was destroyed (vss. 17-24).

These accounts from the Book of Judges remind us that it is God who enables us to be effective in our work for Him. As a matter of fact, Jesus said in John 15:5 that apart from Him we can accomplish nothing. The idea is that as believers remain spiritually united to the Son by faith, His life flows through them, and they continue to bear fruit. Apart from the life-giving resources of a vine, no branch can bear fruit of itself. In the same way, believers are wholly dependent upon the Messiah when it comes to being productive (vs. 4).

SUGGESTIONS TO TEACHERS

The late great classical scholar Frank Bourne taught Roman history at Princeton University. He was fond of saying, "In the age of Pax Americana, there's no more important lesson we can teach young Americans than the rise and decline of Pax Romana." He always began and ended his course with the Latin words *De Nobis fabula narratur*—"Their story is our story."

The same may be said about the lessons from the Old Testament. Our studies of individuals showcased in the Book of Judges must be understood as examples from history that God included in His written Word to encourage us to pursue uprightness (see 1 Cor. 10:6). Be sure to let the class know that this week's lesson concerns the account of how God empowered Ehud to lead his fellow Israelites to victory.

1. SCENE OF DESPAIR. The tribes of Israel had suffered 18 years of harassment and oppression from Eglon, the king of Moab. A sense of hopelessness pervaded the people. Only Ehud seemed to stand as a leader with faith.

2. STRATEGY FOR DELIVERANCE. This left-handed warrior knew that the Lord was the key personality for his fellow Israelites during their time of crisis. Point out that God chooses all sorts of believers to carry out His plans, and remind the class that the individual who trusts in the Lord will be the true leader.

3. SUCCESS FROM DECISIVENESS. Have the students consider the decisiveness it took for Ehud to single-handedly deal with Eglon. Because of the resurrection of the Son, believers are given confidence in the Father's ultimate victory. Regardless of the circumstance, we live in hope because of the Gospel.

4. SUPPORT FOR THE DISHEARTENED. Ehud was able to get his demoralized fellow Israelites to fight against their Moabite adversaries. Ehud's courage inspired even the most timid! Similarly, the person who trusts in God is empowered to stand up to the most negative and disbelieving doubter. Moreover, we Christians may sing with joy when we have Ehud's kind of commitment to God's work.

FOR ADULTS

■ TOPIC: Help from Unexpected Sources

■ QUESTIONS: 1. What circumstance led the Israelites to once again feel desperate? 2. What set apart Ehud as a gifted leader? 3. How might you use the talents God has given you to serve Him more effectively? 4. In what way did Ehud display courage and ingenuity in his dealings with Eglon? 5. What situation are you currently facing for which you especially need God's help?

■ **ILLUSTRATIONS:**

Help from Above. Amy's elderly mother, Susan, wanted to move from the nursing home by the end of the week. Staff members had forgotten her pills, residents had wandered into and out of her room, and she had been receiving little physical therapy after a major fall. To make matters worse, a well-meaning relative had responded to Susan's desire by unwittingly scheduling a move into an equally poor facility.

No one—not even the upbeat social worker of the other excellent home Amy found—believed the necessary paperwork could be completed in time. Susan's records needed to be transcribed and faxed from a busy Chicago hospital and from the office of a physician who had recently had a heart attack.

But as doors closed, a window opened. A sensitive, efficient hospital administrator acquired in one day what Amy was told would take three to four weeks. It became obvious that the Lord was going ahead of Amy and Susan. Just as God had with Ehud and his fellow Israelites (see Judg. 3:15, 28-30), the Lord arranged the battle strategy in this more contemporary situation—and now was winning the war.

Our Ally in Life's Battles. Judges 3:27-30 records a pivotal confrontation in which a Benjamite named Ehud led his fellow Israelites to victory over their Moabite foes. It's easy to look back at epic battles in the Bible and assume that God's strength comes with numbers. So how much does the Lord really care when the battles are the stuff of our everyday life—and there isn't a chariot or battering ram in sight?

"I used to think that God had more important things to do than hold my hand during every little crisis," Eileen says. "But I don't believe that anymore. Little crises start adding up, and they can take a toll on us spiritually and emotionally. Maybe this week it's a car repair that didn't go right. Maybe next week it's an unexpected illness or an awkward job review. In the big scheme of things, though, they aren't so bad. But if you don't remember that God is with you in those little battles, you might forget about Him when the big problems hit. And that would be terrible."

Sometimes, we may not see the glitches, setbacks, and struggles in our everyday experience as "battles." However, these skirmishes are definitely part of a battle for our thoughts, actions, and attitudes—our very lives. Through trial and error, Eileen came to realize that God does care about everything we experience.

Railway Worker Mishap. There once was a railway worker in Russia who accidentally locked himself in a refrigerator car. Because he was unable to escape or to attract attention, he resigned himself to his fate. As the hapless worker felt his body becoming numb, he took a pencil out of his pocket and recorded the story of his approaching death. He scribbled on the walls of the car: "I'm becoming colder . . . still colder . . . I'm slowly freezing . . . feeling half asleep—these may be my last words."

A short while later, after the car was opened, the man was found dead. But oddly enough, the temperature of the car was only about 56 degrees. Officials discovered that the freezing mechanism was out of order and that there was plenty of fresh, warm air available. In fact, there was no physical reason that they could find for the worker to have died. Eventually, it was concluded that he expired because he was convinced he would die.

From a spiritual perspective, we see that what we believe to be true affects us to the core of our being. Indeed, it shapes us and makes us what we are. What we believe either blesses us because it opens us up to the power of God, or it afflicts us because it blinds us to what we could be and what God is trying to do for us.

The Israelites seemed to understand these truths. After all, God's people had sufficient faith to cry out to Him for deliverance from their Moabite oppressors (Judg. 3:15). The Israelites also believed Ehud's declaration that the Lord would give them victory over their foes (vs. 28). Likewise, God is with us in our everyday battles and will help us to overcome them.

| FOR YOUTH | ▇ TOPIC: A Call for Help |

▇ **QUESTIONS:** 1. Why would the Lord raise up a deliverer for His people after they disobeyed Him? 2. What distinctive qualities has God given you to serve Him? 3. What plan did Ehud devise to deal with Eglon? 4. What are some appropriate ways you can be courageous for the Lord? 5. How did God use Ehud to lead the Israelites in victory over their enemies?

▇ **ILLUSTRATIONS:**

Depending on God. All leaders are expected to make decisions. The important choices the teens in your class have to make spotlights their need to develop strong Christian principles. This will help them guard against such vices as greed, covetousness, and sensuality. They need to grow in their ability to discern and avoid choices that will weaken their faith and their Christian testimony.

When faced with a dilemma, teens should not go it alone. As the Israelites did during their time of crisis (see Judg. 3:15), so, too, saved adolescents can call out to the Lord for help. Even as leaders, they can benefit from the advice God provides through their parents, pastors, and youth ministers (to name a few important people). God can use the input of significant others to steer youth away from the harmful tendencies of their peers. Let your students know that it never pays to rush into something without first praying and asking God to direct their paths.

An Employer and Friend. On NPR's *Morning Edition*, Katie Simon tells how Gus Hernandez and Siddiqi Hansoti became friends. Gus worked as a mortgage consultant until 2008, when he was laid off from his job. Soon his dire financial situation led to him being evicted from his home.

After Gus and his family "spent a couple of nights in their car," he used a phone book to find the "El Dorado Motel in Salinas, California." It was an increasingly desperate circumstance when Gus entered the motel and told Siddiqi, the owner, that "he needed a place to stay but only had $50 in his pocket." In response, Siddiqi said to Gus, "Put that away. I'll trust you."

Rather than owe Siddiqi a pile of money, Gus "offered to leave the motel after his family had been there for three weeks." In response, Siddiqi said he "needed a handyman." He proposed that Gus could both have the job and "continue to live in the motel." Gus accepted the offer and now is in charge of maintenance at Siddiqi's motel. Gus noted that "when I had money, I had a lot of friends, but when I didn't, Sid was there."

There's a sense in which Gus was making a plea for help and Siddiqi responded. During the time of the judges, the Israelites cried out to God for deliverance and He provided Ehud (see Judg. 3:15). Perhaps the Lord might use you in a special way to reach out to others in need. When you rely totally on Him, it's hard to imagine how much good He can accomplish through you for His glory!

An Eagle or a Chicken? Experts tell us that what we believe can make a huge difference in how our lives turn out. For instance, if the Israelites had doubted that God cared about them, they would not have looked to Him for deliverance from a Moabite tyrant named Eglon (see Judg. 3:15). God's people would have missed an opportunity for victory had they doubted whether He was working through Ehud (see vs. 28).

The truth of these observations is illustrated by the following fable. Once upon a time, a man found the egg of an eagle. It had been abandoned for some reason by its mother. But because it was still warm, the man took it and put it in the nest of one of his backyard chickens. There it lay along with the other eggs being brooded upon.

After a period of time, the eaglet was hatched. Then, along with the other chicks from its nest, it began to go about the backyard doing what the other chicks did. It scratched the earth for worms and insects. It looked for the corn that the man would throw into the yard. The eaglet clucked as best as it could. And as it grew, it would, like all the chickens around it, thrash its wings, squawk its beak, and hop a few feet in the air.

Years passed in this way, and the eagle grew very old. One day it saw a magnificent bird far above it in the cloudless sky. This creature glided majestically among the powerful wind currents, soaring and swooping, scarcely beating its long golden wings. The old eagle looked up at the bird in awe and asked, "What is that?" A chicken cackled, "Why, that's an eagle! It's the king of the birds! It belongs to the sky and to the high places. We belong to the earth, because we're just chickens." The old eagle was convinced that this statement was true. And so it was that the bird lived and died as a chicken, for that is what it believed about itself.

LET GOD RULE

BACKGROUND SCRIPTURE: Judges 6—8; 21:25
DEVOTIONAL READING: 1 Samuel 2:1-10

KEY VERSE: When Gideon heard the telling of the dream, and the interpretation thereof, that he worshiped, and returned into the host of Israel, and said, Arise; for the LORD hath delivered into your hand the host of Midian. (Judges 7:15)

KING JAMES VERSION

JUDGES 7:2 And the LORD said unto Gideon, The people that are with thee are too many for me to give the Midianites into their hands, lest Israel vaunt themselves against me, saying, Mine own hand hath saved me.
3 Now therefore go to, proclaim in the ears of the people, saying, Whosoever is fearful and afraid, let him return and depart early from mount Gilead. And there returned of the people twenty and two thousand; and there remained ten thousand. 4 And the LORD said unto Gideon, The people are yet too many; bring them down unto the water, and I will try them for thee there: and it shall be, that of whom I say unto thee, This shall go with thee, the same shall go with thee; and of whomsoever I say unto thee, This shall not go with thee, the same shall not go. . . .

13 And when Gideon was come, behold, there was a man that told a dream unto his fellow, and said, Behold, I dreamed a dream, and, lo, a cake of barley bread tumbled into the host of Midian, and came unto a tent, and smote it that it fell, and overturned it, that the tent lay along. 14 And his fellow answered and said, This is nothing else save the sword of Gideon the son of Joash, a man of Israel: for into his hand hath God delivered Midian, and all the host. 15 And it was so, when Gideon heard the telling of the dream, and the interpretation thereof, that he worshiped, and returned into the host of Israel, and said, Arise; for the LORD hath delivered into your hand the host of Midian. . . .

8:22 Then the men of Israel said unto Gideon, Rule thou over us, both thou, and thy son, and thy son's son also: for thou hast delivered us from the hand of Midian. 23 And Gideon said unto them, I will not rule over you, neither shall my son rule over you: the LORD shall rule over you. 24 And Gideon said unto them, I would desire a request of you, that ye would give me every man the earrings of his prey. (For they had golden earrings, because they were Ishmaelites.) 25 And they answered, We will willingly give them. And they spread a garment, and did cast therein every man the earrings of his prey.

NEW REVISED STANDARD VERSION

JUDGES 7:2 The Lord said to Gideon, "The troops with you are too many for me to give the Midianites into their hand. Israel would only take the credit away from me, saying, 'My own hand has delivered me.'
3 Now therefore proclaim this in the hearing of the troops, 'Whoever is fearful and trembling, let him return home.' " Thus Gideon sifted them out; twenty-two thousand returned, and ten thousand remained.

4 Then the Lord said to Gideon, "The troops are still too many; take them down to the water and I will sift them out for you there. When I say, 'This one shall go with you,' he shall go with you; and when I say, 'This one shall not go with you,' he shall not go." . . .

13 When Gideon arrived, there was a man telling a dream to his comrade; and he said, "I had a dream, and in it a cake of barley bread tumbled into the camp of Midian, and came to the tent, and struck it so that it fell; it turned upside down, and the tent collapsed."
14 And his comrade answered, "This is no other than the sword of Gideon son of Joash, a man of Israel; into his hand God has given Midian and all the army."

15 When Gideon heard the telling of the dream and its interpretation, he worshiped; and he returned to the camp of Israel, and said, "Get up; for the Lord has given the army of Midian into your hand." . . .

8:22 Then the Israelites said to Gideon, "Rule over us, you and your son and your grandson also; for you have delivered us out of the hand of Midian."
23 Gideon said to them, "I will not rule over you, and my son will not rule over you; the Lord will rule over you." 24 Then Gideon said to them, "Let me make a request of you; each of you give me an earring he has taken as booty." (For the enemy had golden earrings, because they were Ishmaelites.) 25 "We will willingly give them," they answered. So they spread a garment, and each threw into it an earring he had taken as booty.

Monday, July 18	1 Samuel 2:1-10	*No Holy One like the Lord*
Tuesday, July 19	Deuteronomy 13:1-5	*Follow the Lord Only*
Wednesday, July 20	Judges 6:1-10	*Suffering Oppression*
Thursday, July 21	Judges 6:11-16	*I Will Be with You*
Friday, July 22	Judges 6:25-32	*A First Act of Obedience*
Saturday, July 23	Judges 6:36-40	*Seeking a Sign from God*
Sunday, July 24	Judges 7:2-4, 13-15; 8:22-25	*The Lord Will Rule*

BACKGROUND

Judges 6–8 records the account of Gideon's judgeship over Israel (1162–1122 B.C.). We learn that when the Israelites returned to their evil ways, the Lord allowed the Midianites to oppress them for seven years (6:1). The Midianites were a confederation of desert peoples alternately in alliance and at war with Israel. Jacob's son, Joseph, was sold by his brothers to some Midianite traders (Gen. 37:28, 36). Years later, when Moses fled from the pharaoh of Egypt, he found shelter with Jethro, a priest of Midian (Exod. 2:15-16). When Israel was in the Transjordan and preparing to enter Palestine, the elders of the Midianite and Moabites tried to hire Balaam to curse God's people (Num. 22:4-7). Some Midianite women were evidently involved in leading Israel into apostasy (25:6). Five Midianite kings and their men were slain by the Israelites (31:7-8).

In the days of Gideon, the Israelites were forced to flee to shelters in mountain clefts and caves. When they were totally impoverished, the Israelites cried out to the Lord for help and He sent them a prophet. The spokesperson delivered words reminding them of God's past deliverance and of their failure to obey Him (Judg. 6:2-10). Around that time, Gideon was threshing wheat in a winepress when an angel of the Lord appeared to him. After the emissary explained that Gideon was to lead the Israelites into battle against the Midianites, Gideon noted that his clan was the weakest and he himself was the least in his family. Gideon requested a sign and then left to prepare an offering. When he returned with an offering of meat and bread, the angel told him to place them on a rock. The emissary touched the offering with his staff, and fire consumed it. In response, Gideon built an altar there and called it "The Lord is Peace" (vss. 11-24).

NOTES ON THE PRINTED TEXT

In Judges 6, we see how timid and hesitant Gideon was about going into the battle against the Midianites. In chapter 7, we see him filled with courage to battle these enemies of God and His people. This change in Gideon's behavior is evident in verse 1, which says that Gideon and all his troops established their camp at the spring of Harod.

Though Gideon led the Israelite troops, the Lord was the supreme commander of His people. He told Gideon that he had too many warriors in his army (vs. 2). God wanted to reduce the size of this fighting force so that the Israelites would not brag that their own prowess delivered them from the Midianites. This way Israel would learn that the victory always came from the Lord. Gideon announced to his troops that anyone who trembled with fear at the prospect of fighting was permitted to leave Mount Gilead (vs. 3). As a result of Gideon's offer, 22,000 left and 10,000 remained. The original fighting force, then, numbered 32,000. This was less than one-fourth of the Midianite invasion force, which numbered 135,000 (see 8:10).

Even after Gideon lost two-thirds of his soldiers, the Lord still considered Gideon's army too large. The Lord alone was Israel's defender, and He wanted to ensure that His people understood this. The Israelites were oppressed by the Midianites because of their unfaithfulness. The Hebrews worshiped pagan gods and rejected the Lord as their sole source of power and protection. In order to turn the hearts of the people back to Him, God made it impossible for them to obtain total victory over the Midianites except through His power. Thus the Lord told Gideon to lead the remainder of his troops down to the spring of Harod. There the exalted, supreme commander of Israel's armies was going to sift them some more (7:4). God's filter was going to be the manner by which each soldier drank water from the spring. Some would lap the water from their hands, while others would kneel down and place their mouths directly in the stream to drink the water (vs. 5).

Three hundred soldiers used their hands to bring the water to their mouths, while the rest of the warriors got down on their knees (vs. 6). The Lord told Gideon that He would defeat the massive Midianite invasion force with only the 300 men who lapped from their hands. The rest returned to their homes (vs. 7). God was clearly in charge of the military operation, and Gideon was following His orders. In accordance with the Lord's instructions, Gideon dismissed the 9,700 men. This means that less than 1 percent of the original fighting force returned to battle the horde of Midianites. These 300 Israelites were more than enough to defeat the enemy. In reality, the Lord did not have to use any of them (see 1 Sam. 14:6).

The remaining 300 soldiers took the provisions (which perhaps were stored in jars) and the trumpets that the rest of the troops had left behind. Meanwhile, the Midianite camp was about three and one-half miles north of the Israelite camp, and somewhat lower in elevation (Judg. 7:8). During the middle of the night, the Lord told Gideon to get up and prepare to invade. The Israelites were to attack the enemy camp, for God was about to give His people victory over them (vs. 9). The Lord's sovereign timing of events was perfect and would ensure that the Midianites were defeated at the hands of His people. Gideon may have wondered how he and his small band of men would ever be able to defeat the huge invasion force. The Lord, who knows all things, was aware of Gideon's fears. For this reason, God graciously invited Gideon to take his servant, Purah, and spy out the enemy camp (vs. 10). The Lord told Gideon that when he and his servant came to the enemy camp, they were to listen to what the soldiers were saying. Gideon would be so encouraged by what he heard that his apprehension would disappear (vs. 11).

Gideon and Purah obeyed the Lord and went to the edge of the enemy camp. They discovered that it was swarming with Midianites, Amalekites, and other nomadic peoples from the desert region east of Moab and Ammon. There were so many of them that they seemed as thick as locusts. Likewise, there were so many camels that they appeared to exceed the grains of sand on the seashore (vs. 12). Gideon overheard a man telling his friend about his dream. An enemy soldier had just awakened from a dream in which a stale cake of barley bread tumbled into the Midianite camp. The cake struck a tent so hard that it turned over and fell flat (vs. 13). The man's comrade explained that his dream was about the sword of Gideon. (Interestingly, the Midianites not only knew that Gideon was the person who commanded the Israelite army, but also that he was the son of a man named Joash.) Just as the tent overturned and collapsed from the force of the barley cake, so, too, the army of Midian would be routed by the Israelites. God would enable Gideon and his band of warriors to wipe out the entire invasion force (vs. 14).

Undoubtedly, Gideon was astonished by the conversation he overheard. He bowed down in gratitude and worshiped the Lord (vs. 15). Next, Gideon and Purah returned to the Israelite camp. Gideon's lingering doubts finally vanished. He was now absolutely certain that God would enable His people to triumph over their foes. When Gideon arrived at the camp of Israel, he awakened his men and announced that the Lord had already given them victory over the Midianite coalition. Gideon's newfound trust in the Lord would help to bolster the confidence of his troops and result in their victory of their foes. The Israelites were so grateful to Gideon for rescuing them from their Midianite oppressors that he was invited to become the Israelites' king, with his son and grandson succeeding him (8:22). Perhaps the people thought that a strong leader would prevent them from falling prey to invaders in the future.

Gideon wisely declined the offer to become king and stressed that the Lord was to rule over the Israelites (vs. 23). Gideon understood that God's people were supposed to put their trust in His leadership. Though Gideon turned down the offer to rule the Israelites, he did request that each of the people give him an earring (or possibly a nose ring) from the plunder. The Ishmaelites were known for their gold earrings (vs. 24). The descendants of Ishmael, the son of Abraham and Hagar (see Gen. 16:15), were interrelated with the Midianites and often identified with them (see 37:25, 28). Like the Midianites, the Ishmaelites led a nomadic existence in the desert region east of the Jordan River.

The Israelites were willing to grant Gideon's request. After spreading out the garment, each person tossed an earring from his plunder into it (Judg. 8:25). Altogether the gold rings weighed 1,700 shekels, that is, between 35 and 75 pounds, depending on whether the light or heavy shekel was used (vs. 26). In addition, Gideon received the crescent-shaped ornaments, necklaces, and purple robes that the kings of Midian had been wearing. He also obtained the chains that the Midianite kings had placed around the necks of their camels. Gideon made a terrible decision about how to use his new wealth. He made an ephod of gold from the items he received. This ornate garment, which he placed in Ophrah, became an object of worship for the Israelites. They committed spiritual adultery by bowing down in reverence to it. Ultimately, the object became a moral trap that caused Gideon and his entire family to sin (vs. 27).

SUGGESTIONS TO TEACHERS

One school of historians insists that an understanding of a nation's history comes when one studies its leaders' lives. These personalities shape events. This week's lesson centers on a man who shaped events in ancient Israel—Gideon. The clue to his success was his eventual obedience to God. Your emphasis in this lesson will be to help your class grow more obedient to the Lord.

1. DESPAIR FROM DISOBEDIENCE. The rampaging Midianites and Amalakites had plundered and destroyed the land of the Israelites so frequently and for so long that most felt a sense of hopelessness. The reason for the despair was a lack of trust in the Lord. But God had not given up on His people. In a time when the conditions seem hopeless, remind your class that God calls us to be faithful! Through the Son, the Father pleads with us to be obedient to His ways and His will.

2. DECLARATION BY THE DEITY. God always raises up leaders to carry out His plans. In Judges 6–8, God called Gideon. The task appeared to be overwhelming. But God promised, "I will be with thee" (6:16). With the presence of the Lord, we may move forward with confidence regardless of the opposition against His will.

3. DESIGN FOR DEFEAT. Initially, Gideon was skeptical of God's call and God's power. Finally, after Gideon was convinced to serve God with total obedience, Gideon was given a battle plan for victory. God does more than offer encouragement. He also gives guidance to believers who will listen. And we listen with the aid of the Spirit, especially as we study Scripture and pray.

4. DEMONSTRATION OF DECISION. Gideon was ordered to pare down his huge horde of fighters to a lean strike force of only 300. This elite unit arrayed against the enormous enemy army was to show God's great power. Gideon and other "knowledgeable" strategists probably thought it was foolhardy to strip down the Israelite collection of armed men to a mere 300, but they obeyed God. Victory resulted.

5. DISASTER FROM DISCIPLINE. Those 300 men under Gideon followed his orders completely, thereby routing the opposing army in a nighttime surprise attack. These 300 Israelites brought victory through their obedience to Gideon's commands and thus to God's. Obedience to the Lord turns disaster into triumph.

<table>
<tr><td>

**FOR
ADULTS**
</td><td>

■ **TOPIC:** Following Wise Leaders
■ **QUESTIONS:** 1. What were some of Gideon's fears? How did God
</td></tr>
</table>

address them? 2. What were some of Gideon's strengths that he displayed in the battle against the Midianites? 3. What challenges do you feel God has
called you to accept? 4. How does the Christian faith help a person to deal with feelings of inadequacy? 5. How can Christian leaders encourage their fellow believers to
courageously follow the Lord?

■ **ILLUSTRATIONS:**

Chosen to Win. In contrast to Gideon, the likelihood of our being chosen to lead an
army into battle is not very great. However, God gives us many other opportunities to
win battles for Him and wise Christian leaders to guide us along the way. In fact, each
day is a battle for our love and allegiance. The greatest battles often center around our
thoughts, feelings, and actions.

Sometimes, it seems as if we never get out of the entanglements of moral and spiritual warfare. In our struggles to trust and obey the Lord, He is training us to win the
one great battle that really counts, namely, the fight between Himself and Satan for
our souls.

We know that Jesus is stronger than the devil. When we put our trust in the Lord,
we can depend on Him to help us win the battles we face. Like Gideon, we may feel
overwhelmed. But remember that the Spirit who indwells us is greater than the evil
one who is in the world (see 1 John 4:4).

Faced with Choices. The dad, in his 40s, was earning a comfortable wage and was
advancing in his career. The mom was successfully teaching their three children at
home. Their church life was busy and satisfying. They were happy living in their well-
kept Victorian house in Middle America.

Then it struck. No, it wasn't a midlife crisis. It was something more significant—
midfaith challenge. The dad, who had long prayed for God's direction, felt called to
train for ministry. The family pulled up stakes and moved out of state. They traded
their large Victorian house for a small mobile home. The husband went to class and
worked part-time. The wife worked three-quarter time, while the children attended a
local school nearby.

Like this family, each time our faith is challenged, we are faced with choices: Will
we trust to the point that we obey without doubting? Will we let go of our fears of
what others might think? Will we remember God's track record of faithfulness to us?

Perhaps these are the same sorts of questions Gideon struggled with as he responded to the call of God on his life. Like Gideon, we must choose to step over each stumbling block of hesitation and remember that God provides the strength and resources
to handle the challenges He brings to our lives.

Stepping Up to the Challenge. Seven months after quitting her salaried job to start a home-based craft business, Sharon was beginning to doubt her decision. "I was lugging my stuff to all of the craft shows in the state, spending hours and days driving to malls and fairgrounds." But it didn't seem to be paying off. "When I was making shirts, everyone wanted bears. When I switched to bears, they all asked for Christmas ornaments."

Still, Sharon believed God had helped her dream become a reality. "I figured He didn't bring me this far just to let me flounder. I realized that God had already given me everything I needed to succeed. I just needed to use those gifts and interests and step up to the challenge."

Sharon decided to follow her heart rather than the whims of her customers. "I started carrying decorative bird houses with Bible verses on them. At first, they were so unusual that people didn't know what to make of them. But I kept praying about them, praying about the customers that would put them in their homes, and things started to turn around."

In this week's lesson, we learn about the struggles Gideon had in responding to God's leading. In response to these doubts, God reminded Gideon that he already had his God-given strength and mission. All he needed was a push to meet his challenges head-on and put that strength to use.

■ TOPIC: God Rules!

■ QUESTIONS: 1. Who were the Midianites? 2. What was Gideon's response to God's call? 3. How do you react to impossible odds or jobs? 4. Why was God concerned about the number of soldiers in Gideon's army? 5. How can we be encouraged in the knowledge that God used Gideon, despite his doubts?

■ ILLUSTRATIONS:

Be Obedient. Adolescents are expected to obey their parents. And soldiers are expected to obey their commanding officer. In fact, in every walk of life, obedience is a key principle.

The events recorded in Scripture mostly revolve around the issue of whether God's people would recognize His rule over their lives and obey Him. Paul noted that these narratives serve as a warning to us against craving evil things (1 Cor. 10:6). We also remember the statement of our Savior, who said, "If a man love me, he will keep my words" (John 14:23).

When we put our trust in the Lord Jesus, we are promising to obey Him. The account of Gideon, which is the focus of this week's lesson, encourages us to do God's will even against seemingly insurmountable obstacles.

Keeping Perfect Time. Like the Israelites in Gideon's day, our waiting on God for an answer to our prayers can be challenging. This is especially so after we've prayed about something for a long while. Eventually, though, we learn as Gideon did that God's timing is perfect.

It would be silly to ask a newborn baby to run a marathon. It's not the right timing. It would be odd to see someone saying to a rosebud, "Open up, now!" When the time is right, the baby will walk, then run. The rose will bloom one day, but no one can make it happen any faster. As we learn from God's dealings with Gideon, He has His reasons. While we may not know why God does what He does, we can trust the wisdom behind His rule.

There are many references to a right time or an "appointed time" in the Bible. Here are just a few: God sent His Son to earth at the appointed time. "But when the fullness of the time was come, God sent forth his Son" (Gal. 4:4). Abraham and Sarah had their baby, Isaac, at the appointed time. "Is any thing too hard for the LORD? At the time appointed I will return unto thee, according to the time of life, and Sarah shall have a son" (Gen. 18:14). Jesus died for us at the right time. "For when we were yet without strength, in due time Christ died for the ungodly" (Rom. 5:6). Yes, waiting can be hard. But God is never late. He keeps perfect time.

When the Time Comes. A U.S. Army officer told about the contrast in his pupils during two different eras of teaching at the artillery training school at Fort Sill, Oklahoma. In 1958–60, the attitude was so lax that the instructors had a problem getting the men to stay awake to listen. During the 1965–67 classes, however, the men, hearing the same basic lectures, were alert and took copious notes. The reason? These men knew that in less than six weeks they would be facing the enemy in Vietnam.

One reason that Bible study seems to be irrelevant to many Christians is that they have no interaction with non-Christians, no vital ministry to growing believers, and no personal and internal struggle for godliness, all of which are factors that bring the truths of the Bible to life. Like Gideon, we need to be ready to take action for God when the time comes, including speaking the truth of His Word. God will use our prayers and times of Bible study to prepare us for the battles we will face.

RETURN TO OBEDIENCE

BACKGROUND SCRIPTURE: Judges 10:6–11:33; 21:25

DEVOTIONAL READING: Judges 10:10-18

KEY VERSE: [The Israelites] put away the strange gods from among them, and served the LORD: and his soul was grieved for the misery of Israel. (Judges 10:16)

KING JAMES VERSION

JUDGES 10:10 And the children of Israel cried unto the LORD, saying, We have sinned against thee, both because we have forsaken our God, and also served Baalim. 11 And the LORD said unto the children of Israel, Did not I deliver you from the Egyptians, and from the Amorites, from the children of Ammon, and from the Philistines? 12 The Zidonians also, and the Amalekites, and the Maonites, did oppress you; and ye cried to me, and I delivered you out of their hand. 13 Yet ye have forsaken me, and served other gods: wherefore I will deliver you no more. 14 Go and cry unto the gods which ye have chosen; let them deliver you in the time of your tribulation. 15 And the children of Israel said unto the LORD, We have sinned: do thou unto us whatsoever seemeth good unto thee; deliver us only, we pray thee, this day. 16 And they put away the strange gods from among them, and served the LORD: and his soul was grieved for the misery of Israel. 17 Then the children of Ammon were gathered together, and encamped in Gilead. And the children of Israel assembled themselves together, and encamped in Mizpeh. 18 And the people and princes of Gilead said one to another, What man is he that will begin to fight against the children of Ammon? he shall be head over all the inhabitants of Gilead.

NEW REVISED STANDARD VERSION

JUDGES 10:10 So the Israelites cried to the Lord, saying, "We have sinned against you, because we have abandoned our God and have worshiped the Baals." 11 And the Lord said to the Israelites, "Did I not deliver you from the Egyptians and from the Amorites, from the Ammonites and from the Philistines? 12 The Sidonians also, and the Amalekites, and the Maonites, oppressed you; and you cried to me, and I delivered you out of their hand. 13 Yet you have abandoned me and worshiped other gods; therefore I will deliver you no more. 14 Go and cry to the gods whom you have chosen; let them deliver you in the time of your distress." 15 And the Israelites said to the Lord, "We have sinned; do to us whatever seems good to you; but deliver us this day!" 16 So they put away the foreign gods from among them and worshiped the Lord; and he could no longer bear to see Israel suffer.

17 Then the Ammonites were called to arms, and they encamped in Gilead; and the Israelites came together, and they encamped at Mizpah. 18 The commanders of the people of Gilead said to one another, "Who will begin the fight against the Ammonites? He shall be head over all the inhabitants of Gilead."

9

Monday, July 25	2 Corinthians 7:5-11	*Grief Leading to Repentance*
Tuesday, July 26	1 Kings 8:46-50	*The Path to Forgiveness*
Wednesday, July 27	Ezekiel 18:25-32	*New Hearts and New Spirits*
Thursday, July 28	Luke 13:1-9	*Unless You Repent*
Friday, July 29	Revelation 3:14-22	*God's Loving Reproof*
Saturday, July 30	Luke 24:44-49	*Proclaiming Repentance and Forgiveness*
Sunday, July 31	Judges 10:10-18	*Repentance and Submission*

BACKGROUND

After Gideon died, the citizens of Shechem and Beth Millo made Abimelech their king. Abimelech treacherously murdered his 70 brothers except for Jotham, Gideon's youngest son. From the heights of Mount Gerizim, Jotham used a parable to rebuke the people for making Abimelech their king. After three more years of Abimelech's rule, the citizens of Shechem became disenchanted with him. A man named Gaal came to the city and tried to turn the people against Abimelech. Then he and his soldiers attacked Shechem and routed Gaal's men. After massacring the people of the city, Abimelech's forces destroyed it (Judg. 9:1-49).

During the siege of Thebez (13 miles northeast of Shechem), Abimelech was mortally wounded when a woman in the city's tower dropped a millstone on him. At Abimelech's request, his armor-bearer ended his life. When the Israelites saw that Abimelech was dead, they went home. God thus repaid Abimelech and the citizens of Shechem for all their evil deeds (vss. 50-57). After Abimelech died, a man named Tola from the hill country of Ephraim judged Israel for 23 years (10:1-2). After Tola died, a man named Jair from Gilead judged Israel for 22 years (vss. 3-5).

NOTES ON THE PRINTED TEXT

The cycle of oppression and deliverance is seen again in the events leading up to the judgeship of Jephthah (1078–1072 B.C.). A new generation of Israelites disobeyed God. In addition to serving the idols of Baal and Ashtoreth, the people venerated a host of other pagan deities (Judg. 10:6). The Israelites' false worship represented a wholehearted devotion to idolatry. Rather than exclusively serving the Lord, the people abandoned their commitment to Yahweh. This amounted to spiritual adultery. It is sad to read that the great God of Israel was no longer the sole object of His people's devotion. The Lord's anger was kindled against His wayward people, and He turned them over to the Philistines and the Ammonites (vs. 7). The enemies ruthlessly oppressed the Israelites for 18 years (vs. 8).

The Philistines and Ammonites afflicted the Israelites on the east side of the Jordan River in the region of Gilead. The Ammonites also crossed the Jordan River and invaded the western highlands that belonged to the tribes of Judah, Benjamin, and

Ephraim. God's people suffered greatly during this extended period. It's possible to understand verse 9 to be saying that the Israelites felt hemmed-in by their foes, with the latter leaving no way of escape for those they raided. As the distress and losses experienced by the Israelites piled up from one year to the next, the situation eventually became unbearable. The circumstance became so dire that the Hebrews cried out to the Lord for help. They acknowledged that they had abandoned their commitment to God and venerated the idols of Baal (vs. 10). For a long time, the Israelites tried to worship the Lord on their terms, not His. They wanted a deity who would fulfill their agendas, not the reverse.

In verses 11-12, the Lord recounted that He had rescued His people from those who lived both inside and outside of Canaan. These enemies included Egyptians, Amorites, Ammonites, Philistines, Sidonians, Amalekites, and Maonites. The last group may have lived in the hill country of Judah south of Hebron. (Some ancient Greek manuscripts read "Midianites" instead of "Maonites.") God not only rebuked His people for their apostasy, but also refused to deliver them from their present calamity (vs. 13). Since the Israelites continued to venerate pagan deities, the Lord told them to cry out to those gods for help. Then the Hebrews would see how powerless these lifeless idols were to deliver them in the day of calamity (vs. 14).

The Israelites realized the false gods and goddesses of the Canaanites could not free them from their oppressors. In desperation, they acknowledged that they had "sinned" (vs. 15). The underlying Hebrew verb focuses attention on both violation of the Lord's commands and the resulting guilt and punishment that are incurred. God's people were willing to accept whatever discipline He inflicted. Even so, they petitioned Him for relief from the anguish they suffered at the hands of the Ammonites. The discipline of the Lord, though often hard to endure, always has a definite end, and is always lined with grace. The Israelites showed evidence of their repentance by getting rid of their pagan deities and giving the Lord their exclusive worship. Their wholehearted repentance evoked God's compassion, as seen in His grieving over the suffering His people endured (vs. 16).

At some point, the Ammonites assembled their troops for war and camped in Gilead. This name refers in general to an area on the east bank of the Jordan River that extended from the Arnon River in the south to the Bashan River in the north, and to the desert in the east. In verse 17, the name of Gilead is loosely used to refer to a particular city (perhaps Ramoth Gilead). The Israelites responded by gathering their forces and camping at Mizpah, which in Hebrew means "lookout" or "watchtower." Some experts think this town was located north of the Jabbok River, while others think the town was south of it. A few authorities have suggested that the town was Ramoth Mizpah (see Josh. 13:26), which was located about 18 miles east of Jericho.

The leaders of Gilead recognized the threat posed by the Ammonites. The Israelites searched for people who would courageously lead their warriors to victory against the enemy. To encourage someone to volunteer for the job, a promise was made that the triumphant commander would be made ruler of Gilead's territory (Judg. 10:18). The officials chose Jephthah to marshal their forces. Background information concerning him is found in 11:1-3. He was renowned as a valiant and spirited warrior. He was also the son of a prostitute and a man named Gilead.

Apparently, Jephthah was the only illegitimate child in his family. When Gilead's sons were full-grown, they denied their stepbrother a share in the family inheritance and forced him to leave their father's home. Jephthah became the leader of a group of outlaws and bandits who lived in a desolate area called Tob. This area was east of the Jordan River, north of the hill country of Gilead, and about 15 miles northeast of Ramoth Gilead. Jephthah and his band of misfits may have survived by making raids on settled communities in the Tob district and on caravans of merchants that regularly passed through the area.

When the Ammonites attacked the Israelites, the elders (or leaders) of Gilead came to Jephthah for help (vss. 4-5). They had heard about his exploits and wanted to hire him to lead their fighting men into battle (vs. 6). In those days, it was common for the leaders of a community to hire mercenaries to help them achieve their military and political objectives (see 9:4). Jephthah was surprised that the elders of Gilead wanted to hire him as their field commander. After all, they had played a significant role in forcing him from his father's house. Jephthah wondered why people who despised him so much would now look to him for help in their time of distress (11:7). Gilead's leaders did not debate with Jephthah. Instead, they pledged their loyalty and repeated their request for Jephthah to lead their forces in battle against the Ammonites. This time, however, the elders upped the ante. The former outcast would not only be commander but also a permanent chief over all who lived in Gilead (vs. 8).

This new offer appealed to Jephthah, and so he asked the officials how serious they were. Would they really make him their regional head if the Lord enabled him to rout the Ammonites? Some take verse 9 as an affirmative statement rather than a question. In this case, Jephthah would be repeating the terms of the agreement to officially confirm the intent of Gilead's leaders. Regardless of which option is preferred, it is clear that the city's elders were desperate. They needed someone to effectively lead their troops to victory. Thus, they solemnly called on Yahweh, the God of Israel, as a witness to verify that they would keep their promise to Jephthah (vs. 10).

The officials' vow became a binding oath in which they were legally obligated to fulfill what they had pledged. Jephthah was convinced that the elders of Gilead were serious. He agreed not only to be the field commander, but also to assume the role of tribal chief should he defeat the Ammonites. The negotiations were formally concluded when Jephthah repeated his pledge before the leaders and people of Gilead. Jephthah wanted to be accountable for what he had promised. He made his vow "before the LORD in Mizpah" (vs. 11), which affirms that God was the final arbitrator of the pact being ratified, especially should any grievance arise between Jephthah and Gilead's officials.

SUGGESTIONS TO TEACHERS

This week's lesson spotlights a generation of Israelites who were grieving because they had experienced judgment for their sin. You may have students who are trying to come to terms with the consequences of sinful behavior. Consider using the teaching time to encourage them to take the opportunity to seek the Lord. Also, be sure to encourage everyone to find hope in the Lord, regardless of the circumstances they face in their life.

1. SEVERE JUDGMENT. The Israelites acknowledged that their sins had provoked the wrath of God to the point that the Lord sent foreign invaders as agents of His judgment (Judg. 10:10). Remind your students that the consequences of sin are typically built into the behavior itself. We know that we risk reputation and respect, perhaps even family and career, when we gossip, lie, cheat, steal, commit adultery, or abuse drugs. Experiencing sin's consequence usually is much worse than imagining it.

2. SUPREME SORROW. The Israelites found themselves in great distress as a result of their prolonged sin (vs. 9). The people's extreme sorrow brought them to realize that they had to repent and turn to the Lord again (vs. 15). Encourage your class members to recognize the value of godly sorrow as an emotion that God can use to turn us from sin to righteousness (2 Cor. 7:10-11). Also, be sure to caution your students not to interpret every difficulty of life as a judgment for sin. After all, the Israelites experienced turmoil after provoking the Lord to anger.

3. STEADFAST LOVE. The Lord was not a cruel tyrant. He took to heart the troubles of His people, especially when they threw away the pagan deities they owned (Judg. 10:16). Encourage your students to reflect on the character of God when facing hard times, such as depression, divorce, illness, death, unemployment, loneliness, and age-related limitations. The steadfast love of God can pull us through dark places that seem everlasting but eventually will end.

4. SURE HOPE. The Israelites hoped in God Himself, not just in some abstract characteristic of God. They realized that they still had a covenant relationship with the Lord that let them call out to Him for help (vs. 10). Your students can also hope in the Father as long as they have a personal relationship with Him through faith in the Son as their Savior from sin. All believers can hope in the daily mercies of God and affirm "great is thy faithfulness" (Lam. 3:23).

FOR ADULTS

■ TOPIC: Improving Community

■ QUESTIONS: 1. Why do you think the Israelites repeatedly found themselves struggling with the sin of idolatry? 2. What are some things that might distract your attention from God? 3. What are some ways believers can remind one another of the good things God has done for them? 4. How have you seen God's sovereignty at work in your life? 5. Why did the elders of Gilead decide to search for someone to lead their warriors to victory against the enemy?

■ ILLUSTRATIONS:

Maintaining Hope! Most of your students are probably Christians. No doubt most of them have been exposed to God's love. Despite the many ways God has shown His love to us, we all have areas in our lives where we stubbornly insist on doing what we want to do rather than what God expects us to do.

Although your students are adults, in many ways they may act like little children who are self-centered and spoiled. Remind your students that God views us in the same way as parents view their young children. Just as we expect our children to develop into mature adults, so God wants us to mature as Christians. This is one of the most pivotal ways of improving the quality of life in our faith communities.

Of course, as we grow in the Lord, we will make many childish mistakes and even rebel sometimes, just as the Israelites did during the period of the judges (see Judg. 10:6). One important truth from a study of the life of Jephthah is that even though we often act selfishly and behave stubbornly, God continues to care for us (see vs. 16). It's the presence of His compassion that gives us hope in the midst of despairing circumstances.

True Commitment Shown during Hard Times. In 1921, Evan O'Neill Kane had already practiced surgery for 40 years. He was chief of surgery at a prominent New York City hospital that bore his name, Kane Summit Hospital. For some time, Kane had toyed with the idea of performing many common surgeries under local anesthesia. He wanted to experiment with an appendectomy, but months passed and he could not find a volunteer willing to take the risk.

Then one gray February day, a brave soul came forward. He was wheeled into surgery where Kane prepped him, administered a local anesthetic, deftly opened his abdomen, and removed the troublesome appendix. All the while, the patient was fully alert but feeling no pain, which was a good thing, since Kane was removing his own appendix.

Many Christians profess to trust God's faithfulness, steadfast love, and tender mercies to see them through any trial of life. That is easy to say, but much more difficult to do. In the case of the Israelites, it took a prolonged period of distress to get them to put their trust once more in the Lord (see Judg. 10:9-10, 15). We know our professed faith is genuine when we have relied on God's faithfulness, love, and mercy during an emergency.

Suffering Deepens Empathy. Charles H. Spurgeon, the great 19th century Baptist preacher, delivered a sermon in which he told the story of one of the worst periods in his own life. It was a time when he was discouraged in his work, depressed with his inward progress, and failing in his health. He felt, as the Israelites did during the time of Jephthah, that God was no longer with him (see Judg. 10:11-14).

After the service, a man came up to Spurgeon who was, the preacher said, "one step from an insane asylum." His hands twitched nervously as he shook the great orator's hand. He told Spurgeon that he had come forward because he felt that finally he had met a person who could empathize with his problems. Spurgeon comforted the man as best he could and prayed that God would be gracious in His compassion to him. They departed and the preacher didn't see him again for a while.

Five years later, following another worship service, the same man came again to Spurgeon. This time the man seemed the model of accomplishment and success. From that time forth, Spurgeon pledged to God that he would willingly go through any trial if it might encourage another soul to seek the Lord.

■ **TOPIC:** U-turn Needed!

■ **QUESTIONS:** 1. If you were living among the Israelites, how might you have encouraged them to remain faithful to the Lord? 2. Why is it important for believers to acknowledge to God that they have sinned against Him? 3. What could you eliminate from your life to make it more pleasing to God? 4. Who among your peers needs to know that only God can free them from the bondage of sin? 5. What promise did Gilead's officials make to the individual who led the charge against the Ammonites?

■ **ILLUSTRATIONS:**

Despair and Hope. A teen lost his older brother in an automobile accident. He struggled for three years to find hope. During that time, he could not talk about it. Meanwhile, after the accident, some other students who were not Christians made a spiritual "U-turn" when they came to faith because of his brother's witness on campus.

These converts found that the only way to deal with the tragedy was to commit themselves to the Lord. It's a lesson the Israelites had to learn the hard way. In the midst of their anguish, they decided to abandon their sinful ways and renew their devotion to God (see Judg. 10:9-10, 15).

The world-famous explorer and missionary, Wilfred T. Grenfell, left us with some sound advice when we think about despair and hope. He wrote, "The faith that Christ asks for is not to understand Him, but to follow Him. By that and that alone can we convert the tragedy of human life—full of disappointments, disillusionments, and with death ever looming ahead—into the most glorious field of honor, worthy of the dignity of a son of God."

True Compassion. "Now, pay attention," the voice of Sally's dad gently warned, as her little brother reached up to receive his ice cream cone. Even though it was years ago, Sally could still hear her father's voice telling Jason, "Hold on with both hands."

Jason didn't answer. His eyes were fixed on the two-scoop wonder that was now all his. But within about a minute of getting his treat, his attention had wandered away from the task of keeping his cone upright. Others around him were all suddenly aware of his failure when the sounds of heartbreak filled that little ice cream parlor.

There stood Jason holding an empty cone, ice cream at his feet, and his head thrown back in the very real grief of a toddler. He'd forgotten to pay attention. But his grief could have melted an iceberg as he managed between gasps and sobs to get out, "I-I-I'm s-s-sorry, Dad-dy-y-y!"

The father was there in a heartbeat, picking Jason up, holding him close, and promising it would be OK. There was no need to scold, for the lesson had been learned. Compassion was the only appropriate response.

Our heavenly Father is even more compassionate toward us. Long ago, when His people experienced the consequences of their sin, He was grieved by their misery and took their troubles to heart (see Judg. 10:16). He is just as merciful today toward His spiritual children, especially when their hearts are breaking and their repentance is real.

Trust God in Good and Bad Times. An American man and an Irish woman who had been pen pals since childhood finally realized they had fallen in love. John scraped together enough money to fly to Dublin where Maureen was to meet him wearing a green scarf, a green hat, and a green carnation.

John stepped from the plane and scanned the crowd in the terminal. When he spotted the green scarf, green hat, and green carnation on the homeliest woman he had ever seen, his heart sank. But Maureen was John's dearest friend, so he approached her with a smile to give her a hug.

"Hey! Get away from me," the homely woman cried out when John embraced her. "Is this airport full of crazy people today? That girl over there just paid me 20 pounds to wear all this green."

The prettiest girl John had ever seen stepped forward and held out her hand. "I'm so pleased that you came, John. Please forgive my little trick. I'm just so tired of shallow men who only care about my looks."

How tired God must get of people whose shallow love for Him only lasts as long as the good times. This is the sort of fickleness that plagued the Israelites during the time of Jephthah (see Judg. 10:6-7). Trust the Lord's love and mercy in the bad times, and you'll find out how true a friend He can be.

WALK IN GOD'S PATH

BACKGROUND SCRIPTURE: **Judges 13; 21:25**
DEVOTIONAL READING: **Romans 2:1-8**

KEY VERSES: The woman bare a son, and called his name Samson: and the child grew, and the LORD blessed him. And the Spirit of the LORD began to move him. (Judges 13:24-25)

KING JAMES VERSION

JUDGES 13:1 And the children of Israel did evil again in the sight of the LORD; and the LORD delivered them into the hand of the Philistines forty years. 2 And there was a certain man of Zorah, of the family of the Danites, whose name was Manoah; and his wife was barren, and bare not. 3 And the angel of the LORD appeared unto the woman, and said unto her, Behold now, thou art barren, and bearest not: but thou shalt conceive, and bear a son. 4 Now therefore beware, I pray thee, and drink not wine nor strong drink, and eat not any unclean thing: 5 For, lo, thou shalt conceive, and bear a son; and no razor shall come on his head: for the child shall be a Nazarite unto God from the womb: and he shall begin to deliver Israel out of the hand of the Philistines. 6 Then the woman came and told her husband, saying, A man of God came unto me, and his countenance was like the countenance of an angel of God, very terrible: but I asked him not whence he was, neither told he me his name: 7 But he said unto me, Behold, thou shalt conceive, and bear a son; and now drink no wine nor strong drink, neither eat any unclean thing: for the child shall be a Nazarite to God from the womb to the day of his death.

8 Then Manoah intreated the LORD, and said, O my Lord, let the man of God which thou didst send come again unto us, and teach us what we shall do unto the child that shall be born. . . .

24 And the woman bare a son, and called his name Samson: and the child grew, and the LORD blessed him. 25 And the Spirit of the LORD began to move him at times in the camp of Dan between Zorah and Eshtaol.

NEW REVISED STANDARD VERSION

JUDGES 13:1 The Israelites again did what was evil in the sight of the Lord, and the Lord gave them into the hand of the Philistines forty years. 2 There was a certain man of Zorah, of the tribe of the Danites, whose name was Manoah. His wife was barren, having borne no children. 3 And the angel of the Lord appeared to the woman and said to her, "Although you are barren, having borne no children, you shall conceive and bear a son. 4 Now be careful not to drink wine or strong drink, or to eat anything unclean, 5 for you shall conceive and bear a son. No razor is to come on his head, for the boy shall be a nazirite to God from birth. It is he who shall begin to deliver Israel from the hand of the Philistines." 6 Then the woman came and told her husband, "A man of God came to me, and his appearance was like that of an angel of God, most awe-inspiring; I did not ask him where he came from, and he did not tell me his name; 7 but he said to me, 'You shall conceive and bear a son. So then drink no wine or strong drink, and eat nothing unclean, for the boy shall be a nazirite to God from birth to the day of his death.'"

8 Then Manoah entreated the Lord, and said, "O Lord, I pray, let the man of God whom you sent come to us again and teach us what we are to do concerning the boy who will be born." . . .

24 The woman bore a son, and named him Samson. The boy grew, and the Lord blessed him. 25 The spirit of the Lord began to stir him in Mahaneh-dan, between Zorah and Eshtaol.

Monday, August 1	Romans 2:1-8	*God's Righteous Judgment*
Tuesday, August 2	Numbers 6:1-8	*Separated to the Lord*
Wednesday, August 3	Leviticus 10:8-11	*The Holy and the Common*
Thursday, August 4	Deuteronomy 5:6-10	*Keep the Commandments*
Friday, August 5	Deuteronomy 10:12-21	*Hold Fast to God*
Saturday, August 6	Judges 13:15-23	*Wonders for God's Followers*
Sunday, August 7	Judges 13:1-8, 24-25	*God Prepares a Deliverer*

BACKGROUND

The term "Nazarite" (Judg. 13:5) comes from a Hebrew word that means "set apart" or "devoted." According to Numbers 6:1-21, any Israelite could take a vow to become a Nazarite for a specified period of time (for example, 30 days). Nazarites pledged to abandon worldly pursuits and set themselves apart in whole-hearted commitment to God. Even though they did not withdraw from society, they consecrated themselves for special service. In addition to abstaining from alcoholic beverages (such as wine) and refusing to cut one's hair, the devotee also avoided contact with the dead.

The Lord had specific plans for the son of Manoah. Samson would begin the process of delivering the Israelites from the control of the Philistines. Samson judged Israel for 20 years (1075–1055 B.C.; see Judg. 15:20; 16:31). The work of liberating God's people from Philistine domination was brought to completion by Samuel, Saul, Jonathan, and finally David. Tragically, Samson repeatedly ignored the restrictions of his vow. His lapses into moral and spiritual failure mirrored those of the 12 tribes of Israel throughout the period of the judges.

Many scholars assume that the Philistines originated in the Aegean Sea region (near present-day Greece) and migrated to the land of Canaan. The Philistines that Abraham met when he arrived in Canaan were peaceful and showed few signs of becoming Israel's principal enemy in future generations (Gen. 21:32-34). The Philistines remained unconquered during the times of the judges and served as Israel's main foe during the early monarchy.

The Philistines were subdued during the reign of David and paid tribute to Solomon (1 Kings 4:21, 24), but they existed as a people until the Babylonian king Nebuchadnezzar destroyed their cities hundreds of years later. During Samson's time, the Israelites seemed to accept the Philistine domination. Indeed, at one point, 3,000 men from Judah gathered to capture Samson and turn him over to the Philistines (Judg. 15:11-15). The lasting impact of the Philistines endures in the name "Palestine," which comes from the Greek word for "land of the Philistines."

NOTES ON THE PRINTED TEXT

Perhaps the episode involving Samson and his exploits is the clearest example of the Israelites returning to idolatry right after the death of a judge. Like their predecessors, a new generation engaged in practices God detested. The Hebrew adjective rendered "evil" (Judg. 13:1) denotes actions that are both wicked in character and result in calamity. In this case, the Lord responded by allowing the Philistines to dominate and oppress His people for 40 years. Once again God had to awaken His people from their spiritual stupor and lead them out of darkness. Also, He disciplined them so that they would return to wholehearted devotion.

Details surrounding the birth of Samson are recorded in verses 2-7. His father, Manoah, belonged to a clan from the tribe of Dan. Manoah lived in Zorah, a town located in the western foothills of Judah (vs. 2; see Josh. 15:33). Centuries earlier, Bilhah, a concubine of Jacob, bore the patriarch Dan and Naphtali (Gen. 30:3-8). During the period of the judges, members of the tribe of Dan resettled about 100 miles north of Zorah in the land of Laish (see Judg. 18).

Manaoh's wife was barren, and the couple had been childless for a number of years (13:2). One of the worst situations for a woman in biblical times was to be sterile. The situation not only deprived a husband and wife of personal happiness, but also exposed them to the reproach of their neighbors. The barren woman usually bore the brunt of this shame. Moreover, remaining childless meant a couple would have no children to take care of them in their old age. Also, the family property could be up for grabs when the couple died. Perhaps most tragic of all, the family line would end. This situation undoubtedly grieved Manoah and his wife.

One day, the angel of the Lord appeared to Manoah's wife (vs. 3). This heavenly emissary announced to the woman that even though she was infertile, she would become pregnant and give birth to a son. During her pregnancy, she was not to drink any alcoholic beverages. She was also prohibited from eating ceremonially unclean foods (vs. 4). In Bible times, particular foods were considered ritually defiled and consuming them made one ritually contaminated (see Lev. 11). According to the Mosaic law, everything the Israelites did, both individually and as a covenant community, was to reflect God's moral purity. The angel disclosed to Manaoh's wife that no razor was ever to touch the head of her son, for he was to be a lifelong "Nazarite" (Judg. 13:5). Moreover, God would use Him to bring deliverance to His people.

After the angel of the Lord departed, the wife of Manoah told him about her encounter with a "man of God" (vs. 6), by which she meant a divinely sent messenger and prophet. The woman said the visitor's majestic appearance made her wonder whether he was an angel from God. Perhaps out of fear, Manoah's wife did not ask the heavenly emissary where he was from, and he had not volunteered his name. The woman repeated the essential details of the angel's message to her. This included the conception and birth of a son and his lifelong Nazarite vow (vs. 7). Oddly enough,

Manoah's wife did not (as far as we know) mention that the child would play a significant role in delivering the Israelites from the Philistines. Perhaps the woman was afraid of how her husband would react to this information.

Manoah and his wife felt they needed more instructions on how to properly rear this special child. So Manoah begged the Lord to send back His prophet—referred to as the "man of God" (vs. 8)—so that the divine will might be clearer. There is no element of doubt or unbelief in Manoah's request, only a desire to better understand what God wanted the parents to do with their child, who had a most unusual calling. The Lord responded to Manoah's petition by once again dispatching His emissary to confirm what had been previously declared (see vss. 9-20).

After God's angel departed, he did not appear again to Manoah and his wife. Manoah concluded that the visitor was more than a prophet. He was a messenger from heaven, the "angel of the LORD" (vs. 21). His presence authenticated his pronouncement about the child to be born. Manoah realized he had seen a visible appearance of God and that he had been speaking to the Lord of Israel. Manoah feared he would die from this unusual encounter with Yahweh (vs. 22; see Gen. 32:30; Exod. 33:20).

Manoah's wife recognized, however, that it was unlikely that the Lord was going to take them. She reasoned that the Lord did not mean to kill them, especially since He had accepted their burnt and grain offerings, had displayed marvelous works of power to them, and had personally announced to them His wonderful promise (Judg. 13:23). This Old Testament couple's experience was the exception. During this time, no one could approach God directly and live. Because of Jesus' work on the cross, however, we have unrestricted access to the Lord of the universe. By God's grace, we are able to speak freely with Him with no danger of reproach.

The faith and conviction of Manoah's wife was confirmed when she gave birth to a son and named him Samson (vs. 24). The child's name is derived from a Hebrew word that means "brightness" or "sun." As Samson matured mentally and physically, the Lord blessed him. God enabled him to be productive and prosperous in his endeavors. While Samson was at Mahaneh Dan (which means "the camp of Dan"), the Spirit began to work within him (vs. 25). Samson was being prompted by the Spirit to begin the task of delivering the Israelites from Philistine aggression. This verse says that Mahaneh Dan was located between Zorah and Eshtaol. Both were only a mile and a half apart from one another. Archaeological evidence from the region suggests that Mahaneh Dan may have been a tent camp, not a permanent settlement.

Chapters 14–16 record the highlights of Samson's exploits. For instance, later in his career he went to Gaza and was in the house of a prostitute when the Philistines discovered his presence. They surrounded the house and waited, planning to kill him at dawn. But Samson arose in the middle of the night, lifted the city gate on his shoulders, and carried it to the top of a hill that faced Hebron (16:1-3). After that episode, Samson fell in love with a woman named Delilah. Learning this, the Philistine rulers offered Delilah a large sum of silver if she could find out the secret of Samson's strength. Three times Delilah asked about Samson's strength, and three times Samson gave false answers to her inquiry (16:4-14).

Delilah continued to nag Samson until he told her everything—that he had been a Nazarite from birth and that if his head was shaved his strength would leave him. Delilah called the Philistine rulers, who returned after Samson was asleep on Delilah's lap. One man shaved Samson's head and his strength left him. Not aware that the Lord had left him, Samson awoke and was unable to subdue the Philistines. They gouged out his eyes and forced him to grind grain in prison. But his hair began to grow back (vss. 15-22). The Philistines gathered at their temple to praise the pagan deity Dagon for delivering Samson into their hands. Samson was brought out and placed between two pillars. Samson pushed the pillars down, collapsing the temple. All the Philistines, along with Samson, were killed (vss. 23-31).

SUGGESTIONS TO TEACHERS

Paint me warts and all," Oliver Cromwell instructed the artist painting his portrait. The Bible writers described the personalities in Scripture "warts and all." The leaders of Israel are shown with all their flaws. Our lesson based on Samson makes this clear. But the disclosure that the figures in Israel's history were human shows that God calls and uses flawed people—people like us!

1. A MESSAGE OF HOPE. The era of the judges was a depressing period in Israel's history. Each time the Israelites went through the cycle of sin, oppression, repentance, and deliverance, they seemed to sink deeper into alienation from God. Spiritual compromise was the norm. They kept giving in to the pagan ways of their neighbors, and each time God sent powerful oppressors until they cried out for deliverance. Despite the Israelites' infidelity, a message of hope emerges. Though God's people were unfaithful, He did not abandon them. He allowed His people to experience not only the natural consequences of their sin, but also the joy of His mercy.

2. REBELLION AND DISASTER. There are two main truths from the Book of Judges that are relevant to Christians. First, rebellion against God always leads to disaster. Whenever we value the things of the world (wealth, power, recognition, and so on) more than the things of God, the result is frustration and disappointment. Our disobedience brings spiritual defeat and moral bankruptcy to our lives. Only God's loving discipline can bring us back.

3. FORGIVENESS AND RESTORATION. The second key truth is that when we admit our sin by taking personal responsibility for it, we experience the Lord's forgiveness and restoration. He wants us to examine our lives to make sure that nothing is more important to us than Him. If we discover that we value something more than the Lord, we should turn away from it immediately. When we do, we will find ourselves stunned by God's grace.

■ TOPIC: Preparing for Leadership

■ QUESTIONS: 1. Why did the Israelites engage in wicked activities? 2. When we are faced with prolonged suffering, what can we do to remain strong in our commitment to God? 3. Why would Samson be a lifelong Nazarite? 4. Why did Manoah want the angel to make a return visit? 5. In what ways have you seen the Lord bless you and other believers in your church?

■ ILLUSTRATIONS:

Preparing for Commitment. When a couple gets married, they make a commitment to be faithful to each other. When people join the church, they pledge to be loyal to God and the congregation. Tragically, such promises are easily broken. Often we know married couples who later divorce, and members of the church fail to keep their commitments.

Those who break their commitments to be faithful can give a host of reasons for doing so. Such cases of unfaithfulness should prompt us to ask what we could have done to help prevent the broken promises. Did we fail to note a couple's struggles? Did we refuse to help a friend through difficult circumstances? What steps could we have taken to encourage others in their faith?

Before Samson was born, his parents prepared themselves for the commitment the Lord had placed upon them. In turn, they did all they could to encourage their gifted son to remain faithful to God. Consider how this week's lesson might be used to emphasize these truths to the students, especially as they prepare to take on leadership responsibilities in the church.

Always Faithful. The 1983 suicide bombing attack on the American Embassy in Beirut, Lebanon, took the lives of 241 American servicemen and severely injured 60 others. Shortly after the explosion, General Paul Kelley went to the hospital to visit the wounded. He came to the bedside of a young U.S. marine who had been critically hurt in the attack. Bandages covered the eyes of the American marine, and a tracheotomy had been placed in his throat. General Kelley gently spoke to the young man and leaned over to allow the marine, who could not see or speak, to touch the four stars of the general's rank on his shoulder.

Not long afterward, the general learned that the young marine was going to have a birthday. Kelley visited again, gave the four stars as a present to the man, and told him how proud he and the nation were of him. Unable to say anything and still swathed in bandages, the marine reached for a pad and pencil. On the pad, the marine scrawled in crude letters SEMPER FI, the abbreviated form of the motto of the United States Marine Corps: "Semper Fidelis"—"Always Faithful."

Lifelong fidelity is also what God intended for Samson to demonstrate, and it is what God intends for us to live. He wants us to remember that He is our ultimate source of power to live and triumph over our circumstances.

FOR YOUTH

■ **TOPIC:** Birthing a Leader

■ **QUESTIONS:** 1. Why did the Lord allow the Philistines to oppress the Israelites? 2. How is the compassion of God evident in the appearance of His angel to Manoah's wife? 3. In what ways is your dedication to God evident to others? 4. What details of the angel's message did Manoah's wife relate to her husband? 5. What might the Spirit of the Lord be prompting you to do for His glory?

■ **ILLUSTRATIONS:**

The Ultimate Goal. Early in life we ask students what vocation they want to pursue. Seeking this information may be premature, for often they do not have the knowledge, experience, or maturity necessary to make such a momentous decision.

For believers, more important than the career we choose is the character we develop. For instance, consider how Samson's career as a judge in Israel would have been different had he not disobeyed the Lord. His great potential for leadership was largely wasted because he lived immorally. His character flaws—which were seen early in his life—eventually led to his downfall.

Young people are wise if they ask the Lord to guide them down the right path. Their greatest desire should be to grow in Christlikeness, whether in word or deed, and whether as leaders or followers in the church (2 Pet. 3:18).

Involved and Responsible. Maine fishermen tell the story of a landlubber tourist who insisted on accompanying a crew in a boat heading out to the Georges Bank. A severe storm suddenly arose, and at that time the boat developed engine troubles. The boat began to take on water. Meanwhile, the visitor lounged in the galley, idly drinking a cup of coffee.

The skipper struggled with the wheel to try to keep the boat headed into the wind while the crewmen frantically worked below trying to operate a pump and restart the engine. Noticing the tourist not doing anything, one of the crew shouted, "Hey! Give us a hand here with the pump! We're in trouble and you're not doing anything!" Shrugging, the landlubber-visitor took another sip of coffee and replied, "I don't care. It's not my boat."

Imagine Samson's parents teaching him to be this apathetic to the needs of his fellow Israelites. Samson would not have known the blessing of the Lord as he grew to adulthood. Also, Samson would have been indifferent to the prompting of the Spirit (see Judg. 13:24-25). We're all involved and responsible as fellow crew members on this voyage of life.

Missing Ingredient. Correspondent Jennifer Epstein of *Inside Higher Ed* reported on high blood pressure and obesity among college-age students. According to a recent study she cited, these two issues are "among the health problems plaguing" young people in college. Understandably, the results of the research worry "experts on student health."

The causes for the poor physical shape of America's young people are legion: too much sitting and watching television, poor eating habits, particularly with fast food, and too many sedentary activities with no outdoor activity. Finally, poor role models are to blame. As children, young adults saw their parents flopped in front of a television eating chips and doing little if any physical activities.

For all of Samson's shortcomings, he was a model of activity. He was physically active. However, the missing ingredient in his life was not physical activity, but a dedication to the Lord. Faithfulness had been lost. It had been replaced by a desire to gratify himself and his body. The Lord calls each of us to care for our bodies while maintaining our spiritual commitment to Him.

CHOOSING A COMMUNITY

BACKGROUND SCRIPTURE: Ruth 1:8-18
DEVOTIONAL READING: Romans 10:5-13

KEY VERSE: Ruth said, . . . whither thou goest, I will go; and where thou lodgest, I will lodge: thy people shall be my people, and thy God my God. (Ruth 1:16)

KING JAMES VERSION

RUTH 1:8 And Naomi said unto her two daughters-in-law, Go, return each to her mother's house: the LORD deal kindly with you, as ye have dealt with the dead, and with me. 9 The LORD grant you that ye may find rest, each of you in the house of her husband. Then she kissed them; and they lifted up their voice, and wept. 10 And they said unto her, Surely we will return with thee unto thy people. 11 And Naomi said, Turn again, my daughters: why will ye go with me? are there yet any more sons in my womb, that they may be your husbands? 12 Turn again, my daughters, go your way; for I am too old to have a husband. If I should say, I have hope, if I should have a husband also tonight, and should also bear sons; 13 Would ye tarry for them till they were grown? would ye stay for them from having husbands? nay, my daughters; for it grieveth me much for your sakes that the hand of the LORD is gone out against me. 14 And they lifted up their voice, and wept again: and Orpah kissed her mother-in-law; but Ruth clave unto her. 15 And she said, Behold, thy sister-in-law is gone back unto her people, and unto her gods: return thou after thy sister-in-law. 16 And Ruth said, Intreat me not to leave thee, or to return from following after thee: for whither thou goest, I will go; and where thou lodgest, I will lodge: thy people shall be my people, and thy God my God: 17 Where thou diest, will I die, and there will I be buried: the LORD do so to me, and more also, if ought but death part thee and me. 18 When she saw that she was steadfastly minded to go with her, then she left speaking unto her.

NEW REVISED STANDARD VERSION

RUTH 1:8 But Naomi said to her two daughters-in-law, "Go back each of you to your mother's house. May the Lord deal kindly with you, as you have dealt with the dead and with me. 9 The Lord grant that you may find security, each of you in the house of your husband." Then she kissed them, and they wept aloud. 10 They said to her, "No, we will return with you to your people." 11 But Naomi said, "Turn back, my daughters, why will you go with me? Do I still have sons in my womb that they may become your husbands? 12 Turn back, my daughters, go your way, for I am too old to have a husband. Even if I thought there was hope for me, even if I should have a husband tonight and bear sons, 13 would you then wait until they were grown? Would you then refrain from marrying? No, my daughters, it has been far more bitter for me than for you, because the hand of the Lord has turned against me." 14 Then they wept aloud again. Orpah kissed her mother-in-law, but Ruth clung to her.

15 So she said, "See, your sister-in-law has gone back to her people and to her gods; return after your sister-in-law." 16 But Ruth said,
"Do not press me to leave you
   or to turn back from following you!
Where you go, I will go;
   where you lodge, I will lodge;
your people shall be my people,
   and your God my God.
17 Where you die, I will die—
   there will I be buried.
May the Lord do thus and so to me,
   and more as well,
if even death parts me from you!"
18 When Naomi saw that she was determined to go with her, she said no more to her.

11

Monday, August 8	Romans 10:5-13	*The Lord of All*
Tuesday, August 9	Romans 12:3-8	*Bound Together in Christ*
Wednesday, August 10	Romans 14:1-9	*Seeking Unity in Community*
Thursday, August 11	Genesis 50:15-21	*Restoring Community*
Friday, August 12	Exodus 1:8-21	*Protecting Community*
Saturday, August 13	Ruth 1:1-7	*Seeking Comfort in Community*
Sunday, August 14	Ruth 1:8-18	*Choosing Community*

BACKGROUND

Ruth 1:1 places the account of the book in the period when judges ruled Israel, or about 1375–1050 B.C. Most of the judges did not rule over all of Israel. Deborah and Barak, for example, were unable to gain the cooperation of the tribes of Reuben, Gilead, Dan, and Asher in their war against the Canaanites. Gideon did not include Ephraim in his battles, and almost caused a civil war because of it. Furthermore, the era of the judges was a moral low point in Israel's history.

If we did not have the Book of Ruth, we might think that this time period was about nothing but warfare and that the only people who really mattered then were the great tribal heroes. But thankfully, we do have the Book of Ruth, and it shows us the other side of that era. Instead of having a large scope and telling about battles, it is a relatively brief account about domestic relations. Also, rather than being about heroes and villains, its characters are ordinary, godly individuals, mainly women. Thus, this four-chapter drama shows us that while the fate of tribes and nations was being decided, everyday life was still going on. Better yet, the book shows us that while Israelite society as a whole was caught in a downward spiral of apostasy, there were some individuals who remained loyal and faithful to God.

NOTES ON THE PRINTED TEXT

Throughout history, it was common for families to relocate to a new community because of job or economic circumstances. In Ruth 1:1-2, we learn that a family from Bethlehem in Judah did so. Elimelech, the husband, and his wife, Naomi, had two sons, Mahlon and Chilion. Though the name of the family's hometown, Bethlehem, means "House of Bread," there was a famine in the area that made survival tough. Just as hunger had forced Jacob's sons to seek food in Egypt (Gen. 42:1-2), starvation drove Elimelech and Naomi from Bethlehem to Moab. Moab was an area across the Salt Sea (Dead Sea) from Bethlehem. Moab's territory stretched from the south of the sea to its middle, and the edge of the Syrian desert formed the kingdom's eastern boundary.

Sometime after Elimelech and Naomi's arrival in Moab, tragedy struck. Elimelech's death left Naomi dependent on her sons (Ruth 1:3). Apparently Mahlon and Chilion liked Moab well enough to marry and settle down (1:4). These marriages would have been frowned upon by orthodox Israelites, for whom Moab long represented temptation to immorality. Ten years after Naomi's family had moved to Moab, tragedy struck again. The names of Naomi's sons indicate they were physically weak (perhaps from birth). Mahlon means "weak" or "sick," and Chilion means "failing" or "annihilation." Ruth and Orpah were probably widowed soon after their weddings (Ruth 1:5). After Mahlon and Chilion died, all three women were left without support. In ancient patriarchal societies, women depended on male relatives for protection and care. Sadly, widows were usually ignored and destitute.

Eventually, word came from Bethlehem that the famine had ended (vs. 6). Naomi made the courageous decision to return home. She and her daughters-in-law faced the prospect of crossing about 50 miles of barren desert. The risks of this journey were great: heat exhaustion, starvation, and attacks by beasts or bandits. However, for Naomi, death on the road would be no worse than destitution and loneliness in a foreign land. Naomi's daughters-in-law were determined to go with her, a decision that underscored how much they appreciated her (vs. 7). Soon, however, Naomi told the women to go back to their families, find husbands, and start life over. Despite her need for their support, the older woman unselfishly set her daughters-in-law free (vs. 8).

Naomi could not provide husbands for her two daughters-in-law, and she cared too much for them to let them live as widows, especially since they had been good to her sons and herself. Perhaps Naomi also wanted to protect Ruth and Orpah from abusive discrimination, which they might face in Bethlehem. Naomi softened the blow of her directive by giving Orpah and Ruth a double blessing. In the first part of the blessing, Naomi wished the Lord's kindness on her daughters-in-law. Also, in the process of doing so, Naomi expressed her appreciation for the kindness the young women had shown to her sons and to herself.

In the second part of the blessing, Naomi wished her daughters-in-law rest in a new husband's home (vs. 9). In this case "rest" meant ceasing from toil and trouble and experiencing lifelong protection and blessing from the Lord. We can see from Naomi's double blessing that she did not hesitate to speak about Yahweh, the Israelites' God, in the presence of her Moabite daughters-in-law. Indeed, Naomi's words show that she believed He was the one who had the power to bless them.

Naomi kissed Orpah and Ruth to show her love for them. At this the young women wept. Through the tears, however, both declared their intention to continue with Naomi (vs. 10). Clearly, Naomi's love for them had evidently made a powerful impact on them. While the idealism of youth is inspiring, the experience of age often reveals the most prudent course. Concerning Naomi, she repeated her exhortation to Orpah and Ruth to return home, and this time she was prepared to give them a good reason to obey her (vs. 11). We earlier noted that in Israel it was a man's duty to marry his brother's widow so as to see that she was taken care of. As it happens, Naomi had no more sons to marry Ruth and Orpah. Moreover, Naomi didn't expect to marry again and have more sons (vs. 12). Even if she did bear sons, it would take too long for them to reach a marriageable age (vs. 13). Thus, if the young women traveled to Judah with her, Naomi wouldn't be able to give them more of her sons to marry.

Naomi's attempt to turn the young women back worked—somewhat. After a few more tears and more kissing, Orpah headed home (vs. 14). This decision to return to Moab is not a reproach on her character. Rather, she was showing a practical concern for herself. Also, her tearful parting from Naomi indicates a fondness for the older woman. Here we see that sometimes loyalty means allowing loved ones to do what is best for them, even if such an action means loss for us. In Naomi's case, her prospect for surviving and thriving in Judah was reduced with the departure of Orpah. Yet, despite this, Naomi remained sensitive to the needs of her daughter-in-law.

While Orpah made a commonsense decision, Ruth opted to place Naomi's needs first. This decision is all the more remarkable in light of Naomi's statement about Orpah. Since she was returning to "her people, and unto her gods" (Ruth 1:15), it appeared reasonable for her sister-in-law to follow her back home. Ruth, however, refused to do so and even asked that Naomi stop trying to dissuade her. Ruth was convinced that if she returned to her people, it would mean abandoning Naomi and leaving her more vulnerable than before.

Ruth's clinging to Naomi indicated a love stronger than formal regard. Self-centered choosing wants to know, "What's in it for me?" Loyalty like Ruth's asks, "What can I do for you?" In her pledge of loyalty, Ruth made four choices (vs. 16). First, she decided to forsake the comforts of home to travel across the desert. Second, she would live where Naomi lived, even in poverty. Third, Ruth would identify herself with Naomi's people, even though she knew they might reject her. Ruth's most significant commitment—the fourth one—was to Yahweh, the God of Israel: "thy God [will be] my God."

Ruth's pledge in the name of Israel's God may be paraphrased, "May a severe judgment fall on me if I am not true to this vow" (vs. 17). Naomi not only realized that Ruth was determined to follow her no matter what perils lay ahead, but also Naomi saw that Ruth had a deep faith in the God of Israel. Thus Naomi no longer tried to persuade her daughter-in-law to remain in Moab (vs. 18). Ruth's loyalty must have filled Naomi's heart with joy as they began the long trek together. God calls us to love our family members unconditionally. Though we may not always get along, family ties are not easily broken.

The two women eventually completed the journey to Bethlehem. Their arrival caused quite a stir among Naomi's former neighbors. The women of the town exclaimed, "Is this Naomi?" (vs. 19). Apparently, life had taken its toll on Naomi. Ten years in a foreign culture, the loss of a husband and sons, hard work, and long journeys—all this must have affected Naomi's appearance. It certainly had impacted her attitude. Her name, "Naomi" (1:20), means "pleasant," but she told the other women to call her "Mara," which means "bitter."

This play on words reflected the pain of Naomi's circumstances. She had left in a time of famine and returned in a season of plenty. Nonetheless, she considered herself to have been full before (for then she had a family) and empty now (for her husband and sons were gone; vs. 21). She attributed her misfortune to the Lord, whom Naomi believed was afflicting her (vs. 13). Allegedly, the sovereign one had treated Naomi very harshly (vs. 21). Verse 22 sums up the action so far and looks ahead to what was to come. The two bereaved women arrived in Bethlehem at the barley harvest season, that is, in about April.

SUGGESTIONS TO TEACHERS

In a few verses, several character traits and attitudes are portrayed by one Israelite woman—Naomi—and two Moabite women—Ruth and Orpah. As we take a look at how these three women expressed these traits and attitudes, we would do well to strive to emulate them in our lives as followers of the Lord Jesus Christ.

1. BE KIND. Naomi thanked Ruth and Orpah for the kind way they had treated her husband, her sons, and herself. Indeed, the two younger women were in no way legally bound to Naomi, but they had grown to love her and respect her deeply, and thus they dealt with her in a kind manner. May we, too, treat others with kindness, sensitivity, and compassion.

2. BE THOUGHTFUL. Ruth and Orpah, though widowed themselves, realized that Naomi's circumstances were more grave than their own. Naomi, in one sense, was somewhat stranded in a foreign country. Being thoughtful of Naomi's needs, they did not discourage her from returning to her homeland, but rather began escorting her on her way home. May we, too, be thoughtful of the needs of others.

3. BE CONSIDERATE. Naomi felt that it would be in the best interest of her daughters-in-law to remain in their home country. And even though she would be alone on a dangerous journey, she was considerate enough of her daughters-in-law to encourage them to stay home while she braved the trek home. May we, too, be considerate of the best interests of others—even if it means we may have to face part of our journey alone.

4. BE LOYAL. Both Ruth and Orpah expressed intense loyalty to their mother-in-law. Though Naomi was not of their native land, their native family, their native culture, or their native religion, the two daughters-in-law continually expressed their love and loyalty to their mother-in-law. May we, too, express and act upon our loyalty to our families, church, employers, friends, and (especially) our God.

5. BE COMMITTED. No amount of explanation could convince Ruth to turn away from her mother-in-law. In fact, Ruth "clave unto her" (Ruth 1:14). Ruth's commitment to her mother-in-law could not be dissuaded or deterred. And even if Naomi could only offer Ruth more tragic and desperate circumstances, the young woman was committed to stay with her mother-in-law. May we, too, never be dissuaded or deterred from our commitments.

■ **FOR ADULTS**

■ **TOPIC:** Choosing Community Wisely

■ **QUESTIONS:** 1. What series of tragedies struck Naomi? 2. What sorts of struggles might have Naomi and her two daughters-in-law have faced as they decided to leave Moab? 3. How had Ruth come to be so devoted to the God of Israel? 4. How might God be working in the day-to-day events of your life to bring about solutions to your problems? 5. How might others see from your life witness that God honors steadfastness in family relationships?

■ **ILLUSTRATIONS:**

Commitment to a New Community. What causes waning commitment among adults to the members of their faith community? Each of us struggles with a different set of weaknesses.

Some adults struggle with sexual immorality. Other adults harbor deep anger toward a family member or friend who has hurt them in some way. Still other adults can't seem to help but break the trust of a loved one by relating confidences to others.

Honesty, forgiveness, unselfishness, and loyalty are God-honoring character traits for the new community of God's people. As we study Ruth's loyalty to Naomi, we will be encouraged to examine our own relationships, reshape our loyalties, and overcome grief in our lives.

Commitment Is the Key. Ruth's decision to go with Naomi shows a firmness of purpose. Indeed, her commitment went far beyond personal convenience. The decisiveness of the choice Ruth made is illustrated in the life of Italian operatic tenor Luciano Pavarotti (who died in 2007).

"When I was a boy, my father, a baker, introduced me to the wonders of song," Pavarotti relates. "He urged me to work very hard to develop my voice. Arrigo Pola, a professional tenor in my hometown of Modena, Italy, took me as a pupil. I also enrolled in a teacher's college. On graduating, I asked my father, 'Shall I be a teacher or a singer?'

"'Luciano,' my father replied, 'if you try to sit on two chairs, you will fall between them. For life, you must choose one chair.'

"I chose one. It took seven years of study and frustration before I made my first professional appearance. It took another seven to reach the Metropolitan Opera. And now I think whether it's laying bricks, writing a book—whatever we choose—we should give ourselves to it. Commitment: that's the key. Choose one chair."

Faithful to the Commitment. A young businessman was rushed to a hospital in serious condition. A physician predicted that he might die. Not a religious man at the time, the ailing man did, however, turn on a radio and heard a Christian song being played: "God Will Take Care Of You." He said that he couldn't get that song out of his mind.

The young businessman began to pray and, as he did, he reported a sense of energy flowing in. It was near Christmas, a Sunday morning. He heard a group of nurses having a brief worship service in a nearby room and struggled up out of bed and joined them. While there, he committed his life to Christ. That man recovered. Thereafter, for the rest of his life, he remained as faithful to his commitment as Ruth had been in her lifelong devotion to Naomi and the people of Israel.

That man referred every business and every personal decision to God and was resolute in his ethics, living by the teachings of Jesus. Perhaps you've heard about this man, who told all about this in a book concerning his life. His name was J. C. Penney. He, too, insisted throughout his life that the apostle Paul was quite right in promising divine help for those in whom Christ's Spirit lives.

FOR YOUTH

■ TOPIC: Switching Communities

■ QUESTIONS: 1. How did Naomi respond to the death of her two sons? 2. What does Ruth's response to her situation suggest about her character? 3. How do you see yourself in comparison to Ruth? 4. How does your faith in the Lord affect your loyalty to the people in your life? 5. What are some ways you can openly speak of God before others who may not be used to hearing about Him?

■ ILLUSTRATIONS:

Who's in the Family? Adolescents soon learn that short-term loyalties, like fireworks, blaze intently for a brief time and then vanish. They also come to discover that constant loyalty glows like a lightbulb pointing the way through a dark tunnel.

This week's lesson makes it clear that, as Orpah's loyalty faded, she returned home, but Ruth's commitment was permanent. Even when her initial plans for marriage tragically ended, she switched communities by devoting herself to her mother-in-law, Naomi, and to the God of Israel. Ruth even submitted to His plan for her life.

Jesus' last earthly promise to His disciples in Matthew 28:20 was "And, lo, I am with you alway, even unto the end of the world." Christian love is not commitment by convenience, which disappears when life becomes difficult. Real love says, "I'll be there for you when times are tough for you." Saved teens need Christian fellowship, especially in hard places. The Lord did not intend that any of them should go it alone, but journey with others who belong to the family of God.

Found Greater Happiness. Ruth is not the only person who had to make the tough choice of switching communities. Consider the testimony of John Frank, who played tight end with the San Francisco 49ers from 1984 to 1988.

This two-time Academic All-American had participated in two Super Bowl games and was entering his athletic prime at the age of 27. He had once dreamed of becoming a physician, but had postponed that goal to make big money in professional football. Yet Frank discovered that money could never be the main purpose in life. He also learned that a sense of compassion can bring a person to a deeper joy.

The turning point in John Frank's career came the day when he rushed over to the side of an opponent who appeared to have suffered a serious injury—only to be chewed out by his coach for "giving aid and compassion to the enemy." That was the event that made Frank decide to go full-time to medical school. Frank is now a physician. Walking away from pro football seemed silly to everyone, but Frank says he is happier now in serving the hurting. He has no regrets about giving up fame and fortune in the pro ranks.

A Pivotal Decision. She was a pretty 16-year-old. However, she was heavily into drugs. Though she was only 16, she had been in and out of hospital psychiatric units and detox programs.

One day, during the chaplain's visit, she asked him if he believed in God. He affirmed that he did. She asked if this God was the force who held everything together. "Yes," he responded. "Does this God have a name?" she continued. "Jesus Christ," came the chaplain's reply. The girl looked shocked, apparently unsure whether to believe the chaplain, even though she desperately needed something to hold on to in her life.

God came to earth as Jesus and lived as a human being. This realization filled the 16-year-old with hope, and she trusted in Christ for salvation. She got her life together. Today, many years later, she is a happily married woman, a mother who is continuing to discover each day how God is involved in her life.

This person's experience mirrors that of Ruth, who thousands of years ago as a young person decided to leave one community (Moab) for another community (Israel). Ruth's vow to Naomi was no "pie-crust" promise, that is, easily made and just as easily broken. Ruth's commitment was complete and unselfish.

EMPOWERING THE NEEDY

BACKGROUND SCRIPTURE: Ruth 2–3; Leviticus 19:9-10
DEVOTIONAL READING: Proverbs 22:1-9

KEY VERSE: [Boaz replied to Ruth,] the LORD recompense thy work, and a full reward be given thee of the LORD God of Israel, under whose wings thou art come to trust. (Ruth 2:12)

KING JAMES VERSION

RUTH 2:8 Then said Boaz unto Ruth, Hearest thou not, my daughter? Go not to glean in another field, neither go from hence, but abide here fast by my maidens: 9 Let thine eyes be on the field that they do reap, and go thou after them: have I not charged the young men that they shall not touch thee? and when thou art athirst, go unto the vessels, and drink of that which the young men have drawn. 10 Then she fell on her face, and bowed herself to the ground, and said unto him, Why have I found grace in thine eyes, that thou shouldest take knowledge of me, seeing I am a stranger? 11 And Boaz answered and said unto her, It hath fully been shewed me, all that thou hast done unto thy mother-in-law since the death of thine husband: and how thou hast left thy father and thy mother, and the land of thy nativity, and art come unto a people which thou knewest not heretofore. 12 The LORD recompense thy work, and a full reward be given thee of the LORD God of Israel, under whose wings thou art come to trust. 13 Then she said, Let me find favour in thy sight, my lord; for that thou hast comforted me, and for that thou hast spoken friendly unto thine handmaid, though I be not like unto one of thine handmaidens. 14 And Boaz said unto her, At mealtime come thou hither, and eat of the bread, and dip thy morsel in the vinegar. And she sat beside the reapers: and he reached her parched corn, and she did eat, and was sufficed, and left. 15 And when she was risen up to glean, Boaz commanded his young men, saying, Let her glean even among the sheaves, and reproach her not: 16 And let fall also some of the handfuls of purpose for her, and leave them, that she may glean them, and rebuke her not.

17 So she gleaned in the field until even, and beat out that she had gleaned: and it was about an ephah of barley. 18 And she took it up, and went into the city: and her mother-in-law saw what she had gleaned: and she brought forth, and gave to her that she had reserved after she was sufficed.

NEW REVISED STANDARD VERSION

RUTH 2:8 Then Boaz said to Ruth, "Now listen, my daughter, do not go to glean in another field or leave this one, but keep close to my young women. 9 Keep your eyes on the field that is being reaped, and follow behind them. I have ordered the young men not to bother you. If you get thirsty, go to the vessels and drink from what the young men have drawn." 10 Then she fell prostrate, with her face to the ground, and said to him, "Why have I found favor in your sight, that you should take notice of me, when I am a foreigner?" 11 But Boaz answered her, "All that you have done for your mother-in-law since the death of your husband has been fully told me, and how you left your father and mother and your native land and came to a people that you did not know before. 12 May the Lord reward you for your deeds, and may you have a full reward from the Lord, the God of Israel, under whose wings you have come for refuge!" 13 Then she said, "May I continue to find favor in your sight, my lord, for you have comforted me and spoken kindly to your servant, even though I am not one of your servants."

14 At mealtime Boaz said to her, "Come here, and eat some of this bread, and dip your morsel in the sour wine." So she sat beside the reapers, and he heaped up for her some parched grain. She ate until she was satisfied, and she had some left over. 15 When she got up to glean, Boaz instructed his young men, "Let her glean even among the standing sheaves, and do not reproach her. 16 You must also pull out some handfuls for her from the bundles, and leave them for her to glean, and do not rebuke her."

17 So she gleaned in the field until evening. Then she beat out what she had gleaned, and it was about an ephah of barley. 18 She picked it up and came into the town, and her mother-in-law saw how much she had gleaned. Then she took out and gave her what was left over after she herself had been satisfied.

12

409

BACKGROUND

Last week we learned that Naomi urged her daughters-in-law to return home, for she was too old to have sons who could become their husbands. Orpah returned to her family, but Ruth went with Naomi. The two women continued their journey, arriving in Bethlehem at the beginning of the barley harvest (Ruth 1:11-22). As poor, defenseless widows, they depended on the kindness of friends, relatives, and strangers for their daily bread. Soon help came in the form of harvesttime.

At this point in the narrative, we are introduced to another major character: Boaz. He was a relative of Elimelech and one of the important men in town (2:1). The Hebrew text literally says "a man mighty in substance." Elsewhere in the Old Testament, this phrase is frequently translated as "mighty man of valor." While Boaz might not have been a warrior, he still was a wealthy and influential person in Bethlehem. Though Naomi had sought to send her daughters-in-law back to their homes, Boaz would prove to be a relative who would protect Ruth and Naomi.

The two women had to find a source of income. Since it was the time of the barley harvest, Ruth offered to go into the fields and glean, that is, pick up grain missed or dropped by the harvesters. Ruth might have learned from Naomi that the Hebrew law made provision for the poor to do this (see Lev. 19:9; 23:22). But of course, it was not in the financial interest of farmers to allow gleaning, so Ruth hoped to find someone who would look favorably upon her and allow her to glean (Ruth 2:2). In this way, Ruth, the Moabitess, took the role of a subordinate servant as she sought permission from landowners. In turn, they could decide to show kindness by permitting her to glean in their fields behind their harvest workers. Naomi gave Ruth permission; and so it was that Ruth found herself gleaning in a field belonging to Boaz.

NOTES ON THE PRINTED TEXT

While Ruth was gleaning in the field of Boaz, he approached her and greeted her as "my daughter" (Ruth 2:8). This form of address was friendly and welcoming. It possibly indicates that Boaz was older than Ruth, but by how many years remains unclear. In that era, gleaners might wander from one field to the next in search of food wherever they might find it. Boaz encouraged Ruth to stay in his field and follow the women in his crew closely. By remaining relatively close to the women who worked for Boaz, Ruth would get the first chance at what they left behind and be able to collect considerably more grain than would otherwise be possible. Also, Boaz could better guarantee Ruth's safety. On that score, Boaz reassured Ruth by informing her that he had instructed the men in his work crew to leave her alone. In short, she did not have to fear being sexually molested by them. Moreover, Boaz arranged for Ruth to quench her thirst after hot hours in the fields. By being able to drink from what the men had drawn (most likely carried from a well some distance away), she would save herself the laborious, time-consuming process of having to stop and fetch water for herself (vs. 9).

In response to the unusual kindness shown by Boaz, Ruth knelt down in his presence with her forehead to the ground. This was a sign of extreme humility and gratitude. Boaz had done more for Ruth than the social laws of conduct had required, and Ruth responded accordingly by thanking him in a profound way. Yet, even as Ruth demonstrated her gratitude, she wondered what she had done to merit his actions. "Grace" (vs. 10) renders a Hebrew noun that emphasizes undeserved kindness. The attentiveness of Boaz seemed even more pronounced to Ruth given the fact that she was a "stranger," not an Israelite. The reason for Boaz's thoughtfulness and generosity was straightforward. He was impressed with the kindness and devotion Ruth had displayed toward her mother-in-law (and a relative of Boaz). This included the sacrifice Ruth made to leave her native land and people to remain with Naomi.

Boaz recognized that no law or custom obliged Ruth to do so. Even though she had already fulfilled her duties as a daughter-in-law, she still had chosen to be loyal and devoted to her mother-in-law (vs. 11). In response, Boaz offered a prayer on behalf of Ruth. Boaz asked the Lord to recompense Ruth for her kindness to Naomi. Behind the statement made by Boaz is the belief that God would fully repay Ruth's efforts. At the same time, Boaz acknowledged that Ruth had come to believe in Israel's God for herself. By saying that Ruth had come under the metaphorical wings of the Lord, Boaz was picturing a little bird snuggling under its mother's pinions. Some think Boaz was referring to the fact that Ruth was now living in the territory of God's people. Another possibility is that Boaz believed Ruth had a personal faith in the Lord (vs. 12).

Ruth was deferential and modest when she responded with her own wish that Boaz would continue to look on her favorably. Ruth appreciated the fact that Boaz had both reassured and encouraged her by his considerate, thoughtful words. The Hebrew term rendered "handmaid" (vs. 13) placed Ruth at the lowest rung in the hierarchy of laborers in Israelite society. She drew attention to her humble situation by noting that she did not enjoy the same status as Boaz's "handmaidens." In light of this information, it's no wonder that Ruth went out of her way several times to express thanks to Boaz. It must have been uncommon for a landowner to invite an impoverished widow to join his harvest crew for lunch, but that's what Boaz did for Ruth a little later. He gave her the opportunity to eat bread with sauce. Then Boaz gave Ruth roasted grain, which would have been a treat at harvesttime. Freshly reaped grain was left attached to the stalks and held in the fire, which would burn away the chaff and roast the kernels of grain. Ruth's portion was large, as she had some left over (vs. 14).

After Ruth left the dining place, Boaz instructed his male crew members to make sure Ruth had a lot of grain to pick up. If she gathered among the sheaves—where the poor were not normally allowed—they were not to verbally rebuke her. Singling her out in this way would bring unnecessary reproach on her (vs. 15). Furthermore, the workers were to deliberately leave some grain for Ruth, again without speaking harshly to her (vs. 16).

The provisions made by Boaz were designed to benefit Ruth without robbing her of dignity and self-respect. Under the favorable conditions fostered by Boaz, Ruth gleaned until dusk, when the crew would have finished its work. Then she threshed her barley, which means she separated the valuable kernels from the unwanted chaff, in this case probably by beating it with a stick. The grain that resulted amounted to about an ephah, or about three-fifths of a bushel. This was a good day's yield for a gleaner (vs. 17).

After Ruth returned home, she showed Naomi the ephah of grain and the leftovers from her lunch (vs. 18). This was a greater bounty than Naomi had expected to see. Excitedly, Naomi quizzed Ruth about her work and blessed the person who had helped her (vs. 19). Ruth gave the information Naomi requested. If anything, this increased Naomi's excitement. She again blessed Boaz, noting that he had shown kindness to "the living and to the dead" (vs. 20). This possibly means he had been generous to the family of Elimelech when they had previously lived in Bethlehem. And now Boaz was doing the same out of respect for the deceased husband of Naomi.

Until this point, Ruth had been ignorant about her family relationship with Boaz. So now Naomi explained that he was not only a close relative but also a family guardian. In Israelite custom, the latter was a person who took on the responsibility of caring for a relative. Naomi saw Boaz in that role, and indeed he might have too. That would explain his going out of his way to help Ruth at the field that day. Ruth noted that Boaz had invited her to continue gleaning in his fields until the end of the grain harvest (vs. 21). Naomi encouraged Ruth to take Boaz up on his offer, for she would be safer with his crew than with others (vs. 22).

Consequently, Ruth continued gleaning with the servant women of Boaz throughout the barley harvest and the wheat harvest that followed. In total, this was about a seven-week period. At night, Ruth returned to the place in Bethlehem where Naomi was staying. The lodging might have been with friends or on the land that Naomi still owned in the city (vs. 23; compare 4:3). During this time, Naomi's mind was busy working on a plan to secure the help of Boaz on a more permanent basis.

In ancient Israel, the spring harvest began with reaping. This was accomplished with small, curved sickles. The cut stalks would immediately be bound into sheaves. Next, workers would carry the sheaves to the threshing floor—that is, a large open area, often at the top of a hill. There the stalks would be trampled by oxen or other large animals, sometimes drawing a wooden sledge with sharp studs embedded in the underside. This process separated the kernels from the straw and chaff. After threshing, workers would winnow the grain, using pitchforks to toss it into the evening breeze. The light straw and chaff would blow away, while the heavier kernels would fall to the ground. Then the workers would sift the grain to further remove impurities. To prevent theft, farmers usually would sleep near their grain until they could store it in large clay jars or pits dug in the ground.

SUGGESTIONS TO TEACHERS

In the 1800s, so-called "scientific" writers claimed to show evidence of inequality between races in order to present a justification for slavery. To most of us, such a thing sounds shocking. Yet even in the supposedly enlightened new millennium, racism is still a reality dividing our society—sometimes violently. To help the members of your class weigh their own responses to strangers, have them discuss the following points.

1. RECOGNIZING OUR COMMON GROUND. Despite advances made since the early days of the Civil Rights Movement in America, we continue to divide ourselves from others by income, job status, and so on. There's nothing easier than recognizing our differences. What's hard is recognizing our common ground. Encourage your students to consider ways they can focus less on the perceived differences and more on the things they have in common with their peers.

2. NOTING WHAT'S GOOD IN OTHERS. When Boaz first met Ruth, he could have settled for seeing her just as an alien, a non-Israelite, someone who was different. But Boaz was himself different. He did not blindly give in to cultural prejudices. He realized that there was something special about Ruth. She loved her mother-in-law. Note to the class members that Ruth's devotion to Naomi resonated with Boaz, leading him to want to learn more about this woman from Moab. Have the class members discuss how recognizing the good in others can enable them to treat others kindly, regardless of their gender, race, or economic status.

3. SEEING THE REAL PERSON. The features that the students discover that turn a stranger into a friend might well be different for each person they meet. Of course, not every new person they encounter will become a friend. But when the class members work to note the real person behind the gender difference, beneath the different-colored skin, or behind the expensive (or hole-filled) clothes, they begin to see with God's own eyes. Have the students note that just as Boaz's impression of Ruth led to his performing acts of kindness on her behalf, so the class members' own new understanding can lead them to treat others in humane, godly ways.

■ TOPIC: Depending on Community

■ QUESTIONS: 1. Why do you think Boaz decided to be so kind to Ruth? 2. What individuals in your community could benefit from receiving similar kindness? 3. What are some ways the Lord has honored your efforts to be a blessing to others? 4. Why did Boaz deem it necessary to warn his male laborers not to harass Ruth? 5. In what sense had Ruth sought refuge in the God of Israel?

■ ILLUSTRATIONS:

Barriers to Acceptance. Why do many adults refuse to accept into their community people of another gender, race, or economic status? Fear is one of the greatest barriers for adults to overcome. John Perkins, who has made great strides in bridging ethnic gaps, writes about this fear in his book *With Justice for All.*

What Perkins says about racial relationships can also be extended to relationships between people of different genders and economic status. Adults who stretch across the gap of race, economics, or gender reach into the unknown, and naturally most of us have misgivings about the unknown. Thus, as Perkins suggests, bearing the burdens of others not only erases the unknown factor but also helps us exhibit God's concern for others outside our immediate social network.

Empathy is difficult for adults, especially since it presupposes looking at a situation through the emotions and perspective of another. Yet without empathy we will never achieve reconciliation and begin to treat others with the sort of kindness and respect that Boaz extended toward Ruth, the Moabitess.

Among the Most Despised. This week's lesson dealing with the interactions between Ruth and Boaz encourages members of God's faith community to treat others kindly and respectfully, regardless of their gender, race, or economic status. In turn, this approach has the potential to bear evangelistic fruit.

For instance, 8,000 people, including many Muslims, have become Christians in Ethiopia in recent years as a result of the kindness and generosity shown to them by believers. Active churches have formed throughout Southeast Ethiopia, a group from the mission agency Aktionskomitee für Verfolgte Christen (Action Committee for Persecuted Christians) told Dawn Ministries of *FridayFax.* In one town, the Muslims "sold their small mosque to the Christians, but it is already too small." The missions agency supports 75 evangelists in Ethiopia.

Members of the missions group said they were particularly thankful for God's working in the Manja tribe, "one of the nation's most despised tribes," who live on monkey meat and roots, serve many idols, and yet live in constant fear of evil spirits. Eight churches with more than 900 members were planted among the tribe when a former agricultural engineer evangelized in the region. Acts of charity were a key component of his Christian witness.

Testimonies about Life. In a book titled *A Healing Touch*, Richard Russo tells the stories of those who have journeyed with loved ones struggling with Alzheimer's disease. One of those accounts is that of Lee Duff, a school administrator in Maine. In 1994, his wife, Ann, was diagnosed with Alzheimer's. It would be another nine years before she finally lost her battle with the disease.

According to Russo, playing racquetball with others became for Lee a "kind of an oasis . . . to hit a ball and hit it as hard as you can." The author compared this sort of therapeutic involvement with others as "draining the poison" connected with a "horrific," prolonged experience.

Some might initially think the stories in the book are only about dealing with loss and grief. Instead, one finds testimonies "about life, with lots of laughter and joy." But as Russo explains, "I think for the people who told us their stories and for people who read this book, they're going to come to the conclusion that whatever it is that they may be going through right now, they're not alone."

These sentiments reflect what Naomi and Ruth experienced when they resettled in Bethlehem. In their case, the Lord used Boaz to show kindness and generosity to Ruth and her mother-in-law. Members of Jesus' spiritual body can also join together to unconditionally accept and help their fellow believers in their time of need.

FOR YOUTH

■ TOPIC: Depending on Community

■ QUESTIONS: 1. If you were Ruth, how would you have felt about the kindness shown by Boaz? 2. What are some tangible ways your church can minister God's kindness to people? 3. Why do you think Ruth chose to be so devoted to her mother-in-law? 4. Why is it important for believers to look to God for refuge in times of trouble? 5. What work ethic did Ruth demonstrate as she labored in the fields owned by Boaz?

■ **ILLUSTRATIONS:**

Showing Kindness. Kindness is easily pushed aside in a culture that persists in looking out for number one. With our focus on satisfying our own needs comes an appalling lack of interest in and concern for others in our community. Many social tragedies could be averted if we spent more time developing the habit of welcoming others into our social network and less time on seeking self-fulfillment.

"I'm too busy" is one of the most frequent excuses for not taking the time to help people in need. This is sad, for in many cases people are starving for companionship and encouragement. Elderly people are easily forgotten, and young people complain that their parents do not care about them.

The Book of Ruth shows teens that one person can make a difference. Boaz did not allow his concern for profits to overshadow the needs of a foreign widow. He not only gave her food to eat, but also tried to meet her deeper needs—all at considerable expense to himself. He sets the example for showing kindness to others.

Simple Acts of Kindness. Making a stranger feel welcome is a simple but invigorating act. I recently discovered the benefits firsthand. I have the habit of eating my lunch every Friday in the food court of the local mall. The lunch hour is typically busy, with high-school students, mall employees, and nearby businesspeople all vying for tables.

One Friday, with a full tray of food in hand, I spotted a free table for four. A single cup of soda sat there, but I assumed someone had left it for the cleanup crew. I had just taken a bite of my sandwich when a young mother and her toddler started to sit down beside me. I realized then that the drink had been theirs, left to save their place.

"I'm sorry," I said, suddenly very embarrassed and fumbling with my sandwich. "I didn't realize you were . . ." "No stay," she said, waving me to sit down. "You're welcome to join us." Still embarrassed, I couldn't help thinking how incredible it was that this woman would let a stranger share a table with her and her son. Yet, it probably happens every day in crowded small-town diners. But in a big, impersonal mall? I was touched by the mother's simple gesture. I knew that I might not have made the same offer had our roles been reversed.

I don't know whether my table partner was a Christian. But I know she acted in a Christlike fashion. Without knowing anything about me, she made me feel welcome. It is one thing to act kindly toward family and friends. To step beyond that to act with the grace of Boaz or the kindness of that young mother in the mall is to show the people around us a glimpse of our Creator.

Miracles in Return for Faithfulness. A "small miracle" helped Russian children find God several years ago. Nearly 140 young people and their sponsors were on their way to a Nazarene youth camp in Volgograd when organizers learned that the building they had rented wasn't available, *Nazarene Communications Network* said.

Organizers turned for help to officials at a local school, who in the past had warned students to avoid the Nazarenes, describing the group as a "sect." But something had changed their hearts. Not only did the school open its doors to the students, but cafeteria staff also provided meals and snacks during the two-day event, some giving up a holiday to serve the children. More than 100 children became Christians at the camp, field director Chuck Sunberg said. "Do you know what that means for our church?" he asked. He described the number of professions of faith as "astonishing."

Perhaps at first, Ruth entertained doubts about leaving her homeland to resettle among God's people in Bethlehem. The Lord blessed this foreign widow's decision to put her trust in Him by bringing along Boaz, who showed her unconditional acceptance and generosity. Imagine how differently the account would have been had Boaz decided to either ignore or dismiss Ruth?

FOLLOWING THE RULES

BACKGROUND SCRIPTURE: Ruth 4
DEVOTIONAL READING: Philippians 1:3-11

KEY VERSE: Then said Boaz, What day thou buyest the field of the hand of Naomi, thou must buy it also of Ruth the Moabitess, the wife of the dead, to raise up the name of the dead upon his inheritance. (Ruth 4:5)

KING JAMES VERSION

RUTH 4:1 Then went Boaz up to the gate, and sat him down there: and, behold, the kinsman of whom Boaz spake came by; unto whom he said, Ho, such a one! turn aside, sit down here. And he turned aside, and sat down. 2 And he took ten men of the elders of the city, and said, Sit ye down here. And they sat down. 3 And he said unto the kinsman, Naomi, that is come again out of the country of Moab, selleth a parcel of land, which was our brother Elimelech's: 4 And I thought to advertise thee, saying, Buy it before the inhabitants, and before the elders of my people. If thou wilt redeem it, redeem it: but if thou wilt not redeem it, then tell me, that I may know: for there is none to redeem it beside thee; and I am after thee. And he said, I will redeem it. 5 Then said Boaz, What day thou buyest the field of the hand of Naomi, thou must buy it also of Ruth the Moabitess, the wife of the dead, to raise up the name of the dead upon his inheritance. 6 And the kinsman said, I cannot redeem it for myself, lest I mar mine own inheritance: redeem thou my right to thyself; for I cannot redeem it. 7 Now this was the manner in former time in Israel concerning redeeming and concerning changing, for to confirm all things; a man plucked off his shoe, and gave it to his neighbor: and this was a testimony in Israel. 8 Therefore the kinsman said unto Boaz, Buy it for thee. So he drew off his shoe.

9 And Boaz said unto the elders, and unto all the people, Ye are witnesses this day, that I have bought all that was Elimelech's, and all that was Chilion's and Mahlon's, of the hand of Naomi. 10 Moreover Ruth the Moabitess, the wife of Mahlon, have I purchased to be my wife, to raise up the name of the dead upon his inheritance, that the name of the dead be not cut off from among his brethren, and from the gate of his place: ye are witnesses this day.

NEW REVISED STANDARD VERSION

RUTH 4:1 No sooner had Boaz gone up to the gate and sat down there than the next-of-kin, of whom Boaz had spoken, came passing by. So Boaz said, "Come over, friend; sit down here." And he went over and sat down. 2 Then Boaz took ten men of the elders of the city, and said, "Sit down here"; so they sat down. 3 He then said to the next-of-kin, "Naomi, who has come back from the country of Moab, is selling the parcel of land that belonged to our kinsman Elimelech. 4 So I thought I would tell you of it, and say: Buy it in the presence of those sitting here, and in the presence of the elders of my people. If you will redeem it, redeem it; but if you will not, tell me, so that I may know; for there is no one prior to you to redeem it, and I come after you." So he said, "I will redeem it." 5 Then Boaz said, "The day you acquire the field from the hand of Naomi, you are also acquiring Ruth the Moabite, the widow of the dead man, to maintain the dead man's name on his inheritance." 6 At this, the next-of-kin said, "I cannot redeem it for myself without damaging my own inheritance. Take my right of redemption yourself, for I cannot redeem it."

7 Now this was the custom in former times in Israel concerning redeeming and exchanging: to confirm a transaction, the one took off a sandal and gave it to the other; this was the manner of attesting in Israel. 8 So when the next-of-kin said to Boaz, "Acquire it for yourself," he took off his sandal. 9 Then Boaz said to the elders and all the people, "Today you are witnesses that I have acquired from the hand of Naomi all that belonged to Elimelech and all that belonged to Chilion and Mahlon. 10 I have also acquired Ruth the Moabite, the wife of Mahlon, to be my wife, to maintain the dead man's name on his inheritance, in order that the name of the dead may not be cut off from his kindred and from the gate of his native place; today you are witnesses."

HOME BIBLE READINGS

Monday, August 22	Philippians 1:3-11	*Pray for the Faith Community*
Tuesday, August 23	Psalm 15	*The Blameless Walk*
Wednesday, August 24	1 Kings 9:1-5	*Integrity of Heart*
Thursday, August 25	Psalm 26:1-11	*Walking in Integrity*
Friday, August 26	Proverbs 10:6-11	*Integrity Provides Security*
Saturday, August 27	Job 2:1-9	*Persisting in Integrity*
Sunday, August 28	Ruth 4:1-10	*Following Community Standards*

BACKGROUND

Ruth, following the advice of Naomi, discreetly let Boaz know about her preference for him to fulfill the duties of the kinsman-redeemer (Ruth 3:1-9). Boaz blessed Ruth and praised her for what she had done. Boaz considered this gesture to be a greater act of devotion toward Naomi than her earlier decision to accompany Naomi to Israel (vs. 10; compare 2:11-12). Boaz knew Ruth could have found a man younger than he, perhaps even a richer man. But Ruth desired to remain with Boaz because Ruth knew that as a family guardian he might help take care of Naomi. Expressed differently, Ruth took Naomi's interests into consideration when she pursued a husband.

Boaz assured Ruth that he would try to act as a family guardian to her. He added that her "virtuous" (3:11) character was known throughout the town. Thus, even though Ruth was a foreigner, Boaz's marriage to her would be acceptable to the community. Nonetheless, Boaz did bring up one possible impediment to the plan. There was a man in Bethlehem who was a closer relative to Naomi and Ruth than was Boaz (vs. 12). Accordingly, this person had the greater right to act as a guardian of the family interests. Boaz promised to find out the other individual's intentions in the morning. If this person did not want to act as a kinsman-redeemer, Boaz would do it. With these encouraging words, Boaz urged Ruth to finish her night's sleep where she was (vs. 13).

Ruth got up the following morning before the light was bright enough for anyone to recognize her. Boaz, after waking, told Ruth not to let the public know that she had spent the night at the threshing "floor" (vs. 14). Their precautions were likely meant to avoid leaving any impressions of immoral relations between them. Boaz then gave Ruth six measures of barley by pouring them into her "veil" (vs. 15) or cloak. The measure is not defined, but it was likely the seah. Six seahs of barley would weigh about 60 pounds, which in that day would have been considered a reasonable weight for a young woman to carry. Apparently, Ruth's strength was not just spiritual. Possibly Boaz's gift of grain was a dowry payment in expectation of his marriage to Ruth. But more likely, it was a practical expression to Naomi and Ruth of Boaz's intention to act as their kinsman-redeemer.

NOTES ON THE PRINTED TEXT

Boaz and Ruth now headed for different destinations. Boaz went to Bethlehem to wait for an opportunity to speak with the closest relative of Naomi and Ruth. In turn, Ruth carried the six measures of grain to Naomi. When Ruth arrived home, Naomi asked, "Who art thou?" (Ruth 3:16). This was an idiomatic way of asking whether Ruth was still Mahlon's widow or Boaz's bride-to-be.

We can imagine the excitement of the two women as the daughter-in-law recounted everything done and said that night. Ruth saved for last the account of Boaz's gift of grain and what he said when he gave it (vs. 17). Naomi must have been touched by this display of generosity. Earlier, Naomi had pushed Ruth into action to secure a husband, but now her counsel was for her daughter-in-law to wait and see. Ruth had told Naomi about Boaz's planned negotiations with the closer relative, and now Naomi was convinced the matter would be settled that same day (vs. 18). Perhaps with Boaz's expensive gift of grain lying at Naomi's feet, she was certain that Boaz would come through as their family guardian.

Boaz went to the Bethlehem gate when he wanted to settle with the closer relative (4:1). Before long, that individual passed by, probably on his way to work in his fields. The biblical text literally reads "a certain one." The ambiguity surrounding the man's name stands in sharp contrast to all the other names appearing in this chapter. Perhaps the narrator intentionally chose to keep the relative anonymous to convey a sense of poetic justice. Expressed differently, this individual did nothing memorable to fulfill the role of the family guardian, which would have included preserving the name of Mahlon. In turn, the specific identity of the relative is deliberately omitted from the record. Boaz asked this person, as well as 10 other elders of the city, to sit down (vs. 2). Boaz wanted the village leaders to serve as witnesses and to arbitrate if a dispute arose.

Boaz's strategy was to describe the sale of Naomi's land, then to bring up the matter of marriage to Ruth. Because Boaz was a person of integrity, he wanted to give the other person the opportunity to exercise his rights as the closer relative. Of course, Boaz also wanted to take on the role of the family guardian for Naomi and Ruth. And so, Boaz may have thought this strategy would be more successful. It was normal in Hebrew culture to offer the sale of land to a relative before placing it on the open market. On Naomi's behalf, Boaz offered the closer relative the opportunity to acquire the land that had belonged to Elimelech, Naomi's husband, since before the family went to Moab (vs. 3). Boaz added that he was willing to purchase it if the other individual was not. Then, in the presence of the village elders, the relative affirmed his interest in exercising the right to redeem the property (vs. 4). He may have thought that this was a chance to do his family duty while earning a profit.

In keeping with cultural custom, Boaz informed the nearer relative that he not only was redeeming the property from Naomi, but also obligating himself to act as a family guardian in connection with Ruth, the foreigner from Moab. Boaz explained that Ruth had been married to Mahlon, one of Elimelech's deceased sons. The nearest relative who acquired the property was duty-bound by Hebrew law to preserve the family name by raising up a descendant to inherit the land (vs. 5). This addition to the transaction changed the mind of the would-be family guardian. He withdrew his offer to acquire the property belonging to Elimelech.

Apparently, the expectation of raising up an heir for the deceased would have endangered the inheritance that was left to the purchaser's own children (vs. 6). The Moabite widow was young. She would likely have numerous children. The first son would be considered Mahlon's heir to the property bought from Naomi. The other sons Ruth might have with the unnamed relative would then split his estate with the children he already had, making less for each of them. Up to this point, the anonymous relative may have been thinking that obtaining the land would involve him in marrying Naomi. But she was past childbearing age, and the value and productivity of the property would far outweigh the cost of adding this older woman to his household. With Ruth, though, it was a different matter. So, in order to preserve his holdings the way they were, the relative declined to act as the kinsman-redeemer. In sharp contrast to Boaz, this person evidenced selfishness by disgracefully evading his duties as the family guardian.

The nearer relative told Boaz to purchase Naomi's land. In token of his decision to give Boaz the right to do this, the man gave his sandal to Boaz (vs. 8). Doing so made the act legally binding. By the time the Book of Ruth was written, this custom had already become obsolete. Thus, the writer inserted a comment to explain that the transfer of a sandal had been a way of symbolizing the finalization of a transaction involving the transfer of property (vs. 7). This symbolism appears to have come from the fact that landowners would walk around on their own property wearing their sandals. To make the transaction doubly official, Boaz claimed as witnesses the community leaders and other onlookers (vs. 9). Boaz had redeemed both Elimelech's land and Mahlon's widow as his wife. Boaz and Ruth's first son would be considered Mahlon's offspring and thus the heir of Naomi's land. That meant Elimelech's land would remain in the hands of his descendants. Furthermore, Mahlon's name would be perpetuated (vs. 10).

Next, the people pronounced blessings on the engaged couple. First, they blessed Ruth, asking the Lord to make her like Rachel and Leah, the wives of Jacob who had given birth to the heads of many of the Israelite tribes. Put differently, they hoped that Ruth would have many children who would help build up Israel. Next, the people blessed Boaz, wishing him financial prosperity and social prominence in Bethlehem (vs. 11). Finally, the onlookers blessed Boaz's entire family with a wish of fertility. The Bethlehemites prayed that children might make Boaz's family large. Whereas they had compared Ruth to Rachel and Leah, the well-wishers likened Boaz to Perez (vs. 12). Perez was one of a pair of twin boys born after their widowed mother, Tamar, posed as a prostitute to trick her father-in-law, Judah, into sleeping with her (Gen. 38; 46:12; 1 Chron. 2:3-4).

SUGGESTIONS TO TEACHERS

Just as Naomi and Ruth were unaware of the larger purpose in their lives—that God was preparing for the births of David and even of Jesus—we cannot always know how God's purpose is taking shape in our lives. Certainly, we will not realize the importance and impact of our lives until we look back from the perspective of eternity. Therefore, it is important for us to develop certain traits that will enable us to fulfill God's plan, direction, and will for our lives.

1. DEVELOP AN EXEMPLARY CHARACTER. Ruth had developed an exemplary character. She was consistently loving, faithful, kind, and courageous. She had a reputation for always displaying these admirable qualities. And Boaz, the man who would become Ruth's husband, took notice of all these character traits. Developing an exemplary character takes a lot of work. To be successful in this venture, it is vital that we live out the character qualities we long for—regardless of the people around us or their country or their cultural or religious practices.

2. DEVELOP A STRONG WORK ETHIC. Ruth had developed a strong work ethic. She approached her task of gleaning—though menial, tiresome, and degrading in that it was reserved for the poor—with industriousness and diligence. Can we develop the same kind of strong work ethic so that we approach any task with diligence and devotion? God rewards a strong work ethic.

3. DEVELOP A STRATEGY FOR ACTION. Neither Ruth nor Naomi nor Boaz were the type of people who sat around waiting for something good to happen to them. Each of them are classic examples of good people who developed a strategy for action—and then they acted. Ruth immediately sought work gleaning in the fields, Naomi devised a plan for Boaz to further notice Ruth and become the kinsman-redeemer, and Boaz willingly provided for the needy and fulfilled his role in redeeming the parcel of land that had belonged to Elimelech. We, too, should plan to act, develop a strategy for action, and then act.

FOR ADULTS

■ TOPIC: Caring for One Another

■ QUESTIONS: 1. Why do you think Boaz was so motivated to resolve the issue involving the family guardianship of Naomi and Ruth? 2. If you were Boaz, do you think you would have invested so much effort into the matter? 3. How do you think the residents of Bethlehem felt about Naomi's decision to resettle in the town after being gone for so long? 4. How often do we express our concern for the well-being of others by offering to help them? 5. What might have happened to Ruth and Naomi if Boaz chose not to intervene on their behalf?

■ ILLUSTRATIONS:

Doing God's Work. Mutual care and compassion typified the lives of Naomi, Ruth, and Boaz. Each was willing to sacrifice their personal desires and ambitions for the good of others.

Florence Nightingale (1820–1910) also exemplified this mind-set. At age 17, she felt God calling her to serve Him. She found her place of service in nursing, which in the early 1800s was done mostly by untrained volunteers. During the Crimean War (1853–1856), Nightingale and 38 nurses whom she trained, organized hospitals for 5,000 wounded British soldiers. She established the first real nurses' training, fought for sanitary hospitals in Britain, and helped make nursing the respectable profession it is today.

But Nightingale felt uncomfortable when Queen Victoria and Parliament honored her. She explained that she was doing God's work. "Christ is the author of our profession," Nightingale said of nursing. She later refused a national funeral and burial in Westminster Abbey when it was offered to her. She wanted only to be buried with her family in a rural churchyard in a simple service.

No Ordinary Minister. In 1995, successful entrepreneur Mark Cress left his job, sold his $1.8 million home, and went to seminary to become a pastor. But he's no ordinary minister. He founded Inner Active Ministries, a North Carolina-based nonprofit organization providing pastoral counseling for business employees. He and his staff are chaplains to nearly a dozen small, fast-growing companies.

Each day, Cress visits offices, factories, and warehouses to minister to the emotional and spiritual needs in the workplace. "Roger had foot surgery four weeks ago. Dave here is headed toward nuptials in a few weeks," Cress explains as he shows a visitor around one of the warehouses he visits. But those experiences pale compared with one man's story. This person's 27-year-old wife is dying from a rare blood disorder. His son has the disease, too, and his other son was recently hit by a bus and killed.

Cress believes everyone is at one of three stages in life: either they have a crisis, are in the midst of a crisis, or will soon experience a crisis. He hopes his ministry can provide the compassion people need to make it through life's troubles. In this regard, his caring attitude mirrors that of Boaz. Thousands of years ago, this property owner looked beyond the confines of his relatively comfortable existence to help a family in need. And God used his act of kindness to profoundly impact biblical history.

What Can Be Done? As Jenny walked through downtown Springfield, Illinois, early one Sunday morning while on vacation with her family, the normally busy capital lay sleeping. It felt good to her to get out of the hotel room and great to get away from people for a while.

The children frolicked by the side of Jenny and her husband. Then father and son decided to go in one direction, while mother and daughter went in another. That's when Jenny saw the woman, with her chalky, pale makeup, ruby-red lipstick, and intense green eye shadow. Her cosmetics couldn't cover the gaunt, wrinkled skin and distant, staring eyes of a drug addict.

This person had come down the stairs and out of the door of an apartment building. Meanwhile, Jenny and her daughter had been "window shopping" nearby. When their eyes met that of the woman, Jenny said, "Hi." This person looked at Jenny's daughter, then turned away.

Not long after that encounter, Jenny noticed the woman meeting someone down the street. She glanced at Jenny nervously. It was then that the mother decided to take her daughter back to the hotel. Later, Jenny wondered whether she could have reached out to this individual in some caring way. Jenny recognized that their worlds seemed so different, and she wasn't quite sure what to do.

We can imagine a respected, well-established individual such as Boaz also wondering how he might respond to the presence of a foreigner named Ruth, who one day unexpectedly started gleaning in his fields. The Lord gave Boaz the discernment and fortitude to help this newcomer in need. And He is the same God who can enable contemporary believers like Jenny (along with the rest of us) to make a tangible difference in the lives of those whom we meet.

■ TOPIC: Show Some Respect

■ QUESTIONS: 1. In the transaction involving the near relative, why did Boaz request the presence of 10 of Bethlehem's elders? 2. If you were Boaz, what emotions do you think you would have felt as you negotiated over the family guardianship of Naomi and Ruth? 3. How can we earn a reputation as people who do our duty even when it is unprofitable or inconvenient? 4. In what ways do our words and actions confirm our faith in God? 5. Who are some individuals God has recently brought into your life who could use a special touch of His compassion?

■ ILLUSTRATIONS:

Faithfulness Rewarded. Homeless, hungry refugees often fill our television screens. We watch them clamor and fight for food and clothing being thrown from trucks. Ruth, a refugee of sorts from Moab, found shelter in Bethlehem and eventually earned the respect of its residents.

What kept Ruth going? It was her faith in God and courage to remain devoted to His people. Ruth had no earthly prospects and was reduced to foraging for food. Yet she did not quit, for she knew that trusting and obeying the Lord was her highest goal.

Many adolescents can relate to the struggles Ruth experienced—losing a loved one, moving to a strange place, struggling to make ends meet, and so on. Saved teens also know that peers who do not share their faith in Christ sometimes treat them like outcasts. They should be encouraged to remain loyal to their Christian faith and heritage. They can do so knowing that the Lord will be with them every step of the way.

The Windfall of God's Grace. Newlyweds Brian and Dena had searched for a used car for two weeks. Then, one Saturday this tired and frustrated couple stumbled into a dealership just before closing. The salesman politely spoke to them as if they were people, not just sales prospects. "And with their no-haggle pricing policy, we didn't have to wrangle a 'deal' out of them," Dena says.

After everything else the two had been through, this experience was a welcome surprise. But the real surprise came when the young couple returned to finalize the paperwork and pick up the car. "They had run the car through their 100-point checklist. They even washed it for us," Brian notes.

The 21-year-old husband continued, "What really got to me, though, was when our salesman said, 'Now, I'd like you to meet Jessica, our customer service representative.' When we turned around, Jessica handed Dena two red roses and said, 'Welcome to the family. If there's anything we can do for you, just let us know.'"

God's grace is like that—overwhelming us with surprises we could never have imagined. We spot it in the lives of Naomi, Ruth, and Boaz. And if we look hard enough, we can see evidences of His unconditional favor in our day-to-day experiences, too.

Making the Most of Our Circumstances. Instead of complaining about all the challenges she encountered after relocating to Judah, Ruth made the most of her circumstances. And down through the centuries, there have been others who demonstrated similar levels of commitment and courage. Here are the stories of a few of them.

John Keats was a poet who some said was the equal to Shakespeare, except that he only lived to be 26. Franz Schubert died at the age of 31, but in those few years he wrote more than 110 musical compositions.

One boy was so ugly and poorly clothed that he was the object of constant torment from his schoolmates. At the age of 18, he worked as a bricklayer for modest wages. It wasn't until Ben Johnson captured the attention of the arts world that his talent was recognized and acclaimed. He went on to become one of the most famous playwrights England has ever produced.

This young man had lost most of his hearing by age eight, but Thomas Edison went on to give us the electric light, the phonograph, movies, and more than 100 other useful inventions.

He almost died on several occasions from severe coughing spells due to the terrible hemorrhages in his lungs. Yet, in his invalid state, he directed his energy to write two masterpieces—*Dr. Jekyll and Mr. Hyde* and *Treasure Island*. His name was Robert Louis Stevenson.

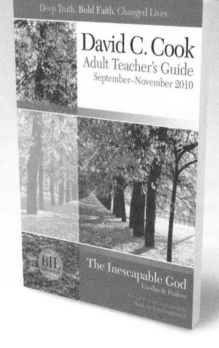